T0329312

INVESTMENT BANKS, HEDGE FUNDS, AND PRIVATE EQUITY

INVESTMENT BANKS, HEDGE FUNDS, AND PRIVATE EQUITY

THIRD EDITION

David P. Stowell

ELSEVIER

ACADEMIC PRESS

An imprint of Elsevier

Academic Press is an imprint of Elsevier
125 London Wall, London EC2Y 5AS, United Kingdom
525 B Street, Suite 1800, San Diego, CA 92101-4495, United States
50 Hampshire Street, 5th Floor, Cambridge, MA 02139, United States
The Boulevard, Langford Lane, Kidlington, Oxford OX5 1GB, United Kingdom

Library of Congress Cataloging-in-Publication Data
A catalog record for this book is available from the Library of Congress

British Library Cataloguing-in-Publication Data
A catalogue record for this book is available from the British Library

ISBN: 978-0-12-804723-1

For information on all Academic Press publications visit our website at
https://www.elsevier.com/books-and-journals

Working together
to grow libraries in
developing countries

www.elsevier.com • www.bookaid.org

Publisher: Candice Janco
Acquisition Editor: Scott J. Bentley
Editorial Project Manager: Susan Ikeda
Production Project Manager: Julie-Ann Stansfield
Designer: Mark Rogers

Typeset by TNQ Books and Journals

For William, Thomas, Henry, Anne, Alexander, Isabel and Oliver

Contents

16. Overview of Private Equity

17. LBO Financial Model

18. Private Equity Impact on Corporations

19. Organization, Compensation, Regulation, and Limited Partners

20. Private Equity Issues and Opportunities

III
CASE STUDIES

Preface

The world of finance dramatically changed following the global financial meltdown of 2007–09, and this change has continued following Brexit in 2016 and the new administration that took over in the United States during 2017. These significant events have caused governments and financial industry to look again at investment banks, hedge funds, and private equity through a new lens. Market participants have been significantly impacted, and attitudes toward risk, transparency, regulation, and compensation have changed. Investment banks, hedge funds, and private equity firms are at the epicenter of a transformed financial landscape, forging new roles and seeking new ways to create value within a paradigm of lower risk and greater regulation. This book provides an overview of investment banks, hedge funds, and private equity firms and describes the relationships between these organizations: how they both compete with and provide important services to each other, and the significant impact they have on corporations, governments, institutional investors, and individuals. Together, they have reshaped global financing and investing patterns, attracting envy and awe, but also criticism and concern. They dominate the headlines of the financial press and create wealth for many of their managers and investing clients. This book enables readers to better understand these heavily interconnected organizations, their impact on the global financial market, historical development, principal activities, regulatory environment, and risks and opportunities.

Ultimately, the objective of this book is to demystify investment banks, hedge funds, and private equity firms, revealing their key functions, compensation systems, unique role in wealth creation and risk management and their epic battle for investor funds, and corporate influence. After reading this book, the reader should better understand financial press headlines that herald massive corporate takeovers, corporate shareholder activism, large capital market financings and the myriad strategies, risks, and conflicts in the financial market landscape. The inclusion of case studies and spreadsheet models provides an analytical framework that allows the reader to apply the book's lessons to real-world financing, investing, and advisory activities.

TARGET AUDIENCE

The target audience for this book includes MBA, MSF, and Executive MBA students, and upper-level undergraduates who are focused on finance and investments. Investment banking classes can use this book as a primary text and corporate finance, and investments classes can use the book either as a secondary text or as a principal text when focused on hedge funds and private equity. In addition, professionals working at investment banks, hedge funds, and private equity firms can use the book to broaden understanding of their industry and competitors. Finally, professionals at law firms, accounting firms, and other firms that advise investment banks, hedge funds, and private equity firms should find this book useful as a resource to better understand and assist their clients.

DISTINGUISHING FEATURES

This book is unique for two reasons. First, it is a product of a long career working for and with investment banks, hedge funds, and private equity firms, in addition to 12 years of teaching students about these institutions. Second, by addressing all three of these institutions in the same book, and focusing on their simultaneous competition and cooperation with each other, the book provides a more holistic view of the changing boundaries and real-world impact of these institutions than has previously been available.

I wrote this book following a 20-year career as an investment banker at Goldman Sachs, JP Morgan, and UBS, and an additional 4 years at O'Connor & Associates, a hedge fund that is now part of UBS. As an investment banker, in addition to completing numerous M&A, debt and equity financing, equity derivative, and convertible transactions with corporate clients, I worked with private equity firms (financial sponsors) as they acquired companies and pursued exit strategies through recapitalizations, M&A sales, and IPOs. Since 2005, I have been a professor of finance at Northwestern University's Kellogg School of Management, where I have had the privilege of teaching what I learned during my preacademic career, while completing ongoing research into the ever-changing landscape of investment banks, hedge funds, and private equity. Teaching these subjects in classrooms has provided greater objectivity and the opportunity to refine concepts and make them more relevant to students. This book is therefore a blend of practitioner's experience and academic experience, creating an educational offering that more fully opens the door to understanding the key participants in the global financial and advisory markets.

CASES

The inclusion of 12 independent cases facilitates greater understanding of the concepts described in the chapters. These cases focus on recent actual financial and advisory transactions and include a summary of risks, rewards, political considerations, impact on corporations and investors, competition, regulatory hurdles, and other subjects that are linked to chapter topics. The cases include questions for students and case notes and teaching suggestions for instructors. In addition, several cases include spreadsheet models that allow readers to create an analytical framework for considering choices, opportunities, and risks that are described in the cases. The cases are assembled together at the end of the book, but all are linked to preceding chapters. As a result, cases are designed to be used in conjunction with chapter reading to reinforce concepts and enhance learning.

THE WORLD HAS CHANGED

During 2008, Bear Stearns collapsed into a fire-sale to JP Morgan, Lehman Brothers declared bankruptcy, Fannie Mae and Freddie Mac were placed into US government conservatorship, the US government assumed majority control over AIG and injected over

$100 billion to keep it afloat, Countrywide and Merrill Lynch both sold themselves to Bank of America under duress, Wells Fargo bought Wachovia at the brink of bankruptcy, Washington Mutual went into receivership with its branches absorbed by JP Morgan, Goldman Sachs and Morgan Stanley became bank holding companies, and banks all over the world had to be rescued by their respective governments. In the United States, this included the rapid provision to banks of over $200 billion of equity capital by the US Treasury as part of a larger $700 billion rescue program, guarantees of debt and asset pools by the FDIC totaling many hundreds of billions of dollars, and an unprecedented expansion of the Federal Reserve's balance sheet by trillions of dollars as it provided credit based on almost any type of collateral. All of this occurred as the world experienced the most significant, globalized downturn since the Great Depression in the 1930s. Between 2008 and 2017, investment banks, hedge funds, and private equity firms have all come under increasing regulation and scrutiny. They have had to derisk their balance sheets and become more transparent. The imperative to improve relationships with governments and with the press has become abundantly clear. Many firms have had to downsize and change their business models as new competition has entered their arena and additional capital requirements have reduced margins and returns to investors. Ongoing debates regarding whether governments have done too little or too much regarding reducing volatility and risk continue to occupy management attention at many financial institutions.

The investment banking business, in many ways, will never be the same. Leverage has been reduced, some structured financial products have ceased to exist, and regulation has increased. However, the fundamental business remains the same: advising corporations and investors; raising and investing capital; executing trades as an intermediary and principal; providing research; making markets; and providing ideas and capital directly to clients. As investment banks reinvent some aspects of their business and learn to live in a world of decreased leverage and increased regulation, new opportunities loom large, while issues such as public perception, compensation, and risk management must be carefully worked through.

Hedge funds and private equity funds suffered significant reversals during 2008, with hedge funds recording investment losses of over 19% on average and private equity firms acknowledging similar potential losses to their investors. Although these results were undesirable and caused some investors to abandon funds, the global equity markets fared even worse, with the major US stock market indices dropping by more than 38% and other equity and nongovernment debt indices throughout the world posting similar, or greater, losses. Hedge funds and private equity have had to adjust to a changing landscape and reexplain their value proposition while contending with slower growth in assets under management and weaker returns. Although hedge fund assets under management has increased dramatically since the global financial crisis, 2016 was a very disappointing year for the industry in relation to returns, and some large investors have backed away from historical investment levels with these asset managers. Private equity funds have shown respectable returns over the past 8 years, and experienced significant growth in assets under management, but many smaller players have left the industry as limited partners search for differentiated platforms and sometimes direct investment opportunities.

Investment banks, hedge funds, and private equity firms have redefined their roles and developed new processes and business plans designed to maintain historical positions of power and influence. The world has changed, but these institutions will continue to have a significant impact on global capital markets and M&A transactions. This book projects how they will achieve this, and the resultant impact on corporations, governments, institutional investors, and individuals.

STRUCTURE OF THE BOOK

The book is divided into three parts. The first part is comprised of 10 chapters that focus on investment banks. The second part includes five chapters that discuss hedge funds and five chapters that review the activities of private equity firms. The third part of the book includes 12 cases that focus on recent transactions and developments in the financial markets. These cases are cross-referenced in the preceding chapters and are used to illustrate concepts that benefit from more rigorous analysis. In addition, there is an M&A case embedded within Chapter 4.

PART ONE: INVESTMENT BANKING

This part includes 10 chapters that provide an overview of the industry and the three principal divisions of most large investment banks, including descriptions of the M&A and financing activities of the banking division; the intermediation and market-making activities of the trading division; and the investment gathering and money management activities of the asset management division. In addition, the other businesses of large investment banks and the activities of boutique investment banks are reviewed. Other chapters focus in more detail on financings, including the activities of capital markets groups and the underwriting function, and discussion of IPOs, follow-on equity offerings, convertibles, and debt transactions. The role of credit rating agencies, prime brokerage groups, research, derivatives, and exchanges is also explored. Finally, regulations, leverage, risk management, clearing and settlement, international investment banking, career opportunities and the interrelationship between investment banks, hedge funds, and private equity are discussed. The capstone chapters in this part of the book drill deeply into M&A, convertible securities, and investment bank innovation.

Part One is designed to be used as the text for a full course on investment banking. It should be used in conjunction with cases in Part Three that are specifically referenced in Part One chapters. Part Two's hedge fund and private equity chapters may be used as supplemental material.

PART TWO: HEDGE FUNDS AND PRIVATE EQUITY

The **first section** of Part Two is comprised of five chapters that focus on hedge funds, including an overview of the industry; a focus on selected hedge fund investment strategies; shareholder activism and impact of hedge fund activists on corporations; risk, regulation, and organizational structure of hedge funds; and a review of performance, risks, threats, and opportunities, as well as the changing value proposition offered by hedge funds to their limited investor partners. Finally, hedge fund competition with investment banks and private equity is reviewed, as well as the symbiotic relationship between all three parties.

The **second section** of Part Two is comprised of five chapters that examine private equity from the perspective of those firms that principally focus on leveraged buyouts (LBOs) and other equity investments in mature companies. These chapters provide an overview of private equity; an explanation of an LBO model and how it drives decision-making; private equity impact on corporations, including case histories of more than a dozen LBO transactions; a description of organizational structures, compensation, regulation, and limited partner relationships; and a discussion of private equity issues and opportunities, diversification efforts, IPOs, historical performance and relationships with hedge funds and investment banks.

Part Two is designed to be used as the text for a full course that focuses on hedge funds and private equity. It should be used in conjunction with cases in Part Three that are specifically referenced in Part Two chapters. Part One's investment banking chapters may also be used as supplemental material.

PART THREE: CASES

This part contains 12 cases that are referenced in different chapters in Parts One and Two. The cases enable students to drill deeper into the subject matter of the chapters and apply concepts in the framework of real transactions and market developments. Case questions (and teaching notes for instructors) are provided, as well as several spreadsheet models that enable students to manipulate data. The cases focus on the following: the dramatic change in the global investment banking landscape that occurred during the 2008 financial crisis; the use of equity derivatives by Porsche and CSX as these two corporations interacted with investment banks and hedge funds in effecting significant corporate change; Cerberus's investments in Chrysler and GMAC (GM's captive finance subsidiary); the divergent CDO investment strategies of two hedge funds, which, in the first case, resulted in excellent returns, and in the second case, caused bankruptcy; Freeport McMoRan's acquisition of Phelps Dodge, which focuses on M&A, risk taking and financing activities; the acquisition through a bankruptcy court process and management of Kmart and Sears by ESL, one of the world's largest hedge funds; Proctor & Gamble's acquisition of Gillette, including the advisory role of investment bankers and discussion of corporate governance and regulatory issues; the LBO of Toys R Us, focusing on the role of private equity funds and investment banks; activist hedge fund investor Pershing Square's impact on the capital and organizational structure of McDonald's Corporation; the acquisition of H.J. Heinz by Berkshire Hathaway and 3G; and the IPO of Quintiles, the world's largest contract clinical research company.

NEW CONTENT IN THE THIRD EDITION

The third edition reflects the most significant developments for investment banks, hedge funds, and private equity funds during 2012–17 in relation to regulatory and tax considerations as part of the ongoing global financial reform. In addition, developments in the global competitive landscape are addressed, and significant new content that focuses on international markets is included in many chapters. All time-sensitive exhibits have been updated, reflecting current information and considerations. Basically, this edition brings the reader up to date through 2017 on all of the key issues and considerations that impact investment banks, hedge funds, and private equity funds as key participants in the global financial markets.

Additional content can be downloaded from the book's companion website https://www.elsevier.com/books-and-journals/book-companion/9780128143520

Acknowledgments

I am very grateful to many who have contributed to this publication. My wife, Janet, and my children (Paul, Lauren, Audrey, Julia, and Peter) have been very patient and supportive during the process of researching and writing this book. When I decided to become an academic, they assumed that my investment banker work-week would drop from 70+hours to less than half that amount. This has not been the case, as I learned that academics work long hours too, and the book added many hours to my schedule. I am also grateful to many finance department colleagues and administrators at Northwestern University's Kellogg School of Management for their support for this project and me over the past 12 years as I transitioned from practitioner to academic. They have been very patient and encouraging during this process.

I am indebted to many colleagues and friends from investment banks, hedge funds, and private equity funds, as well as professionals from law firms, accounting firms, data providers, rating agencies, exchanges, and regulators. Since I have credited them in previous editions, their names will not be repeated here. I am also grateful to students who have given me excellent feedback as I have taught hundreds of classes based on the content of this book, and to those students who helped me update exhibits and improve the organization of chapters. Finally, I appreciate the patience and guidance extended to me by my contacts at Elsevier for their encouragement and support over many years.

SECTION I

INVESTMENT BANKING

Overview of Investment Banking

The material in this chapter should be cross-referenced with the following cases: **Investment Banking in 2008 (A) Case** and **Investment Banking in 2008 (B) Case**.

Investment banking changed dramatically during the 20-year period preceding the global financial crisis that started during mid-2007, as market forces pushed banks from their traditional low-risk role of advising and intermediating to a position of taking considerable risk for their own account and on behalf of clients. This high level of risk-taking, combined with high leverage, transformed the industry during 2008, when several major firms failed, huge trading losses were recorded and all large firms were forced to reorganize their business.

Risk-taking activities of investment banks were reduced following large losses that stemmed primarily from mortgage-related assets, bad loans, and an overall reduction in revenues due to the financial crisis. This led to an industry-wide effort to reduce leverage ratios and a string of new equity capital issuances. By the end of 2008, five US headquartered "pure-play" investment banks (which did not operate deposit-taking businesses, unlike large "universal" banks such as JP Morgan Chase, which operated a large investment bank, a deposit-taking business, and other businesses) had undergone significant transformations: Goldman Sachs and Morgan Stanley converted into bank-holding companies; the US Federal Reserve (Fed) pushed Bear Stearns into the arms of JP Morgan to avoid a bankruptcy; Lehman Brothers filed for bankruptcy protection after the Fed and Treasury Department ignored its pleas for government support; and Merrill Lynch, presumably to avoid a similar bankruptcy filing, agreed to sell their firm to Bank of America at a substantial discount to historical prices (see Exhibit 1.1).

EXHIBIT 1.1 TRANSFORMATION OF PURE-PLAY/ NONDEPOSIT-TAKING INVESTMENT BANKS

- Bear Stearns: sold to JP Morgan on March 16, 2008[1]
- Lehman Brothers: filed for bankruptcy protection on September 14, 2008
  - Sold U.S. operations to Barclays on September 16, 2008
  - Sold part of European and Asian operations to Nomura on September 22, 2008
- Merrill Lynch: sold to Bank of America on September 14, 2008[2]
- Goldman Sachs: converted to bank holding company on September 21, 2008
- Morgan Stanley: converted to bank holding company on September 21, 2008

Note 1: Initial price of sale at $2 per share was increased to $10 under a revised agreement on March 24, 2008.
Note 2: Date of announcement; deal completed on January 1, 2009.

Historically, through 1999, US banks with deposit-taking businesses (commercial/retail banks) were barred from operating investment banking businesses. This rule was created by the Glass–Steagall Banking Act of 1933, which was enacted after the stock market crash of 1929 to protect depositors' assets. In 1999, the Gramm–Leach–Bliley Act overturned the requirement to keep investment banks and commercial banks separate, and led to the formation of US-headquartered universal investment banks, including JP Morgan, Citigroup, and Bank of America. Two of the main arguments for rejoining these two businesses were (1) to provide for a more stable and countercyclical business model for these banks and (2) to allow US banks to better compete with international counterparts (e.g., UBS, Credit Suisse, and Deutsche Bank) that were less encumbered by the Glass–Steagall Act. As a result, Citigroup, which was created through the 1998 merger of Citicorp and Travelers Group (which owned the investment bank Salomon Brothers), did not have to divest the Salomon Brothers business to comply with Federal regulations. JP Morgan and Bank of America followed the lead of Citigroup in combining businesses to create universal investment banks. These universal banks rapidly developed a broad-based investment banking business, hiring many professionals from pure-play investment banks and strategically using their significant lending capability as a platform from which they were able to capture investment banking market share.

POSTCRISIS GLOBAL INVESTMENT BANKING FIRMS

As of 2017, the surviving nine key global firms that encompass both investment banking and deposit-taking businesses and operate throughout the world included JP Morgan, Bank of America, Citigroup, Credit Suisse, UBS, Deutsche Bank, Barclays, Goldman Sachs, and Morgan Stanley. See Exhibits 1.2–1.5 for a summary of financial results, financial measures, and market capitalization for these nine firms.

EXHIBIT 1.2 FINANCIAL RESULTS

Firm	2015 Net Revenue $ in millions	2015 Net Earnings $ in millions	2015 Return on Equity	2015 Price/Tangible Book Value
Bank of America	$ 79,346	$ 15,888	6.4%	1.10x
Barclays[1]	32,909	(73)	0.9%	0.76x
Citigroup	69,246	17,242	8.0%	0.86x
Credit Suisse[2]	23,757	(2,980)	-6.5%	0.98x
Deutsche Bank[3]	35,609	(7,428)	-9.5%	0.53x
Goldman Sachs	33,820	6,083	7.1%	1.11x
JP Morgan	89,716	24,442	10.2%	1.42x
Morgan Stanley	35,226	6,127	8.5%	1.06x
UBS[3]	30,973	6,278	11.4%	1.54x

Note 1: Calculated at September 30th, 2015 GBP/USD rate of 1.4819

Note 2: Calculated at December 31st, 2015 CHF/USD rate of 1.0121

Note 3: Calculated at December 31st, 2015 USD/EUR rate of 0.9146

Source: Capital IQ

EXHIBIT 1.3 CREDIT RATINGS, ASSETS, VaR, AND EMPLOYEES

Firm	Credit rating	2015 Total Assets ($ millions)	Average daily VaR ($ millions)	Number of employees
Bank of America	BBB+	2,144,316	61	210,516
Barclays	A-	1,120,012	17	129,400
Citigroup	A-	1,731,210	86	239,000
Credit Suisse	A	820,805	51	48,200
Deutsche Bank	BBB+	1,629,130	43	101,104
Goldman Sachs	BBB+	861,395	71	34,800
JP Morgan	A-	2,351,698	47	235,678
Morgan Stanley	BBB+	787,465	46	55,802
UBS	A-	942,819	15	60,099

Note 1: S&P rating for long-term debt as of June 2016 according to reports of financial institutions.

Note 2: Barclays, Goldman Sachs, JP Morgan Chase, Morgan Stanley, and UBS' average daily value-at-risk are calculated using 95% confidence level. Morgan Stanley estimates its average daily VaR under a 99% confidence level. Credit Suisse employs a 98% confidence interval, while Bank of America, Citigroup, and Deutsche Bank estimate VaR using a 99% confidence level.

Note 3: The data on average daily VaR and total assets value are presented on the basis of 2015 annual reports.

EXHIBIT 1.4 LEVERAGE AND ROE

Firm	Leverage (Asset/Equity)				Avg. ROE % 2012-2015
	2012	2013	2014	2015	
Bank of America	9.33	9.03	8.64	8.37	3.4725
Barclays	25.21	21.01	20.59	17	-0.4175
Citigroup	9.76	9.12	8.69	7.75	5.635
Credit Suisse	26.04	20.7	20.96	18.23	1.8925
Deutsche Bank	37.44	29.45	24.99	24.09	-1.5875
Goldman Sachs	12.4	11.62	10.34	9.88	10.065
JP Morgan	12.99	11.44	11.1	9.5	9.8025
Morgan Stanley	11.94	12.06	11.12	10.34	4.44
UBS	25.66	20.29	19.54	16.45	5.0425

Note 1: ROE calculated based on the income from continuing operations available to common equity holders divided by average common shareholder's equity.
Note 2: Barclays, Deutche Bank, and UBS financials are presented under IFRS standards. All other banks are presented according to US GAAP. A major difference between IFRS and US GAAP is the accounting for derivatives, nonderivative trading assets, and reverse repos/borrowed securities. The former shows gross exposures while the latter shows values on a net basis.

EXHIBIT 1.5 SHARE PRICE AND MARKET CAPITALIZATION

Firm	End of 2014 Share Price in $	End of 2015 Share Price in $	% change	End of 2014 Mkt Cap $ in billions	End of 2015 Mkt Cap $ in billions
Bank of America	17.89	16.83	-5.93	175.24	173.47
Barclays	324.08	376.03	16.03	55.60	62.52
Citigroup	54.11	51.75	-4.36	154.16	158.03
Credit Suisse	25.08	21.69	-13.52	35.86	41.75
Deutsche Bank	30.02	24.15	-19.55	30.45	35.83
Goldman Sachs	193.83	180.23	-7.02	62.41	81.88
JP Morgan	62.58	66.03	5.51	205.57	225.90
Morgan Stanley	38.80	31.81	-18.02	46.48	71.63
UBS	17.05	19.37	13.61	71.89	63.51

Note 1: Calculated at December 30, 2014, GBP/USD rate of 1.5569, and December 30, 2015, GBP/USD rate of 1.4819.
Note 2: Calculated at December 31, 2014, CHF/USD rate of 1.0116, and December 31, 2015, CHF/USD rate of 1.0121.
Note 3: Calculated at December 31, 2014, USD/EUR rate of 0.8222, and December 30, 2015, USD/EUR rate of 0.9146.
Sources: Capital IQ

OTHER INVESTMENT BANKING FIRMS

In addition to these nine key global investment banks, other large banks compete effectively in regional markets worldwide and, in some countries, have a larger market share for investment banking business than the nine designated global banks. Examples of banks in the category of large regional investment banks include HSBC, Société Générale, BNP Paribas, CIBC, MUFJ, Sumitomo Mitsui, Mizuho, Nomura and Macquarie, etc. Smaller banks that engage in investment banking business are called boutique banks. Boutique banks principally focus on merger and acquisition (M&A)–related activity, although some may provide additional services such as fee-based financial restructuring advice and asset management. Firms that do not participate in M&A, but focus principally on retail client investments in stocks and bonds are called retail brokerage firms. See Exhibit 1.6 for a sampling of banks that compete in each of these areas.

INVESTMENT BANKING BUSINESSES

Although each investment bank takes a somewhat different approach, the basic businesses of most large investment banks consist of an (1) investment banking business managed by the investment banking division that principally focuses on capital raising and M&A transactions for corporate clients and capital raising for government clients; (2) sales and trading business managed by the trading division that provides investing, intermediating, and risk management services to institutional investor clients, research, and also participates in selected direct investing and lending activities; and (3) asset management business managed by the asset management division that is responsible for managing money for individual and institutional investing clients (see Exhibit 1.7).

EXHIBIT 1.6 INVESTMENT BANKING FIRMS

Global Investment Banks	Large Regional Investment Banks	Boutique Investment Banks	Retail Brokerage Firms[1]
• Bank of America	• BNP Paribas	• William Blair	• Charles Schwab
• Barclays	• CIBC	• Evercore Partners	• Commonwealth Financial Network
• Citigroup	• HSBC	• Greenhill & Co.	• E* Trade
• Credit Suisse	• Macquarie	• Houlihan Lokey	• Edward Jones
• Deutsche Bank	• Mizuho	• Jefferies & Co.	• LPL Financial
• Goldman Sachs	• MUFG	• Keefe, Bruyette & Woods	• Royal Alliance
• JP Morgan	• Nomura	• Lazard	• Scottrade
• Morgan Stanely	• Royal Bank of Canada	• Moelis & Co.	• TD Ameritrade
• UBS	• Royal Bank of Scotland	• Perella Weinberg Partners	
	• Société Générale	• Robert W. Baird & Co.	
	• Standard Chartered Bank	• Rothschild	
	• Sumitomo Mitsui		
	• Wells Fargo		

Note 1: Retail brokerage firms generally do not provide a full range of investment banking products and services.

EXHIBIT 1.7 PRINCIPAL BUSINESS OF INVESTMENT BANKS

Investment Banking Business

- Arranges financings for corporations and governments: debt; equity; convertibles.
- Advises on M&A transactions.

Trading Business

- Sells and trades securities and other financial assets as an intermediary on behalf of institutional investing clients.
- Operates in two business units: Equity and Fixed Income, Currency, and Commodities (FICC)[1].
- Provides research to investing clients.

Asset Management Business

- Offers equity, fixed income, alternative investments, and money market investment products and services principally to individual investing clients.
- For alternative investment products, the firm coinvests with clients in hedge funds, private equity, and real estate funds.

Note 1: Fixed income refers to an investment such as a bond that yields a regular (or fixed) periodic return; currency refers to foreign exchange (FX); commodities refer principally to energy- and metals-based commodities.

Within the nine large global investment banks, Goldman Sachs and Morgan Stanley are examples of more narrowly focused investment banks. They operate each of the businesses described above and also offer a limited deposit-taking and lending service. However, they do not participate in certain other noninvestment banking businesses that the other global firms conduct. JP Morgan Chase (whose investment banking business is separately branded as JP Morgan) and Citigroup are examples of more broadly focused financial organizations that operate a large investment banking business, but also conduct many other noninvestment banking businesses. See Exhibits 1.8 and 1.9 for an overview of the principal businesses of Goldman Sachs and JP Morgan Chase, respectively. Note that Goldman Sachs has divided their Sales and Trading business into two separate units—Institutional Client Services, which provides investing, intermediating, and risk management services to institutional investor clients; and Investing & Lending, which invests in equity and debt offerings of clients and provides loans to clients by using the firm's own capital and capital from clients of the Investment Management business. Goldman Sachs calls their Asset Management business "Investment Management". JP Morgan Chase competes directly with Goldman Sachs through their Investment Bank, in combination with their Asset Management business, but the bank also has other businesses that focus on retail and commercial banking, and card, treasury, and securities services.

EXHIBIT 1.8 GOLDMAN SACHS PRINCIPAL BUSINESSES

$ in millions	End of the year			% of 2015 Net Revenues
	2015	2014	2013	
Investment Banking				21%
Net revenues	$ 7,027.00	$ 6,464.00	$ 6,004.00	
Operating expenses	$ 3,713.00	$ 3,688.00	$ 3,479.00	
Pre-tax earnings	$ 3,314.00	$ 2,776.00	$ 2,525.00	
Institutional Client Services				45%
Net revenues	$ 15,151.00	$ 15,197.00	$ 15,721.00	
Operating expenses	$ 13,938.00	$ 10,880.00	$ 11,792.00	
Pre-tax earnings	$ 1,213.00	$ 4,317.00	$ 3,929.00	
Investing & Lending				16%
Net revenues	$ 5,436.00	$ 6,825.00	$ 7,018.00	
Operating expenses	$ 2,402.00	$ 2,819.00	$ 2,686.00	
Pre-tax earnings	$ 3,034.00	$ 4,006.00	$ 4,332.00	
Investment Management				18%
Net revenues	$ 6,206.00	$ 6,042.00	$ 5,463.00	
Operating expenses	$ 4,841.00	$ 4,647.00	$ 4,357.00	
Pre-tax earnings	$ 1,365.00	$ 1,395.00	$ 1,106.00	

Business Segments in Goldman Sachs
(the percentage of 2015 Net Revenues)

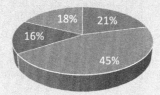

- Investment Banking
- Institutional Client Services
- Investing & Lending
- Investment Management

Investment Banking	**Institutional Client Services**
Investment Banking serves public and private sector clients around the world. We provide financial advisory services and help companies raise capital to strengthen and grow their businesses. We seek to develop and maintain longterm relationships with a diverse global group of institutional clients, including governments, states and municipalities. Our goal is to deliver to our institutional clients the entire resources of the firm in a seamless fashion, with investment banking serving as the main initial point of contact with Goldman Sachs.	Institutional Client Services serves our clients who come to the firm to buy and sell financial products, raise funding and manage risk. We do this by acting as a market maker and offering market expertise on a global basis. Institutional Client Services makes markets and facilitates client transactions in fixed income, equity, currency and commodity products. In addition, we make markets in and clear client transactions on major stock, options and futures exchanges worldwide. Market makers provide liquidity and play a critical role in price discovery, which contributes to the overall efficiency of the capital markets. Our willingness to make markets, commit capital and take risk in a broad range of products is crucial to our client relationships.

(Continued)

I. INVESTMENT BANKING

EXHIBIT 1.8 GOLDMAN SACHS PRINCIPAL BUSINESSES—cont'd

Investing & Lending	Investment Management
Our investing and lending activities, which are typically longer-term, include the firm's investing and relationship lending activities across various asset classes, primarily debt securities and loans, public and private equity securities, and real estate. These activities include investing directly in publicly and privately traded securities and in loans, and also through certain investment funds and separate accounts that we manage and through funds managed by external parties. We also provide financing to our clients.	Investment Management provides investment and wealth advisory services to help clients preserve and grow their financial assets. Our clients include institutions and high net-worth individuals, as well as retail investors who primarily access our products through a network of third party distributors around the world.

EXHIBIT 1.9 JP MORGAN CHASE PRINCIPAL BUSINESSES

JPMorgan Chase						
Consumer Businesses			**Wholesale Businesses**			
Consumer & Community Banking			**Corporate & Investment Bank**		**Commercial Banking**	**Asset Management**
Consumer & Business Banking	Mortgage Banking	Card, Commerce Solutions & Auto	Banking	Markets & Investor Services	• Middle Market Banking	• Global Investment Management

• Consumer Banking/ Chase Wealth Management
 • Business Banking
	• Mortgage Production
	 • Mortgage Servicing
	 • Real Estate Portfolios
		• Card Services
		   – Credit Card
		   – Commerce Solutions
		 • Auto & Student
			• Investment Banking
			 • Treasury Services
			 • Lending
				• Fixed Income Markets
				 • Equity Markets
				 • Securities Services
				 • Credit Adjustments & Other
					• Corporate Client Banking
					 • Commercial Term Lending
					 • Real Estate Banking
						• Global Wealth Management

Source: JPMorgan Chase 2015 Annual Report

INVESTMENT BANKING DIVISION

    The Investment Banking Division of an investment bank is responsible for working with corporations that seek to raise capital through public or private capital markets, risk-manage their existing capital, or complete an M&A-related transaction. In addition, at some firms, this division provides financing through direct investments in corporate equity and debt securities and loans to corporate clients. Finally, this division helps government-related entities raise funds and manage risk. Individuals who work in the Investment Banking Division are called "bankers" and are assigned to work in either a product group or a client coverage group (see Exhibit 1.10). The two key product groups are M&A and Capital Markets. Within the M&A product group, bankers typically specialize by industry (and at some investment banks, they work within the client coverage group). In the Capital Markets Group, bankers specialize by working in either debt capital markets (DCM) or equity capital markets (ECM). Client coverage bankers are usually organized into industry groups, which typically focus on the following industries: healthcare, consumer, industrials, retail, energy, chemicals, financial institutions, real estate, financial sponsors, media and telecom, technology and public finance, among others (see Exhibit 1.11). Exhibit 1.12 provides a summary of the product groups in Morgan Stanley's Investment Banking Division.

EXHIBIT 1.10 INVESTMENT BANKING DIVISION

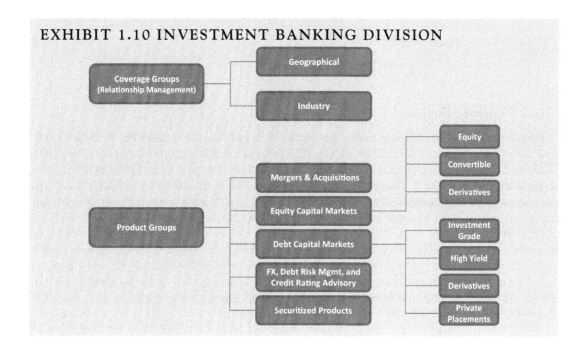

EXHIBIT 1.11 MORGAN STANLEY INDUSTRY COVERAGE

Basic Materials	Industrials
Communications	Power & Utilities
Consumer Products & Retail	Real Estate
Energy	Services
Financial Institutions	Technology
Financial Sponsors	Transportation
Healthcare	

Source: *Investment Banking and Capital Markets.* Morgan Stanley. Web. 17 Jul. 2015

EXHIBIT 1.12 MORGAN STANLEY SERVICES

Merger & Acquisitions

Morgan Stanley's Mergers and Acquisitions (M&A) department devises and executes innovative, customized solutions to our clients' most challenging issues. The M&A team excels in domestic and international transactions including acquisitions, divestitures, mergers, joint ventures, corporate restructurings, recapitalizations, spin-offs, exchange offers, leveraged buyouts and takeover defenses as well as shareholder relations. Morgan Stanley applies its extensive experience with global industries, regions and banking products to meet our clients' short- and long-term strategic objectives.

Global Capital Markets

Morgan Stanley's Global Capital Markets (GCM) division responds with market judgments and ingenuity to clients' needs for capital. Whether executing an IPO, a debt offering or a leveraged buyout, GCM integrates our expertise in Sales and Trading and in Investment Banking to offer clients seamless advice and sophisticated solutions. We originate, structure and execute public and private placement of a variety of securities: equities, investment-grade and non-investment-grade debt and related products.

Source: *Our Services*. Morgan Stanley. Web. 17 Jul. 2015.

Client Coverage Bankers

Bankers assigned to industry teams are required to become global experts in the industry and understand the strategic and financing objectives of their assigned companies. They help CEOs and CFOs focus on corporate strategic issues such as how to enhance shareholder value and reduce corporate risk. This sometimes leads to an M&A transaction in which clients sell the company or buy another company. Bankers also assist companies to achieve an optimal capital structure, with the appropriate amount of cash and debt on their balance sheet. This often leads to a capital markets transaction in which the company issues equity or debt, or repurchases outstanding securities. In short, client coverage bankers develop an in-depth understanding of a company's problems and objectives (within the context of their industry) and deliver the full resources of the investment bank in an effort to assist their clients. They are the key relationship managers and provide a centralized point of contact for corporate clients of the investment bank.

A financing or M&A assignment usually results in a partnership between client coverage bankers and product bankers to execute the transaction for a corporate client. Other investment banking services include risk management and hedging advice in relation to interest rate, energy, or FX risks; credit rating advice; and corporate-restructuring advice. There are product bankers who are responsible for each of these product areas (which are a much smaller source of revenue compared to the capital markets and M&A product areas). Sometimes, the role of the client coverage banker is to encourage a corporate client *not* to complete a transaction if it goes against the best interests of that client. The banker's mission is to become a trusted advisor to clients as they complete appropriate transactions that maximize shareholder value and minimize corporate risk.

For client coverage bankers to be helpful to their corporate clients, bankers must develop strong relationships with CEOs and CFOs, and also with corporate development and treasury groups. The corporate development group usually reports to the CFO, but sometimes directly to the CEO. Their role is to identify, analyze, and execute strategic transactions such as mergers, acquisitions, or divestitures. The treasury group reports to the CFO and focuses on acquiring and maintaining appropriate cash balances, achieving an optimal capital structure for the company and risk managing the company's balance sheet. This group also manages the company's relationship with credit-rating agencies. Exhibit 1.13 summarizes a client coverage banker's template for providing investment banking products and services to corporate clients.

Sometimes clients of the Investment Banking Division prefer being covered by bankers who work in geographical proximity to the client. As a result, some client coverage bankers may be assigned to cover clients based on a geographic coverage model rather than through an industry coverage model. Each investment bank attempts to coordinate the activities of industry coverage and geographic coverage bankers in an effort to meet client preferences and achieve operating efficiency for the bank.

EXHIBIT 1.13 INVESTMENT BANKER'S TEMPLATE[1]

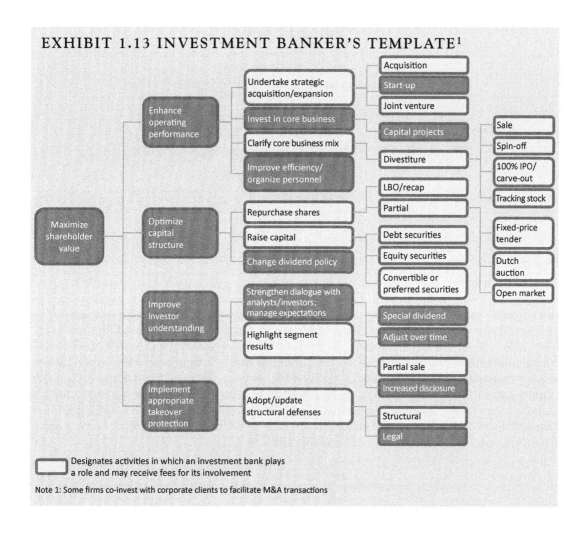

Designates activities in which an investment bank plays a role and may receive fees for its involvement

Note 1: Some firms co-invest with corporate clients to facilitate M&A transactions

Capital Markets Group

The Capital Markets Group is comprised of bankers who focus on either ECM or DCM.[1] At some investment banks, these two groups coordinate their activities and report to the same person, who oversees all capital markets transactions. At other banks, the two groups report to different individuals and remain fairly autonomous. The Capital Markets Group operates either as a joint venture between the Investment Banking Division and the Trading Division or is included solely within the Investment Banking Division. When issuers need to raise capital, they work with a team that comprises a client coverage banker and a capital markets banker. The capital markets banker "executes" the capital raising by determining pricing, timing, size, and other aspects of the transaction in conjunction with sales professionals and traders in the Trading Division who are responsible for creating investment products that meet the needs of their investing clients (see Exhibit 1.14).

EXHIBIT 1.14 CAPITAL MARKETS GROUP

Equity Capital Markets

ECM comprises bankers who specialize in common stock issuance, convertible security issuance, and equity derivatives. Common stock issuance includes initial public offerings (IPOs), follow-on offerings for companies that return to the capital markets for common stock offerings subsequent to issuing an IPO, secondary offerings for major shareholders of a company who wish to sell large "blocks" of common shares for which the proceeds are received by the selling shareholders and not by the company and private placements (which do not require registration with a regulator). Convertible security issuance (see Chapters 3 and 9) usually takes the form of a bond or preferred share offering, which can be converted (either mandatorily or at the investor's option) into a predetermined number of the issuer's common shares. Equity derivatives enable companies to raise or retire equity capital, or hedge equity risks, through the use of options and forward contracts.

---

[1] Banks may subdivide the capital markets group even further, for instance, by having a leveraged finance group that is separate from debt capital markets.

Bankers in ECM work closely with client coverage bankers to determine suitable corporate targets for equity-related products. After helping companies decide to complete an equity financing, ECM assumes primary responsibility for executing the transaction. This involves close coordination with sales and trading professionals in the Trading Division to determine the investment appetite of their client base, which includes institutional and individual investors. In essence, ECM intermediates between the Investment Banking Division's issuing clients who want to sell securities at the highest possible price and the Trading Division's investing clients who want to buy securities at the lowest possible price. This poses a challenge that requires considerable dexterity to balance competing interests and structure an optimal equity-related security.

ECM and client coverage bankers must consider many issues with their corporate clients before initiating a transaction, including credit rating impact and whether the offering will be "bought" by the investment bank (with the resale price risk born by the bank), or sold on an agency basis (with the price risk born by the issuer). In addition, they focus on capital structure impact (including cost of capital considerations), earnings per share dilution, likely share price impact, shareholder perceptions, use of proceeds and, if it is a "public offering", filing requirements with securities regulators, among other things. This process can take several weeks to several months to complete, depending on the vagaries of the market and potential issues raised by regulators.

Debt Capital Markets

Bankers in DCM focus principally on debt financings for corporate and government clients. Their clients can be grouped into two major categories: investment grade and noninvestment grade issuers. Investment grade issuers have a high credit rating from at least one of the major credit-rating agencies (Baa or stronger from Moody's; BBB- or stronger from Standard & Poor's). Noninvestment grade issuers have lower ratings and their debt offerings are sometimes called "junk bonds" or "high yield bonds".

DCM bankers stand between corporate or government issuers (with whom relationships are maintained by bankers in the Investment Banking Division) and investors (covered by sales professionals in the Trading Division). Their role is to find a balance between the competing price objectives of issuers and investors, while facilitating communication and providing execution of transactions.

Bankers in DCM work closely with client coverage bankers to determine suitable corporate and government issuer objectives and help clients decide timing, maturity, size, covenants, call features, and other aspects of a debt financing. Of critical importance is determination of the likely impact that a new debt offering will have on the issuer's credit ratings and investor reaction to a potential offering.

In the United States, DCM helps clients raise debt in the public capital markets through SEC-registered bond offerings or through privately placed 144A transactions (investors limited to qualified institutional investors). They also serve as the conduit through which a bank loan can be secured and provide debt risk management services (using derivatives) and advice regarding the potential credit rating impact of a debt issuance.

Merger and Acquisition Product Group

At some investment banks, the M&A Group is an independent group from the client coverage group while, at other banks, the two are blended. Regardless, most bankers specialize in one or more industries. Unlike the Capital Markets Group, which, at some firms, is a joint venture between the Investment Banking Division and the Trading Division, the M&A Group always falls under the sole responsibility of the Investment Banking Division.

The principal products of the M&A Group include (1) "Sell Side" transactions that involve the sale or merger of an entire company or disposition of a division (or assets) of a company; (2) "Buy Side" transactions that involve the purchase of an entire company or a division (or assets) of a company; (3) restructurings or reorganizations that focus on either carving out businesses from a company to enhance shareholder value or dramatically changing a company's capital structure to either avoid bankruptcy or facilitate a sell side transaction; and (4) hostile acquisition defense advisory services (see Exhibit 1.15).

EXHIBIT 1.15 MERGER & ACQUISITION PRODUCTS

Sell Side assignment	• Involves the sale, merger, or disposition of a company • Highest priority since higher probability of completion
Buy Side assignment	• Involves the purchase of a company • Lower priority since lower probability of completion
Merger of Equals (MOE)	• The merger of two companies of equal assets that have comparable market value
Joint Venture	• Two companies contribute assets and form a new entity to undertake economic activity together
Public Market Separation	• Includes carve-out, spin-off, and tracking stock • Completed in coordination with equity capital markets group
Hostile Defense	• Raid defense: defense against a specific take-over proposal • Anti-raid preparation: work to deter future unsolicited take-over activity • Advice to hostile bidders: strategic and tactical advice on initiating an unsolicited take-over

See Chapter 4 for a detailed description of these products

M&A bankers develop strong valuation analysis and negotiation skills, and they usually work directly with a company's CEO, CFO, and corporate development team. Fees are typically paid to M&A bankers only upon successful completion of a transaction (although in the case of buy side, restructuring, and defense advisory services, a nominal retainer fee may be charged during the period of the engagement).

TRADING DIVISION

The Trading Division is responsible for (1) all investment-related transactions with institutional investors, including financial institutions, investment funds, and the cash management arms of governments and corporations; (b) market-making and clearing activities on exchanges; and (3) subject to regulatory limitations, principal investments in debt, real estate and equity, and loans to clients made both directly and through managed funds. This division typically operates in three different business areas: Fixed Income, Currencies and Commodities; Equities; and Principal Investments and Loans. At some investment banks, Principal Investments and Loan activity is conducted from a different division. Research on economics, fixed income securities, commodities, and equities is also provided by the Trading Division to investing clients (see Chapter 6 for more information on the research function and its regulatory history).

Fixed Income, Currencies, and Commodities

FICC makes markets in and trades government bonds, corporate bonds, mortgage-related securities, asset-backed securities, currencies, and commodities (as well as derivatives on all of these products). At some firms, FICC is also involved in the provision of loans to certain corporate- and government-borrowing clients (in coordination with the Investment Banking Division). Subject to regulatory limitations, the business also engages in selected proprietary (nonclient-related) transactions in the same product areas. Individuals who work in the client-related area of FICC are either traders, who price these products and hold them in inventory as a risk position, or sales professionals, who market trade ideas and bring prices from the traders to investors to facilitate purchases and sales of the products.

Equities

The equities desk makes markets in and trades equities, equity-related products, and derivatives in relation to the bank's client-related activities. The business generates commissions from executing and clearing client transactions on global stock, option, and futures exchanges. Subject to regulatory limitations, equities also engages in selected proprietary (nonclient-related) transactions in the same product areas. As is the case in FICC, individuals who work in the client-related area of Equities are either traders or sales professionals.

Large investment banks typically have a Prime Brokerage business that provides bundled services such as securities borrowing and lending, financing (to facilitate leverage), asset custody, and clearing and settlement of trades to hedge fund clients and other money managers. Although initially an equity-centric business, Prime Brokerage has expanded its capabilities to other asset classes (in step with the diversification of strategies employed by hedge funds). Part of Prime Brokerage—related revenue comes from commissions from executing and clearing client trades by the sales and trading professionals in Equities. Other revenue sources include earning spreads and fees from financing and securities-lending activities. Refer to Chapter 5 for a more detailed discussion of Prime Brokerage and its services.

Investing Directly and With Clients in Private Equity and Hedge Funds

Large investment banks have historically invested in private equity and hedge fund assets either directly or by coinvesting in a fund offered to clients. For example, the Principal Investments and Asset Management businesses within Goldman Sachs historically invested in public and private companies through sponsorship of private equity funds in the same way as KKR, a large private equity firm, and in hedge fund assets in the same way as Och-Ziff, one of the largest hedge funds (see Exhibit 1.16). However, regulators in many countries now limit the amount of private equity and hedge fund investments by investment banks. For example, in the United States, the Dodd-Frank Act, which was passed in 2010, limits investment banks from holding more than 3% of any private equity fund or hedge fund and also requires that a bank's total private equity and hedge fund investments not exceed 3% of Tier 1 Capital.

EXHIBIT 1.16 GOLDMAN SACHS PRINCIPAL INVESTMENTS

Goldman Sachs Principal Investments as of Dec. 2015 $ in millions		
Investments	Fair Value of Investments	Unfunded Commitments
Private Equity Funds	$ 5,414	$ 2,057
Credit Funds	611	344
Hedge Funds	560	-
Real Estate Funds	1,172	296
Total	$ 7,757	$ 2,697

Goldman Sachs Principal Investments as of Dec. 2014 $ in millions		
Investments	Fair Value of Investments	Unfunded Commitments
Private Equity Funds	$ 6,307	$ 2,175
Credit Funds	1,008	383
Hedge Funds	863	-
Real Estate Funds	1,432	310
Total	$ 9,610	$ 2,868

Goldman Sachs Principal Investments as of Dec. 2013 $ in millions		
Investments	Fair Value of Investments	Unfunded Commitments
Private Equity Funds	$ 7,446	$ 2,575
Credit Funds	3,624	2,515
Hedge Funds	1,394	-
Real Estate Funds	1,908	471
Total	$ 14,372	$ 5,561

Source: Goldman Sachs 2015 and 2014 Annual Report

Proprietary Trading

In addition to investing directly and with clients as described above, most major investment banks have historically made short-term, nonclient-related investments in securities, commodities, and derivatives for their own account. This "proprietary" investment activity is similar to the investment activities of hedge funds. Indeed, investment banks' proprietary investing activities used to compete directly with hedge funds for investing and hedging opportunities worldwide.

During 2005 and 2006, investment banks' proprietary investing contributed in a significant way to robust Trading Division earnings. During 2007 and 2008, however, this trading activity caused very large losses at many banks. During the four quarter period ending in April 2008, investment banks suffered over $230 billion in proprietary trading losses. As these losses continued to grow during the rest of 2008, investment banks significantly curtailed their proprietary investment activity. Investment banks have experienced a number of scandals involving rogue traders who lost very large amounts of money while engaging in proprietary trading. For example, Jérôme Kerviel, a trader who had been working for Société Générale, lost approximately $7 billion in January 2008. A proprietary trading mishap also occurred at UBS in September 2011, when a trader lost approximately $2.3 billion from trading in futures contracts. The risk had been concealed by the trader's creation of fictitious hedging positions. In the United States, the Dodd-Frank Act of 2010 significantly curtailed the proprietary trading activities of investment banks, and many other countries have similarly imposed restrictions on this activity.

ASSET MANAGEMENT DIVISION

The Asset Management business offers investment products in the following areas: equity, fixed income, currency and commodity, alternative assets (private equity, hedge funds, and real estate), and money markets investment products to individuals and institutions. Investments are offered in the form of mutual funds, private investment funds, or separately managed accounts and are sometimes commingled with the bank's own investments. Revenues are created principally based on fees that are paid by investors as a percentage of assets under management (AUM), which varies depending on the asset class. At times, investors pay an incentive fee to the investment bank when returns exceed a predetermined benchmark. Most firms have a private wealth management business organized alongside the asset management business that reports to the same division head (see Exhibit 1.17). The professionals in the private wealth management business act as advisors to investors, helping them decide how to invest their cash resources. In most cases (but not all), investors will be encouraged to invest in funds managed by the firm's asset management teams. However, advisors have a fiduciary obligation to direct investments into the funds (internal or external) that best meet the risk and return objectives of investors. Chapter 6 provides a more detailed discussion of the asset management business.

EXHIBIT 1.17 ASSET MANAGEMENT

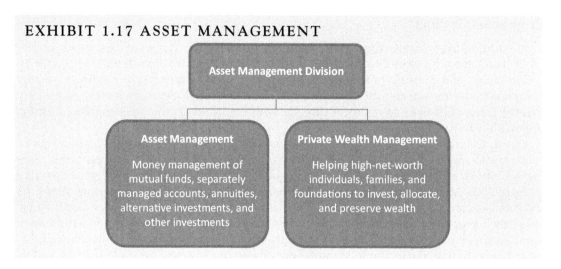

Coinvestments in Asset Management Division Funds

Investment banks make direct investments in certain funds that are managed by their Asset Management Division. Most of these investments are made in the "Alternative Assets" area: (1) private equity (LBOs and other equity control investments), (2) hedge fund-type investments, and (3) real estate. Investment banks typically invest their own capital alongside the capital of their high net worth individual and institutional clients in these funds (and they charge investing clients both management fees and performance fees based on the clients' AUM). This coinvesting activity, however, is limited to 3% of any fund and is subject to total investments in these areas not exceeding 3% of Tier 1 Capital, as described above.

Regulation of the Securities Industry

INTRODUCTION

Activities of investment banks impact the global economy and are very important to the smooth functioning of capital markets. Given their significance, it is no surprise that the business of investment banking has been subject to a great deal of government regulation. This chapter discusses the regulatory environment of investment banking. In US Regulations section, historical investment banking regulation in the United States is discussed. Section Recent Developments in Securities Regulations looks at more recent events and regulations. Section Securities Regulations in Other Countries summarizes the regulatory environment in the United Kingdom, Japan, and China.

US REGULATIONS

Early Investment Banking

The essence of what an investment bank does in its underwriting business is to act as an intermediary between issuers and investors so that one party can gain access to capital, while the other party can preserve and grow wealth. These underwriting services were essential to the foundation and development of the United States. George Washington, the first president of the United States, took office in 1789. Already at this time the federal government had incurred $27 million of debt, and the states had debts totaling $25 million. Alexander Hamilton, the first US treasury secretary, persuaded Congress and President Washington to assume the state debt and issue bonds to finance this obligation, in spite of strong opposition from Thomas Jefferson. Investment bankers played a role in negotiating the terms and conditions of these bonds.

The underwriting function grew significantly after the US revolution. The firms conducting these premodern investment banking activities were referred to as "loan contractors." Their services were to guarantee issuers' security offerings and sell them to investors, hopefully at a profit. The loan contractors' business was performed by speculators, merchants, and by some commercial banks. In addition, professional auctioneers were often intermediaries in the sale of investment products, taking bids from buyers and offers from sellers. Finally, there were private bankers and stockbrokers who also performed the functions of modern day investment banks.

As the new country began to spread over a vast continent, technological innovation fed into the industrial revolution. The benefits from increased economies of scale made large projects essential and profitable. Large-scale implementation of new technologies allowed for the extraction of natural resources, which created a need for trains to transport people and resources between cities. This and many other activities required capital that no individual or firm could afford alone. As a result, a more formal version of investment banking developed to intermediate between firms needing capital and individuals desiring to build wealth. By underwriting securities, investment banks made it possible for many investors to pool together their wealth to meet the great capital needs of a growing nation.

Industrial growth created a new class of wealthy industrialists and bankers who helped finance their empires. During this period, investment bankers operated in a regulatory vacuum and were largely free to respond as they saw fit to changing market forces. The practices they developed brought them power and influence. From 1879 to 1893, the mileage of railroads in the United States tripled, and the financing of railroad bonds and stocks rose from $4.8 to $9.9 billion, keeping investment bankers busy underwriting new issues. At the same time, other industrial growth was emerging that required family-owned businesses with limited resources to incorporate to raise more capital than could otherwise be obtained. This led to the use of investment banking services by an ever-increasing number of companies. The demand for capital had grown, and at the same time, so had the supply of capital, including capital provided by foreigners, which more than doubled from $1.4 to $3.3 billion between 1870 and 1890.

The Growth of Investment Banking

Investment banking practices expanded further in the period between 1890 and 1925. During this era, banks were highly concentrated and the industry was largely run by an oligopoly, which included J.P. Morgan & Co.; Kuhn, Loeb & Co.; Brown Brothers; and Kidder, Peabody & Co. During this period, the United States did not require separation between commercial and investment banks, which meant deposits from the commercial banking side of the business often provided an in-house supply of capital to deploy in the bank's underwriting projects.

From 1926 to 1929 equity issuance jumped from $0.6 to $4.4 billion, while bond issuance decreased, as companies increasingly took advantage of a seemingly unstoppable rise in the stock market by preferring equity issuance over debt.

Limited Regulation

During the investment environment of the first three decades of the 20th century, the lack of regulation, strong demand for securities, and fierce competition resulted in weak internal controls within banks. Despite their previous attempts at self-regulation, banks could not prevent scandals. In response to growing criticism and societal desire for industry regulation, the banking industry formed the Investment Bankers Association of America (IBAA) in 1912 as a splinter group of the American Bankers Association. One of the ideas established by the IBAA was the concept of nonprice discrimination in the sale of securities, regardless of the investor and transaction size. Although there was limited federal regulation of investment banks before the Great Depression started in 1929, banks had to adhere to state securities laws or "blue sky" laws. The first blue sky law was enacted in Kansas in 1911. Among other features, it required that no security issued in the state could be offered without previously obtaining a permit by the state's Bank Commissioner. Between 1911 and 1933, 47 states enacted similar state laws regulating the issuance of new securities (all of the existing states at the time except Nevada). As federal regulations were enacted in the 1930s and 1940s, the state laws remained on the books, whereas the federal laws mostly duplicated and extended the blue sky laws. The passage of the National Securities Markets Improvement Act by Congress in

1996 effectively removed states from securities regulation of investment banks, except for antifraud matters.

On October 28, 1929, referred to as Black Monday, a precipitous fall in the stock market began. In spite of the 1929 crash and the ensuing economic malaise, President Herbert Hoover did not promote any meaningful new regulation of the financial markets. In contrast, Franklin Roosevelt, who became president in 1933, took an active approach to economic difficulties and instituted a variety of regulations that shaped the financial sector, investment banks in particular, for the remainder of the century. At Roosevelt's urging, Congress passed seven pieces of legislation that significantly impacted the business of investment banking.

Three of these laws, the 1933 Securities Act, the 1933 Glass–Steagall Act, and the 1934 Securities Exchange Act, drastically altered the business environment in which investment banks practiced. The next portion of this section will go into detail regarding the regulatory requirements found in these three pieces of legislation. The other four legislative acts that impacted investment banking to a lesser extent will also be briefly covered. Finally, more recent legislation, including the Gramm–Leach–Bliley and Sarbanes–Oxley Acts, as well as the regulatory response to the Bear Stearns collapse, Lehman Brothers' bankruptcy and economic crisis of 2007–09 will be addressed, focusing in particular on the Dodd–Frank Act of 2010.

The Securities Act of 1933

The Securities Act of 1933 was meant to bring stability to capital markets and stop manipulative and deceptive practices in the sale or distribution of financial securities. The Securities and Exchange Commission (SEC) states that the 1933 Act had two purposes: "[to] require that investors receive financial and other significant information concerning securities being offered for public sale; and prohibit deceit, misrepresentations, and other fraud in the sale of securities." To fulfill these objectives, the 1933 Act required investment banks that participated in the distribution of securities to disclose a significant amount of relevant and important details regarding securities and the firms they represented. Prior to the enactment of this law, few investors received basic information regarding their investments. The new law set a minimal requirement for providing information and ensured that all potential investors could access relevant issuer records.

The 1933 Act has four main sections of regulation that impact investment banks. The relevant sections relate to: submitting a registration statement to the SEC; providing an investment prospectus to potential investors; assuming civil and criminal liability for disclosure; and having a postfiling waiting period before selling issues to the public.

The Registration Statement

Before a security can be sold in the United States, certain information regarding the issuer and the securities being issued must be provided to regulators and prospective investors through a filing with the SEC. Exhibit 2.1 is an abridged list of information regarding the issuer and the issuance that must be included in the registration statement.

There are certain exceptions or exclusions from the registration requirements of the 1933 Act. These include: when the issuance will only be offered intrastate, making it solely the jurisdiction of state laws; when the issuance of securities is by a municipality, a state, or the federal government; when the offering is below a certain value cutoff; and when the offering is made privately or is made to a small number of investors. Generally, the 1933 Act provides for certain exceptions based on the type of security that is offered (security-based exceptions) and for certain exceptions based on the type of offering (transaction-based exceptions).

EXHIBIT 2.1 INFORMATION REQUIRED IN THE REGISTRATION BY THE 1933 ACT

- Summary information, risk factors, and ratio of earnings to fixed charges,
- Use of proceeds,
- Dilution,
- Selling security holders (if any),
- Plan of distribution,
- Description of securities to be registered,
- Interests of named experts and counsel,
- Information with respect to the registrant,
  - Description of business,
  - Audited financial information,
  - Description of property,
  - Legal proceedings,
  - Market price of and dividends on the registrant's common equity and related stockholder matters,
  - Management's discussion and analysis of financial condition and results of operations,
  - Changes in and disagreements with accountants on accounting and financial disclosure,
  - Quantitative and qualitative disclosures about market risk,
  - Directors and executive officers,
  - Executive compensation,
  - Corporate governance,
  - Security ownership of certain beneficial owners and management,
  - Transactions with related persons, promoters, and certain control persons,
- Material changes,
- Disclosure of commission position on indemnification for securities act liabilities,

Source: U.S. Securities and Exchange Commission.

The Investment Prospectus

Companies are required to provide investors with a prospectus, which contains certain of the information included in the registration statement. The securities cannot be distributed until after the issue has been registered with the SEC. Any known misstatement or omission of material information from the registration statement is a criminal offense and can leave the issuer and underwriter liable to investor lawsuits.

New Liabilities

Before the 1933 Act, there were no special laws assigning liability to investment bankers beyond those that applied to the activities of all citizens. After the 1933 Act was enacted, investment bankers became liable for securities law violation if "material facts" are omitted from the registration statement, and investors suffer a loss that is attributable to that omission. If this occurs, investors can sue the banks to repurchase their shares at the original price and rescind the transaction. Underwriters' liabilities were broadly defined since, as intermediaries between issuers and investors, banks have more information than do investors regarding a company. To mitigate their liability, bankers seek to be indemnified by the issuers for any losses (including any costs associated with litigation) arising from material misstatements or omissions, resulting in a shared responsibility to provide accurate and complete information to purchasers of securities. See Exhibit 2.2 for sample indemnification language found in underwriting agreements.

EXHIBIT 2.2 SAMPLE INDEMNIFICATION SECTION FROM UNDERWRITING AGREEMENTS

Indemnification

The Company agrees to indemnify and hold harmless the Underwriters and each person, if any, who controls the Underwriters within the meaning of Section 15 of the Securities Act or Section 20(a) of the Exchange Act against any and all losses, liabilities, claims, damages and expenses as incurred (including but not limited to reasonable attorneys' fees and any and all reasonable expenses incurred in investigating, preparing or defending against any litigation, commenced or threatened, or any claim, and subject to subsection [ ] of this Section, any and all amounts paid in settlement of any claim or litigation), joint or several, to which they or any of them may become subject under the Securities Act, the Exchange Act or any other federal or state statutory law or regulation, at common law or otherwise, insofar as such losses, liabilities, claims, damages or expenses (or actions in respect thereof) arise out of or are based on any untrue statement or alleged untrue statement of a material fact contained in the Prospectus, or any amendment or supplement thereto, or arise out of or are based on the omission or alleged omission to state therein a material fact required to be stated therein or necessary to make the statements therein not misleading; provided, however, that the Issuers will not be liable in any such case to the extent but only to the extent that any such loss, liability, claim, damage or expense arises out of or is based on any such untrue statement or alleged untrue statement or omission or alleged omission made therein in reliance on and in conformity with written information furnished to the Issuers relating to the Underwriters by the Underwriters expressly for use therein. This indemnity agreement will be in addition to any liability that the Issuers may otherwise have included under this Agreement.

Source: Jenner & Block LLP.

One impact of the law has been a greater distinction between underwriters and dealers or selling group members. In general, an underwriter refers to the party that works directly with an issuer and agrees to purchase a new securities issue. A dealer is the party that works with the end investors and sells securities that are on an underwriter's books. These functions were originally intertwined, but because dealers are not liable under the 1933 Act, to some extent, the two functions have separated to limit further the entities exposed to liabilities and to reduce the likelihood for a civil liability suit.

Due Diligence

Due diligence is the practice of reviewing information about an issuer in an effort to mitigate risk. Due diligence is conducted in connection with most securities offerings, with most acquisitions and with many other transactions. To avoid being held liable for false or misleading disclosure in a registration statement, an underwriter must conduct an investigation "reasonably calculated to reveal all those facts [that] would be of interest to a reasonably prudent investor." What is appropriate will be determined based on the facts and circumstances of each offering and then only in hindsight. Exhibit 2.3 summarizes six proposed practices to be included in an underwriter's due diligence effort. Exhibit 2.4 summarizes factors considered by courts when they review an underwriter's due diligence activity.

EXHIBIT 2.3 SIX PROPOSED PRACTICES TO BE INCLUDED IN AN UNDERWRITER'S DUE DILIGENCE EFFORT

- Whether the underwriter received the registration statement and conducted a reasonable inquiry into any fact or circumstance that would cause a reasonable person to question whether the registration statement contains an untrue statement of a material fact or omits to state a material fact required to be stated therein or necessary to make the statements therein not misleading;
- Whether the underwriter has discussed the information contained in the registration statement with the relevant executive officers of the registrant (including, at minimum, the CFO or Chief Financial Officer), and the CFO (or his/her designee) has certified that s/he has examined the registration statement and that, to the best of his/her knowledge, it does not contain any untrue statement of a material fact or omit to state a material fact required to be stated therein or necessary to make the statements therein not misleading;
- Whether the underwriter has received Statements on Auditing Standards 100 comfort letter from the issuer's auditors;
- Whether the underwriter received a 10b-5 negative assurance from issuer's counsel;
- Whether the underwriter employed counsel that, after reviewing the issuer's registration statement, Exchange Act filings, and other information, provided a 10b-5 negative assurance; and
- Whether the underwriter employed and consulted a research analyst that:
  - Has followed the issuer or the issuer's industry on an ongoing basis for at least 6 months immediately before the commencement of the offering; and
  - Has issued a report on the issuer or its industry within the 12 months immediately before the commencement of the offering.

Source: Morrison & Foerster LLP.

EXHIBIT 2.4 FACTORS CONSIDERED BY COURTS WHEN REVIEWING AN UNDERWRITER'S DUE DILIGENCE ACTIVITY

- Reasonable reliance on expertized portions of a registration statement (such as certified financial statements)
- Investigation in response to a "red flag," including independent verification (management interviews; site visits; customer calls; receipt of written verification from the issuer, issuer's counsel, underwriter's counsel, and the auditors; familiarity with the issuer's industry; a review of the issuer's internal documents; and an interview with independent auditors)
- Updating information through the offering date, including updating information contained in the issuer's Exchange Act reports (bring-down diligence)
- Documentation of diligence investigation

Source: Morrison & Foerster LLP.

Gun-Jumping Rules

Securities offerings can be divided into three stages under the 1933 Act:

1. The "prefiling period" begins with the decision to proceed with an offering and ends with the filing of the registration statement.
2. The "waiting period" is the period between the filing and effectiveness of the registration statement.
3. The "posteffective period" is the period after the registration statement has been declared effective by the SEC (sales of securities can be made during this period).

Prior to reforms promulgated during 2005, oral and written offers by any issuer were prohibited during the waiting period (that also is called the "quiet period"). During the quiet period, oral or written offers, but not sales, could be made and any offers made in writing could only be made by means of a prospectus that conformed to the requirements of the 1933 Act. This prospectus is typically called a "red herring" prospectus (because of the red legend on the first page that reminds investors that the information contained in the prospectus is "preliminary"). Violations of these basic restrictions are referred to as "gun-jumping" and may result in an SEC-imposed "cooling-off" period, rescission rights to purchasers in the public offering, and class action or other litigation.

The securities offerings reforms enacted in 2005 provide safe harbors for communications made more than 30 days before filing a registration statement that do not reference a securities offering, for the regular release of "factual business information" and, in the case of reporting issuers, for certain "forward-looking information." For certain large issuers that meet minimum size standards and are followed by sophisticated investors and research analysts (called Well-Known Seasoned Issuers, or, "WKSIs"), unrestricted oral or written offers are permitted before a registration statement is filed without violating gun-jumping provisions. For all issuers, the use of "free writing prospectuses" following the filing of a registration statement, which may include information that goes beyond (but may not be inconsistent with) the information in the prospectus, is permitted. This avoids the need to file a more formal and time-consuming prospectus supplement or amendment to the registration statement when new information needs to be disclosed. In summary, with the exception of the favorable treatment given to WKSIs, the regime governing dissemination of information during the offering process remains largely unchanged since 1933, although simplified to reflect technological advances and changes in the capital markets, and issuers must be careful how they communicate before and during the offering process to avoid actions that could be deemed to be conditioning the market. See Exhibit 2.5 for a summary of the 1933 Act.

EXHIBIT 2.5 SECURITIES ACT OF 1933

Often referred to as the "truth in securities" law, the Securities Act of 1933 has two basic objectives:
• Require that investors receive financial and other significant information concerning securities being offered for public sale; and
• Prohibit deceit, misrepresentations, and other fraud in the sale of securities.

Purpose of Registration

• A primary means of accomplishing these goals is the disclosure of important financial information through the registration of securities. This information enables investors, not the government, to make informed judgments about whether to purchase a company's securities. While the Securities and Exchange Commission (SEC) requires that the information provided be accurate, it does not guarantee the accuracy of the information. Investors who purchase securities and suffer losses have important recovery rights if they can prove that there was incomplete or inaccurate disclosure of important information.

The Registration Process

• In general, securities sold in the United States must be registered. The registration forms that companies file provide essential facts while minimizing the burden and expense of complying with the law. In general, registration forms call for:
  • a description of the company's properties and business;
  • a description of the security to be offered for sale;
  • information about the management of the company; and
  • financial statements certified by independent accountants.
• Registration statements and prospectuses become public shortly after filing with the SEC. If filed by US domestic companies, the statements are available on the Electronic Data Gathering, Analysis, and Retrieval (EDGAR) database accessible at www.sec.gov. Registration statements are subject to examination for compliance with disclosure requirements. Not all offerings of securities must be registered with the SEC. Some exemptions from the registration requirement include:
  • private offerings to a limited number of persons or institutions;
  • offerings of limited size;
  • intrastate offerings; and
  • securities of municipal, state, and federal governments.

Source: U.S. Securities and Exchange Commission.

The Glass–Steagall Act (Formally, the Banking Act of 1933)

Another legislative response to the stock market crash of 1929 and the collapse of numerous banks thereafter was passage of the Glass–Steagall Act, which was signed into law on June 16, 1933. The Glass–Steagall Act was a large piece of regulation that, among other things, separated commercial and investment banks and created the Federal Deposit Insurance Corporation (FDIC), which insured depositors' assets in the event of a bank's default (originally for up to $2500; today it is for up to $250,000). This Act had a significant effect on investment banking since it required the industry to alter its operations and the structure of its firms, changed the process for distribution and underwriting of securities, and cut off a key source of capital for new security underwriting.

During the Great Depression, over 11,000 banks closed or merged: one out of every four banks that existed in 1929 was no longer operating by 1934. Before the Glass–Steagall Banking Act, there was no required separation between underwriting, investment, and depository banking services. A bank could (and did) take in deposits from checking account holders and use that money to invest in securities it was underwriting for its own in-house investment activities. Given this situation, the safety of a depositor's assets was in doubt, especially since there was no FDIC insurance to guarantee repayment. The Glass–Steagall Act was a response to this unstable environment.

Separation of Private Banks Into Deposit and Investment Banks

Private banks were able to both accept deposits and perform the functions of an investment bank prior to the Glass–Steagall Act. The Act required private banks to choose to be either a private depository bank or an investment bank.

Separation of Commercial and Investment Banks

Commercial banks, like private banks, were both accepting deposits and engaging in the functions of investment banking. After the Glass–Steagall Act was passed, investment banking functions that a commercial bank could perform were substantially reduced and their underwriting capacity was severely limited. They were only allowed to underwrite or "agent" bond offerings for municipal, state, and federal government bodies. Those banks that chose commercial banking over investment banking either spun off their investment banking business (for example, J.P. Morgan & Co. decided to operate as a commercial bank and spun off its investment banking arm to form Morgan Stanley in 1935), or drastically cut staff. In addition, commercial banks were limited to earning no more than 10% of total income from securities transactions, not including an exemption for the underwriting of government-issued bonds.

Separation of Directors and Officers From Commercial Banks and Security Firms

Partners and officials of firms associated with security investments were restricted from serving as directors or officers of commercial banks.

All of these changes had the same goal: to ensure that resources from depositors were protected from being unknowingly put at risk. However, as described later in this chapter, the Glass–Steagall Act was overturned by the Gramm–Leach–Bliley Act in 1999, which once again allowed banks to conduct both investment banking and commercial banking activities if these activities operated under a holding company structure.

Securities Exchange Act of 1934

A supplement to the Securities Act of 1933, the Securities Exchange Act of 1934 was the third and final expansive law passed during the Roosevelt presidency that reshaped the investment banking industry. This Act is sometimes referred to as the Exchange Act. Passed on June 6, 1934, the new law dealt primarily with the supervision of new security offerings, ongoing reporting requirements for these offerings, and the conduct of exchanges. The law also significantly changed the secondary market for securities by requiring minimal reporting standards and codifying rules for transactions. In addition, it required that exchanges be governed by self-regulatory organizations (SROs). NYSE Euronext and NASDAQ, the two largest US exchanges, are SROs.

The Exchange Act also created the SEC, which took over responsibility of supervising the capital markets, including the supervision of investment banks. To carry out its mission, the SEC was provided with broad powers to enact and enforce new regulations on exchanges, investment banks, broker/dealers, and traders to protect the safety and soundness of the securities business. The SEC is responsible for carrying out and enforcing the Securities Act of 1933; it regulates activities on the exchanges and adopts rules and procedures for its members to follow, and it prohibits manipulative practices such as wash sales and matched orders, while setting strict standards for short-selling and stop-loss orders. The role of the SEC in capital markets cannot be overstated. It continually makes adjustments to prior rules and regulations to minimize the potential for unfair undertakings while promoting the efficiency of the capital markets. In addition, the SEC maintains flexibility to keep up with the regulation of new types of securities and financial products. See Exhibit 2.6 for a summary of the Exchange Act.

EXHIBIT 2.6 SECURITIES EXCHANGE ACT OF 1934

With this Act, Congress created the Securities and Exchange Commission (SEC). The Act empowers the SEC with broad authority over all aspects of the securities industry. This includes the power to register, regulate, and oversee brokerage firms, transfer agents, and clearing agencies as well as the nation's self-regulatory organizations (SROs), including securities exchanges such as NYSE Euronext and NASDAQ.

The Act also identifies and prohibits certain types of conduct in the markets and provides the SEC with disciplinary powers over regulated entities and persons associated with them.

The Act also empowers the SEC to require periodic reporting of information by companies with publicly traded securities.

Corporate Reporting

Companies with more than $10 million in assets whose securities are held by more than 500 owners must file annual and other periodic reports. These reports are available to the public through the SEC's EDGAR database. Other companies that are not required to file may voluntarily choose to do so.

Continued

EXHIBIT 2.6 SECURITIES EXCHANGE ACT OF 1934—cont'd

Proxy Solicitations

The Securities Exchange Act also governs the disclosure in materials used to solicit shareholder votes in annual or special meetings held for the election of directors and the approval of other corporate actions. This information, contained in proxy materials, must be filed with the SEC in advance of any solicitation to ensure compliance with the disclosure rules. Solicitations, whether by management or shareholder groups, must disclose all important facts concerning the issues on which holders are asked to vote.

Significant Ownership Stakes and Tender Offers

The Securities Exchange Act requires disclosure of important information by anyone seeking to acquire more than 5% of a company's securities by direct purchase or tender offer. Such an offer often is extended in an effort to gain control of the company. As with the proxy rules, this allows shareholders to make informed decisions on these critical corporate events. The Act also requires holders of a significant amount of a public security to file certain regular reports to inform nonaffiliated shareholders about potential ownership changes.

Insider Trading

The securities laws broadly prohibit fraudulent activities of any kind in connection with the offer, purchase, or sale of securities. These provisions are the basis for many types of disciplinary actions, including actions against fraudulent insider trading. Insider trading is illegal when a person trades a security while in possession of material nonpublic information in violation of a duty to withhold the information or refrain from trading.

Source: U.S. Securities and Exchange Commission.

Investment Company Act of 1940

The Investment Company Act of 1940 describes what constitutes an investment company (including its best-known form, a mutual fund) and separates the functions of investment banks and investment companies. This Act sets out restrictions on the number of investment bankers

EXHIBIT 2.7 INVESTMENT COMPANY ACT OF 1940

This Act regulates the organization of companies, including mutual funds, that engage primarily in investing, reinvesting, and trading in securities, and whose own securities are offered to the investing public. The regulation is designed to minimize conflicts of interest that arise in these complex operations. The Act requires these companies to disclose their financial condition and investment policies to investors when stock is initially sold and, subsequently, on a regular basis. The focus of this Act is on disclosure to the investing public of information about the fund and its investment objectives, as well as on investment company structure and operations. It is important to remember that the Act does not permit the Securities and Exchange Commission (SEC) to directly supervise the investment decisions or activities of these companies or judge the merits of their investments.

Source: U.S. Securities and Exchange Commission.

who can serve as directors of an investment company and restricts business transactions between investment banks and investment companies. See Exhibit 2.7 for a summary of this Act.

RECENT DEVELOPMENTS IN SECURITIES REGULATIONS

After World War II little happened with regard to major legislation impacting investment banks in the United States for almost 60 years. This section discusses recent changes in regulation, including the Gramm–Leach–Bliley Act, the Sarbanes–Oxley Act, and the Dodd–Frank Act.

Gramm–Leach–Bliley Act

On November 12, 1999 the US Congress passed the Gramm–Leach–Bliley Act, which overturned the mandatory separation of commercial banks and investment banks required by the Glass–Steagall Act of 1933. This legislation is also referred to as the Financial Services Modernization Act. The original reason for the separation was the concern that depositors' holdings would be used aggressively in risky investments by the investment banking side of the firms. The argument for joining the two types of firms is that it would provide a more stable business model irrespective of the economic environment. In poor economic environments, people tend to hold on to cash, which drives up commercial banking deposit revenues, thereby providing a balance to a slow new securities issuance market. On the other hand, in a booming economy, cash deposits are low, but new issuance activity is high.

Another argument for rejoining investment banks and commercial banks was that non-US headquartered universal banks, such as Deutsche Bank, UBS, and Credit Suisse, were not encumbered by the Glass–Steagall Act. These banks had a competitive advantage over US headquartered commercial banks, such as Citigroup, JPMorgan Chase, Bank of America, and stand-alone investment banks, such as Goldman Sachs and Morgan Stanley, because the non-US headquartered banks could participate in both commercial banking and investment banking activities.

The separation of commercial and investment banks had already been gradually weakened over the years, and the Gramm–Leach–Bliley Act was the final step. As early as 1986, the Federal Reserve allowed bank-holding companies to participate in the underwriting of corporate issues, whereas they were previously restricted to only government debt underwriting. The Fed required that this nongovernment underwriting activity could represent no more than 10% of a commercial bank's total revenues. In 1996 this was further weakened by increasing the revenue limit from 10% to 25%. Finally, in 1999 the remaining restrictions were relaxed through passage of the Gramm–Leach–Bliley Act. This Act allowed Citigroup, formed through the merger of Citicorp and Travelers Group in 1998, to keep the investment banking business that was a part of Travelers Group. It also enabled commercial bank Chase Manhattan Bank to merge with J.P. Morgan & Co. in 2000.

The regulatory environment of banks also changed with this Act. Commercial banks were already regulated by the Federal Reserve (among other regulators, depending on the specific type of commercial bank). The Act, however, failed to give the SEC (or any other agency) direct authority to regulate large investment bank-holding companies. Without explicit statutory authority over these institutions, the SEC created the Consolidated Supervised Entities (CSE) program in 2004 pursuant to which investment bank holding companies were subject to voluntary regulation by the SEC, as an attempt to fill this regulatory gap. As a result of the financial crises that led to the conversion of the remaining US pure-play investment banks (Goldman Sachs and Morgan Stanley) into bank holding companies during the fall of 2008, the CSE program was no longer necessary and was, therefore, ended in September 2008. The Federal Reserve now shares with the SEC principal regulatory oversight of all investment banking activities in the United States.

Sarbanes–Oxley Act

The Sarbanes–Oxley Act of 2002 produced a sweeping change in regulation that impacted corporate governance, disclosure, and conflicts of interests. Although this bill was expansive, its impact on investment banking was less significant than its impact on auditors and public companies and their boards of directors.

The principal impact of this Act on investment banking related to research and due diligence. The Act required the SEC to adopt rules to minimize the risk of investment bankers influencing equity analysts' research reports by separating stock analysis from underwriting activities. For example, analysts' compensation could no longer be based on investment banking underwriting revenues and analysts who provided a negative report of a company were protected from retaliation by bankers who are responsible for underwriting activities.

The Sarbanes–Oxley Act had several other broad implications that impacted the regulatory environment of securities markets. It created the Public Company Accounting Oversight Board to set accounting rules and standards and also reduced the influence of auditors on corporate decision-making. Outside auditors' independence was more carefully defined to avoid conflicts of interest. Top executives of the corporations were required to personally certify that information made available to investors was accurate by signing a statement accompanying quarterly and annual filings. Loans to insiders (employees or others with close ties to the firm) were restricted and additional disclosures were required by issuers, including off-balance sheet transactions. In addition, the Act criminalized certain activities and created more responsibilities for the audit committee of the board, while imposing a significant new layer of costs to enable compliance. See Exhibit 2.8 for a summary of the Sarbanes–Oxley Act.

EXHIBIT 2.8 SUMMARY OF THE SARBANES–OXLEY ACT OF 2002

Restoring Confidence in the Accounting Profession

- The Act established the Public Company Accounting Oversight Board
- Section 108(b)—The Securities and Exchange Commission (SEC) recognized the Financial Accounting Standards Board as the accounting standard setter.
- Title II—The SEC adopted rules improving the independence of outside auditors.
- Section 303—The SEC adopted rules forbidding the improper influence on outside auditors.

Improving the "Tone at the Top"

- Section 302—The SEC adopted rules requiring CEOs and CFOs to certify financial and other information in their companies' quarterly and annual reports.
- Section 306—The SEC adopted rules prohibiting company officers from trading during pension fund blackout periods.

EXHIBIT 2.8 SUMMARY OF THE SARBANES–OXLEY ACT OF 2002—cont'd

- Section 402—This section prohibits companies from making loans to insiders
- Section 406—The SEC adopted rules requiring companies to disclose whether they have a code of ethics for their CEO, CFO, and senior accounting personnel.

Improving Disclosure and Financial Reporting

- Section 401(a)—The SEC adopted rules requiring disclosure of all material off-balance sheet transactions.
- Section 401(b)—The SEC adopted Regulation G, governing the use of non-GAAP financial measures, including disclosure and reconciliation requirements.
- Section 404—The SEC adopted rules requiring an annual management report on and auditor attestation of a company's internal controls over financial reporting.

Improving the Performance of "Gatekeepers"

- Section 407—The SEC adopted rules requiring the disclosure about financial experts on audit committees.
- Section 501—The SEC approved new SRO rules governing research analyst conflicts of interest.

Enhancing Enforcement Tools

- Section 305—This section sets standards for imposing officer and director bars and penalties.
- Section 704—The SEC issued a study of enforcement actions involving violations of reporting requirements and restatements.
- Section 1105—This section gives the SEC the authority in administrative proceedings to prohibit persons from serving as officers or directors.

Source: U.S. Securities and Exchange Commission.

Regulation Analyst Certification

The SEC adopted new legislation in 2003 to bring more accountability to research analysts. Regulation Analyst Certification (Regulation AC) requires research analysts to "certify the truthfulness of the views they express in research reports and public appearances, and disclose whether they have received any compensation related to the specific recommendations or views expressed in those reports and appearances," for both equity and debt securities. For research reports distributed to US persons, the analyst must certify that (1) the views expressed in the research report accurately reflect the research analyst's personal views about the subject securities and issuers; and (2) either (a) no part of the analyst's compensation was, is, or will be directly or indirectly related to the specific recommendations or views contained in the research report or (b) part or all of the analyst's compensation was, is, or will be directly or indirectly related to the specific recommendations or views contained in the research report. If the latter, the certification statement must then include the source, amount, and purpose of such compensation and include cautionary language that it may influence the analyst's recommendation in the research report.

Global Research Settlement

On April 28, 2003, the SEC and other regulators (Regulators) announced enforcement actions against the 10 largest investment banking firms (Investment Banks). Regulators charged that the Investment Banking Division of Investment Banks had undue influence over equity research analysts, thereby affecting the objectivity of their investment opinions. In addition, Regulators charged that these conflicts of interest were not adequately managed or disclosed to investors.

The Investment Banks, who did not admit to or deny the charges brought against them, agreed to settle with the Regulators for approximately $1.4 billion. In addition to agreeing to pay this amount, the Investment Banks agreed to a number of reforms:

1. Structural reforms: the Investment Banks would comply with significant restrictions relating to interaction between the Investment Banking Division and equity research department.
2. Enhanced disclosures: additional disclosures would be made to recipients of research reports regarding (among other things) potential conflicts of interest resulting from investment banking activities.
3. Independent research: the Investment Banks would contract with independent, third party research firms to make available to US customers these independent research firms' report.

Finally, outside of research, the Investment Banks also voluntarily agreed to restrict allocations of securities in "hot" IPOs (offerings that begin trading in the secondary market at a premium) to certain company executive officers and directors, a practice known as "spinning." See Chapter 6 for further discussion regarding this enforcement action and the role of equity research.

Dodd–Frank Act

The Dodd–Frank Wall Street Reform and Consumer Protection Act was signed into US law on July 21, 2010, the culmination of a comprehensive legislative reform effort that followed the financial crisis of 2007–08. This Act is the most far-reaching regulatory change to the financial services industry since 1934. It contains 16 provisions and the Volcker Rule and is mainly focused on protecting consumers, ending "too big to fail" bailouts, improving coordination between various regulatory agencies, identifying systemic risk early, creating greater transparency for complex financial instruments, and providing greater transparency for executive compensation, as described in more detail below.

Changes in Financial Oversight

Historically, several government agencies were responsible for regulating financial institutions, which led to regulatory gaps. The newly created Financial Stability Oversight Council is supposed to remedy this situation. One of the main tasks of the Council is to provide an early warning system for possible emerging systemic risks. Moreover, it is supposed to identify regulatory gaps, oversee the various government agencies involved in regulation of the financial industry, suggest priorities for financial market regulation, and promote market discipline.

Consumer Protection

The centerpiece of consumer protection is the Consumer Financial Protection Bureau. The Bureau has independent rule writing power governing banks and nonbanks if they offer financial products to consumers. To protect consumers, the Bureau is able to act without the need for Congress to pass new laws, but it is required to first coordinate with other regulators.

Securitization

Financial firms that engage in securitization and sale of securitized products such as collateralized debt obligations or mortgage-backed securities must retain at least 5% of each debt tranche they create. This retained risk, which firms are not permitted to hedge, motivates more careful assessment of risk in creating securitized debt products. Additionally, securitizers must disclose asset-level data, including individual securities, so that these securities can be linked to the loan originator and the risk retention of the originator. Since credit rating agencies provide ratings for securitized products, they must provide detailed reports documenting the rationale for their rating decisions.

Over the Counter Derivatives

Many over the counter (OTC) derivatives, such as credit default swaps (CDS) were completely unregulated prior to the 2007–08 financial crisis. Through the Dodd–Frank Act, the SEC and the Commodities Futures Trading Commission now have authority to regulate OTC derivatives. New regulation of OTC derivatives in the Act deals mainly with "swaps" and "security-based swaps." Swaps are defined very broadly to cover almost any kind of OTC derivative, including puts, calls, caps, floors, and other options of a similar kind, and risk transfer instruments such as total return or credit default swaps.

The Dodd–Frank Act attempts to mitigate the risk posed by bilateral trading and clearing of OTC derivatives. The regulatory concern is that counterparties can fail and that buy-side firms may not know their exact exposure at any given time. The intent of the Act is to increase transparency and liquidity, reducing the opacity of sell-side trading operations and mitigating counterparty concentration. While the effects on the sell-side are significant, the buy-side will also be impacted as swap execution facilities (SEFs) and central counterparties (CCPs) come on line. The greatest change to trading in OTC derivatives will be the move from collateral bilateral trading into a margin-based arrangement. The new model will use SEFs for execution and price discovery, and an exchange-style CCP to centralize the exchange of collateral. Regulators must determine the specific types of swaps and derivatives that must be cleared through a CCP, and therefore traded through an SEF, to meet transparency requirements dictated by the Act. Central clearing for OTC derivatives is initially limited to CDS and interest rate swaps. The intent of the new reform is to reduce system risk inherent in transactions that fall outside regulatory supervision, as well as to protect asset managers from counterparty exposure. However, what remains undefined is how these instruments will specifically trade, clear, and settle under the new reform. The Act does not specify the execution method or price discovery mechanics of the SEF, but as rules governing the SEF are clarified, these details will become clearer. The rules will have a direct impact on how securities firms connect to SEFs and what functionality is required from investment management systems. The regulation will also drive more buy-side clearing as opposed to bilateral dealer-to-dealer arrangements that exist today. Any OTC transaction involves counterparty risk, with payment of profits and losses being impacted by ability to pay. Historically, counterparty exposure involved aggregating exposures due to trading activity, performing stress tests on likely profits expected, and assessing if any party was overexposed. Now, more transparency is required by incorporating a credit value adjustment directly into the reported fair value of derivatives. This means all fair market or exit values must expressly capture the monetized value of the counterparty credit risk.

Ending Bailouts

One of the main concerns of the Dodd–Frank Act was to put an end to "too big to fail." In an attempt to restrain banks from accumulating too much risk, regulators adopted the so-called Volcker Rule (named for previous Fed Chairman Paul Volcker). Under the Volcker Rule, banks are no longer allowed to engage in proprietary trading. However, the definition of proprietary trading is murky and subject to ongoing debate. In addition, the Volcker Rule limits bank investment in hedge funds and private equity funds to 3% of any such fund, with overall investment in these funds limited to an amount that does not exceed 3% of Tier 1 Capital. The Act also includes "funeral plans" requiring large financial companies to periodically submit plans regarding how they would shut down in an orderly manner if they fail in the future. Additionally, the Act enables preemptive liquidation of a financial institution if it poses substantial systemic risk.

Further Provisions

The Dodd–Frank Act also imposes new rules on credit rating agencies, private equity funds, and hedge funds. Rating agencies are now overseen by the Office of Credit Ratings within the SEC. Furthermore, rating agencies may be held accountable if they fail to conduct a reasonable investigation of credit risk. If a rating agency continuously provides inaccurate ratings, the SEC may deregister the offending agency. Hedge funds and private equity funds are considered to be part of the "shadow banking system." The Act attempts to end this system and essentially requires most hedge fund and private equity advisors to register with the SEC. In addition, they are required to disclose their activities to the SEC so that a potential systemic risk originating in their activity can be addressed at an early stage. Shareholder rights have also been strengthened by the Act. In particular, shareholders are now allowed to vote on executive pay and golden parachutes and nominate directors. The Act also provides an incentive for greater corporate reporting accuracy by allowing for clawbacks if executive compensation is based on inaccurate financial statements.

IMPACT ON INVESTMENT BANKS

The Dodd–Frank Act has had a significant impact on US-based investment banks. The Act requires banks to offset their assets with at least 5% of equity, which represents a ratio of 20 units of assets for every 1 unit of equity. Banks must hold 6% equity relative to assets in their federally-insured subsidiaries, and regulators have the ability to require up to 8.5% equity. For the largest investment banks, the Act empowers the Fed to require an additional layer of capital based on the risk-weighted assets of each bank. Although this capital surcharge is subject to yearly change based on the bank's size, entanglement with other firms and internal complexity, the current capital surcharge is: J.P. Morgan: 3.5%; Citigroup: 3.5%; Bank of America: 3%; Goldman Sachs: 3%; and Morgan Stanley: 3%. For eurozone banks, the new capital requirement is for large banks to maintain Tier 1 (equity) capital ratios of 9.9%, with an additional 0.2% set aside by systemically important banks. Some critics feel that this equity cushion is not enough to prevent future bank solvency, but other critics state that by forcing investment banks to hold ever greater amounts of equity capital, returns suffer and shareholder value is diminished. Furthermore, an increased equity requirement makes banks less competitive and pushes an increasing amount of traditional bank risk-taking (including lending) into nonbank financial institutions, including finance companies and hedge funds that have less regulation. This, ironically, may result in increasing global systemic financial risk, rather than reducing it.

Another important requirement of the Dodd–Frank Act is to require investment banks to have greater liquidity, which means that a larger portion of higher quality liquid assets are required so that, if necessary to maintain solvency, banks can readily sell these assets for cash. It is possible, however, that forcing greater liquidity requirements on banks may result in less regulated firms such as hedge funds picking up the slack in less liquid assets. Here again, the overall global systemic financial risk may therefore increase, rather than decrease. An equally important requirement is for banks to meet an annual stress test in which an economic crash as severe as the crash in 2008 is simulated to see if banks can survive without government assistance. The concern about this test is that banks may not give regulators correct information, causing unreliable results. The opposing concern is that the banks don't fully understand how the test works so they do not know how to improve their practices to pass the test, and that this is a burdensome regulation that adds unnecessary costs without demonstrable benefits.

The Volcker Rule is a particularly problematic part of the Dodd–Frank Act from the perspective of investment banks since it bans internal hedge funds and private equity funds, which has caused investment banks to significantly downsize trading and principal risk activities. The result is to limit bank risk taking in more speculative areas to mitigate solvency questions at institutions that hold government-insured customer deposits. Critics of the Volcker Rule believe that it is difficult to differentiate between risk taking that facilitates liquidity for customers and risk taking that is a speculative position taken solely for the benefit of the bank. To comply with the Rule, banks have become less willing to hold securities in inventory to facilitate customer purchase and sale interests, which may cause an overall reduction in liquidity, which in turn, may result in more expensive and risky financial markets.

EXHIBIT 2.9 SUMMARY OF THE KEY US LAWS AND AGREEMENTS THAT IMPACT INVESTMENT BANKS

The Securities Act of 1933

- Often referred to as the "truth in securities" law, the Securities Act of 1933 has two main objectives: to require that investors receive financial and other significant information concerning securities being offered for public sale; and to prohibit deceit, misrepresentations, and other fraud in the sale of securities.
- In general, securities sold in the United States must be registered with the Securities and Exchange Commission (SEC) (unless qualified for certain exemptions) and must provide a minimum required amount of information regarding the security. After a registration statement is filed with the SEC, investment prospectuses must also be provided to potential investors.

Continued

EXHIBIT 2.9 SUMMARY OF THE KEY US LAWS AND AGREEMENTS THAT IMPACT INVESTMENT BANKS—cont'd

Glass–Steagall Act (1933)

- The Act separated commercial and investment banks and limited the underwriting capabilities of commercial banks. Partners and officials of firms associated with the security investments were restricted from serving as directors or officers of commercial banks.
- The Federal Deposit Insurance Corporation was founded by this Act to insure bank deposits.

Securities and Exchange Act of 1934

- The Act deals primarily with the supervision of new security offerings, ongoing reporting requirements for these and the conduct of exchanges. Companies with >$10 million in assets and >500 owners must file annual and other periodic reports that need to be available to the public throughout the SEC's EDGAR database. Proxy solicitations and the acquisition of significant ownership stakes (>5%) are subject to filing requirements as well.
- The Act required that exchanges be governed by self-regulatory organizations.
- The Act created the SEC, which took over the responsibility of supervising the capital markets, including the supervision and regulation of investment banks, exchanges, broker/dealers, and trader.
- Insider trading is prohibited by this Act.

Gramm–Leach–Bliley Act (1999)

- Also known as the Financial Services Modernization Act, this Act overturned the mandatory separation of commercial and investment banks, as originally required by the Glass–Steagall Act.

Global Research Settlement (2003)

- Investment banks have to comply with significant restrictions relating to interaction between the Investment Banking Division and equity research department. Disclosures must be made to recipients of research reports regarding (among other things) potential conflicts of interest resulting from investment banking activities.
- The practice of "spinning hot IPOs" is restricted.

Dodd–Frank Act (2010)

- Establishes an early warning system for emerging systemic risk, requires liquidation plans for large financial firms and ends "too big to fail" bailouts.
- Increases consumer and investor protection by creating a new independent Consumer Protection Agency and implements tougher rules for credit rating agencies.
- Regulates over the counterderivatives such as credit default swap and other credit derivatives.
- Restrains proprietary trading by investment banks and imposes new regulatory requirements on hedge funds and private equity funds.

SECURITIES REGULATIONS IN OTHER COUNTRIES

The regulatory environment in three important markets outside of the United States will be discussed. The following section provides a broad overview of the regulatory environment in Japan, the United Kingdom, and China.

Japan

The current Japanese system of regulation has some similarities with the US regulatory system. After World War II, the United States directed the rebuilding of Japan, which led to many Japanese regulatory organizations initially resembling US regulatory organizations. As discussed in US Regulations section of this chapter, the most influential regulations for investment banks in the United States were contained in the 1933 Securities Act, the 1934 Securities Exchange Act, and the Glass–Steagall Act of 1933. These codes were transferred almost wholly to the Japanese system in 1948 when the Japanese Diet passed the Securities and Exchange Law. Even so, given the differences between the countries, Japan's system has evolved into a somewhat different regulatory environment.

Japan's regulations differed in the distinction of bank types and the ownership structure of businesses. Similar to the Glass–Steagall Act in the United States, Japanese regulators distinguished banks based on their business activities. Commercial banks, also known as "City Banks," were restricted from underwriting securities until 1999 (banks that accepted consumer deposits and distributed loans were restricted from underwriting securities, with the exception of government bonds or government-guaranteed bonds). Pre-WWII Japanese banks were often controlled by a "Zaibatsu," a large conglomerate of businesses owned by a single holding company. Although the Zaibatsu were banned after WWII, they were later allowed to reintegrate (through share purchases in each other) to expedite the rebuilding of Japan's economy. A Zaibatsu that is formed around a bank is called a "Keiretsu" and has a similar structure as a Zaibatsu but with many owners. Several different banks are owners in a Keiretsu since banks are not allowed to own more than 5% of equity in companies to which they lend. The City Banks have maintained an influential role in Japan's financial and industrial activities through the Keiretsu. Correspondingly, however, the securities market has grown slowly in Japan because of the City Banks' underwriting restrictions. As a result, most companies finance their business through short and medium term loans instead of through the securities market.

The Japanese regulatory environment has gone through three significant periods since the US-assisted restructuring: 1947–1992, 1992–1998, and 1998–Present.

1947–1992

Established in 1947, the Ministry of Finance (MOF) is in charge of regulating the Japanese financial system. It has a large mandate, including the supervision of banks, and shares responsibility for fiscal and monetary policy with the Bank of Japan. Before 1971 foreign securities firms were banned from operating in Japan. The Law Concerning Foreign Securities Firms that was passed in 1971 allowed foreign firms to enter the market for investment banking services.

1992–1998

Like in the United States, Japan also eliminated the separation of investment banking and commercial banking. This process started in 1992 with the Financial Institution Reform Act, which allowed commercial banks, investment banks, and insurance companies to engage in each other's business through subsidiaries. This Act also established the Securities Exchange and Surveillance Commission (SESC), which assumed many of the regulatory responsibilities of the MOF.

1998–Present

Starting in 1998 Japan initiated the "Big Bang" and began to deregulate the financial industry. A key part of the Big Bang was the separation of the SESC from the MOF, and the creation of the Financial Supervisory Agency (that in 2000 turned into the Financial Services Agency), which is the current regulator of Japan's securities industry. During 1999, the Financial System Reform Law allowed commercial banks to own brokerage firms that underwrite equity and debt securities. In addition, a new securities law was passed, called the Law Concerning the Sale of Financial Products, which governs underwriter practices.

In 2006, the Financial Instruments and Exchange Law passed and became the main statute codifying securities law and regulating securities companies in Japan. The law provides for registration and regulation of broker-dealers; disclosure obligations applicable to public companies; tender offer rules; disclosure obligations applicable to large shareholders in public companies; and internal controls in public companies (similar to the controls imposed in the United States by the Sarbanes–Oxley Act).

Japanese banks had considerably lower exposure to subprime mortgage investments compared to US. and European counterparts, and were subsequently not hit as severely by the 2007–08 financial crisis. Although the United States and Europe pursued aggressive new regulation of financial institutions, Japan did not follow suit because Japanese lawmakers were concerned that overregulation would weaken the competitiveness of Japanese banks.

United Kingdom

Founded in 1694, the Bank of England was the principal regulator in the United Kingdom for over 300 years until 1997. Like Japan, the evolution of the regulatory system can be separated into three periods: Pre-1986, 1986–1997, and 1997–Present.

Pre-1986

Until 1986, self-regulation (for example, by members of the London Stock Exchange) prevailed. In 1986 there was a "Big Bang" in the UK's financial industry, which placed the self-regulatory system into a statutory framework. This was the precursor to the Japanese Big Bang; both were meant to shake up the regulatory system.

1986–1997

Sweeping reform in the regulation of the UK investment industry started with the Financial Services Act 1986, which created a comprehensive government regulator called the Securities and Investment Board (SIB). A financial firm had to register with the SIB, unless it was a member of an SRO. The SROs were given enforcement powers (fines, censures, and bans) at this time. Under the Financial Services Act 1986, undertaking any investment business without authorization by the SIB was a criminal offense.

1997–Present

In 1997 an overhaul of the financial regulatory system was announced and the SIB changed its name to the Financial Services Authority (FSA). The FSA consolidated the powers of nine regulatory agencies into a single regulator for the entire industry, and removed the influence of SROs. In the process, the FSA also took over responsibility for regulating banks from the Bank of England. This contrasts with the United States that has several different financial regulators. The FSA has the power to create rules by its mandate, and like the US SEC, FSA's rules are binding without any parliamentary action. In 2001, the Financial Services and Markets Act 2000 replaced the Financial Services Act 1986.

Following the outbreak of the global financial crisis in 2007, the FSA worked with the Bank of England and the UK Treasury (together called the "Tripartite Authorities") to reform and strengthen the existing UK regulatory framework. As a result of this process, financial regulation in the United Kingdom is no longer solely conducted by the FSA. The FSA was split into the Prudential Regulation Authority (PRA), a subsidiary of the Bank of England, focusing on regulation of deposit-taking institutions, insurers and investment banks, and the Financial Conduct Authority, focusing on regulation of retail and wholesale financial markets and the infrastructure that facilitates these markets.

In mid-2010, the Chancellor of the Exchequer announced the creation of the Independent Commission on Banking to make recommendations to the government on how to reform the UK financial system. The main suggestion of the Commission was the "ring-fencing" of retail banking from investment banking so failure of one business will not require government bailout of the other business. In addition, the Commission recommended higher capital requirements and increased competition in the UK banking market.

Owing to perceived regulatory failure of the banks during the financial crisis of 2007–08, the UK government decided to restructure financial regulation and abolish the FSA. The Financial Services Act, which came into force during April, 2013, eliminated the FSA, and its former responsibilities were divided between two new agencies: the Financial Conduct Authority (responsible for policing the financial activities of the City and the banking system) and the PRA of the Bank of England (responsible for regulation of financial firms, including banks, investment banks, building societies and insurance companies). The Act gave the Bank of England responsibility for financial stability, bringing together macro and microprudential regulation, and created a new regulatory structure consisting of the Bank of England's Financial Policy Committee, the PRA, and the Financial Conduct Authority.

Effect of European Union Regulation

As a member state of the European Union (EU), the United Kingdom is also subject to a number of EU banking and securities legislation that seeks to impose a level-playing field in relation to the regulation of financial markets across the EU, particularly for the wholesale markets.

Following the 2007–08 financial crisis, EU regulators initiated a number of new regulatory programs that impacted the financial services industry, including the Alternative Investment Fund Managers Directive, European Market Infrastructure Regulation (EMIR) and the Markets in Financial Instruments Directive. The main changes from these programs include the tightening regulation of hedge funds and private equity funds, stricter rules for trading and clearing of derivatives, the creation of new regulatory agencies and higher capital requirements.

The EMIR is an EU law that aims to reduce the risks posed to the financial system by derivatives transactions in the following three main ways: reporting of derivatives trades to an authorized trade repository; clearing derivatives trades above a certain threshold; and mitigating the risks associated with derivatives trades by, for example, reconciling portfolios periodically and agreeing dispute resolution procedures between counterparties. EMIR impacts market participants in the EEA (European Economic Area) and market participants outside of the EEA trading with an EEA counterparty.

China

Although Hong Kong is now under Chinese rule, it differs significantly from the rest of the country in its investment banking regulation standards because it operated under English control until 1997. This discussion will exclude Hong Kong and focus strictly on the mainland Chinese financial regulatory environment. The Chinese financial regulatory system for investment banking only recently modernized to resemble more closely the standards found in other countries with developed financial systems. The regulatory system can be separated into four periods: Pre-1992, 1992–1998, 1998–2005, and 2005–Present.

Pre-1992

Prior to 1992, China was essentially closed to investment banking. However, economic reforms initiated under Deng Xiaoping's administration set the stage for a market-based economy that opened the doors for foreign trade and investments.

1992–1998

In 1992, the Chinese government implemented two commissions: the State Council Securities Commission (SCSC) and the China Securities Regulatory Commission (CSRC). The SCSC deals with centralized market regulation, whereas the CSRC is the enforcement arm of the SCSC and supervises the securities markets. In 1995 Morgan Stanley became the first and only global investment bank to operate inside of China.

1998–2005

In 1998 the Securities Law of the People's Republic of China was created as the main statute regulating investment banks. The SCSC was merged into the CSRC to form one government body. The new CSRC was a direct government entity of the State Council, the head council of the Central People's Government of China. Under the Securities Law, there was a separation of banks engaging in deposit-taking and securities activities.

2005–Present

In 2005 the Securities Law of the People's Republic of China and the Company Law of the People's Republic of China underwent revisions. The changes in law were extensive: over 40% of the articles were amended, 53 provisions were added, and 27 were deleted. After the 2005 Securities Law update, the restriction on banks and their affiliates engaging in securities activities was relaxed. It also allowed for the creation of derivative markets, whereas previously China restricted the financial markets to only cash markets. In addition, the updated Securities Law took further actions to protect investors dealing with new security issuance. Article 5, for example, states that "[the] issuance and transaction of securities shall observe laws and administrative regulations. No fraud, insider trading, or manipulation of the securities market may be permitted." Finally, the new Law provided securities regulators with additional powers to investigate and gather information, and to control a securities firm's assets if necessary. China's entry into the World Trade Organization (WTO) created opportunities for foreign banks to enter the market. As part of their WTO commitment, the government allowed foreign financial institutions that meet Chinese requirements to engage in local currency retail banking. In 2010 the China Banking Regulator Commission raised the capital requirements for these foreign banks.

CHAPTER
3

Financings

The material in this chapter should be cross-referenced with the following cases: **Freeport–McMoRan: Financing an Acquisition Case and Quintiles IPO Case**.

This chapter focuses on raising financing for corporate and government clients, one of the two key businesses conducted by the Investment Banking Division of an investment bank.

CAPITAL MARKETS FINANCINGS

A capital markets financing is a long-term funding obtained through the issuance of a security in a regulated market. A security is a fungible, negotiable instrument representing financial value. The security can be debt (bonds, debentures, or notes), equity (common stock), or a hybrid (a security with both debt-like and equity-like characteristics, such as preferred shares or convertibles). A capital markets financing is usually underwritten by investment banks, meaning that the banks take on risk when purchasing securities from an issuer and then reselling those securities to investors. This financing process is governed by securities laws that determine disclosure, marketing limitations, and underwriter compensation, among other things. A capital markets offering where investment banks purchase securities at a discount from issuers and then resell them to investors is called a primary offering. The sale of securities through a capital markets offering where the proceeds do not go to the issuer of the security, but to a current large holder of the security, is referred to as a secondary offering.

After securities are sold in the capital markets through either a primary or secondary market offering, subsequent trades are called secondary market trades, which take place on an exchange or in the over-the-counter (OTC) market. In a secondary market trade, cash is received by a seller, the buyer receives the purchased security, and the original issuer of the security does not receive any cash proceeds or issue a new security.

In the United States, a primary market securities offering must either be registered with the Securities and Exchange Commission (SEC) through a registration statement (a portion of which is called a "prospectus") or sold pursuant to an exemption from this registration requirement. The most frequently used exemption is Rule 144A, which allows for the immediate resale of restricted securities among qualified institutional buyers (these institutions, often referred to as "QIBs," manage $100 million or more in discretionary investable assets). The majority of debt offerings and a large portion of convertible offerings in the United States are now completed on a 144A basis. Transactions in securities that are exempt from registration because the securities were not offered or sold in a public offering are called "private placements," and investors in private placements must be contacted without the use of a general solicitation or advertising process (See Exhibit 3.1). A primary market offering that is registered with the SEC is called a "public offering."

EXHIBIT 3.1 PRIVATE PLACEMENTS

Private placements of bonds (that are not of the same class as an exchange-listed security) may be exempt from registration with the Securities and Exchange Commission (SEC) when both initial sale (to an underwriter) and subsequent sales are limited to sophisticated investors who are qualified institutional buyers (QIBs). The terms for private placements are often either more restrictive or more expensive for the borrower because of illiquidity; investors are restricted when reselling the bonds to other QIBs, which usually results in a lower resale price compared to a public market security that has a much broader investor base to tap into. Most bonds and convertible transactions (other than mandatory convertibles) are completed without registration with the SEC based on a Rule 144A exemption.

When a company sells stock to the public for the first time in an SEC-registered offering, this is an initial public offering (IPO). Subsequent sales of stock to the public by the company are called "follow-on" offerings. If major shareholders of a company wish to sell their shares, subject to the company's agreement, the shares can be sold using the company's registration statement, enabling a broad selling effort. This is called a selling shareholder offering (or a secondary offering, as described above) and the agreement to use the company's registration statement is called a "registration rights agreement."

Most public market securities offerings are underwritten by investment banks, where the bank buys the entire issue at a discount and attempts to resell it at a higher price. The difference between the purchase and sale price is called the "gross spread" and represents compensation for the bank for undertaking a distribution effort and certain legal risks. Subject to agreement between the issuer and the bank (called an "underwriting agreement"), the underwriting can be completed either on a best-efforts basis, in which the issuer bears security price risk, or on a firm-commitment basis (bought deal) where the bank bears security price risk. In either scenario, the investment bank still bears closing and settlement risks.

Typically, a group, or "syndicate," of investment banks underwrites a securities offering. In this case, the issuer must decide which banks will act as the "lead bookrunners" of the transaction. The lead bookrunners have responsibility for determining the marketing method and pricing for the transaction and, therefore, receive the highest underwriting allocation and a proportionately higher percentage of the gross spread. Sometimes, one bank will be the dominant bookrunner, while in other cases, the bookrunners operate on an equal basis. Other banks that participate in the syndicate, called "comanagers," take on smaller underwriting allocations. They may provide minor input to the bookrunner(s) on marketing and pricing issues but don't control this process, have less risk and less work to do. As a result, they receive lower compensation. There can be between one and seven comanagers in an underwriting syndicate. In some securities offerings, there may be another group of investment banks that participate in the "selling group" for the offering. These banks don't take any financial risk and receive even lower compensation.

The investment banking industry keeps track of underwriting participations by all banks, and this becomes a basis for comparing banks' underwriting capabilities. This record is called a "league table," and every different type of security (and geographic region) has its own league table. The most important league table is the one that keeps track of a bank's bookrunning underwriting activity. In this table, the bookrunners receive full credit for the entire proceeds of the offering (with the proceeds divided by the number of bookrunners), irrespective of the percentage actually underwritten by the bookrunning banks (see Exhibits 3.2 and 3.3 for equity and debt league table, respectively).

EXHIBIT 3.2 GLOBAL EQUITY AND EQUITY-RELATED, JANUARY 1 TO SEPTEMBER 30, 2016 (FIRST 9 MONTHS 2016)

)Bookrunner	2016 Rank	2015 Rank	Proceeds in $	# of Deals	Fees in $
JP Morgan	1	3	41,812.00	247	779.1
Morgan Stanley	2	2	34,024.00	191	612.4
Goldman Sachs & Co	3	1	33,779.90	195	573.8
Bank of America Merrill Lynch	4	5	25,415.50	169	540.4
Citi	5	6	23,029.80	164	376.9
Deutsche Bank	6	8	21,091.00	116	260.6
Credit Suisse	7	7	20,752.40	156	374.9
UBS	8	4	17,046.20	125	270.7
Barclays	9	9	14,763.40	103	246.4
CITIC	10	12	9,599.60	41	138.5
RBC Capital Markets	11	11	9,241.10	105	225
Wells Fargo & Co	12	13	7,482.20	86	160.2
Nomura	13	10	7,028.40	63	215.3
China International Capital Co	14	19	5,684.60	25	70.6
TD Securities Inc	15	43	5,484.40	41	136.7
Guotai Junan Securities	16	27	5,207.30	42	84.2
China Securities Co Ltd	17	24	5,158.90	29	103
BNP Paribas SA	18	18	5,104.30	40	93.8
Haitong Securities Co Ltd	19	28	5,082.60	35	59.1
BMO Capital Markets	20	22	4,987.10	73	161.3
Industry Total			479,131.10		9,871.80

Source: http://dmi.thomsonreuters.com/Content/Files/3Q2016_Global_Equity_Capital_Markets_Review.pdf.

EXHIBIT 3.3 GLOBAL DEBT, JANUARY 1 TO SEPTEMBER 30, 2016 (FIRST 9 MONTHS 2016)

Bookrunner	2016 Rank	2015 Rank	Proceeds in $	# of Deals	Fees in $
JP Morgan	1	1	349,260.50	1,296	1,305.50
Citi	2	4	310,475.70	1,137	1,157.30
Bank of America Merrill	3	3	299,178.00	1,157	1,229.90
Barclays	4	2	279,534.10	924	860.6
HSBC Holdings PLC	5	8	236,947.40	970	570.4
Goldman Sachs & Co	6	7	223,418.20	707	883.3
Deutsche Bank	7	5	219,317.30	857	801.9
Morgan Stanley	8	6	208,406.80	952	871.9
Wells Fargo & Co	9	10	168,726.10	787	694
BNP Paribas SA	10	11	136,517.30	538	413
Credit Suisse	11	9	136,363.60	543	629.1
Nomura	12	13	119,237.20	518	182.3
Bank of China Ltd	13	38	107,211.30	735	152.4
Mizuho Financial Group	14	18	104,138.00	586	410.7
Industrial & Comm Bank	15	31	104,128.50	730	127.2
China Construction Bank	16	39	103,143.50	723	117.6
RBC Capital Markets	17	12	96,134.30	510	414
Agricultural Bank of China	18	56	91,266.60	587	100.2
TD Securities Inc	19	17	89,817.80	425	188.6
Credit Agricole CIB	20	15	88,093.80	405	207.1
Bank of Communications Co	21	51	87,714.20	601	94.3
Societe Generale	22	16	77,965.20	306	205.6
UBS	23	14	77,245.90	409	344.8
UniCredit	24	20	56,771.20	246	127.2
Mitsubishi UFJ Financial	25	22	46,871.20	236	220.6
Industry Total			**5,517,966.60**	**15,521**	**18,123.20**

Source: http://dmi.thomsonreuters.com/Content/Files/3Q2016_Global_Equity_Capital_Markets_Review.pdf.

The capital markets groups at investment banks are principally responsible for originating and executing capital markets transactions. In this role, they coordinate with client coverage bankers to target likely issuers and with professionals from the syndicate desk to determine appropriate potential pricing. In conjunction with the client coverage banker, the capital markets group enters into a competitive process to receive a "mandate" from an issuer for a financing. Competitive pressures sometimes compel investment banks to undertake considerable risks, such as agreeing to a bought deal, which means buying an entire transaction at a specified price from the issuer, and attempting to resell the security at a higher price to investors. Another risk that investment banks sometimes assume involves committing to provide a large loan to a client as a "bridge" financing for an M&A transaction. This is a contingent loan that the investment bank will actually fund only if a "take-out" financing for the M&A transaction that is underwritten by the bank in the capital markets based on predetermined terms is not able to be completed due to adverse market conditions.

FINANCING CONSIDERATIONS

When investment bankers advise issuers regarding potential financing transactions, the bankers typically focus on liquidity (cash balances, marketable securities, and available lines of credit), cash flow multiples, debt/earnings multiples, cost of capital, and rating agency considerations before recommending whether a client should raise financing and, if so, whether it should be in the form of debt, equity, or a hybrid security like a convertible. Bankers also analyze the company's liquidity as a percentage of market capitalization, total debt, annual interest payment obligations, and other balance sheet and income statement metrics. These metrics are then compared with results from other companies in the same industry to determine whether the client has relatively more or less liquidity than its competitors. This analysis provides a foundation for discussing whether a company needs to increase or decrease liquidity (see Exhibit 3.4). If it is determined that a company needs to increase liquidity, bankers will discuss a range of financing alternatives, as described in Exhibit 3.5.

EXHIBIT 3.4 CORPORATE CAPITAL STRUCTURE

Companies focus on raising cash or reducing cash:

Raise Cash Through:	Reduce Cash Through:
Debt issuance:	Share repurchases:
• public or private bonds, loans or securitization	• open market, auctions, or derivatives
Equity -related issuance:	Asset acquisitions:
• public or private share issuance, convertibles or preferred shares	• M&A
	Retire debt, convertibles or preferred shares
Selling assets:	Increase capital expenditures
• M&A	Dividend payments:
Decrease capital expenditures	• quarterly small payments or one time large special dividend
Cut dividends or eliminate share repurchases	

Key areas of focus that relate to capital structure include earnings per share, credit ratings, financial flexibility, hedging assets and liabilities, tax implications, and maintaining capital structure parity with principal competitors.

EXHIBIT 3.5 FINANCING ALTERNATIVES

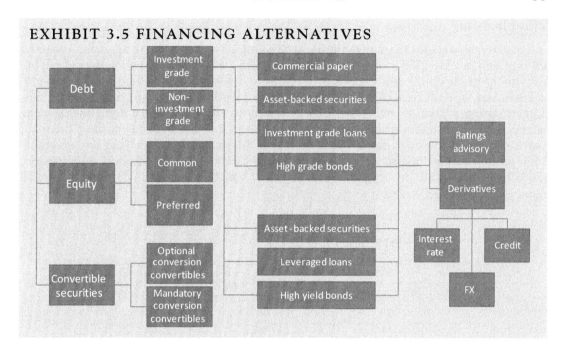

After a company and its banker agree on the need for new financing, they must, in the first case, decide whether to offer debt, equity, or convertible securities. An equity offering generally has a higher cost of capital than a debt financing and will likely cause a drop in earnings per share (EPS) for the issuer, which may negatively impact the company's share price. However, equity will strengthen the company's balance sheet and may lead to a higher bond rating from a credit rating agency, which may result in lower future bond financing costs. A debt offering usually has a lower cost of capital but may weaken the company's balance sheet and reduce financial flexibility. As a result, the company and its banker must consider the risk-adjusted cost of debt when comparing this form of financing with an equity financing. Before issuing new debt, bankers and their clients must consider both the impact of debt on cash flow multiples (to determine if additional interest charges can be adequately covered by cash flow) and the likely impact on credit ratings. They also must decide whether management has the requisite skills to manage a more leveraged company. A convertible security offers a blend of the same costs and benefits as equity and debt securities. In the final analysis, risk-adjusted cost of capital, credit ratings, comparisons with peer companies, equity and debt analyst views, and management comfort with the resulting balance sheet are among the many considerations that determine whether a company raises financing from debt, equity, or convertible markets.

FINANCING ALTERNATIVES

After making a decision regarding the type of financing, the client and the banker consider an array of financing alternatives to determine the optimal financing product.

Debt Financing

If a company decides to issue debt that will be rated by credit rating agencies, the debt offering will be classified as either investment-grade debt or noninvestment-grade debt. Investment-grade debt has bond ratings of BBB- or higher from Standard & Poor's (S&P) or Fitch, and/or Baa3 or higher from Moody's (see Exhibit 3.6). Investment-grade ratings suggest stronger balance sheets and greater ability to withstand large demands on cash balances. Noninvestment-grade ratings start at BB+ or Ba1 and decline based on the relative weakness of the debt issuer. Debt financing alternatives include investment-grade (high-grade) bonds, noninvestment-grade (high-yield or "junk") bonds, investment-grade loans, low-grade (leveraged) loans, asset-backed securities (ABSs), and commercial paper (see Exhibit 3.5).

EXHIBIT 3.6 CREDIT RATINGS

Investment Grade		Below Investment Grade	
Moody's	S&P and Fitch	Moody's	S&P and Fitch
Aaa	AAA	Ba1	BB+
Aa1	AA+	Ba2	BB
Aa2	AA	Ba3	BB-
Aa3	AA-	B1	B+
A1	A+	B2	B
A2	A	B3	B-
A3	A-	Caa	CCC
Baa1	BBB+		
Baa2	BBB		
Baa3	BBB-		

Source: Standard & Poor's, Moody's, and Fitch.

Bonds

A bond is debt in the form of a security, issued as a long-term obligation of a borrower with a specific maturity and coupon. The debt capital markets group at an investment bank underwrites a bond offering by purchasing the security from the issuer and reselling it to institutional investors or individual investors through a registered public offering or through a 144A offering. The underwriting could be in the form of a best-efforts underwriting (issuer bears price risk), a bought deal underwriting (investment bank bears price risk), or a backstop commitment (investment bank commits to a worst-case price). See Exhibit 3.7 for a description of these types of bond underwritings. Bond issuance is in the form of either investment-grade bonds or junk bonds, which are originated through two different teams within the debt capital markets group of an investment bank.

EXHIBIT 3.7 TYPES OF BOND UNDERWRITINGS

Best Efforts	
■ Comprises a majority of transactions ■ Issuer of bond bears price risk	■ Least expensive ■ Market deal
Bought Deal	
■ Investment bank buys the bond at a certain rate ■ Generally seen in competitive markets	■ Investment bank bears the price risk
Backstop Commitments	
■ Rate is "backstopped" or committed to, but issuer will get the lower rate if it clears the market	■ Investment bank commits to a worst case price

Loans

Loans are not securities from a US regulatory perspective and, therefore, there is no registration process with the SEC. The banks and other sophisticated lenders who provide loans require more onerous restrictions (covenants) on the borrower compared to the restrictions imposed by a bond. See Exhibit 3.8 for a description of the principal differences between loans and bonds.

EXHIBIT 3.8 HOW DO COMPANIES CHOOSE BETWEEN LOANS AND BONDS?

- Prepayable versus nonprepayable debt
  - Loans are generally prepayable at anytime at par
  - Bonds are noncallable for some period of time, usually 4–5 years
- Bonds usually have no covenants
  - Incurrence covenants versus maintenance covenants
  - Usually less restrictive on incurring more debts
- Loans require amortization
- Bond investors generally accept more risk and therefore receive higher returns
- Bonds have longer maturities
- Bonds are generally more expensive

Asset-Backed Securities

ABSs are securities whose income payments and value are derived from and collateralized ("backed") by a specified pool of underlying assets such as first mortgage loans, home equity loans, auto loans, credit card receivables, student loans, or equipment leases in a process called securitization. Investment banks participate in the securitization by purchasing the underlying assets and utilizing a special-purpose vehicle (SPV) to purchase assets from the bank, then sell securities, using the proceeds of the sale to pay back the bank that originated the transaction. The SPV bundles underlying assets into a specified pool that fits the risk preferences of investors. When the credit risk of the underlying assets is transferred to investors through the purchase of securities, banks can remove the credit risk of the underling assets from their books. An SPV is designed to insulate investors from the credit risk of the bank by selling pooled loans to a trust, which issues interest-bearing securities that can achieve an independent credit rating based solely on the cash flows created by the assets (see **A Tale of Two Hedge Funds: Magnetar and Peloton Case** for further discussion of ABSs).

Collateralized debt obligations (CDOs) are a type of ABS that divides assets into different tranches: senior tranches (rated AAA), mezzanine tranches (AA to BB), and equity tranches (unrated). Losses are applied in reverse order of seniority, and so lower rated tranches offer higher coupons to compensate for higher default risk. The coupons on each tranche are slightly higher than the coupons on correspondingly rated corporate debt. This "yield pickup" is a principal reason why CDO issuance has rapidly grown, creating significant profits for investment bank underwriters. Collateralized loan obligations are CDOs that are backed by leveraged loans. Collateralized bond obligations are CDOs that are backed by high-yield bonds. The credit crunch that started during mid-2007 dramatically decreased CDO issuance and created huge losses at investment banks that held large CDO underwriting-related and investment inventory. The International Monetary Fund has estimated that all CDO-related losses suffered by global financial firms between mid-2007 and the end of 2008 were approximately $1 trillion. After CDO issuance dropped to a negligible level during 2009, the market has come back slowly (see Exhibit 3.9).

EXHIBIT 3.9 GLOBAL COLLATERALIZED DEBT OBLIGATION ISSUANCE (IN BILLIONS OF US DOLLARS)

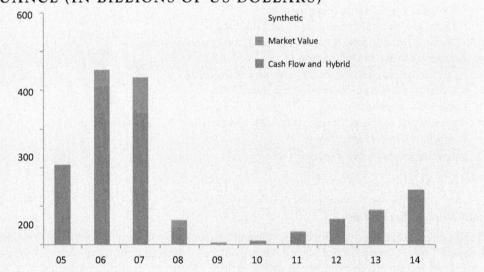

Note: Figures for 2014 are annualized based on data to September. Unfunded synthetic tranches are not included in this analysis.
Source: IMF staff calculations; and the Securities Industry and Financial Markets Association.

One of the main reasons for losses was that many CDO structures were too complicated and not sufficiently transparent, resulting in risks that were not well understood. As a consequence, the Dodd–Frank Act for US capital markets and the markets in financial instruments directive (MiFID) for the European capital markets require that, unless an exemption applies, banks that originate ABS transactions such as CDOs must retain at least 5% of each issuance. Moreover, the regulations do not allow banks to hedge the risk of their ABS retention since regulators want banks to have "skin in the game." Disclosure requirements have been significantly increased to improve transparency.

Commercial Paper

Commercial paper is a short-term US promissory note with a maturity that does not exceed 270 days. Financial companies comprise approximately three quarters of all commercial paper issuance. Commercial paper is exempt from registration with the SEC and is widely marketed and therefore, subject to market conditions, represents a very low-cost vehicle for raising short-term financing.

Equity Financing

Initial Public Offerings

An investment bank's equity capital markets group helps private companies determine if an IPO of stock is a logical decision based on an analysis of benefits and disadvantages (see below). The bank then determines if there is sufficient investor demand to purchase new equity securities offered by the company. Assuming sufficient interest, the investment bank determines the expected value of the company based on comparisons with publicly traded comparable companies or values derived through other methods (including discounted cash flow (DCF) analyses). This is an imperfect process that requires analysis of both historical operating earnings and revenues and forecasts for future earnings and revenues. Because it is sometimes difficult to find good comparable companies, and forecasts can be problematic, the valuation process for some prospective IPO candidates can be more art than science. The Comparable Company Analysis discussion in Chapter 4 provides some insight into this valuation process.

Principal benefits of going public include the following:

1. Access to public market funding: for a US offering, registration with the SEC enables the broadest exposure to investors, not only for the IPO but also for subsequent "follow-on" offerings. This allows the company to have a broad, diverse ownership structure (including retail and institutional ownership) that could help stabilize share prices during market down cycles. The rigorous disclosures required by the SEC create investor confidence and, potentially, a stronger demand for shares.
2. Enhanced profile and marketing benefits: public companies receive more attention from the public media, which can result in heightened interest in company products and increased market share.

3. Create an acquisition currency and compensation vehicle: public stock can be used instead of cash for future acquisitions, which can be very important for companies with high growth opportunities. In addition, stock and stock options can be used as employee incentives and compensation vehicles. This preserves cash, creates greater employee commitment, and facilitates recruiting.

4. Liquidity for shareholders: an IPO allows founders to reduce exposure to their company by selling shares. However, sales by founders and other key employees (selling shareholders) are usually no more than 25% of the IPO offering to maintain a significant risk position (although this percentage can be higher depending on how long selling shareholders have held the stock and the total size of the offering). This provides IPO purchasers with confidence that founders and managers will remain economically motivated to increase shareholder value. In addition, the need for primary capital (cash received by the company for shares sold by the company) to operate and grow the business is a key consideration in determining the mix of primary and secondary shares (shares sold by selling shareholders) offered in an IPO.

Principal disadvantages of going public include the following:

1. Reporting requirements: an SEC registration requires not only up-front accounting and other reporting that conforms to SEC requirements but also quarterly, annual, and other event-related reporting through filing of 10-Qs, 10-Ks, and 8-Ks, respectively. In addition, proxy statements and individual reporting for officers, directors, and principal shareholders are required. Equally important are the compliance requirements for public companies that were created by the Sarbanes–Oxley Act of 2002 (SOX), which imposes a vast array of time-consuming reporting and procedural obligations on a public company and its officers.

2. Costs: the ongoing reporting requirements described above create significant annual costs. These costs include legal, accounting, and tax reporting costs. In addition, the up-front costs for an IPO are considerable. For example, up to 7% (this percentage decreases as the deal size increases) of the IPO proceeds go to investment bankers as a gross spread (fee), and 3% or more of IPO proceeds pay for legal, printing, accounting, and other costs, depending on the size of the transaction. As a result, usually less than 90% of the IPO proceeds are kept by the issuer. Most companies also have to replace or significantly upgrade their corporate information systems, which is very expensive as well. Finally, a cost should be assigned to management time spent launching an IPO. Management will be required to allocate a large amount of time to review documents to be filed with the SEC and then travel to multiple cities to meet with prospective institutional investors during the "road show."

3. Disclosure: the SEC requires companies to share an extensive amount of information in the registration process and some of this may be potentially sensitive information that could benefit competitors.

4. Short-term management focus: the requirement to provide quarterly information to investors through 10-Q filings often diverts management's attention from managing

a business that creates long-term value to managing, redirecting focus to achieving quarterly results expected by the market. Shareholders usually expect steady growth in quarterly earnings, and if this is not achieved, the company's share price may decline. This can create pressure to manage the company for the short-term, at the expense of creating long-term value.

The IPO process starts with a selection by the company of the investment banks they will work with as the lead bookrunners. The selected banks will develop a valuation model to determine the share price range for the offering and recommend the number of shares to be offered. The company also selects other investment banks to act as comanagers of the offering, determines the use of proceeds, and chooses the exchange on which to list its shares. The company then works with its auditing firm to create financial statements that are consistent with SEC requirements. The company's and the investment banks' legal counsels prepare filing documents with the SEC (usually an "S-1" filing) in conjunction with the bankers and company officers. This filing is referred to as the "registration statement," of which a portion is called the "prospectus." The filing notifies the public regarding the potential IPO and provides considerable information regarding the issuer. The registration statement is subsequently amended one or more times based on comments received from the SEC. After all changes requested by the SEC are incorporated and the lead bookrunners and company agree on a share price range (which is usually based principally on either a comparable company valuation or DCF valuation completed by the lead bookrunners), the registration statement is amended for the last time to include the price range.

The company and lead bookrunners decide on a schedule for a road show, which could take up to 2 weeks and starts after a "teach-in" at each of the investment banks participating in the underwriting. The teach-in is an opportunity for research analysts at each bank to provide their views on the company to sales people in the bank's trading division. The equity capital markets and sales teams from the lead bookrunners, together with company management, will then talk with prospective investors during the road show, using a "red herring" prospectus, which is taken from the most recently amended S-1 registration statement filed with the SEC.

Road show discussions focus on the current health of the company, management's plans for the company going forward, comparisons with other companies, and investor reactions to the share price range and expected size of the offering (which is generally less than 25% of shares privately held, although this can vary, depending on the cash needs of the business). During the road show, investors provide the lead bookrunners with indications of interest, or specific prices at which they may buy a designated number of shares. Once the "book" is built and the lead bookrunners believe that they have a strong deal to price, the company asks the SEC to get ready to declare their registration statement "effective" and then the deal is priced (typically within the most recent price range, although approximately a quarter of IPOs end up pricing out of this range). At this point, the SEC declares the registration effective, and the lead bookrunners "allocate" shares to investors (see a sample IPO timeline in Exhibit 3.10).

EXHIBIT 3.10 SAMPLE INITIAL PUBLIC OFFERING TABLE

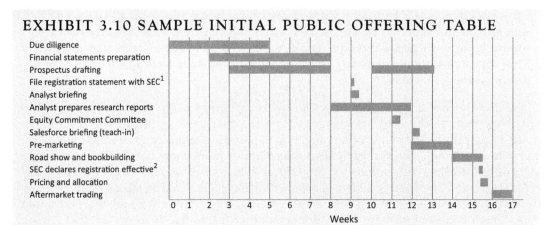

Note 1: Registration statement includes a pricing range.
Note 2: Final registration statement includes the price at which shares are offered to investors. The SEC imposes limitations on the issuer's communications during the "quiet period" that begins when company files a registration statement with the SEC and ends when the final registration is declared effective.
Source: Morgan Stanley.

The period between the beginning of the registration process (which starts when an issuer files the original S-1 prospectus with the SEC) and continuing until the SEC declares a registration effective has historically been called the "quiet period." During the quiet period, the SEC allows a company to disclose their interest in offering IPO shares to investors only by means of a preliminary, red herring prospectus (so called because of a red legend on the cover page that states the preliminary nature of the information provided). In 2005, as a result of reforms enacted by the SEC, companies were allowed to provide free-writing prospectuses (written offers to sell or solicit to buy securities) to investors after filing the registration statement, as long as a copy of the prospectus precedes or accompanies the free-writing prospectus. Further, if the free-writing prospectus is in electronic format, the issuer only needs to provide a hyperlink to the statutory prospectus. Other than this, "offers to sell" are not allowed during the quiet period and publicity initiated by the company that has the effect of "conditioning the market" or arousing public interest in the issuer or its securities is also forbidden. Failure to abide by these rules may result in a "gun-jumping" violation, and the SEC may require the issuer to withdraw its filing. An example of a gun-jumping problem experienced by Google during 2004 in its "Dutch auction" IPO is described in Exhibit 3.11. See Chapter 2 for a more detailed explanation of gun-jumping and other SEC issues associated with an IPO.

EXHIBIT 3.11 GOOGLE'S INITIAL PUBLIC OFFERING

Deal size: $1.7 billion	Date announced: April 29, 2004	Date completed: August 18, 2004

When Google set out to choose the bankers for its initial public offering (IPO), the company organized a working team that was charged with identifying qualified investment banks. The group initially selected 20 firms, requiring them all to sign confidentiality agreements before proceeding.

Each firm was then sent a 21-point questionnaire, asking for its credentials and thoughts on the best way Google could approach its offering.

Google started holding in-person interviews with individuals from 12 firms. Instead of allowing bankers to make their traditional pitches, Google conducted the meetings as question-and-answer sessions, judging each firm's response to their plan to hold a modified Dutch auction for the company's IPO. By using an auction, Google hoped to ensure the greatest distribution possible to retail investors. Following the interviews, the company chose Credit Suisse First Boston and Morgan Stanley as joint bookrunners.

Many investment banks tried to persuade Google to pursue a traditional "book-building" IPO based on a road show that enables bankers to obtain pricing input from large institutional investors. They reasoned that a Dutch auction would alienate these investors since it disenfranchises their pricing input and removed the opportunity to receive a large allocation directed by the bookrunner. However, Google persevered because they wanted a more egalitarian process. They also wanted to avoid some of the excesses that can occur in large IPOs, particularly the large first-day pop in a stock's price.

In a Dutch-auction system, investors weigh in with bids, listing the number of shares they want and how much they are willing to pay for those shares. Bids are stacked with the highest price at the top. Starting at the top of the stack and going down, a final market price is established at which all shares available for sale can be sold. All bidders get the selected lowest price offered. The system, heavily dependent on participation from retail investors, is not popular on Wall Street.

The Google IPO was a conundrum for investment bankers. Their firms wanted the cachet that would come with underwriting the highest-profile offering ever, but they were put off by the auction process and the lower-than-average fees Google was paying.

Banks typically earn commissions as high as 7% of the value of traditional IPOs they help to sell. That arrangement would have netted about $250 million for Google's banks. Instead, the company was offering to pay $97.8 million in commissions and underwriting discounts, or 2.7% of the $3.6 billion it was aiming to raise in its IPO.

When the SEC declared Google's registration effective in early August, bankers found themselves faced with the prospect of not only pricing the offering in a month that is traditionally slow for new issuance but also with the Nasdaq index near a low for the year. Most issuers were pricing their deals below their target range, if not withdrawing their offerings altogether. But unwilling to postpone the deal, Google decided to go ahead, agreeing to cut the target price range to $85–$95 per share, from the initial hopes of $108–$135 per share. The company also cut the number of shares it would offer to 19.6 million from 25.7 million.

In the weeks leading up to the pricing, Google faced another obstacle. First off, its efforts to level the playing field between institutional and retail investors were put under the microscope as Google refused to provide institutional investors with the same sort of in-depth financial guidance about its business that most issuers do.

All this secrecy, along with a unique, very short lockup structure that would allow Google employees to sell shares only 15 days following the IPO, spooked institutions. Then a Playboy magazine interview with Google's founders riled the SEC, leading to speculation that the deal would be pulled for possible quiet-period violations.

Google's management and bankers agreed to push forward, ultimately pricing the deal at $85 per share, with its electronic auction proving enough of a success that investors who placed bids at or above that price were granted at least 74% of their orders. Moreover, despite all the criticism, Google's stock quickly proved a success. Shares closed at $100.34 at the end of the first day of trading. At the end of 2004, it closed at $192.79, a 127% increase over the offering price.

Note: This transaction did not fully meet Google's objectives because there was almost no retail participation (since Google did not allow a selling concession to retail brokers), and the price jumped 18% during the first day of trading, invalidating the principal purpose of the Dutch auction (by leaving money on the table).

Source: Tunick, Britt Erica. "Google goes its own way: Novel Dutch auction had twists and turns all the way to IPO." *IDD*. January 17, 2005.

Follow-On Offerings

After an IPO is completed, subsequent SEC-registered equity offerings by a public company are called follow-on offerings. Follow-on offerings are often referred to as "secondary offerings" to distinguish them from IPOs. For these financings, an investment bank underwriting group is formed, with one or more lead bookrunners and a number of comanagers selected by the issuer. For a US follow-on offering, the company files either an S-1 or S-3 registration statement with the SEC (subject to their meeting the requirements to do so, among which is the requirement that the company must have been public for at least 1 year at the time of the filing), which enables, as is the case with an IPO, a broad-based marketing effort using a red herring prospectus during a road show (if conducted). A final prospectus that has been declared effective by the SEC is then used as the basis for confirming orders from investors. Unlike an IPO, however, a follow-on offering does not include a price range since shares are priced in relation to the market price of the issuer's shares at the exchange on which they are listed. As a result, for follow-on transactions, investment bankers do not go through a valuation process with the company to establish a price range. Instead, they focus on, among other things, the most effective marketing plan for the offering, including the appropriate size, targeted investor base, and the appropriate price to set in relation to the price of outstanding shares at the time of the offering.

The size of a follow-on offering is important because new shares cause dilution to current shareholders in terms of EPS. EPS concerns are mitigated if the company forecasts that future earnings will grow fast enough to offset the dilution associated with issuance of additional shares. If the offering size is too large relative to the growth in projected earnings, declining EPS may negatively impact the company's share price (subject to the use of proceeds and other considerations). Therefore, bankers and their issuing clients must be careful to properly size a follow-on offering. It is unusual for the proceeds of a follow-on offering to be in excess of 25% of the then current stock market value (market capitalization) of the issuing company.

Good targets for follow-on offerings include companies that demonstrate the characteristics indicated in Exhibit 3.12. These companies must always consider the cost of capital associated with an equity offering. For most companies, an equity issuance will have a higher cost of capital compared to the issuance of debt. Consequently, many companies are reluctant to complete follow-on offerings unless the proceeds of the offering can be used to create significant growth opportunities that will, over time, result in an increase in EPS (accretion) as opposed to EPS dilution. However, even in the case of dilution, some companies will still proceed with a follow-on offering if they determine that a financing is essential and that a debt offering would significantly weaken their balance sheet. Too much debt in a company's capital structure may cause rating agencies to reduce their credit ratings, which will likely increase the cost of debt financing. The focus of both the company and its investment bankers, therefore, is on striking a balance between the amount of debt and equity in the company's capital structure. Frequently, bankers advise companies on the likely credit rating that will result from both debt and equity financing alternatives and build models to guide optimal financing decisions.

EXHIBIT 3.12 CHARACTERISTICS OF PROSPECTIVE EQUITY ISSUERS

- Strong stock performance or supportive equity research
- Large insider holdings or small float/illiquid trading
- Overly leveraged capital structure
- Strategic event: finance acquisition or large capital expenditure
- Sum of the parts analysis indicate hidden value
  - Carve-out
  - Spin-off
  - Tracking stock
- Investor focus
  - Road show focuses investors on misunderstood value
  - Brings additional equity research

Convertible Securities

A convertible security is a type of equity offering, even though most convertibles are originally issued in the form of a bond or preferred shares. Most convertible bonds or convertible preferred shares are convertible anytime (after a 3-month period following issuance), at the option of the investor, into a predetermined number of common shares of the issuer. This is called an "optionally converting convertible." The other type of a convertible is a "mandatorily converting convertible," where the investor must receive a variable number of common shares (based on a floating conversion price) at maturity (a mandatory receipt rather than an option to receive).

The issuer's preference regarding equity content of the convertible determines whether the convertible will be issued as an optionally converting convertible or a mandatorily converting convertible. From the perspective of a credit rating agency, an optionally converting convertible bond is considered to have bond-type characteristics since there is no assurance that the security will convert into common shares and there is a fixed coupon payment obligation. As a result, when originally issued, an optionally converting convertible bond weakens a company's balance sheet in almost the same way that a straight bond of the same size and maturity would (although the company's balance sheet will subsequently be strengthened if the convertible security eventually converts into common shares). By contrast, mandatorily converting convertibles (mandatory convertible), from a credit rating agency perspective, are considered to have equity-type characteristics. This is because there is certainty regarding conversion into common stock (and therefore no cash repayment obligation at maturity in the event of nonconversion). In addition, most mandatory convertibles are issued in the form of preferred stock, and there is usually no contractual issuer obligation to pay dividends on preferred shares (compared to a contractual obligation to pay interest coupons for a convertible bond). Therefore, mandatory convertibles strengthen a company's balance sheet in almost the same way that a common share offering of the same size would. Depending on the structure of the mandatory convertible, credit rating agencies generally assign between 50% and 95% equity content to this security.

Rationale for Issuing Convertible Bonds

If a company wants to issue debt, they might consider a convertible bond rather than a straight bond to reduce the coupon associated with debt issuance. For example, if a company could issue a $100 million bond with a 7-year maturity and a coupon of 6%, that same company might be able to issue a convertible bond for the same amount and maturity but with a coupon of 3%. The reason convertible bond investors might accept a coupon that is 3% lower than a straight bond coupon is because the convertible bond gives them the option to receive a predetermined number of common shares of the issuer's stock in lieu of receiving cash repayment. This option is valuable to investors because the future value of the stock might be considerably higher than the $100 million cash repayment value of the convertible bond. Basically, a convertible bond has an embedded call option on the issuer's common stock, and the investor "pays" for this option by accepting a lower coupon.

If the value of the common shares that convertible bond investors have the right to receive does not exceed $100 million during the life of the convertible, they will generally not elect to convert the bond into shares and will therefore receive $100 million in cash at maturity in 7 years. If the value of the shares exceeds $100 million on or anytime before maturity, investors may elect to convert the bond and receive shares (see Exhibit 3.13 to determine the breakeven future share price for the investor to be economically indifferent between purchasing a convertible bond compared to purchasing a bond issued by the same company).

EXHIBIT 3.13 CONVERTIBLE BOND COMPONENT PARTS

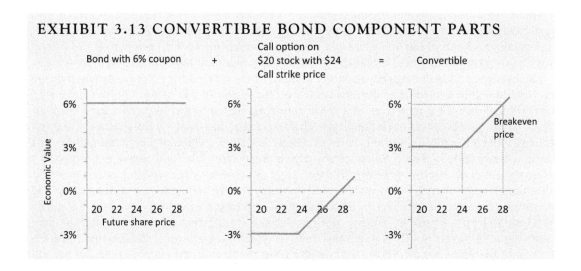

Convertible Bond Example

A company issues a $100 million convertible bond with a 7-year maturity and a 3% annual coupon. Investors are given the right to receive either $100 million repayment at maturity or, at their option, give up receipt of this cash amount in exchange for receiving a predetermined number of shares of the issuer's common stock. On the date of convertible issuance, the company's stock price is trading at $25, and the company agrees to a "conversion price" for the convertible of $31.25, which is 25% above $25. This percentage is called the "conversion premium," because the conversion price is set at a premium (in this case, a 25% premium) to the company's share price on the date of convertible issuance. The conversion price determines the number of shares that the investor has the right to convert into. This determination is made by dividing the total proceeds of the offering by the conversion price. The result, in this example, is $100 million/$31.25 = 3.2 million shares. Convertible investors, therefore, have a choice to make: either take $100 million in cash at maturity or give up the cash right in exchange for receiving 3.2 million shares anytime at or before maturity. If, for example, the issuer's share price increases to $45 at maturity in 7 years, convertible investors might elect to give up the right to receive $100 million in cash in exchange for 3.2 million shares because the value of these shares would be 3.2 million × $45 = $144 million. In practice, most investors wait until maturity to make the conversion decision due to the value of the options embedded in the convertible, but they have the right to convert earlier.

Convertible Market

The global convertible market has historically been a robust market, with proceeds raised typically equal to 20%–50% of proceeds raised through follow-on common stock issuance (see Exhibit 3.14). During September of 2008, the SEC instituted a ban on short selling US listed financial stocks. Because major investors in convertible bonds include convertible arbitrage hedge funds that short the underlying stock to hedge their long

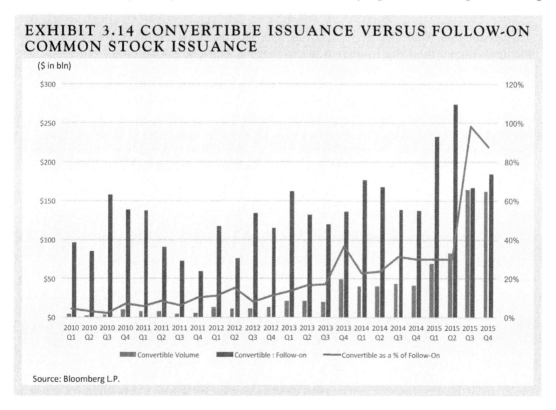

EXHIBIT 3.14 CONVERTIBLE ISSUANCE VERSUS FOLLOW-ON COMMON STOCK ISSUANCE

Source: Bloomberg L.P.

I. INVESTMENT BANKING

position in the convertible security, the short sale ban effectively made this strategy impossible. As a result of this and the severe dislocation experienced by the credit markets following Lehman Brothers' bankruptcy, a large portion of the convertible bond market was essentially shut down during the second half of 2008 and did not show much recovery until 2013.

The two main types of convertible investors are "outright buyers" and "arbitrage buyers." Outright buyers purchase convertibles with the expectation that the company's share price will exceed the conversion price (by an amount in excess of the break-even amount illustrated in Exhibit 3.13). Arbitrage buyers are focused on hedging away share price risk and creating profits in excess of the coupon through "delta hedging" their position. This is described in more detail in Chapter 9. Arbitrage buyers principally consist of hedge funds that leverage their investment by using the convertibles they purchase as collateral for borrowing a significant portion of the purchase price of the convertibles. Historically, more than 70% of all convertibles have been purchased by hedge funds.

FEES TO BANKERS

Investment banks that underwrite capital markets transactions are paid fees in the form of a gross spread (the difference between total proceeds of the offering and cash that the company receives, before paying legal, accounting, printing, and other offering expenses). This fee is broken into three parts:

1. Management fee (typically 20% of the total fee): This compensates the managers of the financing for their role in preparing the offering. The lead bookrunners receive a disproportionate amount of this fee.
2. Underwriting fee (typically 20% of the total fee): This compensates for underwriting risk. The fee is divided proportionally among underwriters based on the actual amount each firm underwrites.
3. Selling concession (typically 60% of the total fee): Usually apportioned based on each firm's underwriting commitment, this compensates underwriters for their selling efforts. Sometimes (although less common now), there is a "jump ball" selling structure in which the selling concession allocations are decided by investors.

See Exhibit 3.15 for a summary of global fees for IPO and convertible underwriting.

EXHIBIT 3.15 EQUITY UNDERWRITING GROSS SPREADS (FEES)

	2014 Total Global Volume	2014 Total Global Fees	2015 Total Global Volume	2015 Total Global Fees
		$ in millions		
IPOs	249,019.2	7,957.8	188,406.7	5,636.5
Convertibles	103,581.5	2,057.9	90,146.1	1,672.4

Source: Thompson Reuters.

The fees associated with convertible financing depend on the type of convertible security (i.e., convertible bond, convertible preferred shares, or mandatory convertible), the maturity, and structural issues. Generally in the United States, convertible financing fees range from 1.5% of proceeds for convertible bonds to 3% of proceeds for mandatory convertibles. Mandatory convertible fees are much higher than convertible bond fees because mandatory convertibles are similar to common stock from the perspective of investor share price exposure and are generally more complicated securities than convertible bonds. By comparison, bond fees range from 0.5% to 0.875% for high-grade bonds to 1.5%–2.0% for high-yield (junk) bonds and equity fees range from 2% to 6% for follow-on equity offerings to 3%–7% for IPOs. For equity deals, the fee percentage is mostly an inverse function of the offering size. Fees for convertibles, IPOs, follow-on offerings, and bonds are somewhat lower outside of the United States.

DISTRIBUTION ALTERNATIVES

A company and its investment bank must decide on how to distribute a capital markets offering. Historically, investment banks have conducted a 3- to 5-day road show for follow-on offerings (in comparison to a 7- to 10-day period for an IPO) since the market is already familiar with a company that initiates a follow-on offering. However, the road show period has recently been shortened to limit issuer price risk. The company's share price is subject to change during the road show for a follow-on offering and so, if the share price drops, the company will receive lower proceeds than they would have if the offering had been completed immediately, without a road show. Sometimes, issuers mitigate this share price risk either by completing an accelerated offering with a shorter road show period of 1 or 2 days, or by carrying out a block trade, in which the investment bank buys the securities without a road show and bears full price risk (see Exhibit 3.16).

EXHIBIT 3.16 HISTORICAL DISTRIBUTION ALTERNATIVES

Fully Marketed	• Issuer bears share price risk • 3-5 day management roadshow • Red herring prospectus delivered • Accesses widest pool of investor demand
Accelerated	• Issuer bears smaller share price risk • 1-2 day management roadshow • Red herring prospectus delivered • Narrower access to investor demand
Block Trade	• Investment bank bears share price risk • Marketing limited to sales calls to potential investors during the evening, with purchase commitment from bank before market opens the next morning • No red herring prospectus • Eliminates market risk for issuer • Requires a discount to market price to accommodate risk taken by the bank

Note 1: Recently, almost all distributions have been completed on an accelerated basis.
Note 2: Regardless of the distribution alternative, investment banks bear the risk settlement: if an investor changes his mind the morning after a verbal commitment to purchase is made, the investment bank must purchase the securities at the offered price.

Because of the increased market volatility associated with the credit crisis of 2007–08, the marketing timeline for offerings decreased significantly in an attempt to help issuers minimize pricing risk. Fully marketed deals are now usually completed in 1–2 days, and some follow-on offerings are conducted exclusively over the phone. One recent innovation is an "over the wall" deal, in which select institutional investors are approached on a confidential basis by investment bankers about a yet-to-be-named issuer. Interested parties are brought "over the wall" and provided with confidential information about the issuer (after which they can no longer trade the company's stock until the deal is completed, regardless of whether they decided to purchase shares from the offering).

SHELF REGISTRATION STATEMENTS

Many large companies that engage in regular US public capital markets financings for equity, debt, and convertible securities file a shelf registration statement (an "S-3" filing) with the SEC at some point at least 1 year after completing their IPO. A shelf registration enables a company to file one registration statement that covers multiple issues of different types of securities (under Rule 415). Once declared effective by the SEC, this registration, which provides much of the same accounting, disclosure, and descriptive information found in an IPO filing, allows multiple offerings of several types of securities over a 3-year period, as long as the company updates the registration with quarterly financial statements and other related required updates. This enables a company to use the registration opportunistically, without having to separately file for each financing and wait for SEC clearance each time. A financing using a shelf registration statement is called a "shelf take-down."

In 2005, the SEC created new rules for "well-known seasoned issuers" (also known as "WKSI" filers), which allow companies that satisfy a number of requirements (among which is a minimum market capitalization of $700 million) to file a shelf registration and have it become immediately effective and useable for offerings, without SEC review. For this reason, the practice of filing a shelf "just in case" is no longer widely used by WKSI's.

"GREEN SHOE" OVERALLOTMENT OPTION

A "Green Shoe" is an "overallotment" option that gives an investment bank the right to sell a short number of securities equal to 15% of an offering the bank is underwriting for a corporate client. The term overallotment is used because the investment bank allocates 115% of the base deal to investors and only takes delivery from the issuer of 100% of the base deal, thus creating a "naked" short position. An investment bank will need to buy shares after the initial offering equal to the 15% overallotment. To do this, the bank either buys shares from the issuer at the offering price (if the share price increases over the coming days or weeks) or buys shares in the market at the prevailing market price to generate demand and support the stock (if the share price decreases during this period). The SEC permits this activity to enable investment banks to stabilize the price of an equity offering following its initial placement. The objective is to mitigate downside share price movement in the secondary market (trades between investors after the initial sale from the issuer) by allowing the underwriting banks to cover their short position by buying shares in the open market if the issuer's share price drops after issuance. This benefits the shareholders, the company, and the investment bank underwriters because it increases demand for the shares in the secondary market if the issuer's share price is falling after the offering is launched, reducing the perception of an unstable or undesirable offering (which can lead to further share price declines). Because of the benefits to the issuer, most companies decide to include a Green Shoe option in their securities offerings. Exhibit 3.17 describes in detail how the Green Shoe option works.

EXHIBIT 3.17 GREEN SHOE OPTION (OVERALLOTMENT OPTION)

To mitigate downside share price risk in a Securities and Exchange Commission registered securities offering and to meet potential investor demand for more securities, an investment bank and the issuer are able to enter into an overallotment option prior to the offering. The overallotment option allows an investment bank to sell short securities that are equal to 15% of the securities sold in a public offering by a company at the time of the offering. The following example shows the outcome of this activity for both the company and the investment bank. Assume that the company agrees to (1) sell 100 shares of common stock through the investment bank at a price of $100 per share, (2) a 15% overallotment option, and (3) pay the investment bank a 2% fee (gross spread) on issuance proceeds.

Outcome

The investment bank sells on behalf of the company 100 shares long at $100 per share = $10,000 proceeds. The investment bank simultaneously sells short 15 of the company's shares at $100 per share = $1500 proceeds.

If the company's share price increases after the offering, the investment bank buys 15 shares from the company at $100 per share and delivers these shares to the initial short sale buyers. In this case, the company receives total proceeds of $11,500 and issues 115 shares. Investor demand has been met for 115, instead of 100 shares, and the company receives more money than they would have if only 100 shares had been issued. The investment bank's short position has been hedged (resulting in no gain or loss), and it receives a fee of 2% of $11,500 = $230.

If the company's share price decreases after the offering, the investment bank buys 15 shares from the market at, say, $99 per share (paying $99 × 15 = $1485) and delivers these shares to the initial short sale buyers. In this case, the company receives total proceeds of only $10,000 and issues only 100 shares. The investment bank's short position has created a profit for the bank of $1500 − $1485 = $15. The bank's purchase of 15 shares in the market mitigates downside pressure on the company's stock (without this purchase, the stock may have dropped to, say $95, which would make both the company and investors unhappy). The investment bank receives a fee of 2% of $10,000 = $200. As a result, the bank is better off if the company's share price increases because they earn more ($230 fee is better than $200 fee plus $15 short position profit).

The company, investment bank, and investors all hope the company's share price increases after the equity offering. However, this means that the company must have board approval for issuing a range of shares between 100 and 115 shares (accepting the negative earnings per share (EPS) consequences of issuing more shares). The quid pro quo for the EPS risk is the stabilizing benefit of the investment bank's purchase of shares from the market if the company's share price decreases after the offering.

Note: The investment bank may purchase less than 15 shares in this example if there is only a modest drop in the company's share price.

The term Green Shoe comes from a company founded in 1919 called Green Shoe Manufacturing Company (now known as Stride Rite Corporation), which was the first company allowed to use this option in an equity offering during 1971.

INTERNATIONAL FINANCINGS

Financial markets have become more integrated internationally, allowing corporations and governments more ways to raise capital by issuing securities outside their domestic markets. Investment banks and legal counsel help issuers consider which country to issue securities in, which legal entity to use as the issuer, market liquidity, foreign laws (including investor protection laws), accounting standards, tax issues, currency risk exposure, and investor demand.

Owing to capital market segmentation, it may be beneficial for a company to issue securities in foreign markets as an alternative to or in addition to issuing securities at home (see Chapter 8 for a description of international security issuance). Bonds issued by a company outside its home country are called Eurobonds. Non-US companies can have their shares listed on a US exchange based on the issuance of American depository receipts that are backed by the company's shares held in a depositary account in their home country.

Investment Banks, Hedge Funds, and Private Equity, Third Edition
http://dx.doi.org/10.1016/B978-0-12-804723-1.00004-9

The material in this chapter should be cross-referenced with the following cases: **The Best Deal Gillette Could Get? Proctor & Gamble's Acquisition of Gillette Case, and H.J. Heinz M&A Case**.

Corporate change of ownership transactions or combinations such as mergers, acquisitions, divestitures, and joint ventures (collectively, "M&A") are important strategic considerations for companies that are contemplating ways to enhance shareholder value or reduce shareholder risk. Investment bankers play a key role in initiating, valuing, and executing M&A transactions. This activity accounts for a substantial portion of revenue generated by the Investment Banking Division within large investment banks and represents most of the revenue at certain boutique investment banks.

M&A is a global business, with approximately half of all transactions completed inside the United States (see Exhibit 4.1). Virtually no major company or industry across the globe is unaffected by M&A transactions.

EXHIBIT 4.1 US COMPLETED M&A

Financial Advisor	2016 Rank	2015 Rank	Value $ (millions)	# of Deals	Fees $ (millions)
Goldman Sachs & Co	1	1	532,089.80	98	1,236.80
Bank of America Merrill Lynch	2	3	405,221.30	66	517.1
Citigroup	3	5	395,394.00	49	399.1
Morgan Stanley	4	6	390,090.30	87	1,004.30
Barclays	5	7	355,801.10	76	461.7
JP Morgan	6	2	353,605.10	101	971.7
Credit Suisse	7	10	323,448.00	52	354.8
Centerview Partners LLC	8	8	258,518.50	32	398.4
Deutsche Bank	9	9	224,771.30	35	175.8
Lazard	10	4	211,627.80	44	297.3
Evercore Partners	11	12	200,008.90	69	355.4
LionTree Advisors LLC	12	38	157,482.50	7	72.9
Guggenheim Securities LLC	13	18	155,799.00	13	132.2
UBS	14	11	117,250.30	26	148
RBC Capital Markets	15	14	104,530.40	41	172.5
Moelis & Co	16	28	101,015.80	56	210.3

EXHIBIT 4.1 US COMPLETED M&A—cont'd

Financial Advisor	2016 Rank	2015 Rank	Value $ (millions)	# of Deals	Fees $ (millions)
Allen & Co Inc	17	13	89,007.80	6	68
Needham & Co LLC	18	79	68,628.60	8	12.2
Wells Fargo & Co	19	16	64,415.40	34	163
Greenhill & Co, LLC	20	20	57,188.00	18	114.9
Rothschild & Co	21	40	43,122.80	20	75.1
PJT Partners LP	22	19	32,616.60	24	106.8
BNP Paribas SA	23	31	31,988.90	4	27.5
Jefferies LLC	24	17	30,357.90	64	263.2
Sandler O'Neill Partners	25	43	26,469.70	47	118
Industry Total			**1,154,484.20**	**6,078**	**11,311.10**

THE CORE OF MERGERS AND ACQUISITIONS

At the core of M&A is the buying and selling of corporate assets to achieve one or more strategic objectives. Before entering into an acquisition, companies typically compare the costs, risks, and benefits of an acquisition with their organic opportunity (often referred to as a "Greenfield analysis"). This buy versus build analysis is an important departure point for a company as it begins to think about an acquisition. Is it better to build a brand, geographic coverage, distribution network, installed base of products or services, and relationships? Or is it better to acquire them? Obviously, time, expense, and assessment of risk play a key role in this decision-making.

The analysis is never static. Strategic decisions must be reevaluated in light of new circumstances. The success or failure of competitors, the changing costs of capital, and pricing of public and private assets all come into play and constantly alter the equations.

The inverse decision—whether to sell—is an analysis that asks whether the benefits of continuing to operate an asset (for oneself or as the fiduciary of shareholders) is a better risk-adjusted option than monetizing the asset (for cash) or other consideration (such as stock of the acquirer). Often, corporate boards refer to the sale of a company for cash at a premium as a "derisking" of the investment for the benefit of shareholders.

The critical component that enables this decision-making begins with a thorough understanding of the asset (for sale or to be acquired). The development of a base operating plan is the starting point. Investment bankers must review previous management forecasts to gain a sense of their predictive ability, and then help management make an honest assessment of the value of the asset.

CREATING VALUE

The global capital markets are significantly impacted by the thousands of M&A transactions that are completed each year. Investment banks, lawyers, accountants, management consultants, public relations firms, economic consultants, and deal magazines are all important participants in this business. However, there is an ongoing debate about whether, apart from enriching the investment bankers and other professionals who advise, execute, and report on the transactions, M&A is beneficial to shareholders. Furthermore, even if a transaction benefits shareholders, there are questions about the potential resulting harm to consumers (if a monopolistic business is created), employees (if they lose their jobs), and communities (if their tax base is impaired).

In determining after the fact whether an M&A transaction was beneficial to shareholders, it is important to consider the change in value following completion of an acquisition compared with share prices of other companies in the same industry over the same interval of time. For example, America Online announced its agreement to acquire Time Warner for about $182 billion in stock and debt during January of 2000. With dominating positions in the music, publishing, news, entertainment, cable, and internet industries, the combined company, called AOL Time Warner, boasted unrivaled assets among media and online companies. This was the largest M&A transaction in history at the time and some analysts heralded it as a "great transaction," an "unprecedented powerhouse," and an "unbeatable alliance." The new company was owned 55% by AOL shareholders and 45% by Time Warner shareholders. However, 2 years later, following the bursting of the technology bubble, the company's share price had dropped over 55%, and some of the same analysts who called the transaction an unprecedented powerhouse were calling it an unprecedented failure.

Although AOL Time Warner's share price drop was indeed remarkable and discouraging to shareholders, a determination of whether this transaction enhanced or destroyed value should be made in the context of comparable company share price movement during the same time period. When looking at share price changes experienced by AOL Time Warner's competitors, criticism that the AOL acquisition of Time Warner was a failure may be somewhat unwarranted. For example, during this same 2-year period, News Corp, a major competitor, saw a drop in its share price of over 50%. Moreover, many pure technology companies during this period suffered share price drops that were even larger.

Acquirer returns vary by characteristics of the acquirer, target, and the form of payment. According to research, smaller acquirers tend to realize higher M&A returns, acquirer returns are often positive for privately owned or subsidiary targets, relatively small transactions may generate higher returns, and the form of payment impacts the returns achieved by acquirers (see Exhibit 4.2).

EXHIBIT 4.2 ACQUIRER RETURNS

Characteristic	Empirical Support
Type of Target: Acquirer Returns	
• US buyouts often provide positive returns when the target is privately owned (or a subsidiary of a privately owned company) and slightly negative returns when the target is a large publicly traded firm, regardless of the country • Cross-border deals generally provide positive returns except for those involving large public acquirers	Jansen et al. (2014) Netter et al. (2011) Capron and Shen (2007) Faccio et al. (2006) Draper and Paudydyal (2006) Moeller et al. (2005)
Form of Payment: Acquirer Returns	
• Acquirer returns for equity financed large public companies are less than for all-cash financed deals in the US • Acquirer returns for equity financed acquisition of public or private firms are frequently better than for all-cash financed deals in European Union countries • Acquirer returns for equity financed acquisitions involving private firms (or subsidiaries of publicly owned firm) often significantly exceed returns for cash deals • Acquirer returns for cross-border deals financed with equity are negative	Fu et al. (2013) Shleifer and Vishny (2003) Megginson et al. (2003) Heron and Lie (2002) Linn and Switzer (2001) Martynova and Renneboog (2008) Netter et al. (2011) Officer et al. (2009)
Acquirer/Target Size: Acquirer Returns	
• Smaller acquirers often realize higher returns than larger acquirers. • Relatively smaller deals generate higher acquirer returns than larger ones • Acquirer returns may be lower when the size of acquisition is large relative to the buyer (i.e., more than 30% of the buyer's market value)	Vijh et al. (2013) Offenberg (2009) Gorton et al. (2009) Moeller et al. (2005) Moeller et al. (2003) Hackbarth et al. (2008) Rehm et al. (2012)

Source: Donald DePamphilis, Mergers, acquisitions, and other restructuring activities: 2015.

STRATEGIC RATIONALE

A company must have a strategic rationale for completing an M&A transaction. This includes a desire to achieve cost savings through economies of scale that come from sharing central services such as legal, accounting, finance, and executive management, as well as through reducing real estate holdings, corporate jets, and other redundant assets. An investment banker works closely with the company's senior management to create a strategic rationale for an M&A transaction and determine the resulting benefit to stakeholders. Ultimately, the goal of an M&A transaction should be to drive either an immediate or a near-term increase in shareholder value. To determine if this can be accomplished, a banker, together with the client, attempts to project an M&A transaction's impact on earnings per share (EPS; accretion or dilution), post-transaction cost of capital, return on equity (ROE), return on invested capital (ROIC), and trading multiple expansion or contraction.

SYNERGIES AND CONTROL PREMIUM

A key component in determining whether or not an M&A transaction is strategically justifiable is the analysis of projected synergies that should be created by the transaction. Synergies in this context refer to expected reduced costs and increased revenues. Cost synergies are most important, and they arise through efficiencies created from elimination of redundant activities, improved operating practices, and economies of scale. Revenue synergies, which are usually given less weight, come from the ability to create greater revenue through a combined company than the sum of the independent companies' revenues. Companies should develop a thorough, realistic process for forecasting synergies by bringing representatives from both companies together to define what needs to be done to capture synergies and the value derived from this capturing process.

Cost synergies can be identified in the following general areas: Administration (exploiting economies of scale in central and back-office functions); Manufacturing (eliminating overcapacity); Procurement (purchasing power benefits through pooled purchasing); Marketing and Distribution (cross-selling and using common sales channels and consolidated warehousing); and R&D (eliminating R&D overlap in personnel and projects). Investment bankers should carefully review a company's forecasted synergies to determine if they are realistic, so that a credible total cost savings amount is included in post-transaction valuation calculations. It may be determined that both revenue and cost synergies should be discounted from management's projections since they are difficult to capture. According to research by McKinsey, 88% of acquirers were able to capture at least 70% of estimated cost savings, while only half of acquirers were able to capture at least 70% of estimated revenue synergies.

A control premium relates to the price that an acquiring company is willing to pay to purchase control over a target company's decision-making and cash flow. This premium equals the difference between a control-based purchase and a minority (non-control) purchase of shares. In many acquisitions, the acquirer is willing to pay a higher price than the current market price for a public company based on consideration of both expected synergies and other benefits associated with control.

CREDIT RATINGS AND ACQUISITION CURRENCY

Companies must consider the credit rating impact of an M&A transaction: a transaction can result in a ratings upgrade, downgrade, or no rating change. A downgrade may lead to a risk-adjusted higher cost of capital, which impacts the benefits of the transaction as well as the company's operating model going forward. As a result, companies and their investment bankers sometimes have confidential discussions with rating agencies before transactions are consummated to determine the probable rating impact of a transaction. This, in turn, can affect the decision regarding whether to use shares or cash as an acquisition currency. Share-based acquisitions have a more salutary effect on the acquirer's balance sheet and so ratings may not be negatively impacted, compared with a cash-based acquisition.

When considering the acquisition currency, acquiring companies should also focus on the transaction's impact on their EPS, balance sheet, cash flow, financial flexibility, and taxes. Although using shares as the acquisition currency can mitigate credit rating concerns, it can also have a negative impact on EPS relative to a cash-based acquisition. In addition, if more than 20% of the outstanding shares of a US public company are to be issued in an acquisition, a shareholder vote is required to support the issuance. Higher P/E (price to earnings) companies use stock as consideration more frequently than lower P/E companies do. However, the cost of issuing equity should always be compared with the after-tax cost of debt when determining whether to use cash or shares as the acquisition currency. If a target firm prefers receiving the acquiring company's shares because it is more tax-effective for selling shareholders (capital gains taxes are deferred until the shares received from the acquisition are sold), the acquirer may need to consider shares as the acquisition currency. In addition, target shareholders might prefer receiving shares to enable their participation in the future share appreciation potential of the postacquisition company. See **The Best Deal Gillette Could Get? Proctor & Gamble's Acquisition of Gillette Case** to review acquisition currency considerations.

When using shares as the acquisition currency, the acquirer and the seller must consider share price risk associated with this payment method. Because there is a meaningful time-lapse from the announcement of the transaction to the actual closing (typically 3–9 months), there is the potential for significant share price movement during this period. Therefore, if shares are to be delivered in an acquisition, a decision must be made to either structure the transaction with a fixed share exchange ratio and floating economic value, or a floating share exchange ratio with a fixed economic value. The exchange ratio is the number of acquiring company shares to be exchanged for each target company share, calculated as follows: offer price for target/acquiring company's closing share price on the last trading day before the deal is announced = exchange ratio. As an example, in an all-stock acquisition where the exchange ratio is 2.0× at closing (which, as indicated, could be 3–9 months after the deal is announced), the acquiring company will deliver to target company shareholders two acquiring company shares for every outstanding target company share. This is a fixed exchange ratio transaction, creating the potential for changing economic value, depending on changes in the acquiring company stock price. In a floating exchange ratio transaction, the exchange ratio moves up or down during the period from announcement to closing, depending on the acquiring company's stock price. This arrangement creates the same economic outcome (from a cash equivalence perspective) regardless of whether the acquirer's share price increases or decreases.

A common adjustment to a fixed exchange ratio is to impose a collar around the ratio that provides for an increase in the exchange ratio if the acquiring company's share price drops below a predetermined floor price and a reduction in the exchange ratio if the acquiring company's share price increases above a predetermined cap price. This collar arrangement creates a cash equivalent economic outcome at closing that has boundaries which, for example, might be 10% above and below the value of the transaction based on the exchange ratio on the date the transaction was announced.

REGULATORY CONSIDERATIONS

Companies, and their legal and investment banking advisors, must analyze the regulatory approvals that are necessary to complete an M&A transaction, focusing on local, regional, national, and international regulators. Approvals required to close a transaction depend on the size of the deal, the location of major businesses, the industry, and the industry regulatory body (if there exists one). In the United States, most public M&A transactions require a Hart–Scott–Rodino filing with the Federal Trade Commission (FTC) and the Department of Justice (DOJ). On filing, there is a 30-day waiting period during which the FTC and the DOJ may request further information. If there are international operations, the companies might also need to file with the European Commission, or with antitrust regulators in other relevant countries. Other US regulatory considerations include filing a merger proxy or a financing registration statement with the Securities and Exchange Commission (SEC), determining whether a report should be filed with the Pension Benefit Guaranty Corporation (if the transaction impacts company pension plans) and, potentially, filing with tax agencies, such as the IRS.

SOCIAL AND CONSTITUENT CONSIDERATIONS

There are numerous social considerations in any potential M&A transaction. For example: what is the quality of the target company's management team and should they be retained or asked to leave? Can two different management teams be combined without unduly disrupting the overall business? How many and who will be on the board of directors? Are there golden parachutes (severance packages payable on termination) that must be accounted for? Will there be large job losses? Are there environmental or political issues that must be addressed? Will the tax base of the communities in which the company operates be affected? Are there significant relocation issues? These social issues are particularly important in stock-for-stock combinations.

The principal constituents that must be considered in any potential transaction include the following:

1. Shareholders, who are concerned about valuation, control, risk, and tax issues
2. Employees, who focus on compensation, termination risk, and employee benefits
3. Regulators, who must be persuaded that antitrust, tax, and securities laws are adhered to
4. Union leaders, who worry about job retention and seniority issues
5. Credit rating agencies, who focus on credit quality issues
6. Equity research analysts, who focus on growth, margins, market share, and EPS, among other things
7. Debt holders, who consider whether debt will be increased, retired, or if there is potential for changing debt values
8. Communities, who may find their tax base and real estate markets impacted

Each of these constituents' concerns must be considered, but since there are many competing concerns, frequently, not every constituent (other than regulators) will be satisfied.

It is imperative that, as constituent priorities are considered, the companies involved in the M&A transaction and their advisors determine the potential reaction of politicians and the media. Not anticipating criticism from these sectors can imperil a deal. Considering criticism in advance and developing strategies for dealing with it is an increasingly important part of the M&A landscape (see **The Best Deal Gillette Could Get? Proctor & Gamble's Acquisition of Gillette Case**).

ROLE OF INVESTMENT BANKERS

Investment bankers help identify potential companies or divisions to be bought, sold, merged, or joint ventured. They create scenarios for successful transactions, including pro-forma projections and analysis of benefits and disadvantages. When a client agrees to proceed with a transaction, investment bankers provide extensive financial analysis, deal structure recommendations, tactical advice and, sometimes, financing (that they provide themselves, or arrange through the capital markets). Bankers work with a company's corporate development group to manage all phases of the transaction process. Bankers also play a key role in negotiating the terms of the transaction and certain parts of the documentation (in conjunction with legal advisors and senior management of the company). In most cases, an investment bank also delivers a fairness opinion (see below) at the time of transaction closing.

Bankers are paid different fees for advising on the transaction and for providing a fairness opinion. The bulk of an advisory fee is usually only paid if the transaction is successfully closed. The fee is normally calculated as a percentage of total consideration, and may vary from 2% for a relatively small transaction (below $200 million) to a fraction of 1% for a very large transaction (above $10 billion). Transactions may have much higher or lower fees, depending on the type and complexity of the transaction.

OTHER MERGER AND ACQUISITION PARTICIPANTS

In addition to investment bankers, there are many other key participants in an M&A transaction. The senior management of the company determines strategy, selects advisors, and makes key deal decisions. The company's corporate development group brings the best ideas presented by investment bankers (or through their own initiatives) to senior management and works on all aspects of deal execution. The board of directors is in charge of either recommending or rejecting proposed transactions and they must act in the best interests of shareholders based on the assumption of certain fiduciary duties. Other key participants include business unit heads (who participate in due diligence, integration planning, and synergy discussions); internal and external legal counsel; internal and external investor relations; human resources; and accountants. Each of these participants plays a role in identifying, analyzing, and advancing an M&A transaction.

FAIRNESS OPINION

Investment bankers are usually asked to render a fairness opinion to the respective boards of companies involved in an M&A transaction (see Exhibit 4.3). The opinion is made publicly available and it states, among other things, that the transaction is "fair from a financial point of view." A fairness opinion is not an evaluation of the business rationale for the transaction, a legal opinion or a recommendation to the board to approve the transaction. The fairness opinion includes a summary of the valuation analysis conducted by the investment bank to show the basis on which the opinion is offered.

A typical fee paid for a fairness opinion in a large M&A transaction is around $1 million, although this amount can vary, depending on the size and complexity of the transaction. This fee is paid separately from the M&A advisory fee (which is paid only if the deal is consummated). A fairness opinion is not a guarantee that a deal is fair, or even good. It is simply a document that reviews a deal's valuation based on standard valuation processes, including comparison of similar deals, and states that it falls within the parameters of the analysis. Boards of directors use fairness opinions as a data point in deciding whether to vote for or against a transaction and to create evidence that they have fulfilled their fiduciary duty in the event that they need to defend against any lawsuit relating to the M&A transaction.

There is division about whether it makes sense for the same investment bank that provides the fairness opinion to also act as the M&A advisor, since the advisory fee will only be paid if the transaction is completed and it will not be completed unless, among other things, the board is advised that the purchase price is fair. Sometimes, to mitigate this concern, companies employ one investment bank to render the fairness opinion and a different bank to provide M&A advice. Alternatively, consulting firms or accounting firms can be hired to provide the fairness opinion. Bringing in a third party to perform the fairness opinion is not without its issues, however. While independent, they will not understand as much about the deal as the party who negotiated it. As a result, it can be a problematic decision to divide up the advisory and fairness opinion roles: there are good arguments for and against both positions.

EXHIBIT 4.3 ORIGINS OF THE FAIRNESS OPINION

Fairness opinions are an outgrowth of a court case that involved the 1981 acquisition of TransUnion by Marmon Group. Defendant Jerome Van Gorkom, who was TransUnion's Chairman and CEO, chose a proposed price of $55 per share without consultation with outside financial experts. He only consulted with the firm's CFO and did not determine an actual total value for the company. A Delaware court was highly critical of his decision, writing that "the record is devoid of any competent evidence that $55 represented the per share intrinsic value of the Company." The court found that the company's directors were grossly negligent, because they quickly approved the merger without substantial inquiry or any expert advice. For this reason, the board of directors breached the duty of care that it owed to the corporation's shareholders. As such, the protection of the Business Judgment Rule was unavailable. Ever since, most public company boards have decided it is best to obtain a fairness opinion for any material M&A transactions.

LEGAL ISSUES FACED BY BOARDS

M&A decisions by a company's board are covered under the "Business Judgment Rule," a legal standard that presumes that board's make decisions that are in the best interests of shareholders. To challenge the decisions of a board in relation to an M&A transaction, a plaintiff must provide evidence that the board has breached their fiduciary duty of good faith, loyalty, or due care. If this cannot be proved in court, a plaintiff is not entitled to any remedy unless the transaction constitutes waste, which is interpreted to mean that the transaction was so one-sided that no business person of ordinary, sound judgment could conclude that adequate consideration was delivered. If a plaintiff is able to prove that the board lacked independence or otherwise breached its fiduciary duties, then the Business Judgment Rule's presumption that the board is acting in the best interests of shareholders is overcome, and a court will apply the "Entire Fairness Doctrine." As a result, the burden shifts to the company and its board to prove that the M&A process followed and the price offered were fair to shareholders. A board must also consider their "Revlon Duties" in relation to M&A sale transactions. If the sale or breakup of a company is inevitable, Revlon Duties are triggered, and the fiduciary obligation of directors of a target company are narrowed significantly: the singular responsibility of the board becomes determining how to maximize immediate shareholder value by securing the highest price possible. This highest price can usually be best obtained through a market test or an auction. As a result of triggering the Revlon Rule, the board's decisions are not evaluated based on the Business Judgment Rule, but instead based on consideration of this singular obligation to obtain the highest price.

ACQUISITIONS

A publicly traded company can be acquired through either (1) a merger; (2) an acquisition of stock directly from the target company shareholders using a tender offer, followed by a merger to acquire any remaining untendered shares; or (3) an acquisition of the target company assets and a distribution of the proceeds to the target company shareholders. The third acquisition method is rarely used since it is usually tax inefficient, and so only the first two methods are summarized below.

Merger

A merger is the most common way to acquire a company. It involves the legal combination of two companies based on either a stock swap or cash payment to the target company shareholders. For a merger to proceed, there must be a shareholder vote that favors the merger by more than 50% (or an even higher percentage, depending on the corporate articles and the state of incorporation). Typically the acquiring firm has principal control of the board and senior management positions. A merger of equals (MOE) is a combination of two companies with approximately equal assets. There is a less obvious designated buyer or seller, and the control premium is either nonexistent or negligible because, in theory, value created through synergies are shared approximately equally by shareholders of both companies. For example, Dow Chemical Co. and DuPont Co. combined during 2017 in an all-stock MOE that was the first step in a plan to create three new businesses. The merger was expected to lead to $3 billion in cost savings. The deal was the largest ever in the chemicals industry, creating a $130 billion company that combined products from both Dow and DuPont in the areas of agriculture, commodity chemicals, and specialty products to create new businesses. The agreement came after 2 years of pressure from activist investors who argued that shareholders of both companies would realize greater value if they were broken up. The merged company, called DowDuPont, was to be owned 50–50 by current shareholders of both Dow and DuPont. Although, in theory, an MOE results in equal representation on the board of directors and within senior management ranks, this seldom occurs. Usually one side or the other is subtly dominant.

Tender Offer

Another way to acquire a company is to purchase stock directly from shareholders, without requiring a shareholder vote, which is easiest if there is a single majority shareholder, or a small group of like-minded shareholders who, together, hold a majority position. If it is difficult to obtain the shares through private negotiations, or if the board is not supportive, a tender offer can be initiated. A tender offer is a public offer by an acquirer to all shareholders of a target company to tender their stock for sale at a specified price during a specified period of time. If less than 100% of shareholders accept the tender offer, a second step is required to gain control of the nontendered shares through a merger. If 90% or more of the shares are tendered, the merger can be effected through a short form merger process, which allows the acquirer to "squeeze-out" the untendered shares, requiring that they be sold without a shareholder vote. Typically a tender offer is initiated if the target company's board is not supportive of the acquisition. However, even with board support, a tender offer is sometimes initiated rather than a merger because, without the need for a shareholder vote, the tender offer can be completed faster than a merger. Tender offers in the United States are governed by the Williams Act, which requires that bidders include all details of their offer in a filing with the SEC. Interpretations of the Williams Act have become more difficult with the increasing use of derivative instruments employed by activist hedge funds in their acquisition efforts (see Chapter 13).

Under certain jurisdictions, a squeeze-out can be accomplished based on a threshold of less than 90% acceptance of a tender offer. For example, in Ireland, there are two thresholds to be considered in relation to a squeeze-out: 80% and 50%. Under Irish Takeover Rules, a compulsory acquisition through a squeeze-out can be effected if at least 80% of the shares are tendered to the prospective acquirer. If greater than 50%, but less than 80% of shares are tendered, the acquiring firm will not be able to effect a compulsory acquisition, but as the largest shareholder, it will control board decisions. See the **M&A Litigation Case** at the end of this chapter for further discussion on squeeze-outs.

Proxy Contest

A proxy contest is an indirect method of acquisition since it is designed to gain minority representation on or control of a board of directors. This strategy is often initiated by a financial agitator, but can also be used by a strategic acquirer to put pressure on senior management and existing board members. If successful, the proxy contest may change the composition of a board, as discussed in the **M&A Litigation Case**.

DUE DILIGENCE AND DOCUMENTATION

To enhance the chances of a successful acquisition, the buyer must carefully review a full range of issues regarding the target company. Every M&A transaction requires a due diligence process that investigates a company's business in detail by reviewing publicly available information and, subject to agreement by the parties, nonpublic information, after signing a confidentiality agreement. It is customary for most transactions to include in due diligence a tour of major facilities, discussion with management regarding their business, an extensive "data room" review (physical or electronic) of confidential documents, discussions with selected customers or suppliers and a follow-up session to ask questions that develop during data analysis. If an acquisition offer is not embraced by the target company and the prospective acquirer pursues a hostile initiative, the amount of information available through a due diligence effort is limited to publicly available information and anecdotal information that may be sourced from comparable companies, venders, customers, and suppliers. It is, therefore, more difficult to uncover all issues and concerns, and more challenging to develop cash flow forecasts and synergy estimates for a hostile takeover transaction.

Documents that are used in an M&A transaction include either a Merger Agreement, if an acquiring company directly purchases the stock of a target company, or a Stock Purchase Agreement, if an acquiring company purchases stock but does not want to complete a merger filing. Mergers involve the legal combination of two companies, are governed by state statutes, and require an affirmative vote of either a majority or a supermajority of the target company shareholders for approval, depending on the company's charter or bylaws (or by state laws if the company's charter or bylaws are silent on this point). If an acquiring company issues more than 20% of its pretransaction shares in a share for share merger, then the acquiring company shareholders also must vote in favor of the transaction. With a Stock Purchase Agreement, rather than merging two companies, an acquiring company can acquire stock directly from majority shareholder(s) in privately negotiated agreements or, through a tender offer, which does not require a shareholder vote if all shareholders sell. If not all shareholders agree to sell, then a merger is required as a second step to gain control of nontendered shares. If only assets are purchased, and not the entire company, an Asset Purchase Agreement is used.

An important provision in M&A documents is the "material adverse change clause" (MAC). A MAC is an event that materially changes the economic substance of the transaction after signing, but before closing. If a MAC clause is triggered, the transaction may be terminated. MAC clauses are carefully negotiated, with a particular focus on what constitutes materiality. This clause, in turn, impacts any payments that may be owed under deal protection provisions, including a breakup fee (see below). See the **M&A Litigation Case** for further discussion regarding a MAC clause. Another key provision in documents relates to whether the target company is allowed to "shop" its deal with an acquiring company to other prospective buyers. If so, there is a "go shop" provision; if precluded, there is a "no shop" provision. See the **H.J. Heinz M&A Case** for further discussion of a go shop provision.

BREAKUP FEE

A breakup fee is paid if a transaction is not completed because a target company walks away from the transaction after a Merger Agreement or Stock Purchase Agreement is signed. This fee is designed to discourage other firms from making bids for the target company since they would, in effect, end up paying the breakup fee if successful in their bid. A reverse breakup fee is paid if the acquiring company walks away from a transaction after signing the agreement. These fees are usually set at 2%–4% of the target company's equity value, but this is the subject of considerable negotiation during the documentation process. In some instances there is no breakup fee, but rather language enabling "specific performance" whereby a court can compel the deal to close. See **The Best Deal Gillette Could Get? Proctor & Gamble's Acquisition of Gillette Case** for further discussion of a breakup fee.

ALTERNATIVE SALE PROCESSES

Investment banks generally give priority to solicitation of M&A assignments that allow them to help sell a company or a division of a company. This is because there is a higher likelihood that a "sell-side" deal will be completed than for a "buy-side" deal. Sell-side processes are somewhat different, depending on the industry; the type of asset being sold; timing, acquisition currency, and tax concerns; impact on the company's business; and employee and confidentiality concerns. However, there are four general ways in which a sell-side assignment can be approached (as described below).

Preemptive

Bankers screen and identify the single most likely buyer and contact that buyer only. This process maximizes confidentiality (disclosing confidential selling company information to only one buyer) and speed, but may reduce the potential for price maximization.

Targeted Solicitation

Bankers identify and contact two to five most likely buyers. By limiting the potential buyers and avoiding public disclosure of the sale effort, this process may eliminate a perception that the deal is being shopped (unless there is an inadvertent disclosure). This process allows for reasonable speed and maintains strong control over confidentiality, while improving the potential for price maximization.

Controlled Auction

Bankers approach a subset of buyers (perhaps 6–20 potential buyers) who have been pre-screened to be the most logical buyers. This process is slower and quickly becomes known in the market, which sometimes creates undesirable share price pressure. Although confidentiality agreements will be signed with any potential buyer that the seller and investment bankers are comfortable with, a significant number of parties will obtain confidential selling company information, and some of these parties are direct competitors. The rationale for taking the risk that competitors will become more familiar with the target company (which is disadvantageous if the company is not ultimately sold) is that this more expanded sale process may result in a higher sale price.

Public Auction

The company publicly announces the sales process and invites all interested parties to participate. This creates potentially significant disruptions in the company's business since there are more moving parts and even greater confidentiality concerns, compared with a controlled auction. In addition, the process may take more time. The benefit of a public auction is that it may result in finding "hidden" buyers, creating the greatest potential for price maximization. See Exhibit 4.4 for a summary of these four alternative sale processes.

EXHIBIT 4.4 ALTERNATIVE SELL-SIDE PROCESSES

Divestiture Strategy	Description	# of Buyers	Advantages	Disadvantages	Circumstances
Preemptive	• Screen and identify most likely buyer	1	• Efforts focused on one buyer • Maximum confidentiality • Speed of execution • Minimum business disruption	• Unlikely to maximize value • Tied to result of one negotiation	• Have very clear sense of most logical buyer • High risk of damage from business disruptions • Have strong negotiating position
Targeted Solicitation	• High-level approach to selected potential buyers • Customized executive summary-type presentation • No pre-established guidelines or formal process • No public disclosure	2 to 5	• Speed of execution • Confidentiality maintained • Limited business disruption • Sense of competition enabled	• Requires substantial top-level management time commitment • Risks missing interested buyers • May not maximize value	• Have limited group of logical buyers • Have key objectives of confidentiality and limiting any business disruption
Controlled Auction	• Limited range of logical potential buyers contacted • Requires formal guidelines on sale process • No public disclosure	6 to 20	• Reasonably accurate test of market price • High degree of control over process • Creates strong sense of competition	• Lack of confidentiality • May "turn off" logical buyers • Potential for disruption due to rumors	• Seek good balance between confidentiality and value
Public Auction	• Public disclosure made • Preliminary materials distributed to wide range of potential buyers	N/A	• Most likely to obtain highest offer • Finds "hidden" buyers	• May limit subsequent options if process fails • Highest risk of business disruption	• Believe business is unlikely to be damaged by public process • Have difficulty identifying potential buyers

CROSS-BORDER TRANSACTIONS

A large number of M&A transactions are completed between companies that are based in two different countries. These transactions are almost always more complicated since there are multiple regulators (focusing principally on antitrust and securities law matters), complex accounting and disclosure considerations, and especially difficult tax matters to resolve. For example, in a transaction where a non-US company acquires a US company in a stock-for-stock arrangement, American Depositary Receipts (ADRs) may need to be used since most US-based shareholders want an acquisition currency that is freely monetizable in the United states, and some institutional investors are not allowed to own foreign stocks (see Chapter 8 for an explanation of ADRs). If an ADR program doesn't already exist for the acquirer's stock, it may need to be organized. In a stock-for-stock transaction where a US company acquires a non-US company, some non-US shareholders may feel compelled to sell their shares immediately because they don't want foreign exchange risk, or are uncomfortable holding a foreign stock. In this case, there may be large amounts of the US company's stock being sold, which puts downward pressure on the stock (see Exhibit 4.5). This phenomenon is called "flow-back."

EXHIBIT 4.5 CROSS-BORDER M&A TRANSACTIONS (STOCK-FOR-STOCK)

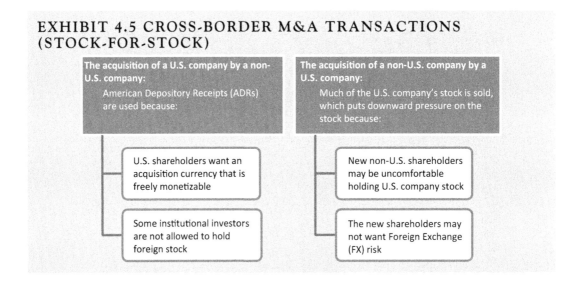

International Market Developments

As global economies are becoming more interconnected, mergers and acquisitions are an increasingly international affair. Deregulation in the United States, Europe, and Japan has led to a period of high merger and acquisition activity both within the United States and internationally. Examples of large international transactions that closed during 2016 are the $81.5 billion acquisition of BG Group by Royal Dutch Shell and the $106 billion acquisition of SAB Miller by Anheuser-Busch InBev. Completion of the EU's Internal Market initiative has eased regulations regarding mergers and acquisitions, enabling an expansion of this activity in Europe. Recently, the growth of emerging economies has resulted in M&A expansion throughout the world.

International M&A deals usually involve more legal complexity, intricate antitrust and tender offer regulations, new accounting rules, protectionism, and currency risk. Cultural differences must also be considered in international transactions.

An example of potential difficulties that can arise in international mergers was Kraft's hostile takeover of Cadbury, a large UK confectionery company. After completion of the deal, UK regulators initiated significant changes in their country's takeover rules, including new disclosure requirements about fees and employee and creditor participation in the merger decision. New regulations also required a 1-year commitment by the acquirer regarding employment following consummation of the transaction and other new employee rights.

In most European countries "creeping takeovers" (acquiring shares in the market before the actual takeover) are not allowed without disclosure. Many European takeover laws require shareholders that have already acquired approximately one-third of the company to make a binding offer for the entire target company.

While many US M&A transactions include a combination of cash and shares, this might be difficult for some cross-border transactions because common share cross-listing hurdles have to be overcome and, in some cases, the legal framework for a mixed cash-and-shares offer is problematic.

The total value of announced M&A activity in the Emerging Markets reached nearly US$1.2 trillion during 2015, a 41.6% increase from totals reached during 2014. Chinese involvement in deals drove M&A activity, with 5751 transactions worth $806 billion, far outpacing South African involvement, which generated the next highest volume with 438 deals worth $51.5 billion. Brazil followed, with $45.4 billion and 623 transactions. High technology led Emerging Market activity during 2015, accounting for 13.4% of M&A volume. Total estimated fees earned from completed Emerging Market M&A transactions during 2015 were US $4.3 billion.

TAX-FREE REORGANIZATIONS

M&A transactions, if structured properly, may be characterized as tax-free reorganizations. In the United States, the Internal Revenue Code provides a tax exemption for the exchange of shares (in a stock-for-stock transaction) that has the objective of reorganizing, or rearranging the company. The interest of the parties involved is to qualify the transaction as a tax-free reorganization that results in no corporate level or shareholder level taxes. However, this does not mean that shareholders will never have to pay taxes. This designation simply delays the taxable event until the target company's shareholders sell the acquirer shares received from the transaction. When target company shareholders receive acquiring company shares, the original basis in the target company shares is passed on to the new shareholding. Whenever the shares are sold, a tax will be paid based on the gain between the basis and the sales price of the shares. In addition, a substantial part of the consideration must consist of stock (at least 40%, or more, depending on the structure of the transaction), which will result in tax-free treatment of the portion of the consideration paid in shares (the cash portion will still be taxable). Finally, the acquiring company must continue to operate or use a significant part of the target company's business or assets.

CORPORATE RESTRUCTURINGS

Corporate restructurings involve either bankruptcy-related concerns or strategic opportunities. This section focuses on the latter, creating strategic opportunities that unlock shareholder value through the separation of a subsidiary from a parent company and not on bankruptcy-related transactions. Senior management and boards of directors must constantly analyze new opportunities to maximize shareholder value. From a strategic opportunity standpoint, this includes determining whether it is possible to create a new publicly traded company from one or more of the parent company's businesses. Sometimes, separating a non-core business from a company's other businesses can create greater clarity in the market and unlock value if the separated business participates in a higher growth industry. In addition, separating a business can improve operating performance, reduce risk profiles (including credit risk), and provide more efficient access to public capital markets. A separation event can either be completed in the private or public market. A private market event involves selling a subsidiary to private investors or to another company. A public market event involves selling or separating part of or the entire subsidiary in a public market transaction such as an initial public offering (IPO), carve-out, spin-off, split-off, or tracking stock transaction.

Initial Public Offering

A subsidiary IPO is the sale of all shares of a subsidiary to new public market shareholders in exchange for cash. This creates a new company with a new stock that trades independently from the former parent company stock. If the cash received by the parent is in excess of the parent's tax basis, then the IPO is a taxable event for the parent.

Carve-out

The sale through an IPO of a portion of the shares of a subsidiary to new public market shareholders in exchange for cash is called a carve-out. This type of transaction leaves the parent with ongoing ownership in a portion of the former subsidiary. In practice, since a large sale might flood the market with too many shares, thereby depressing the share price, usually less than 20% of the subsidiary is sold in a carve-out. Selling a minority position of the subsidiary also enables the parent to continue having control over the business and, importantly, makes it possible to complete a potentially tax-free transaction if less than 20% of the shares are sold. One consideration of a carve-out is the potential conflict of interest between the parent and the separated company. For example, if the separated company is vertically integrated with the parent company (i.e., a supplier), potential conflicts may arise if the former subsidiary pursues business with the parent company's competitors.

Spin-off

In a spin-off, the parent gives up control over the subsidiary by distributing subsidiary shares to parent company shareholders on a pro rata basis. This full separation avoids conflicts of interest between the parent and the separated company (unlike in a carve-out).

No cash is received by the parent company since a spin-off is essentially redistributing assets owned by parent company shareholders to those same shareholders. A spin-off may be accomplished in a two-step process. First, a carve-out is completed on a fraction of the shares to minimize downside pressure on the stock. It also allows the subsidiary to pick up equity research coverage and market making in the stock prior to delivery of the remaining shares to the original parent company shareholders. The carve-out sale is usually on less than 20% of the subsidiary's shares to preserve tax benefits. A spin-off provides the new company with its own acquisition currency, enables the new company management to receive incentive compensation, and unlocks the value of the business if comparable companies trade at higher multiples than the parent company multiple. Negatives include potentially higher borrowing costs and takeover vulnerability. See the **McDonald's, Wendy's, and Hedge Funds: Hamburger Hedging? Case** for a description of McDonald's spin-off of Chipotle.

Split-off

In a split-off, the parent company delivers shares of the subsidiary to only those parent shareholders who are willing to exchange their parent company shares for the shares of the subsidiary. This leaves the original parent company shareholders with either subsidiary shares (and no parent company shares) or parent company shares (and no subsidiary shares). A split-off is preferred to a spin-off when a portion of parent company shareholders prefers to own only the subsidiary's shares and not the parent company's shares. A split-off can be structured as a tax-free event if an initial carve-out of less than 20% of the subsidiary is followed with a split-off transaction. Since a split-off requires parent company shareholders to choose between keeping parent company stock and exchanging this stock for subsidiary stock, to achieve complete separation, sometimes a premium must be offered for the exchange (providing more shares of the subsidiary than a valuation analysis without incentives would suggest). A split-off transaction is much less common than a spin-off transaction.

Tracking Stock

In a tracking stock transaction, a separate class of parent company shares is distributed to existing shareholders of the parent company. The new stock tracks the performance of a particular business (which is usually a higher growth business compared with the parent company's other businesses), but this stock does not give shareholders a claim on the assets of either that business or the parent company. Revenues and expenses of the business are separated from the parent's financial statements and this financial information determines the tracking stock's valuation. Although a tracking stock offers the parent company the advantage of maintaining control over a separated subsidiary, it complicates corporate governance because there is no formal legal separation and a single board of directors continues to operate both businesses. In addition, both entities are liable for each other's debt obligations and so, in a bankruptcy scenario, it is unclear how the assets will be split up. As a result, this is a potentially confusing form of separation, and the logic of this transaction is frequently debated.

TAKEOVER DEFENSES

Companies that either have received or expect to receive a hostile takeover bid often retain investment bankers to assist them. This effort is designed to either fight off the bid and remain independent or negotiate a transaction that maximizes shareholder value. A takeover defense strategy is critically dependant on the specific laws that govern attempts to acquire a company. In the United States, the SEC governs all tender offers, but companies are incorporated based on state laws, and most states have adopted antitakeover statutes as part of their state corporation laws. Delaware has a separate court system for corporate law called the Delaware Chancery Court, which has been a leader in the development of corporate law. Many large US corporations are incorporated in Delaware because of the perceived benefits received from the state's clarity on corporate law matters.

Various defense strategies can be deployed by corporations, based on the advice of their investment bankers and legal counsel. The most actively utilized defense strategy is a shareholder rights plan.

Shareholder Rights Plan

A shareholder rights plan usually does not require a shareholder vote and often has a 10-year maturity. The key feature of this plan involves implementation of a "poison pill," which gives nonhostile shareholders a right to purchase additional shares in the company at a substantial discount (usually 50%). The result of the exercise of this right is that hostile shareholder ownership percentage declines as "friendly" shareholder ownership increases. This dilution of hostile ownership economically compels the hostile party to give up, negotiate a higher price, or launch a proxy contest to gain control of the target company's board and then rescind the poison pill. Poison pills have been a very effective deterrent to hostile takeover attempts for several decades, but since 2001 the number of companies that implemented (or renewed) this defense provision has declined in the face of shareholder activism. Some shareholders believe that a poison pill entrenches ineffective management and boards, resulting in a failure to maximize shareholder value. See Chapter 13 for additional discussion of takeover defenses, shareholder activism, and poison pills.

RISK ARBITRAGE

In a stock-for-stock acquisition, some traders will buy the target company's stock and simultaneously short the acquiring company's stock. The purchase is motivated by the fact that after announcement of a pending acquisition, the target company's share price typically trades at a lower price in the market compared with the price reflected by the Exchange Ratio that will apply at the time of closing. Traders who expect that the closing will eventually occur can make trading profits by buying the target company's stock and then receiving the acquiring company's stock at closing, creating value in excess of their purchase cost. To hedge against a potential drop in value of the acquiring company's stock, the trader sells short the same number of shares to be received at closing in the acquiring company's stock based on the Exchange Ratio.

The participation of these traders (called "risk arbitrageurs" or "risk arbs") is an important consideration in stock-for-stock acquisitions since their trading puts downward pressure on the acquiring company's stock and upward pressure on the selling company's stock.

For example, if an acquiring company agrees to purchase a target company's stock at an Exchange Ratio of 1.5×, then at closing, the acquirer will deliver 1.5 shares for every share of the target's stock. Assume that just prior to when the transaction is announced, the target's stock price is $25, the acquirer's stock is $20, and it will be 6 months until the transaction closes. Since 1.5 acquirer shares will be delivered, the value to be received by target company shareholders is $30 per share. However, because there is some probability the acquisition doesn't close in 6 months, the target company stock will likely trade below $30 until the date of closing. If the target stock trades at, for example, $28 after announcement, for every share of target stock that risk arbs purchase at $28, they will simultaneously short 1.5 shares of the acquirer's stock. This trade enables risk arbs to profit from the probable increase in the target's share price up to $30, assuming the closing takes place, while hedging its position (the shares received by risk arbs at closing will be delivered to the parties that originally lent shares to them to enable their short sales). The objective for risk arbs is to capture the spread between the target company's share price after announcement of the deal and the offer price for the target company, as established by the Exchange Ratio, without exposure to a potential drop in the acquirer's share price. However, if the transaction doesn't close or the terms change, the risk arbs' position becomes problematic and presents either a diminution in profit or a potential loss. Investment bankers keep close track of risk arb activity throughout the transaction period since the prices of both the acquirer and target stocks can be significantly impacted by risk arb trading.

VALUATION

Multiples-Based Valuation

In determining the appropriate value for a public company that is the subject of a potential acquisition or sale, the starting point is the consideration of the company's current share price. This price may represent the best indicator of fair value for a large public company without a control shareholder. To reflect the appropriate value for control of the company, this price must be adjusted upward. In other words, when purchasing a small fraction of the company, the closing market price is the best barometer of value for one share of stock, but if a majority of the company is purchased, there generally should be a control premium added to this closing market price. There are four basic valuation methods that guide investment bankers (and others) in determining the appropriate price for the purchase of a controlling interest in a company: comparable company analysis, comparable transaction analysis, leverage buyout (LBO) analysis, and discounted cash flow (DCF) analysis. In addition, a sum-of-the-parts analysis is often useful if a company has many different (and disparate) businesses, and there is the possibility that individual businesses, if sold independently, could create value in excess of the company's value. For certain industries, other valuation approaches may also be appropriate. For a private company, all, or only some of these valuation methods may be applicable in determining the appropriate value for an acquisition. The key to selecting the best valuation methodologies for public and private companies (or divisions of companies) is to consider the idiosyncrasies of and available information on the industry, and then factor in market precedents for valuing companies in that industry.

Comparable company analysis and comparable transactions analysis are multiples-based methods for determining value in relation to a set of peers. This means that a company's value is calculated as a multiple of a metric such as earnings or, more importantly in most cases, earnings before interest, taxes, depreciation, and amortization (EBITDA). EBITDA is a proxy for cash flow, but they are not identical. In multiples valuation, EBITDA is generally used because it can be calculated using only the income statement, whereas cash flow also requires information from the balance sheet. The most common multiples are enterprise value to EBITDA (EV/EBITDA); price to earnings (P/E); and price to book (P/B).

To obtain meaningful information from a multiples analysis, it is essential to select a peer group of public companies that have the most similar characteristics to the company being valued. This usually means analyzing companies in the same industry by using Standard Industrial Classification codes, or by using the North American Industry Classification System, utilizing a database such as Thompson Financial or Dealogic. However, sometimes a company should be excluded from a comparables peer group if the company competes in the same product area, but also has other large businesses that are unrelated to the key products of the company being valued. Size of comparable companies is also important. A company that has a market capitalization of $50 billion may not be a good comparable to a company that has a market capitalization of $500 million. Also, a thinly traded company that has limited analyst coverage may be removed from a peer group of comparable companies that have robust trading volume and active analyst coverage because its fundamental value is not fully reflected in its share price. Growth is also a very important consideration, and companies that exhibit much lower or higher growth than most other companies in an industry may be excluded for multiples analysis purposes. In addition, for a comparable transactions analysis, there is generally a valuation discount for smaller companies as compared with larger ones. These and many other factors must be considered when determining the best comparables. Coming up with the ideal list of comparables is challenging and, if the wrong companies are included, valuation conclusions may be incorrect. Finally, in addition to selecting the right peers, it is also important to normalize the financials of the peer companies to exclude any extraordinary items, nonrecurring charges, and restructuring charges. This ensures the comparison across peers is on an apples-to-apples basis.

Cash Flow–Based Valuation

DCF analysis and LBO analysis are cash flow–based methods of valuation. Both require projected future cash flows, which are discounted by a company's cost of capital. A DCF analysis attempts to determine the intrinsic value of a company based on future cash flow projections. An LBO analysis attempts to determine an internal rate of return (IRR) for a private equity firm acquirer based on future cash flow projections. The challenge for both DCF and LBO analysis is developing accurate long-term projections for 5–10 years of cash flow (EBITDA), which is industry convention for this valuation method. In an effort to improve the reliability of future EBITDA projections, sometimes, the future compensation and career track of managers who provide forecasts (and are tasked with managing the business going forward) are linked to these projections. Another challenge for DCF and LBO analysis is determining the most accurate discount rate, which varies considerably between companies and between industries, and relies on a number of sometimes difficult to determine assumptions.

Comparable Company Analysis

A comparable company analysis provides a helpful reference point for publicly trading companies, but it is not used as a principal basis for determining the value for an acquisition target since it does not incorporate a control premium. It is a useful exercise to look at companies in the same industry, or companies that have similar business characteristics in terms of growth, profitability, and risk. This analysis relies on the assumption that markets are efficient and current trading values are an accurate reflection of industry trends, business risks, growth prospects, and so forth. A multiples range can be developed for comparable companies and then this range can be applied to the company being valued to determine implied valuation (that doesn't include a control premium). The derived value for the company can then be compared with the company's stock price (which is always the best barometer of value for one share of a company in an efficient market). Discrepancies between the company's stock price and implied value range from this analysis can provide insights into unique challenges or prospects faced by the company. This is a starting point in a valuation analysis, but it is not relevant without utilizing other valuation processes that include a control premium.

Comparable companies in many cases can be analyzed based on their P/E multiple, which is calculated by dividing the current stock price by the annual EPS. The P/E multiple is usually calculated based on both the latest 12-month EPS as well as using forecasted EPS for the next fiscal year. EPS is calculated by dividing net income for a period by the weighted average shares outstanding for the period. When the P/E multiple range has been determined for comparable companies, this range should be applied to the company being valued by multiplying the company's earnings by this multiple range, to arrive at a valuation of the company's equity.

Comparable companies should also be analyzed based on their enterprise value (EV), which represents the total cost of acquiring a company. An EV/EBITDA multiple is most frequently used, but sometimes EV/EBIT (earnings before interest and taxes, without depreciation or amortization) is also considered. Enterprise value is equal to the current market value of equity plus net debt (and minority interests, if they exist). Net debt is comprised of short-term debt + long-term debt + capitalized leases + preferred stock—cash and cash equivalents. Net debt is included in EV because the acquirer of a company's stock has the eventual obligation to pay off debt (and related obligations) and assumes cash on hand will be used in the first case to retire debt, leaving net debt as an addition to equity market value. Because EV takes into consideration the value of equity and net debt, it provides a better comparison across companies with differing capital structures, thereby making the EV/EBITDA multiple a key basis for valuation. When an EV/EBITDA multiple range has been determined for comparable companies, this multiple range can be applied to the company being valued by multiplying the company's EBITDA by this multiple range.

Comparable Transactions Analysis

A comparable transaction analysis focuses on M&A transactions in which comparable companies were acquired. A comparable transaction analysis is similar to a comparable company analysis in relation to using multiples. However, comparable transactions include control premiums (and expected synergies), and so the multiples will generally be higher than for comparable companies and more reflective of a reasonable price to be paid for a controlling acquisition of a target company. In this analysis, as with the previous analysis, it is important to compare only selected companies in the same industry, or companies that exhibit the same business characteristics.

The company being analyzed for a potential takeover should be valued at approximately the same relative value as the comparable transaction companies, if the peer group is appropriately developed. In other words, if the comparable companies that completed transactions in the same industry sold for an EV/EBITDA multiple of 10× to 11×, then this multiple range should be applied to the EBITDA of the target company being considered for an acquisition. If the target company's EBITDA is, for example, $100 million, the logical EV range for the target company is $1.0–$1.1 billion ($100 million × 10 to 11). The equity value of the company would be based on the following formula: Equity Value = EV − net debt. If the target has total debt of $300 million, cash of $100 million and no preferred shares, capitalized leases or minority interests, the company's equity value is $1.0 billion to $1.1 billion − ($300 million − $100 million) = $800 million to $900 million. If the target company has 20 million shares, the value range per share for an acquisition is $40 to $45 ($800 million to $900 million/20 million shares).

Comparable transactions are typically drawn from the previous 5- to 10-year period, although the most recent transactions are generally considered the most representative. It is essential to use the relevant financials for the completed acquisitions based on the year of completion and to use both historical and forecasted EPS and EBITDA multiples from the announcement date. If done properly, a comparable transactions analysis can be very helpful in determining a potential range of prices to offer when purchasing a company, since the multiples for comparable transactions include control premiums and synergies. By looking at similar transactions over an historical period, this analysis is also useful in identifying industry trends such as consolidations and foreign investments, as well as to flag financial crises (such as during 2008–09, where multiples may not be relevant to subsequent periods) and to consider the activity of financial buyers such as private equity firms. After establishing the value of the target company using a comparable transaction analysis, it is important, when possible, to complete at least two other valuation processes and then attempt to triangulate the best price to offer for an acquisition based on multiple reference points. A subset of a comparable transaction analysis is a premium paid analysis, which compares the acquisition premium being considered to the premium paid in previous comparable transactions.

Discounted Cash Flow Analysis

A DCF analysis is considered an essential valuation methodology since it attempts to determine the intrinsic value of a company. This valuation, when it employs a perpetuity method, does not involve the selection of comparable companies, and so is immune to the inherent problems in creating a comparable company list. DCF relies on the projected cash flows of the company. A DCF analysis assumes that the value of a company (the enterprise value) is equal to the value of its future cash flows discounted by the time value of money and the riskiness of those cash flows. The company's value is calculated in two parts in a DCF analysis: (1) the sum of the cash flows during the projection period and (2) the terminal value (TV) (the estimated value of the business at the end of the projection period). Both parts are discounted using the company's weighted average cost of capital (WACC). The end result is determination of the net present value of the company's operating assets. The cash flows used are unlevered, which means that they do not include financing costs (e.g., interest on debt or dividends on stock). Because EV is the value to all capital providers of the company (debt and equity), unlevered cash flows represent the cash available to each of these providers. After establishing the EV of a company, the equity value can be determined by subtracting net debt from EV.

In a DCF analysis, future projections can incorporate changes in a company's long-term strategic plan. As a result, a DCF analysis is flexible enough to incorporate changing assumptions about growth rates and operating margins, while allowing for adjustments for non-operating items. However, a DCF valuation also has limitations. For example, it is critically dependent on accurate projections and, the longer the projected period of time it covers, the less confident one should be in its accuracy. Senior management's projections can be tested or sensitized by the investment banker. In addition, a DCF analysis utilizes WACC, which can be the subject of a wide range of costs estimates. Calculation of the cost of equity requires a number of variable inputs such as the levered beta of the company (which itself is the subject of numerous variables) and the market risk premium (which may also include a size discount or premium). Finally, it is important in a DCF analysis to project cash flows through the period of time covered by a full operating cycle, so that cash flows at the end of the projection period are "normalized." The end of this projection period is often called the "termination value date," which is typically 5–10 years in the future. The TV of a company should be determined as of the termination value date. TV is the present value (for the period into perpetuity that starts as of the termination value date) of all future cash flows, assuming a stable growth rate forever. There are two methods of projecting TV: (1) terminal multiple method, which applies a multiple such as EV/EBITDA to projected EBITDA at the termination value date or (2) perpetuity growth rate method, which is determined based on the following formula: $TV = FCF \times (1+g)/(r-g)$, where FCF is free cash flow projected as of the terminal valuation date; r is equal to WACC; and g is the perpetual growth rate (equal to the expected rate of inflation + the long-term real growth in GDP, historically about 3.25% in the United States). So, for example, if FCF is $100 million as of the terminal valuation date, WACC is 11%, $TV = \$100 \text{ million} \times (1.05)/(0.11 - 0.0325) = \$1.35 \text{ billion}$. It is important to note that because TV represents a significant portion of EV, overall value becomes highly sensitive to TV calculation assumptions.

The three steps that are necessary to complete a DCF valuation are as follows:

1. Determine unlevered free cash flows for a 5 to 10 year period such that the end of this period represents a steady-state condition for the company.
2. Estimate the TV of the company at the time when the company has reached a steady state (which coincides with the end of the cash flow forecast period) and continuing into perpetuity.
3. Determine WACC, which is the blended cost of debt and equity for the company, and then discount the unlevered free cash flows and the TV by WACC to create a present value (enterprise value) of the company.

A DCF analysis can be completed without inclusion of any synergies (Standalone DCF), but a typical DCF analysis usually is sensitized to show the impact of net synergies related to cost savings (Standalone plus cost savings DCF) and, sometimes, inclusion of total synergies, including revenue synergies (Standalone plus total synergies DCF).

Leveraged Buyout Analysis

An LBO analysis is a relevant acquisition analysis when there is the possibility of a financial sponsor buyer. Financial sponsors are private equity firms that purchase companies using equity they have raised in a private investment fund combined with new debt raised to facilitate the purchase. Compared with corporate buyers (strategic buyers), private equity firms (financial buyers) include higher amounts of debt to fund their acquisition. Financial buyers usually include senior secured debt provided by banks, subordinated unsecured debt, and sometimes mezzanine capital in their financing package. Management of the newly acquired company, which can be either the preacquisition team, or a new team brought in by the financial buyers, usually makes an equity investment in the company alongside the private equity firm. See Chapters 16 and 17 for a more complete overview of private equity and LBO transactions.

Targets for private equity firms are typically companies in mature industries that have stable and growing cash flow to service large debt obligations and, potentially, to pay dividends to the financial buyers. In addition, targets usually have low capital expenditures, low existing leverage, and assets that can be sold. Financial buyers generally target an exit event within 3–7 years, which is usually accomplished through either an IPO or M&A sale to a strategic buyer or, sometimes, to another financial buyer. Financial buyers usually target an IRR on their investments of more than 20% (although this target can move down depending on the overall economic climate and financing environment).

An LBO analysis includes cash flow projections, TV projections (the price at which a financial buyer thinks the company can be sold in 3–7 years), and present value determination (the price that a financial buyer will pay for a company today). The analysis solves for the IRR of the investment, which is the discount rate that results in the cash flow and TV of the investment equaling the initial equity investment. If the resulting IRR is below their targeted IRR, the financial buyer will lower the purchase price. Investment bankers run LBO models and assume a minimum IRR required by financial buyers based on risks associated with the investment and market conditions. They can then solve for the purchase price that creates this targeted IRR. If the purchase price is above the current market value of the company, this provides an indication that the company would make an economically viable investment for a financial buyer. In this case, investment bankers will include an LBO analysis as one of several valuation methods they use to determine the appropriate value for a target company and financial buyers will be included in addition to strategic buyers in the list of potential acquirers.

An LBO analysis is similar to a DCF analysis in relation to use of projected cash flows, TV, present value, and discount rate. The difference is that a DCF analysis solves for the present value (enterprise value), while the LBO analysis solves for the discount rate (IRR). Once the IRR is determined in the LBO analysis, the purchase price may need to increase or decrease to align with the targeted IRR (see Exhibit 4.6).

EXHIBIT 4.6 LEVERAGED BUYOUT ANALYSIS AND DISCOUNTED CASH FLOW ANALYSIS

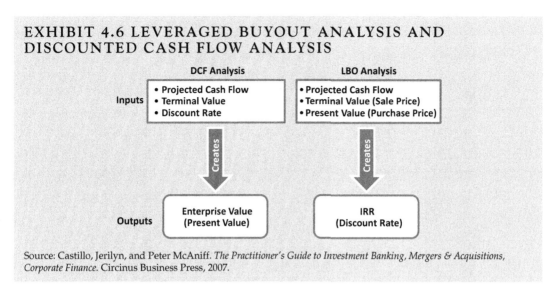

Source: Castillo, Jerilyn, and Peter McAniff. *The Practitioner's Guide to Investment Banking, Mergers & Acquisitions, Corporate Finance.* Circinus Business Press, 2007.

In addition to focusing on IRR, the LBO analysis considers whether there is enough projected cash flow to operate the company and also pay down debt principal and cover interest payments. The analysis also determines if there is sufficient cash flow to pay dividends at some point to the private equity investor. The ability to retire debt and pay dividends results in a higher IRR. Subject to consideration of financial risk, financial buyers will often raise the highest amount of debt that providers of debt will allow to minimize their equity contribution, which, in turn, maximizes the IRR.

Sum-of-the-Parts Analysis

A breakup analysis is a useful additional valuation tool when a company has many different businesses which, when analyzed separately, are worth more than the value of the company as a whole. If the sum of the parts of a company is greater than the current market value of the company, then there may be an opportunity to break up the company and sell it to different buyers, creating incremental value in the sale process. Investment bankers who are working on behalf of a sell-side client might employ a sum-of-the-parts analysis that focuses on EV/EBITDA multiples for each separate business and then add all EVs together to create a case for a higher sale price for the full company. Bankers who are working on behalf of a buy side client might focus on a sum-of-the-parts analysis to determine certain businesses that their client might want to sell postacquisition if those businesses don't fit in well with the acquiring company's existing businesses. In this case, bankers will need to determine business unit values separately and then adjust values based on allocation of assets and liabilities, and consideration of tax issues. Bankers need to determine whether unwanted businesses are best sold in an IPO, carve-out, or spin-off (in which case a comparable company analysis is helpful), sold to another company (in which case a comparable transaction analysis and DCF plus synergies analysis is most helpful), or sold to a private equity fund (in which case an LBO analysis is appropriate).

See Exhibit 4.7 for a summary of the different valuation methods described in this section.

EXHIBIT 4.7 SUMMARY OF VALUATION METHODS

	Publicly Traded Comparable Companies Analysis	Comparable Transactions Analysis	Discounted Cash Flow Analysis	Leveraged Buyout Analysis	Other
Description	• "Public Market Valuation" • Value based on market trading multiples of comparable companies • Applied using historical and projected multiples • Does not include a control premium	• "Private Market Valuation" • Value based on multiples paid for comparable companies in sale transactions • Includes control premium	• "Intrinsic" value of business • Present value of projected free cash flows • Incorporates both short and long-term expected performance • Risk in cash flows and capital structure captured in discount rate	• Value to a financial buyer • Value based on debt repayment and return on equity investment	• Sum-of-the-parts analysis • Liquidation analysis • Break-up or net asset value analysis • Historical trading performance • Discounted future share price • Dividend discount model
Comments	• Similarity of companies (size, growth prospects, product mix) • Placement within peer group • Underlying market / sector trading fluctuations • Market may view firm's outlook differently • Valuing synergies, tax benefits problematic	• Limited number of truly comparable transactions • Dated information due to changes in market • Data missing or hard to find (earnings often unavailable on subsidiary transactions)	• The preferred valuation technique when credible cash flows can be projected and confident in WACC determination • Sensitive to terminal value assumptions	• Usually represents a floor bid because of lack of synergies and high cost of capital and high required return (IRR) • Requires various assumptions on capital structure • May not be a viable option due to size or type of business	• May be more situational and not as relevant as a broad-based valuation technique • Near-term EPS impact may not reflect true value

Valuation Summary

After completing all appropriate valuation methodologies, investment bankers summarize the result by creating what is called a "football field" that shows the valuation ranges for each methodology. This summary, in turn, enables bankers to establish a valuation range for a company that is the subject of an M&A transaction. Normally, a football field will show a comparable company range that is lower than a comparable transaction range because a control premium is included in the comparable transaction analysis. A DCF analysis generally creates a valuation range that is similar to the range for a comparable company analysis (although there are examples where this is not the case). Typically, a company's current acquisition value falls above the overlapping ranges provided by the comparable company analysis and the DCF analysis (although, again, there are examples where this is not the case). This is because an acquirer should pay a control premium, which is not included in either of these valuation methodologies. An LBO analysis usually provides a "floor value" for a company since it represents a price that a financial buyer would be willing to pay based on achievement of their required IRR. Generally speaking, strategic buyers are able to pay more than financial buyers since they can take advantage of synergies with their own company, whereas a financial buyer cannot find synergies because they are usually not combining similar companies. However, if the market allows especially high leverage, which drives higher IRRs, or if there are unique operating strategies that a financial buyer brings to the transaction, then it may be possible for financial buyers to outbid strategic buyers, notwithstanding the lack of synergy benefits. If there are multiple major lines of businesses within a company, then a breakup analysis may be included in the football field. Depending on the company and industry, other valuation methodologies may also be included in the summary.

An example of a football field is included in Exhibit 4.8. Looking at this football field, assuming a company's current share price is $40, a typical comparable company analysis might show a valuation range of $36–$44, which is lower than a comparable transaction valuation range of $42–$51, based on the control premium inherent in the comparable transaction analysis. A DCF analysis might show a valuation range of $38–$45, unless synergies are added, in which case the range might increase to $43–$50, assuming cost synergies of $5. In this football field, it has been determined that financial buyers might be interested in the target company based on the company's strong cash flow, low leverage, and small capital expenditure requirements, and so an LBO valuation was completed, which shows a valuation range of $39–$45, based on an assumed 20% IRR requirement. A breakup analysis was completed because there are several different business lines run by the company and the valuation range based on this analysis is $41–$51, which is the widest range due to uncertainty regarding different business line values after allocating debt and considering tax issues. Based on this football field, investment bankers might determine that the appropriate triangulated value for the target company is $50 (which might be expressed as a range of $48–$52), which represents a 25% premium to the current share price of $40. However, $50 could be adjusted up or down based on the acquisition consideration (shares or cash), probability of completion, and other factors.

EXHIBIT 4.8 MERGERS AND ACQUISITIONS VALUATION SUMMARY (FOOTBALL FIELD)

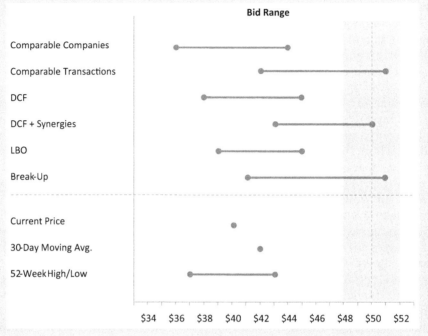

A case is provided in Exhibit 4.9 that summarizes the strategic considerations of a public company that is feeling pressure from some key investors regarding the need to take actions that will enhance shareholder value. In the case, the company asks for advice from an investment bank regarding a range of strategic issues and a valuation analysis to help determine if a sale of the company is the optimal way to enhance shareholder value.

EXHIBIT 4.9 SERVICECO CASE STUDY

This case simulates the experience of an investment banking firm advising a publicly traded client on evaluating strategic alternatives at a time, when the client's operating and stock price performance have been stagnant and the management team and board of directors are getting pressure from certain shareholders, notably hedge funds, to take action that will enhance near-term shareholder value. It requires the reader to determine the value of the Company under a number of strategic alternatives available using traditional valuation techniques including comparable company trading analysis, precedent transactions analysis, discounted cash flow analysis, and leveraged buyout analysis.

EXHIBIT 4.9 SERVICECO CASE STUDY—cont'd

The assignment

Service Company ("ServiceCo" or the "Company"), a publicly traded company, provides services including lawn care, janitorial and maintenance service, and building repair to the consumer and commercial markets. It is October 2016 and hedge funds have recently started building positions in the Company's stock, attracted by the Company's strong and stable cash flows, relatively low valuation, and stagnant stock performance. You are a managing director in your firm's Investment Banking Department. Given your firm's history of advising the Company on past acquisitions and capital market decisions, the Company's board of directors has asked your team to evaluate strategic alternatives for the Company.

The first step in evaluating strategic alternatives is to determine valuation under the following scenarios:

- Continue running the Company as is.
- Change the capital structure.
- Sell the Company to a strategic buyer.
- Sell the Company to a financial buyer.

Owing to the management team's lack of experience in operating a company with significant leverage, the board of directors is not willing to significantly change the capital structure unless the Company is sold.

You have a meeting next week where you will be presenting your preliminary valuation and recommendations to the board of directors, including whether to pursue a broad or targeted sale process.

- Broad "auction" process
  - Likely to achieve the highest price
  - Sale process more likely to become public, leading to greater customer and employee disruption
  - Greater drain on company resources (both management's time and expense)
  - Likely to achieve the highest price
  - Harder control dissemination of competitive information (detailed financials, customer lists, organizational charts, etc.)
  - Likely will take longer for process to be completed
  - Less likely to trigger a shareholder lawsuit
- Targeted process
  - Likely to achieve the highest price
  - More difficult to achieve the highest price
  - Sale process less likely to become public, leading to less customer and employee disruption
  - Lesser drain on company resources
  - Easier to control dissemination of competitive information
  - Can be a faster process
  - More likely to trigger a shareholder lawsuit
  - Requires company and advisors to select the "right" group of buyers

Continued

EXHIBIT 4.9 SERVICECO CASE STUDY—cont'd

Your task is to recommend a potential sale process to ServiceCo's board of directors assuming the following for ServiceCo:

- Hedge funds are advocating a sale at the highest value possible.
- Key employees may defect if the process takes a long time and becomes public.
- Top management is very concerned about dissemination of competitive information.
- Top managers are significant holders of the Company's stock.
- Company employees are spending a large portion of their time focused on the Company's turnaround plan.

Use the provided ServiceCo operating projections (see Fig. 4.1) to compare ServiceCo's operating performance to the operating statistics of ServiceCo's publicly traded comparable companies, and companies that have been acquired in precedent transactions that have taken place in the industry to determine a public trading valuation range and change of control valuation range, respectively, for ServiceCo. In addition, use the provided ServiceCo operating projections and return on equity, average borrowing rate, and tax rate statistics to determine the intrinsic value of ServiceCo using a discounted cash flow (DCF) analysis. Finally, use the provided ServiceCo operating projections, debt structure, interest rate assumptions, and leveraged buyout (LBO) model to determine a purchase price range for ServiceCo assuming a private equity firm will take the Company private.

	2016	2017	2018	2019	2020	2021	2022	2023	2024	2025	2026
	Actual					Projected					
Key Operating Statistics											
Net Sales	6,400	6,600	6,800	7,050	7,300	7,600	7,904	8,220	8,549	8,891	9,247
% Growth	–	3.1%	3.0%	3.7%	3.5%	4.1%	4.0%	4.0%	4.0%	4.0%	4.0%
EBITDA	800	825	884	917	949	988	1,028	1,069	1,111	1,156	1,202
% Margin	12.5%	12.5%	13.0%	13.0%	13.0%	13.0%	13.0%	13.0%	13.0%	13.0%	13.0%
EBIT	750	765	814	827	839	858	892	928	965	1,004	1,044
% Margin	11.7%	11.6%	12.0%	11.7%	11.5%	11.3%	11.3%	11.3%	11.3%	11.3%	11.3%
Investment in Noncash Working Capital	(30)	(5)	(7)	(10)	(12)	(14)	(15)	(16)	(16)	(17)	(18)
% as Change in Net Sales	–	2.5%	3.5%	4.0%	4.8%	4.7%	5.0%	5.0%	5.0%	5.0%	5.0%
Capital Expenditures	(80)	(100)	(110)	(115)	(120)	(130)	(135)	(141)	(146)	(152)	(158)
% of Net Sales	1.3%	1.5%	1.6%	1.6%	1.6%	1.7%	1.7%	1.7%	1.7%	1.7%	1.7%

FIGURE 4.1   Projected financial information: ServiceCo projections as of January 2017.

Your presentation should include the following:

- Preliminary valuation summary ("football field"); see Fig. 4.2.
  - This is a summary of the results of the various valuation techniques and provides a good illustrative summary slide from which to communicate your conclusions to the board of directors.
  - Depending on the results, conclusions drawn, and audience, this slide could come before all of the summary slides for the respective analyses performed.
  - Assume the Company has 250 million shares outstanding, $800 million of debt, and $200 million of cash.
- Comparable company trading analysis; see Figs. 4.3 and 4.4.
  - This analysis provides an indication of the potential implied value of the Company excluding a change of control premium by comparing ServiceCo to similar selected.

EXHIBIT 4.9 SERVICECO CASE STUDY—cont'd

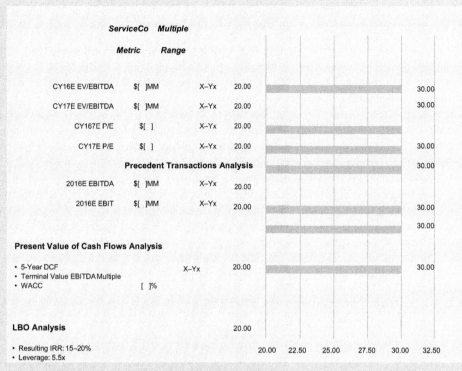

FIGURE 4.2 Preliminary valuation summary ("football field") in $ per share.

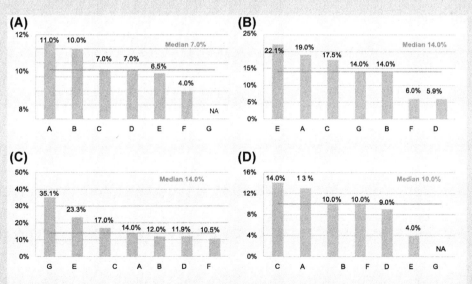

FIGURE 4.3 **Comparable company operating performance comparison.** (A) 2016E–2018E revenue growth, based on Wall Street equity research estimates; (B) last 12 months EBITDA margin, based on last 12 months of reported financial data; (C) last 12 months return on invested capital (ROIC) (ROIC ¼ Tax Effected EBIT ÷ (Net Debt + Shareholders' Equity)—assumes 35% tax rate); (D) long-term EPS growth (median IBES estimates for 5-year projected EPS growth).

Continued

EXHIBIT 4.9 SERVICECO CASE STUDY—cont'd

- Use the provided list of publicly traded comparable companies to ServiceCo and their respective comparable operating performance and trading valuation multiples to develop a view on the appropriate 2016 and 2017 P/E and enterprise value/EBITDA multiples to be used to value ServiceCo.
  - This can be accomplished by taking the ratio of (1) enterprise value, defined as the sum of market capitalization and total debt-less cash and cash equivalents, often referred to as net debt, to (2) EBITDA, defined as estimated earnings before interest, taxes, depreciation, and amortization, for calendar years 2016 and 2017;
  - The ratio of share price to estimated earnings per share for calendar years 2016 and 2017.
- Based on the analysis of the relevant financial multiples and ratios for each of the comparable companies, select representative ranges of financial multiples for the companies and apply these ranges of multiples to the corresponding ServiceCo financial statistics.
- For this exercise, account for how "comparable" the companies are to ServiceCo based on relative size, growth expectations, and profitability margins. Assume (just for the purposes of this analysis) all of the companies compete in the same end markets as ServiceCo.
- Assume ServiceCo's 2016 and 2017 EPS are $1.46 and $1.50, respectively.

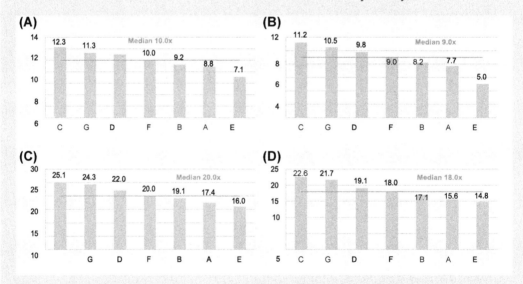

FIGURE 4.4 **Comparable company trading analysis.** (A) CY16 enterprise value EBITDA; (B) CY17 enterprise value EBITDA, based on Wall Street equity research estimates; (C) CY16 PE; and (D) CY17 PE, based on last 12 months of reported financial data.

EXHIBIT 4.9 SERVICECO CASE STUDY—cont'd

				EV Multiple (LTM Data)			LTM Margin	
Date	Acquirer	Target	Transaction Value	Revenue	EBITDA	EBIT	EBITDA	EBIT
11/16/15	Acquirer A	Target A	$897.0	1.9	11.5	19.0	16.5%	10.0%
08/08/15	Acquirer B	Target B1	8,121.8	0.7	8.8	13.9	8.0%	5.1%
03/01/15	Acquirer C	Target C	2,669.4	0.8	9.5	13.5	8.3%	5.8%
01/24/15	Acquirer D	Target D	141.8	1.1	NA	NA	NA	NA
03/29/14	Acquirer E	Target E	5,147.5	0.8	10.6	14.1	7.7%	5.8%
12/22/13	Acquirer F	Target F	113.9	0.2	14.6	49.4	1.4%	0.4%
12/16/13	Acquirer G	Target G	1,837.2	1.0	12.5	NA	8.3%	NA
10/01/13	Acquirer H	Target H	103.5	4.4	NA	9.6	NA	46.2%
03/08/13	Acquirer I	Target I	110.0	1.2	NA	NA	NA	NA
01/05/13	Acquirer J	Target J	629.0	3.5	8.7	NA	40.0%	NA
02/12/11	Acquirer K	Target K	186.0	0.3	NA	NA	NA	NA
10/05/10	Acquirer L	Target L	800.0	0.4	9.8	13.3	4.2%	3.1%
08/07/10	Acquirer M	Target M	170.0	0.3	NA	NA	NA	NA
11/03/08	Acquirer N	Target N	856.9	0.5	5.9	7.3	9.1%	7.3%
10/27/08	Acquirer O	Target O	322.2	0.6	NA	9.7	NA	6.1%
03/23/08	Acquirer P	Target P	260.9	0.5	10.3	20.1	5.0%	2.6%
11/02/07	Acquirer Q	Target Q2	331.0	1.1	NA	16.6	NA	6.6%
08/08/05	Acquirer R	Target R	218.5	1.1	8.6	12.4	13.4%	9.3%
		Mean		1.1	10.1	16.6	11.1%	9.0%
		Median		0.8	9.8	13.7	8.3%	6.0%

Note 1: August 8, 2015, Target B deal represents revised and accepted bid (LTM data as of 6/30/15). Initial proposal dated 5/1/15, based on 3/30/15 data, was valued at 0.7×, 8.6×, and 13.2× of revenue, EBITDA, and EBIT, respectively.
Note 2: EV Multiple based on run-rate volume of $300 million at time of acquisition per Equity Research.

FIGURE 4.5 Precedent transactions analysis (in $ million). *WACC*, weighted average cost of capital.

- Precedent transactions analysis; see Fig. 4.5.
  - This analysis provides an indication of the potential value of the Company, including a change of control premium by reviewing the publicly available financial terms of precedent transactions that share certain characteristics with ServiceCo.
  - Use the provided list of precedent transactions and compare their respective size, operating performance metrics (profitability margins), and transaction valuation multiples to develop a view on the appropriate transaction enterprise value to 2016 EBITDA and EBIT multiples that should be used to value ServiceCo.
  - Assume this is the best list of representative precedent transactions; however, account for how "comparable" the transactions are to a potential ServiceCo transaction based on the relative size and profitability margins of the respective target companies in the data set.
- DCF analysis; see DCF Valuation Model on Elsevier's website.
  - This analysis enables you to determine the long-term intrinsic standalone value of the Company.
  - Use the provided ServiceCo operating projections to determine the DCF value of the Company.
  - Use the enterprise value/EBITDA multiple method to calculate your terminal value; use the comparable company operating and trading statistics to determine an appropriate terminal multiple range.
  - To determine the appropriate discount rates, assume the following information:
    - 10-year US Treasury rate of 4.47%
    - Unlevered forward predicted beta of 1.254
    - Equity market risk premium of 4%–6%
    - Debt/equity ratio of 0.43
    - Cost of debt of 8%
    - Implied tax rate of 39%

Continued

EXHIBIT 4.9 SERVICECO CASE STUDY—cont'd

- Determine whether the discount rate assumption or the exit multiple assumption has a larger impact on the DCF valuation.
- Determine the additional potential value that the Company may be worth for a strategic buyer using the synergy assumptions outlined in the following:
  - Synergies—ServiceCo has identified a broad range of potential synergies that could be available to a strategic buyer, resulting in an increase in EBITDA if those synergies are realized:
    - Cost synergies: potential total EBITDA increase of $50 to $100 million
      - Consolidate headquarters
      - Consolidate purchasing of raw materials
      - Consolidate back-office functions
      - Leverage increased marketing and advertising purchasing power
    - Revenue synergies—potential total EBITDA increase of $200–$300 million (in addition to potential cost synergies)
      - Cross-sell ServiceCo products to the customer base of the buyer
      - Cross-sell buyer products to the ServiceCo customer base; bundle multiple services to increase customer loyalty
      - Increase advertising spend effectiveness by lowering the cost of advertising and coadvertising brands and services
- Evaluate the potential valuation impact of the identified synergies.
- Apply your assumed 2016 EBITDA multiple to the synergy value that you believe that a strategic buyer will conservatively include in their valuation considerations.
- Briefly explain why you believe that a strategic buyer would pay for the synergies you identified.
- Add this "synergy" value to the DCF value to estimate the potential value of the Company for a strategic buyer.
- LBO Analysis; see LBO Valuation Model on Elsevier's website.
  - This analysis enables you to determine what a financial sponsor (private equity firm) could potentially pay for the Company and still achieve its targeted return thresholds.
  - Use the provided ServiceCo operating projections to build an LBO model with an exit in the fifth year (2021).
  - The leveraged finance group at your firm has provided you with the following debt structure and rate assumptions:
    - Bank debt maximum of 2.5×2016 EBITDA at LIBOR + 250 basis points
    - Total debt maximum of 5.5×2016 EBITDA with the remainder of the debt in bonds at 10.0%
  - For the LBO analysis, you will need to calculate the incremental transaction amortization from the purchase accounting adjustment made at the closing of the transaction. The incremental transaction amortization (which is not tax deductible) is calculated as follows:
    - Implied equity purchase price plus transaction fees and expenses (which change based on the purchase price: 1% of new bank debt + 2% of all other new debt) less tangible book value of $800 million (shareholder's book equity less existing goodwill and intangibles).
    - Assume 25% of new goodwill can be amortized.
    - Assume amortization period of 20 years.

EXHIBIT 4.9 SERVICECO CASE STUDY—cont'd

- Given the operating projections, leverage, and rate assumptions, determine the maximum that a financial sponsor could pay per share and still achieve 15%–20% returns in 5 years.
  - Use the comparable company operating and trading multiple statistics and precedent transaction operating and valuation multiple statistics to determine an appropriate exit multiple range for the potential financial sponsor to appropriately exit the ServiceCo LBO investment through either an initial public offering ("IPO") or a sale to a strategic buyer or another financial sponsor; justify the exit multiples you choose to use.
  - Using ServiceCo management's financial forecasts for fiscal years 2016–21, assume that the potential financial sponsor would value its ServiceCo investment in calendar year 2020 at an aggregate value range that represented your chosen exit multiples for calendar year 2021 EBITDA. Then calculate ServiceCo's calendar year end 2020 equity value range by adding ServiceCo's forecasted calendar year end 2020 cash balance and subtracting ServiceCo's forecasted debt outstanding at calendar year end 2020. Based on your calendar year end 2020 equity value range for ServiceCo, assume that the financial sponsor would likely target 5-year internal rates of return ranging from approximately 15%–20%. Based on this, derive estimated implied values per share that the financial sponsor might be willing to pay to acquire ServiceCo.
  - Please note that your exit multiple assumption should not be higher than the entry multiple assumption and could be lower; discuss why this is relevant.
- "Credit crunch" analysis
  - ServiceCo's board is particularly concerned about a downturn in the credit markets.
  - The leveraged finance group at your firm suggests that a credit market downturn would result in the following structure and rates:
    - Bank debt maximum of 2.0×2016 EBITDA at LIBOR$+350$ basis points
    - Total debt maximum of 4.5×2016 EBITDA with the remainder of the debt in bonds at 12.0%
  - Discuss whether the decrease in leverage or increase in rates has a larger impact on ServiceCo's valuation
- Conclusions
  - Provide clear conclusions on the best strategic option and suggested next steps for the Company.
  - Recommend a targeted process or a broad auction and justify your choice.
  - You are being paid to give advice, not calculate numbers!

Overview of ServiceCo

ServiceCo is a national company serving both residential and commercial customers. The services it provides include lawn care, landscape maintenance, termite and pest control, home warranty, disaster response and reconstruction, cleaning and disaster restoration, house cleaning, furniture repair, and home inspection. As of December 31, 2015, ServiceCo offered these services through a network of approximately 5500 company-owned locations and franchise licenses operating under a number of leading brands. Incorporated in Delaware in 1995, ServiceCo is the successor

Continued

EXHIBIT 4.9 SERVICECO CASE STUDY—cont'd

to various entities dating back to 1940. ServiceCo is organized into five principal operating segments: LawnCare, LandCare, Exterminator, Home Protection, and Other Operations and Corporate.

The following table shows the percentage of ServiceCo's consolidated revenue from continuing operations derived from each of ServiceCo's reportable segments in the years indicated:

Segment	2015 (%)	2014 (%)	2013 (%)
LawnCare	31	32	32
LandCare	13	14	14
Exterminator	31	33	33
Home Protection	16	16	16
Other Operations and Corporate	9	5	5

ServiceCo LawnCare Segment

The LawnCare segment provides lawn care services primarily under the ServiceCo LawnCare brand name. Revenues derived from the LawnCare segment constituted 31%, 32%, and 32% of the revenue from continuing operations of the consolidated ServiceCo enterprise in 2015, 2014, and 2013, respectively. The ServiceCo LawnCare business is seasonal in nature. Weather conditions, such as a drought or snow in the late spring or fall, can affect the demand for lawn care services. These conditions may result in a decrease in revenues or an increase in costs.

ServiceCo LawnCare is the leading provider of lawn care services in the United States serving both residential and commercial customers. As of December 31, 2015, ServiceCo LawnCare provided these services in 45 states and the District of Columbia through 225 company-owned locations and 45 franchised locations.

ServiceCo LandCare Segment

The ServiceCo LandCare segment provides landscape maintenance services primarily under the ServiceCo LandCare brand name. Revenues derived from the ServiceCo LandCare segment constituted 13%, 14%, and 14% of the revenue from continuing operations of the consolidated ServiceCo enterprise in 2015, 2014, and 2013, respectively. The ServiceCo LandCare business is seasonal in nature. Weather conditions such as a drought can affect the demand for landscape maintenance services, or declines in the volume of snowfall can affect the level of snow removal services and may result in a decrease in revenues or an increase in costs.

ServiceCo LandCare is a leading provider of landscape maintenance services in the United States serving primarily commercial customers. As of December 31, 2015, ServiceCo's LandCare provided these services in 43 states and the District of Columbia through 102 company-owned locations and had no international operations.

Exterminator Segment

The Exterminator segment provides termite and pest control services primarily under the Exterminator brand name. Revenues derived from the Exterminator segment constituted 31%, 33%,

EXHIBIT 4.9 SERVICECO CASE STUDY—cont'd

and 33% of the revenue from continuing operations of the consolidated ServiceCo enterprise in 2015, 2014, and 2013, respectively. The Exterminator business is seasonal in nature. The termite swarm season, which generally occurs in early spring but varies by region depending on climate, leads to the highest demand for termite control services and therefore to the highest level of revenues. Similarly, increased pest activity in the warmer months leads to the highest demand for pest control services and, therefore to the highest level of revenues.

Exterminator is the leading provider of termite and pest control services in the United States serving both residential and commercial customers. As of December 31, 2015, Exterminator provided these services in 45 states and the District of Columbia through 380 company-owned locations and 127 franchised locations.

Home Protection Segment

The Home Protection segment provides home warranty contracts for systems and appliances primarily under the Home Protection brand name and home inspection services primarily under the Home Inspection brand name. Revenues derived from the Home Protection segment constituted 16%, 16%, and 16% of the revenue from continuing operations of the consolidated ServiceCo enterprise in 2015, 2014, and 2013, respectively. The Home Protection and Home Inspection businesses are seasonal in nature. Sales volume in the Home Protection segment depends, in part, on the number of home resale closings, which historically has been highest in the spring and summer months. Home Protection's costs related to service call volume are highest in the summer months, especially during periods of unseasonably warm temperatures.

Other Operations and Corporate Segment

The Other Operations and Corporate segment provides disaster response and reconstruction services, residential and commercial disaster restoration and clearing services, domestic house cleaning services, and on-site furniture repair and restoration services primarily under the Furniture Medic brand name. In addition, the Other Operations and Corporate segment includes ServiceCo's headquarters, functions. Revenues derived from the Other Operations and Corporate segment constituted 9%, 5%, and 5% of the revenue from continuing operations of the consolidated ServiceCo enterprise in 2015, 2014, and 2013, respectively.

Franchises

Franchises are important to ServiceCo. Total franchise fees (initial and recurring) represented 3.5%, 3.4%, and 3.3% of consolidated revenue in 2015, 2014, and 2013, respectively. Related franchise operating expenses were 2.2%, 2.1%, and 2.1% of consolidated operating expenses in 2015, 2014, and 2013, respectively. Total franchise-related profits comprised 11.3%, 10.5%, and 10.3% of consolidated operating income before headquarters overhead and restructuring charges in 2015, 2014, and 2013, respectively. Franchise agreements made in the course of these businesses are generally for a term of 5–10 years. The majority of these franchise agreements are renewed prior to expiration.

Continued

EXHIBIT 4.9 SERVICECO CASE STUDY—cont'd

Competition

ServiceCo competes with many other companies in the sale of its services, franchises, and products. The principal methods of competition in ServiceCo's businesses include quality and speed of service, name recognition and reputation, pricing and promotions, customer satisfaction, brand awareness, professional sales forces, and reputation/referrals. Competition in all of the Company's markets is strong.

- Lawn care services. Competition in the market for lawn care services comes mainly from local, independently owned firms, and from homeowners who care for their own lawns. ServiceCo continues to expand toward a more national footprint.
- Landscape maintenance services. Competition in the market for commercial landscape maintenance services comes mainly from small, owner-operated companies operating in a limited geographic market and, to a lesser degree, from a few large companies operating in multiple markets, and from property owners who perform their own landscaping services.
- Termite and pest control services. Competition in the market for termite and pest control services comes mainly from thousands of regional and local, independently owned firms, from homeowners who treat their own termite and pest control problems, and from Orkin, Inc., a subsidiary of Rollins, Inc., which operates on a national basis. Ecolab competes nationally in the commercial pest control segment.
- Home warranty contracts for systems and appliances. Competition in the market for home warranty contracts for systems and appliances comes mainly from regional providers of home warranties. Several competitors are initiating expansion efforts into additional states.
- Home inspection services. Competition in the market for home inspection services comes mainly from regional and local, independently owned firms.
- Residential and commercial disaster restoration and cleaning services. Competition in the market for disaster restoration and cleaning services comes mainly from local, independently owned firms and a few national professional cleaning companies.
- House cleaning services. Competition in the market for house cleaning services comes mainly from local, independently owned firms and a few national companies.
- Furniture repair services. Competition in the market for furniture repair services comes mainly from local, independent contractors.

Major Customers

ServiceCo has no single customer that accounts for more than 10% of its consolidated operating revenue. Additionally, no operating segment has a single customer that accounts for more than 10% of its operating revenue.

M&A LITIGATION TOPICS

A. Inversions and Squeeze-outs

A corporate inversion involves changing a US company's legal domicile to another country that has a lower-tax rate, while retaining most of the company's US operations. During

2014–2016, many US companies achieved a corporate inversion through a merger with another company that was domiciled in low-tax countries such as Ireland (12.5% tax rate) or Canada (15% tax rate). Corporate inversions attempt to lower taxes by adopting the low-tax rate of the non-US merger partner, and avoiding the US tax practice of requiring US taxes as high as 39% to be paid on all income, whether earned in the United States or outside of the United States. An inversion through a merger allows the former US headquartered company to limit payment of the high US tax to only profits earned in the United States and enables non-US income to be taxed at the lower rates of the countries in which the income is generated. Basically, this allows large income streams from outside of the United States to avoid double taxation (both in the country in which the income is generated and also in the United States). Another aspect of an inversion is the ability to engage in earnings stripping, a practice in which a US corporation uses loans between different divisions of the same company to shift profits out of high-tax jurisdictions and into lower-tax ones. Earnings stripping is one of the most common tax avoidance techniques facilitated by tax inversions. Furthermore, the US corporation may find additional tax avoidance strategies allowed to corporations domiciled in non-US countries such as ways to define revenue or cost so that they are taxed in lower-tax countries, although the customers may be in higher-tax countries. Mylan and Perrigo, two US companies achieved corporate inversions through mergers with non-US corporations. Both companies' tax rates on average fell by about 20% as a result of their inversions. These two inverted companies were involved in acquisition activities during 2015 that are summarized below.

Mylan

Mylan is a global generic and specialty pharmaceuticals company. Mylan relocated its headquarters to Amsterdam, the Netherlands, after being incorporated originally in Pennsylvania, which is known as "the graveyard of hostile takeovers," because of at least six different antitakeover laws. To effect their inversion, Mylan acquired the nonspecialty and branded generics business of Abbott Labs, which Abbott had previously moved to the Netherlands. Mylan then merged with this business to become a Netherlands-based company. In this transaction, Abbott received 110 million shares of Mylan N.V., giving Abbott 22% ownership of Mylan. To achieve the tax benefits sought, more than 20% of Mylan's stock had to be held by Abbott. Mylan targeted Abbott because it "creates significantly enhanced financial flexibility and more competitive global tax structure for future opportunities." Although being located in the Netherlands did not provide as much antitakeover protection as Pennsylvania provided, Mylan benefited significantly from the much lower-tax rate of 25% in the Netherlands. In addition, this country offers a poison pill equivalent called stitching: a Netherlands company can issue preferred shares to a foundation to enable the foundation to take temporary voting control in an effort to thwart a hostile takeover attempt. While there are many antitakeover options in the United States, this "nuclear" option is unique in the Netherlands. Mylan has no legal control over the foundation—it can act even if Mylan does not want it to, essentially giving significant control over Mylan to an independent third party.

Perrigo

Perrigo is a global generic drugmaker that moved its headquarters to Dublin, Ireland, from Allegan, Michigan, through an inversion process to reduce taxes. Michigan law, such as Pennsylvania, provides some protection against takeovers, including a limitation on parties that acquire 10% or more of a company from acquiring the remaining shares for at least 5 years, allowing a staggered board (which means that only one-third of its directors can be up for election in any given year), and a poison pill defense. Based on these protections, it would take 2 years to replace Perrigo's board with new directors who could remove a poison pill and allow an acquisition to go through. Although Ireland as a corporate headquarters provides significant tax breaks with a corporate tax rate of 12.5%, there is almost no antitakeover protection in this country.

The Attempt by Mylan to Acquire Perrigo Through a Squeeze-out Tender Offer

During April 2015, Mylan offered to buy Perrigo for $205 per share in a cash and stock deal for a total consideration of $29 billion. If the acquisition were completed, the resulting firm would be the largest participant in the global generic medicines business, with a significant position in brands, generics, and over-the-counter nutritional products. The combined company was projected to generate $15.3 billion in sales and achieve significant cost synergies. However, Perrigo turned down the cash-and-shares offer because, although the transaction reflected a valuation of 18.7× forecasted EBITDA (a significant premium to the company's current market value), Perrigo believed it should be valued at greater than 20× forecasted EBITDA based on future growth expectations, and in line with Mead Johnson and Proctor and Gamble, even though its operating margin was about two-thirds of the operating margins of these companies.

Usually, it is very difficult for large companies such as Perrigo to be taken in a hostile acquisition effort because of the takeover protections provided by different states. However, with the less stringent protections available to Perrigo as an Ireland-headquartered company, Mylan had a better chance of success in a hostile takeover. Mylan was able to go directly to Perrigo's shareholders in an attempt to squeeze-out those shareholders who were not supportive of the takeover. Under a hostile tender takeover, it is unlikely that 100% of the shareholders of a target company will support the deal. Under Delaware law and the law of certain other states, if 90% of shareholders agree to the acquisition, the hostile company can squeeze out the remaining shareholders, forcing them to accept the transaction. However, under Irish takeover laws, a squeeze-out can occur if only 80% of shareholders agree. So the inversion related change of domicile by Perrigo from Michigan to Ireland gave Mylan a better shot at a hostile acquisition. However, in spite of the expectation by many shareholders and equity analysts that Mylan would be successful, less than 50% of Perrigo shareholders agreed to the acquisition, and so it failed.

Earlier that year, Mylan had been the subject of a takeover attempt by Teva Pharmaceutical Industries, but Mylan escaped this acquisition by persuading Abbott, their largest shareholder, to oppose the transaction. The Mylan effort to squeeze out Perrigo by launching a tender offer to shareholders was very unusual because hostile takeover attempts are normally neutralized by poison pills that threaten to dilute any hostile suitor who is successful in acquiring a large block of shares. Furthermore, US laws require tender offers to remain open longer, giving targets time to persuade shareholders to reject an offer. As a result, the Mylan hostile tender offer for Perrigo was the first such effort to actually cause a shareholder vote in relation to a hostile takeover attempt in more than 25 years.

B. Staple Financing

A staple financing is the formal financing package offered by a sell-side advisor's lending affiliate as part of an M&A auction process. The term is coined from the prearranged financing terms that are stapled to the back of an acquisition term sheet. In a staple finance, a seller's M&A advisor is also involved in the buyer's financing, potentially allowing the advisor to profit from both sides of a deal—they receive an M&A fee from the seller and a lending fee from the buyer. The buyer is usually a private equity firm that is reliant on a large financing to fund the acquisition. This type of financing not only creates significant revenue opportunities for an investment bank, but also the potential for conflict of interest because the M&A advisor is taking fees from both buyer and seller.

The benefits of staple financing from the perspective of the buyer are that there is no need to shop for acquisition financing and the buyer can have more confidence in firming up an acquisition price based on knowledge of the financing terms. From the seller's perspective, the staple finance may enable a higher acquisition price and a greater number of bidders. This structure may also better preserve confidentiality and facilitate a faster auction process. A staple financing streamlines the acquisition process by providing potential buyers a well-negotiated term sheet that guarantees the availability of financing for their bid.

Although staple financing is undoubtedly a useful tool, the potential for a conflict of interest can mitigate its advantages. In this structure, the seller's financial advisor is involved in both sides of the deal: as a lender to the buyer and as advisor to the seller. As a result, the bank's incentives may be skewed. If the sell-side advisor can receive compensation from a buyer that wants to use its staple financing, the bank might be motivated to push the transaction to that buyer, without running a robust auction that maximizes the selling company's share price. If there are other bidders that are interested in the acquisition, the bank might not bring them forward in the auction process even if they might offer a higher purchase price.

In recent years, there have been a number of staple financing cases that have been questioned by courts, including M&A transactions involving Del Monte, who was advised by Barclays, and Rural/Metro, who was advised by Royal Bank of Canada.

Del Monte

Staple financing garnered attention after the Del Monte Foods Shareholder Litigation, which focused on Del Monte's board of directors and Barclays, their financial adviser. Del Monte is a North American food production and distribution company, with headquarters in Walnut Creek, California. It is one of the country's largest producers, distributors, and marketers of branded food in the United States, with approximately $1.8 billion of annual revenue. In November 2010, Barclays advised Del Monte in a sale of the company to three private equity firms: Kohlberg Kravis Roberts (KKR), Centerview, and Vestar. The transaction amount was $5 billion, a 40% premium above Del Monte's unaffected stock price. Barclays both advised Del Monte on the sale and also provided staple financing for the buyers. However, Barclays' role as a lender to the buyer was not disclosed to the Del Monte board until very late in the acquisition process. Led by NECA-IBEW Pension Trust, an Illinois union pension fund, Del Monte shareholders accused Barclays of not running a proper and fair auction process that focused on obtaining the highest possible price.

Prior to the start of the transaction, Barclays had begun talks with a number of potential buyers, including Vestar, about acquiring Del Monte. However, instead of Vestar making an independent bid, the firm decided to make a joint bid with KKR. Shareholders alleged that Barclays urged this combination to facilitate a successful acquisition by private equity firms that would use the bank's staple financing, without maximizing the sale price through an auction that would have included other bidders who did not need the staple financing. Furthermore, shareholders alleged that if Barclays had kept these two firms from bidding together, competition between them may have resulted in a higher purchase price (and that Barclays did not fully inform the board regarding the joint bidding process). However, regulatory filings showed that Barclays did not, in fact, arrange the partnership between these two firms.

Because Barclays worked on both sides of this transaction, the bank was able to double its fees to $48 million. Before the lawsuit was filed, Del Monte issued a letter to Barclays that stated: "In the event that Barclays Capital is asked to provide acquisition financing to a buyer of the company, the company should expect Barclays Capital to seek to protect its interests as a lender, which may be contrary to the interest of the company." The lawsuit claimed that Barclays failed to adhere to the guidelines of this letter and to the law. The Delaware Court of Chancery determined that Barclays had manipulated the sale of Del Monte to profit from hefty fees. The court took the position that by working with the private equity firms to ensure that the deal was completed, and failing to inform Del Monte of all aspects of the bidding process until it was too late, Barclays had pushed for an unfair deal. As a result, the court required a total payment by Barclays to shareholders of $89.4 million. This was one of the largest settlements ever in the Delaware Court of Chancery. The court required that Del Monte Foods pay $65.3 of this amount, leaving Barclays to pay $23.7 million, which came directly out of the fees earned from the transaction.

Both Del Monte and Barclays denied any wrongdoing. Barclays claimed that it had approached 53 potential buyers for Del Monte, which resulted in a strong premium for shareholders. Del Monte stated that it was pleased with the process, was satisfied with the $19 per share offer, and that shareholder value had been maximized. However, both the court and shareholders did not agree, and the court required this significant settlement to end the dispute.

Rural/Metro

On March 28, 2011, Rural/Metro Corporation, an American emergency services organization, announced it was being acquired by the private equity firm Warburg Pincus LLC in a $437.8 million transaction based on a price of $17.25 per share in cash. Rural/Metro's M&A advisor was Royal Bank of Canada (RBC). In October 2014, the Delaware Supreme Court ruled that RBC owed $76 million to former shareholders of Rural/Metro for pushing the company into an ill-advised sale that secured fees from both the seller and its buyer. RBC allegedly pushed for a quick sale to Warburg Pincus rather than a more extended auction process that might have elicited a higher price.

While advising Rural/Metro, RBC was also providing staple financing to Warburg Pincus. In court proceedings, it was alleged that RBC purposely undervalued Rural/Metro to facilitate a sale to the private equity firm. RBC argued that it ran a rigorous sale process and Warburg Pincus was the highest bidder out of six potential bidders and that the staple financing facilitated their highest bid, which resulted in maximizing value for shareholders. Furthermore, the deal was subject to a postclosing market check for 90 days during which other bidders could have stepped in at a higher price, but they did not. The Delaware Court, however, sided with Rural/Metro shareholders who brought the law-suit, agreeing that RBC's potential conflict of interest became, in fact, an actual conflict that resulted in a sale below a higher price that, but for the conflict, would have been attainable.

C. Force Majeure Financing Out

Cooper Tire and Rubber Company, a Findlay, Ohio tire maker, and Apollo Tyres, an India-based tire maker, announced in June 2013, a $2.5 billion acquisition agreement for Apollo to take over Cooper. However, this transaction was canceled 6 months later after hit-ting major roadblocks, including litigation in the Delaware Chancery Court. After signing a Merger Agreement, Apollo backed away from their acquisition commitment, arguing that Cooper management tried to hide certain labor-related risks associated with the transac-tion. They claimed that Cooper did not disclose that their Chinese joint venture partner, Cooper Chengshan Tire Co. Ltd (CCT), opposed the transaction, had the ability to thwart the deal and demanded as much as $400 million to agree not to. When Cooper declined to pay this amount, the company's joint venture operations in China were disrupted when CCT's employees went on strike, stopped production of Cooper tires and denied Cooper management access to their own facility. In addition, Apollo had to unexpectedly renegoti-ate labor contracts for Cooper's Arkansas and Ohio plants after a union filed grievances over the merger.

As the deal unraveled, Cooper sued Apollo to force it to close at the $35 per share price that had been agreed to. Apollo counterclaimed that it was enjoined from consummating any deal related to the merger until it reached an agreement with the labor union in the United States, and that Cooper hadn't complied with the merger deal by not allowing Apollo to review the books and records of the Chinese JV partner (which had been confiscated by the Chinese employees). As each difficulty was made public, Cooper's stock plummeted, wiping out some $300 million in shareholder value.

Cooper argued that each of its statements released to shareholders and the public made clear the risks involved, and that as labor-related obstacles became evident, they were each promptly disclosed. Apollo disagreed. Morgan Stanley, the M&A advisor to Apollo, also dis-agreed. Morgan Stanley had committed more than $1 billion in financing to support Apollo's bid, and they were about to round up a syndicate of banks to help them with the financing. However, when the Chinese and US labor problems became apparent just before the sched-uled merger closing, the bank cited a force majeure clause in the financing document as a basis for not providing the committed financing.

Force majeure means civil commotions, acts of God, weather, fires, floods, explosions, natural catastrophes, sabotages, accidents, failures of power, riots, invasion, insurrection, or act of terrorism where there is a material adverse effect on a party's ability to perform any of its obligations contemplated by an agreement and which the parties could not reasonably have expected to occur. Morgan Stanley took the position that the two labor problems (and especially the Chinese employee denial of access to the Cooper plant, including access to its books and records) prevented the firm from performing its obligations in their financing agreement. As a result, Morgan Stanley refused to provide the financing, preventing Apollo from accessing needed funding for the acquisition.

Both Apollo and Morgan Stanley refused to follow through and close the merger transaction, causing significant losses for Cooper shareholders and a bruising battle in a Delaware Court that ultimately sided with Apollo.

CHAPTER

5

Trading

The material in this chapter should be cross-referenced with the following cases: **A Tale of Two Hedge Funds: Magnetar and Peloton Case** and **Kmart, Sears, and ESL: How a Hedge Fund Became One of the World's Largest Retailers Case**.

This chapter discusses the trading activities conducted by investment banks, including the focus and organization of the two key trading businesses: Equities Trading and Fixed Income, Currencies, and Commodities (FICC) Trading. The chapter also addresses the new financial organizations that are taking up much of the former proprietary trading and an increasing amount of the credit-taking roles that investment banks used to undertake before the Dodd–Frank Act was implemented in the United States, and similar regulations were imposed in major countries around the world.

Investment Banks, Hedge Funds, and Private Equity, Third Edition
http://dx.doi.org/10.1016/B978-0-12-804723-1.00005-0

SALES AND TRADING

A large investment bank's sales and trading division (often referred to as the trading business) focuses primarily on (1) servicing large institutional investor clients such as mutual funds, hedge funds, pension funds, sovereign wealth funds, insurance companies, and others in the secondary trading markets and (2) working together with the investment banking division to assist corporate and government clients in raising capital through primary issuance or hedging risk.

The sales and trading division at a large investment bank comprises thousands of staff, with significant numbers of traders, sales professionals, and research analysts working closely with risk controllers, compliance officers, lawyers, technologists, and operations specialists. At most of the largest investment banks, this division typically produces substantially more revenue than the investment banking or asset management divisions (see Exhibits 5.1 and 5.2).

EXHIBIT 5.1 2013–15 AVERAGE ANNUAL TRADING AND BANKING REVENUES OF TOP NINE GLOBAL INVESTMENT BANKS ($ BILLIONS)

Bank	Sales & Trading	of which, FICC	of which, Equities	Investment Banking	Revenue split (FICC / Equities / Banking)
JP Morgan Chase	$ 19.4	$ 14.2	$ 5.2	$ 6.3	55% / 20% / 25%
Goldman Sachs	15.3	8.1	7.2	6.5	37% / 33% / 30%
Citigroup	15.0	12.1	2.9	4.6	62% / 15% / 23%
Bank of America	12.5	8.3	4.2	6.2	44% / 22% / 33%
Deutsche Bank	12.5	8.8	3.7	3.5	55% / 23% / 22%
Morgan Stanley	11.5	4.2	7.3	4.9	26% / 45% / 30%
Credit Suisse	10.2	5.4	4.8	3.7	39% / 35% / 27%
Barclays	8.5	5.2	3.3	3.4	44% / 28% / 29%
UBS	5.9	1.8	4.1	2.8	21% / 47% / 32%
Total	$ 110.8	$ 68.1	$ 42.7	$ 41.9	45% / 28% / 27%

Note: Equities revenues may not be directly comparable as some banks include prime brokerage and securities services within reported Equities revenue.

Source: Bloomberg.

To produce this substantial revenue, the trading business takes significantly more risk than the other divisions, as evidenced by large losses in 2008 in many trading-related businesses. Postcrisis regulations require banks to set aside significantly more equity against many trading businesses, leading to lower return on equity (ROE) for trading compared to the smaller investment banking and asset management businesses. Low ROE has been a particular challenge in fixed income businesses (despite high revenues), leading several large banks to intentionally shrink their fixed income business since 2009, including UBS, Barclays, and Morgan Stanley.

Institutional investors manage over $75 trillion of assets, mostly invested in stocks, bonds, and loans. These investors spend much of their time determining which securities they wish to own to meet their objectives and how to manage their risks. Given the huge pool of securities and the thousands of institutional investors making these decisions, on each trading day of the year there are large trading flows as investors reassess and readjust their portfolios.

EXHIBIT 5.2 GOLDMAN SACHS 2015 ANNUAL REPORT— DESCRIPTION OF SALES AND TRADING BUSINESS

Institutional Client Services serves our clients who come to the firm to buy and sell financial products, raise funding, and manage risks. We do this by acting as a market maker and offering market expertise on a global basis. Institutional Client Services makes markets and facilitates client transactions in fixed income, equity, currency, and commodity products. In addition, we make markets in and clear client transactions on major stock, options, and futures exchanges worldwide. Market makers provide liquidity and play a critical role in price discovery, which contributes to the overall efficiency of the capital markets. Our willingness to make markets, commit capital, and take risk in a broad range of products is crucial to our client relationships.

Our clients are primarily institutions that are professional market participants, including investment entities whose ultimate customers include individual investors investing for their retirement, buying insurance, or putting aside surplus cash in a deposit account.

Through our global sales force, we maintain relationships with our clients, receiving orders, and distributing investment research, trading ideas, market information and analysis. As a market maker, we provide prices to clients globally across thousands of products in all major asset classes and markets. At times we take the other side of transactions ourselves if a buyer or seller is not readily available and at other times we connect our clients to other parties who want to transact. Much of this connectivity between the firm and its clients is maintained on technology platforms and operates globally wherever and whenever markets are open for trading.

Institutional Client Services and our other businesses are supported by our Global Investment Research division, which, as of December 2015, provided fundamental research on more than 3400 companies worldwide and more than 40 national economies, as well as on industries, currencies, and commodities.

Institutional Client Services generates revenues in four ways:

- In large, highly liquid markets (such as markets for US Treasury bills, large capitalization S&P 500 stocks, or certain mortgage pass-through securities), we execute a high volume of transactions for our clients;
- In less liquid markets [such as mid-cap corporate bonds, growth market currencies, or certain nonagency mortgage-backed securities (MBS)], we execute transactions for our clients for spreads and fees that are generally somewhat larger than those charged in more liquid markets;
- We also structure and execute transactions involving customized or tailor-made products that address our clients' risk exposures, investment objectives, or other complex needs (such as a jet fuel hedge for an airline); and
- We provide financing to our clients for their securities trading activities, as well as securities lending and other prime brokerage services.

The sales and trading division serves these institutional investors by providing analysis and ideas, market access and execution, financing client positions, and by providing liquidity through "market-making" activities at the bank's risk. Revenues may be earned through explicit fees or commissions, by earning interest on loans to clients and on certain inventory, or by charging and effectively earning spreads between bid and offer prices across large numbers of securities and derivatives bought from and sold to institutional investors as they alter their portfolios.

The market-making function often involves the bank acting as a principal to buy securities from institutional investors and, at some point (perhaps minutes, hours, days, or months later), reselling those securities to other investing clients. The conduct of this risk-taking function is affected by multiple inputs, including research, regulators, litigation, public relations, competitors, bankruptcies, credit rating agencies, arbitrageurs, and myriad other variables. Trading is a highly analytical position that requires a large number of daily decisions, intensive analysis of public and private data, and quick assimilation of information from multiple sources. Regardless of trading specialization, a strong understanding of global economics, interest rates, currencies, credit risks, equity valuation techniques, and even politics is important.

A good trader has the ability to keep track of and synthesize a large volume of information so that intelligent decisions can be made rapidly, including what bid and offer prices to quote to clients on particular transactions. When an investing client wishes to purchase a security, their sales representative will quote an "offer" price. When the client wishes to sell a security, their sales representative will quote a "bid" price. The consequence of decisions can be a quick gain or loss on a security holding, but sometimes it takes months for the result to be known. Banks execute many thousands of principal trades each day, of which a large number turn out to be unprofitable if viewed in isolation. However, if most individual trades are made with a small positive "expected value" then executing thousands of such trades, while managing the aggregate risk of the trades, is likely to lead the business overall to have profits instead of losses on a large majority of days.

As an example of the interaction of risk management and capturing bid-ask spreads, if a trader quotes a bid and offer on $20 million of illiquid high-yield bonds of chemical company ABC maturing in 2025, a mutual fund sells the bonds to the bank at the bid price, and there is no immediate opportunity to resell to another customer at a profit, the trader may slightly reduce his/her bid and offer on other chemical company bonds, making it more likely that this is the "best offer" in the market when investors who are looking to buy such bonds call multiple banks to check prices. As the best (lowest) offer, it is more likely the trader will have the opportunity to sell short another chemical company high-yield bond in the near-term, which would help hedge exposure given the positive expected correlations between high-yield bonds in the same industry. If there are other bonds in ABC (e.g., 2023 and 2026 maturities), the trader may reduce those prices more than on other bonds in an effort to sell short the ABC bonds (or reduce existing inventory)—same-company bonds would provide the best hedge as they have the highest expected price correlation as well as the only securities with the same "jump to default" risk in an unexpected near-term bankruptcy. While it may take weeks or months to find a good opportunity to sell the 2025 ABC bonds, in the interim the trader is aiming to maintain a reasonably "balanced book" of long and short positions in high-yield chemical sector bonds. If across the trader's book he/she is able to do dozens of client trades every day, over time the trader is effectively earning bid-ask spreads in return for providing liquidity (also known as immediacy) to investors, while retaining some risk that the expected correlations between long and short positions don't hold up.

As a general matter, institutional investors are bearing most of the long-term price risk for securities markets as a whole. Trading divisions typically have little expected direct price risk to overall asset classes but may bear significant correlation risk. When markets experience extreme tension such as during the 2007–09 financial crisis, some seemingly "balanced books" can become unbalanced due to changing correlations and thus suffer significant losses. Some markets are liquid and have reliable correlations that assist in building a balanced book, while other markets are illiquid and offer fewer opportunities to reliably manage risk across the book. These differences are major factors in determining the size of spread between bid and offer price (often called the bid-ask spread) that a market maker feels is necessary to earn a sufficient expected profit for the amount of residual risk they expect to bear in the course of facilitating client trading flows.

Regardless of the expected time frame of a holding, a trader must keep track of every risk position's value on at least a daily basis. This is called "marking-to-market." If a trader holds a public company's stock, the "mark" can be taken from the intraday or closing price as reported by an exchange. For securities and derivatives that do not trade on an exchange, depending on the circumstances, the mark may be determined by reference to other trade reporting services, bid and offer quotes available through interdealer brokers or other sources, comparable securities with a more visible or recently updated price, or an internal model that has been developed to predict the realizable value of the position. Irrespective of the valuation method, a trader must mark to market all securities and derivative positions held in inventory each day, which gives rise to a daily profit and loss statement.

A trader must be able to deal analytically and unemotionally with trading losses since even the best traders usually have a number of losing trades in their book, alongside profitable trades. The key is to have more profitable trades than unprofitable trades and for the cumulative mark-to-market trading position to be positive over a quarter or calendar year time frame.

While traders are expected to make reasonably consistent profits in the course of providing liquidity to clients, the sales and trading team have the additional objective of helping investing clients' trade profitably. If a client can't trade profitably with an investment bank, the client may eventually stop trading with that bank. As a result, sometimes traders decide to accept lower trading margins (or even losses) to accommodate client investment objectives and to facilitate greater trading volume. Relationships with the largest institutional investors take time to build and must be carefully guarded to maximize long-term revenue for the bank, sometimes at the expense of short-term revenue. Balancing such considerations in a risk business can be difficult and requires regular discussion between sales, trading, and senior management functions.

Research

Investment banks' research groups are housed within the sales and trading division, and research analysts speak regularly with salespeople and traders. Research analysts publish reports containing their independent analysis and views on a variety of topics including equities valuations, corporate credit risk, and economic developments. Equity analysts will seek opportunities to meet with company management teams and ask questions on quarterly earnings calls. Analysts are also available to institutional investors to explain their views and debate particular questions with regard to their subject matter.

Research publications are typically provided to institutional investors without cost based on the assumption that when investors find research to be useful, they will use the publishing bank to execute relatively low-risk transactions such as risk-free agency or commoditized transactions that are profitable to the bank. An example of this is the many agency (no-risk) equity trades in the United States where investors pay commissions between $0.02 and $0.04 per share, despite having access to other trading methods in which they would pay less than $0.01 per share. Investors' willingness to pay more than the lowest-cost method is largely explained by their desire to keep receiving value-added research that they pay for indirectly through higher commissions.

Within the investment bank, traders rely on extensive research to gain insight into the securities that they trade. They utilize research from their own firm's research teams, research provided by others that is publicly available, and their own independent research. All traders and salespeople should be able to read company filings and presentations, understand a company's business model and risks, and ask relevant questions. Some market-making desks have one or more designated "desk analysts" that conduct research for the benefit of the traders and the desk's clients, which focuses on specific securities traded by that desk instead of the overall equity story which may be covered by the research department.

See Chapter 6 for a more complete description of the research function.

Sales

Sales professionals cover individual and institutional investing clients. Their role is to build and maintain a trusting relationship with investing clients and to learn the specific goals and interests of each client. This understanding allows salespeople to bring clients value-added investing or hedging ideas. A sales professional provides investment ideas developed from research and analysis. The provision of research that provides unique insights and solutions in a timely way is an important part of the sales process. This is especially the case with complex investment transactions where research and analysis is tailored by sales professionals to meet individual client needs.

Every day in the markets there are thousands of pieces of newsflow, data, prices, and trading color potentially of interest to certain investors. Salespeople add significant value by filtering all this information and only calling particular clients regarding the things they are most likely to be interested in, presenting the information in a succinct and compelling way and offering to follow up with more detail (or get the bank's relevant expert on the phone) if the client wishes to dig further.

Salespeople take orders from investors to buy and sell securities on an agency basis and communicate pricing from traders on principal transactions. Sales teams have the dual objective of helping both traders and investing clients create profits, but sometimes it is difficult to meet the objectives of both sides. The best salespeople are adept at managing the expectations of both investors and traders, intermediating fair prices for both, while facilitating communication on a variety of issues. They know the pressure points and priorities of both traders and investors and keep track of wins and losses over an extended period of time. Analytical skills are an essential part of the sales process, but people skills can be equally important.

EQUITY TRADING

Equity traders trade common shares, derivatives on common shares or equity indexes (options, swaps, and forwards), convertibles, and other common share-based products, including exchange-traded funds (ETFs). Each of these is a large business area that requires a high degree of specialization. Each trader focuses on a limited number of securities or derivatives. Sometimes this is a global focus, but usually traders concentrate geographically, since each country has its own unique regulatory regime and stock exchange practices. Examples of a trader's focus area include US technology companies, US health-care companies, emerging market stocks in Asia, and European equity derivatives. There are dozens of other areas of focus for traders, depending on the size of the firm. Generally speaking, most traders have responsibility for between 20 and 100 securities (or "underlying" securities in the case of derivatives).

There are several benefits to being an active trader in a specific stock. When an investment bank solicits underwriting mandates for follow-on equity offerings, Equity Trading may be able to improve the bank's competitive position if it has significant trading activity in the stock of the prospective issuer. Services such as Autex keep track of trading activity in individual stocks, and the information is carefully monitored and included in banker underwriting pitches when the numbers are favorable. Being active in a stock can also lead to more accurate pricing and higher trading-based revenue. This is because more active traders see more bids and offers, become well versed in the trading characteristics of that stock, and have a deeper understanding of who currently holds the stock, the approximate price at which the stock was acquired and which investors are willing to buy or sell.

A sales team is aligned with each trading area in an investment bank to facilitate trades with investing clients. Traders also work closely with the Equity Capital Markets Group to price initial public offering (IPO) and follow-on equity issues and convertibles that are underwritten by the bank.

The relationship between Equity Trading and investing clients is complex. On the bank's side, it involves traders, sales traders, research salespeople, and research analysts. On the institutional client side, it involves portfolio managers, institutional traders, and operations people (see Exhibit 5.3). In addition to facilitating investing clients' purchases and sales of securities, Equity Trading provides other services to their clients, including financing, hedging, securities lending, and development of trading platforms.

EXHIBIT 5.3 EQUITY TRADING

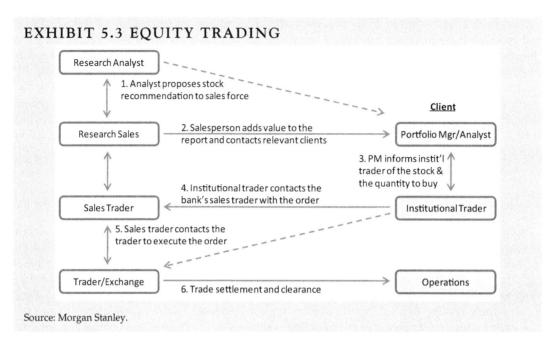

Source: Morgan Stanley.

Prime Brokerage

Most banks house their prime brokerage (or "securities services") business within equities sales and trading. Prime brokerage focuses principally on hedge funds and other clients who borrow securities and cash to support their investment business and other services including trade clearing, custody and settlement, real estate and technology assistance, performance measurement, and performance reporting. Prime brokerage products and services bring in over $1 billion of annual revenue at some banks.

Hedge funds and others sometimes borrow securities from investment banks to enable the fund to sell the securities short (selling a borrowed security, with the obligation to return it after repurchasing the security in the market in the future). Depending on a hedge fund's strategy, shorting is used to create a hedge (e.g., a short stock position to hedge a convertible bond) or to generate a potential gain based on the fund's speculation that a security's price will drop in the future.

Hedge funds also often borrow cash from investment banks' prime brokerage areas to allow the purchase of securities in greater size than the fund's own capital investment would allow. These "margin loans" are typically collateralized by all of the assets held in the fund's prime brokerage account at the bank. If the value of the collateral drops over time, banks will exercise margin calls to receive repayment of a portion of the loan. Sometimes this creates a forced sale of securities to raise cash, causing potential losses for the hedge fund. Cash borrowings enable hedge funds to extract higher returns on their investments, if returns are positive. Conversely, if returns are negative, borrowings (leverage) will create incrementally higher losses.

Prime brokerage is a profitable business for the largest investment banks and historically has experienced few losses. In relation to the lending function, banks provide leverage against a hedge fund's entire portfolio as opposed to on an individual security and risk controllers set lending parameters that require lower leverage and faster margin calls on less diversified portfolios. When combining prime brokerage revenues earned from hedge funds with the commissions earned from these clients, hedge funds at times represent the largest source of client-related revenue within the Equity Trading Division at many large investment banks, despite in aggregate managing much fewer assets than mutual funds or pension funds. Some nonhedge fund institutional investors also borrow securities and cash from the prime brokerage arm of investment banks but in much lesser overall volumes compared to hedge funds.

Securities Lending

Many large institutional investors own sizeable blocks of stock that they expect to hold for an extended period of time. These investors are often willing to lend their shares to investment banks, who relend to other parties. Lenders receive cash collateral from borrowers when they lend shares, and the collateral is adjusted daily, based on a mark-to-market value of the shares lent. Usually the required collateral is 2%–5% greater than the value of the shares. The lenders will pay interest on the cash collateral at a rate less than the overnight market rate, depending on demand and supply conditions for lending of different stocks. If, for example, on a US transaction, the overnight Federal Funds rate is 2% p.a., and there is limited demand for borrowing a particular stock, the lender might pay interest on the collateral to the stock borrower of 1.75% p.a. If, however, demand for the shares initially exceeds the availability of lendable shares, the lender might pay a lower interest rate of 1.00% p.a. The amount of interest paid by lenders to share borrowers is called "rebate." The difference between the rebate amount and the overnight interest income from the cash collateral represents an amount of net investment income that is split between the share lender and the investment bank prime broker who facilitated the stock loan.

As an example, if an investor lent 400,000 shares of IBM stock when the stock traded at $100 (valued at $40,000,000), the borrower might be required to post $40,800,000 in cash collateral with the stock lender when the stock was borrowed. If the loan was outstanding for 3 months, the market interest earned on the $40,800,000 cash collateral at 2% p.a. would be $204,000. Because IBM shares are fairly easy to borrow, the stock lender might pay a rebate to the stock borrower at a rate of 1.75% p.a., or $178,500. The 25 basis point spread, or $25,500 difference between interest earned at a market rate and the rebate paid to the stock borrower, is mostly kept by the stock lender, with a portion paid to the investment bank that facilitated the transaction. (If the investment bank sourced the shares from its own trading desk's holdings instead of from a client, the bank would earn the entire spread.)

Shares of stock can be difficult to borrow under certain scenarios, including the following: a large portion of the stock is held by insiders who are restricted from lending it, investors who might normally lend shares decide they want to sell the shares the next day, or investors who own the shares are concerned about potential negative share price consequences if there is excessive shorting in the stock.

Short selling activity represents an important part of the global capital markets. Hedge funds are the largest participants in short selling and are, accordingly, the most important users of an investment bank's securities lending business. The investment bank sets up security borrowing arrangements with most of its large institutional investing clients and with some large individual investing clients. The borrowing arrangements typically permit the lender to terminate a security loan and recall the security on a few days' notice, although, in practice, most loans continue for months unless the borrower wishes to close out. When supply of a security becomes tight, a repricing of the rebate is usually able to bring supply and demand back into balance, as opposed to causing a "short squeeze." Many investors are willing to lend a portion of their securities to obtain income that enhances the returns of their securities holdings. For some large institutional investors, this can amount to hundreds of millions of dollars a year. In the competitive world of institutional money management, the possibility of earning even an additional 0.1% p.a. while taking substantially no risk (given the excess cash collateralization) is an attractive proposition for many funds. This dynamic leads to oversupply of most large-cap listed stocks in the US securities lending market.

When shares are loaned and shorted, the buyer of those shares becomes the owner from the perspective of the clearing system. This means that the buyer receives dividends if they own the shares on a "dividend record date" and is able to vote if a shareholder election is held. In most cases, the stock loan agreement provides that whenever the company pays a dividend, the stock borrower must pay to the lender a cash amount equal to the dividend.

A significant amount of shorting activity is conducted by investors who want to hedge downside risk in related positions, such as holders of convertible securities or call options, or funds with long stock positions that are hedged by shorting a similar stock (a "pairs trade") or a broad market or sector-specific index or ETF. Another principal reason to short stock is to create a "bearish" position in a company's shares, based on the view that it will be profitable to sell stock short today and then buy stock back in the open market at a lower price if the share price declines in the future. Shares are fungible (completely interchangeable), which enables a borrower of shares to return to the lender different (but equivalent) shares acquired from purchases in the open market.

Naked short selling involves the sale of shares (or other securities) without first borrowing the security or confirming the ability to borrow ahead of the settlement date for the sale. When shares are not borrowed before a closing date, the result is a "failure to deliver," which must be corrected as soon as possible by buying securities in the market to enable delivery. Regulators have banned "abusive naked short selling" as a method to artificially depress security prices. There has been considerable regulatory analysis of naked shorting and its critics claim that this practice can be damaging to companies that are trying to raise capital and in some cases may even contribute to bankruptcies. However, others do not see evidence that naked short selling has created such problems. See Exhibit 5.4 for a discussion of historical issues and regulatory changes that have affected this practice.

In the United States and several other jurisdictions, exchanges track and publicly report the number of shares borrowed and shorted for each listed common stock. The short interest ratio is the number of shares of a publicly traded company that are sold short divided by the average daily trading volume for those shares. It may also be important to consider shares sold short in relation to free float (shares that are not held by owners of more than 10% of the stock or by senior executives and/or insiders). A high short interest ratio may imply that some market participants are bearish on a particular stock. However, this can be misleading since a large portion of the short interest reported for some companies relates to hedge fund purchases of convertible securities. In this scenario, hedge funds short some of the shares that underlie the convertible to hedge share price risk. This type of shorting is therefore usually not an expression of a bearish view on a stock. As a result, an accurate interpretation of short interest ratios must factor in convertibles that have been issued, as well as any publicly known derivative transactions. See Chapter 9 for a more detailed overview of convertibles and related shorting activity.

EXHIBIT 5.4 SHORT SELLING

In a short sale of stock, a trader borrows stock and sells it. If the stock falls in price, then the short seller can buy the stock in the open market at the lower price, return what was borrowed, and pocket the difference.

Through the years, government authorities have occasionally attempted to restrict short selling. Although short selling is a legitimate trading strategy and helps to prevent "irrational exuberance" and bubbles, during 2008 the Securities and Exchange Commission (SEC) restricted certain types of short selling because it worried that these trades, along with false rumors, negatively impacted the financial system.

During September of 2008, the SEC issued an emergency order, which curbed short selling the shares of 19 large financial firms. They subsequently extended this order to include all financial stocks. The order attempted to stop short selling financial stocks as well as "unlawful manipulation through 'naked' short selling" in all stocks. Naked short selling refers to the practice of selling stock short without taking steps to borrow the shares. Historically, a short seller "located" shares (confirmed the availability of borrow supply) and sold the shares short but was not obligated to enter into a contract with the share lender in advance of the settlement date. Sometimes more than one trader was able to locate the same shares and proceeded to execute short sales, which led to failures to deliver. Following the SEC order, a short seller is now required to enter into a contract to borrow the shares on the trade date.

The SEC lifted the financial stock short selling ban after 3 weeks but the new restrictions on naked short selling remained in effect: during July 2009, the SEC made permanent emergency order, requiring traders to complete short sales within 4 days.

Margin Financing

When an investor borrows money to purchase securities and the securities (or other agreed on assets) are posted as collateral, an investor is buying on margin. Investment banks arrange margin accounts for their investing clients when investors want to leverage their investments. The value of the securities held in collateral are marked to market daily and the investor must maintain a predetermined loan to value percentage. If the value of the collateral drops, the investor will be required to deposit additional cash or other collateral. A bank's demand for additional cash or other collateral is called a margin call.

Most margin financing provided by investment banks is "portfolio margin," meaning that the loan is collateralized by a reasonably diversified portfolio held in a prime brokerage account. All else being equal, the more diversified and self-hedged a prime brokerage account is (i.e., if there are short positions as well as long positions), the higher the amount of financing a bank will be willing to provide and the lower the interest rate may be. On the whole, prime brokerage lending represents a relatively low-risk, low-interest rate business for the banks. At some banks, other areas, including equity derivatives trading and structured credit trading, offer higher-risk, higher-rate margin loans against undiversified and illiquid collateral such as individual structured credit or direct lending positions or large insider stakes in restricted common stock.

Margin calls by investment banks have occasionally been a precipitating factor in the blow-up of certain hedge funds. During the financial crisis, this dynamic increased volatility in the market as some hedge funds were forced to rapidly liquidate part or all of their portfolios. See Exhibit 5.5 for a summary of Peloton, a large hedge fund that shut down following margin calls by investment banks. Also refer to **A Tale of Two Hedge Funds: Magnetar and Peloton Case**.

EXHIBIT 5.5 MARGIN CALLS BY PRIME BROKERS AGAINST HEDGE FUNDS

After years of strong growth and outsized returns, during the 2007–09 credit crisis, hedge funds encountered their worst crisis since the 1998 collapse of long-term capital management. Hedge funds rely on prime brokers at investment banks to clear trades, service assets, and perhaps most importantly for their portfolio strategy, provide leverage. Hedge funds take on debt to enhance asset returns and to facilitate certain investment strategies.

However, for some hedge funds that owned mortgage-backed securities (MBS) or collateralized debt obligations in 2007 and 2008, leverage proved to be their downfall. Sharp declines in housing prices reduced the value of these securities' collateral, leading prime brokers to demand additional collateral. As a result, many funds were forced to sell assets to meet margin calls. Some funds such as Carlyle Capital and Peloton Partners were unable to meet requests for additional cash and were forced to unwind their holdings at fire-sale prices.

While high leverage and untimely bets on the housing market were to blame for most of the hedge fund industry's woes, the large subprime losses experienced by investment banks also played a role in the collapse of several hedge funds. With investment banks facing their own asset write-downs and extreme volatility elsewhere in the businesses, the prime brokerage operations within investment banks became more conservative with credit and gave even their best clients little latitude, tightening margin call conditions (i.e., requiring lower loan to value) as the market worsened.

Peloton Partners, a London-based hedge fund started in 2005 by two former Goldman Sachs partners, is a striking example of an otherwise successful hedge fund brought down by margin calls from its prime brokers. In 2007, Peloton's fund posted an 87% return by shorting BB-rated tranches of subprime MBS and going long AAA-rated tranches. However, in January 2008, Peloton revised its strategy after determining that there was little additional downside in subprime securities. Peloton covered their BB short position, while increasing their long position in the higher-rated tranches. As the value of subprime mortgages dropped further with higher default rates, declining housing prices, and ultimately an extremely illiquid market in subprime MBSs , Peloton's losses were great enough to prompt demands for cash from banks. Unable to meet their requests, Peloton shut down its fund and suspended client redemptions, ultimately posting losses of billions of dollars. The implosion of one of London's premiere hedge funds underscores how quickly a fund can go under when margin financing from prime brokerage lenders is tightened or pulled.

FIXED INCOME, CURRENCIES, AND COMMODITIES TRADING

FICC usually focuses on interest rate products, credit products, currencies, and commodities. Traders in these four areas run many different businesses, each of which has its own sales force and research function. FICC has historically been the most profitable division in most of the large investment banks, but many FICC divisions suffered significant losses during the global financial crisis of 2007–08. From 2010 onward, new regulations from a variety of global regulators have required banks to hold significantly more equity against many areas of the FICC business. The result is that while FICC continues to post significant revenues at top banks, it has typically been the lowest ROE business of any division. Accordingly, several top banks have intentionally shrunk their FICC business in recent years (including Barclays, UBS, and Morgan Stanley), while other banks have developed ROE-enhancing strategies including the "juniorization" of staff, increased use of technology in place of personnel, and increased focus on centralized clearing arrangements.

Interest Rate Products

Banks assist clients in trading government bonds in the United States, United Kingdom, German, French, Japanese, and other government and agency bonds and notes. Banks also conduct significant market-making and structuring businesses in interest rate derivatives including swaps, futures, and options. The interest rate business includes some business lines in which the bank acts mostly as agent (e.g., executing agency orders in highly liquid US Treasury bonds and settling and clearing transactions) and other business lines where the bank acts as principal on significant risk positions, including bespoke interest rate derivative transactions. For market-standard derivative structures that trade in high volume, such as interest rate swaps, postcrisis regulations, and advancing technology have increased competition for investment banks from exchanges and certain hedge funds interested in providing electronic market-making services. This is an area where clients or vendors to investment banks can actively compete with banks to the potential detriment of bank profits.

Credit Products

Credit products include corporate bonds (investment grade, high yield, and distressed debt securities), MBS, asset-backed securities (credit card receivables, automobile loans, computer leases, trade receivables, equipment leases, etc.), structured credit, and credit derivatives (primarily credit default swaps).

Corporate Bond Trading

In the United States, over $1 trillion of investment grade corporate bonds have been issued annually in the past several years, while issuance of high-yield bonds has been running at a multiple of the previous high during the 2006–07 leveraged buyout (LBO) boom (see Exhibit 5.6). While publicly traded companies typically have only one common stock, larger companies tend to have many different bonds outstanding, leading to relative illiquidity of any

particular bond. Most corporate bond trading involves an investment bank acting as intermediary between institutional investors. In some cases a bank is able to act solely as agent and
therefore not transact until the other side of a transaction is located. In other cases a bank may
find an opportunity to buy and resell a bond on the same day at a small profit. However, the
most typical case is that a bank must quote a bid and offer and take the risk that they will bear
the resulting position for a period of weeks or longer, similar to the chemical bond example
earlier in this chapter. For some issuers with substantial bonds outstanding, banks also make
markets in credit default swaps (CDSs) (see the later description) linked to reference bonds.

Owing to the distinct trading characteristics and client bases for different types of corporate bonds, large banks typically have separate trading and sales teams focused on investment-grade bonds, high-yield bonds, and distressed debt.

EXHIBIT 5.6 US HIGH-YIELD BOND ISSUANCE ($ BILLIONS)

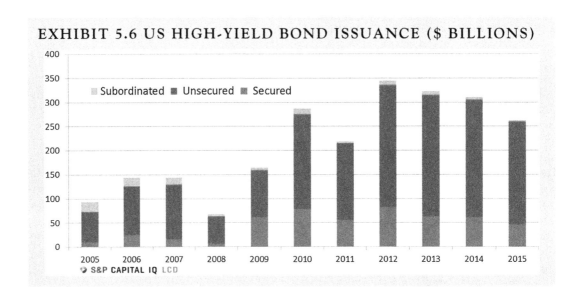

Structured Credit

The Structured credit business focuses primarily on intermediating credit risk between
companies and investors. The investment bank may at different times act as an advisor, structurer, originator, lender, or administrative agent in the course of creating credit instruments
that meet credit investor needs while providing useful funding to borrowers. Significant portions of the business involve securitization (asset-backed securities and MBS), nonsecuritized
pooling or tranching, or other forms of structuring, and splitting risks between the bank and
different investors (see Exhibit 5.7). In many structured credit transactions, the investment
bank will take credit risk on its balance sheet for a period of time while it works to structure
and syndicate down the exposure through its sales force. In some transactions, the bank will
keep significant residual risk on its book indefinitely, while administering a loan, which is
held in part by credit investors. In these transactions, the bank is effectively acting not only
as an intermediary and structurer but also as a traditional bank lender on the portion of the
risk it retains, albeit usually on more complex lending structures than traditional bank loans.

EXHIBIT 5.7 DEUTSCHE BANK'S DESCRIPTION OF ITS STRUCTURED CREDIT BUSINESS

Structured credit is a global market–leading platform focused on illiquid credit, securitizations, hard asset financing, and special situations. Integrated solutions include the following:

- Broad asset-backed securities franchise
- Financing solutions
- Structured credit trading (secondary trading and customized solutions)
- Structured finance advisory (liability management and M&A capital structure advisory)
- Syndicated credit (structuring and syndicating private bank market credit)
- Pension and insurance risk markets

One important area of structured credit is collateralized loan obligations, or CLO. A CLO is a debt security underwritten by an investment bank that is backed by a pool of noninvestment grade loans. Because the pool includes a broadly diversified group of assets, credit rating agencies have given an investment-grade rating to certain tranches in many of these CLOs. In a CLO, a special purpose trust is formed to purchase noninvestment-grade loans and then the trust issues three or more tranches of bonds (each with a different credit rating) to investors who purchase these securities as a means to receive slightly higher coupons than similarly rated securities. While certain CDO structures with underlying subprime mortgage collateral had write-downs even on AAA-rated tranches, CLOs backed by corporate loans to date have never seen a default on AAA-rated tranches (though mark-to-market losses have occurred.) Further information on CLOs is found in Exhibits 5.8 and 5.9.

EXHIBIT 5.8 WHAT IS A COLLATERALIZED LOAN OBLIGATION?

Basic Structure	CLO Balance	
	Assets	Liabilities

- A CLO is comparable to a finance company
  - Borrows money (liabilities)
  - Invests in collateral (assets)
  - Has residual value (equity)
- The equity of a CLO represents an ownership stake in an entity and is the first loss position
- The assets are typically managed by a seasoned asset manager with a strong track record in the respective CLO asset class
- Repayment of liabilities relies on the performance of the underlying collateral pool and asset manager
- Credit enhancement and tranching creates different rating levels, allowing involvement by a wide investor base

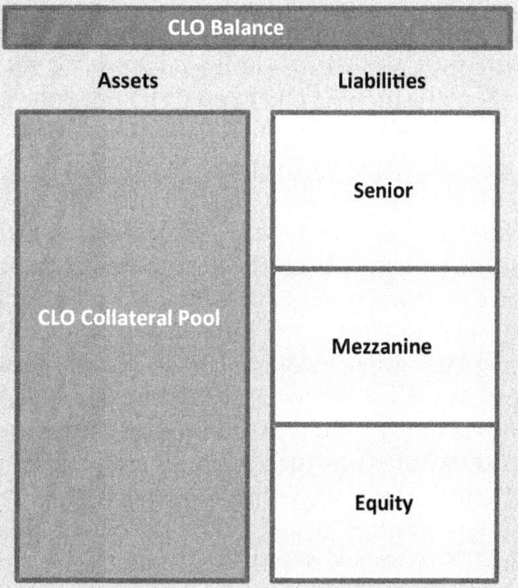

Assets: CLO Collateral Pool

Liabilities: Senior / Mezzanine / Equity

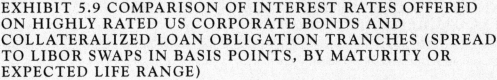

EXHIBIT 5.9 COMPARISON OF INTEREST RATES OFFERED
ON HIGHLY RATED US CORPORATE BONDS AND
COLLATERALIZED LOAN OBLIGATION TRANCHES (SPREAD
TO LIBOR SWAPS IN BASIS POINTS, BY MATURITY OR
EXPECTED LIFE RANGE)

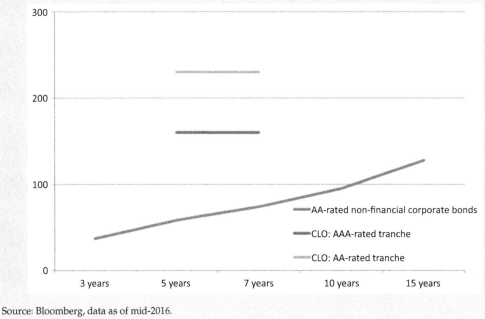

Source: Bloomberg, data as of mid-2016.

During 2007 and 2008, investment banks recorded significant losses on their structured credit positions because of the credit crisis that started during the middle of 2007. The effects of diversification on CLO and CDO portfolios proved to be much less than estimated by ratings agencies and investors. Losses reported by financial institutions approached $1 trillion in relation to this product area by the end of 2008, based on losses from both commercial and residential MBSs.

MBS are debt obligations where the underlying assets (collateral) are mortgage loans. In the case of residential MBS, the loans are purchased from mortgage originators such as banks and mortgage companies and assembled into pools. Securities are then issued to investors who become claimants to the interest and principal payments made by borrowers in the pools of loans. MBS issuers include US government sponsored entities Fannie Mae (Federal National Mortgage Association) and Freddie Mac (Federal Home Loan Mortgage Corporation), the US government agency Ginnie Mae (Government National Mortgage Association), and some private institutions such as banks and brokerage firms.

Historically, many MBS have been used to create CDOs, and many of the buyers (and insurers) of MBS-related CDOs have been financial institutions. They viewed some of these securities as very low-risk investments (the senior tranches typically had AAA credit ratings), with a slightly higher yield than straight AAA bonds. Unfortunately, until 2008 most of these institutions underestimated the risk of these securities and ignored the real estate bubble. Many statistical models utilized by issuers, rating agencies, and investors did not incorporate the possibility of a significant decline in housing prices across the country. As a result of large losses stemming from this product area, as well as losses on loans to fund private equity transactions, an unprecedented number of senior executives of investment banks were asked to step down during 2007 and 2008. CDOs and CLOs have been utilized again in recent years, but investment banks now have much lower risk tolerance for holding pools of assets on their books for any significant period of time while the securitization is completed and the various tranches sold off.

The Dodd–Frank Act of 2010 had a significant impact on structured credit. The act requires banks to retain at least 5% of each CDO tranche they sell and (with minor exceptions) they are not allowed to hedge or transfer this risk. Advocates of this regulation claim that it encourages more careful risk assessment in developing CDO products, whereas critics argue that it increases banks' capital requirements and therefore increases securitization costs.

Exhibit 5.10 summarizes Merrill Lynch's multiyear aggressive buildup of its CDO book, which resulted in huge write-downs and the ultimate sale of the firm to Bank of America.

EXHIBIT 5.10 MERRILL LYNCH

During July 2008, Merrill Lynch agreed to sell more than $30 billion in toxic mortgage-related collateralized debt obligations (CDOs) at a steep loss, hoping to purge its balance sheet of problems that plagued the brokerage giant. The sale was to Lone Star, an affiliate of a private equity firm, which paid $6.7 billion, or 22 cents on the dollar. This created a $5.7 billion write-down for Merrill.

Merrill's move was an effort to stem the tide of losses after more than $46 billion in write-downs during the previous 12 months. Faced with this leak in its balance sheet, Merrill sold $8.5 billion in new common stock, diluting existing shareholders by about 38%.

Many CDOs held by Merrill were viewed as highly likely to default and lose some or most of their principal value. Of the 30 CDOs totaling $32 billion that Merrill underwrote in 2007, 27 had seen their AAA ratings downgraded to "junk."

Merrill had been hit especially hard by the mortgage crisis, largely because of big bets on mortgage-backed securities not long before the market for those securities collapsed. During 2007, Stanley O'Neal, the CEO who oversaw those bets, was forced out and replaced by John Thain, a former Goldman Sachs mortgage and CDO trader who later ran the New York Stock Exchange.

Despite installing new risk controls and a new management team, Thain was unable to steer Merrill out of trouble. During September of 2008, these ongoing troubles, and the near-panic surrounding the bankruptcy of Lehman Brothers, led to the sale of Merrill Lynch to Bank of America for a price that was less than one-half the value of the firm 15 months earlier.

Credit Default Swaps

A CDS is a contract between two counterparties whereby one party makes an upfront payment and periodic payments in return for receiving a payoff if an underlying security or loan defaults. For example, if an investor purchased $10 million of a 5-year investment grade bond issued by Company ABC and later decided to protect their investment risk by entering into a

CDS on $10 million notional in Company ABC, they might pay 2% of $10 million upfront and 1% of $10 million annually for 5 years in exchange for the right to receive a cash payment in the event of a default by Company ABC. The default-contingent cash payment is equal to the difference between the bond's face value and the expected recovery value as determined in an auction conducted by large market-makers soon after the default. The party that receives an annual fee is a credit protection seller; the annual fee payer is a credit protection buyer. None of the cash that flows from the CDS directly involves Company ABC, but ABC's bond is the reference security for the CDS contract. A CDS is essentially an insurance policy to hedge against default. Because there is no requirement to own the actual underlying security or loan when entering into this type of contract, many CDS credit protection buyers engage in this transaction purely for speculative purposes when a CDS buyer believes the market is underestimating the probability of default. Buying CDS is a common method of establishing an effective "short credit" position.

CDS transactions were historically not regulated in the United States because the SEC determined that a CDS contract was not a security and the Commodities Futures Trading Commission determined that CDS was not a commodity. As a result, there was concern about unregulated CDS risk positions that grew substantially over many years. The Dodd–Frank Act addressed this issue by classifying "securities-based" swaps as securities. As a consequence, CDSs are now covered under SEC regulations. The total face value of CDS contracts decreased from an estimated $50 trillion at the end of 2008 to under $15 trillion during 2016 based on the impact of new regulations and credit concerns that arose during the 2008 global financial crisis.

The CDS market came under regulatory scrutiny because of its massive size, lack of regulation, and potential to permit insider-trading activity. An example of the last point follows: The cost of CDS sometimes increases considerably in the weeks prior to the announcement of a corporate takeover by a private equity fund. On completion of a LBO, the target company's credit rating generally deteriorates because the buyout is financed in large part by leveraging the target's balance sheet. Because this increases the riskiness of the company's outstanding bonds, the result is a decrease in the company's bond prices and corresponding increase in CDS spreads. During 2007 and 2008, prior to announcement of a number of acquisitions by private equity funds, CDS pricing for the target company increased substantially, suggesting that CDS credit protection buyers became aware of the acquisition before it was publicly announced. Speculators evidently purchased CDS on private equity target companies before the announcement and then sold CDS after the announcement, creating a substantial profit. Such insider trading would likely be caught, and prosecuted, in the highly regulated stock market, but the CDS market did not have much regulatory surveillance at that time.

A notable disaster involving CDS occurred during late 2008 when AIG, which had previously been one of the world's largest and strongest insurance companies, had to be bailed out by the US government. As a credit protection seller, AIG had approximately $500 billion notional exposure in its CDS positions. After marking-to-market the amount it owed as a credit protection seller on a portfolio of MBS following the collapse of the real estate market, AIG's capital reserves were reduced and, as a result, the company lost its AAA credit rating. Subsequent ratings downgrades triggered requirements to post tens of billions in collateral to AIG's CDS counterparties (primarily investment banks). When AIG could not provide the required collateral, rather than allowing the insurer to fail, the US Federal Reserve in late 2008 provided an emergency $85 billion loan to the company. The total amount of bailout funding available to AIG through various government-related programs grew to over $180 billion, and the US Treasury Department held a controlling stake in the company's common stock for a considerable period.

In response to concerns about the impact of an unregulated CDS market, InterContinental Exchange, CME, and Citadel launched clearinghouses for CDS. By shifting CDS transactions to centralized clearinghouses, transparency was increased and counterparty risk was reduced. In addition, the International Swaps and Derivatives Association (ISDA) pushed forward standardization of CDS contracts (including upfront payments and standard annualized fees) to increase transparency and prevent legal disputes.

Bank Loans

To meet the full financing objectives of selected clients, in addition to arranging capital markets financings, investment banks sometimes provide bank loans for strong credit borrowers and leveraged loans for weaker credit borrowers. One of the largest users of leveraged loans from investment banks are private equity firms. Private equity firms are among the most important clients of the Investment Banking Division since they use many different bank products, including equity underwriting, debt underwriting, leveraged lending, and M&A advisory. Based on its experience underwriting, investing in and trading corporate bonds, the Trading Division collaborates with the Investment Banking Division in providing loans to many other important clients of the firm when there are other revenue opportunities with the client that support the extension of credit.

LBOs require a substantial amount of debt financing. Investment bankers help private equity firms meet the massive debt requirements of their acquisitions either through a bond offering or through a syndicated bank loan in which the investment bank typically tries to sell up to 90% of the loan to other banks, hedge funds, and other investors. For many LBOs, private equity firms require a firm commitment letter from banks to fund the debt portion of the capital structure themselves if they are unable to successfully distribute the planned loans and/or bonds to investors. Unfortunately for the investment banks, during 2006 and the first half of 2007 banks made much more significant LBO commitments than ever before. This resulted in significant large unexpected loan drawdowns from the investment banks when other lenders and investors refused to buy the debt, creating unexpected credit exposures for the banks. Private equity–related bank loans exceeded $400 billion at the end of 2007, and when banks ultimately sold many of these loans to other investors at prices as low as 70 cents on the dollar, the banks recorded very large write-downs.

Foreign Exchange

Every day over $5 trillion worth of foreign exchange transactions are conducted by banks, corporations, governments, investors, and other parties. This volume has increased significantly over time as more corporations operate globally and as world trade grows faster than global economic output. Salespeople and traders within FICC service clients for their FX needs, advising on hedging strategies and conducting agency and principal transactions. Most corporations that operate in multiple currency areas hedge much of their FX exposure by trading FX forwards, which lock in a price at which one currency will be exchanged for another in the future. Corporates and governments often enter into FX swaps that closely match their outstanding debt to effectively move a debt obligation from one currency to another. Banks also make markets in FX options and create customized derivatives where clients find it helpful. At some banks, the FX business is tightly integrated with the interest rate business.

Commodities

Contracts on commodities are traded by investment banks principally in the energy (electricity, natural gas, and oil) and metals (precious metals and base metals) sectors. A number of investment banks trade physical commodities as well and have even owned energy production facilities. Over the past decade, many large investment banks have conducted commodities trading as a substantial part of their business operations, including JPMorgan, Goldman Sachs, Morgan Stanley, Deutsche Bank, and Barclays. However, a number of large banks have recently either exited or substantially reduced their commodities-trading business. For example, Barclays announced its exit from the agricultural, precious metals, and energy businesses, and Deutsche Bank has exited from commodities trading altogether. JPMorgan announced a $3.5 billion sale of its physical commodities-trading division to Swiss-based Mercuria Group, and Morgan Stanley announced the sale of part of its oil-trading business to Rosneft, a state-owned Russian firm.

There are a number of reasons for this reduction in large bank commodities business, including concerns about profitability and ROE, a more difficult trading environment, more stringent regulation, and greater reputational risk. Worldwide regulatory rule changes, such as Basel III regulation, have forced banks to set aside additional capital to support the higher-risk commodities business, and the regulation also limits significant borrowing in support of the business. As banks reduce their commodities exposure, capital is freed up and redirected into other, less risky, business areas.

An additional reason to reduce exposure to commodities may relate to regulators and legislators periodically expressing unhappiness with the idea of bank ownership of physical commodities because of their concern about potential for price fixing when the same party operates physical assets and also trades securities that relate to the products of these assets. A final concern is that physical holdings of commodities and associated operations by banks could lead to environmental catastrophes given that bank senior management is not primarily experienced with operating such businesses.

Clients buy and sell financial contracts on commodities to hedge risk positions arising in the regular course of business (e.g., airlines, distributors, industrial companies, producers, refiners, shipping companies, and utility companies) or to invest in or trade them as part of an investment strategy (e.g., hedge funds may bet that oil or gold prices will increase or decrease). As investment banks reduce their exposure to commodities, new nonbank entities are filling the gap for contracts that cannot be traded on exchanges.

MARKET-MAKING EXAMPLES

As described previously, the client-focused trading activities of large investment banks are often referred to as market-making. The meaning is that the bank stands willing to "make a market" any time it is requested by a client. In other words, the bank will quote a client a bid price or an offer price (or often both simultaneously) on many securities or derivatives at any time.

If the client wishes to buy a security or derivative, the bank will sell it to them, and if the client wishes to sell, the bank stands ready to buy. The difference between the price at which the bank is willing to buy (bid price) and the price at which it is willing to sell (ask, or offer price) is referred to as the "bid-ask spread."

Market-making is the business of "capturing" bid-ask spreads, by continuously buying securities at the bid price and selling securities at the higher offer price. However, to capture bid-ask spreads, market-makers must take risk. The nature of the risk varies greatly depending on the security or derivative, the length of time the risk position is held, and the liquidity of the security or derivative. In general, bid-ask spreads are narrower in liquid markets and less complex products. See Exhibits 5.11 and 5.12 for examples of the business of market-making.

EXHIBIT 5.11 MARKET-MAKING EXAMPLE 1—THE IDEAL: RISKLESS AND UNSOLICITED TRANSACTION

On the high-yield bond trading desk, a salesperson picks up a ringing phone and hears the familiar voice of a pension fund manager. The client says that he/she wants to sell $10 million face amount of ABC Corp 8% bonds due June 2020. (If there is a good relationship with the client, the salesperson may also be able to get additional information, such as why they are selling, whether this represents their whole position in the bond or just a fraction and what they think about the company and the sector generally.)

Simultaneously, a bond portfolio manager at an insurance company calls another salesperson on the same desk. He/she says he/she is adding to his/her energy positions and wants to buy $10 million face amount of the same ABC Corp 8% bonds.

Both salespeople tell their clients they will quickly check the price, put them on hold, and yell over to the trader who handles high-yield energy bonds. These bonds generally only trade several times a week, making this outcome very unusual. Despite the illiquidity, the trader will have already been following the bonds, tracking any reported trades in the market, and adjusting his/her view of the appropriate bid and ask prices many times each day based on factors such as the current yields of Treasury bonds (which define the risk-free interest rate for various maturities), the price movements of high-yield bonds generally on that day, and any sector or company-specific news which has recently come out.

Based on all of this, the trader tells the salespeople to quote the pension fund a bid price of 91.25% of par and quote the insurance company an ask price of 91.75% of par. Both salespeople relay the prices to their clients, and both clients immediately agree to the trade at the price quoted to them.

The desk books a purchase of $10 million bonds at 91.25% and a sale of $10 million bonds at 91.75%. The two salespeople and one trader just earned the desk a $50,000 profit with no residual risk for the bank and with very little effort.

Three important notes on this example:

1. The transaction which occurred turned out to be riskless, but the bank actually had to take substantial risk to get the business. Recall that while the clients had equal, offsetting, simultaneous interest in the bond, unlike the bank, neither of them was obligated to go through with the anticipated transaction. In fact, either of them could have changed their mind after hearing the price or might have called three other investment banks to ensure they got the best price possible. If the bank in this example was "best bid" of three banks quoted by the pension fund but was not the "best offer" of the three banks quoted by the insurance company, then it would have purchased $10 million of bonds at a cost of $9.125 million, with no offsetting sale. In this case, no profit has been locked in, and the bank retains the risk of the bonds declining in price before it can sell them to another client, as well as the more drastic possibility of the issuer's bankruptcy.

(Continued)

EXHIBIT 5.11 MARKET-MAKING EXAMPLE 1—THE IDEAL: RISKLESS AND UNSOLICITED TRANSACTION—cont'd

2. A situation like this is very rare. For illiquid securities with bid-ask spreads of 0.50% or higher, the chances of simultaneous unsolicited offsetting orders are very small. Liquid securities with high trading frequency (on which clients with offsetting orders do sometimes send orders in simultaneously) tend to have much lower bid-ask spreads.
3. Clients are sometimes not willing to tell the bank what they are doing. In many cases they will ask to see a "two-sided" market, or both the bid and offer price, and the bank does not know whether the client plans to buy or sell. In that case, the trader would not know whether his/her worst-case residual risk was being long or short $10 million bonds or $20 million if both clients turned out to be buyers or sellers.

EXHIBIT 5.12 MARKET-MAKING EXAMPLE 2—BLOCK TRADE OF STOCK

A trader at a mutual fund calls a salesperson at a bank at 10:45 a.m. and says he/she wants to sell 500,000 shares of XYZ Corp and is asking two banks for an "at risk" price at 11:00 a.m. The salesperson and the client agree that when the price is quoted, the fund will agree within 2 min if it wants to proceed.

The salesperson walks over to the trader who is responsible for XYZ shares to consider the situation together. XYZ shares on average trade 1.25 million shares per day, so the sale represents 40% of average daily volume. While mutual funds usually trade in and out of shares gradually, accepting the market price and paying very small commissions, this fund wants to get out of its entire position at a guaranteed price, passing the risk on to the bank.

The stock is currently trading at $60, so 500,000 shares represent $30 million of risk for the bank. The trader and salesperson review a shareholder list, call up internal records of clients that have recently been buying or selling the stock, and ask the other salespeople about qualitative comments clients have made about the stock and what they think clients' interest may be in buying the stock if it came in large size and at a slight discount to the market price. The team also checks recent sentiment among research analysts who cover the stock. In conjunction with the trading desk head and a market risk controller, they review recent price moves in the stock and what caused them and study the general volatility profile of the stock. After analyzing all the risks involved, at 10:59 a.m. the trader agrees to bid $59.30 for the 500,000 shares. This represents a 1.17% discount from the current market price of $60.

The salesperson calls the client to commit the price. The client puts him/her on hold for 15 s, then comes back on the line and says, "You're done. I sell 500,000 shares of XYZ to you at $59.30."

The trader and salesperson get the attention of the rest of the salespeople on the desk and tell them about the trade and the need to sell the shares. Together, they formulate a strategy regarding which clients to call and the price and minimum size to offer. Given the risk position, the sales force might decide to only call a handful of trusted clients to minimize the information flowing into the marketplace.

The salespeople tell investors that they have XYZ Corp stock for sale, without mentioning the exact amount, and offer to sell 25,000 shares or more to each investor, at a price of $59.60.

EXHIBIT 5.12 MARKET-MAKING EXAMPLE 2—BLOCK TRADE OF STOCK—cont'd

Two investors express interest in 150,000 shares each, so the bank resells 300,000 shares at $59.60. The bank has made a profit of $90,000 on these shares.

The trader decides that rather than have the sales force make any further calls to less trusted clients, he/she will trade out of the remaining 200,000 shares on his/her own. Using program trading software, he/she inputs an order for the computer to sell 200,000 shares gradually into the flow of market trading, targeting 25% of total market volume. The software will drop a few hundred shares into the market several times per minute, trying to match the frequency and size of the sales as closely as possible to 25% of volume.

The stock begins to trade down rapidly. By 11:30 a.m. the stock is at $59, where it stays for the rest of the trading day. The trader manages to sell the last shares just before the market close. He/she calculates that on the 200,000 shares that the desk wasn't able to place with clients, his/her average sale price was $59.08. This represents a loss of $44,000 on the unplaced shares, making the desk's net profit on the entire trade $46,000.

PROPRIETARY TRADING

Historically, proprietary traders at investment banks traded solely for the benefit of their firm. They had no responsibility to balance their profitability interests with the interests of clients of the firm and therefore were considered competitors to these clients. In the United States, the Dodd–Frank Act of 2010 prohibited most proprietary trading by investment banks and so this activity has been substantially discontinued by US headquartered banks. According to this act, banks are not allowed to "invest in securities as principal." This has been interpreted to include proprietary trading. The separation of proprietary trading from regular banking business is often referred to as the "Volcker Rule," named after former Fed Chairman Paul Volcker. Most other developed countries have taken a similar regulatory approach, which has significantly reduced global proprietary trading by investment banks that also provide depository services to their customers.

Prior to this regulatory change, the proprietary trading business within banks was somewhat similar to the business conducted by hedge funds. During an approximately 10-year period ending in 2007, investment banks became significant competitors to hedge funds (who were the most important clients of the banks' client-related trading business). This sometimes created conflicts and, as a result, some hedge funds limited their trading activity with those investment banks that had the largest proprietary trading businesses.

NEW NONBANK FINANCIAL INSTITUTIONS

Because regulators have forced investment banks to curtail much of their former proprietary trading activity and imposed higher regulatory capital burdens on certain other businesses that are deemed to be too risky, other nonbank financial institutions have stepped up to fill this large gap. These institutions may take a variety of forms including business development companies, commercial mortgage real estate investment trusts, closed-end funds, CLOs, direct lending platforms, and others.

For example, Ares Capital is a publicly traded global alternative asset manager with approximately $94 billion of assets under management. In various vehicles, a few of which are publicly traded, Ares delivers credit, private equity, and real estate investment capital. For almost any form of capital a company might want, from senior debt to common equity, there is likely some Ares vehicle that could provide it without the assistance of a bank, if deemed an attractive investment proposition.

Another example is Citadel, a large hedge fund based in Chicago. As banks have retreated from commodities, Citadel has built a large commodities business, including crude and refined oil products, the North American natural gas market and the European gas and power market. In addition, the firm has developed an automated trading platform, providing execution and market-making services to counterparties who may have previously transacted with investment banks. A number of other hedge funds, private equity funds, and other asset managers have stepped into historical investment banking and "merchant banking" businesses, as many large investment banks have reduced their exposure to riskier areas that require more capital and are the subject of stringent regulatory overview.

INTERNATIONAL TRADING

Regulators around the globe developed new financial regulation following the 2007–08 financial crisis. However, while US legislation provided a comprehensive new set of rules, European regulators developed a somewhat narrower set of regulations that focused on different regulatory objectives. Proprietary trading in the EU is covered by the European Market Infrastructure Regulation (EMIR), which was passed by the European Parliament in September 2010 and became effective in all member states at the end of 2012. EMIR contains a number of new provisions, including regulation of over-the-counter derivatives, short selling, and clearing requirements. However, EMIR does not require the separation of proprietary trading from regular banking activities as is required under the Volcker Rule in the United States. Because most European banks have always been universal banks (commercial banks that have not been separated from investment banks), their regulators have not enforced a separation in these businesses. UK regulators made different proposals in reaction to the 2007–08 financial crisis. The United Kingdom treasury set up the "Independent Commission on Banking" to make recommendations for making the banking system more robust. The commission did not recommend a full separation of investment banking and retail banking in the spirit of the Glass–Steagall Act but instead suggested that banks should "ring-fence" their retail division from their investment banking division. As a result, the United Kingdom has gone well beyond EU regulation.

In Asia, the China Banking and Regulatory Commission issued a new provision during 2011 to restrict banks' proprietary trading activities (domestic and foreign). Under this new provision, nonhedged investments by banks must be limited to 3% or less of the banks' total capital. Other major financial centers in Asia such as Singapore or Hong Kong have not imposed a version of the Volcker Rule.

Canada is a noteworthy example of a country that had limits on bank proprietary trading activities prior to the financial crisis. Before 2008, this seemed like a competitive disadvantage for Canadian banks, but it resulted in much less loss-making for these banks during the crisis.

Retrenching and cost-cutting European investment banks lost market share to US rivals for the 10th straight year during 2015. US banks also outperformed on returns, creating an average ROE of 12.4% that year, compared to 8.3% for European banks. US investment banks restructured and recapitalized sooner and were helped by being based in the world's largest financial market. UBS started its retrenching earlier than other European banks, resulting in a higher ROE than competitors. Deutsche Bank is attempting to bring costs down to 70% of revenue, but this is still significantly higher than US banks that average below 60%. Deutsche Bank's trading business has exited certain fixed income and currencies products where ROE has dropped following adoption of new capital rules. Credit Suisse has restructured, allocating more resources to its wealth management business and away from some of its trading businesses. The bank is reducing its foreign exchange and rates trading products, allowing it to redeploy capital and reduce risk-weighted assets. Barclays embarked on a plan to cut 19,000 jobs, including 7000 in its investment bank, focusing on returns rather than revenue. The bank significantly reduced its trading businesses as it attempted to reduce capital deployment and improve profitability.

RISK MONITORING AND CONTROL

Investment banks have risk committees that review the activities of trading desks, approve new businesses and products, and approve market risk limits and credit risk limits. There is also a capital committee that reviews and approves transactions involving commitments of the firm's capital to support extensions of credit, bond underwritings, equity underwritings, distressed debt acquisitions, and principal investment activities. In addition, investment banks usually have risk monitoring committees that focus on structured products, new products, operational risk, credit policies, and business practices.

VALUE AT RISK

A key tool in measuring an investment bank's trading risk is value at risk (VaR). VaR represents the potential loss in value of trading positions due to adverse market movements over a defined time horizon based on a specified statistical confidence level. Typically, investment banks use a 1-day time horizon and a 95% confidence level in reporting VaR. This means that there is a 1 in 20 chance that daily trading net asset values will show a loss at least as large as the reported VaR. Stated another way, shortfalls from probable trading losses on a single trading day that is greater than the reported VaR would be expected to occur, on average, once a month, assuming 20 trading days in an average month.

Typical implementations of VaR use historical data, with more recent data given greater historical weight. An inherent limitation of VaR is that the distribution of past changes in market risk factors may not produce an accurate prediction of future market risk. In addition, VaR calculated over a 1-day time period does not completely capture the market risk of positions that cannot be liquidated within 1 day.

As an example of how to interpret VaR, if an investment bank reports an interest rate trading business VaR of $50 million, this means that, under normal trading conditions, the bank is 95% confident that a change in the value of its interest rate portfolio would not result in a loss of more than $50 million in a single day. This is equivalent to saying that there is only a 5% confidence level that the value of the interest rate portfolio will decrease by $50 million or more on any given day. A summary of VaR reported by several investment banks is included in Exhibit 5.13.

EXHIBIT 5.13 AVERAGE DAILY VALUE AT RISK

Value-at-Risk measures the worst expected loss under normal market conditions over a specific time interval at a given confidence level.

In the jargon of VaR, suppose that a portfolio manager has a daily VaR equal to $1 million at 1% (or 99% confidence level). This means that there is only 1 chance in 1000 that a daily loss bigger than $1 million occurs under normal market conditions.

Average Daily VaR as of 2014 $ in millions		
Firm	Average Daily VaR	Confidence Level
Bank of America	$ 65	99%
Barclays	34	95%
Citigroup	133	99%
Credit Suisse	43	98%
Deutsche Bank	62	99%
Goldman Sachs	72	95%
JPMorgan Chase	43	95%
Morgan Stanley	47	95%
UBS	50	99%

Sources: Respective 10-K and 20-F filings

Pricing Securities Offerings

Traders work closely with the capital markets group (often a joint venture between the Investment Banking Division and the Trading Division) on pricing for all primary market financing transactions for corporate and government issuers. They also work closely with sales professionals in the Trading Division to sell securities to investing clients, providing those clients with bids and offers on all securities that are underwritten by the investment bank or that the bank chooses to trade in the secondary market.

When the Trading Division and the Capital Markets Group price new securities, they focus on outstanding securities from the same issuer or, if none exist, on outstanding securities from comparable issuers as pricing reference points. Depending on the security, different pricing methods are used:

1. IPOs are principally priced based on a comparable public company valuation methodology (see Chapter 3).
2. Follow-on equity and bond offerings use the prevailing public market prices of the company's securities as a starting point to determine the appropriate offering price. In addition, traders determine whether a pricing discount to the public price is necessary based on the size of the offering and market dynamics.

3. Convertible securities are principally priced based on a convertible valuation model that is similar to the model that convertible arbitrageurs utilize (see Chapter 12).

When traders work with the Capital Markets Group to discuss pricing prior to launching a public offering, the traders are said to be brought "over-the-wall." This means that certain traders will become aware of material nonpublic information regarding an upcoming financing, and they must "wall" themselves off from trading outstanding securities of that issuer. As a result, traders are careful in determining who will work with the Capital Markets Group to finalize pricing. Compliance departments diligently monitor which traders have nonpublic information and on which companies.

Whenever pricing is committed to an issuer in a capital markets financing, over-the-wall traders must make a risk decision regarding pricing, timing, size, and structure. Sometimes the risk associated with these underwritings is considerable. For example, when a company asks an investment bank to complete a bought deal, the bank buys the entire securities offering without a road show that would have provided investors' views on potential pricing and structure. In this scenario, the bank is exposed to the risk that investors won't purchase the underwritten securities at a price equal to or greater than the price at which the bank purchased the securities from the issuer, creating a potential loss for the bank.

Before an underwriting commitment can be made to any issuing client, an investment bank assembles a "commitments committee" to determine the riskiness of the underwriting and whether to proceed with an underwriting transaction. The over-the-wall traders (usually senior traders who manage other traders more so than trade directly themselves) are a key voice in this committee. If they are convinced that the firm will lose money on the underwriting or expose itself to other significant risks, they will likely oppose the transaction. However, if underwriting fees are large and there is a strong push from the Investment Banking Division to support a key issuing client, traders will sometimes accept an underwriting even when the risks are perceived to be higher than normal.

CHAPTER

6

Asset Management, Wealth Management, and Research

OUTLINE

ASSET MANAGEMENT

Asset management refers to the professional management of investment funds for individuals, families, and institutions. Investments include stocks, bonds, convertibles, alternative assets (such as hedge funds, private equity funds, and real estate), commodities, indexes of each of these asset classes and money market investments. Asset managers specialize in different asset classes and management fees are paid based on the asset class and skill of the manager. For alternative assets, additional fees are paid based on investment performance as well. Fees types can be broken down into four major categories, based on asset class:

1. Alternative assets: Management fees can range from 1% to 2% of assets under management (AUM) and additional fees are charged based on the fund manager's performance. Some alternative asset managers receive performance fees of 10%–20% on the annual increase in value of assets. This means that if a high net worth investor entrusted $10 million to an alternative asset manager, and the value of this investment increased to $11.5 million in 1 year (a 15% increase), the asset manager would be paid as much as 2% × $10 million = $200,000 management fee, plus 20% × ($11.5 million − $10 million) = $300,000 performance fee. So total fees paid would be $500,000, which is, in effect, a 5% fee on the original $10 million investment. Although this may seem high, the investor's net return is still 10% after fees. Therefore, despite the high

fee percentage, this may be a suitable fee arrangement for an investor if the net return is better than net returns from other investment choices. Of course, this determination should be made in the context of the riskiness of the investment and diversification objectives of the investor.

2. Equity and convertible investments: Fees are generally lower for this asset class than for alternative asset investments. Management fees typically range from 0.75% to 1.75% of AUM, depending on the type of equity or convertible investment (US domestic, international, large cap, small cap, etc.). Although it is less common for additional fees to be charged based on the fund manager's performance for this asset class, depending on the type of fund and the manager of the fund, performance fees may be paid.

3. Bond and commodity investments: Fees are generally lower for this asset class than for equity and convertible funds. Investment fees typically range from 0.50% to 1.5% of AUM, depending on the type of fund (US high grade, US low grade, distressed debt, international, etc.). Performance fees are unusual in bond or commodity investments, but possible, depending on the risk and complexity of the investment process.

4. Indexes: Fees for managing indexes are usually even smaller, ranging from 0.05% to 0.50% of AUM.

Asset management products are offered through separately managed accounts and through commingled vehicles such as mutual funds and private investment funds. A summary of AUM by some of the largest investment banks is provided in Exhibit 6.1. Invested funds are generally lumped into the following categories when placed in asset management accounts at an investment bank: fixed income, equity, alternative investments (comprised principally of hedge fund, private equity and real estate investments) and money market.

EXHIBIT 6.1 GLOBAL INVESTMENT BANK ASSET MANAGEMENT DIVISIONS

Firm	AUM ($bln)
UBS	$1,737
Bank of America	$1,445
Morgan Stanley	$1,439
Credit Suisse	$687
Citi	$508
J.P. Morgan	$437
Goldman Sachs	$369
HSBC	$261
Wells	$225

Source: Scorpio Partnership's Annual Private Banking Benchmark 2016.

Fund performance is a key metric when evaluating asset management capabilities. Investors measure this by relying on performance measurement firms such as Morningstar and Lipper, who compile aggregate industry data that demonstrate how individual mutual funds perform against both indices and peer groups over time. For alternative asset classes such as hedge funds and private equity, there are specialized industry research firms that track fund performance (for example, Hedge Fund Research and Alpha Magazine track hedge fund performance, while Preqin Global Private Equity Review, among others, track private equity performance). Many funds are ranked into quartiles based on their relative performance each quarter and each year. Inevitably, top quartile funds attract disproportionately more investable funds whenever rankings are announced.

For most asset classes, performance is measured against a benchmark. This benchmark can be either a well-known index for the asset class being managed or a benchmark created by averaging the returns of a peer group of funds. For mutual funds, where the focus is principally on relative returns, performance is compared against indices and peers. For alternative assets such as hedge funds, it is common to measure performance not only on a relative basis, but also on an absolute return basis. Hedge funds attempt to achieve a positive (nonnegative) return (and not just beat a certain benchmark) through the use of derivatives and by creating short positions in different asset classes. However, as demonstrated by the average industry return of −19% in 2008 (the worst ever for hedge funds), it is clear that these funds are not always successful at generating absolute returns.

Performance measurement is often not just focused on returns, but on risk-adjusted returns as well. Modern portfolio theory has established the qualitative link that exists between portfolio risk and return. The capital asset pricing model developed by Sharpe in 1964 highlighted the concept of rewarding risk. This led to the creation of risk-adjusted ratios including the Sharpe ratio, which measures the return of a portfolio in excess of the risk-free rate, compared to the total risk of the portfolio. Subsequent efforts to measure risk-adjusted returns have led to improved performance measurement practices.

Hedge Fund Investments

Most major investment banks have hedge funds housed within their asset management division. Prior to the Dodd–Frank Act, banks frequently invested directly in their own hedge funds, often taking up a 10% position (and sometimes more) in each fund.

The Act limits this investment to no more than 3% of the fund, and total investment in "covered funds," which largely include hedge funds and private equity funds, is limited to an amount that is not more than 3% of the bank's Tier 1 Capital. Goldman Sachs Asset Management (GSAM), the asset management business within Goldman Sachs, has historically had several hedge funds that invest in a wide range of asset classes and strategies, including commodities, equity, fixed income, and emerging markets. Global Alpha was one of the hedge funds, which had assets of approximately $12 billion at its peak in 2006, but shrunk to approximately $2.5 billion by 2008 (after losses and withdrawals). In September 2011, GSAM decided to close and liquidate all of the assets of Global Alpha. Global Equities Opportunities Fund, another Goldman Sachs hedge fund, also encountered difficulties during 2007 and required a $3 billion cash infusion (two-thirds from the parent firm). This fund had about $7 billion in assets at its peak, but shrunk to as low as $1 billion in assets during early 2008 before being closed down in 2010. Other hedge funds managed by GSAM had substantially better results. Overall, at the end of 2015, Goldman Sachs managed six hedge funds within GSAM, with AUM of more than $15 billion, ranking the firm (as a third-party manager of hedge funds) at #29 among global hedge funds. Investors in these funds include high net worth clients, institutional investors, and employees of Goldman Sachs.

J.P. Morgan purchased a majority of hedge fund Highbridge Capital during 2004 (completing the full acquisition during July 2009), creating a flagship hedge fund within the bank's asset management division. Managing several other hedge funds in this division as well, J.P. Morgan's aggregate hedge fund AUM at the end of 2007 stood at $44.7 billion, making the bank the world's largest hedge fund manager. In 2008, however, after suffering from investor redemptions and poor performance at the Highbridge fund, J.P. Morgan saw its AUM drop to $32.9 billion, placing it second, after Bridgewater Associates (a noninvestment bank affiliated hedge fund manager). In 2015, Bridgewater continued to be the largest hedge fund manager with more than $100 billion under management, and J.P. Morgan ranked eighth (as a third-party investor) with approximately $30 billion under management.

Private Equity Investments

Most large investment banks participate in private equity to varying degrees. Investments may include leveraged buyout, mezzanine, real estate, and infrastructure transactions. The Dodd–Frank Act imposes limitations on investment bank direct principal investments or coinvestments in private equity funds. Banks are limited to a maximum of 3% holding in any private equity fund and are further limited to total investments in "covered assets" to an amount that is no more than 3% of the bank's Tier 1 Capital. Goldman Sachs had historically controlled one of the most comprehensive private investment programs. Since 1986, Goldman Sachs' Merchant Banking Division (part of the asset management division) had raised more than $124 billion of capital for private investments, including more than $78 billion for investing in private equity, growth capital, infrastructure, and real estate investments, and more than $46 billion for mezzanine investments (fixed income securities with an associated equity component, which may include an equity warrant), senior security lending, distressed debt, and real estate credit transactions. However, following the passage of the Dodd–Frank Act, Goldman Sachs had to sell most of its private equity investments to meet the asset constraints of the Act.

WEALTH MANAGEMENT

Wealth management refers to advisors who provide investment advice to selected individual, family, and institutional investing clients. Wealth management advisors attempt to identify investors who have a significant amount of funds to invest and then work with these investors to make investments in the asset classes described above. In other words, wealth management professionals create investment advisory relationships with investors and are not directly involved in the management of asset classes (which is the role of asset managers). An investment bank's wealth management advisors help investors define their risk tolerance and diversification preferences. They then either assist investors in self-directed investments or persuade them to entrust the advisor to make investments on their behalf. Wealth management advisors must exercise good judgment in allocating funds to achieve acceptable investment returns and appropriate diversification relative to client risk objectives.

Wealth management services include more than providing investment advice. To a certain extent, advisors are also asset allocators, if they have been entrusted to invest funds on behalf of clients. They are also acting in many cases as a financial planning advisor, helping clients obtain retail banking services, estate planning advice, legal resources, and taxation advice. There is also a growing trend for advisors to provide insurance and annuity products to clients. The wealth management advisor attempts to help investing clients sustain and grow long-term wealth and meet financial goals, and there are many different noninvestment tools that are introduced to facilitate these goals.

Wealth management advisors typically limit their services to clients who have more than $5 million in investable funds. Some banks require an even higher amount of funds to focus attention and limited resources on investing clients. For example, subject to a number of considerations, Goldman Sachs largely limits its wealth management efforts to clients who have more than $25 million in investable funds.

Some banks have created a "private client services" business that brings many, but not all of the services described above to investors who do not meet the investable fund threshold amount required to be covered by wealth management advisors.

Individual investors who have an even lower amount of investable funds are covered by "retail" advisors and brokers who help them invest cash in both the asset management products offered by the bank and products offered from external sources. All of the largest investment banks, with the exception of Goldman Sachs, have a retail team. Merrill Lynch, immediately prior to its acquisition by Bank of America in 2008, had the largest retail business, followed by Wachovia (which was acquired by Wells Fargo in 2008). Citigroup's Smith Barney division established a joint venture with Morgan Stanley during early 2009 (which is now wholly owned by Morgan Stanley). As of December 2015, the largest retail brokerage teams in the United States were controlled by Morgan Stanley, Bank of America, Wells Fargo, and UBS (see Exhibit 6.2).

EXHIBIT 6.2 US BROKERAGE FORCE RANKING, AS OF DECEMBER 2014

Firm	Number of Brokers	Revenue $ in billions	Revenue per Broker	Client Assets $ in billions
Morgan Stanley	16076	$ 15	$ 927,000	$ 2,025
Bank of America	16000	13.3	831,000	1,081
Wells Fargo	15100	9.2	609,000	1,420
UBS (U.S. division)	7000	3.9	557,000	1,032

Sources: Respective 10-K filings.

In summary, the largest investment banks have dedicated "sales forces" that focus on two or three different individual investing customer segments, based on the client's investable asset amount and requirement for noninvestment services.

Since wealth management advisors at investment banks have a duty to help clients achieve the best possible returns in the context of their risk tolerance, in some cases, investing clients may be directed to investment products not provided by the investment bank. Suppose, for example, an investment bank's asset management fund offerings do not include a type of investment that a client wants to invest in, or the performance of an internal fund (from a risk/return perspective) is less than a competing fund at another firm. In this scenario, the wealth management advisor may choose to direct part of a client's investment portfolio to an asset management product provided by a competitor. However, at many banks, incentive systems are designed to keep all client investments within the bank rather than see funds go to a competing firm, which creates a potential conflict of interest. This became a significant issue at Citigroup and at Merrill Lynch, as discussed in Exhibit 6.3.

EXHIBIT 6.3 AVOIDING CONFLICT OF INTEREST IN ASSET MANAGEMENT

During 2005 and 2006, both Merrill Lynch and Citigroup decided to give up control over their asset management business because, among other reasons, they wanted to avoid a potential conflict of interest between the wealth management advisory function and the asset management function. In 2005, Citigroup entered into an arrangement with Legg Mason, Inc, a leading global asset management firm, whereby the brokerage portion of Legg Mason was bought by Citigroup, while the asset management business of Citigroup was bought by Legg Mason.

In 2006, 2 months after the Citigroup–Legg Mason deal closed, Merrill Lynch entered into an arrangement with BlackRock, a large investment management firm that had a particularly strong focus in fixed income securities, whereby Merrill Lynch's asset management business merged with BlackRock, creating a new independent company with nearly $1 trillion in AUM. Merrill Lynch's ownership of the combined asset management company was 49.8%, and it came with a 45% voting interest in a firm that had a majority of independent directors. By giving up control of its asset management business, Merrill Lynch was able to mitigate potential conflict of interest concerns.

Wealth management advisors at each bank work closely with colleagues from the asset management group to bring appropriate investment offerings to investors. In addition, they also work closely with the bank's capital markets teams to place underwritten new offerings with their investing clients. At some banks, wealth management advisors place 10%–30% of underwritten offerings with their investors (the balance of which goes to institutional investors). Finally, wealth management advisors work with some traders in their secondary market making activity, helping to create flow for the traders and meeting the secondary investment interests of their clients.

RESEARCH

Research is provided by all large investment banking firms to selected institutional and individual investing clients on a global basis. This research usually covers equity, fixed income, currency, and commodity markets. Research professionals also focus on economics, portfolio strategy, derivatives and credit issues, offering insights, and ideas based on fundamental research.

Equity research focuses on public company-specific analysis as well as on industries and geographical regions. This research sometimes coordinates with macro, quantitative and derivatives research teams to identify investment ideas. Economic research formulates macroeconomic forecasts for economic activity, foreign exchange, and interest rates based on globally coordinated views of regional economists. Fixed income research focuses on corporate debt in the context of the issuer's industry and is critically dependent on understanding credit risks. Commodities research is a globally focused effort that principally analyzes energy and precious metals. Strategic research groups provide market views, forecasts, and recommendations on asset allocation and strategic investment strategies that could involve other forms of research.

Research is typically (but not always) housed within the trading division of an investment bank and is comprised of two different groups. Research that is provided to investing clients of the firm is called "sell-side" research. Research that is provided to the bank's asset managers, who manage money for investing clients, is called "buy-side" research. This is the same type of research that hedge funds produce for their internal traders, or that large mutual funds such as Fidelity produce for their internal fund managers.

Sell-side research has always been an analytically intense area within investment banks. Equity research analysts produce detailed financial models that help forecast earnings as well as the future value of assets. Revenue and earnings projections are based on several factors, including, but not limited to, company guidance, economic conditions, historical trends, and new information (e.g., product introductions, customer wins/losses, competitive conditions, and analyst judgment). They then use multiples based on revenue, EBITDA, earnings, book value, and cash flow to help assess a company's future share price. In addition, the analyst may also employ other valuation models such as peer comparisons, discounted cash flow analysis, or replacement value. An analyst may then use this information along with other research to formulate an investment opinion, which is then communicated to investors or investment advisors. If a company's forecasted value is above the value implied by the current market price, the analyst might use this information to rate a company "overweight" or "buy." Conversely, if a company's forecasted value is below its implied market value, a rating of "underweight" or "sell" might be given. If the analyst believes the company is trading at or near fair value, then the stock might be given an "equal weight" or "hold" rating.

Equity analysts usually publish research reports quarterly in association with a company's earnings reports. Additional research is published if there are important events announced by a company through a press release, 8-K filing with the Securities and Exchange Commission (SEC) (in the United States), or if the analyst has conducted proprietary research. An example may be a recent interview between the analyst and senior management of the company or an investor field trip. Research is provided in both print and electronic form. Some of a firm's most important investing clients are sometimes given direct access to analysts and are able to discuss models and assumptions on an ongoing basis.

The information provided to investing clients by sell-side equity research analysts includes the following:

1. In-depth initiation reports that introduce investing clients to new industries or new companies.
2. Quarterly performance reports during earnings season when investors need concise and rapid summaries of results.

3. Previews of expected quarterly performance.
4. Analysis of how an investment thesis changes following material events.
5. Creation of financial models and valuation tables.
6. Proprietary research and interpretation of compelling investment considerations.
7. Summary of investor concerns about an industry or individual companies in the industry.
8. Company or industry updates.
9. Surveys of industries based on field checks and industry conferences.
10. Access to company management by arranging investor meetings, conferences, and nondeal roadshows.
11. Due diligence with a company's senior management prior to an IPO, where the bank's investment bankers have an underwriting mandate (if the research team decides to pick up coverage).

Research is usually organized into four main segments: equity research, economic research, commodities research and credit (fixed income) research:

1. Equity research focuses on individual stocks in targeted industries, which may include communication, media and entertainment, consumer products, financial institutions, industrials, technology, transportation, healthcare, retail, education, and other industries.
2. Credit research focuses on corporate debt of issuers in various industry sectors. Teams are divided into investment grade credit and high-yield credit. The focus of this research is on different aspects of a company than what is provided in equity research. In particular, credit research analyzes bond and loan documentation and whether a company's future cash flow is expected to meet all cash payment obligations.
3. Commodities research uses economic models to analyze supply-and-demand fundamentals and creates price forecasts on a range of commodities.
4. Economic research provides macroeconomic forecasts for economic activity, foreign exchange rates, and interest rates.

Paying for Research

Research has historically received revenue from investing clients through an indirect mechanism: part of the commissions paid by investors to sales professionals when they buy securities is redirected to the research department. This "soft dollar" compensation arrangement has been a key part of sell-side research for decades, since investors are generally reluctant to pay direct fees for the use of research. For example, an investor who values equity research provided by a sell-side analyst at an investment bank might be willing to pay a commission of 3 cents per share for common shares the investor purchases through the bank, and a portion of this commission is redirected to the research department. It is estimated that about 60% of the roughly $8 billion in annual brokerage commissions in the United States, and EU is allocated to research departments.

Institutional investors use a system called "broker votes" to budget future aggregate commission payments across investment banks. At the end of every year, these investors determine which research group provided the best research and other services, and then award internal votes to each research group accordingly. These votes are responsive to actions that investment bank research analysts take to communicate with client investors as well as provide insightful research. Investment banks use client-supplied votes as a basis for then compensating individual analysts for contributions to bank-wide commission payments.

Unfortunately, for research departments, estimated revenues from sales commission reallocations dropped by more than 50% in the United States between 2005 and 2016. This drop occurred, in part, because large institutional investors expanded their own buy-side research in response to growing concerns about the independence of sell-side research (questions arose about whether research was biased in favor of companies that were clients of the Investment Banking Division of a bank). In addition, Regulation FD (see the later discussion) made some research marginally less valuable to investors.

Most institutional investors do not want to pay direct fees for research because they are concerned that these fees will negatively impact their investment record. For example, when investors buy stock through an investment bank, the stock acquisition cost is net of commissions that are slightly higher than an investor might otherwise pay (to include some compensation for research). Since investors record returns based on the difference between the purchase cost net of commissions and their eventual sales price, if a separate fee is paid for research, with a correspondingly smaller commission, the net purchase price will be higher (since it does not net out the separate fee paid for research), which corresponds to a lower investment return, assuming an eventual sale at a profit.

Despite efforts to change, the use of soft dollars has actually increased. In the United States, Greenwich Associates has estimated that soft dollar transactions now account for about 40% of total commissions generated. The reasons for continuing this compensation model include the following: it enhances competition for nontraditional research and services by letting independent research providers compete; it gives asset managers more choices; and it helps smaller firms by lowering the barriers to entry. However, the concerns raised against soft dollars include the following: these arrangements may raise overall transaction costs; may also result in inefficient trading where fulfilling a commitment might override best execution; there could be a misallocation of resources by asset managers who end up purchasing marginal research/services; and the hidden cost of active management may make it difficult to evaluate the true cost of obtaining portfolio management services. In addition, investors who prohibit the use of soft dollars may be getting a free ride from the research/services paid for by the soft dollars of other investors.

During 2006, Fidelity, a major institutional investor, completed agreements with several investment banks to pay a separate fee for research and simultaneously reduce commissions. Since Fidelity's decision, other large investors such as Vanguard, MSF Investment Management, Bridgeway Funds, and American Century have reached agreements to pay a separate fee for research. In spite of these new fee arrangements, it is unclear how investment banks will address declining research revenue and the future mechanism for compensating research. In this environment, investment banking research departments have been pared back and compensation has been reduced. At some banks, there has been internal discussion regarding whether the research function should be sold since costs of operation exceed allocated and direct revenue. This problem was exacerbated by the 2003 enforcement action against 10 of the top investment banks operating in the United States that, among other things, took away the Investment Banking Division's ability to make payments to the research team as an inducement to help bankers obtain underwriting mandates from corporate clients (see the discussion below).

A new European Union law requires institutional investors to pay for any analyst research or services they receive. Investment banks are developing new business models to enable them to comply with this law, including adoption of fees in excess of $50,000 a year to receive standard research notes, and significantly higher fees for specific research completed on behalf of investors and direct access to analysts. A potential outcome of these higher fees will be a reduction in research divisions as banks attempt to find customers willing to pay for research. Some banks may end up exiting the research function if investors are unwilling to pay fees for service. This may result in more research business for independent research firms. In the United Kingdom, regulators have also sought to physically separate research analysts from trading activities to guard against traders seeing market-sensitive draft research notes and leaking the information to clients.

Investment managers such as hedge funds and endowments typically get a greater supply of research, and better access to analysts, the more they trade. But the research and trading commissions ultimately are paid for by the investors whose money they oversee. Historically, that gave investment managers little incentive to cap spending. However, the new rule changes are prompting large investment managers to reassess what research is worth buying.

The EU rules require money managers to either pay for research out of their own pockets or set agreed upon research budgets with clients. EU regulators have also banned research payments linked to trading volume. Although some research analysts feel more pressure on their performance from the rules change, many welcome greater transparency in valuing their work and a breakdown in the perception that research is considered free.

Conflicts of Interest

One of the major problems with sell-side research is its alleged lack of independence. Some banks' Investment Banking Divisions have historically put pressure on research analysts to modify negative views on a company when bankers were soliciting a financing or M&A transaction with a company. Negative equity or fixed income research could upset management, making it problematic for bankers to obtain mandates. As a result, some bankers felt it necessary to press research departments to prioritize their research activities based on the Investment Banking Division's underwriting or M&A effort, rather than on the firm's investing clients' priorities for objective research. This created a conflict of interest that had far-reaching repercussions.

During April 2003, the SEC, New York's attorney general, the National Association of Securities Dealers (NASD), and the New York Stock Exchange (NYSE) announced enforcement actions against the following 10 investment banks: Bear Stearns, Credit Suisse, Goldman Sachs, Lehman Brothers, JPMorgan, Merrill Lynch, Morgan Stanley, Citigroup, UBS, and Piper Jaffray. The banks were required to pay a total of approximately $1.4 billion, comprised of $875 million in penalties and disgorgement, $432.5 million to fund independent research, and $80 million to promote investor education. In addition to the monetary payments, the firms were also required to comply with significant requirements that included eliminating any influence by the Investment Banking Division over the research department, increasing supervision and making independent research available to investors.

The enforcement actions alleged that all of the firms engaged in acts and practices that created or maintained inappropriate influence by the Investment Banking Division over research analysts, thereby imposing conflicts of interest on research analysts. The allegations, which were neither admitted to nor denied by the firms, also charged that certain firms issued fraudulent research reports, issued research reports that were not based on principles of fair dealing and good faith, and did not provide a sound basis for evaluating facts. In addition, it was alleged that certain research reports contained exaggerated or unwarranted claims about the covered companies and/or opinions for which there were no reasonable bases, and certain firms received payments from companies for research without disclosing such payments. Finally, it was alleged that certain firms engaged in inappropriate "spinning" of "hot" IPO allocations (selling IPO shares that had significant demand to top executives and directors of a company, in exchange for future investment banking business from that company).

By insulating research analysts from Investment Banking Division pressure, the enforcement action was designed to ensure stock recommendations are not tainted by efforts to obtain investment banking fees. Important reforms required of investment banks included the following:

1. There must be a physical separation between research and investment banking professionals.
2. The firm's senior management must determine the research department's budget without input from the Investment Banking Division and without regard to specific revenues derived from investment banking activity.
3. Research analysts' compensation may not be based, directly or indirectly, on Investment Banking Division revenues or on input from investment banking personnel.
4. Research management must make all company-specific decisions to terminate coverage, and investment bankers can have no role in company-specific coverage decisions.
5. Research analysts are prohibited from participating in efforts to solicit investment banking business, including pitches and roadshows.
6. In addition to providing their own research, investment banks are obligated to furnish independent research to investing clients. This requirement came to an end during the summer of 2009.

Regulation FD

Regulation FD was implemented by the SEC during 2000. FD stands for fair disclosure. This regulation prohibits a company's executives from selectively disclosing material information that could impact a company's share price. This means that prior to discussing any potential "stock moving" information with research analysts, the company must disclose this information through an SEC filing. The benefit of this regulation is that it levels the playing field, enabling all investors to receive the same information at the same time. Prior to the promulgation of this regulation, some large (most favored) institutional investors received stock moving information based on private discussions that a company had with a research analyst before other investors received this information. Regulation FD was an attempt to bring better transparency and fairness when companies decide to communicate with investors by ensuring that all investors are able to make investment decisions based on the same information at the same time. However, critics claim that because companies must now be more careful in what they say to analysts and investors, and when they say it, less information is distributed in a less timely way. In addition, it is usually filtered through lawyers, causing a dilution in the quality of information. Some investors feel that, as a result of Regulation FD, no one in the investment community, including retail investors, has the same quality or depth of information that they used to receive.

Credit Rating Agencies, Exchanges, and Clearing and Settlement

CREDIT RATING AGENCIES

Credit rating agencies play an important role in the business of investment banking by assigning credit ratings to debt issuers and their debt instruments. Debt instruments include bonds, convertible bonds, commercial paper, and loans. In addition, credit rating agencies assign ratings to structured finance securities, which are backed by various types of collateral. Structured finance includes asset-backed securities, residential and commercial mortgage-backed securities, and collateralized debt obligations. Investment banks work closely with credit rating agencies when developing structured finance products to secure targeted ratings for these securities. See Exhibit 7.1 for a summary of the role of credit rating agencies.

EXHIBIT 7.1 RATING AGENCY ROLE

To communicate unbiased opinions on creditworthiness of companies and their debt instruments to the investment community.

Corporate and government finance	Structured Finance
• Bonds/notes/commercial paper • Convertibles • Bank notes	• Collateralized debtobligations (CDO) • Residential mortgage-backed securities (RMBS) • Commercial mortgage-backed securities (CMBS) • Asset-backed securities (ABS)

Source: Standard & Poor's.

Issuers can be corporations, local, state or national governments and agencies, special purpose entities, and nonprofit organizations. The ratings process involves an analysis of business risk, including competitive position within the industry, diversity of product lines, and profitability compared with peers; and financial risk, including accounting, cash flow financial flexibility, and capital structure considerations (see Exhibit 7.2). The rating reflects the issuer's creditworthiness (ability to repay the obligation), which affects the interest rate (or yield) applied to the security being rated. Therefore, the credit rating reflects the probability that a creditor will default on its debt. These ratings are used extensively by investors, banks, and governments as an input into their investment, loan, and regulatory decisions. The importance of ratings is hard to overstate. For example, many pension funds are required to invest only in securities with a rating better than a designated reference rating, and they are required to liquidate securities if holdings are downgraded. Additionally, many financial contracts reference credit ratings. For example, credit default swaps are usually triggered if a credit rating agency has determined a *credit event* such as bankruptcy, failure to repay, restructuring, or moratorium. The ratings are independent of influence by others (although this has become the subject of some controversy, as described below) and create an easy to understand measurement of relative credit risk. This generally results in increased efficiency in the market, lowering the costs for borrowers, investors, and lenders, and expanding the total supply of capital. In most cases, issuers of public market bonds must receive ratings from at least one agency to attract investment interest. In many cases, a bond will be rated by two or three different credit rating agencies based on requests from investors. See Exhibit 7.3 for ratings scales from Standard & Poor's, Moody's, and Fitch (the three largest credit rating agencies) across different levels of credit risk. These rating agencies operate on an issuer-pay model whereby the issuer, and not the investor, pays for the rating services. An exception to this is rating agencies' policy toward "unsolicited ratings," which is intended to protect investors from issuers that withdraw their ratings when performance begins to suffer. If a company has enough debt outstanding to be considered "widely held," and requests a rating withdrawal, rating agencies reserve the right to assign ratings on an unsolicited basis (so that investors remain informed about credit risk).

Ratings issued by "approved" credit rating agencies have historically been referenced explicitly by the Securities and Exchange Commission (SEC), the Federal Reserve Bank, or the Basel Committee on Banking Supervision, giving the rating agencies almost regulatory power. However, following the 2007–08 financial crisis, lawmakers passed the Dodd–Frank Act, which mandated federal agencies to remove references to credit rating agencies in regulation where appropriate. The SEC has adopted new rules pursuant to the Act that requires rating agencies to report internal controls over the ratings process, provide more transparency of ratings performance and third-party retention to conduct due diligence in relation to ratings for asset-backed securities. In the European Union, credit rating agencies are now supervised by the European Securities and Markets Authority.

EXHIBIT 7.2 THE RATING PROCESS

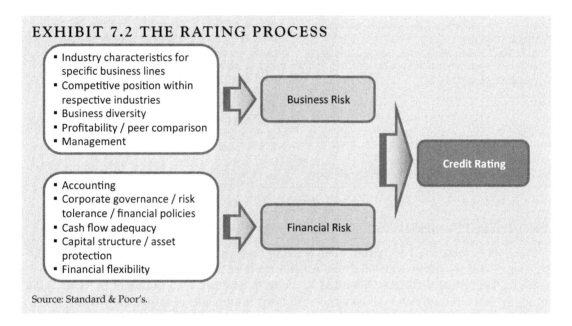

- Industry characteristics for specific business lines
- Competitive position within respective industries
- Business diversity
- Profitability / peer comparison
- Management

Business Risk

- Accounting
- Corporate governance / risk tolerance / financial policies
- Cash flow adequacy
- Capital structure / asset protection
- Financial flexibility

Financial Risk

Credit Rating

Source: Standard & Poor's.

EXHIBIT 7.3 CREDIT RATING SCALES

Standard & Poor's and Fitch Credit Rating Scales

Investment Grade	Non-Investment Grade (High Yield, Junk Bonds)
AAA: the best quality companies, reliable andstable	**BB+, BB, BB-**: more prone to changes in the economy
AA+, AA, AA-: quality companies, slightly higher risk than AAA	**B+, B, B-**: financial situation varies noticeably
A+, A, A-: economic situation can affect financings, but still strong	**CCC+, CCC, CCC-**: currently vulnerable and dependent on favorable economic condition to meet its commitments
BBB+, BBB, BBB-: medium class companies, which are satisfactory at the moment	**CC**: highly vulnerable, very speculative bonds
	C: highly vulnerable, perhaps in bankruptcy or in arrears but still continuing to pay out on obligations
	D: has defaulted on obligations and expected that will generally default on most or all obligations
	NR: not publicly rated

(Continued)

EXHIBIT 7.3 CREDIT RATING SCALES—cont'd

Moody's Credit Rating Scales

Investment Grade	Non-Investment Grade (High Yield, Junk Bonds)
Aaa: Obligations of the highest quality, with minimal credit risk **Aa1, Aa2, Aa3**: Obligations of high quality and subject to very low credit risk **A1, A2, A3**: Obligations upper-medium grade and subject to low credit risk **Baa1, Baa2, Baa3**: Obligations subject to moderate credit risk: medium-grade and possess certain speculative characteristics	**Ba1, Ba2, Ba3**: Obligations are judged to have speculative elements and are subject to substantial credit risk **B1, B2, B3**: Obligations speculative and subject to high credit risk **Caa1, Caa2, Caa3**: Obligations of poor standing and are subject to very high credit risk **Ca**: Obligations highly speculative and are likely in or very near default, with some prospect of recovery of principal and interest **C**: Obligations are the lowest rated class of bonds and are typically in default, with little prospect for recovery of principal or interest **NR**: Not Rated

Source: Standard & Poor's, Fitch, and Moody's.

Asset-Backed Securities

Moody's, Standard & Poor's, and Fitch actively rated mortgage-backed securities, providing many such securities with their highest ratings until 2007, when a portion of the mortgages backing these securities defaulted, causing the securities to plummet in value. As a result, the big three agencies felt compelled to downgrade most securities in this asset class, which exacerbated their decline in value, causing investors and insurers hundreds of billions of dollars in losses during 2007 and 2008.

Investment banks consult with credit rating agencies to determine the optimal structure for different tranches of mortgage-backed securities (and other asset-backed securities). During this process, banks submit contemplated structures and expected ratings to the credit rating agencies for feedback. If there is a divergence between the banker's and the credit rating agency's view on expected ratings, then the process repeats again, with the banker modifying the structure (which could involve increasing the collateral base of the senior tranche or modifying the mix of assets) and resubmitting for feedback. The process repeats until the targeted rating can be achieved. Frequently, rating agencies will express opinions on the types of assets that must be used to secure the debt offered by an asset-backed security to obtain desired credit ratings. There are typically different tranches representing different levels of credit risk in an asset-backed security, based on the cash flow, maturity, and credit support vehicles embedded in each tranche. It is common, for example, to have three separate tranches rated AAA, BBB, and BB, representing low risk, medium risk, and speculative risk, respectively. Investors require higher interest rates (or yields) for the more risky tranches.

Rating agencies state that their ratings suggest the likelihood a given debt security will fail to pay principal and interest over time, but they are not expressing opinions regarding the volatility of the rated security or the wisdom of investing in that security. Historically, the most highly rated debt exhibited low volatility and high liquidity. This means that the price of the debt did not change much on a day-to-day basis and that there were almost always other buyers willing to purchase the debt. Unlike straight bonds and loans, however, asset-backed securities may sometimes have hundreds or thousands of individual securities embedded in each tranche. These similarly rated securities concentrate risk in such a way that even a small change in the perceived risk of default can mushroom in scale and dramatically affect the security's market price. During the 2007 and 2008 credit crisis, this led to very significant drops in the price of many mortgage-backed securities, especially those backed by subprime mortgages.

Criticism Against Credit Rating Agencies

Credit rating agencies have been heavily criticized for their role in working with investment banks to create mortgage-backed securities that had higher ratings than they deserved. They are also criticized for not downgrading mortgage-backed securities as early as they should have. Many investors thought that the agencies were both wrong in the first place and slow to make corrections.

Other criticisms of rating agencies relate to their relationship with corporations that issue straight bonds and other nonasset-backed securities. Although investors are the principal users of the credit ratings, they do not pay for this service. Instead, it is the issuer of the debt security that pays for the rating. It has been suggested by some investors (especially those who invest in securities that experience a ratings decline) that the agencies are susceptible to undue influence from corporations or are vulnerable to being mislead. On the other hand, corporate treasury staff sometimes feel that they have an adversarial relationship with credit rating agencies. When receiving a rating that they believe is unjustifiably low, companies sometimes claim that the rating agencies don't understand their business.

Credit Rating Advisory Services Provided by Investment Banks

Most companies and governments that issue bonds want credit ratings assigned to their bonds to facilitate investor purchases of the securities at the lowest possible yield. Although most issuers pay for this service, there are a few companies that do not. These companies generally have actively traded debt and unassailable credit strength, which makes demand for their bonds far greater than supply. Companies and governments that pay for credit ratings spend considerable time and resources to provide information that helps the agencies build financial models that best reflect their financial strength.

Investment banks provide credit rating advisory services to companies by suggesting the potential credit rating outcome from the issuance of different kinds of financings (bonds, loans, convertibles, preferred shares, or common shares). Bonds and loans weaken an issuer's balance sheet and, subject to the use of proceeds, may reduce cash flow. As a result, rating agencies might consider downgrading a company if the company initiates a large loan or bond transaction. However, if the bond or loan proceeds are used to repay existing debt or to fund an acquisition or new business that is expected to generate significant cash flow (which could be used to pay the coupons on the debt offering), then there may not be a downgrade. Furthermore, if the bond or loan obligation is small relative to the company's capital structure, there may not be a downgrade.

If a company issues convertibles, the transaction could positively or negatively impact ratings depending on maturity and conversion features. If a company issues common shares, this will have a positive impact on ratings if the size of the issue is sufficiently large. Typically, issuers are careful to not raise financing that results in a credit rating agency downgrade of their debt obligations, unless there are favorable results that come from the financing, such as an accretive M&A transaction or an improvement in risk adjusted weighted average cost of capital.

Investment bankers help prepare clients for an annual or semiannual pilgrimage to New York to meet with the agencies to review the client's business and any material changes that could impact ratings. Sometimes, investment bankers and their issuing clients miscalculate rating agency reaction to a new security issuance or changing business fortunes of a company. When this leads to an unexpected downgrade, there is considerable frustration and anxiety. Normally, investment banks are able to avoid surprises by attempting to replicate the models built by credit rating agencies and advising corporations (or governments) on ratios that they need to meet in relation to interest coverage, total debt, cash flow, and other credit-related metrics. Nevertheless, it is not a perfect process and surprises still occur.

To help rating agencies build models that accurately reflect the business and financial risks of companies, senior management from companies (and investment bankers, if retained for this purpose) sometimes provide material nonpublic information regarding a potential financing to rating agencies prior to initiating the new financing. This enables the agency to incorporate information into their models in advance of the financing, which allows a rating to be issued on the same day as the financing. This is beneficial to investors who want to know the ratings impact of all new securities before they commit to invest in these securities. It is incumbent on rating agencies to not disclose any material nonpublic information to anyone who can use the information to trade securities of the company prior to the company's announcement of the financing.

Investment bank credit ratings advisors are frequently former employees of Moody's or Standard & Poor's and have an in-depth understanding of the models used by their former employers (as well as the personalities and analytical perspectives of their former colleagues). This is helpful in advising companies regarding the probable ratings outcome from different financing alternatives. Investment bankers provide a narrower range of credit rating advisory services to governments.

EXCHANGES

Investment banks actively trade stocks, bonds, and derivatives on exchanges around the world. Exchanges enable buyers and sellers to anonymously buy and sell securities at agreed-upon prices principally through an electronic medium.

Intercontinental Exchange Group (ICE), a futures exchange based in Atlanta, acquired The New York Stock Exchange (NYSE) Euronext during early 2016, following a shareholder vote and approval by the European Commission and the SEC. ICE was founded in 2000 and expanded rapidly through acquisitions. The combined company operates 16 global exchanges and 5 central clearing houses and is the third largest exchange group globally, behind Hong Kong Exchanges and Clearing and CME Group Inc., parent of the Chicago

Board of Trade and the New York Mercantile Exchange. Intercontinental Exchange Inc. and NYSE Euronext are now subsidiaries of ICE.

The largest stock exchanges in the world by value of shares trading (turnover) are NASDAQ and NYSE Euronext (US) in the United States; London Stock Exchange, Frankfurt Stock Exchange (Deutsche Börse), and NYSE Euronext (Europe) in Europe; and Tokyo Stock Exchange and Shanghai Stock Exchange in Asia. See Exhibit 7.4 for the ranking of the top 20 exchanges.

EXHIBIT 7.4 TOP 20 STOCK EXCHANGES

Rank	Exchange	Economy	Headquarters	Market cap (USDbn)	Monthly trade volume (USDbn)
1	New York Stock Exchange	United States	New York	19,223	1,520
2	NASDAQ	United States	New York	6,831	1,183
3	London Stock Exchange Group	United Kingdom	London	6,187	165
4	Japan Exchange Group–Tokyo	Japan	Tokyo	4,485	402
5	Shanghai Stock Exchange	China	Shanghai	3,986	1,278
6	Hong Kong Stock Exchange	Hong Kong	Hong Kong	3,325	155
7	Euronext	European Union	Amsterdam Brussels Lisbon London Paris	3,321	184
8	Shenzhen Stock Exchange	China	Shenzhen	2,285	800
9	TMX Group	Canada	Toronto	1,939	120
10	Deutsche Börse	Germany	Frankfurt	1,762	142
11	Bombay Stock Exchange	India	Mumbai	1,682	11.8
12	National Stock Exchange of India	India	Mumbai	1,642	62.2
13	SIX Swiss Exchange	Switzerland	Zurich	1,516	126
14	Australian Securities Exchange	Australia	Sydney	1,272	55.8
15	Korea Exchange	South Korea	Seoul	1,251	136
16	OMX Nordic Exchange	Northern Europe	Stockholm	1,212	63.2
17	JSE Limited	South Africa	Johannesburg	951	27.6
18	BME Spanish Exchanges	Spain	Madrid	942	94
19	Taiwan Stock Exchange	Taiwan	Taipei	861	54.3
20	BM&F Bovespa	Brazil	São Paulo	824	51.1

In 2015, Hong Kong was the world's top stock exchange for initial public offerings (IPOs), followed by the New York Stock Exchange (see Exhibit 7.5). Exhibit 7.6 shows total equity funds raised per exchange, Exhibit 7.7 shows market value of domestic shares per exchange, and Exhibit 7.8 shows value of share trading per exchange.

EXHIBIT 7.5 INITIAL PUBLIC OFFERING FUNDS RAISED DURING 2015

Rank	Exchange	IPO Equity Funds Raised (US$ million)
1	HKEx	33,708.45
2	NYSE	19,687.31
3	NASDAQ	18,042.63
4	London SE Group	17,500.36
5	Shanghai	17,472.34
6	Japan Exchange Group - Tokyo	15,672.60
7	Madrid Stock Exchange	9,376.06
8	Shenzhen SE	8,045.14
9	Deutsche Börse	7,835.16
10	Euronext - Amsterdam	7,712.83

Note: Real Estate Investment Trusts are included. Funds raised by alternative market(s) operated by the same exchange are grouped under the exchange.
Source: Dealogic.

EXHIBIT 7.6 TOTAL EQUITY FUNDS RAISED DURING 2015

Rank	Exchange	Total Equity Funds Raised (US$ million)
1	NYSE	127,254.1
2	Shanghai Stock Exchange	126,422.2
3	HKEx	125,020.8
4	Euronext	98,677.2
5	Shenzhen Stock Exchange	75,104.4
6	London SE Group	60,132.7
7	Australian Securities Exchange	44,916.6
8	BME Spanish Exchanges	43,762.3
9	TMX Group	42,327.6
10	Japan Exchange Group	19,755.7

Source: World Federation of Exchanges (WFE) Monthly Statistics (not including exchanges for which statistics are not available). Figures are provisional.

EXHIBIT 7.7 MARKET VALUE OF SHARES OF DOMESTIC-LISTED COMPANIES (MAIN AND PARALLEL MARKETS)

Exchange	Rank	November 2015 Market value (US$ million)	Rank	December 2014 Market value (US$ million)	% Change
NYSE	1	18,486,204.3	1	19,351,417.2	-4.5
Nasdaq	2	7,449,205.2	2	6,979,172.0	6.7
Japan Exchange Group	3	4,909,983.6	3	4,377,994.4	12.2
Shanghai Stock Exchange	4	4,459,835.5	5	3,932,527.7	13.4
London SE Group	5	3,974,658.8	4	4,012,882.3	-1.0
Shenzhen Stock Exchange	6	3,424,262.3	9	2,072,420.0	65.2
Euronext	7	3,379,584.6	6	3,319,062.2	1.8
HKEx	8	3,165,127.9	7	3,233,030.6	-2.1
Deutsche Boerse	9	1,737,886.3	10	1,738,539.1	0.0
TMX Group	10	1,697,501.1	8	2,093,696.8	-18.9

Source: WFE monthly statistics (not including exchanges for which statistics are not available). Market value excludes investment funds. TMX Group includes TSX Venture market cap. Percentage changes are calculated based on rounded figures.

EXHIBIT 7.8 VALUE OF SHARE TRADING (MAIN AND PARALLEL MARKETS) DURING 2015

Rank	Exchange	Value of Share Trading (US$ million)
1	Nasdaq	30,173,610.2
2	Shanghai Stock Exchange	20,268,840.6
3	NYSE	18,289,607.1
4	Shenzhen Stock Exchange	17,922,423.5
5	BATS Global Markets-US	12,987,297.6
6	BATS Chi-x Europe	7,753,998.6
7	Japan Exchange Group	5,664,806.9
8	London SE Group	4,104,240.1
9	Euronext	3,033,419.9
10	HKEx	2,141,292.9

Source: WFE monthly statistics (not including exchanges for which statistics are not available). Figures are the sum of the values of electronic order book trades, negotiated deals, and reported trades as reported separately in WFE statistics. They are not entirely comparable across exchanges because of different reporting rules and calculation methods.

Specialists

Historically, a portion of the business conducted on the NYSE Euronext trading floor was through a specialist system, whereby an individual acts as the official market maker for a given security, providing liquidity to the market, taking the other side of trades when there are buy/sell imbalances, and preventing excessive volatility. However, as electronic communications networks (ECNs) have become more efficient, the specialist system has diminished in importance. In addition, there had been rising objections to certain aspects of the specialist system. Some of the objections include the possibility of a special interest profit at the expense of investors, higher cost (relative to ECNs), and the possibility of front running (traders using knowledge of a customer's incoming large order to place their own order ahead of it to benefit from a change in market direction that a large order may induce).

In 2008, in response to these concerns and shifts in the market structure of securities trading, NYSE Euronext moved to eliminate specialists and replaced them with DMMs. A key difference between the new DMMs and specialists is that the issue of front running is eliminated as DMMs no longer get first look at electronic orders. In addition, some of the privileges enjoyed by specialists are no longer available, and some restrictions under the specialist format have been removed to allow greater flexibility. In general, the new structure is designed to modernize the market making function and make it more competitive and effective.

NYSE Euronext provides the following information regarding the human dimension of trading on their exchange in the midst of electronic matching tools.

Designated Market Makers

Designated market makers (DMMs) have obligations for maintaining fair and orderly markets for their assigned securities. They operate both manually and electronically to facilitate price discovery during market openings, closings, and during periods of substantial trading imbalances or instability. This approach is helpful for improving prices, dampening volatility, adding liquidity, and enhancing value. DMMs apply judgment to knowledge of dynamic trading systems, macroeconomic news, and industry specific intelligence to make their trading decisions. DMMs provide regular communication to customers, commit capital during special situations, and attempt to maintain market integrity. DMMs include the following firms: Barclays, Brendan E. Cryan & Co., IMC Financial Market, J Streicher & Co. LLC, KCG, and Virtu Financial Capital Markets LLC.

Floor Brokers

Floor brokers are employees of member firms who execute trades on the exchange floor on behalf of the firm's clients. There are about 274 floor brokers among the 169 NYSE member firms (97 Electronic, 7 DMMs, and 65 Brokerage) on the NYSE. They act as agents, buying and selling stock for the public (institutions, hedge funds, broker/dealers). Floor brokers are physically present on the trading floor and are active participants during the trading day. They also have the ability to participate electronically and are able to access all markets and trade multiple asset classes to provide clients with a complete trading picture.

Supplemental Liquidity Providers

Supplemental Liquidity Providers (SLPs) are electronic, high-volume members who are incented to add liquidity. All of their trading is proprietary, and they do not act for public customers or trade on an agency basis. Every NYSE stock is eligible, but not all stocks have SLPs, who focus principally in more liquid stocks with greater than 1 million shares of average daily volume. SLPs must maintain a bid or offer at the National Best Bid and Offer in each assigned security at least 10% of the trading day. SLPs that post liquidity in an assigned security that executes against incoming orders are awarded a financial rebate by the NYSE. SLPs include the following firms: HRT Financial LLC, Latour Trading, LLC, Tradebot Systems, Inc., Virtu Financial BD LLC, Citadel Securities LLC, KCG Americas LLC, Goldman, Sachs & Company, and IMC Chicago LLC.

Each company that has publicly traded stock must determine the exchange on which to list their securities. Each exchange has its own requirements that a company must meet to obtain and maintain a listing. Requirements are imposed for financial reporting and disclosure standards as well as minimum trading volume and stock price standards. If these standards are not met, shares will be delisted (assuming the infractions are not rectified after a certain "grace period"). Listing requirements for NYSE Euronext include at least 1.1 million shares of stock worth $40 million and earnings in excess of $10 million over the last 3 years. NASDAQ requirements include 1.25 million shares worth at least $70 million and aggregate 3-year earnings of at least $11 million. The London Stock Exchange requires a minimum market capitalization of £700,000, a minimum public float of one quarter of this amount, and a minimum working capital amount.

Derivatives Exchanges

CME Group (CME), headquartered in Chicago, is the world's largest and most diverse derivatives exchange. Derivatives include options, futures, and swaps. Futures are contracts to buy or sell an asset on a specific date (in the future) at a price determined today. This is in contrast to spot contracts, which are for immediate delivery. Options are contracts between a buyer and seller that give the buyer the right, but not the obligation, to buy or sell a designated asset at a future date at an agreed-upon price. Swaps are contracts in which two counterparties agree to exchange one stream of cash flows for another stream of cash flows. Since launching an IPO in 2002, the market capitalization of CME has grown to be the largest of any derivatives exchange in the world and was approximately double the value of NYSE Euronext before its acquisition by ICE, a large derivatives exchange. Following this acquisition in early 2016, CME's market capitalization of approximately $33 billion was still higher than the market capitalization of ICE (stock market value of the ICE business combined with NYSE Euronext) by about 10%.

Instead of stocks and bonds, only derivatives are traded on the CME. With customers utilizing a nearly 24-hour electronic trading platform for some products, remarkable trading volume is generated at the CME. The exchange offers futures and options based on benchmark products available across all major asset classes including interest rates, equity indexes, foreign exchange, energy, agricultural commodities, metals, and alternative products such as weather and real estate. The futures and options contracts for these asset classes enable counterparties a means for hedging, speculation, and asset allocation in relation to risks associated with interest rate sensitive instruments, equity market exposure, changes in the value of foreign currency, and changes in the prices of commodities.

The largest agricultural commodities product is corn, where on average over 300,000 futures and options contracts trade daily. The largest interest rate product is Eurodollars, where over 2 million futures contracts trade daily, and interest rate futures on 10-year US treasury notes, where over 1 million contracts trade daily. The largest equity product is the E-mini S&P 500 futures contract, which trades over 2.5 million contracts daily and other equity index futures and options, where over 1 million contracts trade daily. In addition, there is daily trading of more than 1.4 million energy futures and options contracts, 600,000 FX futures and options contracts, and 230,000 metals futures and options contracts.

CME is now largely an electronic exchange. All major investment banks trade at the exchange for their own account and on behalf of their investing and hedging clients. All trades require the posting of margin that changes daily based on the value of the futures and options contracts that counterparties enter into. The margin positions must be adjusted daily to manage risk properly. Margin obligations are met by cash or performance bonds and vary according to product and associated volatility. The effect of the margin system is to prevent failures to deliver value at contract expiration.

Futures exchanges (a subset of derivatives exchanges) are regulated in the United States principally by the Commodity Futures Trading Commission (CFTC) since futures contracts are not deemed to be securities, which fall under the regulatory scope of the SEC. Other large international futures/derivatives exchanges include Eurex (operated by Deutsche Börse), BM&F Bovespa, and ICE.

There has been an attempt to consolidate stock and derivatives exchanges around the world. One reason for this is the increasing computerization of trading. Because computers can essentially trade nonstop, exchanges are competing globally for market share as each exchange attempts to promote their trading model beyond national borders. Evidence of this consolidation is the 2016 acquisition of NYSE Euronext by ICE.

DARK POOLS

Dark pools have gained considerable popularity and importance. Dark pools are trading platforms that are created away from public exchanges by brokers/dealers for institutional investors. Large transactions such as block trades are often completed through these platforms. Dark pools were developed as a more private trading platform that helps large institutional investors trade with greater anonymity and without moving the price of shares when large blocks are traded. High-frequency traders have been active users of this trading platform. Unlike trading on conventional exchanges, dark pools conduct trading without publishing buy and sell orders. One of the dark pools is Goldman Sachs' Sigma X, which has expanded operations within the United States and Canadian markets. While the name suggests opacity, trading on a dark pool is very similar to a normal exchange in terms of order books and order prioritization. In addition, dark pools offer features such as negotiated pricing, which is unavailable at exchanges. It is estimated that approximately 8% of US equities transactions are now conducted via dark pools.

Credit Suisse and Barclays paid over $150 million in fines to US regulators during 2016 in relation to their alleged inappropriate communications with high-frequency traders who used their dark pools. These cases focused in part on whether the banks misled some clients about how the bank-owned dark pools prioritized certain buy and sell orders, including whether they withheld information that might have led clients to route orders elsewhere. In spite these fines and criticism from some customers, dark pool trading continued to grow, as demonstrated in Exhibit 7.9.

EXHIBIT 7.9 DARK POOL TRADING PLATFORMS

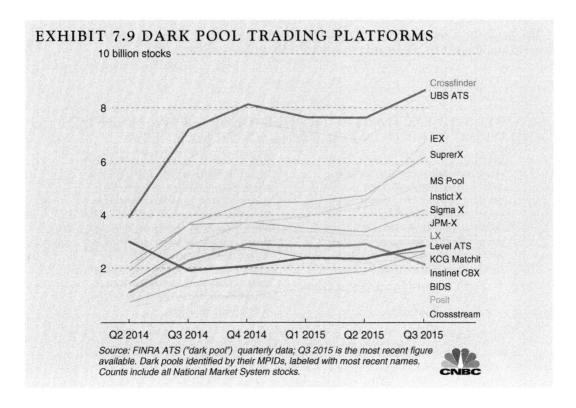

Source: FINRA ATS ("dark pool") quarterly data; Q3 2015 is the most recent figure available. Dark pools identified by their MPIDs, labeled with most recent names. Counts include all National Market System stocks.

CNBC

OVER-THE-COUNTER MARKET

Securities and derivatives that are listed and traded on an exchange are called listed instruments. Securities and derivatives that trade directly between two parties, without an exchange as intermediary, are called over-the-counter (OTC) instruments. Unlike listed trades, OTC trades are not in the public domain and, unless reported by the parties to the trade, remain confidential. OTC stock trades in the United States are sometimes reported by investment banks to either the OTC Bulletin Board (OTCBB), if the relevant company files required reports with the SEC, and/or to Pink Sheets (so named because stock quotes are printed on pink sheets), if the relevant company does not file required reports with the SEC. With the exception of a few foreign issuers that have issued American depositary receipts (ADRs), companies quoted in the

Pink Sheets are generally smaller and have thinly traded stock. These companies are usually much riskier than listed companies or OTCBB-traded companies.

The OTC market for derivatives is much larger than the market for listed derivatives. Derivatives are financial instruments whose value changes in response to changes in an underlying security or other asset. Derivatives have two uses: reducing risks and allowing speculation. They are tied to many different types of assets, including stocks, bonds, interest rates, exchange rates, commodities, and indexes.

Owing to exceptional growth experienced by the global OTC derivatives market, regulators are increasingly concerned about the potential systematic risk posed by this market.

The Bank for International Settlements estimates that as of 2014, the total outstanding notional amount of OTC derivatives was $630 trillion (see Exhibit 7.10).

EXHIBIT 7.10 EXCHANGE-TRADED DERIVATIVE MARKETS AND OVER-THE-COUNTER DERIVATIVE MARKETS

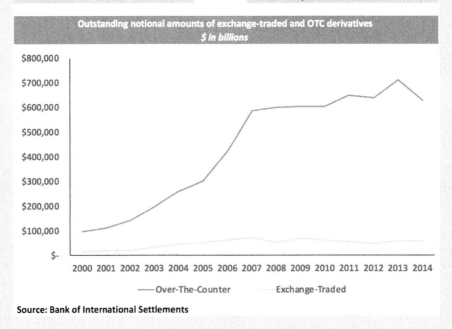

Exchange Traded

Futures exchanges such as CME Group and NYSE Euronext trade standardized derivative contracts. These contracts are either options contracts or futures contracts on a range of underlying products. The total notional amount of all outstanding exchange-traded derivative contracts as of 2014 was $65 trillion.

Over-the-Counter

Derivatives contracts that do not trade on a futures exchange are known as over-the-counter (OTC) contracts. Counterparties to OTC contracts principally include investment banks, hedge funds, commercial banks, and government sponsored enterprises. OTC products include swaps, forward rate agreements, options, forward contracts, and credit derivatives. The notional amount of all outstanding OTC derivative contracts as of 2014 was $630 trillion.

Source: Bank of International Settlements

Because regulators and politicians believed that financial institutions' involvement in OTC derivatives contributed to the financial crisis in 2008, US regulators promulgated increased federal regulation of the previously underregulated OTC market. The new financial regulatory reforms attempt to increase transparency and promote market discipline by requiring many standard OTC derivative contracts to be cleared through regulated central counterparties. These contracts are to be guaranteed by the exchange, mitigating the risk of systemic failure from the collapse of one large counterparty (see additional discussions on transaction clearing in the next section). New reporting requirements for firms with significant positions in complex derivative transactions is now required in an effort to bring a higher level of disclosure across all major players in the derivatives market. Regulators in many of the world's major capital centers have adopted similar regulations in an effort to create greater disclosure and reduce systemic risk.

End users such as companies, farmers, and utilities utilize derivatives as a key tool to protect against risks that are inherent to their businesses. For example, an electric utility can use derivatives to protect against the risk of future price increases on the specific quantity of fuel it needs to serve customers and protect against cost increases. Derivatives also allow financial institutions to hedge their exposure to credit risk, which helps them expand their lending and investment capabilities.

Examples of derivatives which are subject to new regulation include interest rate, credit default swaps, and equity swaps. Regulators, including the CFTC and the SEC, have created new rules designed to meet G20 objectives of increasing transparency and reducing systemic risk in the derivative markets, including reporting swap transactions to a swap data repositories; clearing sufficiently liquid and standardized swaps on central counterparties; trading many standardized swaps on trading platforms; and setting higher capital and minimum margin requirements for uncleared swaps. The CFTC has established regulatory oversight for many new entities, including swap intermediaries known as "Swap Dealers" and "Major Swap Participants," as well as clearing houses and trading platforms. The SEC has implemented requirements covering security-based swaps that require standardized derivatives transactions to be centrally cleared, and the most liquid of those are required to be executed on platforms. However, some derivatives still fall into the OTC category, which means that their terms are privately negotiated between two parties and will remain uncleared. These noncentrally cleared swaps are subject to new margin requirements based on international standards developed by the Basel Committee on Banking Supervision and International Organization of Securities Commissions.

CLEARING AND SETTLEMENT

Investment banks are inextricably linked with exchanges in clearing and settling listed securities and derivatives transactions. Clearing and settlement starts with an effort to capture trade data between counterparties and make sure the terms of buyers' and sellers' trade records match perfectly. This is the "front end" of the trade. Clearing also involves novation, in which the central counterparty clearing house (CCP) substitutes for the original counterparties in relation to future performance of all remaining obligations. For each transaction that is to be cleared, the original contract is replaced with two contracts with the CCP, one where the CCP is the buyer, and one where the CCP is the seller. CCPs use a risk management system that includes the posting of collateral to support a guarantee that is provided by the CCP to transacting parties in a trade. Each exchange has its own clearing house where all members of the exchange are required to clear their trades and postcollateral.

Securities Settlement

Securities are accounted for electronically by "book-entry" in an electronic table. Transfer of ownership of a security is based on the simultaneous transfer of funds to pay for the security, which is called "delivery versus payment." Once title to the security has been passed to the buyer, the clearing and settlement process ends and the custody process begins. Bank CDs and commercial paper settle on the same business day ("for cash"); US Treasury securities settle the next business day ("for regular"); and FX settles two business days after the trade ("T+2"). US equity securities settle three business days after the trade ("T+3").

Settlement risk default arises from two sources. First, the seller either does not have or does not properly deliver securities on the settlement date. This is called a "short fail." Second, the buyer fails to pay for the security, which is called a "long fail." Exchanges have automatic procedures that temporarily mitigate both long and short fails, including cash collateral and netting arrangements.

To reduce the number of transactions that must be settled, exchanges have a multilateral netting system. Since most settlements with an exchange are completed between an investment bank and an exchange and since banks typically have many purchases and sales of the same security, their net delivery obligation is determined by the exchange. All details of settlement obligations must be resolved before the close of business the day after the trade was originally consummated. The funding side of settlement is netted down to a single payment made either by the exchange to an investment bank or by the bank to the exchange.

Derivatives Settlement

Derivatives are also accounted for electronically through a book-entry system. Other than this initial similarity, clearing and settlement of derivatives is quite different from that of securities. Instead of clearing and settling within 3 days, derivatives often remain outstanding for a much longer time—sometimes months and years. Unlike securities, where the security is delivered and simultaneously paid for in full, derivatives represent an obligation (if a futures or swap contract) or an option (if an option contract) to buy or sell a financial instrument or asset at a future date, which can be weeks, months, or years in the future. As a result, the buyer and seller pose financial risks to an exchange for an extended period of time. Because of this large risk, exchanges require daily mark-to-market posting and adjustment of collateral based on the changing value of the derivatives contract. Derivatives, therefore, require substantially more complex risk management systems than are required for securities.

As is the case with securities, for exchange-traded derivative transactions, investment banks that initiate trades (on their own behalf or for clients) novate the transactions by substituting the exchange's clearing house as the counterparty to the trade. This results in the creation of two new contracts with a guarantee of closing provided by the exchange on both contracts. Novation also allows the liquidation of derivative contracts prior to maturity, which is not possible for a security.

In addition to providing risk management, margining and collateral management services to investment banks and other users of an exchange, the exchange also provides a performance guarantee and anonymity between counterparties. To protect itself from financial loss that will occur if an investment bank or other counterparty fails to deliver against their trading obligations, exchanges require all counterparties to deposit performance collateral. Generally speaking, this performance collateral is set at levels that should cover at least 1 day's expected market movement for the instruments that underlie each trade.

International Clearing and Settlement

Through the ongoing integration of financial markets, cross-border clearing houses have emerged that allow clearing and settlement of securities and commodities across national borders. Following the implementation of the Markets in Financial Instruments Directive in 2004, the European Multilateral Clearing Facility was created to promote competition among clearing houses. LCH Clearnet, a European clearing house, has cooperated with NYSE Euronext to enable more efficient transatlantic clearing. In the United States, clearing is mostly conducted through the Automated Clearing House network.

Treasury and Securities Services

Treasury and Securities Services (TSS) has become a significant business unit for many investment banks. TSS professionals advise clients on a variety of matters such as working capital management, custody, securities lending, and fund accounting. Clients can be small businesses, large multinational corporations, and government entities. These services help clients conduct financial transactions in a more efficient manner. This can be an important source of revenue for banks.

In 2015, J.P. Morgan reported revenue in treasury services of approximately $2.6 billion and over $20 trillion in assets under custody. Since this business represents consistent fees that are largely independent of cyclical fluctuations and a low-risk business model, many banks are attempting to grow TSS operations. According to consulting firms and J.P. Morgan analysis, the Treasury Services revenue pool is expected to grow from $144 billion as of 2014 to around $280 billion by about 2024.

International Banking

Investment banking is a global business, with most of the largest firms operating in more than 20 countries. This chapter focuses on (1) Euromarkets; (2) financing and advisory activity in Japan, China, and emerging markets; (3) the global initial public offering (IPO) market; (4) international capital requirements; and (5) selected other international banking topics.

EUROMARKETS

Euromarkets is the generic term used in international capital markets for securities issued and held outside the issuer's country of origin. Bonds that trade in this market are called

Investment Banks, Hedge Funds, and Private Equity, Third Edition
http://dx.doi.org/10.1016/B978-0-12-804723-1.00008-6

Eurobonds. Euromarkets exist to facilitate cross-border financings by corporations and sovereign entities and were originally created in response to the Cold War during the 1950s. The Soviet Union at that time was concerned that holding US dollar deposits (largely generated from sale of oil) in the United States would enable the US government to freeze these assets. As a result, they deposited their US dollars with European banks in Europe, outside of the control of the US government. Due to restrictions on dollar lending activities to foreign companies and ceiling limits on interest rates offered for deposits, US banks also moved significant dollar balances to their banking offices in Europe. All of this gave rise to a very large amount of US dollars deposited mostly in London and has led to remarkable growth in the Euromarkets, especially after OPEC countries began depositing US dollars received from oil sales outside of the United States during the 1980s.

Although London is the unofficial center of the Euromarkets, Frankfurt and Paris are large centers as well. One reason European cities tend to dominate this market is due to their geographic convenience to markets in the Americas and Asia. Euromarkets can also be considered to include certain Caribbean countries such as the Cayman Islands, which have significant foreign deposits as well. The Euromarkets are attractive because they are, for the most part, unregulated and sometimes offer higher yields to investors. This market has become a significant source of global liquidity.

Eurobonds are debt instruments that are listed on an exchange in bearer form (i.e., owned by whoever is holding the security instead of in registered form with registered owners). They are issued and traded outside the country whose currency the Eurobond is denominated in, and outside the regulations of a single country. Interest income from these bonds is exempted from withholding tax and the bonds are generally not registered with any regulatory body. For example, while a US corporation's domestic bonds are subject to SEC oversight, its Eurobonds are not (unless offered concurrently to US investors). The market is self-regulated through the International Capital Markets Association (ICMA). Eurobonds are generally issued by multinational corporations or sovereign entities of high credit quality. An international syndicate of banks typically underwrites a Eurobond issuance and distributes the bonds to investors in a number of countries (other than the country of the issuer).

Eurobonds can be issued in many forms, including fixed-rate coupon bonds (interest is usually payable annually and principal is due in full at maturity, without amortization), convertible bonds, zero-coupon bonds, and floating rate notes. Eurobonds issued in US dollars are called Eurodollar bonds; Eurobonds issued in Japanese yen are called Euroyen bonds. There are many other currencies in which Eurobonds are issued, including pound sterling, euro, and Canadian dollar, among others. In each case, the Eurobond is named after the currency in which it is denominated. Almost all Eurobonds are owned "electronically" rather than in physical form and are settled through either Euroclear or Clearstream, two global electronic depository systems.

London's Financial Market

One quarter of the world's largest financial companies have their European headquarters in London. There are more than 550 banks and 170 global security firms that have London offices, more than any other city in the world. The London foreign exchange (FX) market is the largest in the world, with average daily trading in excess of $5.5 trillion, which represents more than 40% of all global FX transactions. The London market has captured more than one-third of the OTC derivatives market and manages almost half of European institutional equity capital. The London Inter-Bank Offer Rate (LIBOR), which represents the interest rate that banks charge each other for short-term loans, is recorded every day in London and disseminated worldwide as the most used base rate in the world for determining loan pricing.

A number of international banks had traders who allegedly falsely inflated or deflated their bank's reported LIBOR to profit from trades, or to give the impression that their bank was more creditworthy than other banks. LIBOR underpins approximately $350 trillion in derivatives, so the impact of "rigging" LIBOR is very important. Banks are supposed to submit the actual interest rates they are paying, or would expect to pay, for borrowing from other banks. Settlements by Barclays Bank revealed significant fraud and collusion by member banks connected to the rate submission process. In August 2015, UBS trader Thomas Hayes was the only person convicted in connection with the LIBOR scandal. Six bankers accused of LIBOR rigging were cleared in the United Kingdom during 2016.

JAPAN'S FINANCIAL MARKET

During the 1980s, Japan's stock market skyrocketed to remarkable levels. The price to earnings (PE) ratio for the Nikkei 225 stock index reached above 70×, nearly four times higher than the US S&P 500 stock index PE ratio of approximately 18×. This market was buoyed by high real estate prices and an interlocking corporate ownership structure that was common in Japan. Unfortunately, after reaching a high of almost 39,000 in January 1990, the Nikkei 225 index fell more than 50% during that year. Although the market has since seen considerable volatility, it has never returned to the historical high, and by mid-2016, was below 18,000. An innovative investment banking transaction that relates to Japan's financial market crash is summarized in Chapter 9, under the Nikkei Put Warrant section.

The principal banking institutions in Japan have changed dramatically through mergers over the past 20 years. There are currently three large banks: Mitsubishi UFJ Financial Group, Mizuho Financial Group, and Sumitomo Mitsui Financial Group. Each of these banks operates principally as a commercial bank, with somewhat limited securities activities. However, during 2008, in the wake of the credit crisis that weakened many of Wall Street's investment banks, Mitsubishi UFJ Financial Group made a significant investment in Morgan Stanley, acquiring approximately 21% of the US firm's stock. The largest pure-play securities firms in Japan are Nomura Securities and Daiwa Securities. When Lehman Brothers failed during 2008, Nomura Securities acquired most of Lehman's businesses in Asia and Europe, substantially bolstering its global investment banking presence.

M&A in Japan

Due to a restrictive regulatory environment, the M&A market in Japan had been slow to develop. However, new legislation passed in the last decade helped to accelerate the pace of deal making in Japan. In 2003, a new law passed that permitted non-Japanese companies to use their own stock to acquire Japanese companies that were under Japanese bankruptcy court protection. This was followed by a 2007 law that further extended the ability of foreign companies to use their stock to acquire Japanese companies, as well as other laws that lowered the threshold shareholder approval requirement for an acquisition.

One of the most successful foreign acquisitions in Japan was initiated by Ripplewood, a US-based private equity firm. Ripplewood led the buyout of Long-Term Credit Bank (LTCB) in 2000, which was suffering a severe financial reversal. As part of the acquisition agreement, the Japanese government agreed to purchase any LTCB assets that fell by 20% or more post-acquisition. As a result, the bank sold its worst assets at above market prices to the government immediately following the acquisition. LTCB was renamed Shinsei Bank, and with new management and Ripplewood's ongoing support, the bank became profitable. Ripplewood subsequently monetized its investment by taking Shinsei Bank public in 2004, achieving a reported profit of over $1 billion for its 4-year holding.

The median premium paid by Japanese companies for overseas acquisitions during 2015 was about 35%, which was almost twice the premium paid by US buyers during the same year. However, the average EV/EBITDA multiple paid by Japanese buyers was comparable to the multiple paid by US buyers. Japanese companies have a longer investment horizon and, as a result, sometimes pay higher acquisition premiums. In addition, Japanese transactions often emphasize revenue and products more than price, and there is a lesser focus on increasing shareholder value and a greater focus on strengthening the company and employment opportunities over the long term. In relation to synergies, while US companies mainly focus on cost savings, Japanese acquirers prioritize the ability to expand market share and product profile. Some Japanese companies, including Bridgestone, which acquired US tire-maker Firestone during 1988, are willing to wait 10–15 years to fully recover acquisition costs. During 2015, Japanese overseas M&A was principally focused on the United States (almost 40% of volume) and the United Kingdom (about 11% of volume).

Equity Financing in Japan

Approximately 85% of equity underwriting in Japan is conducted by Nomura Securities, Sumitomo Mitsui Financial Group, Mitsubishi UFJ Securities, Daiwa Securities and Mizuho Financial Group. Although foreign investment banks can also underwrite Japanese securities, they have limited distribution networks and therefore most of their underwriting activities are directed to companies whose stocks trade on the Second Section of the Tokyo or Osaka stock exchanges (midsized companies trade on the Second Section while large-cap companies trade on the First Section). However, foreign investment banks sometimes are able to act as a colead bookrunner in partnership with one of the big three Japanese securities firms when First Section–listed companies desire a strong distribution capability outside of Japan.

Trading Securities in Japan

Japanese government bonds are issued in the form of short-term treasury bills and longer-term coupon bonds and zero-coupon bonds ranging from maturities of 2–30 years. Bond auctions are conducted by the Ministry of Finance (MoF) and can be bid for by Japanese banks and securities firms, as well as by qualified foreign firms.

Japanese corporations have historically relied principally on bank borrowings for their debt financings. As a result, the Japanese corporate bond market is small relative to the country's GDP, when compared to the US or UK corporate bond markets. However, over the past 20 years, which has been a difficult time for the Japanese banking sector, the Japanese corporate bond market has grown substantially. Banks are increasingly applying stricter covenants in their loans to corporations and are encouraging many clients to allow them to underwrite bonds, rather than complete bank borrowings. This trend has recently allowed several US and European firms to break into the top bond underwriter rankings in Japan.

Trading in equity securities is largely centered on the Tokyo Stock Exchange (TSE), which accounts for over 80% of all trading volume in the country. In addition to Japanese firms, a limited number of non-Japanese companies list their shares on the TSE. The remainder of the trading volume in Japan is generated from four other equity exchanges: Osaka, Nagoya, Fukuoka, and Sapporo.

CHINA'S FINANCIAL MARKET

China's financial market has seen dramatic growth and increasing sophistication as regulatory barriers have been reduced and the country's economy has grown rapidly (see Exhibits 8.1 and 8.2). This growth has been facilitated in part by the government's relaxation of its foreign exchange controls in 1996. Under relaxed regulations, current account renminbi (RMB) became convertible (subject to certain restrictions) into other currencies. This was followed in 2002 with the creation of the Qualified Foreign Institutional Investor (QFII) program, which allowed qualifying foreign investors to participate in the Chinese equity market via domestic A-shares and in the Chinese debt market. Many non-Chinese financial institutions have since obtained the QFII designation, enabling them to participate in these markets.

The International Monetary Fund decided to include yuan as a reserve currency during 2016, which bolstered China's position in the global financial markets. The IMF determined that the yuan meets the standard of being "freely usable" and so it has joined the dollar, euro, pound, and yen in the IMF's Special Drawing Rights basket, with the yuan having a 10.92% weighting in the basket. Weightings are now 41.73% for the dollar, 30.93% for the euro, 8.33% for the yen, and 8.09% for the British pound. Renminbi is the "peoples currency" in China, and yuan is the basic unit of the renminbi. This distinction is similar to sterling, which is the British currency and pound, which is its basic unit.

M&A in China

Non-domestic M&A activity in China has historically been limited. However, because of China's accession to the World Trade Organization in 2001, there are now more opportunities for foreign investment. China has restructured many of its state-owned assets and is encouraging some of these enterprises to consolidate into larger companies. As a result, a large number of state-owned enterprises are being made available for restructuring or partnering with foreign companies. There is a high level of government participation in all M&A transactions in China, with the Ministry of Commerce and the State Development and Reform Commission focusing on not only antitrust issues, but also on economic and social consequences. In addition, the Ministry of Commerce is the principal foreign investment regulator and has general supervisory and approval authority over M&A transactions. Finally, the State-Owned Assets Supervision and Administration Commission and the China Securities Regulatory Commission are also involved in approving, monitoring, and regulating state-owned or listed company M&A transactions.

Foreign companies are not permitted to operate business directly in China. To conduct business in China, a company must operate through a foreign investment enterprise (FIE).

The percentage of foreign ownership allowable in an FIE depends on the industry: 100% ownership is permitted for some industries, but for others, the percentage of foreign ownership is restricted. FIEs can be set up as joint ventures (JVs), wholly owned foreign enterprises, or foreign-invested companies limited by shares.

Equity Financing in China

The Shanghai Stock Exchange and the Hong Kong Stock Exchange are the two largest exchanges in China. The market capitalization of domestic shares trading on both exchanges exceeded $7 trillion during 2015, ranking them #5 and #6, respectively, in the world. The next largest exchange in China is the Shenzhen Stock Exchange. The market capitalization of shares trading on this exchange was $2.3 trillion during 2015, a dramatic increase over the previous years. The Shenzhen Stock Exchange has been designated as a growth enterprise market for China. This market is similar to NASDAQ in the United States, specializing in smaller-market capitalization and predominantly high-tech companies.

Chinese companies may issue A-shares or B-shares on the Shanghai or Shenzhen exchanges. A-shares are limited to purchases by only Chinese residents and QFIIs, and are denominated in renminbi. B-shares can be purchased by foreign investors, and as of 2001, by Chinese residents as well. These shares cannot be converted into A-shares and are denominated in renminbi, but traded in either US dollars (in Shanghai) or Hong Kong dollars (in Shenzhen). Dividends and capital gains from B-shares can be sent outside of China, and foreign securities firms can act as dealers for these shares.

Foreign investors can also invest in Chinese shares through purchasing shares listed in Hong Kong (H-shares). These shares are listed to facilitate offshore financing by Chinese companies and can only be traded by foreign investors or Hong Kong residents (and not by mainland Chinese residents). H-shares are denominated in Hong Kong dollars. Hong Kong–headquartered companies (which can be incorporated in Hong Kong or certain offshore jurisdictions) that are controlled by mainland Chinese companies or derive significant revenue from mainland China customers issue "Red Chip" stock.

The growth and popularity of the H-share and Red Chip markets in Hong Kong has led to a decline in the B-share markets. Today, there are more than 10 times as many A-shares as B-shares trading on the two mainland exchanges and the aggregate market value of all B-shares is less than 1% of the aggregate market value of A-shares. This decline has led to a gradual withdrawal of foreign institutional funds as the liquidity in the B-share markets continues to dwindle. The majority of B-share investors are now domestic retail investors. Due to the diminishing utility of having a separate A- and B-share market, there is speculation that Chinese regulators are considering merging the B-share market into the A-share market.

UBS, Goldman Sachs, and Morgan Stanley have historically dominated the equity underwriting league tables in Hong Kong for H-shares, but market share has recently been taken away by a group of Chinese securities firms. In mainland China, Chinese firms, including China International Capital Corp. and China Galaxy Securities Co. dominated the rankings for A-share underwriting. Most recently, additional Chinese firms have controlled most of the A share market, including CITIC Securities, China Merchants Securities, Guotai Junan Securities, Guosen Securities, and Haitong Securities. Many of these firms now dominate all equity underwriting for Chinese companies, crowding out most large international firms.

Shanghai–Hong Kong Stock Connect

The Shanghai–Hong Kong Stock Connect was started during 2015 when it connected the Shanghai Stock Exchange and the Hong Kong Stock Exchange electronically, enabling investors in each market to trade shares on the other market using their local brokers and clearing houses. Eligible investors in Mainland China can now purchase eligible shares listed on the Hong Kong Stock Exchange through their own local broker, and investors in Hong Kong and international investors can purchase eligible Shanghai-listed shares through their local broker. All Hong Kong and overseas investors are allowed to trade eligible shares listed in Shanghai, but only Mainland institutional investors and individual investors who have RMB500,000 in their investment and cash accounts are eligible to trade Hong Kong–listed stocks. Mainland investors are able to trade the constituent stocks of the Hang Seng Composite LargeCap Index and Hang Seng Composite MidCap Index, and all H-shares that are not included as constituent stocks of the relevant indices but which have corresponding A-shares listed in Shanghai, with some exceptions.

Trading Bonds in China

China has two bond markets: the Interbank bond market, which is regulated by the People's Bank of China (PBoC) and the Exchange bond market, which is regulated by the China Securities Regulatory Commission (CSRC). The interbank market is much larger than the exchange market, accounting for more than 95% of total trading volume. Trading activity has grown rapidly and the market is very liquid, with more than $60 trillion in total trading volume in 2015. This represents the world's third largest bond market, after the United States and Japan.

There are four main types of bonds in the Chinese market: government bonds, central bank notes, financial bonds, and nonfinancial corporate bonds. Government bonds are issued by the MoF to finance government spending. Local governments also issue bonds, similar to municipal bonds in the United States. Central bank notes are short-term securities issued by the PBoC as a tool for implementing monetary policy. Financial bonds are the most actively traded bonds in China and are issued by policy banks, which are backed by the central government (including China Development Bank, Export–Import Bank of China, and the Agricultural Development Bank of China), commercial banks, and other financial institutions. Nonfinancial corporate bonds include "enterprise" bonds, which are issued by entities affiliated with the central government or states. Issuers in this market include companies such as China National Petroleum, China Petrochemical, and China Telecom. Private companies of any size can also issue corporate bonds, short-term commercial paper, and medium-term notes.

China's government has been trying to expand its domestic bond market because Chinese corporations still rely primarily on equity issuance and bank loans for financing. Because of this heavy reliance on bank loans, the government has encouraged corporations to raise funds by bond issuance. Infrastructure development is another important reason for the growth of China's bond market.

China has established programs that allow foreign investors access to the bond market. The QFII program allows foreign investors access both the Exchange bond market and the Interbank bond market. This program was launched in 2002 to allow licensed foreign investors to buy and sell yuan-denominated equities and bonds in China's mainland stock exchanges (in Shanghai and Shenzhen). In July 2012, new regulations granted QFIIs access to the Interbank bond market.

Prior to that, QFIIs could only access the Exchange bond market. QFIIs can transfer an approved amount of US dollars to a special QFII-qualified custodian account and convert to RMB under the supervision of the State Administration of Foreign Exchange (SAFE). QFIIs are allowed to invest in (1) publicly listed shares on the Shanghai or Shenzhen Stock Exchange other than B-shares; (2) bonds traded on the exchange market and interbank market; (3) open-ended funds and close-ended funds; and (4) other approved financial instruments. RMB QFII (RQFII) was also introduced as an extension of QFII program in December 2011. RQFII2 allows qualified financial institutions to establish yuan-denominated funds in Hong Kong, Singapore, Taiwan, and London for investment in Mainland China. Another pilot program was launched in 2010 to allow three types of offshore institutions to invest in China's largely closed Interbank bond market. The qualified institutions include foreign central banks, lenders in Hong Kong and Macao that have already conducted renminbi clearing, and overseas banks involved in renminbi cross-border trade settlement. The permitted funding sources of investment in the interbank bond market include currency cooperation between central banks, cross-border trades and onshore RMB businesses.

Over 200 bond products trade on the Shanghai Stock Exchange, including treasury bonds, enterprise bonds, corporate bonds, and convertible bonds. There are also over 1000 listed companies, more than 25 securities investment funds, and 20 warrants listed on the exchange.

The corporate bond market in China is very small, compared to the US and European corporate bond markets. Chinese banks provide almost all of the debt financing required by corporate borrowers. Only 6% of all Chinese bonds are issued by nonfinancial enterprises, providing just 1.5% of the total financial needs of corporations in China. 84% of all capital for corporations comes from bank loans and 14.5% comes from equity offerings.

Chinese government bonds trade both on exchanges and in the over-the-counter market. The MoF issues treasury bonds, construction bonds, fiscal bonds, and other "special" bonds. Policy banks such as Export–Import Bank and China Development Bank issue bonds to support infrastructure projects and strategic industries. These bonds are considered to be only slightly riskier than government bonds. Bonds issued by the government and by policy banks are important tools for the central bank in managing the country's monetary and fiscal policies.

International Investment Banking Activity in China

Most major investment banks have actively pursued business opportunities in China. However, tight regulatory controls by the Chinese government have limited the entry of these banks to only certain areas of the domestic market. In addition, depending on when the bank entered the Chinese market, the level of authorization varied according to the legislation in place at that time. In general, these banks can only participate in domestic securities underwriting through JVs set up with Chinese securities firms whereby the foreign bank owns no more than a one-third share in the entity. Goldman Sachs and UBS set up their JV's in 2004 and 2005, respectively, and are the only two foreign banks that have been allowed management control over their JVs. The three other major foreign banks that have domestic securities underwriting approval (Morgan Stanley, Credit Suisse, and Deutsche Bank) only have passive ownership in their JV entities. A summary of major foreign investment bank investments in China is provided in Exhibit 8.1. A summary of foreign and domestic investment bank revenues in China are summarized in Exhibit 8.2. UBS increased ownership of its Chinese securities joint venture during 2015 from 20% to just under 25%. The largest shareholder in this JV (called UBS Securities) is Beijing Guoxiang Asset Management Co., an entity controlled by the Beijing government. Goldman Sachs Gao Hua Securities Co. is the name of the Chinese JV controlled by Goldman Sachs. Other foreign investment banks have securities joint ventures but lack control. Foreign investment banks seeking to do business on the country's domestic yuan-denominated exchanges are required to do so through such joint ventures, with foreign ownership capped at 49%. The joint ventures allow foreign banks to underwrite A-share offerings in Shanghai and Shenzhen and to arrange domestic bond offerings.

EXHIBIT 8.1 FOREIGN EQUITY INVESTMENTS IN CHINA

- Morgan Stanley cofounded China International Capital Corporation (CCC), the first Sino-foreign securities joint venture in China, together with Construction Bank in 1995. After selling its stake in CCC, the company established an RMB private equity fund JV with Hangzhou Industrial & Commercial Trust, as well as an equity JV with Huaxin Securities in 2011. Morgan Stanley holds an 80% stake in the RMB private equity fund JV and 33.3% in the equity JV.
- Citigroup bought 5% of Shanghai Pudong Development Bank for $67 million in 2002. Later on, the company launched Citi Orient Securities Co. Ltd., a JV with Orient Securities Company Ltd. in 2011, holding a 33.3% share.
- Goldman Sachs set up a JV called Goldman Sachs Gao Hua Securities, in which it owned 33.3%, in 2004.
- In 2006, Goldman Sachs, Allianz, and American Express combined to buy a 10% stake of Industrial Commercial Bank of China (ICBC). Goldman sold 1% of its holding in ICBC in 2009 and excited its position during 2013.
- Goldman Sachs bought 12.02% of Tai Kang Life in 2011, an insurance company in China.
- UBS acquired 20% of Beijing Securities and renamed it MUBS Securities in 2005, giving the bank license to underwrite domestic securities. The company purchased an additional 4.99% stake in UBS Securities from International Finance Corporation in 2015.
- Bank of America (then Merill Lynch) entered into a JV agreement with Huaan Securities in 2005, with 33% stake in the venture. However, in 2007, after failing to get approval from the Chinese government, the bank canceled the agreement with Huaan.
- Bank of America bought in a 9% stake in China Construction Bank (CCB) for $3 billion in 2005 and later on increased the holding to 19.1% with an additional $7 billion investment in 2008. Later on, Bank of America started selling its position in CCB: a 5.7% stake in May 2009, 13.1 billion shares in August 2011, 10.1 billion shares in November 2011, and all remaining shares in September 2013.
- Credit Suisse entered into a joint venture with Founder Securities in October 2008 and held 33% of this firm. The joint venture, named Credit Suisse Founder Securities Limited, received regulatory approval to underwrite domestic securities in 2009 and was allowed to provide securities brokerage services in Shenzen Qianhai in 2015.
- Deustche Bank entered into a joint venture called Zhong De Securities with Shanxi Securities in 2009, and the new Venture has obtained regulatory approval to underwrite domestic securities.
- Citigroup established Citi Orient Securities Co. Ltd. in 2011, a joint venture with Orient Securities Company Ltd., and owned a 33.3% share.
- JP Morgan entered into a joint venture with First Capital Securities in June 2011 and named it JP Morgan First Capital Securities Company Ltd. JP Morgan owned a 33.3% stake and the venture received a permit to underwrite securities.

Source: Company press releases.

I. INVESTMENT BANKING

EXHIBIT 8.2 INVESTMENT BANK SECURITIES REVENUE IN CHINA

Firm	2015				2014	
	Rank	Market share (%)	Volume ($ Millions)	Deal Count	Rank	Market share (%)
China International Capital Corp Ltd	1	14.1	91,396	53	1	15.6
Morgan Stanley	2	11.2	72,63	44	3	14.4
CITIC Securities Co. Ltd	3	10.8	70,058	58	2	14.6
JPMorgan Chase & Co.	4	7.7	50,042	26	11	5.4
Goldman Sachs & Co.	5	7.1	45,699	32	5	11.7
Huatai Securities Co. Ltd	6	6.7	43,086	43	17	3.9
Somerley Group Ltd	7	5.4	34,66	29	6	10.3
Bank of America (Merrill Lynch)	8	4.8	31,18	13	4	13.0
China Securities Co. Ltd	9	4.1	26,746	37	10	6.3
HSBC Bank PLC	10	4.0	25,585	10	32	0.9

Source: Global M&A Financial Advisory Rankings.

EMERGING FINANCIAL MARKETS

Emerging market countries are countries that are in a transitional phase between developing and developed status. Examples include India, Mexico, China, most of Southeast Asia, and countries in Eastern Europe and the Middle East (countries included in MSCI Barra's Emerging Market Index are listed in Exhibit 8.3).

Conducting investment banking activities in emerging market countries represents both significant potential revenue opportunities and correspondingly large risks. Some investment banks have prioritized activities in these countries and have been very successful. Included among the most successful banks are Citigroup, Goldman Sachs, UBS, JP Morgan, Morgan Stanley, Deutsche Bank, and Credit Suisse. These firms have focused on a broad array of business activities, including securities underwriting, syndicated lending, M&A, and a significant number of trading and investing initiatives.

Incremental risks associated with investment banking business in these countries include currency, political, liquidity, accounting, tax, and volatility risks. Currencies in some of these countries are subject to rapid, sometimes unanticipated changes based on significant dislocations in a country's credit or stock markets. Political risk can have a major impact on a securities market if a government expropriates property or if there is a political coup. A country's securities market can also be significantly impacted if liquidity dries up. This can happen based on government limitations on foreign investments or if large blocks of shares are held by founding investors who refuse to share control or profits. Accounting and tax policies can sometimes change in a preemptive, unexpected manner in emerging market countries, putting investing and underwriting activities at risk. Finally, high volatility is part and parcel of most emerging market countries, with occasional wild swings in securities and currency prices that are difficult to anticipate and hedge.

In spite of these risks, most large investment banks have prioritized development of their emerging market business since these countries are expected to grow significantly and develop more efficient and predictable capital markets. Many of these countries are improving their legal system to better support enforcement of contracts. They are also improving disclosure requirements and corporate governance practices. Finally, they are increasing privatization of previously government-owned businesses, allowing individual ownership of shares. All of this suggests that investment banks will be able to profitably expand their activities in these countries if they properly monitor and control risk procedures.

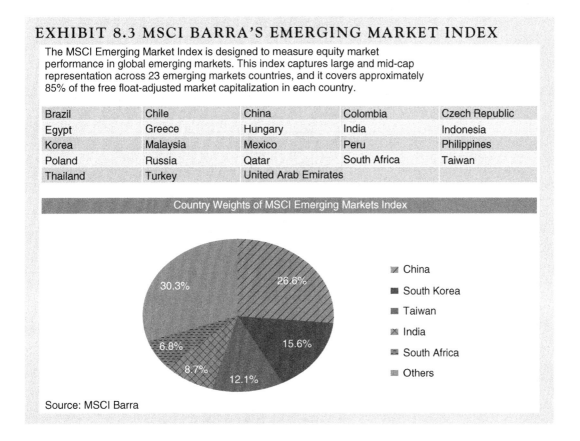

EXHIBIT 8.3 MSCI BARRA'S EMERGING MARKET INDEX

The MSCI Emerging Market Index is designed to measure equity market performance in global emerging markets. This index captures large and mid-cap representation across 23 emerging markets countries, and it covers approximately 85% of the free float-adjusted market capitalization in each country.

Brazil	Chile	China	Colombia	Czech Republic
Egypt	Greece	Hungary	India	Indonesia
Korea	Malaysia	Mexico	Peru	Philippines
Poland	Russia	Qatar	South Africa	Taiwan
Thailand	Turkey	United Arab Emirates		

Country Weights of MSCI Emerging Markets Index

30.3%
26.6%
15.6%
12.1%
8.7%
6.8%

- China
- South Korea
- Taiwan
- India
- South Africa
- Others

Source: MSCI Barra

Bonds

Credit ratings for bonds issued by emerging market countries and for the countries themselves are important considerations in the development of robust securities markets. Credit ratings are provided by rating agencies such as S&P, Moody's and Fitch, as well as by specialty publishers such as Institutional Investor (see Exhibit 8.4). In addition to affecting a country's currency, country rankings and credit ratings can also have an important impact on the universe of investors able to invest in the country. Since most institutional investors cannot invest in countries below a certain credit rating, a ratings upgrade can potentially increase the pool of investors for a country's securities.

EXHIBIT 8.4 GLOBAL CREDIT RANKING FOR EMERGING MARKET COUNTRIES

RANK March 2016	Country	Institutional Investor Credit Rating
18	Taiwan	82
23	Chile	77.3
24	Estonia	76.8
26	China	76
27	Kuwait	74
28	Poland	73.8
35	Mexico	71
36	Israel	71
37	Malaysia	69.5
40	Lithuania	67.8
43	Peru	66.9
44	Colombia	65.2
47	Thailand	61.5
48	India	61.4
49	Philippines	61.4
55	Romania	57.2
56	Portugal	57.1
57	Indonesia	57
60	Bulgaria	55.9
61	Brazil	55.5
62	Costa Rica	55.1
65	South Africa	54
70	Turkey	52.6
71	Morocco	51.7
91	Nigeria	36.9
98	Kenya	33.4

Annual secondary market trading of emerging market bonds (and other emerging market debt securities) is estimated to exceed $6 trillion. Emerging market debt securities include

Brady bonds (see below), sovereign and corporate Eurobonds, local market debt, and sovereign loans. Approximately 50% of this trading volume is represented by trading in debt instruments denominated and traded in the issuer's home country.

Syndicated Loans

Syndicated loans have historically been the key source of new capital for emerging market countries. Unfortunately, during the 1980s, most of these loans defaulted. To mitigate losses that banks were accruing, Brady bonds were created in 1989: bonds that were issued to banks in exchange for their nonperforming loans. In most cases these bonds were tradable and came with guarantees from various governments. In addition, the bonds were usually collateralized by US Treasury 30-year zero-coupon bonds purchased by the debtor country using a combination of IMF, World Bank, and the country's own foreign currency reserves. This allowed the banks to remove the bonds from their balance sheets and the borrowers to regain the ability to pay off existing debt and issue new debt. A large share of all Brady bonds has now been repaid.

Equity

Many emerging market countries have removed most barriers to foreign investor purchases of equity. However, there are still some restrictions that limit the trading activities of international investment banks in most of these countries. Principal equity trading in emerging market countries involves ADR (American Depositary Receipt) and GDR (Global Depository Receipt) issues by some of the larger companies in the emerging markets. Another important trading activity of the investment banks is in emerging market exchange–traded funds. These funds, usually benchmarked off of indices created by MSCI Barra (a spin-off of Morgan Stanley), enable investors to purchase US dollar–based exposure to different emerging market countries based on indexes in individual countries (MSCI Brazil Index Fund, MSCI South Africa Index Fund, MSCI Taiwan Index Fund, etc.). MSCI Barra also has a broad-based index called MSCI Emerging Index Fund, which captures equity market exposure to the emerging market countries listed in Exhibit 8.3.

M&A

Most large investment banks have reasonably active emerging market M&A businesses. Risks must be carefully balanced against expected returns to be successful in this market. Risks that are especially important to consider include intellectual property, political, legal, currency, operational, and financing risks. All of these risks are much higher in emerging market countries and should be factored into deal considerations. For example, in an M&A DCF valuation, WACC should be adjusted higher for companies that are headquartered in emerging market countries, compared to companies from developed countries. It is also important to consider a wide range of potential growth rates, depending on the countries involved. League tables for M&A activity in Latin America and Eastern Europe emerging market countries are provided in Exhibit 8.5.

EXHIBIT 8.5 EMERGING MARKET M&A LEAGUE TABLES RANKING

(A) Latin America Deals between 01/01/2015 and 12/31/2015

Firm	2015				2014	
	Rank	Market share (%)	Volume ($ Millions)	Deal Count	Rank	Market share (%)
Banco Itau BBA SA	1	23.9	16,956	51	4	25.6
Rothschild Ltd	2	23.7	16,79	18	8	21.6
Banco Bradesco BBI SA	3	19.4	13,722	21	13	8.6
Goldman Sachs & Co.	4	19.1	13,522	17	2	29.0
Banco Santander SA	5	18.6	13,174	16	10	15.5
JPMorgan Chase & Co.	6	13.1	9,258	11	5	25.5
Deutsche Bank AG	7	13.0	9,174	7	3	27.3
Banco BTG Pactual SA	8	11.6	8,226	20	9	20.4
Credit Suisse Group AG	9	11.5	8,154	13	1	29.8
HSBC Bank PLC	10	9.4	6,682	6	25	2.7
TOTAL			70,832	860		125,352

(B) Eastern Europe Deals between 01/01/2015 and 12/31/2015

Firm	2015				2014	
	Rank	Market share (%)	Volume ($ Millions)	Deal Count	Rank	Market share (%)
JPMorgan Chase & Co.	1	20.8	12,507	11	11	3.8
VTB Capital ZAO	2	12.8	7,704	13	14	1.4
Morgan Stanley	3	11.1	6,675	7	2	20.2
Lazard Ltd	4	10.1	6,039	3	22	0.6
Credit Suisse Group AG	5	9.6	5,76	1	12	3.1
Citigroup Inc.	6	8.5	5,089	16	7	6.7
Goldman Sachs & Co.	7	5.6	3,367	7	3	20.0
Societe Generale SA	8	4.9	2,955	8	27	0.5
BNP Paribas SA	9	4.8	2,899	8	5	7.3
Renaissance Capital Holdings Ltd	10	4.8	2,873	2	48	-
TOTAL			60,025	1,093		59,225

GLOBAL INITIAL PUBLIC OFFERING MARKET

During 2007, global IPO financings raised nearly $300 billion in proceeds, with Brazil, Russia, India, and China ("BRIC" countries) accounting for $105 billion (or 35%) of this volume. Three years earlier, in 2004, this same group of countries comprised just 11% of total global IPO proceeds. BRIC's share of the global IPO market temporarily decreased to 22% in 2008, mostly stemming from the ongoing uncertainty and market turmoil caused by the global credit crisis. By 2009, however, BRIC IPOs regained much of their prior momentum and comprised more than half of global IPOs. In 2010, global IPOs raised over $280 billion in proceeds and BRIC countries accounted for over 40% of this market. China, by far, represented most of the activity that year among BRIC countries and over one-third of the global IPO market. Other Asian countries such as South Korea have also shown a strong increase in IPO activity, accounting for almost 3% of worldwide IPOs. In 2015, 43% of IPOs came from emerging countries in the Asia–Pacific region and total global IPO proceeds were less than half the level recorded during 2010 (see Exhibit 8.6).

EXHIBIT 8.6 TOTAL FUNDS RAISED BY EMERGING MARKET INITIAL PUBLIC OFFERINGS

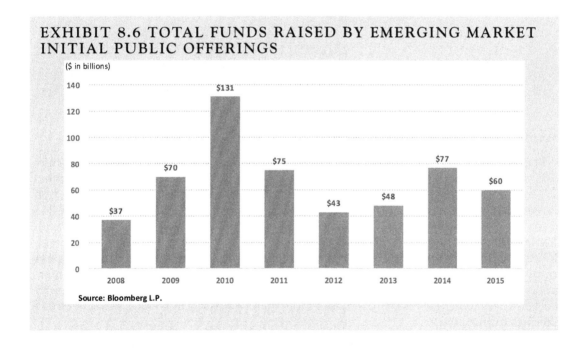

Source: Bloomberg L.P.

Because of the US regulatory restraints, GAAP reporting requirements, high US costs, and development of other equity capital markets, 80% of the world's IPOs are now launched outside of the United States (see Exhibit 8.7).

EXHIBIT 8.7 TOTAL GLOBAL INITIAL PUBLIC OFFERING RAISED DURING 2015

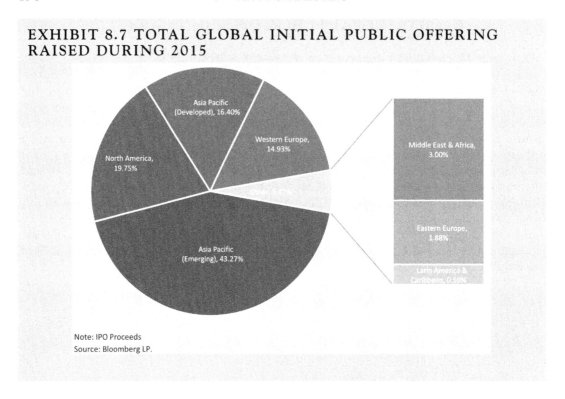

Note: IPO Proceeds
Source: Bloomberg LP.

Brazil's Initial Public Offering Market

Brazil became the third largest IPO market in the world in 2007, contributing to more than 10% of global IPOs by funds raised. 64 companies worth $27.3 billion tapped the Brazilian IPO market, a 251% rise from the previous year. Almost all of these companies listed on the Sao Paolo stock exchange (BOVESPA), which went public in 2007, raising $3.2 billion in the country's largest ever IPO at the time. The BOVESPA then went on to merge with the Brazilian Mercantile and Futures Exchange (BM&F) in 2008 to create the new BM&F BOVESPA. US style corporate governance standards, one-share/one-vote rules, greater transparency, minority shareholder protection, and enhanced quality of disclosed information all combined to draw a record amount of foreign capital into the Brazilian equity market. These foreign investors purchased more than two-thirds of all local Brazilian share offerings during 2007.

The typical business plan for a family-run Brazilian enterprise is to take in private equity or hedge fund money for 25%–30% of the company to enable growth through acquisitions, and then when a sufficient size is achieved, an IPO is the next source for capital. This, in turn, enables further growth since the company now has a liquid acquisition currency. Since the record IPO activity in 2007, there has been a significant decline in Brazilian IPOs.

In 2016, Standard & Poor's reduced Brazil's credit rating to BB (with a negative outlook) and Moody's downgraded the country's rating to Ba2 (with a negative outlook). As a result Brazil's credit rating is in the "junk bond" category.

Russia's Initial Public Offering Market

Russia's capital markets developed rapidly between 2000 and 2007, with the stock market value increasing more than 10-fold during this period. Russia's IPO market in 2007 saw fundraising totaling $19 billion, with 20 IPOs at an average deal size of $948 million. The new issuances primarily came from financial services, real estate, and energy and power sectors. The $8 billion offering from Vneshtorgbank, Russia's second largest state-owned bank, was the largest IPO in the world that year. In all, Russia represented 7% of the global IPO market during 2007. Similar to Brazil, Russia's IPO market slowed down significantly in 2008 (as did the rest of the global capital markets) due to the global credit crisis. In 2009, Russian IPO activity dropped to only $100 million. In 2010, IPO activity increased to $4.4 billion, accounting for roughly 1.6% of IPOs in the world. However, oil and ruble volatility and an economic slowdown resulted in no fully marketed IPOs during 2015 and early 2016.

Russian companies are legally required to list locally at least 30% of their equity. However, the local Russian market retains only enough liquidity to support smaller IPOs below $500 million. The Moscow Exchange provides limited liquidity and an opaque pricing system, although many improvements are underway to improve the listing process, market infrastructure, and trading systems. These changes should improve the appeal of this exchange to issuers and investors over time.

The most popular way for large Russian companies to raise equity is to list a GDR issue in London, combined with a Moscow listing, giving companies exposure to both local and international investors. Some international investors are apprehensive about the ambiguity of certain Russian regulations, especially relating to tax, financial statements, and legal restructuring. Until these uncertainties diminish, there may be limited international demand for Russian GDR issues. As an alternative to listing in London, some Russian companies are listing in Hong Kong. In addition, companies in Ukraine and Kazakhstan have listed IPOs in both London and Hong Kong.

Private equity and hedge fund investments have provided important pre-IPO financing for smaller transaction sizes of up to $200 million. As Russian banks withdrew funding drastically with the advent of the credit crisis that began in 2007, these alternative investors filled the funding gap, enabling Russian companies to continue financing acquisitions. The companies that are able to grow via these acquisitions have also positioned themselves to access the IPO market. Once public, many companies have used their shares as an acquisition currency to facilitate further growth.

India's Initial Public Offering Market

India's IPO market saw 106 deals during 2007, raising an aggregate $8.8 billion, which represents the largest volume raised in 1 year for the country. Average deal size was

$83 million, which is much smaller than in either the Brazilian or the Russian markets. However, during 2008, Reliance Power completed a $3 billion IPO, creating a foundation for future large offerings. The most active Indian IPO issuers come from the industrial, energy and power, financial, and real estate sectors. As India continues to build up its roadways, power plants, and ports, it is expected that the industrial and power sectors will see the most IPO volume going forward, as these industries are direct beneficiaries of infrastructure projects. In 2008 and 2009, IPO activity declined to $4.5 and $4.1 billion, respectively. After dropping further during the following 5 years, in 2015, India's IPO market experienced significant growth, with 22 initial public offerings which raised approximately $2.1 billion.

Due to strict regulatory limits, a foreign institutional investor can invest in no more than 10% of total issued capital of a listed Indian company. However, in aggregate, foreigners provide approximately three quarters of the capital coming into the IPO market. Indian companies seeking to complete an IPO are required by law to list on a local exchange such as the Mumbai Stock Exchange or the National Stock Exchange. They are, however, also allowed to dual list on international exchanges. There are two principal routes taken for dual listings. High-tech Indian companies whose customers might be principally US-based will dual list in the United States since US investors may have a better understanding of the issuer's value proposition. For metals and mining companies, it is common to dual list in the United Kingdom on the AIM market section of the London Stock Exchange since it attracts many of the global players in this industry. Most Indian IPOs that raise more than $125 million include a Rule 144A component that enables some funding from qualified institutional buyers in the United States.

In 2007, both the Mumbai Stock Exchange and the National Stock Exchange became 20% owned by foreign investors that included NYSE Euronext, Deutsche Bourse, and the Singapore Exchange. The resulting sharing of management and regulatory practices has facilitated many improvements in these large Indian exchanges. India's growing GDP and high savings rates of approximately 35% have made a huge pool of investible funds available.

During 2015, total Indian household savings allocated to equities was less than 2% (compared to 45% in the United States). The proportion of retail investors in India's equity markets is strikingly low. Less than 1.5% of the population invests in stocks, compared with almost 10% in China and 18% in the United States. Approximately 70% of the Indian stock market is controlled by foreign institutional investors, who between 2009 and 2015 made net purchases of more than $50 billion. In the same period, domestic investors made net sales of $16 billion. This is an interesting dichotomy because India's equity markets achieved a return of 17% compounded annually during the 10 years ending in 2015, which is about twice the return that was paid during this period from bank deposits, which hold most of the country's household savings. The proportion of retail investment in India's stock markets dropped significantly during these years for a number of reasons, but the biggest issue may have been the country's weak IPO market. During 2003 through 2014, of the 394 IPOs that were launched, only 164 were trading over their offer price at the end of this period, and so 60% of investments in this sector lost money over a decade.

There's also a lingering perception that India's stock markets are controlled by a small number of participants, and there have been several high-profile scams. While India's stock market regulators have been fairly effective in rooting out bad practices, confidence still lags. Also, India's dominant family-run companies, as well as listed public sector companies, have not offered enough of their stock to the public. Many companies have been unwilling to comply with the requirement that at least a quarter of shares be publicly held.

Hedge funds, private equity, and venture capital firms have all invested in pre-IPO companies in India and these firms have been the key driver for the country's IPO market in recent years. International investor interest in smaller Indian companies should continue to grow following the government's announcement that any fund that is regulated in its home country is welcome to invest in India.

China's Initial Public Offering Market

During 2007, Greater China led the world in both IPO funds raised ($66 billion) and number of transactions (259). Proceeds raised that year were almost twice the $34 billion raised in the US IPO market. Under the government's new policy of promoting Shanghai's stock exchange, about two-thirds of funds raised in Shanghai were H-share issues (first-time domestic IPOs by China's biggest companies which had previously listed in Hong Kong). In addition, many mid-sized IPOs were listed in mainland China, with an average deal size of $255 million. The top four Chinese industries by funds raised during 2007 were financial services, industrials, real estate, and metals and mining. The largest ever Chinese IPO was a $22 billion offering from ICBC during 2006: the IPO raised $16 billion in Hong Kong and another $6 billion in mainland China through a dual-listed transaction. This even eclipsed the largest ever US IPO, which was an offering by VISA that raised proceeds of $19.6 billion during 2008. Similar to most IPO markets in the world, Chinese IPO activity declined in 2008 to 97 deals, accounting for $17 billion. In 2009, IPO activity rose to $51 billion (159 transactions) and soared in 2010 with a total volume of almost $130 billion and 440 individual transactions. The Hong Kong Stock Exchange, the only Chinese exchange fully open to foreign investors, raised $57 billion during 2010. This exchange benefited from Chinese companies going public and also from foreign issuers that choose to establish a listing easily accessible to Chinese investors. The most prominent example of this was RUSAL, the world's largest aluminum producer. Companies from Mainland China often went public on both the stock exchange in Hong Kong and the Shanghai or Shenzhen exchanges. In 2011, Chinese exchanges accounted for the vast majority of IPOs in the world, raising over $77 billion, accounting for 41% of global IPO activity. After dropping to $43.4 billion in IPO proceeds during 2014, the Chinese IPO market saw 381 transactions during 2015, with total proceeds raised of $58.8 billion.

Mainland Chinese companies listed on the Shanghai Stock Exchange (A-shares) have historically traded at a premium to Mainland Chinese companies listed on the Hong Kong Stock Exchange (H-shares). This is often true for the same company that lists both A-shares and H-shares. An index was launched in 2007 (the Hang Seng China AH Premium Index) to track the price disparity between A-shares and B-shares of dual-listed companies. The premium tracked by this index has been as high as over 100%. The reason for this anomaly is because of strict capital controls in China that create a supply and demand imbalance. Although the wealth of individuals in China has grown rapidly, capital controls prevent average Chinese investors, who have a very limited range of companies that they can invest in within Mainland China, from investing in shares in Hong Kong or in any non-China market overseas. As a result, the limited numbers of investment opportunities available to Mainland Chinese investors are bid up through heavy demand. The Chinese government recently allowed Mainland Chinese individuals to purchase H-shares (Red Chips) for the first time, which has reduced the price disparity between Hong Kong–listed and Shanghai-listed Chinese companies.

Historically there have been a number of overseas Chinese listings. However, as part of an effort to develop the Shanghai Stock Exchange into an international financial center, the Chinese government passed provisions in 2006 that made it more difficult for Chinese companies to list anywhere outside of the Mainland. Only a limited number of domestic companies may be allowed to dual list in China and on an international exchange, and the process for approval is not very transparent. During 2007, the Chinese e-commerce company Alibaba was the first major Asian technology company not to list on NASDAQ (which historically receives the majority of listings from overseas technology companies). Alibaba achieved a very high PE multiple when it raised $1.7 billion through a listing solely on the Hong Kong exchange. In 2009, China decided to allow qualified foreign companies to float shares and issue GDRs on the Chinese exchange.

Compared with the mainland exchanges, the Hong Kong exchange offers the advantages of better access to global capital, greater brand recognition, higher corporate governance standards, and less volatility. While this exchange caters to foreign investors and settles in HK dollars, the Shanghai and Shenzhen exchanges focus on local retail investors, operate under an exchange control regime, and use the renminbi as the settlement currency. As a result, the Hong Kong and mainland exchanges are not fully comparable and neither is in a dominant position.

Private Chinese companies that are incorporated offshore can choose where to list their shares (other than in Mainland China). Usually, they prefer to list in Hong Kong to access global institutional investors and include Regulation S or Rule 144A provisions to access European and US institutional markets. Smaller private Chinese companies that are incorporated offshore usually consider listing in Singapore or on London's AIM market. Because of the provisions passed in 2006, Chinese companies incorporated offshore need to receive approvals from a number of Chinese regulatory agencies, including preapproval to list from China's securities regulatory body, before they can list on a foreign exchange.

AMERICAN DEPOSITORY RECEIPT

An ADR represents US investor ownership of non-US company shares. ADRs are issued by US depositary banks and deposited with a custodian (an agent of the depositary bank) in the country of issuance. An ADR represents the right for an investor to obtain the non-US shares held by the bank (although in practice investors usually never receive the shares). ADRs are priced in US dollars and pay dividends in US dollars. Although convenient for investors, this results in currency risk embedded in the security. Individual shares of a non-US company represented by an ADR are called American Depositary Shares (ADS).

ADR investors can obtain ADRs by either purchasing them on a US stock exchange or by purchasing the non-US shares in their original market of issuance and then (1) depositing them with a bank in exchange for a new ADR or (2) swapping the shares for existing ADRs.

Investment banks are actively involved in helping non-US companies list their shares in the United States in the form of ADRs. Foreign companies utilize the ADR program to raise capital, increase liquidity, and expand US market awareness of the company. Sometimes issuers also use ADRs as an acquisition currency.

An ADR that trades in the US market is priced based on the non-US company's share price in their home market. This price is constantly adjusted for changing FX spot rates and so there is a high degree of volatility in ADR prices. ADR prices are also impacted by home country accounting, legal and political differences. Although most non-US companies provide GAAP-based financial information, caution is necessary because of the use of estimates, uncertain tax implications, and other adjustments that are unique to the home country.

ADRs are registered with the SEC through Form F-6 based on certain exemptions that are available to qualified non-US companies.

A GDR is similar to an ADR except that a GDR is offered in two or more markets outside the non-US issuer's home country. A number of other depositary instruments exist as well, such as EuroDRs, which trade within the Euro zone and represent ownership of shares in a company headquartered outside of the Euro zone, and SDRs, which trade within Singapore and represent ownership of shares in a company headquartered outside of Singapore.

INTERNATIONAL FINANCIAL REPORTING STANDARDS

During 2002, the European Union agreed that all listed companies within Europe should report using one financial reporting framework, called International Financial Reporting Standards (IFRS). IFRS, finally adopted in Europe in 2005, has become the key contender to be the global financial reporting language. Canada, India, Brazil, China, Korea, and Japan are expected to either adopt or converge to IFRS, and when this occurs, approximately 65% of Fortune 500 companies will be reporting their financial results under IFRS. The SEC has announced that foreign private issuers preparing their financial statements in accordance with IFRS will no longer have to include reconciliation to US GAAP. It is now likely that the SEC will also adopt IFRS as a standard financial reporting framework for US companies. Although there is strong global acceptance of IFRS, some believe that US GAAP is the gold standard, and that a certain level of quality will be lost with full acceptance of IFRS. Furthermore, some US companies that do not have significant customers or operations outside the US resist IFRS because they do not have a market incentive to prepare IFRS financial statements and believe that the significant costs associated with adopting IFRS outweigh the benefits.

A remaining complication with IFRS relates to the fact that, although IFRS applies to listed (public) companies, it does not apply in some countries to unlisted companies. As a result, unlisted companies must use their national standards, and not IFRS, when preparing financial statements. For example, in Germany, listed companies prepare their financial statements in accordance with IFRS, but unlisted companies prepare their financial statements in accordance with German GAAP. Therefore, if an unlisted German company initiates an IPO, the company may have to spend considerable resources to convert its financial information from local GAAP to IFRS.

Despite the initial conversion expense, one global financial reporting language means that the cost of doing business across jurisdictions becomes lower, transparency and comparability increase, and global capital raising initiatives become more compelling. The end result is improved efficiency in global capital markets, lower costs of capital, and enhanced shareholder value. IFRS will enable a harmonization of international regulations and will allow international investors to make more informed decisions, resulting in an expansion of capital available for the world's capital raisers.

Until the Securities and Exchange Commission issues a rule allowing or requiring US public companies to adopt IFRS, companies must continue to prepare their financial statements under US GAAP. The timeline for conversion is uncertain and there remain a number of significant hurdles to overcome before the US joins most of the rest of the world in adopting IFRS.

INTERNATIONAL INVESTORS

Sovereign Wealth Funds (SWFs) have become a major source of funding for international capital raising. Assets under management of SWFs now exceed $6 trillion, and there is an additional amount of more than $7 trillion held in other sovereign investment vehicles, such as pension reserve funds, development funds, and state-owned corporations' funds, as well as more than $8 trillion in other official foreign exchange reserves. As a result, governments of SWFs have control over a pool of funds in excess of $20 trillion. SWFs are significant participants in the global M&A market, investing more than $50 billion in 2015 transactions. These deals involved more than 100 investments, including large corporate, infrastructure, and real estate transactions. Some state-owned wealth funds had come under domestic pressure after losing an estimated $80 billion at the height of the financial crisis by investing in troubled banks. The surge in recent SWF M&A has resulted from increasing confidence as markets have improved, the need to diversify from previous financial institution investments as these investments have run their course, and a build-up of expertise as the funds have hired outside M&A expertise and bolstered internal training. Most large investment banks actively meet with SWFs in an effort to complete transactions with buyers who can write large checks.

Despite their deep pockets, some governments have restricted SWF investment in key companies. For example, Germany prevented a Russian SWF fund from making a major investment in Deutsche Telekom. In an effort to foster closer and more cooperative relationships, the United States signed agreements with Abu Dhabi and Singapore that established a basic code of conduct for SWFs and the countries in which they invest. One of the major principles established in this agreement was the idea of investment decisions driven solely on commercial grounds and not geopolitical motives. Until similar actions are adopted worldwide to resolve these largely political considerations, the long-term impact of SWFs on the global equity (and M&A) markets is difficult to predict. The largest SWFs are listed in Exhibit 8.8.

EXHIBIT 8.8 LARGEST SOVEREIGN WEALTH FUNDS

		Sovereign Wealth Funds Rankings - December 2015 $ in billions			
Rank	Country	Fund	Assets	Inception	Origin
1	Norway	Government Pension Fund - Global	$ 824.9	1990	Oil
2	UAE - Abu Dhabi	Abu Dhabi Investment Authority	773.0	1976	Oil
3	China	China Investment Corporation	746.7	2007	Non-Commodity
4	Saudi Arabia	SAMA Foreign Holdings	668.6	N/A	Oil
5	Kuwait	Kuwait Investment Authority	592.0	1953	Oil
6	China	SAFE Investment Company	547.0	1997	Non-Commodity
7	China - Hong Kong	Hong Kong Monetary Authority Investment Portfolio	417.9	1993	Non-Commodity
8	Singapore	Government of Singapore Investment Corporation	344.0	1981	Non-Commodity
9	Qatar	Qatar Investment Authority	256.0	2005	Oil & Gas
10	China	National Social Security Fund	236.0	2000	Non-Commodity
11	Singapore	Temasek Holdings	193.6	1974	Non-Commodity
12	UAE - Abu Dhabi	Investment Corporation of Dubai	183.0	2006	Non-Commodity
13	UAE - Abu Dhabi	Abu Dhabi Investment Council	110.0	2007	Oil
14	Australia	Australian Future Fund	95.0	2006	Non-Commodity
15	Kazakhstan	Samruk-Kazyna JSC	85.1	2008	Non-Commodity
16	South Korea	Korea Investment Corporation	84.7	2005	Non-Commodity
17	Kazakhstan	Kazakhstan National Fund	77.0	2000	Oil
18	Russia	National Welfare Fund	73.5	2008	Oil
19	UAE - Abu Dhabi	International Petroleum Investment Company	66.3	1984	Oil
20	UAE - Abu Dhabi	Mubadala Development Company	66.3	2002	Oil
21	Libya	Libyan Investment Authority	66.0	2006	Oil
22	Russia	Reserve Fund	65.7	2008	Oil
23	Iran	National Development Fund of Iran	62.0	2011	Oil & Gas
24	US - Alaska	Alaska Permanent Fund	53.9	1976	Oil
25	Algeria	Revenue Regulation Fund	50.0	2000	Oil & Gas

* Assets for SAFE Investment Company is a best guess estimation

Source: Sovereign Wealth Fund Institute

International Capital Requirements

A key part of bank regulation is to make sure that banks hold enough capital to ensure continuation of a safe and efficient market and are able to survive foreseeable problems. The principal international effort to establish global capital requirements has been the Basel Committee on Banking Supervision, which published the Basel Accords. Their purpose is to impose a framework on banks for holding and calculating capital. Based on the Accords, banks must determine capital ratios and capital adequacy. In 1988, the Committee introduced a capital measurement system commonly referred to as Basel I, which was replaced in 2004 by Basel II, a much more complicated capital determination framework, which was followed after the 2008 global financial crisis by Basel III, which is phased in through 2019. One of the key bank ratios is the capital ratio, which represents the ratio of a bank's capital to its risk weighted assets. Weights are defined by risk-sensitivity ratios, which are calculated based on the Accords. Basel II requires that the total capital ratio must be no lower than 8%. However, each country has a slightly different way of calculating bank capital, which creates some disparity when comparing banks from different countries.

Examples of national regulators that implement the Accords include the Office of Comptroller of the Currency and the Federal Reserve in the US, the FSA in the UK, OSFI in Canada, and BaFin in Germany. In the European Union, member states have enacted capital requirements based on the Capital Adequacy Directive.

Under the Basel II Accord bank capital has been divided into two "tiers," each with some subdivisions:

Tier 1 Capital

Tier 1 Capital consists largely of shareholders' equity and disclosed reserves. This is the amount paid up to originally purchase the stock (or shares) of the Bank (not the amount those shares are currently trading for in the market), retained profits, subtracting accumulated losses, and other qualifiable Tier 1 capital securities. Shareholders equity and retained earnings are now commonly referred to as "Core" Tier 1 capital, whereas Tier 1 is core Tier 1 together with other qualifying Tier 1 capital securities.

Tier 2 Capital

Tier 2 capital is comprised of undisclosed reserves, revaluation reserves, general provisions, hybrid instruments, and subordinated term debt. Undisclosed reserves result when a bank has made a profit, but the profit has not appeared in normal retained profits or in general reserves. A revaluation reserve generally relates to reappraising assets held on the bank's books that has increased in value. A general provision is created when a company is aware that a loss has occurred, but is not certain of the exact nature of that loss. Hybrid debt instruments are financings that combine certain characteristics of equity as well as debt. They can be included in supplementary capital if they are able to support losses on an ongoing basis without triggering liquidation, sometimes even if the financing carries a debt interest obligation as long as it can be converted into equity capital in the future. Subordinated debt usually has a maturity of at least 10 years and ranks senior to Tier 1 capital, but subordinate to senior debt, and requires other structural enhancements.

The Basel Committee is the primary global standard-setter for the regulation of banks and provides a forum for cooperation on banking supervisory matters. Its mandate is to strengthen the regulation, supervision, and practices of banks worldwide with the purpose of enhancing financial stability. The Committee reports to the Group of Governors and Heads of Supervision (GHOS) and operates out of the Bank for International Settlements in Basel, Switzerland, staffed mainly by professional supervisors on temporary secondment from member institutions.

"Basel III" is a comprehensive set of reform measures developed by the Basel Committee that attempts to improve the banking sector's ability to absorb shocks arising from financial and economic stress; improve risk management and governance; and strengthen banks' transparency and disclosures. The reforms target bank-level regulation, which helps raise the resilience of individual banking institutions to periods of stress and system-wide risks that can build up across the global banking sector over time. Basel III was developed in response to the deficiencies in financial regulation revealed by the financial crisis of 2008. Basel III is intended to strengthen bank capital requirements by increasing bank liquidity and decreasing bank leverage. Unlike Basel I and Basel II, which focus primarily on the level of bank loss reserves that banks are required to hold, Basel III focuses primarily on the risk of a run on the bank, requiring differing levels of reserves for different forms of bank deposits and other borrowings. Therefore, Basel III does not, for the most part, supersede Basel I and II, but works in companion.

In the United States, during October 2013, the Federal Reserve Board of Governors approved an interagency proposal for the US version of the Basel Committee on Banking supervision (BCBS)'s Liquidity Coverage Ratio (LCR). The ratio applies to certain US banks and other systemically important financial institutions.

The LCR proposal by the United States is more challenging than BCBS's version, especially for larger bank holding companies because it requires high-quality liquid assets (HQLA) that can be quickly liquidated to meet liquidity needs over a short period of time. Banks with more than $10 billion in assets must meet a ratio test based on a numerator that is the value of HQLA and a denominator that equals total net cash outflows over a specified stress period (total expected cash outflows less total expected cash inflows).

Large Bank Holding Companies (BHC) with over $250 billion in consolidated assets in on-balance sheet foreign exposure, and systemically important, nonbanking financial institutions must hold enough HQLA to cover 30 days of net cash outflow based on the peak cumulative amount within the 30-day period. Regional firms with between $50 and $250 billion in assets are subject to a "modified" LCR at the (BHC) level only, requiring enough HQLA to cover 21 days of net cash outflow. The net cash outflow parameters are 70% of those applicable to the larger institutions and do not include the requirement to calculate the peak cumulative outflows. Smaller BHCs with under $50 billion have no incremental net cash outflow tests beyond current parameters.

The US Federal Reserve decided to implement substantially all of the Basel III rules and made clear they would apply not only to banks but also to all financial institutions with more than US$50 billion in assets:

Basel III principally focuses on risk-based capital and leverage requirements, liquidity stress tests, single counterparty credit limits to cut credit exposure of a covered financial firm to a single counterparty as a percentage of the firm's regulatory capital, reducing credit exposure between the largest financial companies, implement early remediation requirements to ensure that financial weaknesses are addressed in a timely way, compensation, and capital raising or asset sales.

Convertible Securities and Wall Street Innovation

CONVERTIBLE SECURITIES

Most convertibles[1] are underwritten by large investment banks on a best-efforts basis. This means that the issuer bears share price risk during the period of time when the security is being marketed to prospective investors. In the United States, convertibles are typically sold based on a 144A exemption from registration with the Securities and Exchange Commission (SEC). These securities, if held for 180 days (and assuming the issuer is current in their required SEC filings), can be freely sold, as can be the underlying common shares, without the need for a registration statement. Investors, therefore, have confidence that, when and if they decide to convert into common shares, the shares will be freely tradable.

Hedge Funds and Delta Hedging

The principal investors in most convertible securities are hedge funds that engage in convertible arbitrage strategies. These investors typically purchase the convertible and

[1] For a general description of convertible securities, please refer to Chapter 3.

simultaneously sell short a certain number of the issuer's common shares that underlie the convertible. The number of shares they sell short as a percent of the shares underlying the convertible is approximately equal to the risk-neutral probability at that point in time (as determined by a convertible pricing model that uses binomial option pricing as its foundation) that the investor will eventually convert the security into common shares. This probability is then applied to the number of common shares the convertible security could convert into to determine the number of shares the hedge fund investor should sell short (the "hedge ratio").

As an example, assume a company's share price is $10 at the time of its convertible issuance. A hedge fund purchases a portion of the convertible, which gives the right to convert into 100 common shares of the issuer. If the hedge ratio is 65%, the hedge fund may sell short 65 shares of the issuer's stock on the same date as the convertible purchase. During the life span of the convertible, the hedge fund investor may sell more shares short or buy shares, based on the changing hedge ratio. To illustrate, if 1 month after purchasing the convertible (having established a 65-share short position) the issuer's share price decreases to $9, the hedge ratio may drop from 65% to 60%. To align the hedge ratio with the shares sold short as a percent of shares the investor has the right to convert the security into, the hedge fund investor will need to buy five shares in the open market from other shareholders and deliver those shares to the parties who had lent the shares originally. "Covering" five shares of their short position leaves the hedge fund with a new short position of 60 shares. If the issuer's share price 2 months after issuance increases to $11, the hedge ratio may increase to 70%. In this case, the hedge fund investor may want to be short 70 shares. The investor achieves this position by borrowing 10 more shares and selling them short, which increases the short position from 60 shares to 70 shares. This process of buying shares when the share price drops and selling shares when the share price increases continues until the convertible either converts or matures.

The end result is that the hedge fund investor is generating trading profits throughout the life of the convertible by buying stock to reduce the short position when the issuer's share price drops and borrowing and selling shares short when the issuer's share price increases. This dynamic trading process is called "delta hedging," which is a well-known and consistently practiced strategy by hedge funds. Since hedge funds typically purchase between 60% and 80% of most convertible securities in the public markets, a significant amount of trading in the issuer's stock takes place throughout the life of a convertible security. The purpose of all this trading in the convertible issuer's common stock is to hedge share price risk embedded in the convertible and create trading profits that offset the opportunity cost of purchasing a convertible that has a coupon that is substantially lower than a straight bond from the same issuer with the same maturity.

For hedge funds to invest in convertible securities, there needs to be a substantial amount of the issuer's common shares available for hedge funds to borrow and adequate liquidity in the issuer's stock for hedge funds to buy and sell shares in relation to their delta hedging activity. If there are insufficient shares available to be borrowed or inadequate trading volume in the issuer's stock, a prospective issuer is generally discouraged from issuing a convertible security in the public markets or is required to issue a smaller convertible, because hedge funds may not be able to participate. Alternatively, an issuer could attempt to privately place a convertible with a single nonhedge fund investor. However, it may be impossible to find such an investor, and even if found, the required pricing for the convertible is likely to be disadvantageous for the issuer.

When a new convertible security is priced in the public capital markets, it is generally the case that the terms of the security imply a theoretical value between 102% and 105% of face value, based on a convertible pricing model. The convertible is usually sold at a price of 100% to investors, and is therefore underpriced, compared to its theoretical value. This practice provides an incentive for hedge funds to purchase the security, knowing that, by delta hedging their investment, they should be able to extract trading profits at least equal to the difference between the theoretical value and "par" (100%). For a public market convertible with atypical characteristics (e.g., an oversized issuance relative to market capitalization, an issuer with limited stock trading volume, or an issuer with limited stock borrow availability), hedge fund investors normally require an even higher theoretical value (relative to par) as an inducement to invest.

Convertible pricing models incorporate binomial trees to determine the theoretical value of convertible securities. These models consider the following factors that influence the theoretical value: current common stock price; anticipated volatility of the common stock return during the life of the convertible security; risk-free interest rate; the company's stock borrow cost and common stock dividend yield; the company's credit risk; maturity of the convertible security; and the convertible security's coupon or dividend rate and payment frequency, conversion premium, and length of call protection, among other inputs.

Zero-Coupon Convertibles

A zero-coupon convertible (ZCC) is similar to a coupon-paying convertible except, instead of paying interest coupons each year, the issuer increases the principal amount of the convertible over time by an amount equal to the unpaid coupon, creating an "accretion" of the bond. Accordingly, as is the case with a zero-coupon bond that does not have a conversion feature, the principal amount increases each year until the maturity of the bond. Notwithstanding the zero-coupon feature, the conversion premium, which determines the underlying shares the security can convert into, is approximately the same for both a coupon-paying convertible and a ZCC of the same issuer (assuming identical maturity and call provisions).[2]

Given the fact that there is approximately the same number of underlying shares for a ZCC and a coupon-paying convertible, and ZCCs' unpaid coupons are "paid" by increasing the principal amount of the convertible, why might a prospective issuer prefer a ZCC to a coupon-paying convertible? The reasons include the following:

1. A US issuer is able to receive tax deductions in relation to the annual accretion of the convertible, creating a positive cash flow bond financing (no cash payments for coupons, but tax deductions equal to the deductions the issuer would receive if a coupon-paying convertible had been issued).
2. If the convertible converts, the tax deductions received based on the annual accretion are not reimbursed to the Internal Revenue Service (IRS) even though the coupons are, in

---

[2] Depending on the credit rating of the issuer, a ZCC might have a slightly lower conversion premium to compensate investors for greater credit risk associated with not receiving annual coupon payments.

effect, never paid because the accreted bond price is never paid by the issuer (although this tax treatment is also available for a coupon-paying convertible).

3. There is a lower probability of conversion on the portion of the convertible that is not purchased by hedge funds[3] because an unhedged investor will usually (assuming no credit or illiquidity concerns) only convert into common shares if the value of those shares exceeds the principal cash redemption value of the bond's accreting principal amount, which increases each year.

A ZCC is, therefore, a positive cash flow bond financing with a lower chance of earnings per share (EPS) dilution since conversion is somewhat less likely. Given these benefits, why don't all potential convertible issuers complete ZCC transactions? One reason is that based on tax law symmetry, since issuers receive tax credits based on the accretion, investors must pay income taxes in relation to this annual accretion (or "phantom income"). As a result, typically only nontaxable investors will consider ZCC investments. Another reason is that because coupons are accreted into the bond principal amount instead of paid annually, investors have more credit exposure to a ZCC issuer at maturity. Depending on the issuer, investors may require a small economic benefit as compensation for this risk (such as an up to 1/8% higher yield compared to a conventional coupon-paying convertible or, as described in Footnote 2, a slightly lower conversion premium).

Mandatory Convertibles

Unlike an optionally converting convertible where the investor has the right, but not the obligation, to convert their bond holding into a predetermined number of the issuer's common shares, a mandatory convertible requires conversion. In an optionally converting convertible, the decision to convert at maturity is based on the company's share price. If the share price does not exceed the conversion price, the investor will require the company to pay off the convertible's principal amount with cash at maturity. As a result, from a credit rating agency perspective, on its issuance date, an optionally converting convertible is considered to be similar to debt. In a mandatory convertible, however, because an investor does not hold the right to demand cash repayment in the future (shares will always be delivered instead), credit rating agencies consider this security to be similar to equity. Because of this, a company seeking to issue equity may consider a mandatory convertible as an alternative to a common share issuance. Issuing a mandatory convertible has the benefit of receiving almost the same equity content from rating agencies as from a common share issuance but with fewer shares delivered to investors if the company's share price is higher on the maturity date (which is usually 3 years following issuance).

---

[3] Hedge funds generally do not convert their holding into common stock based on the value of shares (unless this value has increased significantly) since they have delta hedged their position by selling short a percentage of the shares they can convert into.

A mandatory convertible has, in effect, a floating conversion price that changes based on the company's share price at maturity. The formula for determining the shares delivered at maturity is as follows:

1. If, at maturity, the issuing company's share price (Maturity Price) is at or below the share price on the convertible issuance date (Issuance Price), the shares delivered to investors will be identical to the shares that would have been delivered if common shares had been issued instead of the convertible (Shares Issued).
2. If, at maturity, the company's share price has risen but is less than the conversion price (usually set at 20%–30% above the share price on the issuance date), the number of shares delivered to investors is equal to: Shares Issued × Issuance Price/Maturity Price.
3. If, at maturity, the company's share price exceeds the conversion price, the number of shares delivered to investors is equal to: Shares Issued × Issuance Price/conversion price (see the Freeport–McMoRan (FM) Case to review application of the floating conversion price formula).

Suppose, for example, that company ABC is seeking to raise $100 million. If ABC decides to raise the funds through a $100 million mandatory convertible that has a conversion price of $31.25 (25% conversion premium) when its common stock price is $25, ABC will be obligated to deliver 3.2 million shares at maturity if its share price equals or exceeds the conversion price at maturity ($100 million/$31.25 = 3.2 million shares). This is also the same number of shares that would be delivered if the convertible had been an optionally converting convertible with the same conversion price. If the company had decided to issue common shares when the stock was at $25 per share instead of a mandatory convertible, it would have had to sell 4 million shares to raise $100 million. Assuming ABC's share price at the maturity of the mandatory is equal to or higher than the conversion price, the common share issuance would have resulted in the delivery of 25% more shares compared to a mandatory convertible offering of the same issuance size. If, however, ABC's share price is $25 or lower at maturity of the mandatory convertible, the company will deliver 4 million shares, which is the same number of shares that would have been issued in a common share offering. If the share price is between $25 and $31.25 at maturity, the company will deliver somewhere between 3.2 million shares and 4 million shares, depending on the share price.

Despite the certainty of eventual conversion into common stock, from the perspective of issuers, investors, and rating agencies, a comparison between a mandatory convertible and common shares is somewhat complex. For example, the equity content for one form of mandatory convertible is less than the equity content for a straight common stock offering if the issuer wishes to receive tax benefits from the mandatory convertible issuance (see details in the following paragraph). In addition, the dividend associated with a mandatory convertible is higher than the issuer's common stock dividend. This is because, although mandatory convertible investors bear the same downside risk as common share investors, they do not have the same upside share price benefit (the number of shares received at conversion is lower than the shares that would be received in a common stock offering if the mandatory convertible issuer's share price is higher on the maturity date than on the issuance date).

Mandatory convertibles are issued in two forms. The first one is a Unit Structure, which has two components: (1) 30-year subordinated debt and (2) a 3-year stock purchase contract issued by the company to the same investors, which results in a variable share delivery mechanism after 3 years. For US regulated banks, the Unit Structure has an additional layer, whereby the subordinated debt is issued to a trust vehicle and a simultaneous subordinated trust stake is issued to investors by the trust (including a provision for remarketing the trust stake to other investors after 3 years). See Exhibit 9.1 for an overview of a Unit Structure mandatory convertible issued by Marshall and Ilsley (M&I). The second form of a mandatory convertible is a Non-Unit Structure, which provides for issuance of preferred stock and a variable common share delivery mechanism in 3 years that is linked to the issuer's share price at delivery and with simultaneous retirement of the preferred shares once common shares are delivered (see Exhibit 9.2).

Unit Structure

A Unit Structure mandatory convertible is described in Exhibit 9.1.

M&I's security is divided into two components: a trust, which purchases M&I subordinated debt and a stock purchase contract, which requires investors to make a payment in 3 years to receive M&I stock. The subordinated bonds have a 30-year maturity, and they reprice after 3 years when investment bank underwriters of the convertible conduct an auction to sell the trust stake held by investors to new investors. The yield on the trust stake

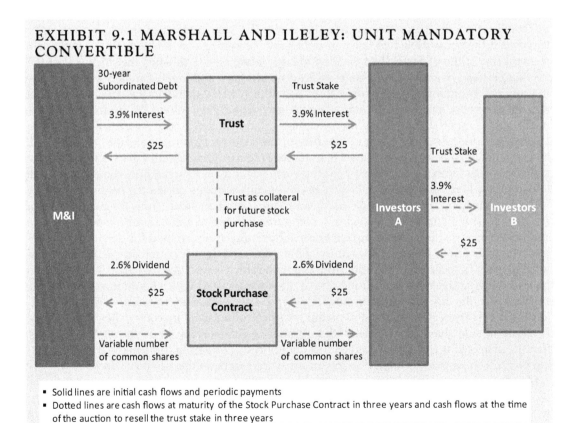

EXHIBIT 9.1 MARSHALL AND ILELEY: UNIT MANDATORY CONVERTIBLE

- Solid lines are initial cash flows and periodic payments
- Dotted lines are cash flows at maturity of the Stock Purchase Contract in three years and cash flows at the time of the auction to resell the trust stake in three years

Source: McDonald, Robert L. *Derivatives Markets*. Prentice Hall, 2006. Auction added by David Stowell.

will be reset at the time of the auction so that it will trade at par. The original investors who purchased the trust stake also enter into the stock purchase contract, which requires them to pay cash for common shares in 3 years. The cash amount payable under the stock purchase contract is exactly equal to the cash that the same investors receive from auctioning the trust stake in 3 years. As a result, investors achieve the same risk/return profile that exists for other mandatory convertible investors, as described above and under Exhibit 9.2 below (for Non-Unit Mandatory Convertibles).

Depending on the terms, the Unit Structure provides a company with equity credit of 50% or 75% from rating agencies. The issuer also receives tax deductions on the interest payments associated with the subordinated debt (equivalent to approximately 60% of the annual cash payment obligation of the company, with the remaining 40% relating to dividends paid pursuant to the stock purchase contract). The Unit Structure also receives favorable accounting treatment that results in less EPS dilution on the date of issuance compared to a common stock offering (based on the treasury stock method of accounting).

Non-Unit Structure

A Non-Unit Mandatory Convertible Structure is preferred by companies that either cannot benefit from tax deductions and/or want even higher (up to 100%) equity content. A description of this structure is in Exhibit 9.2.

In 2007, FM issued a $2.9 billion Non-Unit Structure mandatory convertible underwritten by joint bookrunners J.P. Morgan and Merrill Lynch. FM also simultaneously issued $2.9 billion of common equity, generating total proceeds for the company of $5.8 billion. These transactions, in conjunction with $17.5 billion in debt financing, funded the cash portion of FM's acquisition of Phelps Dodge, which created the world's largest publicly traded copper company.

EXHIBIT 9.2 NON-UNIT MANDATORY CONVERTIBLE

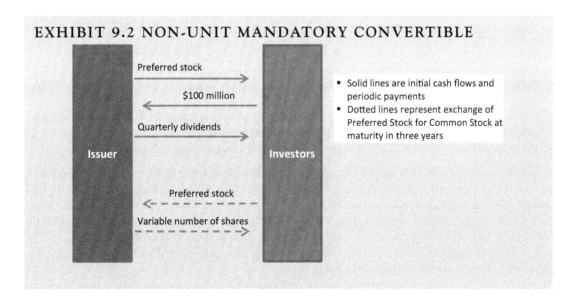

The mandatory convertible financing achieved a number of objectives for FM:

1. It enabled the company to obtain a larger equity financing than would have been available from sale of common stock only due to limited demand for the company's common shares beyond $2.9 billion (most of the mandatory convertible investors were funds that would not have purchased the common stock).
2. It provided FM with almost 100% equity credit for the offering, even though common shares would only be issued after 3 years, upon the mandatory conversion of the convertible from its initial preferred share form.
3. For the same amount of proceeds raised, there would be fewer common shares delivered to investors upon conversion in 3 years compared to the simultaneous common stock offering, assuming FM's share price rises during this period, which provides a permanent benefit to EPS reporting.

FM chose the Non-Unit Structure mandatory convertible for its ability to maximize equity credit and was willing to give up tax deductions that are only available in the Unit Structure because the company operated principally outside of the United States and therefore had no US tax obligations. By contrast, M&I chose the Unit Structure to take advantage of tax deductions, even though this structure provided less equity credit.

The FM mandatory convertible was issued in the form of 28.75 million preferred shares offered at $100 per share, with a 6.75% dividend and a 3-year maturity. The preferred shares were mandatorily convertible into FM's common shares based on the following schedule:

If FM's share price at maturity is

- less than or equal to $61.25, the investor receives 1.6327 FM shares
- between $61.25 and $73.50, the investor receives $100/current FM share price
- equal to or greater than $73.50, the investor receives 1.3605 FM shares

The payoff graph for delivery of FM shares as a function of the company's share price on the maturity date in 3 years is shown in Exhibit 7 of the FM case.

This mandatory convertible, at maturity, provided investors with the following:

1. The same number of FM common shares in 3 years as they would have received by buying the company's common stock on the date of the simultaneous offering (with the purchase price in both cases at $61.25), assuming FM's stock price is equal to or less than $61.25 in 3 years.
2. No participation in the upside of any FM share price appreciation in 3 years if FM's stock price falls in the range of $61.25–$73.50 during this period.
3. Participation in 1/1.2 (83%) of the appreciation in FM share price above $73.50 in 3 years.

Investors in the FM convertible assumed all of the downside risks of owning FM stock over a 3-year period but did not participate in the first 20% appreciation (from $61.25 to $73.40) and participated in only 83% of the appreciation above 20%. As a result, they had to be compensated for the opportunity cost of buying the mandatory convertible compared to purchasing common stock. Compensation was paid, in effect, through 6.75% p.a. dividend payments for 3 years, which was 5.15% p.a. above FM's common stock dividend of 1.6% p.a. at the time of issuance.

Comparison of Mandatory Convertibles Issued by M&I and Freeport–McMoRan

There are both differences and similarities between FM's Non-Unit Structure and M&I's Unit Structure. Both securities pay annual cash flows that are greater than the underlying stock's dividend. M&I's security pays an annual cash flow of 6.5% (2.6% dividend under the stock purchase contract and 3.9% coupon for the subordinated bond component, which was tax deductible for M&I), and FM's security pays 6.75% in annual dividends. Both securities have a similar common share payoff structure at maturity. However, M&I's security was divided into two components: a trust, which contained M&I subordinated bonds and a stock purchase contract, which required investors to make a payment in 3 years to receive M&I stock. The subordinated bonds have a 30-year maturity, and reprice after 3 years so that they trade at par. This enabled investors to sell the subordinated bonds to other investors through an auction conducted by investment banks, receiving the exact amount of cash from this sale necessary for investors to purchase M&I's shares pursuant to the stock purchase contract.

M&I (unlike FM) had US tax obligations, and so chose the Unit Structure over the Non-Unit Structure because of the tax deductions received on the 3.9% coupons. Under the Unit Structure, tax-deductibility arises in part because 30-year debt is issued rather than preferred shares. The debt is remarketed to new investors at the end of a 3-year period (when common stock is delivered under the stock purchase agreement). The detached nature of the debt and stock repurchase agreement are evidenced by separate documents. Although the investor must pledge the debt against their obligation to purchase M&I stock in 3 years, the investor can substitute treasury securities as collateral. As a result, the two documents and related obligations operate independently.

WALL STREET INNOVATION

As evidenced by the complexity of convertible securities, investment banks are creative in achieving the varying objectives of both their issuing and investing clients. New forms of securities must take into account not only client economic priorities, but also consider legal, tax, accounting, and political issues. All large investment banks have new product development teams that work with internal and outside advisors, including lawyers, accountants, tax experts, and regulatory experts. This is a very time consuming and complicated process and often includes false starts. Significant resources can be invested in creating a new structure only to conclude at the end that, although it resolves economic, legal, and tax issues, there is a disadvantageous tax outcome. Or if the tax outcome is acceptable, sometimes regulatory or accounting difficulties may arise. The challenge is making sure all potential issues have been considered and resolved before presenting new products to clients.

When developing new products, a firm must also take its reputation into consideration. Even if all of the key areas are thoroughly analyzed, and all issues seem to be resolved, any negative press coverage of the new product (or the client involved in the new product) can be problematic for the bank. In addition, despite strong favorable opinions provided by the bank's legal, accounting, tax, and other advisors, regulators may disagree in the future with one or more of these opinions, creating unforeseen complications for the product. As a result, all banks have a very careful vetting process where committees must approve any new product prior to its launch. Even when all advisors are supportive, clients are interested in the product, and considerable resources have been used to develop it, these committees may veto the product if there are reputational concerns.

Although some of the most innovative products are developed in the convertible securities market, there have been many other successful products developed in other areas, including structured finance, municipal securities, pension funds, M&A, and others. Two examples of investment banking product innovations are discussed in the following sections: Nikkei put warrants and accelerated share repurchase (ASR) programs.

NIKKEI PUT WARRANTS

The Nikkei put warrants program, developed by Goldman Sachs and other firms, exemplifies an investment banking innovation that not only meets the global needs of both issuing and investing clients but also involves principal risk-taking by investment banks.

In 1990, put warrants on the Nikkei 225 stock index (Nikkei Puts) were sold in the United States for the first time. Nikkei Puts enabled US retail investors to receive a cash payment if the Japanese stock market fell. This market had increased by almost 50% every year in the preceding 4 years, reaching its historical high of 38,915.90 on the last trading day of 1989, 2 weeks prior to the launch of a Nikkei Put offering in the US public market by Goldman Sachs on January 12, 1990. By June of that year, the Japanese stock market had crashed, dropping by more than 50%.

Put warrants (essentially the same as put options) give their holders the right, but not the obligation, to sell an underlying asset by a certain date for a predetermined price. In the case of Nikkei Puts, a decline in the Japanese stock market would increase the value of Nikkei Puts, and the investor would receive a cash payment equal to the difference between the Nikkei 225 stock index market price and the higher predetermined strike price (a cash-settled option). The first Nikkei Puts were listed on the American Stock Exchange and principally underwritten by Goldman Sachs, with the Kingdom of Denmark as the issuer. At the time a private partnership, Goldman Sachs did not have registration capability with the SEC and therefore could not issue the Nikkei Puts directly. The Kingdom of Denmark had the ability to register with the SEC, which enabled them to sell the Nikkei Puts at the request of Goldman Sachs. Simultaneous to selling the puts to US retail investors, the Kingdom of Denmark also entered into a Nikkei Put purchase contract with Goldman Sachs, thereby fully hedging its exposure (see Exhibit 9.3). The proceeds from the Nikkei Put sales exceeded the cost of purchasing the hedge, and so the remaining proceeds were contributed into a Eurobond transaction, which the Kingdom of Denmark simultaneously sold in London through Goldman Sachs, thereby creating low-cost financing.

US companies with registration statements could have been asked to issue the Nikkei Puts, but the unfavorable accounting consequences of matching Nikkei Put purchase and sales contracts precluded their involvement. The Kingdom of Denmark, on the other hand, had no such accounting concerns. Multiple other Nikkei Put transactions took place in the United States during the first half of 1990, until the Japanese government asked investment banks to discontinue these transactions, following the sharp reversal in Japan's stock market. Prior to this shutdown, US investors actively purchased and traded the Nikkei Puts, making them among the most actively traded instruments on the American Stock Exchange. Investors saw the value of their Nikkei Put investment skyrocket as the Japanese stock market crashed (see the Nikkei 225 stock index history in Exhibit 9.4).

EXHIBIT 9.3 NIKKEI PUT WARRANTS

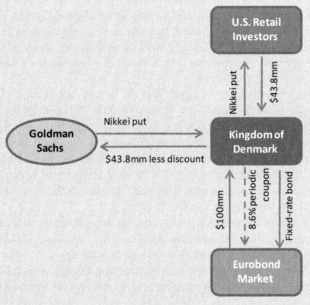

Source: Francis, Jack Clark, William W. Toy and J. Gregg Whittaker. *The Handbook of Equity Derivatives*. John Wiley and Sons, 1999.

EXHIBIT 9.4 NIKKEI PUT WARRANTS: NIKKEI 225 INDEX PERFORMANCE

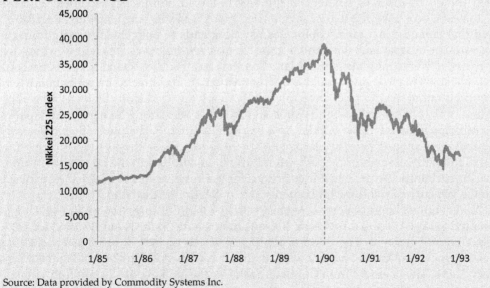

Source: Data provided by Commodity Systems Inc.

The Nikkei Put sales in the United States marked the tail end of a series of transactions arranged by Goldman Sachs in Japan, which also involved the firm's offices and clients in both New York and London. The front end of this story started 2 years earlier in 1988 when Japanese insurance companies purchased hundreds of high-coupon Nikkei-linked bonds from high-quality European issuers. These bonds offered investors above-market coupons in return for accepting the risk of principal loss if the Nikkei 225 Index dropped below a designated level at the maturity of the bonds.

Economically, these bonds can be analyzed as yen-denominated bonds in which the Japanese investor sold an embedded put warrant on the Nikkei 225 Index to the issuer of the bond (see Exhibit 9.5). The issuer of the bond then sold the embedded put warrant to Goldman Sachs (see Exhibit 9.6 and discussion below). A conventional fixed-rate yen bond from an issuer might have carried a coupon of 5%, but Nikkei-linked bonds often had a coupon of at least 7.5%. The amount by which the Nikkei-linked bond coupon exceeded a conventional coupon represented the warrant (option) premium the Japanese investor received for selling the embedded put warrant to the issuer.

If the Nikkei 225 Index dropped below a designated level at maturity (e.g., 32,000 in Exhibit 9.5), the bond's principal amount paid to the Japanese investor decreased. The amount by which it decreased is equivalent to the settlement value for the embedded put warrant. Therefore, if the Nikkei Index's average dropped below the designated level (strike price), the European issuer repaid the original principal amount through two settlements:

1. The reduced amount of principal is paid to the Japanese investor.
2. An amount equal to the difference between the original principal amount of the bond and the reduced payment to the Japanese investor is paid to Goldman Sachs. This difference is equal to the cash settlement value of the put warrant sold to Goldman Sachs.

Japanese investors were obviously bullish on their domestic stock market when they accepted the downside risk inherent in the Nikkei-linked bonds. Beyond their optimism of the domestic economy, regulatory factors also motivated these investments. Regulations required that Japanese insurance companies pay dividends to policyholders only from current investment income and not capital gains from stock holdings. Therefore, while dividends received from equity investments and coupons received from bond investments could be paid out, stock market gains could not. This created an incentive to invest in bonds with high coupons rather than in stock investments with very low dividends (below 1% average).

Because of the Nikkei-linked bonds' higher yield, there was strong demand from Japanese insurance companies for these bonds. As a result, Goldman Sachs (and other investment banks) actively arranged private placements of these bonds for the insurance companies, finding high-quality issuers principally from Europe. In addition to the bond underwriting, the investment banks also arranged transactions for the bond issuers to hedge their exposure to both the yen currency and the high interest rate obligation of the bond.

The Nikkei-linked bond issuers were mostly AAA-rated European banks and sovereigns, who wanted to raise US dollar proceeds at a low interest rate (in the example provided in the exhibits, a 3-year bond with a net coupon of LIBOR-35 basis points). To achieve this objective, the issuer stripped out the Nikkei put warrant that was embedded in the bond and sold it to Goldman Sachs. The payment from Goldman Sachs for the Nikkei put warrant fully compensated the issuer for the difference between the coupon they paid on the Nikkei-linked bonds

EXHIBIT 9.5 NIKKEI PUT WARRANTS: NIKKEI-LINKED BONDS

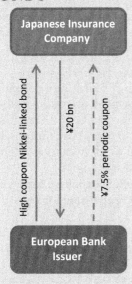

Bond Terms

- Security: high-coupon Nikkei-linked bond
- Maturity: 3 years
- Coupon: 7.50%
- Currency: Japanese Yen
- Redemption payoff structure:
  - If Nikkei 225 Index > 32,000 then Par
  - If Nikkei 225 Index ≤ 32,000 then:

$$\text{Par} \times 1 - \left[\frac{(32{,}000 - \text{Nikkei}) \times 200\%}{32{,}000} \right]$$

Where Nikkei = closing price of the Nikkei 225 Index at maturity. Minimum redemption set at a floor of zero.

Source: Francis, Jack Clark, William W. Toy and J. Gregg Whittaker. *The Handbook of Equity Derivatives*. John Wiley and Sons, 1999.

EXHIBIT 9.6 NIKKEI PUT WARRANTS

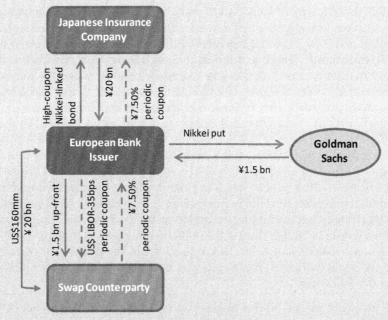

Source: Francis, Jack Clark, William W. Toy and J. Gregg Whittaker. *The Handbook of Equity Derivatives*. John Wiley and Sons, 1999.

(7.5% in the example) and the substantially lower floating rate payment that was their target (LIBOR-35 basis points in the example). In addition, the payment covered the cost of hedging the issuer's currency exposure from yen to US dollars. The issuer was left with a fully hedged US dollar–denominated financing with a coupon that was below their normal borrowing cost (see Exhibit 9.6).

Goldman Sachs' role in the Nikkei-linked bond transaction was manifold:

1. They located investors (Japanese insurance companies) that were interested in yen-denominated bonds that provided a higher-than-market coupon (7.5% in the example) in exchange for accepting principal repayment risk based on downside exposure to the Nikkei Index.
2. They found highly rated issuers from Europe that were willing to accept a complicated financing structure to achieve US dollar fully hedged funding at a below-market interest rate (in the example, approximate annual coupon savings of 35 basis points).
3. They arranged a swap counterparty for the issuer to hedge currency exposure from yen to US dollars, with an up-front payment to the counterparty to compensate for risks and costs associated with the swap.
4. They purchased the Nikkei put warrants embedded in the Nikkei-linked bond from the issuer, paying a price equal to the up-front payment required by the swap counterparty to the issuer.

Goldman Sachs paid a price for the Nikkei put warrants that was considerably below the theoretical value of the warrants, creating potential future profit opportunities. With an approximate 2-year gap between when the first Nikkei-linked bonds were originated (resulting in Nikkei put warrant purchases by Goldman Sachs) and when Nikkei put warrants were sold to US retail investors by the Kingdom of Denmark (after purchasing like-warrants from Goldman Sachs), the investment bank had to manage its exposure to the Japanese stock market. Goldman Sachs did this by buying Japanese stocks or futures on these stocks in amounts equal to a portion of the exposure represented by the purchased Nikkei puts and then "delta hedging" their exposure by buying more shares (or futures) on any future day that the Japanese equity market declined and selling shares (or futures) when the market increased. As a result of this daily delta hedging, Goldman Sachs was able to transform their exposure from Japanese share price exposure to Japanese stock market volatility exposure, which was easier to manage, until the time when the Nikkei put warrants were sold in the US market (see Exhibit 9.7).

By purchasing Nikkei put warrants at a below theoretical market cost from the Nikkei-linked bond issuer and delta hedging this risk position, Goldman Sachs created the opportunity for significant trading profits (buying when stock prices dropped and selling when they increased) that exceeded the Nikkei put warrant purchase cost. Goldman Sachs was able to succeed in its strategy because it had accurately estimated that the future volatility of the Nikkei 225 Index would be higher during the delta hedging period than the implied volatility of the Japanese stock market at the time of the purchase of the Nikkei put warrants.

A summary of the activities of Goldman Sachs in relation to the Nikkei put warrant program includes the following:

1. Investment arranger: placed Nikkei-linked bonds with Japanese insurance company investors and Nikkei put warrants with US retail investors.

EXHIBIT 9.7 NIKKEI PUT WARRANTS

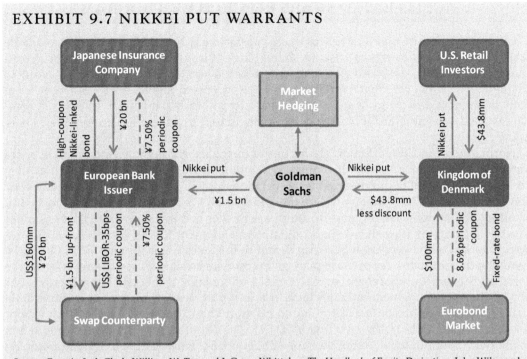

Source: Francis, Jack Clark, William W. Toy and J. Gregg Whittaker. *The Handbook of Equity Derivatives.* John Wiley and Sons, 1999.

2. Financing arranger: raised fully hedged low-cost financings for European issuers of the Nikkei-linked bonds and Eurobonds for the Kingdom of Denmark and other issuers.
3. Swap arranger: developed the strategy for hedging the Nikkei-linked bond and found swap counterparties.
4. Risk manager: acted as principal in pricing the Nikkei put warrants both in Japan and in the United States, delta hedged the Nikkei put warrant risk position, and hedged currency exposure between the yen-denominated Nikkei put warrants purchased and the US dollar–denominated Nikkei put warrants sold.
5. Regulatory catalyst: worked with legal counsel and stock exchange officials to obtain Japanese and US regulatory approvals for the first Nikkei put warrant transaction in the United States.

The Nikkei put warrants transactions created by Goldman Sachs (and several other firms that participated in this effort) offered innovative financing and investing solutions for the firm's issuing and investing clients. By working with its network of offices and clients throughout the world and undertaking considerable principal risks, the investment bank was able to meet client needs while creating significant risk-adjusted profits.

ACCELERATED SHARE REPURCHASE PROGRAM

Corporations must make decisions each quarter regarding how to allocate available cash. One option is to return cash to shareholders through dividends or share repurchases. Historically, dividend payments represented up to 90% of the total payout to shareholders. However, share repurchases have increased significantly and now, cash paid to shareholders from share repurchases exceeds cash paid in dividends, as companies have become more focused on EPS increases as a vehicle to support their share price.

Normally in the United States, shares are repurchased through an open market share repurchase program whereby the company announces through an SEC filing that they have board approval to purchase either a specified number of shares or a specified dollar amount of shares. The company has no obligation, however, to purchase shares, notwithstanding this announcement, and in some cases never completes the purchases (similar to when a company files an S-3 shelf registration statement that covers future securities issuances, but may never issue securities from the registration statement). Assuming the company does initiate a repurchase plan, an investment bank is typically employed as the company's agent to repurchase shares. To take advantage of the safe harbor provisions of SEC Rule 10b-18, which mitigates legal risk in repurchases, the agent must limit daily share purchases (with some exceptions) to no more than 25% of the of the stock's prior 4-week average daily trading volume (ADTV). The result of repurchases is a reduction in the share count in the denominator for EPS reporting. However, with the limitation on daily purchases, it can take more than a year for some companies to purchase the number of shares that the board has authorized, resulting in a slow capture of the EPS benefit from repurchases.

An ASR program is designed to capture the EPS benefit of a repurchase program up-front, rather than waiting for the benefit to be realized over time. This is accomplished by a contract under which a company purchases a large block of its shares from an investment bank at the closing market price on the date of the purchase, with a cash adjustment to follow at the end of the contract (which might be, e.g., 1 year later). The investment bank borrows the shares it sells to the company from existing shareholders, creating a short position, which it covers through daily open market purchases that are limited to 25% of the company's ADTV. Assuming it takes 1 year for the investment bank to purchase enough shares to cover its short position, the total cost for the purchases of shares over this period is determined at the end of the year. If the total purchase cost is higher than the payment received by the investment bank from the short sale of shares to the company 1 year earlier, the company reimburses the investment bank for the difference. If the total purchase cost for the investment bank is less than the payment they received 1 year earlier, the investment bank reimburses the difference to the company. This adjustment amount after 1 year is modified based on the returns that the investment bank achieves from investing cash they received from the company up-front (factoring in a reducing cash position each day as cash is used to purchase shares over the 1-year period). A further modification to the cash adjustment is made to compensate the bank for their service. See Exhibit 9.8 for a summary of the ASR program.

EXHIBIT 9.8 ACCELERATED SHARE REPURCHASE PROGRAM

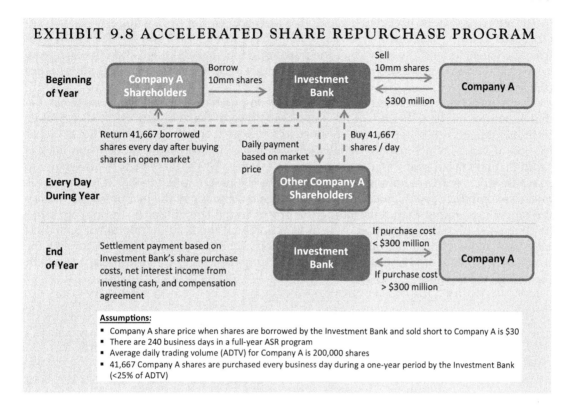

Assumptions:
- Company A share price when shares are borrowed by the Investment Bank and sold short to Company A is $30
- There are 240 business days in a full-year ASR program
- Average daily trading volume (ADTV) for Company A is 200,000 shares
- 41,667 Company A shares are purchased every business day during a one-year period by the Investment Bank (<25% of ADTV)

An ASR program does not create any greater EPS benefit after 1 year than if the company purchased its own shares every day over this period. However, the ASR program accelerates the EPS benefit to the first day of the 1-year period, rather than waiting for the full benefit at the end of the year. This is what motivates some companies to utilize the program. An ASR program also can be linked to equity derivative strategies that create additional potential benefits to the company. For example, call spreads or collars can be included in an ASR program to enable a share repurchasing company to limit the maximum settlement payment they will make at the end of the program.

In addition to creating an earlier EPS benefit, investment banks added an interesting (but short-lived) tax benefit to the ASR, in conjunction with IBM. IBM announced that it had completed a $12.5 billion ASR agreement with three investment banks, under which the company repurchased 118.8 million shares (8% of the company's outstanding shares) at $105.18 per share from the investment banks for immediate delivery to the company. The banks were expected to purchase an equivalent number of IBM shares in the open market during the following 9 months, with an adjustment paid (settlement payment) at the end of this period, as described above.

The repurchases were executed through IBM International Group, a wholly owned subsidiary based in the Netherlands, which used $1 billion of its own cash and an $11.5 billion loan from the banks to fund the balance of the purchase. Principal and interest on the loan were to be paid with cash generated by IBM International Group's non-US operating subsidiaries (see Exhibit 9.9).

As a result of this ASR program, IBM was able to purchase $12.5 billion in stock (immediately improving its EPS) and, at the same time, lower its tax obligations by using funds from its foreign units to repay the loan instead of repatriating these funds to the US repatriation of funds, which usually results in a US tax obligation if the money sent back is profit that was taxed overseas at a lower rate. In essence, IBM's use of their overseas unit to purchase stock, with a simultaneous borrowing by the unit, implied that as IBM's overseas businesses produce profits, these profits would be used to repay the loan raised to finance the repurchase, rather than repatriating the profits to the United States and paying withholding taxes on this repatriation. Assuming a potential repatriation tax rate of 35%, IBM may have reduced their tax bill by approximately $2 billion by applying this rate to the overseas borrowing of $11.5 billion and then reducing the result by an estimated 17% credit for foreign taxes paid.

EXHIBIT 9.9 IBM'S ACCELERATED SHARE REPURCHASE PROGRAM

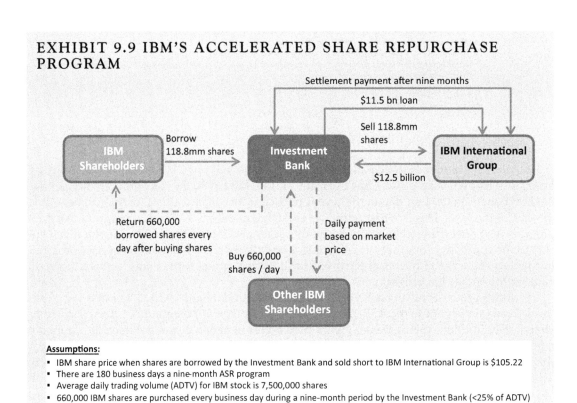

Assumptions:
- IBM share price when shares are borrowed by the Investment Bank and sold short to IBM International Group is $105.22
- There are 180 business days a nine-month ASR program
- Average daily trading volume (ADTV) for IBM stock is 7,500,000 shares
- 660,000 IBM shares are purchased every business day during a nine-month period by the Investment Bank (<25% of ADTV)

Subsequent to the completion of the IBM ASR transaction and several other similar transactions that reduced repatriation-related taxes, the IRS issued new rules under Section 957(c) that effectively shut down this ASR-related structure. The IRS position was immediately challenged by several corporations.

10

Investment Banking Careers, Opportunities, and Issues

Investment banking focuses on (1) giving financial advice to corporate or government-related clients and helping them raise, retire, or risk manage capital; (2) giving strategic advice to corporate clients to enhance shareholder value through acquisitions, divestitures, mergers, or restructurings; (3) taking trading risk positions in financial instruments to provide investment opportunities and liquidity for investing clients; (4) providing financing, risk management, and other securities services to investing clients; (5) providing research for investing clients; (6) selectively investing a small portion of the firm's own capital on a proprietary basis; (7) providing loans to large corporations that use other investment banking services; (8) managing money for investing clients; and (9) providing support functions for all aforementioned areas of focus.

Each of these different areas is separately managed and has different responsibilities and compensation systems. Each requires a separate analysis to determine whether there is a career fit. Most investment banking jobs are time-consuming, intense, and well compensated but vary considerably in terms of content and required skills. The nine focus areas described above generally fall into five main business areas: (1) Investment Banking, (2) Trading and Sales, (3) Wealth Management, Asset Management (AM), and Research, (4) Principal and Credit Investments, and (5) Other investment banking functions such as Operations and Finance.

INVESTMENT BANKING

The Investment Banking Division is responsible for (1) giving financial advice to corporate or government-related clients and helping them raise, retire, or risk manage capital and (2) giving strategic advice to corporate clients to enhance shareholder value through acquisitions, divestitures, mergers, or restructurings. All bankers in this division have strong analytical and communication skills, but some are better at marketing and others are better at focusing on the technical aspects of transaction execution. Bankers with greater marketing skills tend to work in a client relationship management area, and bankers with greater technical skills often work in a product area such as merger and acquisition (M&A) or capital markets. Of course, there are many exceptions to this general statement, and sometimes bankers move between these areas during their career. In addition, some banks combine M&A and client relationship management into a single area.

This division requires long hours, hard work, and strong analytical skills. Fellow employees and clients are intelligent and demanding, and there is a strong focus on teamwork. The first few years provide an apprenticeship environment where the "trade" is taught and skills are developed. Some of the work during this period is somewhat mundane and some work is highly analytical and creative. Banking operates on a meritocracy system, and those who have or can develop the requisite skills and demonstrate a strong work ethic can do very well. There is stiff competition to succeed and not everyone does since there is a culling process to determine the weakest performers every year, who leave the firm either through self-selection or the firm's edict. Depending on the year and the firm, this could be between 5% and 15% of employees. Although compensation generally does not vary much during the first few years, in subsequent years, it can vary dramatically, depending on performance.

There are different entry points into the Investment Banking Division. Analyst positions are available for college graduates. Associate positions are available for a selected group of third year analysts, MBAs, JDs, and, occasionally, professionals from other industries. It is sometimes (infrequently) possible for professionals from other industries or PhDs to be hired as Vice Presidents (VPs) or Managing Directors (MDs), if they have a unique skill set that is needed at the firm, but mostly, these positions are filled through internal promotions or hires from other investment banks. At some firms, there are additional levels such as Senior VPs and/or Directors (see Exhibit 10.1).

EXHIBIT 10.1 INVESTMENT BANKING DIVISION POSITIONS

Position[1]	Source	Period in Position
Analyst	College graduates	2 – 3 years
Associate	3rd year analysts, MBAs, JDs, other industries	3.5 – 5 years
Vice President	Experienced associates, other industries	4 – 10 years
Managing Director	Experienced vice presidents, other industries	

Note 1: Some investment banks also have a Director and/or a Senior Vice President position between Vice President and Managing Director.

Analysts

Prospective candidates for analyst positions should develop skills with spreadsheets during their undergraduate years and, ideally, take accounting and economics classes. Finance or investing classes are not essential but could be valuable preparation as well. Although difficult to obtain, since investment banks limit their summer recruiting to a small number of universities, it is very helpful to secure a summer internship at an investment bank after the sophomore or junior year of college. Analyst positions typically are for a 2- or 3-year period, and most analysts will be asked to leave after this period to pursue an MBA, other academic interests, or to work elsewhere. Depending on the year and the firm, 20%–50% of analysts will be asked to stay, with the promise of promotion to Associate.

An analyst principally runs analytical models, gathers information, analyzes the information so that it can be incorporated in presentations, and develops presentation materials for Associates, VPs, and MDs. They usually have multiple projects to work on and are essential members of a client or deal team. Projects generally relate to either M&A or financing transactions. A typical week can involve 80–100 hours in the office, sometimes including all-nighters and almost always including work during the weekends. A good attitude, strong analytical skills, attention to detail, and a strong work ethic are essential, as is an ability to work well in a team.

Investment banks have historically offered 2-year positions to analysts, with less than 20% asked to stay a third year and only some of the third year analysts asked to stay on as Associates. Firms are generally expected to keep most of these analysts during this period. However, during recent years, an increasing number of analysts have left their firms after one or 2 years to join private equity firms, other financial competitors, or tech start-ups. As a result, many investment banks have revamped their analyst programs, offering a full 3-year period for all analysts, a significantly higher number of promotions at the end of the analyst period to associate, limitations on some weekend work and the overall number of work hours per week, rotations through multiple business units, faster pay raises, and more reliance on technology to take away some of the routine work such as preparing pitch books.

Associates

MBAs are the principal candidates for the Associate position, although an increasing number of third year analysts are being promoted into this position. MBA students should focus on developing strong analytical, negotiation, and teamwork skills while in school. A broad array of finance and investing classes are important, as are classes that focus on investment banking, derivatives, securities analysis, tax planning, restructuring, private equity, and M&A. The best MBA candidates have a strong background of extracurricular and leadership activities and have demonstrated the ability to work well in a group.

Associates manage the day-to-day details of most banking projects and have the principal responsibility to create presentations. They check all analyst work, including financial modeling, and run some of the more complicated models themselves. There is frequent client contact and, for some smaller deals, an Associate may be responsible for executing the transaction, as well as directly communicating with the client. In addition to managing multiple projects, training analysts and recruiting future bankers is also required. Work hours are generally not much less than for analysts: 70–100 hours on average, although there are some differences based on the city and the size of the firms (e.g., outside of New York and/or smaller firms sometimes require fewer hours).

Vice Presidents

Associates are generally promoted to VP after 3.5–5 years, depending on the firm. VPs are responsible for managing most deals and managing both Associates and Analysts who work on deal teams. They are a principal source of communication with clients and are involved in new business development and client relationship management activities. Negotiating and creating solutions for client problems are a core part of their responsibility. VPs also mobilize resources within the firm to meet client needs, and so they need to initiate communication and coordination with different banking teams and other divisions in the firm.

In addition to deal work, VPs are responsible for recruiting, mentoring, and promoting the firm's overall business activities. They understand internal relationships, resource allocation issues, legal issues (in relation to specific transactions), and ethical standards of the firm. VPs may manage 5–10 projects at a time and bear the responsibility for execution of existing transactions and development of new revenue-producing transactions.

Managing Directors

MDs are generally promoted after 4–10 years at the VP (or equivalent) level. MDs manage VPs, Associates, and Analysts and have the most senior responsibility for managing client relationships. In addition, they have the greatest burden for developing new business and are asked to achieve a minimum revenue level each year. They must be team-oriented and possess the ability to obtain all the firm's resources necessary to complete deals and meet client needs. They have access to the firm's senior management and frequently call on them to meet with clients. They also have access to resources provided both internally and externally from outside legal, tax, and accounting professionals.

Negotiating with clients and internally for resources is a key part of an MD's job. Proper resource allocation and internal political issues are important areas of focus. Ultimately, MDs are running fairly large businesses with associated revenue that could fall in the range of $10–$100 million (or more) a year, depending on the function and the firm. MDs also determine compensation levels and career development paths for members of their team, make capital allocation decisions, and focus on recruiting and training. They usually manage between 5–10 revenue-based client projects at a time, while balancing the needs of other clients who are not currently completing transactions but are expected to in the future.

TRADING AND SALES

The Trading Division usually has the following focus: (1) taking trading risk positions in financial instruments to provide investment opportunities and liquidity for investing clients; (2) providing financing, risk management, and other securities services to investing clients; (3) providing research for investing clients; and (4) investing a limited amount of the firm's own capital on a proprietary (short-term) basis or through longer-term principal and credit investments. Usually, the same titles described above for the Investment Banking Division apply to the Trading Division. However, the period of time it takes for promotion could be accelerated for particularly capable employees. Compensation in this division may initially be comparable, or slightly lower than for the Investment Banking Division. However, over time, for especially high-performing employees, the compensation could be higher for Trading Division professionals since they may have the ability to create greater revenue for the firm.

The entry points into the Trading Division are similar to the Investment Banking Division: Analyst positions are available for college graduates; Associate positions are available for Third Year Analysts (with many more promoted, compared to the Investment Banking Division), MBAs, and, occasionally, professionals from other industries. PhDs are also hired as Associates in quant-heavy areas such as fixed-income strategy. Sometimes (infrequently), PhDs and others are hired as VPs or MDs if they have a unique analytical skill that is needed by the firm.

Descriptions of careers in this division are best provided based on job function, rather than job title. The key job functions include trading, institutional sales, and research.

Client-Related Trading

Client-related traders function as equity, fixed income, currency, or commodity traders. In addition, there is a separate group of derivative traders in each of these areas. Traders have the responsibility to commit the firm's capital in support of purchasing and selling securities with investing clients of the firm. They need to have an inventory of securities at all times to actively make bids and offers in reasonable volume for targeted securities. Hedging decisions regarding their inventory and forecasting future valuations are key responsibilities. The ability to make quick, accurate analytical decisions and synthesize myriad risks, including political, regulatory, interest rate, credit, and volatility risks is important. A trader must be able to accept periodic losses and manage a portfolio in an efficient and logical manner. Most of a trader's key decisions are made before noon, when the market is most active, and so a good trader must be able to start early (sometimes 7 a.m. or so) and make numerous clear-headed decisions before lunch. Hours are usually shorter than for bankers: often 50–60 hours/week. However, time spent on a trading floor can be quite intense.

Client-related traders must be able to work as a team with sales professionals, on whom they are critically dependent for information and trades. In addition, they must be able to absorb both internal and external research and synthesize this information to build analytical models that facilitate good trading decisions. This is a very fast-paced environment set on a crowded trading floor with, often, hundreds of other traders sharing a large trading area that might have thousands of computer screens and a high noise level. The ability to isolate oneself from the surrounding tumult and rely on carefully built analytical models to guide trading decisions is a key to success in this business.

Proprietary Trading

Proprietary trading used to be a very profitable part of investment banking until the beginning of the 2008 financial crisis. During this crisis, many investment banks incurred large losses in their proprietary trading business. The future of this trading is diminished based on regulations such as the Dodd–Frank Act, which limits proprietary trading within investment banks. In reaction to this new regulation, many investment banks, including Goldman Sachs and Morgan Stanley, have substantially reduced or eliminated their proprietary trading groups.

Institutional Sales

Institutional sales is divided into equity, fixed income, currency, and commodity areas. There are also separate sales professionals focused on derivative products that relate to these areas. Institutional sales people work directly with client-related traders in an effort to bring reasonable bids and offers in required sizes to their institutional clients, which include pension funds, endowments, family funds, corporate treasury funds, insurance companies, hedge funds, banks, and mutual funds. Of these clients, hedge funds are the most active traders. Hedge fund trading represents a significant amount of all NYSE Euronext, NASDAQ, and London Stock Exchange trading.

Equity Sales

Equity sales comprises four segments. Research sales professionals make stock recommendations to investors based on analysis of internal or external research. Portfolio managers are their client contacts. Sales traders recommend stock trading ideas that are not solely research-based and focus on technical issues that are important to their principal contact, the trader at the institutional investor. Sales traders have direct contact with their firm's client-related traders to price and execute trades with the institutional investor's trader (see Exhibit 5.3 from Chapter 5). Convertibles sales professionals focus exclusively on selling convertible securities to targeted convertible investors. Equity derivative sales professionals cover investing clients who are interested in derivatives transactions.

Sales professionals must always keep abreast of market developments, possess a solid ability to keep track of client's perspectives and priorities, and be creative in finding securities and strategies that help their investing clients achieve good, risk-adjusted trading profits. They stand between internal traders and the investing client, trying to balance the competing interests of both parties.

Fixed-Income Sales

Fixed-income sales is divided into many different product areas, including (1) investment grade corporate bonds, (2) high yield corporate bonds, (3) securitized products, (4) distressed debt, (5) bank loans, (6) US and other sovereign securities, (g) emerging market bonds and loans, (7) municipal securities, (8) preferred stock and commercial paper, (9) money market instruments, (10) foreign exchange, and (11) commodities. Each of these areas is highly specialized and institutional investors expect focused coverage that provides timely ideas, creative solutions, liquidity, and excellent execution.

This is a very fast moving market and volume is the key to achieving profitability, since the margins on many of these products are razor thin. In addition, fixed-income sales includes a separate group of derivatives sales specialists who, in many cases, have overlapping client coverage responsibility. Proper client coverage requires a lot of coordination and good communication. Depending on the firm, a commodities sales team may focus on spot, forward and futures markets in any or all of the following commodities: metals (base and precious), agricultural products, crude oil, oil products, natural gas, electric power, emission credits, coal, freight, and liquefied natural gas.

Prime Brokerage Sales

Hedge funds are the principal clients of the prime brokerage sales effort. The main products of the prime brokerage area are securities lending and the provision of debt financing based on sophisticated collateral mechanisms. This group also coordinates securities clearing and provides custody and reporting services. In addition to facilitating trades in stocks, bonds, and convertibles through lending activities, the group also focuses on foreign exchange, precious metals, and derivatives prime brokerage activities. A sales position in prime brokerage requires extensive knowledge of the securities market and the ability to work closely with internal sales and trading professionals, as well as with hedge fund clients, who demand excellent service.

PRIVATE WEALTH MANAGEMENT

Private Wealth (PW) professionals secure, develop, and manage relationships with high net worth individuals, their families, family offices, and foundations. PW helps investing clients build and preserve their financial wealth by creating and implementing long-term asset allocation strategies based on client risk parameters. They also provide clients with access to investment ideas, private banking services, and trust company services. This job requires strong people skills, as well as analytical ability, networking ability, and an understanding of a global array of investment opportunities. Investing clients can make every investment decision and ask the PW sales professional to execute these decisions. Alternatively, investing clients can turn over many decisions to the PW sales team, who will allocate assets according to the client's risk preferences. In this case, the sales effort is a careful balance between introducing clients to investment products offered internally and products offered by external sources. At some investment banks, the PW business is combined with the AM Business in a single division that comprises the two separate business functions. At other firms, the PW business is separate from the AM business. In addition, some firms have a very large "retail" business that works with individual investing clients who have smaller investment portfolios.

ASSET MANAGEMENT

AM professionals specialize principally in one of the following different areas:

1. Fundamental Equity Investments, which conducts bottom-up research across a broad range of public companies, including both developed and emerging markets globally. This group focuses on both growth equity and value equity investments.
2. Fixed-Income Investments, which locates fixed-income investing opportunities either locally or throughout the world, focusing in particular on credit risks. This group looks at all maturities, including short-term money market instruments and 30-year bonds.
3. Quantitative Investments, which employs advanced quantitative methods to systematically find sources of alpha (risk-adjusted returns in excess of "market returns"). This group utilizes proprietary risk models that actively manage risk and allocations. All securities across all types of investment styles are included in this investment area.
4. Alternative Investments, which includes hedge fund, private equity, fund of fund, and real estate strategies.

AM professionals manage a broad array of funds, including customized investment portfolios and discretionary funds for institutions, corporations, pension funds, governments, foundations, and individuals. They also design and manage families of mutual funds and develop new investment products.

The entry points into the AM Division are slightly different from the Investment Banking Division: there are generally fewer positions available and AM typically has more lateral hires, with candidates coming from consulting, accounting, or investment banking sell-side research. Some AM positions target candidates who have obtained their Chartered Financial Analyst certification. PhDs are also hired in areas such as economic research and quantitative research.

College graduates start at the Junior Analyst/Junior Associate level (title varies depending on firm), which supports the research efforts of buy-side Research Analysts. Some Junior Analysts/Junior Associates leave to pursue MBAs, while others are promoted to Associates. Successful Associates are promoted to buy-side Research Analysts (who provide investment recommendations to Portfolio Managers) and then some eventually become Portfolio Managers.

RESEARCH

Research is a globally focused business. It covers fundamental research and analysis of selected company debt and equity securities, industries, commodities, and economies. This group provides investment and trading recommendations and strategies for institutional and individual investors, as well as for the Trading Division of the firm. In addition to conducting research and writing reports, research professionals interact with investing and issuing clients and host conferences and meetings between investors and corporate or government issuers.

Research professionals develop analytical models that capture relevant information (while filtering out noise) and interpret events so that compelling research themes can be developed. In addition to analytical skills, writing skills are essential to facilitate communication. In depth, nonsuperficial and timely analysis and reporting is essential to perform well in this function.

PRINCIPAL AND CREDIT INVESTMENTS

Principal and Credit Investments comprise professionals who focus on (1) acquiring public companies or divisions of companies through leveraged buyout transactions (private equity); (2) infrastructure investments in transport-related projects (toll roads, airports, and ports) and in regulated gas, water, and electrical utilities; (3) mezzanine finance (subordinated debt or preferred shares with equity warrants or conversion rights); (4) private equity fund of funds (investing in multiple different external private equity funds as an asset allocator); and (5) real estate investments; and long-term credit-based investments.

In the aftermath of the global financial crisis, the equity-related principal investing activities at most investment banks is significantly diminished. However, credit-based activities have increased, resulting in less bank exposure to equity investments and more exposure to loans and other credit-based investments.

Professionals who work in the Principal and Credit Investments area have a strong investment and credit background and aptitude. Their analytical and negotiation skills are well developed by running financial models and developing comprehensive credit analysis.

OTHER INVESTMENT BANKING FUNCTIONS

The other activities conducted by an investment bank are characterized as service areas designed to facilitate revenue production in the previously described businesses. Included among these service areas are Finance, Operations, Compliance, HR, Legal, Building and Security Management, and Technology. Each of these areas is important for the successful operation of an investment bank. The Operations and Finance areas are summarized below:

Operations

The operations activities at an investment bank sometimes represents up to 15% of all employees at a firm. This area assists all of the revenue-generating businesses, serving as internal consultants who develop processes and controls and help specify systems that deliver accurate and timely reporting and execution. This group is involved in risk management and execution activities that protect both the firm's and the client's capital and reputation. It is also a party to the innovation and process improvement activities that create the systems, tools, and workflows that support the firm's transactions, while improving productivity and competitive advantage. This group is also involved in process management activities that create best practices within the firm and solutions to problems faced by clients, the firm, and the industry.

Finance

Members of an investment bank's finance team are responsible for (1) tracking and analyzing the firm's capital flows; (2) managing relationships with regulators; (3) preparing the firm's statutory financial information and statements for each region; (4) measuring, analyzing, and controlling the risk exposures of the firm; and (5) coordinating with each of the firm's business areas to ensure there is sufficient funding and appropriate allocation of capital. Finance is organized into separate groups that focus on different functions. The controller's group is responsible for safeguarding the firm's assets. The corporate tax team ensures compliance with the tax laws of all countries in which the firm operates. Corporate treasury manages the firm's liquidity and capital structure. The credit department protects the firm's capital against counterparty default. The strategy group develops and executes long-term strategic plans (often working closely in conjunction with the heads of the bank's lines of businesses). Market risk management focuses on measuring, analyzing, and controlling the market risk of the firm. Finally, operational risk management analyzes the risk assessment frameworks that identify, measure, monitor, and manage risk exposures.

INVESTMENT BANKING OPPORTUNITIES AND ISSUES

Mortgage Securitization

Mortgage securitization is the process of combining mortgages into pools and then dividing them into portions (tranches) that can be sold as securities in the capital markets. This process breaks with the tradition of commercial banks holding mortgages on their balance sheets. Instead, banks that originate US mortgages can unwind risk and add liquidity by selling pools of mortgages to government-sponsored enterprises—the Federal National Mortgage Association (or Fannie Mae), the Federal Home Loan Mortgage Corporation (or Freddie Mac), or the Government National Mortgage Association (or Ginnie Mae)—in addition to private conduit-type customers. By creating a market for previously illiquid mortgages, securitization offers more efficient pricing of mortgages, which lowers interest rates for borrowers and contributes to greater home ownership. The act of pooling mortgages into different tranches, ranging from high coupon to low coupon or short-term to long-term securities, has also improved the marketability of these investment products by catering to investors with different risk tolerances. Investors can invest in securitized mortgages ranging from senior (low risk) securities that pay low interest rates to subordinated (high risk) securities that pay high interest rates.

Despite the benefits, the complex nature of securitization can also mask some of the risks involved in owning mortgage-related investments. By immediately selling the mortgages they have originated, commercial banks transfer credit and interest rate risk onto institutional and individual investors, thereby giving lenders little incentive to adhere to strict mortgage underwriting standards. This agent–principal problem contributed to the development of negative amortizing loans, zero principal loans, and no documentation mortgages, as well as the explosion of subprime loans. In an attempt to mitigate the agent–principal problem, regulators now mandate that banks retain 5% of each collateralized debt obligation tranche they create and sell to investors. Additionally, banks are not allowed to hedge these positions, with limited exceptions.

Subprime mortgages accounted for over 20% of all mortgage originations in 2007, up from 6% in 2002. Securitized mortgages were at the epicenter of the credit crisis of 2007–08, creating trillions of dollars in investment losses and contributing to significant changes in the investment banking industry landscape. Since the financial crisis, the market for securitized products has weakened and mortgage securitization has dropped considerably. In the future, there will still be a need for securitization, but it is unlikely that the market for mortgage securitization will reach precrisis levels.

Short-Term Financing by Investment Banks

Investment banks have historically relied on large amounts of short-term financing to fund their operations. The most popular forms of short-term financing are commercial paper and repurchase (repo) agreements. In a typical repo agreement, a financial institution receives overnight financing by selling securities and repurchasing them when the agreement matures (often overnight, or in 1 week or 1 month). In this exchange, the buyer receives securities as collateral to protect against default. Should these assets tumble in value, the seller is forced to come up with additional cash to meet margin calls or risk losing access to credit. Almost 25% of total assets at investment banks were financed by overnight repos in 2007, an increase from about 12.5% in 2000.

Commercial paper is different from repos in that it is generally unsecured and matures within 1 to 270 days (although most paper matures within 90 days). Investment banks typically refinance or "roll over" maturing paper with new commercial paper issuance.

Short-term financing provides four principal benefits for investment banks:

1. Funding is cheap (below bank loan rates) because historical default risk is low.
2. Availability of funding is typically high.
3. This funding provides considerable flexibility to meet cash needs as they change from day to day.
4. In a normal upward sloping yield curve environment, the assets purchased with short-term liabilities carry returns above funding costs, creating earnings based on an asset/liability mismatch.

While short-term financing offers investment banks many benefits, it also exposes them to interest rate and liquidity risk. Specifically, should the banks' assets experience a significant drop in value, the interest rate charged by investors can increase and the availability of short-term financing can evaporate. Investment banks found themselves in this position during October of 2008 (following the collapse of Lehman Brothers), when the amount of their commercial paper outstanding shrank to just 25% of its former volume virtually overnight. Instead of issuing more paper to pay back investors, when the market dried up, banks were forced to dump assets at significant discounts. The credit crisis also caused significant value reductions in the collateral backing repo agreements (as well as a general crisis of confidence), resulting in the refusal by many investors to roll over repos. This refusal forced banks to unload more assets at fire sale prices, exacerbating the drop in securities values across the globe. After the credit markets ravaged investment banks during 2007 and 2008, these institutions were forced to significantly reduce their reliance on short-term financing and limit their asset/liability mismatch. The end result was higher funding costs, less flexibility, and lower earnings potential.

Leverage at Investment Banks

Banks are heavily leveraged compared to other businesses. The average commercial bank has a leverage ratio (defined as total assets/book equity) in the range of between 10 and 15 to 1, compared to between 1 and 3 to 1 for the average nonfinancial company. Investment banks historically took on more debt than commercial banks, with average leverage ratios of between 20 and 30 to 1. Investment banks use leverage to enhance their return on equity (a closely watched metric for financial services companies). When business plans are realized, leverage boosts returns and profits. However, when losses occur, banks' high leverage can cause outsized losses that reduce equity and deplete capital cushions. During 2007, leverage at investment banks approached (or reached, in several cases) historical heights.

Investment banks frequently adjust their leverage in response to liquidity conditions and the macro economy. As a result, leverage is typically high during business cycle peaks and low during business cycle troughs. During the first half of 2007, investment banks were enjoying a strong period of growth marked by impressive proprietary trading profits. Despite rising value at risk estimates, which measure an investment bank's "worst case" losses, if conditions quickly deteriorate, investment banks continued to build up leverage to augment their investment returns. Such excessive leverage, however, worked against the banks when the credit markets collapsed during the second half of 2007. At that time, trading losses piled up, and asset prices plunged in response to worries about the value of underlying collateral. Consequently, many investment banks moved from appearing overcapitalized to undercapitalized over the span of 6 months. During 2008 and 2009, investment banks all significantly reduced their leverage following substantial losses and the imposition of regulatory requirements that restricted leverage, and this leverage continued to decline through 2015 (see Exhibit 10.2).

EXHIBIT 10.2 LEVERAGE AT INVESTMENT BANKS

Firm	Leverage (Assets/Equity)			
	2012	2013	2014	2015
Bank of America	9.33	9.03	8.64	8.37
Barclays	25.21	21.01	20.59	17.00
Citigroup	9.76	9.12	8.69	7.76
Credit Suisse	26.04	20.70	20.96	18.23
Deutsche Bank	37.44	29.45	24.99	24.09
Goldman Sachs	12.40	11.62	10.34	9.88
J.P. Morgan	12.99	11.44	11.10	9.50
Morgan Stanley	11.94	12.06	11.12	10.34
UBS	25.66	20.29	19.54	16.45

Sources: Respective 10-K and 20-F filings.

Capital Ratios

Some investors have become increasingly skeptical regarding investment banks' capital ratios. Tier-1 ratios are reported by investment banks based on either Basel I or Basel II guidelines. These ratios compare shareholder's equity to risk-adjusted assets. However, deciding on the proper risk weighting for assets leaves the process open to subjective judgments. Historically US investment banks compiled assets based on Basel I guidelines and under supervision by the SEC, while commercial banks compiled assets based on Basel II and under the supervision of the Federal Reserve. During late 2008, however, all investment banks shifted to compiling assets under Basel II. Unfortunately, Basel II allows for management judgment and management control over models that determine the risk weighting of assets, which, in effect, gives banks some latitude to set their own capital requirements. As a result, there is a concern that these ratios may not provide reliable information about bank capital. See Exhibit 10.3 to compare Tier-1 ratios as of December 31, 2015.

As described in Chapter 8, Basel III, which was promulgated during 2011, and adopted during a phase-in period through 2019, focuses on risk-based capital and leverage requirements, liquidity stress tests, single counterparty credit limits to cut credit exposure of a covered financial firm to a single counterparty as a percentage of the firm's regulatory capital, reducing credit exposure between the largest financial companies, implementing early remediation requirements to ensure that financial weaknesses are addressed in a timely way, compensation, and capital raising or asset sales. Basel III is intended to strengthen bank capital requirements by increasing bank liquidity and decreasing bank leverage. Unlike Basel I and Basel II, which focus primarily on the level of bank loss reserves that banks are required to hold, Basel III focuses primarily on the risk of a run on the bank, requiring differing levels of reserves for different forms of bank deposits and other borrowings. Therefore, Basel III does not, for the most part, supersede Basel I and II but works in companion.

EXHIBIT 10.3 CAPITAL CUSHIONS: BANK TIER-1 RATIOS

Global Investment Banks Tier-1 Ratios As of 2015	
Bank of America	11.30%
Barclays	18.10%
Citigroup	14.80%
Credit Suisse	18.00%
Deutsche Bank	14.70%
Goldman Sachs	14.10%
J.P. Morgan	13.50%
Morgan Stanley	17.40%
UBS	21.00%

Sources: Capital IQ.

Compensation

Historically, investment banks have targeted compensation as a percent of total net income to be at or below 50%. At J.P. Morgan's investment bank, this percentage was 41% in 2006, 44% in 2007, and 63% in 2008, but by 2015, this percentage had dropped to 35%. Bonuses usually make up more than half of a firm's compensation expense. During profitable years, a year-end bonus might be more than three times the size of salary for a successful VP or MD. Following the financial crisis of 2007–08, governments around the world attempted to influence certain investment banks in their compensation decisions in an effort to reduce excessive risk-taking that led to losses during these years. France, Germany, and the Netherlands limited the size of bonuses paid to senior bankers if their bank had received "bail-out" funds from the government. In the United States, firms that received Troubled Asset Relief Program funding from the government were forced to reduce senior management and trader bonuses. However, efforts to remake broad-based financial rules regarding compensation became bogged down amid infighting between federal regulators and opposition from lawmakers who believed that further expanding the government's reach would only create new problems. An industry consensus emerged nonetheless that multiyear employment contracts should be avoided, and up to 50% of bonus compensation should be paid in the form of stock, which vests over multiple years, and becomes unrestricted only if legacy risk positions remain profitable over time. As of 2016, US regulatory requirements imposed on investment banks included mandatory deferral of 40%–60% of incentive compensation for 1–4 years; clawbacks for at least 7 years in relation to misconduct, fraud, or misrepresentations; and limiting incentive compensation to no more than 150% of targeted compensation established at the beginning of a performance period.

Credit Default Swaps

Credit default swaps (CDS) are derivative contracts designed to spread risk and reduce exposure to credit events such as default or bankruptcy. In a CDS, one party (the protection buyer) makes periodic payments to a second party (the protection seller) in exchange for a payoff in the event a third party (the reference entity) defaults on its debt obligations. For protection buyers, a CDS resembles an insurance policy as it can be used to hedge against a default or bankruptcy by the reference entity. For protection sellers, a CDS creates annual income in exchange for the risk they undertake.

Unlike most other financial products, CDS contracts have historically been unregulated. Although contracts specify the identity of protection sellers and the scheduled termination date of default protection, some contracts have not required the seller to hold assets as collateral for the transaction. Without a self-regulatory organization to mandate standard terms and practices, there is no universal way of valuing the securities involved in these contracts. Furthermore, CDS contracts are heavily traded, with one contract changing hands several times over the course of its life. As a result, the protection buyer often does not know whether the protection seller has sufficient capital to cover a security's loss and provide payment to the protection buyer.

According to the International Swaps and Derivatives Association (ISDA), the CDS market exploded over the past decade to more than $54 trillion notional amount in mid-2008, which is more than twice the market capitalization of the US stock market. CDS emerged as a popular portfolio management tool due to its flexibility in customizing exposure to corporate credit. Investors could effectively establish a short position without making an initial cash outlay. These instruments also allowed investors to exit credit positions during periods of low liquidity.

The strong economy of the mid-90s drove the growth of the CDS market. Protection sellers believed the odds of corporate default were low and viewed the premiums received as an easy way of enhancing investing returns. For many years, this was the case and investment banks, commercial banks, some insurance companies (notably AIG) and hedge funds profited from the CDS market.

However, returns quickly evaporated with the onset of the subprime crisis. Credit spreads widened significantly, negatively impacting the performance of CDS contracts that were increasingly used to hedge against default for poor quality companies. According to Fitch Ratings, 40% of CDS protection sold worldwide in July 2007 was on companies or securities that were rated below investment grade, up from 8% in 2002. With bond defaults rising, investors began to worry about counterparty risk and questioned whether sellers had adequate reserves to cover losses. This concern precipitated the Fed's bailout of Bear Stearns and AIG (both active sellers of CDS). Counterparties to Bear and AIG began withdrawing cash from these firms, and regulators feared the repercussions of large-scale bankruptcies.

In response to these events and concerns that the CDS market could unravel, the Dodd–Frank Act classified CDS as securities during 2010 to give the SEC regulatory jurisdiction over these financial instruments. The Financial Accounting Standards Board issued a list of new disclosures to be included in financial statements beginning fiscal year 2009. The rules require CDS protection sellers to disclose the nature and terms of the credit derivative, the reason it was entered into, and the current status of its payment and performance risk. In addition, the seller is required to disclose the amount of future payments it might be required to make and the fair value of the derivative and whether there are provisions that would allow the seller to recover money or assets from third parties to pay for the insurance coverage it has written.

The notional amount of traded swaps reached a peak of more than $62 trillion in 2007, with naked CDS (no long position in the underlying credit instrument) representing as much as 80% of this amount. In the aftermath of the financial crisis and the regulations that followed, the net amount of credit default swaps outstanding globally fell 20% between October 2008 and November 2010 as investors waited to see the impact of regulatory restrictions on the market. The ISDA estimated the total amount of outstanding credit default swaps in 2009 to be $30.4 trillion, due in part to measures taken to cancel contracts that offset each other. As of March 2016, this amount had dropped to $13.1 trillion.

Title VII of the Dodd–Frank Act has given US regulators (primarily the CFTC and the SEC), a mandate to regulate derivatives markets. The definition of "swap" in Section 721(a) (21) includes CDS, as well interest rate, currency, total return, equity, and commodity swaps. CDS, like most other swaps, are now subject to clearing, trading, and reporting requirements with exemptions based on the nature of the parties themselves and the purpose of the trade (for example, end users hedging only their own commercial risks are exempt from most requirements). One of the most controversial provisions of the Act is the swaps "push-out" rule, which requires systemically significant financial institutions to transfer their swap trading into separately capitalized affiliates. This does not apply to centrally cleared CDS.

Bridge Loans

Investment banks have made large bridge loan commitments to M&A clients to fund cash acquisitions, with the expectation that the loans will only be funded if a long-term securities offering a high-yield bond transaction or a secured syndicated loan is not completed. The bridge loan often has a commitment fee, a takedown fee when the loan is drawn down, and a significant credit spread over either LIBOR or Prime as the floating interest rate. In addition, the provider of the bridge loan generally secures the right to arrange the take-out financing, which includes underwriting and placement fees.

Although participating in bridge loans helps investment banks secure more additional lucrative business from private equity firms (such as debt underwriting and M&A advisory), there can also be considerable risk. For example, during 2006 and 2007, private equity firms pushed investment banks to provide large bridge loans to fund many large acquisitions from which the investment banks were receiving M&A advisory fees. When the credit crunch hit, a large number of buyout-related bridge loans were fully drawn down at a time when the capital markets were unable to provide take-out financing in the form of high yield bonds or long-term syndicated loans. As a result, investment banks unexpectedly had to fund what turned out to be long-term loans that tied up considerable bank capital and caused significant losses for the banks as credit conditions deteriorated. As of the end of August 2007, it was estimated that nine largest investment banks held more than $250 billion of unwanted "hung" bridge loans provided to private equity clients to fund their leveraged buyouts (see Exhibit 10.4).

EXHIBIT 10.4 LEVERAGED BUYOUT BRIDGE LOANS

- A large volume of mega private equity deals in 2007 combined with an escalating credits crisis starting in the second half of 2007 created a significant amount of hung bridge loans stuck on bank's balance sheets. By Q3 of 2007, there was an estimated $300 billion in outstanding bridge loans.
- Although not a lucrative business for banks, the intense competition for M&A and financing fees from private equity clients persuaded most large banks to participate in this lending practice.
- Ironically, although pressure from the private equity firms caused this predicament for the banks, private equity firms were also among those that took advantage of lender's woes, by raising dedicated funds to purchase these loans at discounted prices from banks.

Hung Bridge Loans (Q3 07)		Dedicated Hung Bridge Funds	
Company	Estimated Outstanding "Hung Bridges"	Fund	Fund Size
Citigroup	$51 billion	Goldman Sachs Fund	$1 billion
J.P. Morgan	$41 billion	Lehman Brothers Special Situations	$2 billion
Goldman Sachs	$32 billion	Oaktree Fund	$4 billion
Deutsche Bank	$27 billion	TPG Credit Fund	$1 billion
Credit Suisse	$27 billion	Apollo	$1 billion
Lehman Brothers	$22 billion	Blackstone	$1 billion
Morgan Stanley	$20 billion		
Bank of America	$18 billion		
Merrill Lynch	$16 billion		

Source: Reuters Loan Pricing Corp.; Deponte, Kelly: "Hung Bridge" Funds, Probitas Partners, September 2007; company filings; author's estimates.

Investment Banking Future

Investment banking industry revenue tumbled during 2007 and 2008 due to weak financing and M&A markets, reductions in leverage available to support proprietary trading, and massive write-offs from mortgage-related businesses, bridge loans, and structured investment vehicle arrangements. During the first half of 2009 through 2017, a recovery in the M&A and financing markets bolstered revenue and provided a foundation for stabilizing the industry. Goldman Sachs, J.P. Morgan, and Morgan Stanley sit at the top of global investment banking revenue rankings and they have momentum to maintain this lead. The other six largest global firms should be able to maintain their competitive position overall, while boutique investment banks may be able to make inroads in the M&A advisory market.

Equity, equity derivatives, FX, and prime brokerage businesses, which have been somewhat less affected by the credit crunch, should be able to perform well going forward. Some businesses that have been more directly affected, such as securitization and credit derivatives, will require portfolio adjustments and a strengthened talent base to produce required returns in the future. The fixed-income business will need to become less reliant on leverage in general and short-term financing in particular. Due to new regulations, investment banks can no longer rely on proprietary trading as a key source of income. Instead, they will need to build a solid profit base in their core client investing business and develop new sources of revenue.

Going forward, there will be reduced appetite for risk and leverage in the investment banking industry. This will keep returns on equity for most banks centered around 10%, unless firms can make technological progress in driving costs down, more fully capture share-of-wallet opportunities with clients, and create new sources of revenue from products and services that have yet to be developed. Historically, the industry has been remarkably resourceful in reinventing itself and driving earnings through new products and services. In spite of tighter regulations, including greater control over balance sheets and compensation practices, the industry should be able to continue creating value for clients and acceptable returns on invested capital.

International Investment Banking Issues and Opportunities

The career paths in investment banks outside the United States are generally similar to the paths outlined in the previous sections. In both the United States and Europe, the best way to secure an analyst or associate position is by completing a summer internship at an investment bank (some banks even offer year round off-cycle internships). In the United States, most analysts will be asked to leave the firm after 2 or 3 years to pursue an MBA or other academic interests or to work elsewhere. However, in Europe it is much more common for analysts to be promoted to associate (unless they have performed poorly), without leaving the firm. Consequently, most associates are former analysts, and not MBAs. A contributing factor in this practice is the fact that MBA degrees are generally not as common in Europe as they are in the United States. Due to the "Bologna Process," an educational reform plan of the European Union, this is likely to change in the future. The Bologna Process has already started to transform European universities in terms of the degrees they award. The first standard degree now is a bachelor's degree, as is the case in the United States. Before this change, most European universities ran integrated programs in which students would study longer but leave universities with the equivalent of a master's degree. With this change in place, students will more commonly graduate with a bachelor's degree, start working, and then consider returning to school to obtain a master's degree from one of the rapidly developing MBA programs. As a result of this change at European universities, career paths at European investment banks will become more comparable to the career paths at US investment banks.

HEDGE FUNDS AND PRIVATE EQUITY

Overview of Hedge Funds

The Securities and Exchange Commission (SEC) in the United States has stated that the term hedge fund "has no precise legal or universally accepted definition."[1] But most market participants agree that hedge funds have the following characteristics: (1) almost complete flexibility in relation to investments, including both long and short positions; (2) ability to borrow money (and further increase leverage through derivatives) in an effort to enhance returns; (3) minimal regulation; (4) somewhat illiquid since an investor's ability to get their money back is restricted through lock-up agreements (that may prevent any liquidity during the first 1 or 2 years of a hedge fund's life) and quarterly disbursement limitations thereafter (subject to "gates" which may further limit disbursements); (5) investors include only wealthy individuals and institutions such as university endowments, pension funds, and other qualified institutional buyers (except for fund of fund investments, which are available to a broader array of investors); and (6) fees that reward managers for performance.

[1] "Implications of the Growth of Hedge Funds." Staff Report to the United States Securities and Exchange Commission, 2003.

Investment Banks, Hedge Funds, and Private Equity, Third Edition
http://dx.doi.org/10.1016/B978-0-12-804723-1.00011-6

A typical fee structure for hedge funds includes both a management fee and a performance fee, whereas a typical mutual fund does not require a performance fee and has a smaller management fee. Hedge fund management fees are usually around 2% of net asset value (NAV) and performance fees are approximately 20% of the increase in the fund's NAV. This "2 and 20" fee structure is significantly higher than for most other money managers, with the exception of private equity fund managers, who enjoy similarly high fees.

Hedge funds target "absolute returns," which are investment returns that are positive and that theoretically don't depend on the performance of broad markets and the economy, unlike the returns associated with mutual funds. The historical claim by hedge funds that their returns are "uncorrelated" with market returns for traditional investments such as stocks and bonds was dramatically disproved during 2008, when large losses occurred. A lack of correlation is an attractive characteristic for investors who are attempting to either lower risk in their investment portfolio while keeping returns unchanged or increase returns in their portfolio without increasing risk. Although many hedge funds are successful in limiting (if not eliminating) correlation with the market, others are less successful, and overall, the hedge fund industry has followed the market to losses in certain years.

This category of investment management started during 1949 when Alfred W. Jones created a fund that utilized short selling of assets to hedge other assets that were purchased to create an investment portfolio. His fund neutralized the effect of changes in the general market by buying assets that were expected to increase in value and selling short assets that were expected to fall in value. This created a hedge that was designed to remove overall market risk. Others followed Jones in using hedging strategies within an investment fund, creating the investment fund category called hedge funds.

However, many funds that don't use hedging in their investment strategy are still called hedge funds if they exhibit the characteristics described in the first paragraph. Most hedge funds, in fact, are not hedged, as established by several academic studies on the subject. For example, a 2001 study showed that broad hedge fund exposure to the S&P 500 (measured in 1-month intervals) had a beta of 0.84 when adjusting for stale pricing (when pricing does not accurately reflect current values) of assets held.[2] A study in 2009 using more recent market data (and further adjusting for illiquidity) led to similar conclusions. However, individual hedge fund strategies can have significantly lower betas.

Hedge funds have been exempted from some securities regulations in the United States and in many other countries based on the fact that they invite investment from only sophisticated institutional investors and high net worth investors. In addition, there are limitations in some cases on the total number of investors in a fund. As a result, hedge funds have been exempted from regulations that govern leverage, the use of derivatives, short selling, fees, reporting, and investor liquidity. Mutual funds, by contrast, are not exempted from these regulations. This freedom from some regulation enables hedge funds to participate in a broad variety of investment strategies and allows them to change courses and strategies opportunistically and rapidly, taking advantage of changing market circumstances. In the United States, hedge funds are not subject to some of the regulations that are designed to protect investors. Depending on the amount of assets in

[2] Asness, C., R. Krail, and J. Liew. "Do Hedge Funds Hedge?" *Journal of Portfolio Management*. 28 (2001): 6–19.

the hedge funds advised by a manager, some hedge fund managers may not be required to register or to file public reports with the SEC. Hedge funds, however, are subject to the same prohibitions against fraud as are other market participants, and their managers owe a fiduciary duty to the funds that they manage. The Dodd–Frank Act requires SEC registration of advisers who manage private funds with more than US $150 million in assets. Registered managers must provide information regarding their assets under management and trading positions.

European lawmakers have also undertaken regulatory changes affecting hedge funds in recent years. In 2010 the European Union (EU) approved the Directive on Alternative Investment Fund Managers (AIFMD), the first EU directive focused specifically on alternative investment fund managers. AIFMD requires hedge funds to register with national regulators and increases disclosure requirements and frequency for fund managers operating in the EU. Furthermore, the directive increases capital requirements for hedge funds and places restrictions on leverage utilized by the funds.

LEVERAGE

Hedge funds frequently borrow (creating "leverage") to increase the size of their investment portfolio and increase returns (if asset values increase). For example, if a hedge fund received $100 million from investors, the fund might purchase securities worth $400 million by borrowing $300 million from banks, using the $400 million of purchased securities as collateral against the $300 million loan. This is called a margin loan. Another form of leverage used by hedge funds is created through repurchase agreements, where a hedge fund agrees to sell a security to another party for a predetermined price and then buy the security back at a higher price on a specified date in the future. In addition, leverage is provided by selling securities short and using the proceeds to purchase other securities and through derivatives contracts that enable hedge funds to create exposure to an asset without using as much capital as would be required by buying the asset directly (see Exhibit 11.1).

EXHIBIT 11.1 HOW HEDGE FUND LEVERAGE WORKS

Hedge fund investor capital can be leveraged in several ways to enhance overall returns.

Direct Forms of Leverage
Bank Borrowings

Hedge funds can take out margin loans (buying securities on margin) from banks. For example, assuming a 20% margin on security ABC, a hedge fund could buy $10 worth of securities by paying only $2 upfront and having the bank supply the remaining $8 in the form of a loan. To protect its loan balance, the bank requires the hedge fund to deposit an agreed amount of securities as collateral. If the market value of the ABC securities drops, the bank can require additional collateral from the hedge fund (margin call) to further protect itself.

continued

EXHIBIT 11.1 HOW HEDGE FUND LEVERAGE WORKS—cont'd

Repossession Agreements ("Repos")

Usually used by hedge funds to finance debt security purchases, a repo transaction involves one party agreeing to sell a security to another party for a given price and then buying it back later at a higher price.

Implicit Forms of Leverage

Short Selling

Short selling is the practice of selling securities borrowed from banks or other counterparties. Funds raised from the sale of these borrowed securities are used to buy other securities—a practice known as long/short trading.

Off-Balance-Sheet Leverage Through Derivatives and Structured Products

Derivatives include options, swaps, and futures. Investors can gain much larger risk exposures to an asset class through the use of derivatives than from buying the assets directly. Investments in the high-risk portions of structured products such as collateralized debt obligations (CDOs) also provide implicit leverage.

Through the first half of 2008, total hedge fund industry leverage was estimated to be three to four times investor capital.

Source: Farrell, Diana, et al. "The New Power Brokers: How Oil, Asia, Hedge Funds and Private Equity Are Shaping the Global Capital Markets." McKinsey Global Institute October 2007.

When hedge funds borrow money, their losses, as well as their gains, are magnified. For example, if a hedge fund receives $100 million from investors and then borrows $300 million to make investments totaling $400 million, a 25% fall in the value of its $400 million investment portfolio would result in a total loss of the investor's capital if the hedge fund closed down. If, alternatively, the investment portfolio increased by 25%, investors would receive a 100% return on their investment, before subtracting management fees and operating costs.

Hedge funds had over $1.9 trillion in investor capital (which is called assets under management) at the end of 2007. When including leverage obtained through debt and derivative positions, total hedge fund investable assets were $6.5 trillion, which is a 3.4 times implied leverage ratio. This amount was slightly less than one-third of the total investments controlled by insurance companies and slightly more than one-fourth of the investments held by pension funds. In the aftermath of the 2007–08 credit crisis, however, hedge fund leverage decreased significantly to just two times investor capital by the first quarter of 2009 and remained at this level through 2010. Total investable assets decreased in the years 2009 and 2010 from the 2008 highs. In 2011, leverage increased again and total investable assets grew to $4.8 trillion. Asset under management (AUM) for hedge funds at the end of 2015 was almost $3.2 trillion. Assuming that hedge funds used an average leverage of 2.5 times when making investments, investments during 2015 may have almost reached $8 trillion. Hedge fund leverage varied during 2015 between 2.9 times and 1 time, depending on the investment strategy, as shown in Exhibit 11.2. Relative value arbitrage employed the highest leverage and event-driven and credit strategies such as distress debt investing used the lowest leverage.

EXHIBIT 11.2 FINANCIAL LEVERAGE DURING 2015 BY STRATEGY (MEDIAN)

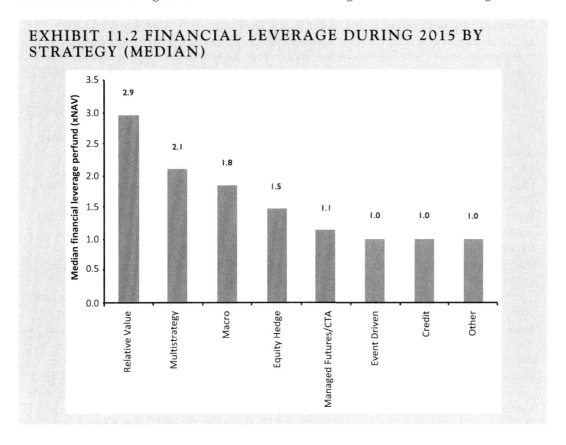

GROWTH

Hedge funds have grown at a remarkable rate since 1990, from 530 funds with under $39 billion in AUM to more than 8000 funds in 2016, with almost $3 trillion in AUM (see Exhibits 11.3–11.5). Between 2010 and 2015, the number of funds grew each year, but then started to drop during 2016, ending the year with about 340 fewer hedge funds worldwide.

Industry growth resulted from the following developments:

1. **Diversification**. Investors were looking for portfolio diversification beyond "long-only" investment funds. Hedge funds provided this portfolio diversification to investors through exposure to a broader range of assets and risks.
2. **Absolute returns**. Investors found the absolute return focus of hedge funds appealing. Most traditional investment funds try to beat market averages such as the S&P 500 index, claiming excellent management skills if their fund outperforms the relevant index. However, if the index return is negative, the outcome would be inferior to a hedge

fund that achieves an absolute return (meaning a return greater than 0%). Of course, notwithstanding the absolute return focus, some hedge funds have, in fact, achieved negative returns.

3. **Increased institutional investing**. After seeing several university endowments such as Yale's endowment achieve spectacular returns from investing up to 50% of their entire portfolio in alternative assets such as hedge funds, private equity, real estate, and commodities (achieving an average annual return of over 23% between 2001 and 2007), many large institutional investors such as pension funds and petrodollar funds (as well as other university endowment funds) substantially increased their exposure to hedge funds.

4. **Favorable market environment. When markets are favorable, hedge funds capitalize on available credit and low interest rates.** Since hedge funds rely on leverage to augment returns, low interest rates, the availability of credit, and flexibility in credit terms, in combination with accommodating tax and regulatory conditions, have fueled hedge fund growth.

5. **Human capital growth**. Some of the best financial and investing talent in the world moved into the hedge fund arena. Hedge funds were able to draw talent from investment banks and asset managers because of very high compensation and the opportunity to be more independent. During 2006, 26 hedge fund managers earned more than $130 million, including James Simons, founder of Renaissance Technologies, who earned an estimated $1.5 billion. This amount was topped during 2007 and 2008, when John Paulson, President of Paulson & Co, was estimated to have earned over $3.7 billion, after directing his firm to take bearish positions in mortgage-backed securities. Paulson's record was beaten in 2009, when David Tepper of Appaloossa Management earned an estimated $4 billion from investing in preferred shares and bonds of big US banks. Tepper correctly predicted that the government would not permit these institutions to fail. That year, the top 25 highest-earning managers were paid a collective $25.3 billion. In 2010, Paulson reclaimed the title of highest-paid hedge fund manager, earning $4.9 billion, while the top 25 managers took home a collective $22.07 billion. During 2015, the highest-paid hedge fund managers were Ken Griffin of Citadel: $1.7 billion; James Simons of Renaissance Technologies: $1.65 billion; Steven Cohen of SAC Capital Advisors: $1.55 billion; David Tepper of Appaloossa Management: $1.2 billion; and David Shaw of D.E. Shaw & Co.: $700 million.

6. **Financial innovation**. Hedge funds' ability to execute increasingly complex and high-volume trading strategies has been made possible by product and technology innovations in the financial market and by reductions in transaction costs. Electronic trading platforms for futures and swaps and "direct market access" tools allowed hedge funds to profitably trade a broad range of financial assets, while at the same time, more effectively manage their risks.

EXHIBIT 11.3 ESTIMATED TOTAL NUMBER OF HEDGE FUNDS AND FUND OF FUNDS

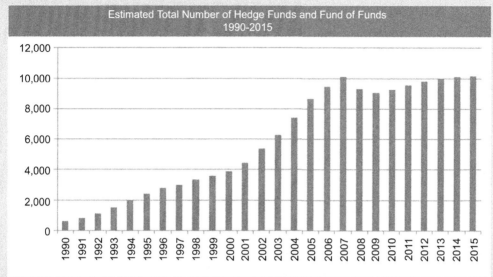

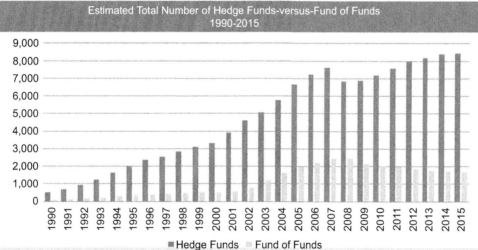

Source: Hedge Fund Research, Inc.

EXHIBIT 11.4 ESTIMATED GROWTH OF ASSETS FOR HEDGE FUNDS AND FUND OF FUNDS

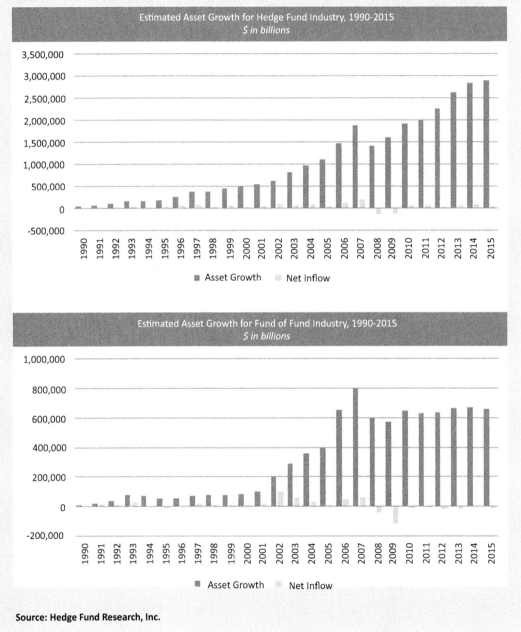

Source: Hedge Fund Research, Inc.

EXHIBIT 11.5 GLOBAL HEDGE FUND INDUSTRY MAP

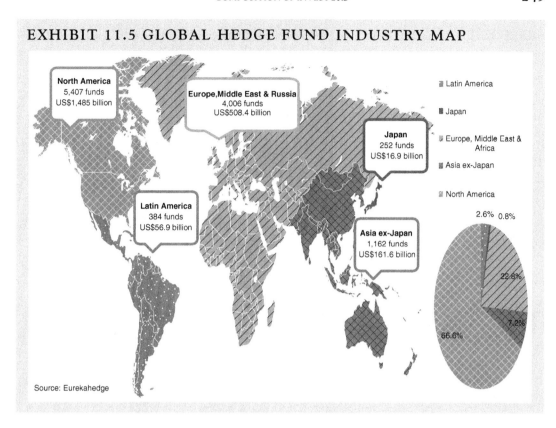

Source: Eurekahedge

COMPOSITION OF INVESTORS

Endowments and foundations are the largest investors in hedge funds, with a 31% share, and pensions (including public and private sectors) are the next largest investors, with a 15% share. Fund of hedge funds, which had a historically high share of 32% during 2008, fell to a 15% share during 2015 (see Exhibit 11.6).

EXHIBIT 11.6 HEDGE FUND INVESTORS

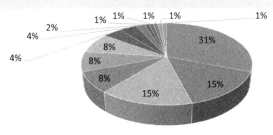

- Endowments/Foundations - 31%
- Public Pension Fund - 8%
- Asset Manager - 4%
- Investment Company - 1%
- Fund of Hedge Funds Manager - 15%
- Wealth Manager - 8%
- Insurance Company - 4%
- Bank - 1%
- Private Sector Pension Fund - 15%
- Family Office - 8%
- Superannuation Scheme - 2%
- Corporate Investor - 1%

Source: blackrock.com.

EXHIBIT 11.7 TOP HEDGE FUNDS BY ASSETS UNDER MANAGEMENT AS OF JANUARY 1, 2016

Firm	Region	AUM($bln)
Bridgewater Associates	United States	104.2
JP Morgan Asset Management	United States	50.0
AQR Capital Management	United States	47.2
Och-Ziff Capital Management Group	United States	44.6
Millennium Management	United States	34.0
Winton Capital Management	Europe	33.8
D. E. Shaw & Co.	United States	33.1
Viking Global Investors	United States	33.1
Man Group	Europe	31.8
BlackRock Advisors	United States	31.1
Two Sigma Investments	United States	30.6

Note: Figures are as of January 31, 2016 or are based on the latest available numbers.
Source: *Institutional Investor's Alpha*.

INDUSTRY CONCENTRATION

The hedge fund industry is dominated by the largest participants. The 11 largest hedge funds as of January, 1 2016 are listed in Exhibit 11.7. At the beginning of 2016, the largest hedge funds (6% of all firms) controlled 77% of all hedge fund assets (see Exhibit 11.8).

EXHIBIT 11.8 HEDGE FUND ASSETS ARE HIGHLY CONCENTRATED

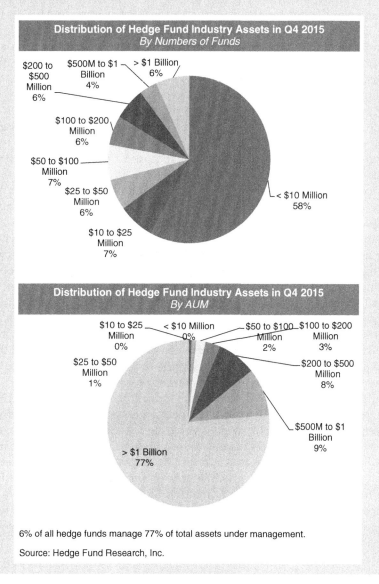

Distribution of Hedge Fund Industry Assets in Q4 2015
By Numbers of Funds

$200 to $500 Million 6%
$500M to $1 Billion 4%
> $1 Billion 6%
$100 to $200 Million 6%
$50 to $100 Million 7%
$25 to $50 Million 6%
$10 to $25 Million 7%
< $10 Million 58%

Distribution of Hedge Fund Industry Assets in Q4 2015
By AUM

$10 to $25 Million 0%
< $10 Million 0%
$50 to $100 Million 2%
$100 to $200 Million 3%
$25 to $50 Million 1%
$200 to $500 Million 8%
$500M to $1 Billion 9%
> $1 Billion 77%

6% of all hedge funds manage 77% of total assets under management.

Source: Hedge Fund Research, Inc.

PERFORMANCE

The average annual returns (after fees are deducted) by hedge funds between 1996 and 2006 was only slightly higher than broad equity market returns during this period. For example, Hedge Fund Research's HFRI Fund Weighted Composite Index (HFR index) showed average annual returns during this period of 10.6%, compared to an average annual return for the MSCI-World Equity Index (MSCI index) of 8.1% over the same period. However, the standard deviation of returns in the HFR index was lower: 2.1% for the HFR index compared to 4.2% for the MSCI index.[3] During 2007 and 2008 (a period of significant market dislocation), the average annual return for the HFR index was −5%, compared to −20% for the MSCI index. From 2002 to 2008, median returns of top performing hedge funds were significantly higher than industry-wide returns: the top deciles of hedge funds outperformed the HFR Fund Weighted Composite Index by an average of 45.8%. As a result, the average hedge fund slightly outperforms the broad equity market in a normal market environment (and with lower risk), but substantially outperforms during unstable markets. For those investors who have money invested in the top performing hedge funds, overall returns are substantially better than average hedge fund returns.

Unfortunately, because hedge funds are not required to follow any prescribed reporting protocol by regulators, hedge fund databases have a number of biases than can skew returns. One example is survivorship bias: some funds are dropped from the database when they are liquidated or failed. Another is backfill bias: when new funds are added to the database they may only report positive past returns. If these biases are excluded, hedge fund returns may be lower. For example, it has been determined that when excluding biases during a survey period of January 1995 through April 2006, the compound annual returns of hedge funds was 9% (net of fees), compared to the S&P 500 return of 11.6% during the same period.[4] However, during this period, it was also found that hedge funds created "alpha" returns (returns that are uncorrelated with the broad market) of 3% p.a. This means that hedge funds provided beneficial diversification, excluding biases, even though they underperformed the S&P 500 during the survey period. During the financial crisis that started in the mid-2007, the correlations between hedge fund returns and the returns of broad-based equity indexes increased, reducing the diversification benefit seen in previous years that were not characterized by extreme market events.

Average hedge fund returns have been positive during every year except 1998, 2008, and 2015 over the period 1995–2016. Their overall performance has been especially strong during bull markets (see Exhibit 11.9). When comparing risk-adjusted returns over the period of 1994–2015, hedge fund strategies have garnered higher average annual returns than both all-equities and all-bonds portfolios (see Exhibit 11.10). In addition, returns from top-quartile hedge funds are higher than returns generated from US equities and bonds (see Exhibit 11.11). As the hedge fund industry continues to mature, increasing amounts of data will become available to assess the industry's performance. A number of academic papers have analyzed hedge fund returns to determine whether hedge funds really deliver alpha. See Exhibit 11.12 for a summary of these findings.

---

[3] Ferguson, Roger and David Laster. "Hedge Funds and Systemic Risk." Banque de France Financial Stability Review, 2006.

[4] Ibbotson, Roger and Peng Chen. "The A, B, Cs of Hedge Funds: Alphas, Betas and Costs." 2006.

EXHIBIT 11.9 HEDGE FUND RETURNS

Monthly Hedge Fund Returns, 1997-2016
Barclay Hedge Fund Index

EXHIBIT 11.10 HEDGE FUND STRATEGIES HAVE OUTPERFORMED BOTH BONDS AND EQUITIES (EVEN ACCOUNTING FOR RISK)

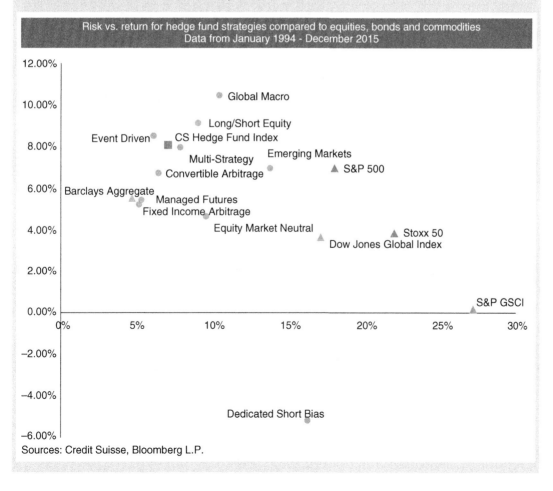

Sources: Credit Suisse, Bloomberg L.P.

EXHIBIT 11.11 HEDGE FUND RETURNS BY STRATEGY

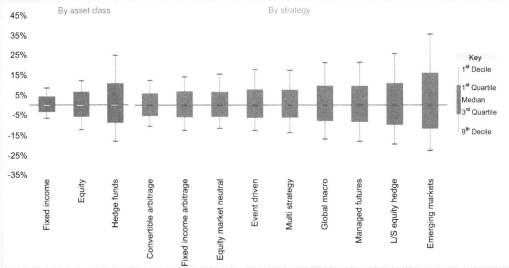

[1]Source: Morningstar (Equity and Fixed Income data), Thomson Reuters Lipper/TASS Database (Hedge Fund and Strategy Data), and BAA (analysis), Strategy classifications are derived from the Lipper TASS Database, Return differentials are defined as the quartile and decile level returns less the median return for each class of funds in order to represent the dispersion of manager returns within that class. As of Q42015.

Past performance is not an indication of future results

EXHIBIT 11.12 ACADEMIC RESEARCH ON HEDGE FUND PERFORMANCE

Due to limitations in the availability of hedge fund performance data, a clear assessment of industry performance is difficult to obtain. However, based on what is available through the small but growing number of academic papers on hedge funds, a number of observations can be made.

- Hedge funds in aggregate have slightly outperformed the public equities market.
  - Top-quartile hedge funds significantly outperform equities.
- Hedge funds in aggregate are slightly less volatile than the public equities market.
- Absolute returns ("alpha" or returns uncorrelated with the broader market) have been more elusive:
  - For many hedge fund strategies, over 70% of returns reflect returns of common market indices (Note 1).
  - Fund of funds delivered no alpha (Note 2).
  - Three percent of annual hedge fund returns can be attributed to alpha (Note 3).
  - Top-quartile hedge funds are able to achieve outsized alphas (as high as 15% annually), based on data from a period of a few years (Note 4).

EXHIBIT 11.12 ACADEMIC RESEARCH ON HEDGE FUND PERFORMANCE—cont'd

These findings suggest that investing in market indices can be a reasonable and less expensive alternative to expensive hedge funds (with the exception of top performing hedge funds).

It is important to note that there are limitations to these observations as imperfect data can create a number of biases:

- Selection bias: participation in hedge fund databases is voluntary.
- Survivorship bias: unsuccessful funds that have folded are not included in most hedge fund databases.
- Backfill bias: once a hedge fund registers with a database, returns from years prior to registration are provided and incorporated into the database as well. Funds are typically included in databases after they have accumulated a good performance track record.
- Liquidation bias: returns are no longer reported before a fund enters into final liquidation.

Although difficult to aggregate the effect of all of these biases, by some estimates, survivorship and backfill bias together can inflate industry returns by as much as 4% (refer Note 5).

Note 1: Hasanhodzic, Jasmina and Andrew W. Lo, "Can hedge-fund returns be replicated?: The linear case." *Journal of Investment Management*, Q2 2007, Vol. 5, No. 2.
Note 2: Fung, William, et al. "Hedge funds: Performance, risk, and capital formation." AFA 2007 Chicago Meetings paper, July 19, 2006.
Note 3: Ibbotson, Roger G. and Peng Chen. "The A, B, Cs of hedge funds: Alphas, betas and costs." Yale ICF working paper, September 2006.
Note 4: Kosowski, Robert, et al. "Do hedge funds deliver alpha? A Bayesian and bootstrap analysis." *Journal of Financial Economics*, Vol. 84, No. 1, April 2007, pp. 229–64.
Note 5: Fung, William and David Hsieh. "Hedge funds: An industry in its adolescence." *Federal Reserve Bank of Atlanta, Economic Review*, Q4 2006, Vol. 91, No. 4.
Source: Farrell, Diana, et al. "The New Power Brokers: How Oil, Asia, Hedge Funds and Private Equity Are Shaping the Global Capital Markets." McKinsey Global Institute, October 2007.

2008 SLOWDOWN

During 2008, an unprecedented decline in global equity and credit markets caused many financial assets, including convertible bonds and bank debt, to fall out of favor and become dislocated in either price or liquidity (or both). A growing uncertainty about the stability of the global financial sector caused counterparties (including prime brokers) to reevaluate the amount and terms of credit they extended to hedge funds, resulting in a broad-scale reduction in leverage and subsequent liquidations of many hedge fund portfolios. An unprecedented number of requests from investors for withdrawals during the third and fourth quarters of 2008 resulted from their own sudden liquidity needs, which forced many hedge funds to liquidate out of favor positions and portfolios into already dislocated markets, exacerbating security mispricings and subsequently causing further erosion to already poor fund performance results.

The Credit Suisse/Tremont Hedge Fund Index was down 19.1% in 2008, making it the worst year ever for hedge funds. However, this decline compared favorably with the 38.5% decline in the S&P 500 index over the same period. Therefore, although 2008 was a bad year for hedge funds, as a group, they outperformed the S&P 500 index by over 19%. Refer to Exhibit 11.13 for a performance comparison. Because of significant losses in 2008, over 900 hedge funds closed, reducing the total number of hedge funds by year end 2008 to 9176 (including fund of funds) and assets under management to $1.4 trillion (down by over $500 billion from a peak of over $1.9 trillion, recorded during mid-2008). During the fourth quarter of 2008, hedge funds saw $152 billion in redemptions. Both poor and well-performing funds experienced net asset outflows as investors looked to raise cash from all possible sources. Investors in funds who were experiencing liquidity problems were unable to withdraw money from those funds and they turned to other funds with "friendly" gate policies as a source for liquidity. This meant that even strong performers, such as Caxton Associates, which saw its largest fund gain 13%, but overall assets drop by 27% in 2008, were not completely immune to the outflow. See Exhibit 11.14 for a discussion of the travails of the hedge fund market during 2008.

EXHIBIT 11.13 COMPARISON OF HEDGE FUND RETURNS TO THE S&P 500 INDEX'S RETURNS, 2000–15

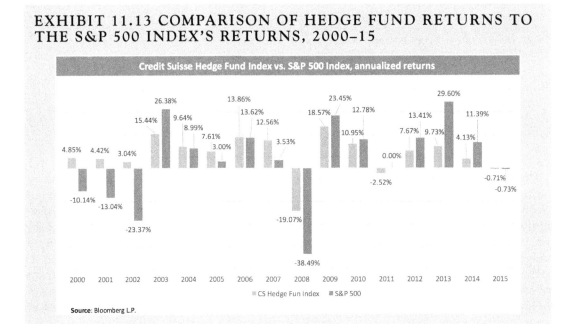

Source: Bloomberg L.P.

EXHIBIT 11.14 TRAVAILS OF THE HEDGE FUND MARKET IN 2008

Hedge funds are supposed to thrive in rough markets, but not in 2008. A historic decline in stocks, and troubles in almost every part of the bond market, dealt hedge funds their worst year on record. By the end of the year, investors were scrambling to get out, bringing an end to years of industry growth and creating uncertainty about the future of major components of the business. Part of the reason for investor redemptions from hedge funds was the desire to find cash to place directly into equity investments when equity allocation benchmarks were breached as the equity market tumbled.

Through December 2008, hedge funds globally lost 19% on average, according to Hedge Fund Research, a Chicago firm that tracks the industry. Although that's better than the 38.5% loss on the Standard & Poor's 500-stock index (including dividends) over the same period, it's far from the gains most funds posted for more than a decade. Long-short funds, the biggest hedge fund category, were down 27% on average. Funds that invest in emerging markets dropped 37%.

Fund managers and their investors tried to figure out what went wrong. One conclusion: Too many funds bought the same assets. As markets fell in September and October, and hedge funds came under pressure, many moved to sell investments, sending prices even lower and causing losses for other funds that hadn't yet sold. Part of the reason that hedge funds had to sell a portion of their portfolio was that some institutions had to redeem hedge fund investments in an effort to raise case to invest directly in equities when the equity market decline caused minimum equity allocation benchmarks to be breached, triggering a need to make additional direct equity investments.

Stocks favored by hedge funds performed even worse than the overall market, according to data from Goldman Sachs. An index of 50 stocks "that matter most" to hedge funds lost nearly 45%, including dividends, compared with a loss of 38.5% on the S&P 500.

One problem for many hedge funds was the amount they held in hard-to-trade assets, such as loans, real-estate holdings, and stakes in small, private companies. These illiquid investments at one time accounted for 20% of some fund portfolios, estimated to total about $400 billion. As financial markets come under pressure, it became harder to get out of these investments, or even to value them accurately.

Another problem for the industry was the fallout from December 2008's arrest of Bernard Madoff for a multibillion dollar Ponzi scheme. While Madoff wasn't a hedge-fund manager, his business of overseeing private accounts for wealthy individuals in tight-knit social circles from Palm Beach, to Long Island, as well as for charities and private-banking clients all across Europe, rattled investor trust in private-investment managers in general.

The scandal also tainted fund of funds, the professional investment firms that raise money from clients to invest in a portfolio of other investment funds. Several such firms channeled billions of dollars to Madoff through feeder funds, raising questions about how much due diligence those firms performed and whether clients' investments are as diversified and safe as they should be.

Source: Zuckerman, Gregory and Jenny Strasburg. "For Many Hedge Funds, No Escape." *Wall Street Journal* January 2, 2009.

MARKET LIQUIDITY AND EFFICIENCY

Hedge funds have a significant impact on global capital markets. Because they actively trade securities, hedge funds account for a large portion of trading in many of the largest equity and debt markets. Hedge fund trading has significantly increased liquidity in markets around the world and increased financial options for institutional investors, corporations, governments, and individuals. Active trading by hedge funds has also created greater price discovery in financial markets, which has led to a reduction in pricing inefficiencies.

Hedge funds have significantly augmented the growth of credit derivatives. According to the McKinsey Global Institute, hedge funds have historically been responsible for over one-third of contracts sold. In addition, hedge funds have been large buyers of asset-backed securities (ABS) and collateralized debt obligations (CDOs) created from ABS. As a result of this activity, banks were able to originate more loans and take credit risks off their own balance sheet. This, in turn, enabled both consumers and companies to access new sources of capital.

Hedge funds have provided many loans to private equity funds in support of their leveraged buyout activity. S&P estimates that hedge funds committed over $70 billion in leveraged loans to private equity firm portfolio companies and below-investment grade companies during previous years.

FINANCIAL INNOVATION

Hedge funds have been significant users of new products developed by investment banks and others that allow exposure to different asset classes more efficiently, at a lower cost and with less transparency. This has given rise to an increase in quantitative trading activities (using computers to analyze anomalous financial prices and then engaging in automated trading to exploit the anomalies) and more robust arbitrage trading activity (investing in two related financial instruments in an effort to exploit price inefficiencies). The newly created financial products are available on exchanges and in the over-the-counter market. These products have given hedge funds the opportunity to acquire, among many new assets, consumer loans, mortgages, and credit card debt that were previously only held by banks.

New products also include total return swaps, credit default swaps, and other synthetic products that create exposures to asset classes that were previously not accessible to hedge funds, as well as hedging vehicles that promote expansion of risk taking. In addition, hedge funds have been the beneficiaries of significant improvement in reporting and risk management systems, which has enabled them to engage in ever more complex and robust trading activities. However, the complexities of many of these products have also led to some unanticipated risks, resulting in increased concerns among regulators and practitioners of the possibility for enhanced losses. There is substantial disagreement about whether the benefits of this innovation have been outweighed by the systemic and individual risks that innovation has created (see Chapter 14).

ILLIQUID INVESTMENTS

Hedge funds have historically limited their participation in illiquid investments, preferring to match their investment horizon to the typically 1-year lock-up periods that their investors agree to. However, many hedge funds have increasingly invested in illiquid assets in an effort to augment returns. For example, they have invested in private investments in public equity, acquiring large minority holdings in public companies. Their purchases of CDOs and CLOs (collateralized loan obligations) and other ABS are also somewhat illiquid, since these fixed income securities are difficult to price and there is a limited secondary market during times of crisis. In addition, hedge funds have participated in loans (Och-Ziff provided a large loan to finance the takeover of Manchester United, one of the world's most popular football/soccer teams) and invested in physical assets (purchasing Indonesian oil rigs). Sometimes, investments that were intended to be held for less than 1 year have become long-term, illiquid assets when the assets depreciated and hedge funds decided to continue their holding until values recovered, rather than selling at a loss (see side pockets below). It is estimated that more than 20% of total assets under management by hedge funds are illiquid, hard to price assets. This makes hedge fund asset valuation difficult and has created a mismatch between hedge fund assets and liabilities, giving rise to significant problems when investors attempt to withdraw their cash at the end of lock-up periods.

LOCK-UPS, GATES, AND SIDE POCKETS

Hedge funds generally focus their investment strategies on financial assets that are liquid and able to be readily priced based on reported prices in the market for those assets or by reference to comparable assets that have a discernable price. Since most of these assets can be valued and sold over a short period of time to generate cash, hedge funds permit investors to invest in or withdraw money from the fund at regular intervals and managers receive performance fees based on quarterly mark-to-market valuations. However, to match up maturities of assets and liabilities for each investment strategy, most hedge funds have the ability to prevent invested capital from being withdrawn during certain periods of time. They achieve this though "lock-up" and "gate" provisions that are included in investment agreements with their investors.

A lock-up provision provides that during an initial investment period of, typically, 1–2 years, an investor is not allowed to withdraw any money from the fund. Generally, the lock-up period is a function of the investment strategy that is being pursued. Sometimes, lock-up periods are modified for specific investors through a side letter agreement. However, this can become problematic because of the resulting different effective lock-up periods that apply to different investors who invest at the same time in the same fund. Also, this can trigger "most favored nations" provisions in other investor agreements.

A gate is a restriction that limits the amount of withdrawals during a quarterly or semi-annual redemption period after the lock-up period expires. Typically, gates are percentages of a fund's capital that can be withdrawn on a scheduled redemption date. A gate of 10%–20% is common. A gate provision allows the hedge fund to increase exposure to illiquid assets without facing a liquidity crisis. In addition, it offers some protection to investors who do not attempt to withdraw funds because if withdrawals are too high, assets might have to be sold by the hedge fund at disadvantageous prices, causing a potential reduction in investment returns for remaining investors.

Hedge funds sometimes use a "side pocket" account to house comparatively illiquid or hard-to-value assets. Once an asset is designated for inclusion in a side pocket, new investors don't participate in the returns from this asset. When existing investors withdraw money from the hedge fund, they remain as investors in the side pocket asset until it either is sold or becomes liquid through a monetization event such as an initial public offering (IPO). Management fees are typically charged on side pocket assets based on their cost, rather than a mark-to-market value of the asset. Performance fees are charged based on realized proceeds, when the asset is sold. Usually, there is no requirement to force the sale of side pocket investments by a specific date. Sometimes, investors accuse hedge funds of putting distressed assets that were intended to be sold during a 1-year horizon into a side pocket account to avoid dragging down the returns of the overall fund. Investors are concerned about unexpected illiquidity arising from a side pocket and the potential for even greater losses if a distressed asset that has been placed there continues to decline in value.

Fund managers sometimes use even more drastic options to limit withdrawals, such as suspending all redemption rights (but only in the most dire circumstances).

COMPARISON WITH PRIVATE EQUITY FUNDS AND MUTUAL FUNDS

Hedge funds are similar to private equity funds in a number of ways. They are both private pools of capital that pay high management fees and high performance fees based on the fund's profits (2 and 20) and both are lightly regulated. However, hedge funds generally invest in relatively liquid assets, purchase minority positions in company stocks and bonds and in many other assets (taking both long and short positions for investments). Private equity funds, by contrast, typically purchase entire companies, creating a less liquid investment that is often held for 3–7 years. Although there is an intention to create liquidity after this period, since exit events often include an IPO, where only a portion of the investment is sold, or an M&A sale, where the consideration could be in shares of another company, rather than cash, liquidity is not assured even then.

Hedge funds are pools of investment capital, as are mutual funds. However, the similarity stops there. Mutual funds must price assets daily and offer daily liquidity, compared to the typical quarterly disclosure of asset values to hedge fund investors and liquidity that is subject to certain limitations, as described in the previous section. In the United States, hedge funds are limited to soliciting investments only from accredited investors, but mutual funds have no such limitation. Mutual funds are heavily regulated in the United States by the SEC, while hedge fund regulation, although subject to change (see Chapter 14), is limited. The hedge fund fee structure is also significantly different: mutual funds usually receive management fees that are substantially lower than fees paid to hedge funds, and mutual funds generally do not receive the performance fees that hedge funds receive. While mutual funds typically do not use leverage to support their investments, leverage is a hallmark of hedge funds. Finally, hedge funds engage in a much broader array of trading strategies, creating both long and short investment positions, utilizing derivatives and many other sophisticated financial products to create the exposures that they want. Mutual funds generally have less investment flexibility and, unlike hedge funds, are required to distribute a significant portion of their income.

Recently, a small number of mutual funds have introduced performance-based fees and some mutual funds are pursuing more aggressive, flexible trading strategies in an effort to keep investors from defecting to hedge funds.

HIGH WATER MARKS AND HURDLE RATES

A high water mark relates to payment of performance fees. Hedge fund managers typically receive performance fees only when the value of the fund exceeds the highest NAV it has previously achieved. For example, if a fund is launched with an NAV of $100 per share and NAV was $120 at the end of the first year, assuming a 20% performance fee, the hedge fund would receive a performance fee of $4 per share. If, however, at the end of the second year, NAV dropped to $115, no performance fee would be payable. If, at the end of the third year, NAV was $130, the performance fee would be $2, instead of $3, because of the high water mark (($130 - $120) \times 0.2$). Sometimes, if a high water mark is perceived to be unattainable, a hedge fund may be incented to close down. See Chapter 15 for more discussion of high water marks. In addition, most hedge funds agree to a hurdle rate whereby the fund receives a performance fee only if the fund's annual return exceeds a benchmark rate, such as a predetermined fixed percentage, or a rate determined by the market, such as LIBOR or a T-bill yield.

PUBLIC OFFERINGS

In Europe, Man Group PLC launched the first ever hedge fund IPO in 1994. On February 9, 2007, Fortress Investment Group (FIG), which is an alternative asset manager that includes hedge fund, private equity, and real estate investment businesses, launched an IPO in the United States at a price of $18.50. Their shares closed on the first trading day at $31, which reflected a price that was 40 times the previous year's earnings per share. This contrasted with Goldman Sachs' price/earnings ratio of 11 times and Legg Mason, a mutual fund, which had a price/earnings ratio of 24 times. FIG's very high price/earnings ratio prompted other US hedge funds and private equity funds to consider an IPO. In June 2007, GLG Partners, a large European hedge fund, launched an IPO in the United States, raising $3.4 billion. Och-Ziff, one of the largest US hedge funds, launched an IPO on November 12, 2007, at a price of $32. All of the hedge fund IPOs offered a stake in a management company, and the offerings were organized through a master limited partnership that gave public investors limited say in the firm's governance. Citadel was the first US hedge fund to file a registration statement with the SEC to enable a public bond offering. In December 2007, they sold a $500 million bond to institutional investors. Several other hedge funds considered, but aborted, US IPO initiatives after seeing the share price of Fortress and Och-Ziff fall precipitously as the market turned negative during 2008 and remained low through 2015 (see Exhibit 11.15).

EXHIBIT 11.15 HEDGE FUND INITIAL PUBLIC OFFERINGS HAVE UNDERPERFORMED THE BROADER MARKET

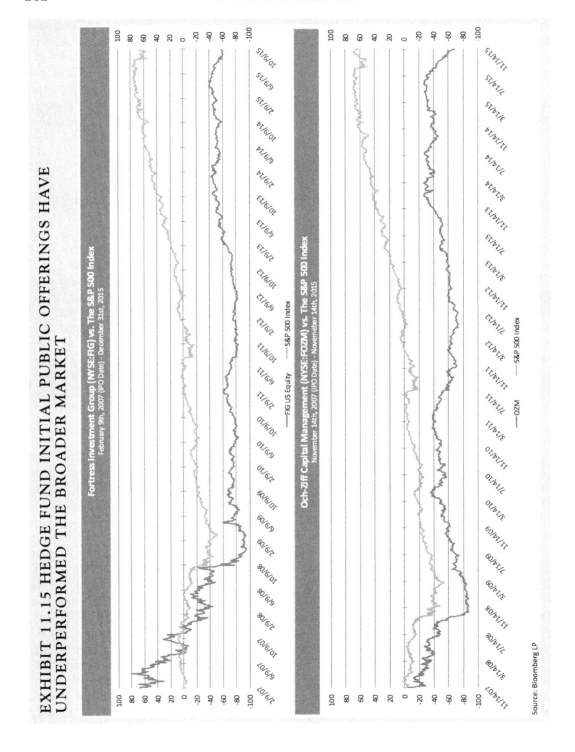

Fortress Investment Group (NYSE:FIG) vs. The S&P 500 Index
February 9th, 2007 (IPO Date) - December 31st, 2015

FIG US Equity — S&P 500 Index

Och-Ziff Capital Management (NYSE:FOZM) vs. The S&P 500 Index
November 14th, 2007 (IPO Date) - November 14th, 2015

OZM — S&P 500 Index

Source: Bloomberg LP

FUND OF FUNDS

A "fund of funds" is an investment fund that invests in a portfolio of other investment funds, rather than investing directly. A fund of hedge funds attempts to provide a broad exposure to the hedge fund industry and risk diversification. They typically charge a management fee of 1%–1.5% of AUM and also receive performance fees that range from 10% to 20%. As a result, if a fund of funds invests in a dozen hedge funds that charge "2 and 20" fees on average, total management and performance fees paid by fund of fund investors could be about 3.25% and 35%, respectively. For some investors, these fees outweigh the benefits of investing in hedge funds. However, many investors who may not qualify to invest in hedge funds because they have insufficient capital to invest, or are not recognized as qualified investors in the United States by the SEC, will invest in a fund of funds as the only vehicle through which they can invest in hedge funds. In addition, since many fund of funds have investments in 10 or more different hedge funds, they provide more diversification than some investors might achieve directly due to limited amounts of investible capital.

Some high net worth and institutional investors will channel money through a fund of funds because they value the "due diligence" process by which fund of funds weed out poor hedge fund managers. However, there are many recent examples of inadequate due diligence, where fund of funds have performed at or worse than hedge fund indexes, based on poor investment decisions that reflect inadequate investigation of hedge fund practices and investment strategies. For example, many investors were distraught when they were told that their fund of funds at Goldman Sachs and Man Group had invested in Amaranth Advisors, a hedge fund that declared bankruptcy in 2006. Another example is the Madoff Ponzi scheme: during December 2008, a number of fund of funds acknowledged that they invested in Bernard Madoff's funds, which resulted in overall investor losses of multiple billions of dollars. Even though Madoff's funds were not considered hedge funds, hedge funds were nonetheless tainted by this disaster. Allegations of poor due diligence by fund of funds has created more intense scrutiny of the investigation practices of these funds (see Exhibit 11.16).

EXHIBIT 11.16 WHY USE A FUND OF FUNDS FIRM?

- Diversification and access
  - Immediate diversification with relatively modest capital investment
  - Access to certain managers who might otherwise be closed for investment
- Value-added investment process
  - Fundamental knowledge of many different investment strategies
  - Network of industry relationships assists in filtering manager universe
  - Staffing resources and expertise necessary for manager due diligence and monitoring
  - Understanding of quantitative and qualitative portfolio construction issues
  - Dynamic process that requires constant attention
- Operational efficiencies
  - Legal due diligence and document negotiation
  - Consolidated accounting, performance, and financial reporting
  - Cash flow management

Source: Grosvenor Capital Management.

Some hedge funds welcome fund of fund investments because it gives them a new source of cash and the investment amount is typically large. Other hedge funds limit fund of fund investment because they worry that fund of funds take a short-term view and are quick to withdraw money if performance declines.

The fund of hedge funds industry is dominated by Blackstone, which has twice as much assets under management as UBS, the second largest firm. The 2015 rankings (see Exhibit 11.17) based on fund of hedge funds assets under management includes Blackstone Alternative Asset Management: $67.260 billion; UBS Hedge Fund Solutions: $34.516 billion; and Goldman Sachs Asset Management: $29.248 billion. During 2016, fund of funds represented more than 28% of all investments in hedge funds. See Chapter 15 for additional discussion of fund of funds.

EXHIBIT 11.17 HEDGE FUND OF FUND MANAGERS

Rank	Manager	Assets (in millions) as of June 30, 2015)
1	Blackstone Alternative Asset Management	$67,260
2	UBS Hedge Fund Solutions	$34,516
3	Goldman Sachs Asset Management	$29,248
4	GCM Grosvenor	$27,373
5	Blackstone Alternative Asset Management	$21,849
6	J.P. Morgan Asset Management	$19,790
7	Permal Group	$18,783
8	Mesirow Advanced Strategies	$14,215
9	Entrust Capital	$12,462
10	Man Group	$11,300

Hedge Fund Investment Strategies

OUTLINE

The material in this chapter should be cross-referenced with the following cases: **Kmart, Sears, and ESL: How a Hedge Fund Became One of the World's Largest Retailers and Porsche, Volkswagen, and CSX: Cars, Trains and Derivatives**.

Hedge funds employ dynamic investment strategies designed to find unique opportunities in the market and then actively trade their portfolio investments (both long and short) in an effort to maintain high and diversified absolute returns (often using leverage to enhance returns). By contrast, most mutual funds only take long positions in securities and are less active in trading their portfolio investments (usually without leverage) as they attempt to create returns that track (and ideally outperform) the market. Some hedge funds attempt to exploit price anomalies in the market by, for example, taking advantage of a pricing mismatch between two related bonds. Other funds use computer models to identify anomalous relationships between different equity securities. There are also hedge funds that simply make unhedged directional bets on market movements, after analyzing macroeconomic fundamentals. In addition, some hedge funds use extensive bottom-up research to pick stocks or bonds that show appreciation or depreciation potential and then buy, sell short, or use derivatives to capitalize on their research. Regardless

Investment Banks, Hedge Funds, and Private Equity, Third Edition
http://dx.doi.org/10.1016/B978-0-12-804723-1.00012-8

of their strategy, most hedge funds are much more active traders, compared to mutual funds. As a result, hedge funds account for a significant share of all financial asset trading activities worldwide.

There are four broad groups of hedge fund strategies: arbitrage, event driven, equity related, and macro. The first two groups in many cases attempt to achieve returns that are uncorrelated with general market movements. Managers of these strategies try to find price discrepancies between related securities, using derivatives and active trading based on computer driven models and extensive research. The second two groups are impacted by movements in the market, and they require intelligent anticipation of price movements in stocks, bonds, foreign exchange, and physical commodities based on extensive research and model building. A summary of the four broad groups of hedge fund strategies is found in Exhibit 12.1.

EXHIBIT 12.1 HEDGE FUND STRATEGIES CAN BE GROUPED INTO FOUR MAIN CATEGORIES

	Subcategory	Description
Arbitrage	Fixed income–based arbitrage	Exploits pricing inefficiencies in fixed income markets, combining long/short positions of various fixed income securities
	Convertible arbitrage	Purchases convertible bonds and hedges equity risk by selling short the underlying common stock
	Relative value arbitrage	Exploits pricing inefficiencies across asset classes, e.g., pairs trading, dividend arbitrage, yield curve trades
Event Driven	Distressed securities	Invests in companies in a distressed situation (e.g., bankruptcies, restructuring) and/or shorts companies expected to experience distress
	Merger arbitrage	Generates returns by going long on the target and shorting the stock of the acquiring company
	Activism	Seeks to obtain representation in companies' board of directors in order to shape company policy and strategic direction
Equity Based	Equity long/short	Consists of a core holding of particular equity securities, hedged with short sales of stocks to minimize overall market exposure
	Equity non hedge	Commonly known as "stock picking"; invests long in particular equity securities
Macro	Global macro	Leveraged bets on anticipated price movements of stock markets, interest rates, foreign exchange, and physical commodities
	Emerging markets	Invests a major share of portfolio in securities of companies or the sovereign debt of developing or "emerging" countries; investments are primarily long

Source: McKinsey Global Institute; Hedge Fund Research, Inc.; David Stowell.

Hedge fund strategies have become more diversified to reduce investment risk. For example, in 1990, macro investments by hedge funds comprised 39% of all hedge fund assets. By 2015, this strategy comprised only 19% of hedge fund assets. During the same period of time, arbitrage and event-driven strategies combined grew from 24% to 52% of all hedge fund assets (see Exhibit 12.2).

EXHIBIT 12.2 HEDGE FUND STRATEGIES HAVE BECOME MORE DIVERSIFIED

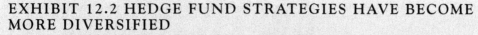

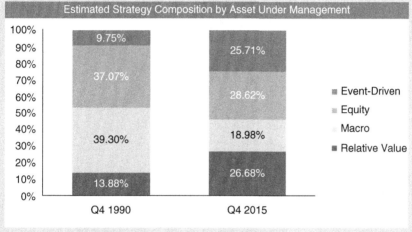

Estimated Strategy Composition by Asset Under Management

* Hedge Fund Research's 'Relative Value' classification is comparable to the 'Arbitrage' classification used in the book.

Source: Hedge Fund Research, Inc.

EQUITY-BASED STRATEGIES

Equity Long/Short

A hedge fund manager who focuses on equity long/short investing starts with a fundamental analysis of individual companies, combined with research on risks and opportunities particular to a company's industry, country of incorporation, competitors, and the overall macroeconomic environment in which the company operates. Managers consider ways to reduce volatility by either diversifying or hedging positions across industries and regions and hedging undiversifiable market risk. However, the overall risk in this strategy is determined by whether a manager is attempting to prioritize returns (by having more concentration and leverage) or low risk (by creating lower volatility through diversification, lower leverage, and hedging). The core rationale of a long/short strategy is to shift principal risk from market risk to manager risk, which requires skilled stock selection to generate alpha. To do this, a manager concurrently buys and sells similar securities in an attempt to exploit relative mispricings, while decreasing market risk. An overview of a long/short strategy is found in Exhibit 12.3.

EXHIBIT 12.3 LONG/SHORT STRATEGY OVERVIEW

Strategy Overview

- **Definition**: Strategy by which the manager concurrently buys and sells similar securities or indexes in an attempt to exploit relative mispricings, while neutralizing a risk common in those securities
- **Examples**: Equities (Long JP Morgan, Short Citigroup); Yield curve (Short 2-year Treasuries, Long 10-year Treasuries); CDOs (Long equity Tranche, Short mezzanine Tranche), etc.
- **Direction**: Can be neutral, net long, or net short
- **Rationale**: Shifts principal risk from market risk to manager risk based on the premise that skilled stock selection generates alpha

Mechanics of a Long / Short Strategy (Equity):

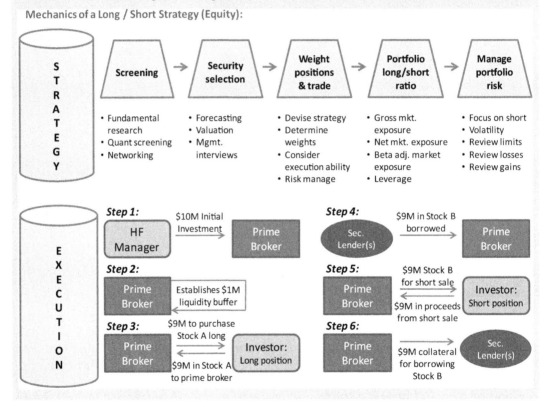

EXHIBIT 12.3 LONG/SHORT STRATEGY OVERVIEW—cont'd

Long/Short Strategy Return Sources and Costs

Return Sources

- Performance
  - Alpha on long position plus alpha on short position
- Interest rebate
  - Short sale proceeds invested by prime broker in short-term securities
  - Rebate = interest on short-sale proceeds – prime broker lender fee and expenses
  - Rebate is usually = 75%–90% of interest on short-sale proceeds
- Liquidity buffer interest
  - Liquidity buffer posted to pay for daily mark to market adjustments and to pay dividend to stock lenders (arranged by prime brokers)
  - Liquidity buffer earns short-term interest

Costs

- Share borrow costs
- Dividend costs on short position
- Transaction costs

Return Attribution:

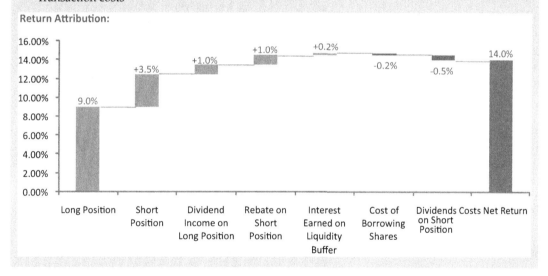

Nonhedged Equity

This strategy is common to hedge funds, mutual funds, and other investors. There is usually no hedge involved and investments are long only (not short). This stock-picking strategy relies on fundamental research on individual companies and industries.

MACRO STRATEGIES

Global Macro

A macro-focused hedge fund makes leveraged bets on anticipated price movements in stock and bond markets, interest rates, foreign exchange, and physical commodities. A macro strategy also takes positions in financial derivatives such as forwards, options, and swaps on assets such as stocks, bonds, commodities, loans, and real estate, and on indexes that are focused on these same assets. A macro-focused fund considers economic forecasts; analysis about global flow of funds; interest rate trends; political changes; relations between governments; individual country, political, and economic policies; and other broad systemic considerations. A well-known practitioner of a global macro investment is George Soros, who sold short more than $10 billion of pound sterling in 1992, successfully profiting from the Bank of England's reluctance to either raise its interest rates to levels comparable to rates in other European countries or to float its currency. Although the Bank of England resisted both initiatives, market forces ultimately forced it to withdraw its currency from the European Exchange Rate Mechanism and to devalue the pound sterling. Soros earned an estimated $1.1 billion from his bearish macro position on the pound sterling.

Emerging Markets

An emerging market–focused hedge fund invests most of its funds in either the securities of companies in developing (emerging) countries or the sovereign debt of these countries. Emerging markets is a term used to describe a country's social or business activity that is characterized by rapid growth and industrialization. Typically, investors demand greater returns because of incremental risks.

ARBITRAGE STRATEGIES

Arbitrage is possible when one of the three conditions are met: (1) the same asset does not trade at the same price in all markets; (2) two assets with identical cash flows do not trade at the same price; or (3) an asset with a known price in the future does not trade today at its future price discounted by the risk-free interest rate.

Fixed Income–Based Arbitrage

Fixed income–arbitrage funds attempt to exploit pricing inefficiencies in fixed income markets by combining long/short positions of various fixed income securities. For example, historically, because of the limited liquidity of the Italian bond futures market, the currency-hedged returns from this market in the short term were lower than the short-term returns in the very liquid US Treasury bond market. However, over a longer period of time, the hedged returns became nearly identical. Fixed income arbitrageurs benefited from the eventual convergence of hedged yields between currency-hedged Italian bond futures and US Treasury bonds by shorting relatively expensive US Treasury bonds and purchasing relatively cheap Italian bond futures.

Another example involves 30-year on-the-run and off-the-run US Treasury bonds. Liquidity discrepancies between the most recently issued 30-year Treasury bonds (called on-the-run bonds) and 29.75-year Treasury bonds that were originally issued one quarter earlier (called off-the-run bonds) sometimes cause a slight difference in pricing between the two bonds. This can be exploited by buying cheaper off-the-run bonds and shorting the more expensive on-the-run bonds. Since the price of the two bonds should converge within 3 months (both bonds becoming off-the-run bonds), this trading position should create a profit for the arbitrageur.

Convertible Arbitrage

A convertible bond can be thought of as a fixed income security that has an embedded equity call option. The convertible investor has the right, but not the obligation to convert (exchange) the bond into a predetermined number of common shares. The investor will presumably convert sometime at or before the maturity of the bond if the value of the common shares exceeds the cash redemption value of the bond. The convertible, therefore, has both debt and equity characteristics and, as a result, provides an asymmetrical risk and return profile. Until the investor converts the bond into common shares of the issuer, the issuer is obligated to pay a fixed coupon to the investor and repay the bond at maturity if conversion never occurs. A convertible's price is sensitive to, among other things, changes in market interest rates, credit risk of the issuer, and the issuer's common share price and share price volatility.

Analysis of convertible bond prices factors in three different sources of value: investment value, conversion value, and option value. The investment value is the theoretical value at which the bond would trade if it were not convertible. This represents the security's floor value or minimum price at which it should trade as a nonconvertible bond. The conversion value represents the value of the common stock into which the bond can be converted. If, for example, these shares are trading at $30 and the bond can convert into 100 shares, the conversion value is $3000. The investment value and conversion value can be considered, at maturity, the low- and high-price boundaries for the convertible bond. The option value represents the theoretical value of having the right, but not the obligation, to convert the bond into common shares. Until maturity, a convertible trades at a price between the investment value and the option value.

A Black-Scholes option pricing model, in combination with a bond valuation model, can be used to price a convertible security. However, a binomial option model, with some adjustments, is the best method for determining the value of a convertible security. See Chapters 3 and 9 for a more complete description of convertible securities, which includes a discussion of convertible preferred shares and mandatory convertibles.

Convertible arbitrage is a market neutral investment strategy that involves the simultaneous purchase of convertible securities and the short sale of common shares (selling borrowed stock) that underlie the convertible. An investor attempts to exploit inefficiencies in the pricing of the convertible in relation to the security's embedded call option on the convertible issuer's common stock. In addition, there are cash flows associated with the arbitrage position that combine with the security's inefficient pricing to create favorable returns to an investor who is able to properly manage a hedge position through a dynamic hedging process. The hedge involves selling short a percentage of the shares that the convertible can convert into based on the change in the convertible's price with respect to the change in the underlying common stock price (delta) and the change in delta with respect to the change in the underlying common stock (gamma). The short position must be adjusted frequently in an attempt to neutralize the impact of changing common share prices during the life of the convertible security. This process of managing the short position in the issuer's stock is called "delta hedging."

If hedging is done properly, whenever the convertible issuer's common share price decreases, the gain from the short stock position should exceed the loss from the convertible holding. Equally, whenever the issuer's common share price increases, the gain from the convertible holding should exceed the loss from the short stock position.

In addition to the returns produced by delta hedging, the investor will receive returns from the convertible's coupon payment and interest income associated with the short stock sale. However, this cash flow is reduced by paying a cash amount to stock lenders equal to the dividend the lenders would have received if the stock were not loaned to the convertible investor and further reduced by stock borrow costs paid to a prime broker. In addition, if the investor leveraged the investment by borrowing cash from a prime broker, there will be interest expense on the loan. Finally, if an investor chooses to hedge credit risk of the issuer, or interest rate risk, there will be additional costs associated with credit default swaps and a short treasury position. See Exhibit 12.4 for a more thorough review of the convertible arbitrage strategy.

EXHIBIT 12.4 MECHANICS OF CONVERTIBLE ARBITRAGE

A convertible arbitrageur attempts to purchase undervalued convertibles and simultaneously short a number of common shares that the convertible can convert into (the "conversion ratio"). The number of shares sold short depends on the conversion ratio and the delta. The delta measures the change in the convertible's price with respect to the change in the underlying common stock price, which represents the convertible's equity sensitivity for very small stock price changes. The arbitrageur's objective is to create an attractive rate of return regardless of the changing price of the underlying shares. This is achieved by capturing the cash flows available on different transactions that relate to the convertible as well as directly from the convertible and by profiting from buying a theoretically cheap convertible. Many convertibles are originally issued at a price below their theoretical value because the stock price volatility assumed in the convertible pricing is below the actual volatility that is expected during the life of the convertible. A summary of potential convertible returns is as follows:

1. **Income generation**
   The arbitrageur tries to generate income while hedging the risks of various components of a convertible bond. Income from a convertible hedge comes from the following: coupon + interest on short proceeds − stock dividend − stock borrow cost. This income is increased if the arbitrageur leverages the investment (two or three times leverage is common). However, costs associated with hedging interest rate and credit risks reduce the income. An example of income generation, which is linked to Fig. 12.2, is given as follows:
       Assuming that an issuer's common stock price is $41.54 and dividend yield is 1% when a $1000 convertible is issued and the convertible has a 2.5% coupon, a conversion ratio of

EXHIBIT 12.4 MECHANICS OF CONVERTIBLE ARBITRAGE—cont'd

21.2037, 53% average short stock position (with 2% interest income available from this position), and a stock borrow cost of 0.25% on the short proceeds, over a 1 year horizon, the total income from a delta hedged convertible would be $28.50, which is equal to 2.9% of the $1000 convertible:

Coupon	2.5% on $1,000 convertible	= $25.00
+ Short Interest	2% on $466.83* short proceeds	= $9.34
- Stock Dividend	1% on $466.83* short proceeds	= ($4.67)
- Stock Borrow Cost	0.25% on $ 466.83* short proceeds	= ($1.17)
Total		= $28.50

* The $1,000 convertible can convert into 21.2037 shares (the conversion ratio). $41.54 (current share price) x 21.2037 = $880.80. Since there is a 53% short position, the value of the shares sold short is $880.80 x 0.53 = $466.83

2. Monetizing volatility

Because of the nonlinear relationship between prices for the convertible and for the underlying stock, there is an additional gain potential in creating a delta neutral position between the convertible and the stock. This is explained in Fig. 12.1. At point 1, the green line represents the long convertible position, whereas the dotted line represents the delta neutral exposure. Therefore, if the stock price were to fall from position 1, the gain on the short stock position is greater than the loss from the long convertible position (position A). However, if the stock were to gain, the loss on the short would be less than the gain on the convertible (position B). To demonstrate this, consider Fig. 12.2.

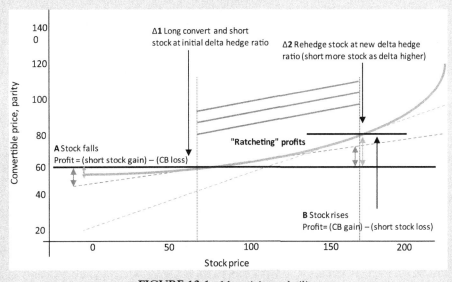

FIGURE 12.1   Monetizing volatility.

continued

EXHIBIT 12.4 MECHANICS OF CONVERTIBLE ARBITRAGE—cont'd

	Convertible arbitrage fund
Stock Px = $41.54	**initial case** Long convertible 101.375 par = $1,013.75
Convertible delta = 53%	Amount of short shares 21.2037*53% = 11.24
Conv. Ratio = 21.2037 shares	Short value = 11.24 (shares)*41.54 (price) = $466.82
Convertible Px = 101.375% par	Net cash outlay = $546.93
	+5% scenario Current share price = $43.617
	Loss from short = $466.82 − (11.24*43.617) = $23.34
	Gain from convertible = $(1,038.07^{1} − 1,013.75) = 24.32
	Net gain = 24.32-23.34 = $.98
	New hedge delta = 58.11%
	−5% scenario Current share price = $39.463
	Gain from short = $466.82 − (11.24*39.463) = $23.34
	Loss from convertible = $(1,013.75 − 991.78^{2}) = 21.97
	Net gain = 23.34-21.97 = $1.37
	New hedge delta = 46.75%

Note: calculations are not rounded.

FIGURE 12.2   Convertible arbitrage trade.

This convertible trades at a price of 101.375% of par, has a delta of 53%, and is convertible into 21.2037 shares per $1000 convertible security. Fig. 12.2 describes the process for "monetizing the volatility," or generating trading profits by rehedging the position as the stock moves. It would cost $1013.75 to purchase the convertible, and there would be $466.83 in short stock proceeds, resulting in a net cash outlay of $546.93. If the stock price subsequently increases by 5%, because of the nonlinearity of the convertible, the convertible appreciated more than the loss on the short position, creating profit of $.98. At this point, the convertible delta exposure is neutralized at the new hedge delta level by shorting more stock, since the delta has increased. Conversely, if the stock decreases by 5%, the convertible depreciates less than the gain on the short position, creating a profit of $1.37. The convertible delta exposure is neutralized at the new delta level by purchasing stock to reduce the short position because the delta is lower at this point. And so, the investor makes a profit, regardless of whether the stock goes up or down. Assuming that there is, on average, a $1.17 annual profit from monetizing volatility [($1.37 + .98)/2] for every 5% change in share price, and assuming there are monthly 5% changes, this represents a hypothetical profit of 12 × $1.17, which is equal to 1.4% of the $1000 convertible. Transaction costs are not included in this analysis, which will reduce the profits in both directions.

See Fig. 12.3 to compare a convertible arbitrage trade with an unhedged (long-only) convertible purchase. For a convertible arbitrage trade, if the underlying stock increases by 5%, the profit is $.98, compared with an unhedged convertible purchase profit of $24.32. If the underlying stock decreases by 5%, a convertible arbitrage trade produces a profit of $1.37, compared to a loss of $21.97 for an unhedged convertible.

EXHIBIT 12.4 MECHANICS OF CONVERTIBLE ARBITRAGE—cont'd

Stock Px = $41.54

Convertible delta = 53%

Conv. Ratio = 21.2037 shares

Convertible Px = 101.375% par

	Long-only fund	
initial case	Long convertible 101.3755 par = $1,013.75	
	Net cash outlay = $1,013.75	
+5% scenario	Current share price = $43.617	
	Gain from convertible = $(1,038.07^1 - 1,013.75) = \$24.32$	
	Coupon for 1 year = 2.5	
	Net gain = $26.82	
-5% scenario	Current share price = $39.463	
	Loss from convertible = $(1,013.75 - 991.78^2) = \$21.97$	
	Coupon for 1 year = 2.5	
	Net loss = $19.47	

Note: calculations are not rounded.

FIGURE 12.3   Long-only trade (1 year).

3. **Purchasing an undervalued convertible**

The purchase of a convertible at a price below its theoretical value should enable a trader to capture this mispricing through the monetization of volatility described in (2). When this happens and the convertible exposures are properly neutralized through delta hedging, incremental profits will be created over time based on the below-market purchase. These profits will be even higher if there is an increase in volatility during the holding period. However, if volatility decreases, this potential profit opportunity can turn into a potential loss. If a convertible is purchased at a 2% discount to theoretical value, this could result in a profit of $20 (2% of the $1000 convertible).

4. **Summary of returns**

The total 1-year convertible return in this hypothetical hedged convertible is comprised of income generation (2.9%) and monetizing volatility (1.4%), which results in a hypothetical return of 4.3%.

If 75% of this convertible is purchased with $750 borrowed from a prime broker at 2%, the total 1-year return from this investment would be approximately ($1000 × 4.3% = $43. $43 − $15 interest cost = $28. $33/$250 = 11.2%).

Notes 1 and 2: The value of the convertible is based on changes in the underlying share price as determined by a convertible pricing model.
Source: Basile, Davide. "Convertible bonds: Convertible arbitrage versus long-only strategies." *Morgan Stanley Investment Management Journal*, Issue 1, Volume 2, 2006.

This strategy attempts to create returns that exceed the returns that would be available from purchasing a nonconverting bond with the same maturity issued by the same issuer, without being exposed to common share price risk. Most convertible arbitrageurs attempt to achieve double-digit annual returns from convertible arbitrage.

Relative Value Arbitrage

Relative value arbitrage exploits pricing inefficiencies across asset classes. An example of this is "pairs trading." Pairs trading involves two companies that are competitors or peers in the same industry that have common shares that have a strong historical correlation in daily stock price movements (or the same company has issued both common and preferred shares, which have a strong correlation). When this correlation breaks down (one stock increases in price while the other stock decreases in price) a pairs trader will sell short the outperforming stock and buy the underperforming stock, betting that the "spread" between the two stocks will eventually converge. When, and if, convergence occurs, there can be significant trading profits. Of course, if divergence occurs, notwithstanding the strong historical correlations, this trade can lose money.

Another example of a relative value arbitrage involves the New York Stock Exchange (NYSE) and the Chicago Mercantile Exchange (MERC). A stock trading on NYSE should have a strong correlation with the futures price for that stock trading on the MERC. If the prices for the stock and its futures contract unexpectedly diverge, fast computers operated by highly quantitative traders recognize the divergence and immediately initiate trades. When the stock outperforms the futures contract, the trade is to short the stock and buy the futures contract. When the futures contract outperforms the stock, the trade is to short the futures contract and purchase the stock. In the case of a stock and its futures contract, the two prices will almost always converge, creating a trading profit. This profit will likely be very small (and fleeting) since many traders/computers will see the same divergence and quickly set up this arbitrage. As a result, for the arbitrage position to be profitable, traders/computers need to look for small pricing discrepancies and then quickly create a large volume of long and short trades in the stock and futures contract to make an adequate trading profit.

EVENT-DRIVEN STRATEGIES

Event-driven strategies focus on significant transactional events such as M&A transactions, bankruptcy reorganizations, recapitalizations, and other specific corporate events that create pricing inefficiencies. Refer to Exhibit 12.5 for a summary of the type of events and catalysts fund managers look for when generating investment ideas.

EXHIBIT 12.5 EVENT-DRIVEN INVESTMENT OPPORTUNITIES: CATALYSTS AND EVENTS

Strategic (Hard Catalysts)

Risk Arbitrage
Strategic Alternative Reviews
Spin-Offs / Break-up Candidates
Activist Shareholders / Proxy Contests
Holding Company Discounts / Stub Trades
Takeover Candidates

Financial

Liquidity Events / Credit Reratings
Recapitalizations
Primary Equity and Debt Offerings
Bankruptcy Reorganizations
Accounting Changes / Issues

Operational

Merger / Synergy Benefits
Restructuring Programs / Turnaround Stories
Senior Management Turnover

Legal / Regulatory

Litigation
Regulations
Legislation

Technical

Broken Risk Arbitrage Situations
Secondary Equity and Equity-Linked Offerings

Source: Highbridge Capital Management, LLC

Activist

Activist shareholders take minority equity or equity derivative positions in a company and then try to influence the company's senior management and board to consider initiatives that the activist considers important to enhance shareholder value. Activist investors often attempt to influence other major investors to support their recommendation to the company, which sometimes leads to proxy solicitations designed to change the management composition of the company. Activist investors commonly push for lower costs, lower cash balances, greater share repurchases, higher dividends and increased debt, among other things. Chapter 13 provides a more complete explanation of activist shareholder activities and their impact on corporations.

Merger Arbitrage

Merger arbitrage, which is also called risk arbitrage, is an investment strategy that attempts to achieve gains based on the spread between an acquirer's purchase price offer and a target's stock price after announcement of the intended acquisition or merger. See Exhibit 12.6 for a summary of the basic strategy for a share for share merger arbitrage transaction.

EXHIBIT 12.6 MERGER ARBITRAGE SUMMARY

- The concept of risk arbitrage involves "betting" that an announced merger or acquisition will ultimately close
- When a company (acquirer) announces the potential merger or acquisition of another public company (target), there is a time lag between the announcement and the actual closing of the deal
  - The price of the target's stock moves up close to the value of the takeover bid, but almost always to a price slightly lower than the announcement price
- The spread between the target's stock price after announcement and the price offered is the "arbitrage spread" and represents the risk that the deal will not be completed
- An arbitrageur will
  - buy shares of the target
  - short the shares of the acquirer (if it is a stock deal)
- If the deal is closed at the offered price, the arbitrageur will then receive the spread plus any dividends received as profit

In a merger, where the acquirer has agreed to deliver its own stock as consideration (a share for share merger, as described above), an arbitrageur will sell short the acquirer's stock and simultaneously buy the stock of the target. If the merger is completed, the target's stock will be converted into the stock of the acquirer based on an exchange ratio that is usually determined at the time of the merger announcement (unless there is a collar established, as described below). Upon receiving the acquiring company's stock in exchange for the target company stock, an arbitrageur will deliver the acquiring company stock to the party who lends shares to create the short position (covering the short).

Sometimes, a share for share merger includes a collar arrangement whereby the number of acquirer shares delivered at closing is subject to change depending on whether the acquirer's share price has increased or decreased between the announcement date and closing date, and if so, by how much. Collar provisions make the merger arbitrage process more complicated, depending on the structure of the collar. Sometimes, mergers also include preferred stock, warrants, or other securities, which makes the arbitrage activity even more challenging.

In a merger where the consideration is cash, an acquirer offers to purchase the shares of the target company for a fixed cash price. During the period of time until the merger closes (which could be 1 month to 1 year, or longer), the target company's stock typically trades below the bid price since there is some probability that the merger does not close. An arbitrageur who thinks that the merger will be consummated will simply buy the target company stock after the merger announcement and achieve profits equal to the difference between the arbitrageur's purchase price and the higher price paid by the acquiring company if the transaction closes.

The upside and downside of a share for share merger arbitrage transaction is summarized in Exhibit 12.7. See Exhibit 12.8 for a comparison of cash and share for share merger arbitrage transactions. See Exhibit 12.9 for a summary of merger arbitrage spreads for both successful and unsuccessful merger arbitrage efforts. The expected return of a cash merger arbitrage is summarized in Exhibit 12.10.

EXHIBIT 12.7 SHARE FOR SHARE MERGER ARBITRAGE

Upside: *The Deal Closes*	Downside: *The Deal Does NOT Close*

• The arbitrageur gains
  ○ The arbitrage spread (difference between Target stock when acquisition announced and bid price when closes)
  ○ Dividends paid on Target stock
  ○ Interest on proceeds of short selling (less borrow costs and dividends paid on shorted Acquirer stock)
• The arbitrage spread can be accentuated if the bid is repriced higher, possibly through the presence of another bidder
	• The target stock will drop to the pre-announcement price (or below), causing losses
	• The Acquirer stock price might increase, causing a loss on the short position

In most cases, the amount an arbitrageur will lose if the deal does not close far outweighs the gain if the deal closes

EXHIBIT 12.8 COMPARISON OF CASH AND SHARE FOR SHARE TRANSACTIONS

Cash Transactions

- Arbitrageur only buys the target company's stock
  - Stock sells at a discount to the acquisition price
  - Arbitrageur holds the target until merger consummation and receives cash

Share for Share Transactions

- Arbitrageur will buy the shares of the target as in a cash transaction, but will also sell short the stock of the acquirer
  - The amount to be shorted is based on the exchange ratio in the bid:
    - If the proposed exchange ratio is 1:2 (one share of the acquirer will be issued for every two shares of the target), then
    - If the arbitrageur buys 1000 shares of the target, there would be a simultaneous shorting of 500 shares of the acquirer
  - Arbitrageur holds the target shares until the acquisition is consummated and then receives acquirer stock, which is used to cover the short position

EXHIBIT 12.9 MEDIAN ARBITRAGE SPREAD

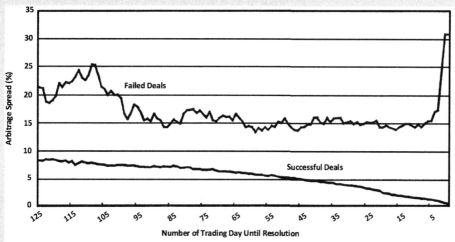

This figure plots the median arbitrage spread versus time until deal resolution. The arbitrage spread spread is defined to be the offer price minus the target price. For failed deals, the deal resolution date is defined as the date of the merger termination announcement. For successful deals, the resolution date is the consumation date.

Source: Mitchell, Mark L. and Todd C. Pulvino. "Characteristics of Risk and Return in Risk Arbitrage." *Journal of Finance* 56: 2135–2176.

EXHIBIT 12.10 EXPECTED RETURN FOR CASH MERGER

Expected return = [C*G-L(100%-C)]/Y*P

where:
- C is the expected chance of success (%)
- G is the expected gain in the event of a success (usually takeover price – current price)
- L is the expected loss in the event of a failure (current price – original price)
- Y is the expected holding time in years (usually the time until the acquisition takes place)
- P is the current price of the security

Example:
Company A makes a tender offer at $25 a share for Company B, currently trading at $15. The deal is expected to close in 3 months. The stock of Company B immediately increases to $24

- C = 96%
- G = $1.00
- L = $9.00 ($24–$15)   **Exp. Return = [0.96*$1 - $9*(1 – 0.96)]/(0.25*$24) = 10%**
- Y = 25% (3/12 months)
- P = $24

Distressed Securities

Distressed securities investment strategies are directed at companies in distressed situations such as bankruptcies and restructurings or companies that are expected to experience distress in the future. Distressed securities are stocks, bonds, and trade or financial claims of companies in, or about to enter or exit, bankruptcy or financial distress. The prices of these securities fall in anticipation of financial distress when their holders choose to sell rather than remain invested in a financially troubled company and there is limited demand from buyers. If a company that is already distressed appears ready to emerge from this condition, the prices of the company's securities may increase. Due to the market's inability to always properly value these securities, and the inability of many institutional investors to own distressed securities, these securities can sometimes be purchased at significant discounts to their risk adjusted value. See Exhibit 12.11.

EXHIBIT 12.11 DISTRESSED SECURITIES RETURN

Capitalize on the knowledge, flexibility, and patience that creditors of a company do not have.

Bonds	Many institutional investors, such as pension funds, are barred by their charters or regulators from directly buying or holding below investment-grade bonds (Ba1/BB+ or lower)
Bank debt	Banks often prefer to sell their bad loans to remove them from their books and use the freed-up cash to make other investments
Trade claims	Holders of trade claims are in the business of producing goods or providing services and have limited expertise in assessing the likelihood of being paid once a distressed company files for bankruptcy

As shown in Exhibits 12.12 and 12.13, an investor can purchase and hold the securities of a company that is about to enter into a restructuring process until the company emerges from this process and the value of the security increases. As shown in Exhibit 12.14, an investor can also purchase the securities held by creditors in a bankruptcy. Alternatively, an investor can capitalize on the mispricing between different securities of the same issuer that have stronger or weaker positions in the company's capital structure. When a distressed situation occurs, stronger securities should appreciate in value relative to junior securities. This suggests that an investor should purchase the stronger (senior claim) securities and sell short the weaker (junior claim) securities. The success of distressed securities strategies usually depends on negotiations with other investors and lenders who have claims on the company and decisions made by bankruptcy court judges and trustees.

EXHIBIT 12.12 RESTRUCTURING PROCESS

Hedge funds invest in distressed securities to arbitrage information asymmetries, risk appetite, and investment horizon between investors

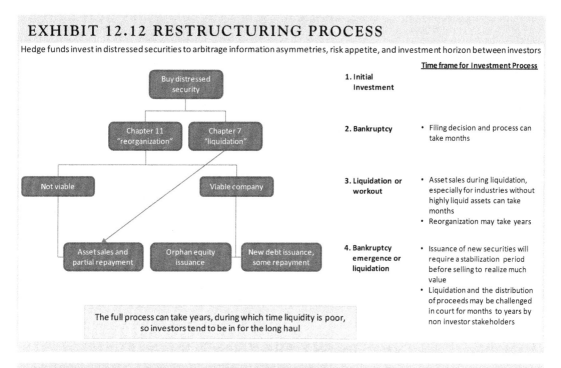

EXHIBIT 12.13 PREBANKRUPTCY STRATEGY

Buy discounted bonds and/or sell stock short.

Expectation

- Prefiling coupon payments + liquidation value of assets = more value than cost of trade
- Stock value will be eliminated

Problems

- Liquidation value may be lower than expected
- Additional debt may be raised, creating more claims on the assets
- Time period for monetization may be extended

continued

EXHIBIT 12.13 PREBANKRUPTCY STRATEGY—cont'd

Challenges

- Determining which tier of debt has a senior enough claim to be repaid
- Understanding bankruptcy law and the bankruptcy process
- Comparing ability to be repaid with trading value, taking into account the time value of money and asset deterioration

EXHIBIT 12.14 INBANKRUPTCY STRATEGY

Purchase shares issued to creditors in bankruptcy or buy junior debt securities in anticipation of shares being issued during reorganization.

Expectation

- Lack of analyst coverage and sales by impatient creditors creates undervalued shares
- Value will climb as firm emerges from bankruptcy

Problems

- Firm liquidates and shares become worthless
- Firm goes back into Chapter 11 a second time ("Chapter 22") and shares become worthless

Challenges

- Difficult to determine that the core business is viable and valuable

A successful distressed securities investment strategy uses an investment process that focuses on fundamental analysis, historical performance, causes of distress, capital structure, debt covenants, legal issues, trade execution, and the nature of claims and liabilities in the target's capital structure (see Exhibit 12.15).

EXHIBIT 12.15 INVESTMENT PROCESS

Analyze:

- Fundamental/quantitative analysis
- Historical performance and cause of distress
- Capital structure
- Debt structure covenants
- Legal issues
  - Bankruptcy proceedings
  - Tax issues
  - Public documents
  - Rights of subordinated creditors
  - Enforceability of derivatives

EXHIBIT 12.15 INVESTMENT PROCESS—cont'd

- Trade execution
  - Understand market trading dynamics
  - Arbitrage risk models that analyze individual relationships among securities
  - Liquidity analysis to understand how long it takes to liquidate a position
  - Potential politics involved in bankruptcy proceedings
  - Multiscenario valuation models
- Nature of claims and liabilities in target's capital structure
  - Size of claims
  - Relative seniority
  - Composition of claims
  - Security liens
  - Guarantees
  - Relationship agreements among equity holders
  - Contingent liabilities
  - Intrinsic value

Distressed securities investment strategies can be active or passive. Active investors will try to influence the restructuring and the refinancing process through participation in a creditor committee and taking a "hands-on" approach to ensure that the workout process is handled on a fair basis and that the investor's interests are protected or augmented. Active investors will get involved with many legal aspects of the workout and will attempt to reorganize the company in a way that is most beneficial to their interests. In contrast, passive investors are less proactive and look for less complicated, time intensive investments in distressed situations (see Exhibit 12.16).

EXHIBIT 12.16 ACTIVE VERSUS PASSIVE DISTRESSED INVESTING

Active		Passive
Control	**Non-Control**	**Passive**
• Requires 1/3 block and 1/2 to control: may require partners	• Senior secured/senior unsecured	• Invest in undervalued securities trading at distressed levels
• Heavy lifting, private equity style investing, restricted	• Influence process, sometimes restricted	• Trading oriented; long, short, and capital arbitrage
• Exit: 2–3 years	• Exit: 1–2 years	• Exit: 6–12 months
• Mid/small cap focus	• Mid/small cap focus	• Large cap focus
• Opportunities: all credit environments	• Opportunities: all credit environments	• Opportunities: cyclical

An example of a distressed securities investment is Barney's, a large clothing retailer, which is summarized in Exhibit 12.17. Another example of a distressed securities investment is found in the **Kmart, Sears and ESL: How a Hedge Fund Became One of the World's Largest Retailers Case**. A summary of downside risks and opportunities for distressed securities investment is provided in Exhibit 12.18.

EXHIBIT 12.17 EXAMPLE TRANSACTION

- When Barney's filed Chapter 11 bankruptcy protection in early 1996 after it was unable to make the rent payments on its stores, many clothing designers chose to sell their trade claims and recoup a portion of their money
- Two hedge funds, Bay Harbour Management and Whippoorwill Associates Inc., acquired the company's distressed unpaid bills in secondary markets for $240 million—Bay Harbour paid about 30 cents on the dollar and Whippoorwill paid about 50 cents on the dollar—and subsequently rejected bids from retailers interested in buying Barney's:
  - Saks Fifth Avenue offered $290 million in 1997
  - Dickson Poon, a Hong Kong entrepreneur, whose Dickson Concepts also owns Britain's Harvey Nichols department store, bid $280 million in 1997
  - DFS Group, airport duty-free store operator, bid approximately $280 million in 1998
- In January 1999, a bankruptcy court handed control over to the creditors: Bay Harbour and Whippoorwill became the two largest shareholders of common stock, collectively holding 85% of the shares
  - The bankruptcy process was lengthy (3 years) and complicated due to a JV partnership with Isetan Company Limited, a Japanese department store operator that had funded Barney's expansion strategy with over $600 million
  - Isetan came away with a stake of about 7% as well as various concessions
  - Other equity holders included the company's President and CEO (6%) and the Pressman (founding) family (2%)
- Barney's was sold to Jones Apparel Group, Inc. for $401 million in December 2004

EXHIBIT 12.18 RISKS AND OPPORTUNITIES

Downside Risks

- High exposure to company/sector risks
- Miscalculation of firm liquidation value
- Timing of market and short-term losses
- Company fraud or misrepresentation
- Debt can turn into worthless equity
- Other creditors are uncompromising
- Reorganization lasts longer than expected
- Securities are not liquid
- At mercy of bankruptcy court
- Increased competition
- Regulatory changes
- Management motivation for a low exit value (when they receive low-strike options)

Opportunities

- Ability to influence the distribution process, new equity issuance, and future of new company
- Forced selling leads to discounted prices
- Many distressed firm not "covered" by Wall Street
- Can adapt style to particulars of deal and are not constrained by ratings
- Replace management/implement cost controls

Argentina and four hedge funds ended a 15-year battle during March 2016 when the country agreed to pay $4.65 billion to settle a number of long-standing lawsuits that the hedge funds brought against Argentina. Argentina agreed to settle with the hedge funds who held euro-denominated bonds that were defaulted on during 2001.

One fund, Bracebridge Capital from Boston, made about $950 million return on its original principal amount of $120 million. That's about an 800% return. Billionaire Paul Singer and his firm NML Capital—the leading firm in the case—received $2.28 billion in principal and interest payments. That's a huge payday considering NML's original amount of only $617 million, resulting in a 370% return, according to the terms of the agreement and a court document filed by Argentina. Argentina offered to pay about 75% of the total claims from the hedge funds, including 100% of the principal and 50% of accrued interest on the bonds they hold.

Resolving the dispute is a big win for Argentina too—it can finally return to foreign capital markets after effectively being shut out since it defaulted on $95 billion of debt in 2001. Singer and the other hedge fund managers are called "vultures" in Argentina.

The hedge fund strategy was simple: they bought the country's debt at a very large discount and then sued the country for full repayment. During 2010, Argentina had settled its debt problems with 92% of its creditors. But Singer and other funds—representing the bulk of the other 8%—held out. A New York judge, Thomas Griesa, agreed with them. He ordered that Argentina couldn't pay any creditors until it paid Singer and other holdouts. The battle finally ended with Argentina's agreement to pay the negotiated amount, subject to the Argentine Congress approval of the payment and changing laws that prevent the country from paying holdouts.

Argentina issued about $15 billion in new bonds to obtain the cash needed to pay the hedge funds and other creditors. Argentina paid the bondholders in cash, saving the country about 20% compared with paying with other bonds. In addition to paying the hedge funds, Argentina had to pay around $4 billion to other creditors who previously owned defaulted Argentine bonds.

SUMMARY

Hedge fund investment strategies attempt to increase returns, reduce volatility of returns, and achieve positive returns even in difficult markets. Sometimes, they are successful in achieving these objectives and sometimes unsuccessful. This chapter has summarized some of the most actively utilized investment strategies, but there are many other strategies that are also employed by hedge funds. These strategies may involve short selling, use arbitrage techniques, employ derivatives, involve significant corporate events, and incorporate sophisticated trading and financial vehicles, which are principally supplied by the prime brokerage, trading, and credit providing desks of investment banks.

To facilitate greater understanding of specific investment strategies, Exhibits 12.19–12.22 provide simplified numerical examples for transactions involving merger arbitrage, pairs trading, distressed investing, and global macro strategies.

EXHIBIT 12.19 MERGER ARBITRAGE

Rationale

- Widget Makers Inc. (WMI) has offered to purchase Sofa Makers Inc. (SMI) for two shares of WMI stock per share of SMI. Just prior to announcement of the offer, WMI was trading at $52 per share and SMI was trading at $74 per share (the offer was at an approximately 40% premium to SMI's share price)
- WMI and SMI both do not pay dividends
- We expect that the offer will be accepted by SMI shareholders and will be completed in the next 2 – 3 months
- Post announcement, WMI is trading at $50 per share and SMI is trading at $95 per share

Trade

- Buy 100 shares of SMI at $95
- Sell short 200 shares of WMI at $50

Expected Result

- The merger will complete and we can close the short position in WMI through the exchange of SMI shares, making a profit of $5 per SMI share purchased over a 3 month period
- *Example*: If WMI rises to $60 per share and SMI rises to $120 upon completion, we do not have any additional cash flow in the future and make $5 per share from the initial investment
- *Example*: If WMI falls to $45 per share and SMI falls to $90 upon completion, we again do not have any additional cash flow in the future and make $5 per SMI share from the initial investment

Additional Upside

- If a competitive bidding situation arises for SMI, we may see the price of SMI increase (and potentially WMI further decrease as it works to sweeten its bid)
- *Example*: If WidgeFactory (WF), comes in and bids $120 per share in cash for SMI, we could see SMI increase up to $118 per share (or even higher as WMI may be expected to counter bid) and WMI stay at $50 per share. If we close the position, we would enjoy a profit of $23 per share on SMI or $2300 from our trade

Downside Risk

- If the transaction fails to complete, we may see SMI's price fall and WMI's price rebound, causing a potentially significant loss
- *Example*: If the transaction is blocked by regulators, we could see SMI's price revert to $74 and WMI return to $52 per share. In this case, we would lose $21 per share on SMI and $2 per share on WMI for a loss of $2500

Mitigating Risk Position Part Way Through

- If we grow concerned regarding the prospects of the merger, we may consider closing our position or purchasing options to limit our downside risk
- *Example*: If WMI stays at $50 per share and SMI rises to $98, we may consider closing our position, rather than waiting for completion
- *Example*: If WMI stays at $50 per share and SMI rises to $98, we may consider purchasing out of the money puts for SMI at for example $95 to lower the loss in case the merger does not complete. If these options cost $1, in case of completion we would make $4 per SMI share or a profit of $400. If the merger does not complete and SMI's price reverts to $74 and WMI returns to $52 per share, we would lose $2 per share on WMI, and nothing on SMI, and would have paid for the put, for a loss of $500 (much better than the $2500 expressed above)

EXHIBIT 12.20 PAIRS TRADING

Rationale

- Widget Makers Inc (WMI) has developed a new product which we believe will make Widget Makers's product much more desirable than that of its main competitor WidgetFactory (WF)
- We expect WMI will take more market share from WF
- WMI and WF both do not pay dividends

Expected Result

- We expect that over time the spread between WMI and WF will widen
- *Example:* If we think that in 1 year WMI will rise to $65 per share and WF will rise to $50 per share → make $13 per WMI share and lose $5 per WF share → make $800 profit from our trade (returns $1500 on $700 investment)
- *Example:* If WMI falls to $40 and WF falls to $30, we lose $12 per share on WMI and we make $15 per share on WF → make $300 from our trade (returns $1000 on $700 investment)

Trade

- Buy 100 shares of WMI at $52
- Sell short 100 shares of WF at $45

Additional Upside

- The upside in this trade comes from the spread widening – it may be more than we expect

Downside Risk

- We may be incorrect in our belief that the new product will be liked by the market (think "New Coke") and we may see the spread tighten or even WM overtake WMI
- For example, if WMI increases to $55 and WF increases to $54, we would gain $3 per share from WMI and lose $9 per share from WF for a loss of $600 on a $700 investment

Mitigating Risk Position Part Way Through

- If we grow concerned regarding the prospects for the new product, we may consider closing our position or purchasing options to limit our exposure
- *Example:* We may consider buying puts and selling calls on WMI and selling puts and buying calls on WF. While this will limit our upside potential, it will also limit our downside risk based upon the spreads we bake into these option positions and their net cost

II. HEDGE FUNDS AND PRIVATE EQUITY

EXHIBIT 12.21 DISTRESSED INVESTING

Rationale

- Investment Power Producer (IPP) operates in the unregulated segment of the highly regulated energy market
- With its input costs increasing at a faster rate than its output revenue over the last several years, IPP has had negative cash flow and negative earnings for the last few years and may be forced into bankruptcy in the near term
- IPP is financed primarily with $10 billion of 5% debt which matures in 10 years, and is trading at a deep discount of 30 per 100 face – IPP's debt has a below investment grade rating
- IPP's stock is trading at $3 per share with 100 million shares outstanding
- IPP has sufficient cash for approximately 2 years of operation and debt service at current cash burn rates ($1.5 billion per year of which $0.5 billion is debt service)
- IPP's debt covenants impose that significant asset sales can trigger a put on the bonds (at the bondholder's discretion)
- We expect IPP will be forced into bankruptcy after 2 years
- In liquidation, we expect the assets could be sold for $3.5 billion (which would take roughly 1 year from the time bankruptcy is entered)

Expected Result

- As our initial portfolio is zero cost by construction, let us examine the cash flows from the trade: we will get coupon payments of $50 per year for the first two years, and then the company will be liquidated resulting in payment of $350 ($35 per $100 face to bondholders)
- The shares will be worthless, creating an economic gain of $300 and no future cash flow

Mitigating Risk Position Part Way Through

- Given the risks associated with this position, it may be difficult to attach additional instruments to limit risk exposure. Given that the equity is already behaving like an option, it is unlikely that there will be a liquid market in equity options in which to transact which would offer any advantages versus transacting in equity
- We may consider going long the credit default swap index for non-regulated power producers to hedge since CDS spreads typically increase with rising stock volatilities
- We may consider closing our stock position

Additional Upside

- If the company looks to negotiate with bondholders sooner than expected, we may see better returns as there will be more assets left to distribute to claimants – for example – if the company liquidates in one year, the value of assets would be $3.5B plus the additional $1.5B in cash remaining, leaving the bondholders $50 per $100 face

Trade

- Buy 1 bond ($1000 face) of IPP at $30 per $100 face
- Sell short 100 shares of IPP at $3

Downside Risk

- Given the regulated nature of the industry, we may see a shift in regulation which could lead to a generally worse scenario with much greater volatility for IPP (for example, regulated utilities must now purchase a set percentage of their power from unregulated power producers such as IPP and newly purchased assets will be subject to additional environmental requirements, thus lowering the value of assets in a sale)
- *Example:* This change in regulation could mean that the assets are worthless. But if a regulated power producer buys its energy from IPP and the company's enterprise value is $20 billion (which happens with a probability of 10%), then the share price would increase to $10 per $100 face (get paid back in full with 10% probability and worthless otherwise) → this would make our trade lose $200 per bond and $7 per share for a loss of $900

EXHIBIT 12.22 GLOBAL MACRO

Rationale

- Elbonia is a developed, industrialized country with a stable government
- Although commodity and Elbonian stock markets have been rallying for the past few quarters, the Elbonian market remains focused on the risks of deflation and continued deterioration of the Elbonian economy
- The Elbonian central bankers have stated that they will "do whatever needs to be done" in order to inflate the economy
- We believe that the market has not accurately priced market implied inflation rates in Elbonia given the relatively low Elbonian CPI readings of 2%
- Current prices are in line given inflation expectations of 1% going forward
- We expect inflation will stay at 2% going forward

Expected Result

- *Example:* our long position is expected to generate a payoff of $1,217 [(1+.02 Real Yield +.02 Inflation)^5] for gains of $217 over 5 years while our short position is expected to grow $1,159 [(1+.03 Nominal Yield)^5] over the 5 years for a net gain of $57

Trade

- Buy 1 Elbonian National Bond Inflation-Protected Security (ENBIPS) maturing in 5 years at 2% at 1000
- Sell short 1 Elbonian National Bond (ENB) at 3% at 1000
- ENB is a Nominal Note so its yield is Nominal Yield = "Real" Yield + Expected inflation
- ENBIPS provides a "Real" Yield
- → ENB Yield minus ENBIPS Yield = Market-Implied Inflation

Additional Upside

- Given the macroeconomic environment and the central bank's stated policy, it is possible that inflation will increase more than expected
- *Example:* If inflation increases to 4% over the lifetime, the value of our long position will grow to $1,338 [(1+.02 Real Yield + .04 Inflation)^5] while our short position remains at $1,159 [(1 + .03 Nominal Yield)^5] creating a gain of $179

Downside Risk

- If deflation does occur, we could experience losses
- *Example:* If we experience deflation of 1% per year, the value of our ENBIPS would increase only to $1,051 [(1+.02 Real Yield -.01 Inflation)^5] over time while our ENB would still grow to $1,159 [(1+.03 Nominal Yield)^5], causing a net loss of $108

Mitigating Risk Position Part Way Through

- *Example:* We may consider purchasing an option which would allow us to enter into a forward contract on the ENBIPS to reduce our loss in case deflation is worse than initially expected

CHAPTER

13

Shareholder Activism and Impact on Corporations

The material in this chapter should be cross-referenced with the following cases: **McDonald's, Wendy's, and Hedge Funds: Hamburger Hedging?** and **Porsche, Volkswagen, and CSX: Cars, Trains, and Derivatives**.

Certain hedge funds focus on shareholder activism as a core investment strategy. An activist shareholder acquires a minority equity position in a public corporation and then applies pressure on management to increase shareholder value through changes in corporate policy. Some of the common changes advocated by activist shareholders include reducing corporate costs, repurchasing common shares, increasing corporate leverage, increasing dividends, reducing CEO compensation, reducing cash balances, and divesting certain businesses. In addition, activist shareholders will sometimes campaign against proposed acquisitions or allocation of cash for purposes that are not perceived to create shareholder value. Activists sometimes also pursue a sale of a target company or a breakup of the company through a piecemeal sale or spin-off of significant operations (see Exhibit 13.1).

Investment Banks, Hedge Funds, and Private Equity, Third Edition
http://dx.doi.org/10.1016/B978-0-12-804723-1.00013-X

EXHIBIT 13.1 SHAREHOLDER ACTIVISM

- Some corporations are vulnerable to hostile initiatives by activist shareholders.
- Hedge funds can be vocal investors who demand change in the corporate governance landscape in a number of ways:
  - Publicly criticizing/challenging boards and managements;
  - Nominating board candidates and pursuing their agenda through proxy contests;
  - Supporting other activists.
- Hedge funds' activist strategy has been successful by taking advantage of:
  - Like-minded hedge funds' herd mentality;
  - Ability to overcome reputation for short-term focus;
  - Ability to skillfully use a deep arsenal of securities and financial instruments;
  - Familiarity with M&A and legal regulations and rights;
  - Readiness to go to battle and devote significant resources to full-blown public relations battles.

Source: Morgan Stanley.

Activist shareholders usually acquire between 1% and 10% of a target company's shares or create an equity exposure by entering into equity derivative transactions, such as purchasing call options on the company's stock, simultaneously purchasing call options and selling put options on the company's stock, entering into forward transactions to purchase the company's stock, or entering into equity swaps in relation to the company's stock. These derivative alternatives will be discussed later in this chapter and are described in the referenced cases. A relatively small shareholding or equity derivative position established by an activist shareholder may enable the investor to launch a campaign to make significant changes in the company, without the added cost, risk, and time required by a complete acquisition. To be effective, however, the activist shareholder generally must secure the support of other large shareholders. To achieve their objectives, activists may initiate large-scale publicity campaigns, shareholder resolutions or, in the extreme, proxy battles for control over the board of directors.

Shareholder activism became an active force during 1985, when the Supreme Court of Delaware ruled on four cases relating to corporate governance: Unocal, Household, Van Gorkom, and Revlon. Pension funds, mutual funds, and activist hedge funds joined the movement at that time, and activity increased slowly every year until 2002, when shareholder activism gained considerable momentum because of the Enron and WorldCom corporate blowups and the subsequent passage of the Sarbanes–Oxley Act of 2002.

SHAREHOLDER-CENTRIC VERSUS DIRECTOR-CENTRIC CORPORATE GOVERNANCE

A key issue in corporate governance is whether the corporate board of directors will survive as the governing organization of the public corporation, or if shareholder activism will ultimately invalidate the role of the board. In other words, will corporations become more shareholder-centric and less director-centric in their governance?

Some critics of shareholder-centric governance indicate that this movement is causing a shift in the board's role from guiding strategy and advising management to ensuring compliance and performing due diligence. This shift can create a wall between the board and the CEO, removing the "trusted advisor" role of board members, as CEOs become increasingly wary of sharing concerns with investigative and defensive boards. Based on concern about litigation, directors sometimes become so focused on their individual committee responsibility that they are less able to focus on the broad objectives of maximizing shareholder value. They become "Balkanized" into powerful committees of independent directors, unable to broadly coordinate the focus of the entire board. Even when the board is able to focus on the business of the corporation in cooperation with the CEO, activist investors create pressure on boards to manage for short-term share price performance rather than long-term value creation. This may result in short-changing the company's relationships with its employees, customers, suppliers, and communities, as well as reducing investment in R&D and capital projects that are critical to a company's long-term success.

Another criticism of shareholder-centric governance is that shareholder activists could ultimately wrest substantial control from boards, causing companies to bring almost every important decision to a shareholder vote. This would largely shut down the normal operating procedures of the company, slowing down decisions, and creating competitive disadvantages, as previously confidential decisions that were made by the board are put in the public domain. There is also concern that activist shareholders can create inappropriate pressure on boards through nondocumented alignments between different activists to achieve their objectives. Activists take advantage of the ambiguity of concepts such as "group," "acting in concert," and "investment intent," testing the limits of securities, reporting, and antitrust rules. This activity is explored in more detail in the **Porsche, Volkswagen, and CSX: Cars, Trains, and Derivatives Case**.

RiskMetrics Group (RMG), through its Institutional Shareholder Services (ISS) division, focuses on corporate governance and proxy voting among institutional investors. This organization, which influences the thinking of institutional investors, has increasingly supported shareholder-centric initiatives. RMG recommends that its institutional investor clients "withhold votes" whenever they disapprove of company policies. For example, RMG has recommended a withheld vote whenever a board "lacks accountability and oversight," coupled with "sustained poor performance" relative to the company's peers. RMG has for many years attacked shareholder rights plans (poison pills), pushing for a 20% or higher triggering threshold and a shareholder redemption feature, which substantially reduces the effectiveness of a rights plan. RMG's policy is to recommend withholding votes against an entire board of directors if the board adopts or renews a rights plan without shareholder approval, does not commit to putting the rights plan to a shareholder vote within 1 year of adoption, or reneges on a commitment to put the rights plan to a vote. This policy could be challenging for corporations that are the subject of potential hostile or unsolicited takeover attempts.

Corporate boards and CEOs are increasingly focused on the threat of activist shareholders and the frequently adversarial positions of organizations such as RMG. They turn to investment bankers and outside law firms for direction in shoring up their defenses against hostile takeovers and unfriendly activist shareholder initiatives. See Exhibit 13.2 for a corporate checklist of matters to be considered by a company regarding how to prevent or respond to hedge fund activism.

EXHIBIT 13.2 DEALING WITH ACTIVIST HEDGE FUNDS

- Create team to deal with hedge fund activism
  - A small group (2–5) of key officers plus lawyer, investment banker, proxy soliciting firm, and public relations firm;
  - Ensure ability to convene special meeting of board with 24–48 h;
  - Continuing contact and periodic meetings of the team are important;
  - A periodic fire drill with the team is the best way to maintain a state of preparedness;
  - War list of contacts updated regularly.
- Shareholder relations
  - Review dividend policy, analyst presentations, and other financial public relations;
  - Prepare fiduciary holders with respect to takeover tactics designed to panic them;
  - Review trustees for various company plans and determine if changes required;
  - Monitor changes in institutional holdings on a regular basis;
  - Plan for contacts with institutional investors (including maintenance of an up-to-date list of holdings and contacts) and analysts and with media, regulatory agencies and political bodies;
  - Remain informed about activist hedge funds and activist institutional investors and about corporate governance and proxy issues;
  - Role of arbitrageurs and hedge funds.
- Prepare the board of directors to deal with takeovers
  - Maintaining a unified board consensus on key strategic issues is essential to success;
  - Schedule periodic presentations by legal counsel and investment bankers to familiarize directors with the takeover scene and the law and with their advisors;
  - Company may have policy of continuing as an independent entity;
  - Company may have policy of not engaging in takeover discussions;
  - Directors must guard against subversion by raider and should refer all approaches to the CEO;
  - Avoid being put in play; psychological and perception factors may be more important than legal and financial factors in avoiding being singled out as a takeover target;
  - Review corporate governance guidelines and reconstitution of key committees.
- Monitor trading
  - Hedge fund accumulation, Schedule 13(f) filings;
  - Monitor analyst reports;
  - Watch for Schedule 13D and Hart–Scott–Rodino filings.
- Responses to casual passes/nonpublic bear hugs
  - No duty to discuss or negotiate;
  - No duty to disclose unless leak comes from within;
  - Response to any particular approach must be specially structured; team should confer to decide proper response; meeting with potential bidder or activist may be best strategy;
  - Keep the board advised; participation by independent directors may be critical.

EXHIBIT 13.2 DEALING WITH ACTIVIST HEDGE FUNDS—cont'd

- Response to Public offers/public bear hugs
  - No response other than "will call you back";
  - Call war list and assemble team; inform directors;
  - Call special board meeting to consider bidder proposal;
  - No press release or statement other than "stop-look-and-listen";
  - Consider trading halt (NYSE limits halt to short period);
  - Determine whether to meet with raider (refusal to meet may be a negative factor in litigation);
  - In a tender offer, Schedule 14D-9 must be filled within 10 business days and must disclose board's position (favor; oppose; neutral) and reasoning, negotiations, and banker's opinion (optional).

Source: Wachtell, Lipton, Rosen & Katz, "Takeover Response Checklist", November 2011.

ACTIVIST HEDGE FUND PERFORMANCE

Activist shareholders have been very active and effective in pushing companies to change policies to meet shareholder demands, including Dell, DuPont, Apple, and Microsoft. Hedge fund activists have attracted significant funding and have been able to advance their playbook to secure board seats, push stock buybacks and higher dividend, and cut costs. The significant increase in shareholder activism following the global financial crisis has had a profound impact on strategic and financial decision-making among major companies worldwide. Activist funds managed less than $12 billion in 2003, but these funds had expanded to more than $115 billion by 2016. Generally good returns followed the growth of the activist funds until late in 2015, when significant reversals occurred, which continued into 2016. Returns plummeted, ideas didn't work and some of the companies largely control by activists floundered.

A train wreck at Valeant Pharmaceuticals was a glaring example. Shares of the company dropped more than 45% in 2015, and then continued dropping in 2016. Activist ValueAct Capital helped create the company, hire its CEO, and has two seats on the company's board. Another activist, Bill Ackman, became Valeant's second biggest shareholder. In large part because of this single investment, Ackman's Pershing Square fund dropped more than 20% during 2015, and this decline continued during 2016.

Carl Icahn, another activist, saw his investment fund fall during 2015. Barry Rosenstein's Jana Partners, Richard McGuire's Mercato Capital, Nelson Peltz's Trian Fund, and Dan Loeb's Third Point all had bad years in 2015 and beyond. In addition, a number of activist hedge funds were forced to shut down during this period based on poor results. However, the activism model remained in full gear as a historically high number of activist campaigns were launched during 2015 and 2016.

Exhibit 13.3 shows performance of activist funds and all hedge fund strategies.

EXHIBIT 13.3 PERFORMANCE OF ACTIVIST FUNDS VERSUS ALL HEDGE FUND STRATEGIES (AS OF JULY 2016)

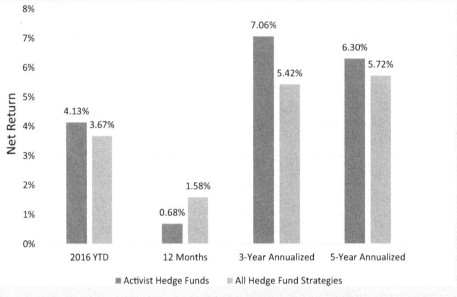

According to academic studies, the number of public companies targeted for poor performance by hedge funds grew more than 10-fold between 1994 and 2006. Despite the prevalence of hedge fund activism, however, the studies identified an apparent contradiction in the notion that a hedge fund portfolio manager with a short-term financial goal would have the time, energy, or expertise to improve the long-term performance of a public company. When examining the effectiveness of hedge fund activism in producing value for shareholders, the studies found that, unless a target company was ultimately sold following activist investment, there was little change (during the 18 months following the first activist filing) in the company's stock price or financial results. This was true even when the company took other steps urged by the activists, such as replacing the CEO, changing the composition of the board or buying back stock. The studies also confirmed that investments by activist funds increase the likelihood that target companies will get sold.

After reaching a record high in 2015, campaigns by activist hedge funds started to recede during 2016, dampened by turbulent markets and portfolio losses. In keeping with recent trends, settlements with insurgents continued to prevail over full-fledged proxy fights. Prolonged market volatility and large portfolio losses during early 2016 dampen hedge fund activism during the year. According to FactSet SharkRepellent, 355 activist campaigns were announced against US companies in 2015, of which 127 resulted in the dissidents obtaining at least one board seat or the right to appoint a new independent director. The trend toward settlements over protracted proxy battles was demonstrated in some of the biggest campaigns during 2016 (see Exhibit 13.4). Xerox and American International Group (AIG) capitulated to Carl Icahn, resulting in several board seats for the dissident and a breakup of Xerox. Yahoo! ceded two board seats to Starboard Value. Eric Jackson of Spring Owl Asset Management pushed Viacom to overhaul its board and management and to spin-off Paramount into a tracking stock. His concerns over board independence, excessive CEO compensation, and poor returns were echoed by Viacom shareholder Mario Gabelli, as well as proxy advisors ISS and Glass Lewis, which urged investors to vote against the compensation committee members. Real Estate investment Trusts (REITs) and retailers with extensive real estate assets were also a focus for activists who wanted to monetize real estate holdings or push restructurings or sales. Other firms in activists' crosshairs during 2016 included Ashford Hospitality Prime, Macy's, and Stratus Properties. In addition to demands for divestitures, hedge funds continued to be catalysts for M&A activity, the most notable being the mega-merger and subsequent three-way split of Dow Chemical and DuPont, which was induced by Trian Fund Management and Third Point. Another initiative involved Canadian Pacific Railway's (CP) hostile pursuit of Norfolk Southern, backed by CP's second largest shareholder, Pershing

EXHIBIT 13.4 MANAGEMENT PROXY FIGHTS

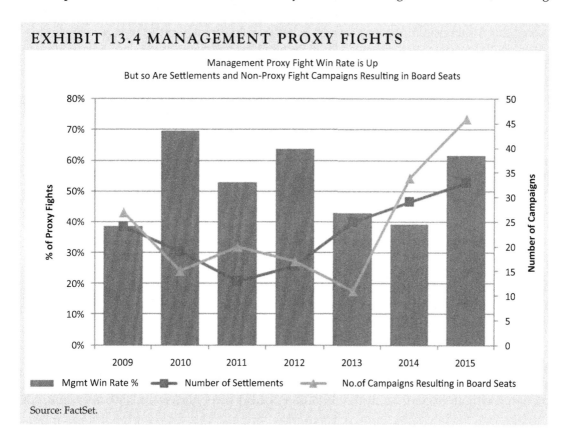

Source: FactSet.

Square Capital Management. Rather than nominate a board slate, CP took a softer approach by submitting a nonbinding resolution asking the Norfolk Southern board to engage in good faith discussions on a merger.

ACTIVIST HEDGE FUND ACCUMULATION STRATEGIES

For an activist investor, timing is everything. Their objective is to accumulate enough ownership in a targeted company to influence change, but they want to secure shares without drawing attention from the target and without attracting tag-along investors, whose purchases can drive up the stock price, making it too expensive to accumulate additional stock. Some activist investors have utilized derivatives to help them create a large exposure to a company, without alerting either the target or other potential investors.

The Securities and Exchange Commission (SEC) requires investors that own 5% or more of a company's equity to disclose their ownership through a 13D filing within 10 days of acquisition (a number of organizations have petitioned the Senate Banking and House Financial Services Committees, urging that Congress take action to shorten the 10-day filing period applicable to Schedule 13D). To avoid tipping their hand regarding holdings of shares that exceed this 5% threshold, some activist investors have used cash-settled equity swaps to create an equity exposure to the target. Under certain interpretations, these derivative contracts do not require 13D disclosure (see CSX Versus TCI section in the **Porsche, Volkswagen, and CSX: Cars, Trains, and Derivatives Case**).

An equity swap is typically entered into with an investment bank counterparty, which causes the bank to buy shares as a hedge against their obligation to pay the returns of the stock ownership (appreciation or depreciation, plus dividends) to the activist hedge fund in exchange for payments that are based on a floating rate of interest (typically LIBOR) plus an appropriate credit spread. In some equity swaps, the hedge fund has the right to purchase the underlying shares from the counterparty under certain circumstances, at which point the hedge fund would disclose ownership of the shares (but not before those shares are delivered). The key question under this arrangement is who controls votes attached to the shares that are the subject of the equity swap? Since the hedge fund does not own the shares, it technically does not own the voting rights and, therefore, may not be required by the SEC to disclose ownership under 13D rules. However, since it might be able to receive these shares before a future vote on the election of directors, the activist can theoretically own the shares when it matters most. It is important to note, however, that some banks expressly refuse to deliver shares to activist investors to close out their equity swap position, or to vote in favor of the activist investor in proxy contests.

Sometimes activist hedge funds have acted in concert with other hedge funds to both buy shares and enter into equity swaps. For example, two funds could each purchase 4.9% of a company's shares without entering into any written agreement to act together, and each could also enter into an equity swap on 4.9% of the company's shares. Even though this may mean that, at the time of a critical corporate event such as election of directors, the two hedge funds might effectively control a combined 19.6% of a company's stock and vote their shares in the same way at that time, neither fund must disclose their position until immediately before the election. In this case, the two hedge funds will enjoy the benefit of surprise and could wield significant influence on the outcome of an election. It is important to note that if, in fact, hedge funds act in concert, there may be legal complications (see CSX Versus TCI section).

CSX VERSUS TCI

Equity swaps have enabled hedge funds to participate in activist shareholder initiatives for many years, creating the following benefits: (1) maximizing the activist's profit potential by avoiding the bidding up of shares in anticipation of a control contest; (2) allowing the activist to strategically time the disclosure of their intent to influence corporate policy (potentially permitting the activist to ambush a company with an undisclosed holding greater than 5%); and (3) enabling an activist to swiftly acquire shares by unwinding the swaps through physical settlement (if the counterparty consents to do so), allowing the activist to potentially acquire the common shares held by swap counterparties as a hedge.

During 2007, The Children's Investment Fund (TCI), a major European-based hedge fund, acquired a 4.2% ownership in CSX, the fourth largest US rail operator. TCI then announced its intent to propose a slate of directors for CSX's board at the company's annual meeting during June 2008. Subsequent to this announcement, the two parties battled in court and in the court of public opinion, with CSX launching a lobbying campaign among US legislators. In March 2008, CSX accused TCI and another hedge fund (3G Capital Partners) of violating disclosure laws by building up a coordinated stake through equity swap contracts. The two hedge funds at that time held a combined 8.7% shareholding in the company and an economic exposure to the stock, based on the equity swaps, equal to an additional 11.5% of outstanding shares. In April, TCI filed a countersuit against CSX, alleging the company withheld material facts and violated insider-trading policies.

Although investors that hold 5% or more of a US company's stock are required to report stock holdings with the SEC, investors who create exposure to the stock through derivatives don't face the same requirements in some situations. Since equity swaps are derivatives that don't grant direct voting rights to the swap counterparty, the hedge funds believed that they had no disclosure obligation. The International Swaps and Derivative Association Inc. and the Securities Industry and Financial Markets Association filed a legal brief supporting the hedge funds and their position regarding nondisclosure. Moreover, during June, 2008, the SEC also sided with the hedge funds, stating that there is no 13D disclosure requirement for holders of cash-settled equity swaps.

Ultimately, TCI and 3G Capital Partners entered into swaps with eight bank counterparties, which in aggregate gave them economic exposure to more than 14% of CSX's shares, with a notional value in excess of $2.5 billion. It was alleged by CSX that most, if not all, of the swap counterparties hedged their exposure by accumulating an equal position in CSX shares. The

SEC ruled that "standard cash-settled equity swap agreements" do not confer either voting or investment power to the swap party over shares acquired by its counterparty to hedge the relevant swaps, a conclusion that is not changed by the presence of economic or business incentives that the counterparty may have to vote the shares as the other party wishes or to dispose of the shares to the other party. The SEC therefore rejected CSX's position that TCI and 3G Capital Partners had acquired beneficial ownership over the CSX shares purchased by counterparties to hedge their exposure to the swaps. As a result, the SEC ruled that the hedge funds were therefore not subject to reporting requirements under Rule 13D (see Exhibit 13.5).

Shortly after the SEC ruling, however, a federal judge found that the two hedge funds had consciously avoided securities laws in their proxy battle with CSX, a decision that has reshaped how activist investors move on their corporate targets. The judge rebuked the funds by saying they sought to justify their actions "on the basis of formalistic arguments," even when they had "defeated the purpose of the law." The court's decision gave ammunition to CSX as it continued its proxy fight based on the judicial view that the hedge funds had together plotted a bid for control of the company, but consciously, and illegally, failed to disclose their intentions. The court also found that the hedge funds delayed publicly disclosing that they were coordinating their CSX-related actions. Finally, the court noted that, although TCI had no legal right to vote or dispose of the hedged shares, as an important client of the investment bank counterparties, they could possibly influence the voting decision of the banks that held CSX shares as a hedge to their equity swap position.

This federal ruling was not a complete victory for CSX, however, since the Judge said that it was too late to reverse their actions, and that he was legally prevented from "sterilizing" or neutralizing their votes when shareholders chose new members of their board of directors on June 25, 2008, including representatives from the hedge funds.

The Federal Court position appears to be at odds with the SEC's position. However, the Federal ruling represents a challenge to hedge funds who attempt to conceal their true economic position through the use of derivatives. See the **Porsche, Volkswagen, and CSX: Cars, Trains, and Derivatives Case** for further discussion of this topic.

EXHIBIT 13.5 EQUITY SWAPS ON CSX SHARES

Assume CSX share price of $40 when equity swaps were executed on 62.5 million shares (a notional amount of $2.5 billion).

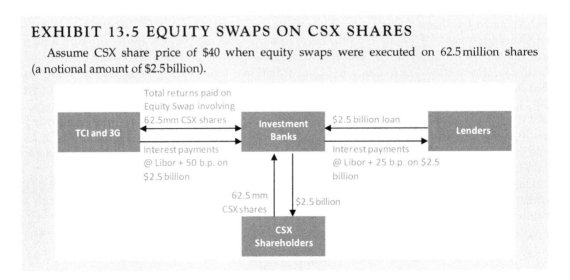

EXHIBIT 13.5 EQUITY SWAPS ON CSX SHARES— cont'd

The outcome of this transaction is as follows:

- TCI and 3G receive economic exposure to 62.5 million CSX shares since they receive/pay total returns from/to investment bank counterparties (quarterly appreciation/depreciation of CSX share price + dividends).
- Since TCI and 3G don't own shares (investment banks purchased 62.5 million CSX shares to hedge their equity swap position) the hedge funds may not need to report beneficial ownership of these shares to the Securities and Exchange Commission.
- The investment banks receive a spread of 25 basis points between their cost of borrowing $2.5 billion and the payments received from TCI and 3G under the equity swap.
- The hedge fund may have the right to unwind the equity swap in the future before a proxy vote by paying $2.5 billion to the investment banks in exchange for 62.5 million CSX shares.

Another attempt to use derivatives to avoid 13D disclosure of shareholdings is Carl Icahn's effort to control enough shares of Yahoo to get elected to the board, as depicted in Exhibit 13.6. Icahn entered into equity collars on Yahoo stock, enabling him to achieve economic control over 49 million shares of the company's stock, without disclosing this strategy or paying cash for shares, since the value of the calls purchased equaled the cost of puts sold.

EXHIBIT 13.6 EQUITY COLLARS ON YAHOO STOCK

- Assume Yahoo share price of $25.15 when the equity collar is executed.
- Put options on 49 million Yahoo shares at a strike price of $19.15 and an 18-month maturity can be sold for proceeds of:
  (i) $2.14/option
- Call options on 49 million Yahoo shares at a strike price of $32.85 and an 18-month maturity can be purchased for a cost of:
  (ii) $2.14/option
- Total cost for a "Cashless Equity Collar" = (i) – (ii) = $2.14/option – $2.14/option = $0.

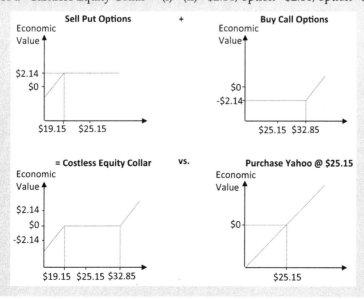

CHANGING RULES THAT FAVOR ACTIVISTS

Activist investors have become adept at initiating proxy contests to obtain shareholder votes in support of the activist's platform. There are many factors that influence shareholder votes, including the makeup of a company's institutional shareholder base, the extent to which these investors are susceptible to influence by third-party advisory services such as RiskMetrics/ISS or Glass Lewis, and the involvement of the retail investor base and their associated broker discretionary votes. In 2009, the SEC decided to eliminate broker discretionary voting for the election of directors, which shifts additional power to activists in director elections. Additionally, due to the Dodd–Frank Act, brokers may no longer vote on executive compensation or other significant matters using uninstructed shares. Historically, brokers have been allowed to vote on behalf of their retail clients who hold shares in public companies if the shareholder fails to vote. Brokers typically vote these shares in-line with management's recommendations, including for incumbent directors. With the SEC elimination of the NYSE rule that allowed for the broker discretionary voting in director elections, there are fewer votes in favor of management.

During 2012, the NYSE announced changes to the application of Rule 452 to certain management-supported corporate governance proxy proposals. These changes limit the discretionary authority of brokers to vote their customers' shares without specific voting instructions. Whether the broker may vote its customer's shares depends upon the nature of the proposals, and, generally, a broker may vote shares in its discretion only on "routine matters." When a proposal is not a routine matter and a broker has not received voting instructions from a customer with respect to that proposal, the broker cannot vote the customer's shares on that proposal. This results in a "broker nonvote."

In the past, the NYSE has permitted broker discretionary voting authority on certain management-supported corporate governance proposals, deeming such proposals "routine matters." In light of congressional and public policy trends disfavoring broker voting of uninstructed shares, the NYSE determined that it will no longer continue its previous approach under Rule 452 of classifying management-supported corporate governance proxy proposals as "routine matters," including the following:

- destaggering the board of directors,
- adopting majority voting in the election of directors,
- eliminating supermajority voting requirements,
- providing for the use of written consents,
- providing rights to call a special meeting, and
- providing for certain types of antitakeover provision overrides.

As a result, companies have found it more difficult to pass these types of proposals, particularly where a majority of the outstanding shares is required for approval, which is typically required to amend a company's charter. This in large part is because a "broker nonvote" will have the same effect as a vote against the proposal. A proposal requiring the lesser standard of a majority of the votes present and entitled to vote on the matter, or a majority of the votes cast on the matter, to pass also may be affected (although likely to a lesser extent) as brokers that generally vote uninstructed shares in accordance with management's recommendation on routine matters are now prohibited from doing so.

The elimination of broker discretionary voting is particularly important since almost 45% of S&P 500 companies have adopted a majority vote election standard, replacing plurality voting. In plurality voting, the nominees for available directorships who receive the highest number of votes cast are elected, irrespective of the number of votes cast, including withheld votes. Under this system, a nominee could theoretically be elected as a director based on receiving, for example, two affirmative votes in an election where there was one vote cast against the director and millions of withheld votes. For companies that have adopted the majority vote requirement for directors, nominees are typically required to receive the affirmative vote of at least 50% of the votes of all shareholders to remain in office for another term. Previously, the broker discretionary voting rule change would have had limited impact since nearly all companies had a plurality voting system. But, with a majority voting standard, disgruntled investors, including activist hedge funds, may be more successful in "just vote no" campaigns to remove incumbent directors.

The Dodd–Frank Act contains several new provisions that increase shareholder activism. The most important ones are the "Say on Pay" and "Say on Golden Parachutes" rules. The first provision mandates public companies to have a nonbinding shareholder vote on executive compensation at least once every 3 years. The second provision requires a nonbinding shareholder vote on the "clear and simple" disclosure and approval of executive compensation related to a transaction (such as a merger). Moreover, companies must disclose the median annual compensation of all employees excluding the CEO, the total annual compensation of the CEO, and the ratio of the two numbers.

DANIEL LOEB AND 13D LETTERS

Daniel Loeb is a hedge fund manager and founder of Third Point LLC. He is well known for writing public letters in which he expresses disapproval of the performance and decision-making of senior management of selected companies. His letters are a form of shareholder activism. These letters are often sent directly to a company's CEO or board, and sometimes are attached to 13D filings with the SEC when Loeb's holdings in a company exceed 5%. Loeb's goal is to shame companies into replacing their CEOs, shaking up their boards, or doing other things that will boost the value of his investment. After Loeb bought shares in Potlatch Corporation and the share price dropped, he branded CEO Pendleton Siegel a "CVD"—chief value destroyer. He wrote to Star Gas Partners L.P. CEO Irik Sevin: "Do what you do best. Retreat to your waterfront mansion in the Hamptons where you can play tennis and hobnob with your fellow socialites." Sevin subsequently resigned from the company. See Loeb's letter to the CEO of InterCept, Inc. in Exhibit 13.7.

EXHIBIT 13.7 DANIEL LOEB 13D LETTER

Mr. Scott Thompson
Chief Executive Officer
Yahoo! Inc.
701 First Avenue
Sunnyvale, CA 94089

March 28, 2012

Dear Scott:

As we discussed, Third Point LLC ("Third Point"), Yahoo!'s largest outside shareholder, was disappointed that you and the Board of Directors did not agree to the reasonable compromise we proposed regarding nominees to the Board.

We were pleased that the Board acknowledged that Harry Wilson would be a valuable Director. However, the way you treated our other nominees confirmed Third Point's fear that the Board's evaluation of our candidates would make a mockery of good principles of corporate governance. You will hear more on that from us in the future.

Our view of the nomination process is further reinforced by your explanation on Sunday as to why I would not be an acceptable Director. You told me that the Board felt my experience and knowledge "would not be additive to the Board" and that as Yahoo!'s largest outside shareholder, I would be "conflicted" as a Director.

Am I conflicted to advocate for the interests of other shareholders because we are owners of 5.8% (over $1 billion) of Yahoo! shares (unlike the non-retiring and proposed board members who have never purchased a single share of Yahoo! except for subsidized shares issued through option exercises and shares "paid" by the Company in lieu of fees)? Only in an illogical Alice-in-Wonderland world would a shareholder be deemed to be conflicted from representing the interests of other shareholders because he is, well, a shareholder too. This sentiment further confirms that Yahoo!'s approach to Board representation is "shareholders not welcome."

When asked to explain this apparent "conflict," you theorized that as a large shareholder, Third Point's interest might be focused only on the short-term. This theory appears, seemingly like many of the Board's conclusions, to have been arrived at by whimsy and emotion. I have never been asked about this alleged short-term bias nor was there any evidence to indicate that our investment model is predicated on short-term trading. On the contrary, a review of our record would indicate that we frequently hold positions for many years at a time (we have held our current position in Delphi Automotive since June 2008 and we held our Dade Behring position for nearly half a decade before it was sold to Siemens in 2007, as just two examples of many long-term investments). In any event, this "long-term vs. short-term" excuse is a canard and particularly inapt in the case of Yahoo!. If there ever was a company in need of a sense of *urgency*, it is this one.

Was it "short-term" thinking that led Third Point to push for the resignations of Jerry Yang, Roy Bostock, Arthur Kern and Vyomesh Joshi? If so, is there a Yahoo! shareholder on the planet who thinks this "short-term" thinking was bad for the Company? Was it "short-term" thinking that led Third Point to speak up for shareholders by questioning the fairness of the attempt by the Company to give away control to private equity funds – without receiving a premium – to entrench Roy Bostock and Jerry Yang? Or to suggest, as Third Point has, that the Company's stake in Alibaba is more valuable than generally understood, and that the Company should hold on to it unless it can

EXHIBIT 13.7— cont'd

get fair value? Was it "short-term" thinking to point out the lack of media and advertising expertise on the Board and nominate extraordinarily qualified nominees to fill that gaping hole?

To the contrary, an unbiased observer might find Third Point's thinking quite "additive." Third Point has been a driving force standing up for shareholders since we disclosed our position in Company shares in September. In fact, the Company's own actions are inconsistent with your assertions, since Yahoo! has adopted many of our recommendations.

At the risk of beating a dead horse, we suppose that, by the Board's analysis, it would have been this dreaded "short-term" thinking to have allowed Microsoft's $31 per share offer four years ago to be presented to shareholders. The real issue is not short-term versus long-term but about Board representatives who have skin in the game and will exercise sound business judgment.

By seeking four seats, Third Point does not look to control the Board, and any individual voice in the room would be only one of 11 or 12. If one director has too "short-term" an approach for other members, a healthy debate will ensue and all directors as a group will decide the issue in a fully informed and deliberative manner. It is absurd to assert a "conflict" that would render a Board Member unqualified based either on ownership or a sense of urgency to repair a company that has been – by your own admission – languishing for years.

We remain willing to engage further with you but will not deviate from our demand for badly-needed shareholder representation.

Sincerely,

/s/ Daniel S. Loeb

Daniel S. Loeb
Chief Executive Officer
Third Point LLC

BILL ACKMAN VERSUS MCDONALD'S, WENDY'S, CERIDIAN, TARGET, MBIA, AND VALEANT

Bill Ackman launched Pershing Square Capital Management (considered to be an activist hedge fund) in 2004. This fund has purchased common shares (or call options to purchase common shares in the future) in many companies, including Wendy's, McDonald's, Ceridian, Barnes & Noble, Borders, Sears, Sears Canada, Dr. Pepper Snapple, General Growth Properties, Longs Drug, Target and Valeant. The fund has also purchased a number of financial company stocks, including Greenlight Capital, Visa, MasterCard, AIG, and Wachovia.

Pershing Square's experience with McDonald's and Wendy's is described in the **McDonald's, Wendy's, and Hedge Funds: Hamburger Hedging? Case**. In the Ceridian investment, Ackman acquired 15% of the company's shares and tried to fill the company's board with his own independent nominees, while pushing for a spin-off of its strongest division. The company ultimately sold itself to a private equity firm and a private insurer for $36 a share, a price that was about double Pershing Square's purchase price.

Ackman set up Pershing Square IV during 2007 to invest solely in Target Corporation, the second largest US discount retailer. The investment totaled $2 billion, creating economic exposure to more than 10% of the company through purchase of common shares and through swap and option positions. Target's stock price dropped by approximately 21% during the fund's 2007 holding period, and this resulted in an over 43% loss in the fund's value because of leverage. During 2008, because of further drops in Target's share price, combined with the fund's leveraged position, the value of Pershing Square IV dropped an additional 68%.

Based on his fund's large position, Ackman pushed Target to buy back shares, sell its credit card unit, and extract more value through its real estate holdings (Ackman wanted Target to spin off the land on which the company's stores were built into a REIT, with the REIT to lease attached buildings to Target for 75 years). The company resisted any real estate initiatives, but ultimately, agreed to purchase $10 billion in shares and sell almost 50% of its credit card portfolio for $3.6 billion.

Valeant's stock fell 51% during a single day in March 2016 after the drug maker reduced its 2016 guidance and warned it may breach debt agreements from a delay in filing its annual report on time. Ackman's Pershing Square Capital Management publicly traded fund lost about $764 million on the common shares it owned on that day, adding to the total year to date fund losses of over 26%. As a result, Standard & Poor' decided to lower its ratings on the debt of the fund. Criticism of Valeant's pricing and drug distribution methods began during 2015, with fallout ranging from restated earnings to a special board committee investigation of a relationship with a mail-order pharmacy.

In addition to investing in the stock of underperforming companies, Pershing Square created large short positions in a number of companies, including Fannie Mae, Freddie Mac, MBIA, and Herbalife. MBIA is the largest provider of financial guarantees to states and municipalities. In addition, MBIA has provided a significant amount of guarantees in support of subprime mortgages and related obligations. Ackman established a large short position in MBIA's stock after flagging the company's over $18.7 billion in subprime exposure through guarantees of mortgage-backed securities and collateralized debt obligations (CDOs), which represented more than 280% of the company's statutory capital. Embedded within this exposure were guarantees of $9 billion in support of CDO-squared obligations (a riskier form of CDOs). This short position was one of the principal drivers for Pershing Square's strong performance in several funds during 2007–08, as MBIA's share price dropped from over $70 to under $4. During this period, Moody's reduced the company's credit rating from Aaa to Baa1. Ackman's short positions in the stocks of both Fannie Mae and Freddie Mac during 2008 also produced significant profits for Pershing Square funds, after these two stocks both dropped in value by over 90%.

Ackman very publicly crusaded against Herbalife, which sells weight loss shakes and nutritional supplements. Ackman contended that the company operates as a "pyramid scheme" that targets poor people, especially in the Latino community, and he promised to take this "to the end of the earth." Herbalife has repeatedly denied Ackman's allegations. In December 2012, Ackman announced Pershing Square's massive "billion dollar" short of Herbalife when shares traded around $47. Shortly thereafter, Carl Icahn and other prominent investors took the other side of the trade. Throughout 2013, the stock rose and eventually made new all-time highs. In October 2013, to avoid a "short squeeze," Ackman announced that Pershing Square had covered 40% of his short position and bought an unspecified number of "long-dated put options." Pershing Square lost money covering their short and had to pay a premium to purchase the long-dated put options. During August 2014, as the put options were coming closer to expiry without meaningfully being "in the money," Ackman announced that he was "extending" by effectively selling the January 2015 options and replacing them with more expensive January 2016 options. The market's expectation is that Ackman's position may ultimately have a range of outcomes, from a potential gain of about $1 billion to a potential loss of over $4 billion, based on Ackman's stated the breakeven price of "something in the mid-30's." By mid-2016, with Herbalife's share price trading above $60, the ultimate outcome looks more like a large loss than a reasonable gain.

SUMMARY

There is disagreement on whether hedge fund shareholder activism makes companies stronger or merely generates short-term gains that principally benefit the activist at the expense of long-term shareholders. During 2016, there were more than 80 hedge funds dedicated to event-driven, activist-style investing, and these funds managed more than $130 billion in assets. See Exhibit 13.8 for a list of notable activist hedge funds. Some significant institutional investors have lined up with these hedge funds to push boards to be more responsive to shareholders. In a number of cases, it appears that improvements have been made in companies that, in the absence of shareholder activism, may not have occurred. In other cases, large share repurchases pushed by activists and executed by companies created substantial opportunity costs when the repurchases occurred before subsequent steep share price drops. In addition, a number of acquisitions pushed by activist shareholders have seen significant share price drops since closing.

Although the outcome is mixed, activist hedge funds have benefited from longer lockups than most hedge funds (typically 3–4 years, compared to traditional hedge fund lockups of approximately 1 year), reasonable returns during certain years and from the increasing support of some large institutional shareholders and from institutional shareholder focused organizations such as ISS and Glass Lewis.

EXHIBIT 13.8 NOTABLE ACTIVIST INVESTORS

Fund	AUM ($bn)	Key Individual(s)	Selected Investments	Comments
Icahn Associates	$12	Carl Icahn	• Time Warner • Motorola • Kerr-McGee • Yahoo • Biogen • Genzyme	• Most prolific activist • Frequently seeks Board seats • Not deterred by market capitalization of target • Access to significantly more capital through Icahn's personal wealth
Harbinger Capital Partners	9	Philip Falcone	• New York Times • Cleveland Cliffs • LightSquared • Terrestar	• Successfully added two directors to the New York Times Board • Opposed Cleveland Cliffs' proposed acquisition of Alpha Natural Resources
Children's Investment Fund (TCI)	7	Chris Hohn	• CSX • Euronext / Deutsche Borse • ABN AMRO • Mittal Steel • Arcelor	• Corporate governance focus • Historically European-focused, but recently active in U.S. • Violations of securities laws in CSX situation did not prevent success story in proxy fights • Opposed Deutsche Borse's bid for the London Stock Exchange
JANA Partners	8	Barry Rosenstein	• Time Warner • Kerr-McGee • CNET	• Regularly partners with Icahn • Managed by former protégé of Asher Edelman
Pershing Square Capital Management	9	William Ackman	• Borders • McDonald's • Wendy's • Ceridian • Target	• Recent focus on retail/real estate plays
Trian Fund Management	3	Nelson Petz Peter May	• Heinz • Wendy's • Chemtura • Cadbury's	• High-profile given Peltz's background • Experience of principals suggests likely focus on consumer/retail sector
Relational Investors	6	David Batchelder Ralph Whitworth	• Sprint • Home Depot • SPX • Sovereign Bancorp	• Corporate governance focus; very targeted • Exceptionally high incidence of CEO change at targets
Steel Partners	7	Warren Lichtenstein	• United Industrials • KT&G Corp • Brinks • Handy & Harman	• Has partnered with Icahn • Recent focus has been more international, particularly Asia

Source: Morgan Stanley, Press Reports.

Risk, Regulation, and Organizational Structure

The material in this chapter should be cross-referenced with the following case: **A Tale of Two Hedge Funds: Magnetar and Peloton**.

INVESTOR RISKS

Hedge fund investors are exposed to portfolio-level risks and investment-level risks at each hedge fund they invest in, as summarized in Exhibit 14.1.

Another way of looking at hedge fund investor risk is to focus on five incremental risks that are more pronounced in hedge funds than in many other investment funds. These incremental risks relate to leverage, regulation, short selling, transparency, and risk tolerance.

EXHIBIT 14.1 RISKS IN HEDGE FUND INVESTING

Portfolio Level Issues		
Liquidity	Survivorship Bias	UBTI[1]
Transparency	Complexity	Headline Risk
Benchmarking	Leverage	Terms and Conditions

Investment Level Issues			
Business	People	Investment Process/Strategy	Systemic
Operational Controls	Key-Person	Strategy Failure	Regulatory Change
Client Composition	Integrity/Behavior	Style Drift	Failure of Prime Broker
Changes in Capital Base	Focus, Drive Motivation	Leverage	Correlation Spike in Stressed Markets
Counterparty Risk	Depth & Breadth of Team	Liquidity	
Conflicts of Interest		Concentration	Failure of Major Financial Institution
Compensation Structure		Unstable Correlations	

Note 1: Unrelated business taxable income is income regularly generated by tax-exempt entities by means of taxable activities. In the case of hedge funds, it includes debt-financed income, on which tax-exempt investors would then need to pay taxes. This issue can be circumvented through the use of offshore hedge funds.
Source: Grosvenor Capital Management.

Leverage

Most, but not all, hedge funds use leverage to increase their returns. In addition, many hedge funds utilize a significant amount of off-balance sheet leverage through derivatives. Exhibit 14.2 shows leverage on balance sheets of hedge funds. This exhibit shows that leverage used in the Macro investment category was 1.8 × NAV (net asset value/equity capital), meaning that investments in this category were funded by 1.8-part leverage and 1.0-part equity capital. Leverage works well when returns are positive, but it backfires when returns are negative. The average leverage applied depends on the investment strategy and the hedge fund. Assuming a hedge fund borrows $70 after receiving $30 from investors and a $100 investment is made with the total proceeds, if the investment declines by 10%, investors suffer a loss of 33%. By the same token, if the investment increases by 10%, investors gain 33%. Some investors are uncomfortable with the variability in potential returns represented by a leveraged hedge fund investment strategy. Leverage is also cited as a significant factor in increasing the risk of a systemic disturbance, since hedge fund leverage creates more vulnerability to liquidity shocks (see Systemic Risk section). Before 2008, the average leverage employed by hedge funds ranged from 40% for many equity long/short strategies to over 400% for some fixed income arbitrage strategies. During 2016, the average leverage applied for equity long/short strategies was approximately 50%, and the average leverage for relative value strategies was almost 200%. This means that the equity long/short strategy used one-part debt for two-part equity capital and the relative value strategy used almost two-part debt to one-part equity to fund investments.

It should be noted that a large proportion of hedge fund leverage is collateralized by assets and so, although notional leverage amounts can be very large, marginal leverage (uncollateralized by assets) is much smaller.

EXHIBIT 14.2 HEDGE FUND LEVERAGE BY INVESTMENT STRATEGY

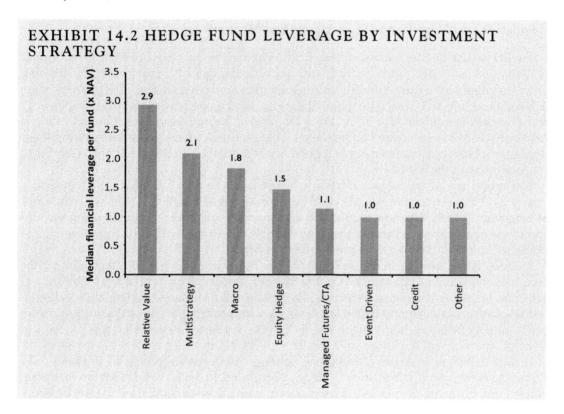

Regulation

US hedge funds have historically been able to rely on the "private adviser exemption" to reporting under the Investment Advisers Act of 1940 ('40 Act), as long as a hedge fund adviser "has fewer than 15 clients and neither holds himself out generally to the public as an investment adviser nor acts as an investment adviser" to a registered investment company. Since nearly all hedge fund advisers manage fewer than 15 separate hedge funds, they were not compelled to register under the '40 Act. As a result, US hedge funds were not subject to as much direct oversight from financial regulators, compared with mutual funds and most other investment managers who are not exempt from the '40 Act. Similarly, non-US–based hedge funds generally had less regulation compared with most other investment funds in their respective countries. However, banks (the principal counterparties to hedge funds in trading and lending transactions) are highly regulated and therefore "indirect" regulation (including the US Fed's Reg T limitations on margin) applies to hedge funds. Moreover, with the implementation of the Dodd–Frank Act of 2010, all hedge fund advisers above $150 million are required to register with the Securities and Exchange Commission (SEC), maintain extensive records about their investment and business practices, provide this information to the SEC, hire a chief compliance officer to design and monitor a compliance program, and be subject to periodic SEC examinations and inspections.

Regulation of Hedge Funds in International Markets

The EU passed the Alternative Investment Fund Managers Directive (AIFMD) on November 11, 2010, putting hedge funds and private equity funds under EU supervision for the first time. The main provisions of the AIFMD include mandatory registration, limits on leverage, detailed reporting and disclosure requirements (including compensation to key employees), and a marketing guideline for EU and non-EU funds. The European Securities and Markets Authority (ESMA) was created on January 1, 2011, and is responsible for interpreting these regulations. However, enforcement of regulations is the responsibility of national agencies in cooperation with the ESMA.

Singapore, one of the major centers for hedge funds in Asia, adopted new regulations during 2010 that require large funds (>$250 million) to register with the Monetary Authority of Singapore (MAS). The new regulations also mandate quarterly (unaudited) reports and annual audited reports to investors and the MAS. Furthermore, hedge fund managers must obtain a Capital Markets Services license from the MAS.

In Hong Kong, another major center for hedge funds in Asia, firms are regulated by the Securities and Futures Ordinance (SFO). The SFO defines several types of hedge fund business activities, including dealing in securities, leveraged foreign exchange trading and dealing in futures contracts, and requires hedge fund managers to apply for the license that is most appropriate for their business. Additionally, the SFO gives recommendations about best practices in terms of reporting and disclosure, and also strongly limits marketing activities to investors.

In China, hedge funds are classified as either government supported or private funds. Private hedge funds are still in an early stage of development, with the first fully privately run hedge fund approved during 2011 by the government. More generally, the market environment in China is not particularly well-suited for running hedge funds. The China Securities Regulatory Commission (CSRC) allows only short sales in about 50 stocks of the CSI 300 Index. Brokers cannot use customers' shares for facilitating short sales and thus the cost for short selling stocks amounts to approximately 10% per year. Additionally, hedge fund managers cannot use leverage to run their fund.

Hedge funds increased in popularity in China during 2015 as wealthy individuals sought to profit from the country's buoyant and volatile markets. According to the data released by Asset Management Association of China, the total number of hedge fund managers registered in China showed a 69% increase during that year. However, regulators are working to improve oversight of hedge funds and related parties. The CSRC stated that, because of unstable markets, tougher penalties for disseminating false information and other financial improprieties would be punished and some hedge funds shut down. As the CSRC clamped down on the country's hedge fund industry, another regulatory body, the China Insurance Regulatory Commission (CIRC) prepared insurance companies to take on more risk and fill the void left if hedge fund activity reduces based on regulatory restrictions. During 2016, the CIRC announced measures to encourage insurance companies to launch debt investment plans, equity investment plans, and mezzanine funds with an objective of encouraging insurance assets to be invested in infrastructure projects and small/median sized businesses.

Moreover, the CIRC encouraged insurance companies to set up new asset management firms. These actions follow the CIRC's encouragement to insurance companies to raise the proportion of investments in equity markets, peer-to-peer lending platforms, real estate investing, and hedge fund-type investing.

Short Selling

Many hedge funds sell securities short as a way to express a bearish view. This short selling action creates a theoretically limitless exposure if the shorted security increases in value. A long position in a security has a loss potential that is limited by the value of the security, but there is no such limit in a short position. However, short sale positions that are hedges against a long holding are considered risk mitigators, rather than risk augmenters.

Transparency

Hedge funds frequently engage in investment and hedging activities that attempt to arbitrage pricing inefficiencies in the market. To the extent that many funds identify the same opportunities, the profitability of an arbitrage strategy can be impaired. As a result, some hedge funds are very secretive about their investment strategies to protect the sources of alpha they have identified and, as a result, provide limited information to investors. Investors therefore have limited ability to monitor hedge fund activities that could potentially impair investment values. In addition, even if investors had more transparency, gates and other liquidity limitations minimize investor alternatives.

Risk Tolerance

Many hedge funds managers are inherently more comfortable taking risks compared with nonhedge fund managers. They are willing to consider a much broader array of investment alternatives and new, innovative transactions. In addition, hedge funds frequently use derivatives, which sometimes carry risks that are problematic to analyze and value. However, derivatives can also mitigate risk, if used properly.

SYSTEMIC RISK

Systemic risk is typically defined as a financial shock that brings with it the reality—or the clear and present danger—of inflicting significant damage on the entire financial system and the economy. In other words, systemic risk relates to the possibility that many financial institutions fail simultaneously in response to a single major event. Hedge funds can create systemic risk in two ways: (1) the failure of several large hedge funds at the same time could create contagion across many classes of financial and real assets as the failing funds are required to unwind all of their investment positions at fire sale prices and (2) hedge funds can potentially create large losses for the banks that lend to them if collateral is inadequate or valuation methodologies are inaccurate. Large losses incurred by banks from their exposure to hedge funds could have a cascading effect on other financial institutions.

The activities of hedge funds were heavily scrutinized following the failure of Long-Term Capital Management (LTCM), which was bailed out during 1998 by 14 major investment banks, operating under the coordination of the US Federal Reserve. These banks and the Fed took the view that excessive leverage employed by LTCM, in combination with a misguided liquidity expectation, caused the fund's collapse and that many other financial institutions would have been dragged into bankruptcy if the bailout had not occurred.

The main themes that emerged from analyzing the LTCM debacle and the subsequent hedge fund failures are the importance of liquidity and leverage, and the correlations among instruments and portfolios that would be considered uncorrelated in normal market environments, but that, under extreme stress, would not be independent.

The failure of Amaranth Advisors in 2006, combined with increasing bank exposure to hedge funds, refocused attention on whether hedge funds posed substantial risks to the general market. Some regulators and central banks, including the Bank of England, concluded that, although hedge funds can create systemic risk, there are even bigger systemic risks posed by other financial market participants. The Bank's Deputy Governor for Financial Stability stated in 2006 that traditionally central banks and regulators believed that the greatest risk to financial stability was posed by the key intermediaries at the center of the financial system. In his view, hedge funds were not even among the top 12 main sources of vulnerability in the system. He also stated that, in fact, hedge funds allowed for the transfer of risk from parties who do not want it to parties who do, potentially reducing systemic risk as a result.[1]

There are many who disagree with this position. For example, in a study that was referred to in the Federal Reserve Bank of Atlanta's Economic Review, the study's authors concluded, among other things, that massive fund inflows have had a material impact on hedge fund returns and a corresponding increase in risks, and that risks facing hedge funds are nonlinear and more complex than those facing traditional asset classes. The study determined that because of the dynamic nature of hedge fund investment strategies and the impact of fund flows on leverage and performance, hedge fund risk models require more sophisticated analytics and are susceptible to greater error.[2] This study and similar studies conclude that hedge funds create systemic risk that alters the risk/reward landscape of financial investments. These studies support the view that, although hedge funds have historically outperformed, on a risk adjusted basis, many other forms of investment management, they have also created corresponding risks that differ in important ways from more traditional investments. Such differences may have implications in the consideration of systemic risk.

Actions initiated by hedge funds' bank counterparties can also create systemic risk. As a result of substantial losses suffered during the 2007–08 credit crisis, banks were forced to shore up their capital base and drastically reduce the amount of credit provided to their borrowing clients, including hedge funds. Many hedge funds were put at risk when banks went bankrupt or reduced funding available to the funds through margin calls (in an effort to strengthen their own balance sheets).

In a scenario where several large and highly leveraged hedge funds experience a significant dislocation in the market and are forced by their lenders to quickly unwind positions,

---

[1] Sir John Gieve, Deputy Governor, Bank of England, October 17, 2006 speech on Hedge Funds and Financial Stability given at the HEDGE 2006 Conference.

[2] Chan, Getmansky, Haas, and Lo. "Do Hedge Funds Increase Systemic Risk?," Federal Reserve of Atlanta Economic Review, 4th Quarter (2006).

there could be a significant drop in prices for the securities being sold. This could, in turn, cause contagion across other, normally uncorrelated, asset classes, which ultimately might create significant losses for other investors and spark a flight to safety, as investors panic and sell many securities at a loss to mitigate investment risk. This scenario was played out to a certain extent during the two-year period starting mid-2007. For example, during August 2007, several large quantitative arbitrage hedge funds experienced significant losses when the credit market became troubled, and stress from this market bled into the equity market. The leverage employed by a number of these funds, combined with the rapid, massive, computer-driven selling of similar securities by the quantitative hedge funds caused billions of dollars of losses for these funds. This, in turn, prompted fund of hedge funds to redeem their investments in hedge funds, which caused more liquidations of hedge fund positions to raise cash to meet these redemptions, which further exacerbated equity and fixed income market declines. Throughout 2007 and 2008, hedge funds continued to sell assets based on margin calls from counterparties, increased investor redemptions and declining risk appetite. The result was to put further downside pressure on securities that were already suffering pricing erosion from the effects of the subprime mortgage asset debacle. See Exhibit 14.3 for an example of how leverage can accelerate forced selling. In this example, if a stock price drops by 5%, a hedge fund will need to sell $20 worth of stock to maintain a required leverage ratio. However, a lender might also ask for a lower leverage ratio, causing sale of an additional $15 worth of stock. This selling activity might put more downside pressure on the stock. See **A Tale of Two Hedge Funds: Magnetar and Peloton Case**.

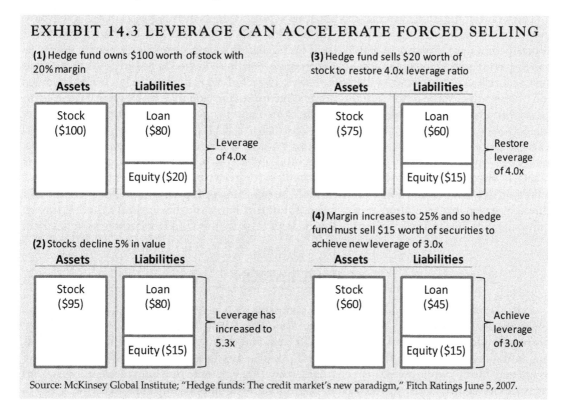

EXHIBIT 14.3 LEVERAGE CAN ACCELERATE FORCED SELLING

Source: McKinsey Global Institute; "Hedge funds: The credit market's new paradigm," Fitch Ratings June 5, 2007.

Bank Exposure to Hedge Funds

A number of large banks carry significant exposure to hedge funds. This exposure includes revenue exposure since hedge funds are the single most important commission-based clients of the trading division of these banks. Services provided by banks to hedge funds include trading securities, clearing and custody, securities lending, financing (including margin loans, repos, and sometimes, permanent capital), and customized technology and reporting tools. The large fees gained from providing these services leaves certain large banks vulnerable to significant reductions in revenue if a number of their largest hedge fund clients fail. In addition, some banks have a very large exposure to credit risk in relation to their cash loans to hedge funds. Although these loans are collateralized, margin adjustments sometimes do not keep up with the changing value of the underlying collateral. In spite of their large credit exposure to hedge funds, historically, banks have suffered minimal losses because of the assets that backed their loans to the funds.

Finally, a number of large banks are the principal counterparties to hedge funds in derivative contracts. For example, hedge funds have entered into a massive amount of credit default swaps (CDS) with banks. A CDS is a privately negotiated agreement that explicitly shifts credit risk from one party to the other. Banks are also exposed to hedge funds through equity swaps and other derivative contracts.

Mitigating Systemic Risk

The key to mitigating systemic risk associated with hedge funds is for (1) banks to employ more conservative lending strategies; (2) hedge funds to become less leveraged and more diversified in their investment activity; and (3) regulators to apply good judgment in efforts to increase regulation of hedge funds. Severe regulatory action directed at hedge funds to mitigate systemic risk is not necessarily the best answer. In fact, if regulation of hedge funds becomes too burdensome, some of the liquidity that hedge funds provide may evaporate. This, in turn, could eliminate important sources of capital when capital markets freeze up. For example, when investors are forced to sell distressed securities to meet liquidity requirements, the buyers of these securities are frequently hedge funds. Without a bid from hedge funds for distressed assets there might not be any buyers, which could further push down the price of the distressed assets. In effect, hedge funds have become "lenders (or investors) of last resort," helping to put a floor on declining asset values. Efforts should be made to appropriately mitigate systemic risk through reasonable regulation of hedge funds, but regulators must be careful to avoid a sharp curtailment in the liquidity that hedge funds provide, since this could exacerbate systemic risk.

REGULATION

In the United States, a public investment company such as a mutual fund is required to register with the SEC under the Investment Company Act of 1940 ('40 Act). After registration, they are required to report information on a regular basis and are subject to many limitations, including limitations on leverage, short selling, and performance fees. Hedge funds, by contrast, are not deemed to be public investment companies since they operate pursuant to exemptions from registration requirements, and so do not have the same limitations imposed on them.

The exemptions utilized by hedge funds are included in Sections 3(c)1 and 3(c)7 of the '40 Act, which are available for funds that have 100 or fewer investors and funds, where the investors are "qualified purchasers," respectively. A qualified purchaser is an individual who has investment assets that exceed $5 million. A 3(c)1 fund cannot have more than 100 investors, but a 3(c)7 fund can have unlimited number of investors, although more than 499 investors would subject the fund to registration under the Securities Exchange Act of 1934.

In addition, managers of hedge funds maintain exemption from registration as investment advisers under the Investment Advisers Act of 1940 (Advisers Act) by advising fewer than 15 funds. For this purpose, an individual hedge fund counts as a single fund, regardless of the number of underlying investors in the fund. Finally, to avoid "plan assets" issues under the Employee Retirement Income Security Act of 1974, most funds limit benefit plan participation to less than 25% of total fund assets.

To obtain exemptions from registration, hedge funds are sold through private placement offerings, which mean that funds cannot be offered or advertised to the general public and are normally offered under Regulation D. This process basically limits hedge fund offerings to accredited investors. An accredited investor is an individual with a minimum net worth of $2.5 million or, alternatively, a minimum income of $250,000 in each of the previous 2 years and a reasonable expectation of reaching the same income level in the current year.

There have been a number of attempts to change the regulatory landscape for hedge funds. In December 2004, the SEC issued a rule change that required most hedge fund advisers to register with the SEC under the Advisers Act by February 1, 2006. This requirement applied to firms that managed in excess of $25 million and that had over 15 investors. However, the rule was challenged in the US Court of Appeals for the District of Columbia and, in June 2006, the court overturned the SEC rule. The SEC has subsequently examined how to address this ruling, but has not mounted a successful challenge. During February 2007, the President's Working Group on Financial Markets rejected further regulation of hedge funds and recommended that the industry should instead adopt voluntary guidelines. However, after significant hedge fund and fund of fund losses that occurred during 2007 and 2008 (including the billions of dollars in losses associated with former NASDAQ Chairman Bernard Madoff's investments business), active regulatory and congressional discussion about imposing new regulations on the hedge fund industry was renewed. This led to the adoption of Section IV of the Dodd–Frank Act in 2010. The main changes promulgated by this act are the closing of exemptions to register with the SEC, increasing disclosure requirements, and the imposition of recordkeeping by investment advisers. See Exhibit 14.4 for a summary of US laws and regulations that impact hedge funds.

Although regulation has historically been minimal in the United States and in the United Kingdom, politicians in continental Europe have actively pursued greater regulation in the aftermath of the global financial crisis. The EU has promulgated a heavy regulatory framework for hedge fund managers. The first piece of legislation, the AIFMD, which became effective during 2013, was vigorously criticized by the hedge fund industry for its inadequate approach to regulation, not responding to the specific needs of the industry and for curtailing its market operations. The Directive covers any person whose regular business is managing one or more hedge funds, but an exemption is given to managers managing smaller funds with a portfolio not bigger than 100 million or 500 million euros when unleveraged and having limited redemption rights. To be authorized under the Directive, managers have to provide a significant amount of information concerning their investment strategies, risk, and leverage positions. Moreover, managers fall under supervision regarding authorization of management, capital, conduct of business, delegation, marketing, and leveraging requirements. However, EU hedge fund managers benefit from the EU Passport, which allows them to manage and market authorized funds in each Member State.

In the aftermath of the financial crisis, short selling became much more difficult in an effort to achieve better transparency through disclosure of net short positions on shares admitted to trading on an EU regulated market. To mitigate the risk of settlement failure, regulation requires a buy-in procedure combined with "locate" conditions that make the executions of naked short sales more difficult. In relation to over-the-counter markets, hedge funds, and other participants are required to clear derivatives through a recognized central counterparty. A further cornerstone of recent regulation is the mandatory reporting of every derivative transaction concluded by all hedge funds as a way to enhance risk transparency. Other regulations influence the ways in which hedge funds trade and the choice about where to trade, as well as slowing down high-frequency trading and pure speculative trading.

EXHIBIT 14.4 SUMMARY OF HEDGE FUND LAWS AND REGULATIONS

- Securities Act of 1933
  - Interest in a fund are "securities"
  - Regulation D "safe harbor"
    - Rule 506
      - No limit on amount of sales
      - Generally only sold to "accredited investors" ($1 million net worth or $200K in income in last two years)
      - Can have up to 35 non-"accredited investors"
    - No general advertising
    - File Form D with SEC within 15 days of sale
- Securities Exchange Act
  - Funds with 500 investors and $10 million in equity must register
- Investment Company Act of 1940
  - Hedge funds exempted under Section 3(c)(1) and 3(c)(7)
    - Section 3(c)(1) funds:
      - No more than 100 investors
      - Accredited investor
      - Qualified client (natural person with net worth of >$1.5 million)
    - Section 3(c)(7) funds:
      - <500 investors (if >500, would have to be registered)
      - Qualified purchaser (natural person with liquid net worth of $5 million)
- Investment Advisors Act of 1940
  - Requires investment advisors to register with the SEC
    - <$25 million AUM: state registration only
    - $25–$30 million AUM: SEC or state registration
    - >$30 million: SEC registration
  - Exemption under Section 203(b)(3) for advisors who have less than 15 clients over a 12-month period

EXHIBIT 14.4 SUMMARY OF HEDGE FUND LAWS AND REGULATIONS—cont'd

- Dodd–Frank Wall Street Reform and Consumer Protection Act
  - Eliminates the <15 clients exemption rule under Section 203(b)(3) of the Investment Advisors Act of 1940
  - Creates three exemptions from registration for:
    - Advisers solely to venture capital funds
    - Advisers solely to private funds with less than $150 million AUM in the United States
    - Foreign advisers without a place of business in the United States with less than $25 million AUM attributable to less than 15 US clients
  - Raises the threshold for SEC registration from $25 million AUM to $100 million AUM
  - Grants the SEC the authority to craft a new regulatory regime for the derivatives market
  - Requires certain noncommercial participants in the derivatives market to trade via exchanges and/or register the transaction with CFTC-registered "Swap Data Repositories"
  - Volcker Rule
    - Prohibits insured depositary institutions and their affiliates from engaging in proprietary trading
    - Prohibits banking entities from sponsoring or having any equity, partnership, or ownership interest in hedge funds or private equity funds

Source: Mallon P.C.; Morrison & Foerster LLP.

Alternative Regulatory Approaches

Regulators worry about three main issues:

1. The possibility of hedge funds defrauding investors—To combat this potential problem, regulators have tried to limit the kind of investors allowed to invest in hedge funds to sophisticated investors who can perform their own assessment (or pay someone else to do this for them).
2. Trading by hedge funds using insider information—To address this problem, regulators generally apply the same rules that they apply to other investment firms in relation to market abuse.
3. Hedge fund destabilization of the financial system and, by extension, the economy— To address this problem, regulators have principally focused on timely and accurate collateral valuations and on the overall level of borrowing by hedge funds, as well as limiting such borrowing by applying more stringent lending standards on banks, which they directly regulate.

However, in spite of common concerns, each country takes a somewhat different regulatory approach. For example, in Portugal, the use of derivatives is carefully controlled, whereas in France there is less focus on derivatives, but more focus on leverage. French regulators have also been very concerned about potential collusion by hedge funds in attempts to push companies to agree to takeover bids. In Russia, regulators are substantially more restrictive than in other G8 countries. UK regulators have been fairly consistent with the regulators in the United States, but have taken a particularly strict view on side letters in an effort to avoid favoring some investors over others.

For many, the best answer is self-regulation. An organization called Alternative Investment Management Association has published the Guide to Sound Practices for Hedge Fund Valuation, which suggests, among other things, the appointment of an independent valuation service provider, the use of multiple pricing sources, and the disclosure of any material involvement by a hedge fund manager in the determination of a fund's NAV.

As an increasing number of hedge funds become public companies, allowing any investor to invest in their stock (for example, Och-Ziff Capital Management in the United States and Man Group in the United Kingdom), a laissez-faire attitude of regulators to hedge funds may come under pressure. As less sophisticated investors gain exposure to hedge funds by investing in public hedge fund stock, some regulators may feel compelled to step up the pressure for more stringent regulation. The counter to this concern is that, by filing the required registration statement with regulators before launching IPOs, hedge funds are already subjecting themselves to additional regulation as a publicly reporting company.

ORGANIZATIONAL STRUCTURE

A hedge fund's organizational structure is generally developed with a principal focus on how to minimize taxes and regulatory constraints. See Exhibit 14.5 for an overview of a typical hedge fund investment partnership.

EXHIBIT 14.5 HEDGE FUND INVESTMENT PARTNERSHIP

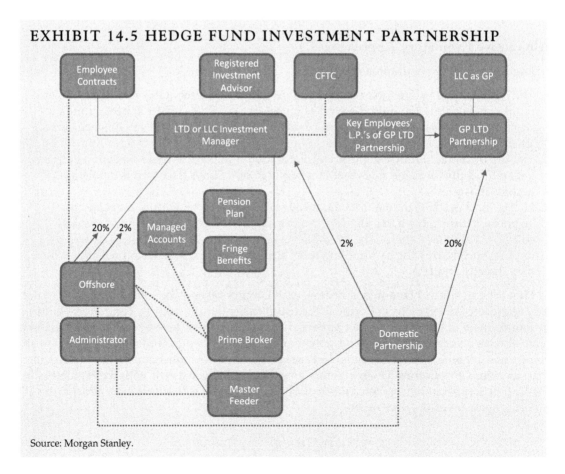

Source: Morgan Stanley.

Domicile

Many hedge funds are registered offshore. The principal offshore locations include the Cayman Islands (55%), British Virgin Islands (15%), and Bermuda (10%). Onshore hedge fund registrations are principally in the United States (65% mostly in Delaware) and in Europe (31%). The chosen domicile depends on the tax and regulatory environment of the fund's investors. By creating an offshore domicile, the fund can avoid paying taxes on the increase in the value of its portfolio. However, investors in the fund will still pay individual taxes on any profit realized in their investment with the fund. In addition, the hedge fund manager will pay taxes on management fees.

Legal Entity

Hedge funds usually organize as a limited partnership for US-based taxable investors. The general partner of the limited partnership is usually the hedge fund investment manager, and investors are limited partners. Offshore investors who are non-US entities and US entities who do not pay taxes (such as pension funds) invest through a separate offshore vehicle. Both onshore and offshore funds usually invest in a master feeder fund, which then coinvests in a master fund. The assets of the master fund are managed by the hedge fund investment manager. This structure creates optimal tax and regulatory advantages for both onshore and offshore investors, while enabling the investment manager to manage all invested funds together. The hedge fund investment manager does not retain an interest in the master fund. If organized properly, this structure enables taxable investors to avoid paying taxes twice, and also enables tax-exempt investors to participate in the same investment management pool as taxable investors.

To create an optimal legal structure, a hedge fund will employ the services of accountants, lawyers, auditors, an administrator (who completes reports and arranges issuance and redemption of interests), an independent valuation party (who determines the NAV of the fund), and a prime broker (who lends money and securities, acts as derivatives counterparty, and provides trade execution, clearing, and settlement services).

Open-Ended Partnership

Hedge funds typically operate as open-ended partnerships. An open-ended fund is able to periodically issue additional partnership interests or shares directly to new investors at a price that is equal to NAV/share or interest. Investors are able to redeem their interests or shares at the prevailing NAV/share or interest on the date of redemption. Shares or interests in open-ended funds are typically not traded. Profits associated with these shares or interests are usually not distributed to investors before redemption. By contrast, a closed-end fund distributes profits to shareholders and allows shares to be traded.

Taxes

Hedge funds based in the United States are organized as investment partnerships and general partners are both the investors and managers of the fund. By contrast, offshore funds, which can be formed in various locations, including the Cayman Islands and Bermuda, are organized as limited duration companies, or in the form of nonpass through vehicles. The offshore funds are advised by an investment advisor under contract (who has ownership in the funds). This section focuses only on US tax matters and is subject to change as the laws change. Other countries have different tax laws that may provide different tax outcomes.

US domestic partnerships pay annual management fees to the management company, which is usually formed as a limited partnership or a limited liability company, and performance fees are allocated to the general partner. For offshore funds, the fund pays management and performance fees to the management company (which is taxed as ordinary income). For US-based managers, the management fee is taxed as ordinary income. The tax characterization for performance fee allocation is more complex. If the fund's profits are from the sale of capital assets held for more than 1 year (it is estimated that less than one-third of investments are held for more than 1 year), the profits will "flow through" to the limited partner investors and the general partner as long-term capital gains. This enables US-based limited partners to pay the lower capital gains tax rate, as opposed to the higher maximum tax rate on ordinary income. The performance fee paid to the general partner is either an unrealized gain or is taxed in the same tax category as a partnership, including dividend interest and long-term gains. In addition, since the partnership is not a business, it therefore does not pay payroll taxes (or the 2.9% in Medicare taxes on performance fees that qualify as long-term capital gains). As a result, under certain circumstances, US-based hedge fund managers may, in effect, pay total taxes on their performance income that equals the lower long-term capital gains tax rate for assets held for more than 1 year, compared with higher marginal taxes, that, with a less permissive tax regime, would be payable. This is known as the so-called "carried interest loophole." According to a study put together by the committee on taxation at the US House of Representatives, these performance fee–related tax savings projected across a 10-year period could exceed $30 billion (this amount includes private equity funds, whose performance fees are subject to the same benefit).

In addition to benefitting from the low tax rate on performance fees, US-based hedge fund managers had historically enjoyed tax benefits in relation to management fees. In 2008, however, the US government eliminated a tax benefit that allowed for the deferral of income taxes on deferred compensation, which impacted all taxpayers, including hedge fund managers. Prior to the enactment of this code (Internal Revenue Code Section 457), hedge fund managers had been able to defer management fees for income tax purposes, whereby no current income was recognized on deferred fees or interest and investment return attributable to deferred fees. Managers recognized income only when, at the manager's election, cash was received based on the deferred amount plus investment return on this amount. Through this arrangement, managers had been able to limit income received each year to only the amount needed to spend or invest outside the hedge fund. The remainder was saved on a tax-deferred basis.

The Alternative Minimum Tax Relief Act of 2008 contained a provision that would have taxed performance fees at ordinary income rates. That act passed the House of Representatives in June 2008, but failed to pass in the Senate. As a result, hedge fund managers continue to have a reduced tax burden for all assets they manage that can be characterized as capital assets held for over 1 year. Some or all of this tax advantage is expected to be eliminated at some point by Congress. However, it is useful to point out that any changes in the US tax policy may affect a relatively small portion of profits since most hedge funds generate the majority of their income from short-term investments.

Hedge Fund Issues and Performance

HEDGE FUND PERFORMANCE

In the hedge fund industry, 2008 was a watershed year. Assets under management (AUM) by hedge funds dropped to unprecedented levels and the concept of managing for absolute returns (positive returns) was, in part, invalidated by significant losses (see Exhibit 15.1). As a result of these losses, investor withdrawals increased substantially. This withdrawal activity, combined with reductions in asset values, resulted in a drop in AUM by approximately 25%, from almost $1.9 trillion at the end of 2007 to just over $1.4 trillion by the end of 2008. Part of the problem during 2008 was that too many funds bought the same assets. As markets fell, many hedge funds sold these assets to gain liquidity, pushing prices even lower.

Hedge funds that invested in Russia and China, which provided big gains during previous years, were among the worst performers in 2008, with losses of 70%–90% during the year. Contrasting with these losses were a few hedge funds such as Paulson Advantage Plus, which was up more than 35% during 2008, based on bearish positions in toxic mortgage-related securities.

The Fund Weighted Composite Index tracked by Hedge Fund Research (HFR) fell by 19% during the year compared to the drop in Standard & Poor's 500 stock index of 38.5%, including

EXHIBIT 15.1 A DIFFICULT YEAR FOR THE INDUSTRY

HFRIndex	2008 Returns
HFRI Fund Weighted Composite Index	**–19.0%**
HFRI Convertible Arbitrage Index	–33.7%
HFRI Distressed /Restructuring Index	–25.2%
HFRI Equity Hedge Index	–26.6%
HFRI Equity Market Neutral Index	–6.0%
HFRI Event Driven Index	–22.1%
HFRI Macro Index	4.8%
HFRI Merger Arbitrage Index	–5.0%
HFRI Relative Value Arbitrage Index	–18.0%

Source: Hedge Fund Research, Inc.

dividends. Therefore, even though hedge fund losses were significant, they were substantially less than the broader equity market. 2008 marked only the second calendar year of negative returns for hedge funds since 1990. Approximately two-thirds of the decline in assets during 2008 was a result of poor hedge fund performance. The remaining one-third came from clients withdrawing their assets. Funds of hedge funds, operating under the premise of greater asset diversification, underperformed hedge funds, losing 21.3% for the year. Emerging market funds and many other funds also performed poorly. With very few exceptions, hedge funds returned negative results for the year, regardless of investment strategy. Despite the overall poor performance, however, it is important to reemphasize that hedge funds (both in aggregate and across the major investment strategies) still outperformed the broader market.

Hedge funds underperformed global markets during the years following the global financial crisis, but AUM grew considerably because many investors viewed hedge funds as a safer, low-volatility option in a challenging investment landscape. The US and European pension funds, searching for more predictable returns during a period of very low interest rates and unpredictable markets, increasingly turned to hedge funds. By 2013, hedge funds managed nearly 30% more money than in 2007. A closer look at this growth shows, however, that the money hedge funds have made—beyond what their clients could have earned from investments tracking the main asset classes—has plunged since the financial crisis. This return, known as "alpha," even turned negative in 2011. Although total returns recovered, average hedge fund risk-adjusted performance actually dropped. The average fund made 5.32% more than the so-called "beta" return delivered by a basket of the major bond, stock, commodity, and currency indexes between 1994 and February 2012. But that headline number hides significant variations in hedge fund returns over time. Over 36 months, hedge fund "alpha" returns reached almost 10% in 2001, but by early 2012, investors were worse off by between 1% and 2% than if they had invested in the basket of major asset class indexes. As a result, it appears that investors are turning to hedge funds to help them manage volatility and ensure steady—if low—returns, rather than hoping for outperformance when markets are strong. From 2007 to 2012, average annual hedge fund volatility was 9.8% according to the HFRI index while the MSCI Global Equity Index was almost twice as volatile at 18.2%. Volatility in the S&P 500 was 16.6%. Many investors increasingly focused on Libor plus 300–500 basis points returns, while others sought returns similar to equity markets but with lower volatility. This is particularly true for pension funds because steady returns help them map out how much they need to pay out to retirees. Whereas, prior to the financial crisis, hedge fund managers built their reputations on high-risk, contrarian bets backed by lots of debt, now many are recasting themselves in a more conservative mold, using less leverage and taking fewer risks.

During 2015, hedge funds lost more than 1% on average (see Exhibit 15.3), even as AUM grew to the highest level in history (see Exhibit 15.2), while the S&P 500 returned 1.4%, including dividends. Managers made numerous mistakes, including bad bets on energy and currencies and overreliance on selected stocks. But the industry continued its reliance on leverage, which accentuates mistakes, and during 2016, use of leverage increased further.

EXHIBIT 15.2 ANNUAL GROWTH OF ASSETS/NET ASSET FLOW

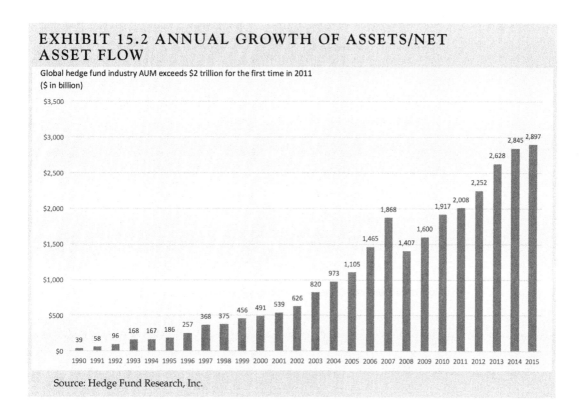

Global hedge fund industry AUM exceeds $2 trillion for the first time in 2011
($ in billion)

Source: Hedge Fund Research, Inc.

Many hedge funds do not want to have their performance compared to equity markets only because they trade not only in stock markets, but also in many other markets. But even as the stock market slowed down during 2015, some of the industry's most successful managers were not able to take advantage. For example, activist investors were on the wrong side of a number of high profile stock bets (both long and short). And the collapse in energy pushed other firms to huge losses. During 2015, a number of well-known funds shut down, including BlackRock Inc. and Fortress Investment Group LLC, while other funds such as Claren Road Asset Management and Stone Lion Capital Partners received redemption requests from nearly all of their investors at year-end, but declined to return investor funds.

Exhibit 15.3 shows the returns of various hedge fund strategies and the S&P 500 Index during 2015.

Exhibit 15.4 shows the outperformance of most hedge fund investment strategies compared to the S&P 500 Index over the past 25 years.

EXHIBIT 15.3 2015 RETURNS OF ALL HEDGE FUNDS, ALL FUNDS OF FUNDS, AND SELECT STRATEGIES

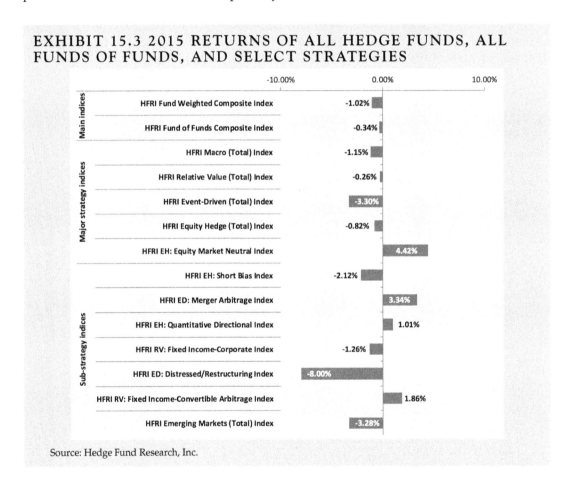

Source: Hedge Fund Research, Inc.

When looking at hedge fund performance at the top and bottom deciles, the extreme market volatility of 2008 translated to the most significant dispersions in returns since HFR started tracking this data. During 2015 the dispersion between the median returns of top and bottom deciles was 39%, a significant drop from the dispersion of 97% during 2009 (see Exhibit 15.5).

EXHIBIT 15.4 THE VALUE OF $1000 INVESTED ON JANUARY 1, 1990

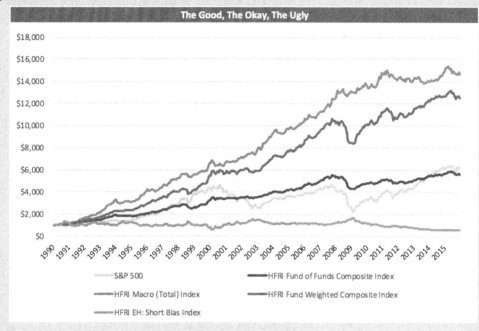

Source: Bloomberg L.P.

EXHIBIT 15.5 DISPERSION BETWEEN TOP AND BOTTOM DECILE MEDIAN FUND PERFORMANCE, 2000–15

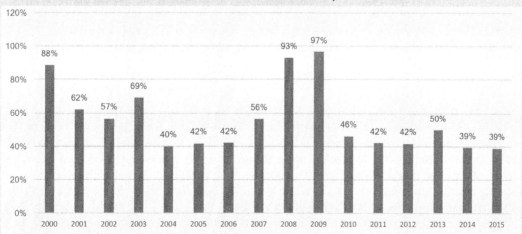

Note: Dispersion calculated as median fund performance of the top decile less the median fund performance of the bottom decile.
Source: Hedge Fund Research, Inc.

An analysis of whether the length of a manager's experience is any indication of expected returns brings interesting results. Comparing the performance of new managers (as defined by those in operation for less than 24 months) against established managers, new managers consistently outperform, even when adjusted for backfill. See Exhibit 15.6.

EXHIBIT 15.6 NEW MANAGERS VERSUS ESTABLISHED MANAGERS

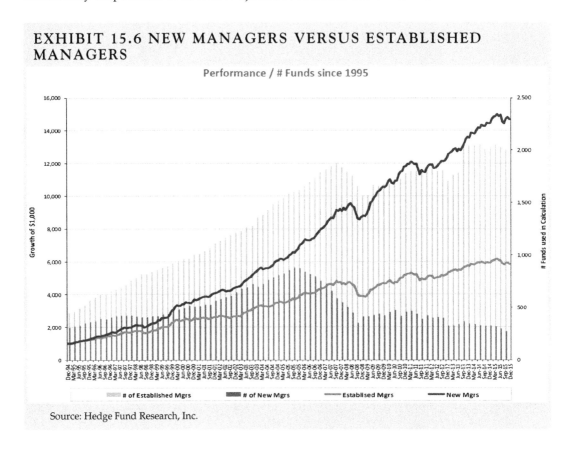

Source: Hedge Fund Research, Inc.

FUND OF FUNDS

The year 2008 ended on a bad note with the disclosure of billions of dollars in losses experienced by those who invested in Bernard Madoff's investment funds. Although Madoff was not a hedge fund manager, a number of fund of funds that allocate investor money to hedge funds also allocated money to Madoff through feeder funds. This created concern about the quality of fund of funds' due diligence processes. The ensuing crisis of confidence in fund of funds resulted in many investors withdrawing money from these funds, which in turn, caused money to be taken out of hedge funds.

Fund of funds have sold themselves to investors on the basis that they offer three key benefits: diversification, access to sought-after managers, and due diligence. The financial crisis weakened the first two benefits from the perspective of many investors. The Madoff scandal significantly undermined the third benefit. As a result, assets under management by fund of funds dropped during 2008 from a high of $826 billion at the end of June 2008 to $593 billion by the end the year, according to HFR.

Compounding the difficulties of fund of funds was the leverage employed by these funds. Many fund of funds borrowed money to supplement investor money when they made investments in various hedge funds. Since most of the hedge funds they invested in were already leveraged, this doubling up of leverage created enhanced losses beyond the losses of the underlying funds. In part, because of this leverage, average losses from fund of hedge funds during 2008 were 21%, compared to average losses for hedge funds during the year of 19%.

ABSOLUTE RETURN

Historically, many investors have viewed hedge funds as an investment class that created absolute returns through the use of sophisticated hedging vehicles and by investing (both long and short) in a very diverse array of global assets. However, the financial crisis of 2007 and 2008 forced investors to reconsider this view. Although the flexibility and skill of hedge funds kept the industry from suffering losses as large as the overall market, it is clear that the concept of achieving consistent positive returns is not always sustainable. In the face of extreme market duress, hedge funds are carried downstream along with relative return investment managers (although at a slower pace).

It is increasingly problematic for hedge funds to market themselves as absolute return funds. Instead, they now have to focus more on delivering diversification as a key benefit. In other words, they are now perceived increasingly as relative value funds, but because of the broad array of investment and hedging tools at their disposal, are still able to apply a partial braking mechanism in bad markets. In a down market, many hedge funds may not produce positive returns, but most will outperform other investment managers because they produce "diversified beta," defined by Partners Group, a Swiss-based alternative asset manager, as "diversification across a large spectrum of return drivers that balances the investment risk of each individual underlying risk."

TRANSPARENCY

Hedge fund investors historically have not required a significant amount of investment transparency from hedge fund managers. However, many investors are now pushing for greater position-level transparency. There will be ongoing pressure for more transparency, but a corresponding pushback from some managers based on their concern that disclosure of strategies will benefit competitors and cause arbitrage opportunities to disappear.

Managers are generally willing to provide organizational and process transparency regarding assets under management, profit and loss attribution, key investment themes, new product initiatives, and personnel. In addition, risk transparency is usually provided through disclosure of credit exposure, volatility exposure, long versus short positions, leverage, geographic focus, portfolio concentration, industry focus, and market capitalization focus.

However, hedge fund managers will attempt to keep specific investment strategies, ideas, and short positions confidential. Investors must therefore decide whether the level of overall transparency provided is adequate in the context of the risks and benefits associated with investing in hedge funds.

FEES

The notion that hedge funds all collect a stereotypical management fee of 2% and a performance fee of 20% has been dying a slow death in recent years, especially for smaller, newer funds. Average performance fees for newly launched funds last touched 20% in 2007 and fell to about 14% during 2015 (see Exhibit 15.7).

EXHIBIT 15.7 PERFORMANCE FEES FALL

New hedge funds aren't commanding the same fees they once did.

■ Performance Fees   ■ Management Fees

Source: Bloomberg, Eurekahedge

Based on new funds launched in each year. Data for 2015 is as of August.

There are two main trends behind the drop in performance fees. One of them is obvious and the other not-so-obvious. First, even though hedge funds as a group outperformed underlying markets during the financial crisis, they still racked up nasty losses. As a result, their fees came under scrutiny. The other trend has been a preference among big institutional investors to place money in larger hedge funds, causing smaller startups to lower their fees to attract investors.

At the end of 2008, Citadel Investment Group gave back about $300 million in fees it had previously collected, after completing a money-losing year. Other firms also gave back fees and remained committed to not receiving performance fees until they reached their high-water marks. At most funds, fee cuts came principally from performance fees, rather than management fees. As a result, 1%–2% management fees continue to be the norm. Hedge funds maintain that, when poor performance eliminates performance fees, management fees are essential to keeping the funds operational.

HIGH-WATER MARK

A hedge fund high-water mark is a mechanism that is implemented to make sure that managers do not take a performance fee in the current period when the fund has had negative performance over previous performance fee periods. The high-water mark is the colloquial term for a "cumulative loss account." A cumulative loss account starts with a zero balance at the beginning of any performance period (quarterly, or yearly, as determined by the firm), and it records net losses during that period. See Exhibit 15.8 for an example of high-water mark calculation.

EXHIBIT 15.8 HIGH-WATER MARK EXAMPLE

An example of the mechanical application of the cumulative loss account and high-water mark calculation is below:

Hedge fund NAV 01/01/06: $1,000,000

Hedge fund NAV 12/31/06: $1,200,000 (total after expenses, including the management fee expense)
Gain: $200,000
Less Performance fee: $40,000 [20% of $200,000]
Cumulative loss account: $0

Hedge fund NAV 01/01/07: $1,160,000

Hedge fund NAV 12/31/07: $1,000,000 (total after expenses, including the management fee expense)
Gain: ($160,000)
Less Performance fee: $0
Cumulative loss account: $160,000

Hedge fund NAV 01/01/08: $1,000,000

Hedge fund NAV 12/31/08 $1,100,000 (total after expenses, including the management fee expense)
Gain: $100,000
Less Performance fee: $0
Cumulative loss account: $60,000

Hedge fund NAV 01/01/09: $1,100,000

Hedge fund NAV 12/31/09 $1,300,000 (total after expenses, including the management fee expense)
Gain: $200,000
Less Performance fee: $28,000 [20% of $140,000]
Cumulative loss account: $0

EXHIBIT 15.8 HIGH-WATER MARK EXAMPLE—cont'd

The concept of the high-water mark is theoretically similar to the "claw-back" provision found in many private equity funds in which its purpose is to make sure the manager is not overcompensated for underperformance. However, the high-water mark is distinctly different in which it is prospective in nature (whereas the claw-back is retrospective in nature). The high-water mark is applied to a hedge fund manager on a going forward basis and so the manager will need to get the fund's account back up to the high-water mark before a performance fee can be taken.

The high-water mark is designed to benefit investors by preventing a manager from taking a performance fee on the same gains more than once. However, the high-water mark also creates a perverse incentive for the hedge fund manager to either take extra risk to generate returns high enough to deplete the cumulative loss account so that a performance fee will be paid, or to close down the fund and start again. Both of these actions could be damaging to investors, forcing them to either request redemptions at inopportune times, or continue with their investment, with a potentially higher risk profile. If a hedge fund manager shuts down a fund, the investor might suffer disproportionate losses as assets are sold in a fire sale environment. However, to keep money invested in the fund under a higher risk profile may also not be in the investor's best interest. Moreover, taking money out to invest with another manager might subject the investor to the same high-water mark issue.

As a result of this conundrum, in some cases, it might make sense for investors to consider modification of the high-water mark. A modified high-water mark resets the high-water mark to the current fund level under circumstances where to do so better aligns everyone's interests. A modified high-water mark may create value for investors by keeping a manager in the game and reducing the incentive of the manager to take excessive risk. As a quid pro quo, some hedge fund managers may be willing to accept lower performance fees.

SEARCHING FOR RETURNS

Hedge funds have traditionally been associated with "alpha-based" returns that are independent of market conditions, but, increasingly, hedge funds participate in the same investment activity as traditional fund managers. To differentiate themselves, hedge fund managers have had to search for new sources of returns in new markets. This search has pushed them into less liquid investments, including private equity investments and other private transactions. This activity extends their investment horizon, requires longer lock-ups, and results in the need to hire new managers who have long-term investment expertise. Hedge funds have become active participants in leveraged bank loans, mezzanine financings, insurance-linked securities, and in LBO transactions. In other words, hedge funds have moved a significant amount of their investment base from public transactions to private transactions, in their search for alpha-based returns.

MERGING OF FUNCTIONS

Hedge funds, private equity funds, and investment banks compete against one another and are, at the same time, major sources of revenue for one another. Prior to the Dodd–Frank Act, competition between hedge funds, private equity funds and investment banks was pronounced, as many investment banks operated their own hedge and private equity funds and ran large proprietary trading desks. Since the implementation of this Act, competition between hedge funds and private equity funds on one side and investment banks on the other has declined significantly. Hedge funds and private equity firms continue to be the largest clients of major investment banks such as Goldman Sachs. Goldman Sachs has an industry leading investment banking business, providing M&A and underwriting services to corporate and municipal clients and to private equity firms. The firm also has an industry leading sales and trading business, providing trading and lending services to institutional and individual investors, including hedge funds. In fact, private equity funds and hedge funds are the two most important clients of Goldman Sachs' investment banking division and trading division, respectively. Due to the Dodd–Frank Act, investments by investment banks in their own hedge funds and private equity funds have been sharply curtailed. Additionally, proprietary trading has been significantly diminished.

Citadel Investment Group is an alternative asset manager that principally focuses on hedge fund investments, but their investment portfolio has broadened beyond traditional hedge fund investments. Citadel has also developed a large hedge fund administration business that competes with the prime brokerage operations of major investment banks by providing securities loans, and reporting and administrative services to other hedge funds. In addition, Citadel expanded beyond its traditional trading-based businesses when it launched an investment banking advisory division in May 2009. Citadel launched a swaps market-making business to take advantage of the retreat by investment banks from this business due to global banking rules that focus on making the financial system safer.

Morgan Stanley's Alternative Investments Partners (AIP) is a fund of funds business that is focused on real estate, private equity and opportunistic investment strategies. As of December 31, 2015, AIP managed total assets of $37 billion. J.P. Morgan controls Highbridge Capital Management, a diversified investment platform consisting of hedge funds, traditional asset management products and credit and equity investments with longer-term holding periods. Highbridge has $21 billion in assets under management.

INTERNATIONAL HEDGE FUND INITIATIVES

Although most hedge funds have principal offices in the United States and the United Kingdom, many hedge funds are also domiciled in one of the following countries: Cayman Islands, Luxembourg, Singapore, Ireland, Malta, Australia, Hong Kong, or the British Virgin Islands. Fund managers have chosen to domicile their funds in these countries due to favorable legal and tax jurisdictions and lower administrative burdens. Due to strong economic growth, some emerging economies have attracted interest from investors and, in these countries, lawmakers have responded by changing laws to make it easier for hedge funds to operate. This is especially true in Asia. Although many Asian governments have been skeptical of hedge funds in the past, the business climate for hedge funds in Asia has steadily improved. Hong Kong and Singapore now offer attractive jurisdictions with limited administrative burdens and more flexible regulation. Other Asian countries such as South Korea and China have also created favorable environments for hedge funds by changing local regulations, encouraging local hedge funds as well as major US hedge fund managers to establish operations in their country.

Other emerging economies are also becoming increasingly attractive for hedge funds. For example, Morgan Stanley opened a prime brokerage office in Brazil to better serve emerging hedge funds in the Brazilian markets. Dubai is another example of a country that has loosened regulations for both domestic and foreign fund managers, inviting hedge funds in.

BENEFITS REVISITED

Historically, hedge fund managers have articulated the following benefits for investors who place money in their funds:

1. Attractive risk-adjusted returns, focusing on positive returns, low volatility, and capital preservation.
2. Low correlation with major equity and bond markets.
3. Investment flexibility to invest long or short, using a variety of instruments, investing in segments of the market that suffer from structural inefficiencies and in smaller asset pools.
4. Focus on marketable securities.
5. Structural advantages including performance-based compensation (focus on performance instead of asset gathering), managers' personal investment (which aligned interests), and the ability to attract the "best and brightest."

An analysis of these benefits in light of the major dislocations of the market suggests the following about hedge funds:

1. Achievement of positive (absolute) returns has become a problematic objective during periods of major market dislocation.
2. Achievement of low correlation with major equity and bond markets is difficult to obtain during periods of major market dislocation.
3. Investment flexibility continues to be a major benefit of hedge funds.
4. Some hedge funds have invested a portion of their assets in nonmarketable securities, creating a mismatch between asset maturities and investor withdrawal requirements.
5. Structural advantages continue, including performance-based compensation and aligned interests.

FUTURE DEVELOPMENTS

Hedge funds suffered significant pain during 2007–09: redemptions created loss of income and forced sales of assets that compounded losses, fees were reduced as performance waned, regulators reached toward greater regulation and more taxes, and many investors became concerned with the hedge fund model. While hedge funds gained in terms of assets under management during 2010 through 2016, their performance was weak compared to broad stock market indices. Moreover, they could not deliver the diversification many investors required.

As a result, a number of significant, lasting developments have occurred:

1. Hedge funds have more limited access to leveraged financing, which, in particular, impacts convertible arbitrage, fixed income arbitrage, and statistical arbitrage investment strategies.
2. The ability to maintain confidentiality over investment strategies has been reduced as investors demand more transparency and liquidity. Losses, gates, and fraud have forced hedge funds to become more open in their activities and more willing to share details of their business and associated risks with investors.
3. Fees have been reduced from the typical 2/20 schedule to a lesser fee system that allows greater returns to investors and acknowledges the lower return environment. Many funds now offer a sliding fee schedule for larger investment commitments.
4. The decline in alpha is well documented and many hedge funds are now viewed as creating diversified beta instead of finding significant returns from market inefficiencies. This still represents value added, but differentiation from many well-managed traditional investment funds is more difficult.
5. Hedge funds are subject to additional regulatory constraints, which limit somewhat their flexibility, especially in long/short equity, event driven and other equity based strategies.
6. A less favorable tax environment will result in reduction in after-tax compensation received by hedge fund managers.
7. As hedge funds adjust to the new realities of the market they are developing longer lock-up arrangements that better match the lengthening maturity profile of their investments. This enables them, in turn, to expand long-term investment activity to take advantage of higher yields available for patient capital.
8. The balance of power has shifted from general partners to limited partners. The result is that limited partners have been successful in obtaining better transparency, improved liquidity (or better match with assets), and the other benefits described above.
9. New regulation through the Dodd–Frank Act in the United States and the Alternative Fund Managers Directive (AIFMD) in the EU adds a considerably increased administrative burden (especially for smaller hedge funds).
10. There will be consolidation among smaller funds as they face both higher administrative cost due to new regulation and pressure on fees.

FORECASTS FOR HEDGE FUND INDUSTRY[1]

1. Reduced Return Expectations

   Hedge fund performance is driven by a combination of manager skill and market-driven returns—alpha and beta. From 2009 to the beginning of 2015, as both the fixed income and equity markets experienced strong bull markets, beta propelled hedge fund performance that rewarded managers with net long market exposure. Over this period, investors' return expectations for new managers steadily declined from the midteens in 2009 to just above 10% in 2014 and to mid-to-high single digits during 2015–2017. These reduced return expectations stem mainly from many investors' belief that beta will add very little value over the next few years as the capital markets trade near all-time highs.

2. Demand for Low-Correlation Strategies

   Lower return expectations for hedge funds will strongly influence hedge fund strategy selection. Investors will perceive higher beta strategies as having higher—and unnecessary—risk. They will increasingly demand strategies such as relative value fixed income, market neutral long/short equity, CTAs, direct lending, volatility arbitrage, reinsurance and global macro, perceiving these as able to generate alpha regardless of market direction and as a hedge against a potential market sell-off.

3. Hedge Fund Assets to Reach All-Time High

   Hedge fund industry assets are expected to increase, but at a lower rate. The climb to a new all-time high will be fueled by pension funds reallocating assets out of long-only fixed income to enhance forward-looking return assumptions, and by other investors shifting some assets away from long-only equities to hedge against a potential market sell-off.

4. Smaller Managers Will Outperform

   Smaller hedge funds, which often produce stronger performance than larger ones, should find the investing landscape particularly attractive. In moving to a performance environment increasingly dependent on alpha, security selection becomes ever more important, especially in less efficient markets where smaller managers have a distinct advantage over their bigger counterparts, many of which are past the optimal asset level to maximize returns for their investors. In addition, large fund managers, whose clients often are big pension funds run by risk-averse investment committees, have an incentive to reduce risk in their portfolios to maintain assets, and thereby increase the probability of continuing to collect large management fees.

5. Pension Funds Will Allocate to Smaller Managers

   As pensions struggle to enhance returns to meet their actuarial assumptions, their hedge fund investment process has evolved to the point where hedge funds are no longer considered a separate asset class, but are incorporated throughout the pension fund's portfolio. Historically, a hedge fund typically needed to have billions of dollars under management to be considered by pension funds, while today this has declined to $750 million and is expected to go lower over time.

---

[1] ThinkAdvisors.com and David Stowell.

6. Building the Brand

   Having a high-quality product offering with a strong track record will no longer ensure success in a marketplace awash in some 15,000 hedge funds. In 2016, hedge fund assets will continue to flow into a small percentage of managers, with 5% of funds attracting 80%–90% of net assets within the industry. To raise capital, hedge funds with robust product offerings must also have a best-in-breed sales and marketing strategy—and a top-flight team to execute it—that deeply penetrates the market and builds a high-quality brand. A firm can either build out an internal sales team, leverage a leading third-party marketing firm or do a combination of both.

7. Marketing Activity Outside the United States

   Marketing activity outside of the United States has declined significantly over the past few years as AIFMD requirements have gone into effect within the eurozone. This has prompted a growing number of US-domiciled funds to direct marketing efforts to US investors, thus making the US marketplace more competitive. Many non-US firms are also targeting US investors. This trend will reverse as hedge fund managers start to realize that investors outside the United States are significantly less covered, and that the registration burden of selling in many non-US countries is less complex than they perceived. In addition, many Europe-based investors are willing to invest in smaller managers because of their higher return potential.

8. Relentless Pressure on Fees

   Pressure on hedge fund fees is coming from several directions. Institutional investors are successfully negotiating big reductions from standard fees for large mandates, and this is likely to increase as big institutions' allocations represent a larger percentage of the market. Small hedge funds (generally those with less than $100 million under management) often have to offer a founder's share class with a 25%–50% discount to standard fees as an incentive to invest in their fund. The "small fund" threshold is now trending up toward $200 million.

9. More Hedge Funds Will Shut Down

   Several factors indicate that hedge funds will shut down at an increased pace. With 15,000 funds currently in the market, the abundance of managers has reduced the average quality of hedge funds, and many lower-quality managers will close down. In addition, increased capital market volatility increases the divergence in overall return between good and bad managers, increasing the turnover of managers as bad ones get fired, and money is reallocated to those who outperform. And with the competitive landscape for small and midsize managers becoming increasingly difficult, these firms are being squeezed from both the expense and revenue side of their businesses. Having a superior quality product alone is not enough to generate inflows of capital. As a result, the closure rate will rise for small and midsize hedge funds.

10. More Illiquid Investing and Longer Lock-ups

   Many sophisticated investors understand the benefits of illiquid investments, but demand fund liquidity provisions that match the underlying liquidity of the portfolio. Longer lock-ups, longer redemption notice periods, gates, and private equity structures for illiquid strategies are expected.

Private equity can be broadly defined to include the following different forms of investment:

1. **Leveraged buyout:** Leveraged buyout (LBO) refers to the purchase of all or most of a company or a business unit by using equity from a small group of investors in combination with a significant amount of debt. The targets of LBOs are typically mature companies that generate strong operating cash flow.

2. **Growth capital:** Growth capital typically refers to minority equity investments in mature companies that need capital to expand or restructure operations, finance an acquisition, or enter a new market, without a change of control of the company.

3. **Mezzanine capital:** Mezzanine capital refers to an investment in subordinated debt or preferred stock of a company, without taking voting control of the company. Often these securities have attached warrants or conversion rights into common stock.
4. **Venture capital:** Venture capital refers to equity investments in less mature nonpublic companies to fund the launch, early development, or expansion of a business.

Although private equity can be considered to include all four of these investment activities, it is common for private equity to be the principal descriptor for LBO activity. Venture capital, growth capital, and mezzanine capital are each considered a separate investment strategy, although some large private equity firms participate in all four investment areas. This chapter principally focuses on LBO activities of private equity firms. See Exhibit 16.1 for a summary of LBO deal flow.

EXHIBIT 16.1 QUARTERLY NUMBER OF PRIVATE EQUITY-BACKED BUYOUT DEALS

Quarterly Number of North American Private Equity-Backed Buyout Deals, Q1 2006 -Q3 2015 TD (As at 19 August 2015)

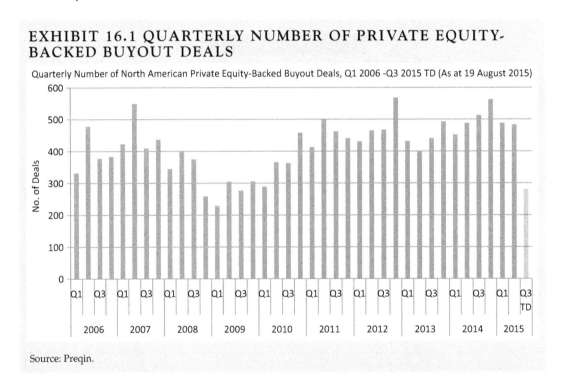

Source: Preqin.

Investment firms that engage in LBO activity are called private equity firms. These firms are also called buyout firms or financial sponsors. The term financial sponsor comes from the role a private equity firm has as the "sponsor," or provider, of the equity component in an LBO, as well as the orchestrator of all aspects of the LBO transaction, including negotiating the purchase price and, with investment banker assistance, securing debt financing to complete the purchase.

Private equity firms are considered "financial buyers" because they usually do not extract synergies from an acquisition, as opposed to "strategic buyers," who are generally competitors of a target company and will benefit from synergies when they acquire or merge with the target. As a result, in auctions conducted by targets, strategic buyers are usually able to pay a higher price than the price offered by financial buyers. However, there are many examples in which financial buyers won auction bids because of antitrust issues or because financial buyers used aggressive assumptions regarding future cash flow (based on a more leveraged capital structure and more effective management direction), favorable debt financing terms, and aggressive exit strategies.

CHARACTERISTICS OF A PRIVATE EQUITY TRANSACTION

Key characteristics of a private equity transaction include the following:

1. In a private equity transaction a company or a business unit is acquired by a private equity fund that has secured debt and equity funding from institutional investors such as pension funds, insurance companies, endowments, and fund of funds, or from high net worth individuals, sovereign wealth funds, hedge funds, or banks. The equity investment portion of an acquisition has historically represented 30%–40% of the purchase price, with the balance of the acquisition cost coming from debt financing.
2. Relatively high debt levels utilized to fund the transaction increase the potential return on equity for the private equity buyer (although this debt can increase losses if the value of the asset declines). There are different types of debt used: senior debt, which is provided by banks and is usually secured by the assets of the target company, and subordinated debt, which is usually unsecured and raised in the high-yield capital markets.
3. If the target company is a public company (as opposed to a private company or a division of a public company) the buyout results in the target company "going private," with the expectation that this newly private company will be resold in the future (typically 3–7 years) through an initial public offering (IPO) or private sale to another company (or to another private equity firm).
4. The private equity firm's targeted internal rate of return (IRR) during the holding period for their investment has historically been above 20%, but actual IRR depends on the amount of leverage, the ability of the target's cash flow to pay down some of the debt, dividend payouts and the eventual exit strategy. The expected IRR should be risk-adjusted to reflect a high use of leverage in the transaction.
5. The "general partners" of the private equity fund commit capital to the transaction alongside "limited partners". In addition, management of the target company usually also have a meaningful capital exposure to the transaction. This combined capital represents the equity funding.

TARGET COMPANIES FOR PRIVATE EQUITY TRANSACTIONS

For an LBO transaction to be successful, the target company must generate a significant amount of cash flow to pay high debt interest and principal payments and, sometimes, pay dividends to the private equity shareholders. Without this ability, the investors will not obtain acceptable returns and the eventual exit strategy may be impaired. To achieve strong cash flow, management of the target company must be able to reduce costs while growing the company. The best potential target companies generally have the following characteristics:

1. **Motivated and competent management:** It is important that management is willing and able to operate a highly leveraged company that has little margin for error. If existing management is not capable of doing this, new management must be brought in. Some private equity firms have a cadre of operating executives who are asked to either take over or supplement management activities to create value and grow the company.

2. **Robust and stable cash flow:** Private equity funds look for robust and stable cash flow to pay interest that is due on large amounts of debt and, ideally, to also pay down debt over time. The fund initially forecasts cash flow that incorporates cost savings and operational initiatives designed to increase cash flow postacquisition. This forecast includes the risk-adjusted maximum amount of debt that can be brought into the capital structure, which leads to determination of the amount of equity that must be invested, and the corresponding potential return based on the equity investment. The greater the projected cash flow, the greater the amount of debt that can be utilized, creating a smaller equity investment. The lower the equity investment, the greater the potential return.

3. **Leverageable balance sheet:** If a company already has significant leverage and if their debt is not structured efficiently (e.g., not callable, carries high interest payment obligations and other unfavorable characteristics), the company may not be a good target. An ideal target company has low leverage, an efficient debt structure, and assets that can be used as collateral for loans.

4. **Low capital expenditures:** Since capital expenditures use up cash flow available for debt service and dividends, ideal target companies have found a balance between making capital expenditures that provide good long-term returns on investment and preserving cash to pay interest and principal payments on debt and potential dividends. As a result, many private equity firms steer away from high-tech, biotech, and other companies that require high capital expenditures (with a few notable exceptions that have resulted in questionable return opportunities, as described in Chapter 18).

5. **Quality assets:** A good target company has strong brands and quality assets that have been poorly managed or has unrealized growth potential. Generally speaking, service-based companies are less ideal targets compared to companies that have significant tangible assets of high quality because a service company's value is significantly linked to employees and intangible assets such as intellectual property and goodwill. These types of assets don't provide collateral value for loans, compared to assets such as inventories, machinery, and buildings.

6. **Asset sales and cost cutting:** A target company may have assets that are not used in the production of cash flow. For example, the company might have too many corporate jets or unproductive real estate used for entertainment or other less productive uses. A private equity firm focuses on any assets that don't facilitate growth in cash flow, and sales of these assets are initiated to create cash to pay down acquisition debt. Another reason to sell assets is to facilitate diversification objectives. The ability to cut costs is also important to create incremental value. Sometimes this leads to a reduction in personnel,

or in entertainment and travel budgets. However, for certain target companies, the principal focus is on facilitating growth rather than cutting costs.

PRIVATE EQUITY TRANSACTION PARTICIPANTS

The key participants in a private equity transaction include the following:

1. Private equity firm (as noted previously, this firm is also called a financial sponsor, buyout firm or LBO firm): The private equity firm (1) selects the LBO target (often with the assistance of an investment bank); (2) negotiates the acquisition price, secures senior and subordinated debt financing (again, often with the assistance of an investment bank); (3) completes the acquisition through a closing event; (4) as owner and controlling member of the board of directors, operates the acquired company through either existing management or new management; (5) oversees the activities and decision-making of senior management; (6) makes all major strategic and financial decisions; and (7) decides when and how to sell the company (by initiating an exit strategy—usually with the assistance of an investment bank).

2. Investment banks: Investment banks (1) introduce potential acquisition targets to private equity firms; (2) help negotiate the acquisition price; (3) often either provide loans (as a participant in a syndicated bank loan facility) and/or underwrite high-yield bond offerings; (4) occasionally assist in recapitalizations by underwriting debt or providing loans that fund the distribution of a large dividend to the private equity owner; and (5) assist in the eventual sale of the company through either an M&A related sale or an IPO transaction. As a result, private equity funds represent a significant source of revenue for investment banks.

3. Investors: Institutional and high net worth investors become limited partners in a fund organized by a private equity firm, as opposed to investing directly in the firm. Fund of funds are also limited partners based on their significant investing capacity. Investors sign investment contracts that lock up their money for as long as 10–12 years. Typically, however, distributions are made to investors as soon as investments are turned into cash through completion of an exit strategy such as an IPO or sale of the company. Limited partners commit to provide capital over time, rather than in a single amount upfront. The general partner's draw on this capital depends on when investment opportunities are identified (both to acquire companies and to expand company operations through acquisitions or product extensions). As a result, it may be a number of years after the original commitment of capital before all of the limited partner funds are drawn down.

4. Management: Management of companies coinvest with the private equity fund in the equity of the acquired company, which aligns management's interests with the interests of the fund. In addition, management usually receives stock options. This effectively eliminates agency issues and provides the incentive to work hard and create significant value. The end result is wealth creation for management if they are successful in managing the company until a successful exit is completed (usually 3–7 years after acquisition). If problems develop during the holding period or if exits are significantly delayed, management will not only forego significant exit-related compensation, but may also lose their job.

5. Lawyers, accountants, tax experts, consultants, and other professionals: There is a significant amount of work by professionals who advise private equity funds and investment banks in the full array of private equity activities described above. As a result, there are many professional service firms that have dedicated staff who focus principally, or only, on private equity transactions.

STRUCTURE OF A PRIVATE EQUITY FUND

Private equity firms are usually organized as management partnerships or limited liability partnerships that act as holding companies for several private equity funds (and sometimes other alternative asset funds) run by general partners. At the largest private equity firms, there may be 20–40 general partners. These general partners invest in the fund and also raise money from institutional investors and high net worth individuals, who become limited partners in the fund.

General partners at private equity firms receive cash from several sources. They receive an annual management fee from limited partners that generally equals about 2% of the fund's assets under management (see Exhibit 16.2). They also receive a portion of the profits generated by the fund, which is called "carry" or "carried interest." The carry is typically approximately 20% of profits, which provides a strong incentive for the private equity firms to create value for the fund. The balance of profits is paid out to limited partners. Finally, the companies that the fund invests in (called "portfolio companies") sometimes pay transaction fees to the fund in relation to various services rendered, such as transaction and consulting services, which are typically calculated as a percentage of the value of the transaction, and sometimes, "monitoring fees." Some (but not all) funds credit these fees against management fees payable by limited partners.

Partnership agreements between the general partners and limited partners are signed at the inception of each fund, and these agreements define the expected payments to general partners. The management fee resembles fees paid to mutual funds and hedge funds (higher than mutual funds and about the same level as hedge funds). The carry has no analog among most mutual funds and is similar to the performance fee received by hedge funds (although hedge fund managers receive performance fees annually based on the value of assets under management, whereas private equity fund general partners only receive carry when their investment is monetized, which often is after a 3- to 7-year holding period). Successful private equity firms stay in business by raising a new fund every 3–5 years. Each fund is expected to be fully invested within 5 years and is designed to realize an exit within 3–7 years of the original investment.

EXHIBIT 16.2 GENERAL PARTNER FEE STRUCTURE, EXCERPT FROM "THE ECONOMICS OF PRIVATE EQUITY FUNDS"

GPs [General Partners] earn the bulk of fixed revenue – which is not based on the performance of the fund – through *management fees*. To see how management fees are calculated, we need to define several terms. Over the lifetime of the fund, some of the committed capital is used for these fees, with the remainder used

EXHIBIT 16.2 GENERAL PARTNER FEE STRUCTURE, EXCERPT FROM "THE ECONOMICS OF PRIVATE EQUITY FUNDS"—cont'd

to make investments. We refer to these components of committed capital as *lifetime fees* and *investment capital*, respectively. At any point in time, we define the invested capital of the fund as the portion of investment capital that has already been invested into portfolio companies. *Net invested capital* is defined as invested capital, minus the cost basis of any exited investments. Similarly, *contributed capital* is defined as invested capital plus the portion of lifetime fees that has already been paid to the fund, and *net contributed capital* is equal to contributed capital minus the cost basis of any exited investments. The typical fund has a lifetime of ten years, with general partners allowed to make investments in new companies only during the first five years (the *investment period*), with the final five years reserved for follow-on investments and the exiting of existing portfolio companies.

Most funds use one of four methods for the assessment of management fees. Historically, the most common method was to assess fees as a constant percentage of committed capital. For example, if a fund charges 2 percent annual management fees on committed capital for ten years, then the lifetime fees of the ten-year fund would be 20 percent of committed capital, with investment capital comprising the other 80 percent. In recent years, many funds have adopted a decreasing fee schedule, with the percentage falling after the investment period. For example, a fund might have a 2 percent fee during five-year investment period, with this annual fee falling by 25 basis points per year for the next five years.

The third type of fee schedule uses a constant rate, but changes the basis for this rate from committed capital (first five years) to net invested capital (last five years). Finally, the fourth type of fee schedule uses both a decreasing percentage and a change from committed capital to net invested capital after the investment period. For any fee schedule that uses net invested capital, the estimation of lifetime fees requires additional assumptions about the investment and exit rates…

…The most common initial fee level is 2 percent, though the majority of funds give some concessions to LPs after the investment period is over; e.g., switching to invested capital basis [84.0 percent], lowering the fee level [45.1 percent], or both [38.9 percent]. Based on these facts, we should expect lifetime fees to be less than 20 percent of committed capital for most funds…

Source: Metrick, Andrew and Ayako Yasuda. "The Economics of Private Equity Funds (June 9, 2009)". Review of Financial Studies, Forthcoming.

CAPITALIZATION OF A PRIVATE EQUITY TRANSACTION

A private equity portfolio company's capital structure has up to 70% debt. This debt includes collateralized bank borrowing through revolving credit facilities and term loans, mezzanine debt, high-yield bonds sold in the public capital markets and subordinated notes placed principally with banks and institutional investors (see Exhibit 16.3). The amount of debt that is included in capital structures increased through mid-2007 and then decreased as the market's tolerance for leverage diminished during the credit crisis that started at that time. See Exhibit 16.4 for a summary of average LBO equity contribution. See Exhibit 16.5 for a summary of Enterprise Value/EBITDA acquisition multiples and Debt/EBITDA multiples for US and European LBO transactions.

EXHIBIT 16.3 PORTFOLIO COMPANY CAPITALIZATION

- Debt (~50%–70% of overall cap structure)
  - Senior bank debt, two types:
    - Revolving credit facility (revolver), which can be paid down and reborrowed as needed
    - Term debt (senior and subordinated) with floating rates
  - Junior debt, two types:
    - High yield (typically public markets)
    - Mezzanine debt (subordinated notes, typically sold to banks, institutions, and hedge funds)
    - Other key features:
      - Warrants
      - Payments-in-kind (PIK) toggle allows no interest payment and increase in principal
- Equity (~30%–50% of overall cap structure)
  - Preferred stock
  - Common stock

EXHIBIT 16.4 AVERAGE EQUITY CONTRIBUTION FOR LEVERAGED BUYOUTS

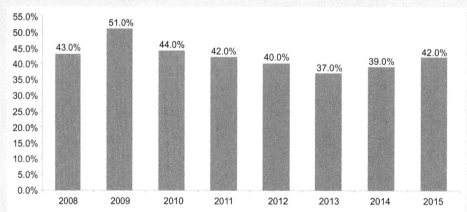

Source: Private Equity Growth Capital Council, S&P Leveraged Commentary & Data.

ASSETS UNDER MANAGEMENT

Assets under management (AUM) increased significantly from a negligible amount in 1995 to almost $2.5 trillion in 2016 (see Exhibit 16.6 and 16.7). Assuming that the average equity fund has employed two parts debt to one-part equity, it is estimated that the total capitalization controlled by private equity funds was approximately $7.5 trillion as of 2016.

EXHIBIT 16.5 AVERAGE LEVERAGED BUYOUT PURCHASE PRICE MULTIPLES (ENTERPRISE VALUE/EBITDA)

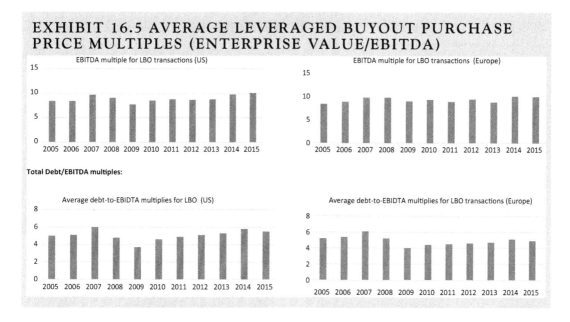

Total Debt/EBITDA multiples:

EXHIBIT 16.6 ASSETS UNDER MANAGEMENT IN PURE LEVERAGED BUYOUT FUNDS

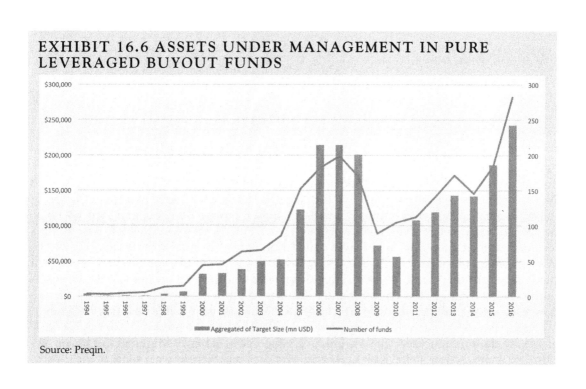

Source: Preqin.

II. HEDGE FUNDS AND PRIVATE EQUITY

EXHIBIT 16.7 PRIVATE EQUITY PARTNERS

- Globally Representative survey of 113 limited partners
- Data as of 2015

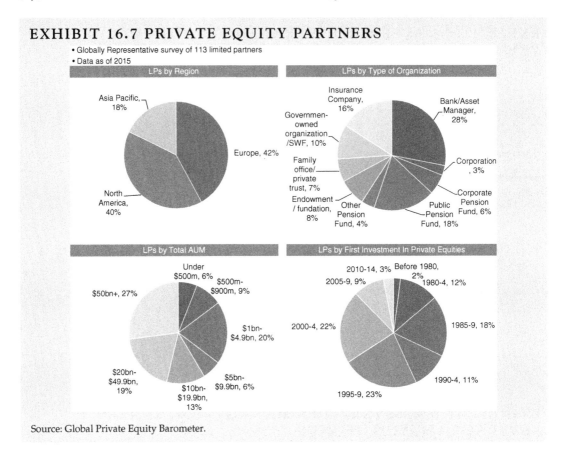

Source: Global Private Equity Barometer.

HISTORY

The first LBO transaction was completed in 1955, using a publicly traded holding company as an investment vehicle to borrow money and then acquire a portfolio of investments in corporate assets. This activity gained momentum during the 1960s when Warren Buffet (through Berkshire Hathaway) and Nelson Peltz (through Triarc) made leveraged investments. During the 1970s a group of bankers at Bear Stearns, including Jerome Kohlberg and Henry Kravis, completed a number of leveraged investments, and in 1976 these bankers left Bear Stearns to organize their own firm, which was called Kohlberg Kravis & Roberts (KKR). In 1982, William Simon (a former US Treasury Secretary) completed an LBO of Gibson Greetings, a producer of greeting cards, for $80 million using a minimal amount of equity and then sold a portion of the company less than 18 months later for $290 million. The significant media attention received by this transaction brought many other investors into this fledgling market.

During the 1980s, many LBO transactions were labeled by the press as "corporate raids," especially those transactions that featured a hostile takeover, asset stripping and major lay-offs. Carl Icahn, Nelson Peltz, Kirk Kerkorian, and T. Boone Pickens were some of the notable "raiders" during this period. The largest and last major LBO during the 1980s was the $31.1 billion takeover of RJR Nabisco by KKR, which attracted significant attention because of the enormous size of the transaction (which was not matched in size until 2006). By the end of the 1980s a number of large buyouts ended in bankruptcy, including Federated Department Stores and Revco. A few years later, KKR was forced to contribute an additional $1.7 billion in equity to RJR Nabisco in a recapitalization designed to salvage this investment. One of the principal reasons for the growth in LBOs during this period was the development of the high-yield bond (junk bonds) market that was propelled by Drexel Burnham Lambert (Drexel). Drexel's junk bond effort was led by Michael Milken, who was indicted in 1989 on charges of racketeering and securities fraud as the result of an insider trading investigation. Drexel filed for bankruptcy protection in 1990 and Milken served 2 years in prison. These events virtually closed down the junk bond market and substantially reduced LBO activity during the first half of the 1990s.

In 2002, the stage was set for remarkable growth in the LBO market. A period of benign interest rates, a resurgent junk bond market, a robust bank loan market, and remarkably lenient lending standards opened the door to an explosive market. The passage of the Sarbanes–Oxley Act in the United States during July 2002 added to growth of the LBO market as a large number of companies recognized the benefits of avoiding increasingly burdensome regulations that were imposed on public companies based on this Act. By "going private," companies were not required to file all of the information required by the Act (and by other securities regulations) and were relieved of millions of dollars of legal and accounting costs that were necessary to remain in compliance. In addition, many companies recognized the benefit of being able to manage their business on a long-term basis as a private company, instead of managing to meet public company quarterly analyst expectations.

Between 2002 and mid-2007, a remarkable number of transactions were completed, many of which were in excess of $30 billion. During 2006, private equity firms bought 654 US companies, spending $375 billion. Globally, private equity firms raised $281 billion during the year, and another $301 billion in the following year. In July 2007, the credit crisis that started earlier in the mortgage markets spilled over into the junk bond and leveraged loan markets, substantially reducing the appetite of the debt markets for private equity transactions. Credit spreads widened considerably during the second half of 2007, and the entire leveraged finance market came to a near standstill. By the end of 2007, there was virtually no debt available to support large private equity transactions (see section Impact of Financial Services Meltdown on Private Equity at the end of this chapter).

FINANCING BRIDGES

Bridge Loans

A bridge loan is an interim financing for a private equity fund to facilitate an acquisition until permanent debt financing can be obtained. Bridge loans are typically more expensive than permanent financing to compensate for the additional risk of the loan. The bridge loan commitment won't be drawn down unless permanent debt funding is not available, creating the need for a bridge in a troubled capital market. Investment banks generally provide bridge loans to private equity firms when they are confident that the bridge funding will not be necessary because they expect to be able to either syndicate a term bank credit facility or successfully place a high-yield bond offering in the capital markets. During 2007 and 2008, because of the global financial crisis, many bridge loans were unexpectedly funded when investment banks were unsuccessful in securing permanent debt financing. See Chapter 10 for more information on bridge loans provided by investment banks to facilitate private equity acquisition activity.

Equity Bridges

A target company requires private equity funds to provide an equity commitment letter prior to signing a purchase agreement. If the fund is unable to cover the entire equity commitment at that time or is waiting for a limited partner to make a coinvestment, but the timing for this coinvestment doesn't coincide with the purchase agreement signing date, the private equity firm might ask banks that are receiving fees from underwriting debt, providing loans and/or advising on the acquisition to provide an equity bridge to the private equity firm to cover the gap. To put an equity bridge in place, the private equity firm enters into a separate commitment with the bank that provides for fees, including utilization fees if the bridge equity is funded, and additional fees if the lenders' equity has not been purchased within a specified period of time. The expectation is that the bridge is a short-term commitment and will be rapidly sold down to permanent equity sources. The equity bridge provider usually has the right to collect a pro rata portion of any breakup fee that might be paid by the target if the deal is terminated, but may resist payment of any reverse breakup fee if the private equity firm walks away from the deal. In some cases, banks are asked to essentially take equity exposure to target companies that approaches or exceeds the equity committed to by private equity funds. The worst-case outcome for banks occurs if they can't sell down the equity exposure they've assumed and are left holding equity stakes in companies that they otherwise have no intention of investing in, with no near-term source for repayment. Because private equity firms have historically paid investment banks billions of dollars in fees each year, fierce competition for future fees has persuaded many banks to participate in this highly risky practice.

During 2007, banks that had provided equity bridges to support large LBO transactions found themselves unable to sell their equity exposure to others. This, combined with bridge loans unexpectedly provided to private equity portfolio companies when capital and loan markets froze up, resulted in hundreds of billions in "hung" loans and deteriorating equity stakes held by banks. Some of these positions were eventually sold at discounts of more than 50%.

COVENANT-LITE LOANS AND PAYMENTS-IN-KIND TOGGLES

During the permissive loan environment of 2006 through mid-2007, a large number of private equity transactions were completed using covenant-lite loans. These loans lacked the financial triggers that historically allowed banks to shut off credit and force loans to become due and payable. This type of loan reduces the likelihood of a loan default, but at the same time, delays the ability of banks to intervene because they are prevented from acting on early warning signs of a problem.

Covenant-lite loans come in many forms, including elimination of covenants that require a borrower to maintain certain financial ratios, leaving lenders to rely only on covenants that restrict a company from "incurring," or actively engaging in certain actions. For example, a covenant that requires a company to maintain a ratio of debt to EBITDA that does not exceed a designated level can be breached if the financial condition of the company deteriorates when the covenant is measured quarterly. In a typical covenant-lite package, this maintenance is eliminated and replaced with a covenant that only restricts a company from incurring new debt, which cannot be violated simply based on a deteriorating financial condition. Rather, the company has to take affirmative action by raising new debt to breach it. Another alternative in a covenant-lite package is a carve-out in a traditional maintenance covenant that forgives in advance predetermined deviations from the covenant. A related benefit often attached to covenant-lite loans are "equity cure" provisions that enable a private equity firm to cure a covenant deficiency by adding more equity into a deal and calling the equity EBITDA, thereby curing the breach.

A "PIK toggle" feature in high-yield bonds and leveraged loans provides a borrower with a choice regarding how to pay accrued interest for each interest period: (1) pay interest completely in cash; (2) pay interest completely "in kind" by adding it to the principal amount (or by issuing new debt having a principal amount equal to the interest amount due); or (3) pay half of the interest in cash and half in kind.

Covenant-lite loans and PIK toggle features allowed private equity firms to secure more favorable debt transactions in support of their acquisition activity during the height of the private equity boom. Default rates were at historically low levels (less than 1% during 2006) and the supply of debt exceeded demand (banks were emboldened by the low default rate, and the opportunity to secure high fees from completing underwriting and M&A transactions with private equity firms, while hedge funds brought a new source of debt financing to private equity firms, creating competition for the banks). As a result, private equity funds were able to secure low-cost financing with very favorable covenant and interest payment packages. This came to an abrupt halt during the second half of 2007 as the credit crisis gained momentum and default rates jumped substantially.

During 2007, as the global financial crisis came into focus, approximately 30% of all loans included covenant-lite and PIK toggle provisions. This percentage dropped to less than 5% during 2009, but then increased every year, topping out at over 70% during 2015.

CLUB TRANSACTIONS AND STUB EQUITY

When the size of a potential acquisition by a private equity firm exceeds around 10%–15% of the capital in a fund sponsored by the firm, the possibility of a "club transaction" is considered. In a club deal, two to five different private equity firms coordinate to coinvest in a target company. The benefits that club transactions create include spreading economic risk, sharing expertise, pooling of relationships with financing sources, reduction of costs per firm, and reduction in competition. The challenges include increasing exposure to a single large transaction for limited partners who have capital invested in more than one of the club members, politics regarding which advisors to hire (investment banks and law firms), determining which firm will coordinate the bidding process, determining the price that all club members accept, agreeing on coinvestors sponsored by each club member (usually from their limited partner pool), regulator antitrust concerns, and the ultimate exit strategy. During 2005–07, when many transactions exceeded $5 billion, formation of clubs was common. Since mid-2007, when most transactions have been for smaller amounts, fewer clubs have been formed.

"Stub equity" refers to the practice of letting public shareholders of a target continue to own equity in a company that is purchased by private equity funds. Stub equity is usually only offered when major shareholders of a target company are unwilling to sell their shares because they believe the offered price is too low. Stub equity allows these shareholders to participate in valuation growth alongside the private equity funds. Usually, stub equity is limited to no more than 30% of postacquisition equity and, if a US transaction, is Securities and Exchange Commission (SEC) registered, but won't be listed on an exchange (substantially reducing the liquidity of the shares). Importantly, unlike the general partners in the fund, owners of stub equity do not participate in carry.

The advantages of stub equity include reduced litigation risk for the private equity sponsor; smaller equity investment required; limitation on governance rights for the stub holders; and sometimes improved accounting results from a recapitalization since the company may qualify for recapitalization accounting, which avoids the write-up of the target's fixed assets or identified intangibles and subsequent depreciation and amortization of these assets (which reduces earnings). The disadvantages of stub equity include SEC disclosure requirements; ongoing SEC reporting requirements; fiduciary duty to minority shareholders; lower leverage applied to the private equity firm's investment; and the potential for future mark-to-market valuations in the event that shares (which are not traded on an exchange) become listed on "pink sheets" and are traded over-the-counter, potentially giving rise to mark-to-market valuations that do not reflect true value for the private equity funds based on the illiquidity of a pink sheet market.

TEAMING UP WITH MANAGEMENT

Private equity firms typically make arrangements with management of a target company regarding terms of employment with the surviving company, postclosing option grants and rollover equity (the amount of stock that management must purchase to create economic exposure to the transaction) prior to executing definitive agreements with the target. When the target is a US public company, these arrangements with management are problematic because of securities law regulations that govern such arrangements. For example, the first question is whether a special committee of the board of the target company is needed to oversee agreements with management. The firm must be careful that the transaction does not lose the benefit of the presumption of fair dealing. In a transaction where a private equity fund teams up with a "controlling" shareholder to take a public company private, the actions of the target's board become subject to the "entire fairness" test, a standard of review that is more exacting than the traditional business judgment rule. There is no bright-line test regarding whether a shareholder is controlling. For example, a Delaware court found that a 40% holder who was the target's CEO fell into the category of controlling. Other courts, however, have applied smaller percentages in determining controlling interest. If a transaction's fairness is challenged, the burden of proof is held by the target. However, if a special committee of independent directors has been formed to review the transaction, then the burden of proof may shift to a plaintiff challenging the fairness of the deal. Even when there is no controlling shareholder involved, a target board will frequently decide to create a special committee to forestall challenges to the transaction, especially when senior management has a significant equity stake in the target (see Exhibit 16.8, Exhibit 16.9).

Teaming up with management can potentially trigger a target's takeover defenses, including poison pills, if management owns more than 15% of the target's stock. Another problem that can arise relates to disclosure. Presigning arrangements with management might require mandatory early disclosure of the transaction, based on Section 13(d) of the Securities Exchange Act. Counsel for the target must determine whether preannounced disclosure is required if the private equity fund does not enter into a presigning voting agreement with management and does not hold equity in the target.

Public company acquisitions are normally either structured as a one-step merger or as a tender offer followed by a back-end merger. However, tender offers have become rare for transactions that include management participation because, according to US securities laws, the bidder in a tender offer is required to pay all of the holders of the target's stock the highest price paid to any single holder. Since private equity transactions that include management participation usually involve negotiation at an early stage regarding employment agreements, rollover equity and postclosing option grants, the issue arises whether these arrangement run afoul of securities laws that require a common price paid to all holders of equity.

When the management of a company approaches a private equity fund to team up on a buyout and management assumes the leading role in orchestrating a going private transaction, this is called a management buyout (MBO). The same issues described above apply to an MBO. However, there are even more issues that complicate the transaction because management's horizon for the investment is usually longer than for a private equity firm and return objectives may be different as well.

EXHIBIT 16.8 DELL MANAGEMENT BUYOUT

During 2013, Dell Inc. announced it had signed a definitive merger agreement under which Michael Dell, Dell's Founder, Chairman and Chief Executive Officer, in partnership with global technology investment firm Silver Lake, would acquire Dell. Under the terms of the agreement, Dell stockholders were to receive $13.65 in cash for each share of Dell common stock they hold, in a transaction valued at approximately $24.4 billion. The price represented a premium of 25% over Dell's closing share price of $10.88 on January 11, 2013, the last trading day before rumors of a possible going private transaction were first published. The buyers acquired for cash all of the outstanding shares of Dell not held by Mr. Dell and certain other members of management.

A Special Committee was formed after Mr. Dell first approached Dell's Board of Directors in August 2012 with an interest in taking the company private. Led by Lead Director Alex Mandl, the Special Committee retained independent financial and legal advisors J.P. Morgan and Debevoise &

Continued

EXHIBIT 16.8 DELL MANAGEMENT BUYOUT—cont'd

Plimpton LLP to advise the Special Committee with respect to its consideration of strategic alternatives, the acquisition proposal and the subsequent negotiation of the merger agreement. The Special Committee also engaged a leading management consulting firm to conduct an independent analysis, including a review of strategic alternatives for Dell and opportunities for the company as a public entity, and thereafter engaged Evercore Partners.

The merger agreement provided for a 45 day go-shop period, during which the Special Committee, with the assistance of Evercore Partners, sought and evaluated alternative proposals from other prospective buyers. Any successful competing bidder would bear a breakup fee of between $180 million to $450 million, depending on whether they qualified during the early or late stages of the go-shop period, respectively. Since no superior buyer was found, the sale to Dell and Silver Lake was completed, and Dell continued to lead the company as Chairman and Chief Executive Officer, maintaining a significant equity investment by contributing his shares of Dell to the new company, as well as making a substantial additional cash investment.

The transaction was financed through a combination of cash and equity contributed by Mr. Dell, cash funded by investment funds affiliated with Silver Lake, a cash investment by an investment fund affiliated with MSDC Management, L.P., a $2 billion loan from Microsoft, rollover of existing debt, as well as debt financing that was provided by BofA Merrill Lynch, Barclays, Credit Suisse, and RBC Capital Markets, and cash on hand.

Many management-led buyouts like the Dell transaction have enriched management, but some question whether this has happened at shareholder expense. The first issue is price. In such a buyout, a company's executives have an incentive to pay the lowest price possible, yet they are also supposed to represent the interests of shareholders. That's a fundamental conflict. As a result, there is sometimes a suspicion that the top executives are timing the buyout to pay a discounted price or are otherwise taking advantage of their unique knowledge to underpay.

On the one hand, Michael Dell had a duty to secure the best price for shareholders. On the other, too rich an offer could make it harder for the buying group, which he was an integral part of, to pay down debt and see a meaningful return on investment. Any time you have an insider trying to buy out the public shareholders the opportunity presents itself for an unfair transaction. That's why it was essential for Dell's management and board to protect itself and reassure shareholders by installing safeguards such as an independent committee and a go-shop process.

Mindful of their obligations to shareholders, CEOs at companies on the verge of being sold would normally negotiate aggressively for the best possible price. But if the purchase price for Dell got too high, significant risk would be created for the surviving company because the higher purchase price would be funded by additional debt, making it harder for Dell and Silver Lake to cash out in the future at a meaningful price. Because of this dilemma, there's an incentive in management-led buyouts for management to low ball the sale price. The management is essentially on both sides of the transaction, creating a potential conflict of interest.

In an effort to allay shareholder concerns, Dell created an independent committee that had its own investment bankers, legal team, and final say on the transaction. This special committee included board members who didn't have a significant ownership stake in the company and weren't part of the management team.

EXHIBIT 16.8 DELL MANAGEMENT BUYOUT—cont'd

Another way to avoid conflict-of-interest accusations is by creating a go-shop period where the target company can seek out better offers from prospective buyers in an effort to demonstrate to shareholders that the agreed price is fair. This is what Dell did, with a 45 day go-shop period. However, the concern always is that this process doesn't work well because management buyers always have more information than any potential competing bidder, and these bidders must pay a termination fee, which adds to their overall purchase price. Ultimately, if the sale process for a management buyout does not look fair to shareholders, they have the right to sue the management team and board in an effort to recover a fair price, or even stop the deal from going forward.

The Dell management buyout began in June of 2012, when the investment firm Southeastern Asset Management, a longtime Dell investor and until recently its No. 2 shareholder, first contacted Michael Dell about the possibility of going private. Dell held his first conversations with people from Silver Lake at a technology industry conference in Aspen, Colorado, the following month.

Ironically, Southeastern became one of the leading voices in opposition to the transaction that ultimately emerged. Soon, the activist investor Carl Icahn had picked up the torch and bought out much of Southeastern's stake, and became Dell's No. 2 investor, after Michael Dell himself.

Icahn and Southeastern proposed their own alternative transaction, which they described as a structured recapitalization. Under their plan, they would have bought up 72% of Dell shares and left the remaining stake as a publicly traded stub. They further proposed to take on new debt, pay a special dividend to shareholders, and issue warrants for the purchase of additional shares within a 7-year window. They argued that the Dell–Silver Lake proposal undervalued the company and locked out current investors from benefiting from any future turnaround of the company that might occur.

For months, the wrangling took the form of a prolonged proxy fight, as neither side had sufficient support among shareholders to take full control.

Icahn took his fight against the transaction public through numerous open letters to shareholders and his relatively new Twitter account. Icahn eventually lost the battle to take control of Dell. However, based on the size of his holdings, he probably achieved a profit of more than $70 million.

EXHIBIT 16.9 KINDER MORGAN LEVERAGED BUYOUT

Background:

- Kinder Morgan management approached Goldman Sachs in February 2006 for a strategic alternatives review to enhance shareholder value.
- Among the options considered were share repurchase programs, a going private transaction and a leveraged buyout (LBO).
- During April, Goldman requested to become the principal investor in a buyout transaction. Top management at Kinder, including President C. Park Sharper and founder, Chairman and CEO Richard Kinder (who owned 18% of the shares of the company) were to be members of the buyout group.
- From April through mid-May, management at Goldman (both the advisory and investment arms) worked together to explore the viability of the buyout option and counseled with outside legal and ratings advisors.

Continued

II. HEDGE FUNDS AND PRIVATE EQUITY

EXHIBIT 16.9 KINDER MORGAN LEVERAGED BUYOUT—cont'd

- On May 13, the board was notified for the first time of the current strategic review and on May 28, a $100 per share offer was presented. Subsequent to receipt of the offer, the board of directors formed a special committee and enlisted the help of Morgan Stanley and Blackstone to evaluate the proposal and seek higher offers.

Issues:

- There is an inherent potential conflict of interest when management joins with the acquiring party
  - While the board is most concerned with maximizing shareholder value through increasing the number of bidders, the management team may prefer having its own bid succeed.
  - As a member of the buyout group, management can participate in the future upside potential of the company through an equity rollover in the transaction, but other shareholders cannot participate when they sell their shares.
- Goldman's role in the transaction also presents potential concerns:
  - The firm stands to earn large fees through its role as the advisor and also as the lead loan arranger on the transaction. It would also potentially achieve significant gains in its investment in Kinder.
- Because the offer was already announced and there were no other buyers that had already performed the amount of diligence that Goldman and the management had completed, initiating an auction for competing bids was risky. If Kinder had started an auction but no interested parties had come forward, the special committee's ability to negotiate with the buyout group would have been hindered.

Outcome:

- Morgan Stanley and Blackstone contacted 35 parties, but none were interested in putting in a competing bid. The board was very unhappy with how Goldman and management developed the transaction, but they were able to leverage that displeasure in a negotiation for a higher offer price of $107.50 per share, which shareholders ultimately approved. The deal closed on May 30, 2007, and ranked as the largest LBO since Kohlberg Kravis Roberts & Co. bought RJR Nabisco in 1989.
- On February 10, 2011, Kinder Morgan raised $2.9 billion in an initial public offering (IPO). At the time, the offering ranked as the largest private equity-backed IPO in history and the largest IPO by a US oil and gas company since Conoco Inc. raised $4.4 billion in 1998. The ownership group sold a 13.5% share in the company at $30 per share, with all of the shares coming from the Carlyle Group, Goldman Sachs, Highstar Capital LP, and Riverstone Holdings LLC. The group retained 50.1% of the ownership of the company, while Richard Kinder's stake remained unchanged at 30.6%. Goldman Sachs and Barclays Plc served as underwriters for the IPO.
- On October 16, 2011, Kinder Morgan agreed to acquire the El Paso Corporation for approximately $21.1 billion in cash and stock. The combined entity would become the largest North American midstream energy company. According to Richard Kinder, the genesis of the deal lay in Kinder Morgan's IPO. While management of the two companies had held merger talks for years, Kinder Morgan needed public stock to use as currency in an acquisition. The deal closed during 2012.

Source: Press reports.

PRIVATE INVESTMENT IN PUBLIC EQUITIES

When the leveraged loan and high-yield markets are not healthy or control investing opportunities are limited, private equity firms sometimes turn to private investments in public equities (PIPEs) investments. These are minority investments in 5%–30% of the stock of a publicly traded company and investments are made without using debt financing. As a result, the return potential of these investments depends on the actions of the management of the company, who are not controlled by the private equity fund, and incremental leverage is not available as a vehicle to enhance returns for the investor. However, sometimes the company will secure additional leverage from the market simultaneous with, but independent of, the equity investment from a private equity firm. Examples of large PIPEs investments by private equity firms include Blackstone's acquisition of a 4.5% equity stake in Deutsche Telekom for $3.3 billion, KKR's purchase of a $700 million convertible bond from Sun Microsystems, and a $1 billion investment by General Atlantic in Bolsa de Mercadorias & Futuros, a Brazilian financial exchange, as part of an IPO offering. A PIPE investment allows private equity firms to influence (rather than control) senior management in their decision-making, and the investment is designed to help management make good long-term decisions based on the injection of long-term patient capital.

LEVERAGED RECAPITALIZATIONS

A leveraged recapitalization of a private equity fund portfolio company involves the issuance of debt by the company sometime after the acquisition is completed, with the proceeds of the debt transaction used to fund a large cash dividend to the private equity owner. This action increases risks for the portfolio company by adding debt, but enhances the returns for the private equity fund. Although the provider of the debt in a leveraged recapitalization is undertaking considerable risk, they are generally paid for this risk through high interest payments and fees. However, the new debt can cause the value of outstanding debt to decline as the company's risk profile increases. The stakeholders that can be harmed by leveraged recapitalizations (in addition to current debt holders) are employees and communities. If the increased leverage results in destabilization of the company because of inability to meet interest and principal payment obligations, employees can lose their jobs (and, potentially, their pensions can be impacted), and communities can lose their tax base if the company is dissolved through a bankruptcy process.

A notable example of a leveraged recapitalization occurred when Hertz, the car rental company, was purchased from Ford Motor Co. in a $15 billion buyout by Clayton, Dubilier & Rice, Merrill Lynch Global Private Equity, and The Carlyle Group. The private equity firms invested $2.3 billion, with the balance funded by debt. Six months after the deal was completed, Hertz borrowed $1 billion and used this cash to pay a dividend to the private equity investors, reducing their exposure by almost half. These firms then completed an IPO of Hertz, resulting in a significant gain for a holding period that amounted to approximately 1 year (see Exhibit 16.10).

EXHIBIT 16.10 RETURN ON INVESTMENT FOR HERTZ' BUYOUT CONSORTIUM

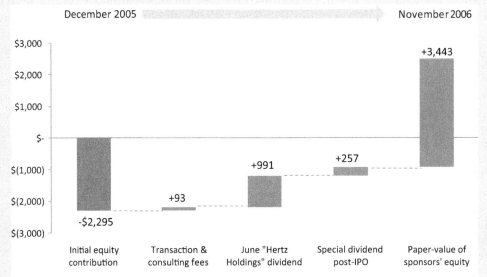

Note: Transaction and consulting fees include a transaction fee of $25 million to each sponsor, a consulting fee of $1 million to each sponsor, and a termination fee of $5 million to each sponsor. Special dividend and paper-value of sponsor's equity calculated based on IPO offer price of $15 per share.

Source: Hertz Global Holdings' SEC registration.

SECONDARY MARKETS FOR PRIVATE EQUITY

A secondary market has developed for private equity to facililate sale of limited partnership interests in private equity funds. Secondary market sales fall into one of two categories: the seller transfers a limited partnership interest in an existing partnership that continues its existence undisturbed by the transfer, or the seller transfers a portfolio of private equity investments in operating companies. Sellers of private equity investments sell both their investments in a fund and also their remaining unfunded commitments to the fund. Buyers of secondary interests include large pooled investment funds and institutional investors, including hedge funds. In addition, the private equity fund that originally invested in a company will sometimes purchase secondary market offerings. In most cases, the consent of the general partner is required to transfer a partnership interest. The principal tax issue in a secondary transfer is determining whether the transfer will cause the fund to become a "publicly traded partnership" that is taxable as a corporation for US federal income tax purposes. This can generally be avoided if an exchange is not used and if there are a number of partners that remain invested.

During 2008, more than $30 billion in secondary market transactions were completed, with an average price for the second half of 2008 at 61%, reflecting a significant decline in net asset value. Sellers came principally from three different groups: distressed parties such as large banks and insurance companies that needed to sell assets to raise cash; quasidistressed investors such as funds of funds, hedge funds, and other direct investors that are no longer self-funding because private equity distributions stopped by mid-year 2008; and other non-distressed sellers including endowments, whose long-term view of the private equity market had changed. The principal buyers included specialist funds that are raising large pools of capital to take advantage of favorable pricing, including funds set up by Goldman Sachs, Credit Suisse, Coller Capital, and Pomona Capital. The market is fragmented, but leading secondary investment firms include Coller Capital, Lexington Partners, AXA Private Equity, HarbourVest Partners, and Partners Group. In addition, major investment banks, including Goldman Sachs, JPMorgan, Morgan Stanley, and Credit Suisse have active secondary market investment programs.

Secondary sales of private equity funds totaled approximately $47 billion in 2014, an increase of about 80% above the previous year, which was the highest volume in 7 years. A robust stock market, combined with low interest rates increased the value of private equity funds, and many investors took the opportunity to capture returns earlier than available by waiting for the funds to mature. About half of all secondary sales were motivated by active portfolio management, as opposed to regulatory pressure or a state of distress. Buyers of stakes in these funds had roughly $55 billion of available capital to spend as of the end of 2015.

Buying through the secondary market presents a lower risk for many buyers because they can evaluate existing assets, as opposed to investing in a classic fund-raising, where the investor commits to a blind pool that as yet holds no assets. Buying older funds in the secondary market becomes an even more attractive diversification proposition if there is concern that new funds are paying too much for assets. During 2015, secondary market private equity purchases were completed at an average discount of 6% to market value. However, a number of secondary transactions were completed at market value, or slightly higher, based on occasional unique high demand.

FUND OF FUNDS

A private equity fund of funds consolidates investments from many individual and institutional investors to make investments in a number of different private equity funds. This enables investors to access certain private equity fund managers who, they otherwise may not be able to invest with, diversifies their private equity investment portfolio and augments their due diligence process in an effort to invest in high-quality funds that have a high probability of achieving their investment objectives. Private equity fund of funds represent about 15% of committed capital in the private equity market. The largest private equity fund of funds includes Adams Street Partners, HarbourVest Partners, Panteon Ventures, and Partners Group (see Exhibit 16.11).

EXHIBIT 16.11 TOP 10 FIRMS BY TOTAL FUND OF FUNDS CAPITAL RAISED 2007–16

Firm Name	Total Fund of Funds Capital Raised 2007-2016 $ in millions	Region
Adams Street Partners	17,077.5	US
HarbourVest Partners	10,776.7	US
Pantheon	10,461.4	Europe
Partners Group	9,126.2	Europe
Goldman Sachs AIMS Private Equity	8,691.0	US
Commonfund Capital	8,249.0	US
Siguler Guff	7,847.0	US
LGT Capital Partners	7,564.9	Europe
Ardian	7,409.0	Europe
BlackRock Private Equity Partners	7,021.3	US

Source: Preqin.

PRIVATE EQUITY GOES PUBLIC

Both The Blackstone Group and Fortress Management Group completed IPOs during 2007, listing shares for their management companies on the New York Stock Exchange. Blackstone raised $7.3 billion, and Fortress raised $2.2 billion. Apollo Management completed a listing of a closed-end debt fund on NASDAQ during 2004, raising $2.2 billion and then completed a listing for a feeder to its US-based fund on Euronext during 2006, raising $1.6 billon. Also during 2006, KKR completed a listing for a feeder to its US-based fund on Euronext, raising $3.9 billion. Although several other firms, including KKR, attempted to issue IPOs in the United States for their management companies during 2007 and 2008, market conditions forced these firms to abort their efforts.

In July 2009, as the markets stabilized and KKR returned to profitability, the firm resumed its attempt to go public via a reverse merger with KKR Private Equity Investors (KPE), its Euronext-listed affiliate. Under terms of the transaction, KKR would own 70% of the combined business while KPE investors would own the remaining 30%. In July 2010, KKR completed the IPO and its shares now trade on the NYSE.

Apollo Management completed an IPO in the United States during April 2011, raising over $550 million. Similar to Blackstone and KKR, Apollo had planned to go public earlier (2008), but as market conditions worsened, the firm delayed their offering.

During 2012, The Carlyle Group launched its IPO in the United States, selling 30.5 million shares at $22 per share to raise proceeds of $671 million. Based on this price, the firm had a market value of $6.7 billion. Oak Tree Capital Group also issued an IPO during 2012. As a result, there are six large private equity firms that are public companies: Apollo Management, KKR, Blackstone, Carlyle Group, Oak Tree Capital Group, and Fortress Management (although Fortress is also considered a hedge fund since the firm has hedge fund AUM that is slightly larger than the firm's private equity AUM). See Exhibit 16.12 for share price performance for these private equity firms compared to the S&P 500 performance.

EXHIBIT 16.12 SHARE PERFORMANCE OF APOLLO MANAGEMENT, KOHLBERG KRAVIS & ROBERTS (KKR), BLACKSTONE, CARLYLE GROUP, OAK TREE CAPITAL GROUP AND FORTRESS MANAGEMENT

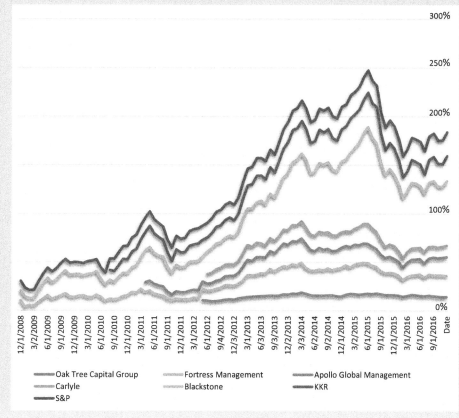

PRIVATE EQUITY EXHIBITS (16.13–16.24)

From 2002 through 2005, LBO activity boomed, but leverage levels and acquisition multiples remained reasonable. Most deals completed during this period provided strong returns for their investors. From 2006 through mid-2007, a bubble developed in the private equity market, with debt and acquisition multiples rising above historical norms. Most of the deals completed during this period have experienced difficulties and produced lower returns. Following mid-2007, after the credit crisis hit, many deals experienced significant problems. Investment banks could not syndicate LBO debt, creating a backlog of around $390 billion. Many transactions were pulled and others were renegotiated. In addition, a significant number of transactions became the subject of large lawsuits. As a result,

EXHIBIT 16.13 PRIVATE EQUITY INVESTMENTS 2000–05

The first half of the 2000s was characterized by a robust leveraged buyout (LBO) market. Because leverage levels and acquisition multiples were at reasonable levels, most deals completed during this period proved to be resilient through the global economic slowdown and credit freeze that began in the second half of 2007.

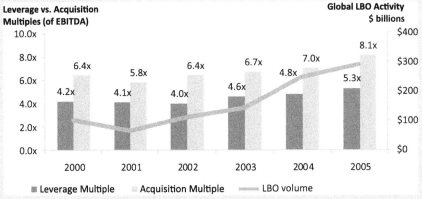

Source: Dealogic; Standard & Poor's.

EXHIBIT 16.14 PRIVATE EQUITY INVESTMENT DURING 2006–07

- A bubble developed in the private equity market during this period, with leverage and acquisition multiples rising considerably above historical norms.
- As a result, many companies acquired during this period experienced financial difficulties.

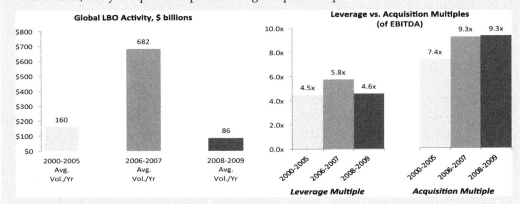

Source: Rubenstein, David: "The Impact of the Financial Services Meltdown on the Global Economy And The Private Equity Industry", Super Return Dubai October 15, 2008, The Carlyle Group, print; Dealogic, Standard & Poor's; Morgan Stanley Financial Sponsors Group.

the nature and structure of private equity transactions changed: smaller in size, more equity contribution, less favorable debt terms, lower number of transactions, less debt dependent transactions, more coinvestments with corporate partners, and longer holding periods. The result of these changes has been lower investment returns and lower risk transactions, with lower amounts of capital committed to this asset class. However, in spite of these significant changes, the private equity market has expanded, and generally higher-quality and lower-risk investments have been pursued in recent years.

EXHIBIT 16.15 PRIVATE EQUITY INVESTMENTS POST-MID-2007: BUSTED AND RESTRUCTURED DEALS

- Many deals experienced difficulty in closing after the onset of the credit crisis
- Investment banks were unable to syndicate leveraged buyout debt, which led to a significant $370 billion debt backlog at its peak in the fall of 2007.
- As a result, many deals were pulled ("busted") while others were renegotiated on more favorable terms to the buyers and lenders.

Busted Deals		Restructured Deals	
Company	Value	Company	Value
Bell Canada	$48.8 billion	Clear Channel Communications	$27.3 billion
Sallie Mae	$25.5 billion	First Data	$26.3 billion
Huntsman Corp	$10.6 billion	Harrah's Entertainment	$26.2 billion
Harman International	$8.2 billion	Biomet	$11.4 billion
Affiliated Computer Systems	$8.0 billion	HD Supply	$8.5 billion
Alliance Data	$7.8 billion	Thompson Learning	$7.8 billion

Source: Rubenstein, David: "The Impact of the Financial Services Meltdown on The Global Economy and The Private Equity Industry," Super Return Dubai October 15, 2008, The Carlyle Group, print; Morgan Stanley Financial Sponsors Group; Press report.

EXHIBIT 16.16 HUNTSMAN VERSUS APOLLO—THE AFTERMATH OF A COLLAPSED PRIVATE EQUITY TRANSACTION

- May 2007—Huntsman puts itself up for sale, contacting, among others, Apollo-owned Hexion Specialty Chemicals and Basell, a subsidiary of Access Industries.
- June 2007—Huntsman signs a merger agreement with the Dutch chemical company Basell for $25.25 per share, with a $200 million termination fee.
- July 2007—After increasingly higher offers from Hexion, Huntsman finally agrees at $28 per share to go with Apollo/Hexion, with a $325 million deal termination fee. The higher offer is made in spite of greater closing risks due to a longer anticipated regulatory approval process, especially given the deteriorating credit environment.
- May 2008—Huntsman reports Q1 2008 profits were down by 31%.

Continued

EXHIBIT 16.16 PRIVATE EQUITY INVESTMENTS POST-MID-2007: BUSTED AND RESTRUCTURED DEALS—cont'd

- June 2008—Hexion is informed by its financial advisors that based on the new financials, the merged entity would not be solvent. Hexion subsequently sues Huntsman, claiming it has met the requisite conditions for terminating the deal without incurring the $325 million termination fee.
- June 2008—Huntsman countersues Hexion's parent, Apollo Management, as well two of the private equity firm's founders, Leon Black and Josh Harris, for pursing "a strategy designed to cause [Huntsman] to terminate with Basell and accept promises [Apollo] never intended to keep." In the suit with Apollo, Huntsman seeks $3 billion in damages and $100 million to cover its half of the Basell breakup fee.
- September 2008—A Delaware judge issues an opinion that refuses to allow Apollo/Hexion from walking away from the deal and orders them to use best efforts to close the deal at the original $28 per share offer price (or pay the $325 million breakup fee to walk away). The judge believed that deteriorating financial performance did not qualify as a material adverse effect.
- December 2008—Huntsman agrees to settle with Apollo for $1 billion in payments:
  - $325 million breakup fee (Hexion has commitments from the original lenders of the deal, Deutsche Bank and Credit Suisse, to fund the fee).
  - $425 million in cash payments from Apollo's affiliates.
  - $250 million payment from Apollo affiliates in exchange for 10-year convertible notes of Huntsman.
  - Huntsman sues Deutsche Bank and Credit Suisse for withdrawing their commitment to finance the deal and conspiring with Apollo to interfere with Huntsman's prior pact with Basell.
- June 2009—Huntsman reaches agreement with Deutsche Bank and Credit Suisse for the banks to pay $632 million in cash and provide $1.1 billion in loans to resolve their dispute. Following announcement, Huntsman's share price dropped to $5, less than one-fifth the original $28 offer price from Apollo/Hexion.

Source: Press reports.

EXHIBIT 16.17 PRIVATE EQUITY DEBT DURING CREDIT CRISIS: MORE EXPENSIVE DEBT

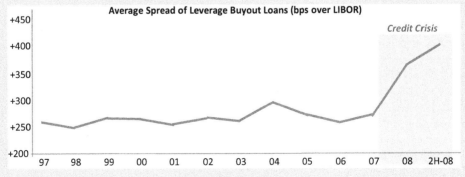

Average Spread of Leverage Buyout Loans (bps over LIBOR)

EXHIBIT 16.18 PRIVATE EQUITY DEBT-TO-EBITDA MULTIPLES

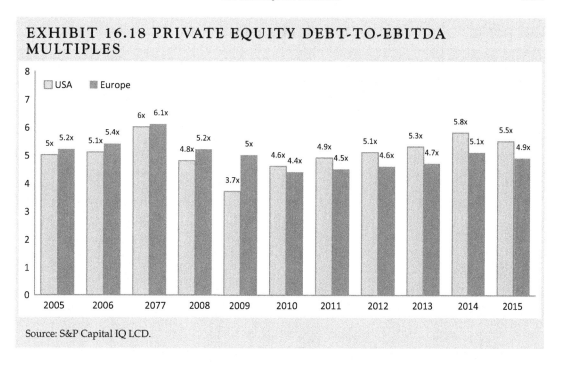

Source: S&P Capital IQ LCD.

EXHIBIT 16.19 AVERAGE DEAL SIZE PER QUARTER
($ MILLION)

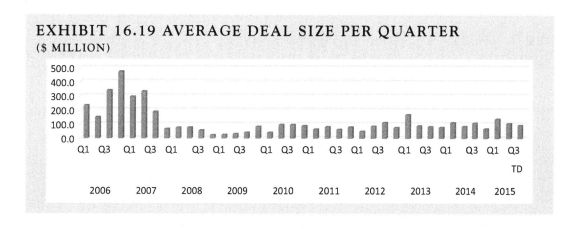

EXHIBIT 16.20 PRIVATE EQUITY DEALS

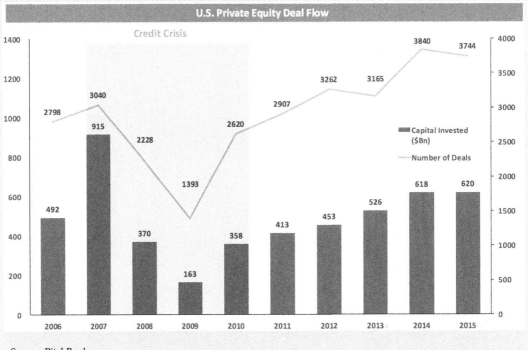

Source: PitchBook.

EXHIBIT 16.21 LARGE PRIVATE EQUITY FUNDS HAVE BECOME MORE ACTIVE IN PURSUING MINORITY BUYOUTS

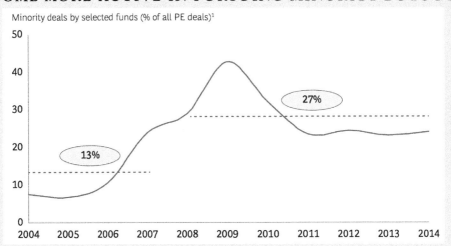

Source: Fund reports; Preqin; BCG analysis. [1]Funds include Apax, Blackstone, BC Partners, Cinven, CVC, KKR, and Warburg Pincus.

EXHIBIT 16.22 PRIVATE EQUITY DEALS POST-CREDIT CRISIS TRENDS

- Strategic alliances: Instead of club deals with multiple private equity funds, there have been an increasing number of private equity firms coinvesting with corporate partners.
  - For example: Blackstone and Bain Capital joined NBC Universal (a unit of General Electric Co.) in a $3.5 billion acquisition of The Weather Channel.
- Equity buyouts: Some funds are turning to equity buyouts, which enable private equity firms to achieve control over companies by purchasing most, but not all, of a target company. The goal is to take out a large dividend in the future, when the credit markets recover, to reduce overall equity exposure.
  - For example: Advent International acquired the card processing business of Experience France in an all cash deal of $260 million.
- Longer investment holding periods: As private equity firms focus more on building value by improving the operational performance of their portfolio companies, many exits will by delayed to achieve targeted exit values

EXHIBIT 16.23 PRIVATE EQUITY DRY POWDER: UNINVESTED COMMITTED CAPITAL

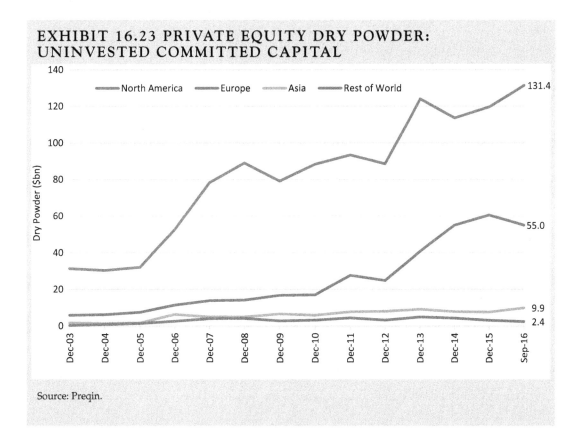

Source: Preqin.

EXHIBIT 16.24 GLOBAL PRIVATE EQUITY BUYOUT FUND-RAISING

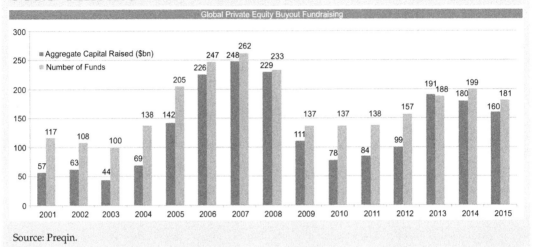

Source: Preqin.

The material in this chapter should be cross-referenced with the following case: **Toys "R" Us LBO**.

As previously discussed, targets for leveraged buyout (LBO) transactions are typically companies in mature industries that have stable and growing cash flow that can be used to service large debt obligations and, potentially, pay dividends to the financial buyers. In addition, targets usually have low capital expenditures, low leverage, and assets that can be used as collateral for debt or sold. Financial buyers generally target an exit event within 3–7 years, which is usually accomplished through either an initial public offering (IPO) or M&A sale to a strategic buyer or, sometimes, to another financial buyer. Financial buyers have historically targeted an internal rate of return (IRR) on their investments of above 20%. The possibility of achieving a high return is augmented by purchasing a company at the lowest possible price using the maximum amount of leverage that is available and, correspondingly, minimizing the equity contribution.

Management of the target company will be asked to grow the company's market share and improve margins, creating growth in free cash flow. Sometimes, as a result of operating improvements, the company can achieve an enterprise value/EBITDA multiple expansion (see Chapter 4), but this is unusual. To realize a target IRR return for a private equity investor, the company must grow cash flow to pay down debt over the holding period (resulting in an increase in equity), and then a sale must be accomplished in the future at a multiple of the increased cash flow level (see Exhibit 17.1). Exhibit 17.2 shows three potential ways to achieve IRR returns by deleveraging, improving margins, and/or through multiple expansion.

EXHIBIT 17.1 LEVERAGED BUYOUT OBJECTIVE: PAY DOWN DEBT DURING HOLDING PERIOD

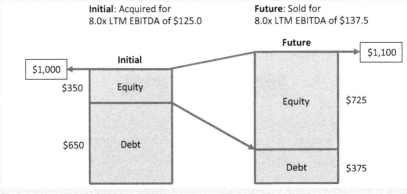

Source: Training the Street, Inc.

EXHIBIT 17.2 LEVERAGED BUYOUT: THREE WAYS TO CREATE RETURNS

Assume the Target company was acquired for 8.0x LTM EBITDA of $125.0

	1. Deleveraging	2. Deleverage & Improve Margins	3. Deleverage, Improve Margins & Multiple Expansion
Sources of Funds			
Total Debt	$650.0	$650.0	$650.0
Total Equity	350.0	350.0	350.0
Total	$1,000.0	$1,000.0	$1,000.0
Year 5 Assumptions			
Cumulative Excess Cash to Repay Debt	$167.6	$212.3	$212.3
Projected EBITDA	125.0	164.5	164.5
Assumed Exit Multiple	8.0x	8.0x	9.0x
Transaction Value	1,000.0	1,316.0	1,480.5
+/-Net Debt [1]	(482.4)	(437.7)	(437.7)
Equity Value	$517.6	$878.2	$1,042.8
IRR Returns (5-YrExit)	8.1%	20.2%	24.4%

Note 1: Total Debt - Cumulative Excess Cash to Repay Debt = Net Debt
Source: Training the Street, Inc.

An LBO analysis includes cash flow projections, terminal value projections (the price at which a financial buyer thinks the company can be sold in 3–7 years) and present value determination (the price that a financial buyer will pay for a company today), and the analysis solves for the IRR of the investment (the discount rate applied). LBO models require an assumption of a minimum IRR required by financial buyers, based on risks associated with the investment and market conditions. The model solves for the purchase price that creates this targeted IRR. Basically, the LBO analysis answers the question: What is the highest purchase price that can be paid for a company to earn a compound annual rate of return that meets the investor's risk-adjusted return requirement?

The LBO analysis considers whether there is enough projected cash flow to operate the company and also pay debt principal and interest payments. In addition, the analysis determines if there is sufficient cash flow to pay dividends at some point to the private equity investor. An ability to retire debt and pay dividends results in a higher IRR.

DETERMINING CASH FLOW AVAILABLE FOR DEBT SERVICE AND DEBT SOURCES

The starting point in an LBO analysis is to determine the cash flow available to service a target company's future debt obligations. This can be done by starting with a determination of net income; adding depreciation and amortization; and then either adding or subtracting amounts for changes in deferred taxes, other noncash charges, and changes in net working capital. The result is cash flow from operations, which should be reduced by capital expenditures to create cash flow available for debt service (see Exhibit 17.3). When cash flow available for debt service has been calculated, the total debt available to purchase the target can be determined through discussion with investment bankers who will advise regarding the market's tolerance for debt, given the cash flow and risk characteristics of the target company and the target company's industry (see Exhibit 17.4). Bankers and their financial sponsor clients sometimes scale back the amount of debt they attempt to secure if associated risks seem too high. When the maximum appropriate amount of debt to finance an acquisition is determined, investment bankers and the financial sponsor can then determine the sources of debt, which include senior credit facilities, second lien loans, high-yield debt, and mezzanine financing (see Exhibits 17.5 and 17.6).

EXHIBIT 17.3 DETERMINING CASH FLOW AVAILABLE FOR DEBT SERVICE

      Net Income
 +   Depreciation and amortization
+/– Changes in deferred taxes
+/– Other non-cash changes
+/– Changes in net working capital
 =   Cash flow from operations
 –   Capital expenditures
 =   Cash flow available for debt service

EXHIBIT 17.4 WHAT DETERMINES DEBT CAPACITY?

Industry Risk	Company Risk	Structural Risk

• Growth rate and size
• Cyclicality
• Barriers to entry
• Capital intensity
• Relative strength of suppliers and customers
• Rate of technological change/threat of substitution
• Environmental issues
• Regulatory risk
	• Competitive position
	• Historical performance
	• Achievability of projections
	• Depth and quality of management
	• Qualitative:
	  o Information quality
	  o Ownership support
		• Quantitative
		  o Size
		  o Leverage
		  o Coverage
		• Security (second way out)
		• Sources of repayment
		  o Are assumptions credible?
		• Valuation/equitycushion
		• Comparable transactions
		• Other successful LBOs in that industry
		• Growth capability given leverage constraints

Source: Training the Street, Inc.

EXHIBIT 17.5 TYPICAL CAPITAL STRUCTURE

- Senior credit facility
  - Revolver
  - Term loans
- Second lien loans
- High-yield debt
  - Senior notes
  - Senior subordinated notes
- Mezzanine/Payment-in-Kind/warrants/preferred stock
- Common equity

Source: Training the Street, Inc.

EXHIBIT 17.6 COMMON FINANCING PARAMETERS

- Key credit statistics:
  - Total debt/EBITDA
  - Senior bank debt/EBITDA
  - EBITDA/interest coverage
  - EBITDA—CapEx/interest coverage
  - Bank debt payoff
  - Equity contribution

- Typical range:[1]
  - 3.5–5.5×
  - 2.5–3.5×
  - >2.0×
  - >1.6×
  - 6–8 years
  - At least 20%–35%

- Factors affecting credit statistics:
  - EBITDA determination
  - Maintenance versus growth in CapEx
  - Average versus peak working capital requirements
  - Off-balance sheet financing

Note 1: These ranges applied prior to the credit crisis, which started during the second half of 2007. Subsequently, market conditions worsened, resulting in lower debt ratios, higher interest coverage ratios, and higher equity contribution requirements. For a few transactions during 2006 to mid-2007, total debt/EBITDA multiples reached 8×. Source: Training the Street, Inc.

EXHIBIT 17.7 COMPARISON OF INTERNAL RATE OF RETURN (IRR) VERSUS MULTIPLE OF INVESTMENT

Initial Equity Invested	Investment Holding Period	IRR	Value of Equity at Exit	Profit	Multiple of Investment
$1,000	2 years	30%	$1,690	$690	1.69x
$1,000	4 years	25%	$2,441	$1,441	2.44x
$1,000	6 years	20%	$2,986	$1,986	2.99x

DETERMINING FINANCIAL SPONSOR INTERNAL RATE OF RETURN

The next step in an LBO analysis is to calculate the IRR. This is done by determining the equity portion of the purchase price, dividend payments to be made, if any, during the investment horizon, and the expected market value of the equity on the exit date. Usually, a range of purchase prices is considered along with a corresponding equity investment amount (which is determined after calculating the maximum debt amount available for the purchase, as described above). The equity amount must, in combination with the projected cash flow and the final projected equity value on the exit date (factoring in the risks associated with cash flow and equity exit value projections), create an IRR that is acceptable to the financial sponsor. If the resulting IRR is below an acceptable level, the financial sponsor must either lower the purchase price or lower the equity contribution, while increasing the debt component of the purchase price, subject to the additional debt being accessible. In other words, this is an iterative process, which sometimes requires the financial sponsor to either reduce their minimum IRR level, or give up the investment opportunity, depending on the price expectations of the target company and pricing from competing buyers. The IRR accepted by the financial sponsor depends on the risk of the investment: lower risk investments allow lower IRR targets and higher risk investments require higher IRR targets.

Ultimately, financial sponsors are principally focused on the profitability of an investment, its risk, and the time it takes to exit the investment. They consider the multiple of the expected equity at the time of exit relative to the initial equity invested and attempt to strike a balance between maximizing IRR and maximizing the total cash amount taken out of the investment when the exit is achieved. For example, even if an IRR of 30% is achievable after 2 years, a sponsor may choose a 25% IRR alternative based on an exit in 4 years if the "profit" of the transaction (equity value at exit—equity invested at inception = profit) is substantially higher in the 4-year exit alternative (see Exhibit 17.7). By holding the investment for 4 years, the sponsor gives up IRR, but increases the multiple of investment from 1.69× to 2.44×. The IRR give-up is caused principally by investor's desire to remain invested based on their aversion to new risks and costs associated with redeployment of funds and financial buyer interest in achieving high multiples of investment (which creates an effective marketing metric for future fundraising).

DETERMINING PURCHASE PRICE AND SALE PRICE

Financial sponsors generally determine a purchase price for a target based on a multiple of enterprise value to EBITDA. In consultation with investment bankers, they determine purchase price multiples that strategic buyers might apply to an acquisition and then decide if they are able to offer a higher multiple based on their targeted IRR (normally, financial buyers cannot pay as high a multiple as strategic buyers can because they lack synergies, but leverage can level the playing field). The IRR, in turn, is determined largely based on the amount of debt financing available and the cash flow available for debt service. The decision regarding a purchase price is therefore based on an iterative process. Financial sponsors usually project a future sale price based on the same multiple used in the initial purchase price determination if an M&A sale is considered the most likely exit strategy. Sometimes, however, a comparable company multiple is used if the ultimate sale is expected to be initiated through an IPO. In addition, the sale multiple could be increased if positive changes in the industry or in management are expected, or decreased if negative changes are expected. See Chapter 4 for a more complete discussion of valuation multiples.

LEVERAGED BUYOUT ANALYSIS EXAMPLE

A simplified example of an LBO analysis is provided below based on the acquisition of Toys "R" Us (Toys) by a consortium of buyers consisting of KKR, Bain Capital, and Vornado Realty Trust during 2005. This consortium will be referred to as "KKR."

Forecast Revenue, Margins, D&A, CapEx, Working Capital, Interest Rate, and Tax Rate

The LBO analysis starts with a review of the target company's financial statements. See Toys financial statements in Exhibits 17.8–17.10. KKR would have completed a summary similar to Exhibit 17.11 to determine historical sales growth and margins. They would have then performed due diligence to determine the likelihood that Toys would be able to continue producing similar (or better) margins and sales growth. KKR would also have completed a forecast of Toys' balance sheet, income statement, and cash flow statement for their expected investment horizon in an effort to determine cash flow projections that would be utilized to establish the future value of the company. This future value would be calculated by multiplying projected EBITDA on the date of a future sale by the expected enterprise value/EBITDA multiple that would be relevant at that time.

As part of the creation of future expected balance sheets, income statements, and cash flow statements, KKR would have made assumptions regarding growth in revenues. When these projections are made, other parts of the income statement (including cost of goods sold; selling, general and administrative expenses; and depreciation and amortization) are expected to remain constant (or to decline slightly) as a percentage of revenues (see Exhibit 17.12).

For CapEx, it is commonly assumed that annual CapEx is equal to annual depreciation to keep the asset base constant.[1] However, KKR may have decided to improve Toys' asset base by increasing CapEx above depreciation or, they might have decided to decelerate CapEx, allowing Toys' asset base to reduce.

Although working capital can be set at a percentage of revenues, KKR probably calculated working capital based on individual balance sheet items, with changes in Toys' working capital resulting from the projected balance sheet (see Exhibit 17.13). Toys FYE 2005 federal tax rate of 35% (state and local taxes might increase the tax rate to as much as 38%) was used as

[1] To account for inflation, however, CapEx is often projected to increase at a higher rate than depreciation so that the real value of physical capital like plant and equipment does not decline.

a base from, which KKR could project future tax rates (which could be constant, increasing or decreasing, depending on known and future expected tax developments). The interest rate assumption used for Toys was higher than the company's historical rate to reflect higher leverage and correspondingly higher risk to lenders (see Exhibit 17.14).

EXHIBIT 17.8 CONSOLIDATED FINANCIAL RESULTS ($ IN MILLIONS, EXCEPT PER SHARE DATA)

	For the Year Ended		
	2/1/2003	1/31/2004	1/29/2005
Net sales	$11,305	$11,320	$11,100
Growth		0.1%	−1.9%
Cost of sales	(7,799)	(7,646)	(7,506)
Gross margin	$3,506	$3,674	$3,594
Growth		4.8%	−2.2%
Margin	31.0%	32.5%	32.4%
SG&A	($2,724)	($3,026)	($2,932)
Growth		11.1%	−3.1%
Margin	−24.1%	−26.7%	−26.4%
Reported EBITDA (pre-restructuring charges)	$782	$648	$662
Growth		−17.1%	2.2%
Margin	6.9%	5.7%	6.0%
D&A	($339)	($368)	($354)
Restructuring and other charges	0	(63)	(4)
EBIT	$443	$217	$304
Growth		−51.0%	40.1%
Margin	3.9%	1.9%	2.7%
Interest expense	($119)	($142)	($130)
Interest and other income	9	18	19
Pretax income	$333	$93	$193
Growth		−72.1%	107.5%
Margin	2.9%	0.8%	1.7%
Income tax (expense)/benefit	(120)	(30)	59
Net income	$213	$63	$252
Growth		−70.4%	300.0%
Margin	1.9%	0.6%	2.3%
Diluted EPS	$1.02	$0.29	$1.16
Growth		−71.6%	300.0%
Adjusted consolidated EBITDA			
Reported EBITDA (pre-restructuring charges)	$782	$648	$662
Add-back of one-time items in Toys "R" Us —U.S. [a]	0	0	118
Adjusted consolidated EBITDA	$782	$648	$780
Growth		−17.1%	20.4%
Margin	6.9%	5.7%	7.0%

EXHIBIT 17.9 CONSOLIDATED BALANCE SHEET ($ IN MILLIONS)

	For the Year Ended	
	1/31/2004	1/29/2005
ASSETS		
Cash and cash equivalents	$1,432	$1,250
Short-term investments	571	953
Accounts and other receivables	146	153
Merchandise inventories	2,094	1,884
Net property assets held for sale	163	7
Current portion of derivative assets	162	1
Prepaid expenses and other current assets	161	159
Total current assets	$4,729	$4,407
Property, plant, and equipment		
Real estate, net	$2,165	$2,393
Other, net	2,274	1,946
Total PP&E	$4,439	$4,339
Goodwill, net	348	353
Derivative assets	77	43
Deferred tax asset	399	426
Other assets	273	200
Total assets	$10,265	$9,768
LIABILITIES AND STOCKHOLDERS' EQUITY		
Short-term borrowings	$0	$0
Accounts payable	1,022	1,023
Accrued expenses and other current liabilities	866	881
Income taxes payable	319	245
Current portion of long-term debt	657	452
Total current liabilities	$2,864	$2,601
Long-term debt	2,349	1,860
Deferred income taxes	538	485
Derivative liabilities	26	16
Deferred rent liability	280	269
Other liabilities	225	212
Minority interest in Toysrus.com	9	0
Total liabilities	$6,291	$5,443
Stockholders' equity		
Common stock	$30	$30
Additional paid-in capital	407	405
Retained earnings	5,308	5,560
Accumulated other comprehensive loss	(64)	(7)
Restricted stock	0	(5)
Treasury shares, at cost	(1,707)	(1,658)
Total stockholders' equity	$3,974	$4,325
Total liabilities and stockholders' equity	$10,265	$9,768

EXHIBIT 17.10 CONSOLIDATED STATEMENT OF CASH FLOW ($ IN MILLIONS)

	For the Year Ended		
	2/1/2003	1/31/2004	1/29/2005
CASH FLOWS FROM OPERATING ACTIVITIES			
Net earnings	$213	$63	$252
Adjustments to reconcile net earnings to net cash from operating activities:			
Depreciation and amortization	$339	$368	$354
Amortization of restricted stock	0	0	7
Deferred income taxes	99	27	(40)
Minority interest in Toysrus.com	(14)	(8)	(6)
Other non-cash items	(9)	1	2
Non-cash portion of restructuring and other charges	0	63	4
Changes in operating assets and liabilities:			
Accounts and other receivables	8	62	(5)
Merchandise inventories	(100)	133	221
Prepaid expenses and other operating assets	(118)	28	76
Accounts payable, accrued expenses, and other liabilities	109	117	(45)
Income taxes payable	48	(53)	(74)
Net cash provided by operating activities	$575	$801	$746
CASH FLOWS FROM INVESTING ACTIVITIES			
Capital expenditures, net	($395)	($262)	($269)
Proceeds from sale of fixed assets	0	0	216
Purchase of SB Toys, Inc.	0	0	(42)
Purchase of short -term investments and other	0	(572)	(382)
Net cash used in investing activities	($395)	($834)	($477)
CASH FLOWS FROM FINANCING ACTIVITIES			
Short-term borrowings, net	$0	$0	$0
Long-term borrowings	548	792	0
Long-term debt repayment	(141)	(370)	(503)
Decrease/(increase) in restricted cash	(60)	60	0
Proceeds from issuance of stock and contracts to purchase stock	266	0	0
Proceeds from exercise of stock options	0	0	27
Net cash (used in)/provided by financing activities	$613	$482	($476)
Effect of exchange rate changes on cash and cash equivalents	($53)	($40)	$25
CASH AND CASH EQUIVALENTS			
(Decrease)/increase during year	$740	$409	($182)
Beginning of year	283	1,023	1,432
End of year	$1,023	$1,432	$1,250

EXHIBIT 17.11 FINANCIAL PERFORMANCE BY SEGMENT ($ IN MILLIONS)

	For the Year Ended						GROWTH / MARGIN BY SEGMENT (%) For the Year Ended		
	2/1/2003	% of Total	1/31/2004	% of Total	1/29/2005	% of Total	2/1/2003	1/31/2004	1/29/2005
NET SALES BY SEGMENT							*GROWTH BY SEGMENT (%)*		
Toys "R" Us —U.S.	$6,755	59.8	$6,326	55.9	$6,104	55.0		-6.4	-3.5
Toys "R" Us —International	2,161	19.1	2,470	21.8	2,739	24.7		14.3	10.9
Babies "R" Us	1,595	14.1	1,738	15.4	1,863	16.8		9.0	7.2
Toysrus.com	340	3.0	371	3.3	366	3.3		9.1	-1.3
Kids "R" Us	454	4.0	415	3.7	28	0.3		-8.6	-93.3
Consolidated net sales	$11,305	100.0	$11,320	100.0	$11,100	100.0		0.1	-1.9
OPERATING EARNINGS BY SEGMENT							*MARGIN BY SEGMENT (%)*		
Toys "R" Us —U.S.	$256	49.4	$70	20.4	$4	0.9	3.8	1.1	0.1
Toys "R" Us —International	158	30.5	166	48.4	220	51.9	7.3	6.7	8.0
Babies "R" Us	169	32.6	192	56.0	224	52.8	10.6	11.0	12.0
Toysrus.com	(37)	-7.1	(18)	-5.2	1	0.2	-10.9	-4.9	0.3
Kids "R" Us[1]	(28)	-5.4	(67)	-19.5	(25)	-5.9	-6.2	-16.1	-89.3
Segment operating earnings	$518	100.0	$343	100.0	$424	100.0	4.6	3.0	3.8
Corporate/other expenses[2]	(75)		(63)		(116)				
Restructuring charges	0		(63)		(4)				
Reported operating earnings	$443		$217		$304		3.9	1.9	2.7
ADJUSTED EBITDA BY SEGMENT							*MARGIN BY SEGMENT (%)*		
Toys "R" Us —U.S.[3]	$447	55.1	$264	39.3	$322	37.4	6.6	4.2	5.3
Toys "R" Us —International	210	25.9	227	33.8	295	34.3	9.7	9.2	10.8
Babies "R" Us	197	24.3	223	33.2	262	30.5	12.4	12.8	14.1
Toysrus.com	(33)	-4.1	(16)	-2.4	1	0.1	-9.7	-4.3	0.3
Kids "R" Us[1]	(10)	-1.2	(27)	-4.0	(20)	-2.3	-2.2	-6.5	-71.4
Adjusted segment EBITDA	$811	100.0	$671	100.0	$860	100.0	7.2	5.9	7.7
Corporate/other expenses[2]	(75)		(63)		(116)				
Add-back: other D&A	46		40		36				
Consolidated adjusted EBITDA	$782		$648		$780		6.9	5.7	7.0

Note 1: Includes markdowns of $49 million and accelerated depreciation of $24 million in 2003 related to the closing of all stores.

Note 2: Includes corporate expenses, the operating results of Toy Box, and the equity in net earnings of Toys "R" — Us/Japan. Increase in amount is due to ourstrategic review expenses and Sarbanes-Oxley Section 404 compliance totaling $29 million. In addition, we incurred charges of $8 million relating to our 2004 restructuring of the Company's corporate headquarters operations, and a $19 million increase in incentive compensation costs.

Note 3: EBITDA for FY 2005 adjusted by adding back $132 million in inventory markdowns and excluding $14 million related to a lawsuit settlement — $118 million net add-back in FY 2005.

Source: Toys "R" Us FYE 2005 10-K Filing

EXHIBIT 17.12 INCOME STATEMENT ($ IN MILLIONS)

Base Case

| | Actual | | | Projected | | | | | | | | | |
For the FYE January 31	2003	2004	2005	2006	2007	2008	2009	2010	2011	2012	2013	2014	2015
Consolidated Net Sales	$11,305.0	$11,320.0	$11,100.0	$10,875.2	$10,456.3	$10,405.8	$10,741.8	$11,140.9	$11,554.9	$11,984.2	$12,429.4	$12,891.2	$13,370.2
Growth		0.1%	-1.9%	-2.0%	-3.9%	-0.5%	3.2%	3.7%	3.7%	3.7%	3.7%	3.7%	3.7%
COGS & SG&A by Segment	$10,494.0	$10,649.0	$10,240.0	$9,986.4	$9,569.5	$9,501.9	$9,799.4	$10,155.5	$10,532.8	$10,924.1	$11,330.0	$11,750.9	$12,187.5
Margin	92.8%	94.1%	92.3%	91.8%	91.5%	91.3%	91.2%	91.2%	91.2%	91.2%	91.2%	91.2%	91.2%
EBITDA by Segment	$811.0	$671.0	$860.0	$888.7	$886.9	$903.9	$942.5	$985.5	$1,022.1	$1,060.1	$1,099.4	$1,140.3	$1,182.7
Margin	7.2%	5.9%	7.7%	8.2%	8.5%	8.7%	8.8%	8.8%	8.8%	8.8%	8.8%	8.8%	8.8%
Corporate / Other Expenses	29.0	23.0	80.0	27.9	26.8	26.7	27.6	28.6	29.6	30.7	31.9	33.1	34.3
Margin	0.3%	0.2%	0.7%	0.3%	0.3%	0.3%	0.3%	0.3%	0.3%	0.3%	0.3%	0.3%	0.3%
Consolidated EBITDA	$782.0	$648.0	$780.0	$860.8	$860.0	$877.2	$914.9	$956.9	$992.4	$1,029.3	$1,067.6	$1,107.2	$1,148.4
Growth		-17.1%	20.4%	10.4%	-0.1%	2.0%	4.3%	4.6%	3.7%	3.7%	3.7%	3.7%	3.7%
Margin	6.9%	5.7%	7.0%	7.9%	8.2%	8.4%	8.5%	8.6%	8.6%	8.6%	8.6%	8.6%	8.6%
D&A by Segment	293.0	328.0	318.0	304.4	288.5	284.6	293.2	303.8	315.1	326.8	339.0	351.5	364.6
Margin	2.6%	2.9%	2.9%	2.8%	2.8%	2.7%	2.7%	2.7%	2.7%	2.7%	2.7%	2.7%	2.7%
Other D&A	46.0	40.0	36.0	35.3	33.9	33.7	34.8	36.1	37.5	38.9	40.3	41.8	43.4
Margin	0.4%	0.4%	0.3%	0.3%	0.3%	0.3%	0.3%	0.3%	0.3%	0.3%	0.3%	0.3%	0.3%
Restructuring Charges	0.0	63.0	4.0	0.0	0.0	0.0	0.0	0.0	0.0	0.0	0.0	0.0	0.0
Consolidated EBIT	$443.0	$217.0	$422.0	$521.1	$537.6	$558.9	$586.8	$616.9	$639.9	$663.6	$688.3	$713.9	$740.4
Growth		-51.0%	94.5%	23.5%	3.2%	4.0%	5.0%	5.1%	3.7%	3.7%	3.7%	3.7%	3.7%
Margin	3.9%	1.9%	3.8%	4.8%	5.1%	5.4%	5.5%	5.5%	5.5%	5.5%	5.5%	5.5%	5.5%
Interest Expense													
Assumed Debt				$139.0	$116.8	$100.3	$88.2	$74.1	$57.8	$39.4	$18.7	$3.9	$0.0
Senior Secured Credit Facility				47.3	50.8	54.3	57.8	61.3	64.8	66.5	66.5	54.5	22.5
Unsecured Bridge Loan				209.0	209.0	209.0	209.0	209.0	209.0	209.0	209.0	209.0	209.0
Secured European Bridge Loan				90.0	90.0	90.0	90.0	90.0	90.0	90.0	90.0	90.0	90.0
Mortgage Loan Agreements				64.0	64.0	64.0	64.0	64.0	64.0	64.0	64.0	64.0	64.0
Total Interest Expense				$549.2	$530.5	$517.5	$509.0	$498.3	$485.6	$468.9	$448.2	$421.4	$385.5
Interest Income on Cash Balance				40.5	46.8	53.0	59.2	65.5	71.7	77.9	77.9	77.9	77.9
Pre-Tax Income				$12.4	$53.9	$94.3	$137.1	$184.1	$226.0	$272.7	$318.0	$370.4	$432.8
Use of NOLs				0.0	0.0	0.0	0.0	0.0	0.0	0.0	0.0	0.0	0.0
Taxes 35.0%				4.3	18.9	33.0	48.0	64.4	79.1	95.4	111.3	129.7	151.5
Net Income				$8.1	$35.0	$61.3	$89.1	$119.6	$146.9	$177.3	$206.7	$240.8	$281.3
Growth					334.2%	75.1%	45.3%	34.3%	22.8%	20.7%	16.6%	16.5%	16.8%
Margin				0.1%	0.3%	0.6%	0.8%	1.1%	1.3%	1.5%	1.7%	1.9%	2.1%
Proceeds from Store Sales (After-Tax)				217.7	185.8	0.0	0.0	0.0	0.0	0.0	0.0	0.0	0.0
Dividends				0.0	0.0	0.0	0.0	0.0	0.0	0.0	0.0	0.0	0.0
Retained Earnings				$225.8	$220.8	$61.3	$89.1	$119.6	$146.9	$177.3	$206.7	$240.8	$281.3

EXHIBIT 17.13 BALANCE SHEET ($ IN MILLIONS)

Base Case

For the FYE January 31	Actual							Projected					
	2003	2004	2005	2006	2007	2008	2009	2010	2011	2012	2013	2014	2015
ASSETS													
Cash and Cash Equivalents			$1,247.0	$1,247.0	$1,247.0	$1,247.0	$1,247.0	$1,247.0	$1,247.0	$1,247.0	$1,247.0	$1,247.0	$1,247.0
Accounts and Other Receivables			153.0	149.9	144.1	143.4	148.1	153.6	159.3	165.2	171.3	177.7	184.3
Merchandise Inventories			1,884.0	1,837.3	1,760.6	1,748.2	1,802.9	1,868.4	1,937.9	2,009.9	2,084.5	2,162.0	2,242.3
Other Current Assets			167.0	163.6	157.3	156.6	161.6	167.6	173.8	180.3	187.0	193.9	201.2
Total Current Assets			$3,451.0	$3,397.9	$3,309.1	$3,295.2	$3,359.6	$3,436.6	$3,518.0	$3,602.4	$3,689.9	$3,780.6	$3,874.8
Net, PP&E			4,339.0	$4,216.8	$4,103.5	$3,993.3	$3,880.0	$3,762.9	$3,641.4	$3,515.4	$3,384.8	$3,249.2	$3,108.6
Goodwill, net			0.0	0.0	0.0	0.0	0.0	0.0	0.0	0.0	0.0	0.0	0.0
New Goodwill			2,684.0	2,684.0	2,684.0	2,684.0	2,684.0	2,684.0	2,684.0	2,684.0	2,684.0	2,684.0	2,684.0
Other Assets			669.0	669.0	669.0	669.0	669.0	669.0	669.0	669.0	669.0	669.0	669.0
Total Assets			$11,143.0	$10,967.7	$10,765.6	$10,641.5	$10,592.7	$10,552.5	$10,512.4	$10,470.8	$10,427.6	$10,382.8	$10,336.4
LIABILITIES & STOCKHOLDERS' EQUITY													
Accounts Payable			$1,023.0	$997.7	$956.0	$949.3	$979.0	$1,014.6	$1,052.2	$1,091.3	$1,131.9	$1,173.9	$1,217.6
Accrued Expenses & Other Current Liabilities			1,126.0	1,098.1	1,052.3	1,044.8	1,077.5	1,116.7	1,158.2	1,201.2	1,245.9	1,292.1	1,340.2
Total Current Liabilities			$2,149.0	$2,095.8	$2,008.3	$1,994.1	$2,056.5	$2,131.3	$2,210.4	$2,292.6	$2,377.7	$2,466.1	$2,557.7
Assumed Debt			$2,312.0	$1,964.1	$1,628.7	$1,457.4	$1,257.1	$1,022.6	$756.4	$455.4	$120.3	$0.0	$0.0
Senior Secured Credit Facility			700.0	700.0	700.0	700.0	700.0	700.0	700.0	700.0	700.0	446.4	27.0
Unsecured Bridge Loan			1,900.0	1,900.0	1,900.0	1,900.0	1,900.0	1,900.0	1,900.0	1,900.0	1,900.0	1,900.0	1,900.0
Secured European Bridge Loan			1,000.0	1,000.0	1,000.0	1,000.0	1,000.0	1,000.0	1,000.0	1,000.0	1,000.0	1,000.0	1,000.0
Mortgage Loan Agreements			800.0	800.0	800.0	800.0	800.0	800.0	800.0	800.0	800.0	800.0	800.0
Total Debt			$6,712.0	$6,364.1	$6,028.7	$5,857.4	$5,657.1	$5,422.6	$5,156.4	$4,855.4	$4,520.3	$4,146.4	$3,727.0
Deferred Income Taxes			485.0	485.0	485.0	485.0	485.0	485.0	485.0	485.0	485.0	485.0	485.0
Other Liabilities			497.0	497.0	497.0	497.0	497.0	497.0	497.0	497.0	497.0	497.0	497.0
Total Liabilities			$9,843.0	$9,441.9	$9,019.0	$8,833.5	$8,695.6	$8,535.8	$8,348.8	$8,129.9	$7,880.1	$7,594.5	$7,266.7
Stockholders' Equity													
New Preferred Stock			$0.0	$0.0	$0.0	$0.0	$0.0	$0.0	$0.0	$0.0	$0.0	$0.0	$0.0
Sponsor Equity			1,300.0	1,300.0	1,300.0	1,300.0	1,300.0	1,300.0	1,300.0	1,300.0	1,300.0	1,300.0	1,300.0
Retained Earnings			0.0	225.8	446.6	508.0	597.1	716.7	863.6	1,040.9	1,247.6	1,488.4	1,769.7
Total Stockholders' Equity			$1,300.0	$1,525.8	$1,746.6	$1,808.0	$1,897.1	$2,016.7	$2,163.6	$2,340.9	$2,547.6	$2,788.4	$3,069.7
Total Liabilities & Stockholders' Equity			$11,143.0	$10,967.7	$10,765.6	$10,641.5	$10,592.7	$10,552.5	$10,512.4	$10,470.8	$10,427.6	$10,382.8	$10,336.4
Check			$0.000	$0.000	$0.000	$0.000	$0.000	$0.000	$0.000	$0.000	$0.000	$0.000	$0.000

EXHIBIT 17.14 INTEREST RATE AND WORKING CAPITAL ASSUMPTIONS ($ IN MILLIONS)

Base Case

For the FYE January 31	2003	Actual 2004	2005	2006	2007	2008	2009	2010	2011	2012	2013	2014	2015
Interest Rate Assumptions													
LIBOR			2.75%	3.25%	3.75%	4.25%	4.75%	5.25%	5.75%	6.00%	6.00%	6.00%	6.00%
Interest Earned on Cash			2.75%	3.25%	3.75%	4.25%	4.75%	5.25%	5.75%	6.25%	6.25%	6.25%	6.25%
Cash Interest Rate on Debt		LIBOR Spread	Fixed Rate										
Assumed Debt			6.50%	6.50%	6.50%	6.50%	6.50%	6.50%	6.50%	6.50%	6.50%	6.50%	6.50%
Senior Secured Credit Facility		3.50%		6.75%	7.25%	7.75%	8.25%	8.75%	9.25%	9.50%	9.50%	9.50%	9.50%
Unsecured Bridge Loan			11.00%	11.00%	11.00%	11.00%	11.00%	11.00%	11.00%	11.00%	11.00%	11.00%	11.00%
Secured European Bridge Loan			9.00%	9.00%	9.00%	9.00%	9.00%	9.00%	9.00%	9.00%	9.00%	9.00%	9.00%
Mortgage Loan Agreements			8.00%	8.00%	8.00%	8.00%	8.00%	8.00%	8.00%	8.00%	8.00%	8.00%	8.00%
Workings Capital Assumptions													
Accounts and Other Receivables		$146.0	$153.0	$149.9	$144.1	$143.4	$148.1	$153.6	$159.3	$165.2	$171.3	$177.7	$184.3
Days Outstanding		4.7	5.0	5.0	5.0	5.0	5.0	5.0	5.0	5.0	5.0	5.0	5.0
Merchandise Inventories		$2,094.0	$1,884.0	$1,837.3	$1,760.6	$1,748.2	$1,802.9	$1,868.4	$1,937.9	$2,009.9	$2,084.5	$2,162.0	$2,242.3
Turns		5.1	5.4	5.4	5.4	5.4	5.4	5.4	5.4	5.4	5.4	5.4	5.4
Other Current Assets		$486.0	$167.0	$163.6	$157.3	$156.6	$161.6	$167.6	$173.8	$180.3	$187.0	$193.9	$201.2
Days Outstanding		15.7	5.5	5.5	5.5	5.5	5.5	5.5	5.5	5.5	5.5	5.5	5.5
Accounts Payable		$1,022.0	$1,023.0	$997.7	$956.0	$949.3	$979.0	$1,014.6	$1,052.2	$1,091.3	$1,131.9	$1,173.9	$1,217.6
Days Outstanding		35.0	36.5	36.5	36.5	36.5	36.5	36.5	36.5	36.5	36.5	36.5	36.5
Accrued Expenses & Other Current Liabilities		$1,185.0	$1,126.0	$1,098.1	$1,052.3	$1,044.8	$1,077.5	$1,116.7	$1,158.2	$1,201.2	$1,245.9	$1,292.1	$1,340.2
Days Outstanding		40.6	40.1	40.1	40.1	40.1	40.1	40.1	40.1	40.1	40.1	40.1	40.1
Total Current Assets		$2,726.0	$2,204.0	$2,150.9	$2,062.1	$2,048.2	$2,112.6	$2,189.6	$2,271.0	$2,355.4	$2,442.9	$2,533.6	$2,627.8
Total Current Liabilities		2,207.0	2,149.0	2,095.8	2,008.3	1,994.1	2,056.5	2,131.3	2,210.4	2,292.6	2,377.7	2,466.1	2,557.7
Working Capital		$519.0	$55.0	$55.1	$53.8	$54.1	$56.1	$58.4	$60.5	$62.8	$65.1	$67.5	$70.0
(Increase)/Decrease in Accounts and Other Receivables			($7.0)	$3.1	$5.8	$0.7	($4.6)	($5.5)	($5.7)	($5.9)	($6.1)	($6.4)	($6.6)
(Increase)/Decrease in Merchandise Inventories			210.0	46.7	76.7	12.4	(54.7)	(65.5)	(69.4)	(72.0)	(74.7)	(77.4)	(80.3)
(Increase)/Decrease in Other Current Assets			319.0	3.4	6.3	0.8	(5.1)	(6.0)	(6.2)	(6.5)	(6.7)	(6.9)	(7.2)
Increase/(Decrease) in Accounts Payable			1.0	(25.3)	(41.7)	(6.7)	29.7	35.6	37.7	39.1	40.5	42.1	43.6
Increase/(Decrease) in Accrued Expenses & Other Current Liabilities			(59.0)	(27.9)	(45.9)	(7.4)	32.7	39.2	41.5	43.0	44.6	46.3	48.0
(Increase in) Reduction of Working Capital			$464.0	($0.1)	$1.3	($0.3)	($2.0)	($2.3)	($2.2)	($2.2)	($2.3)	($2.4)	($2.5)
(Increase)/Decrease in Long-Term Assets				0.0	0.0	0.0	0.0	0.0	0.0	0.0	0.0	0.0	0.0
Increase/(Decrease) in Long-Term Liabilities				0.0	0.0	0.0	0.0	0.0	0.0	0.0	0.0	0.0	0.0

Calculate Acquisition Multiples

On March 17, 2005, Toys announced that it had reached a definitive agreement to sell the entire company to KKR for $26.75 per share in a $7.7-billion transaction, including all transaction fees. The purchase price represented a total transaction value (enterprise value + transaction fees) that was 9.9× Toys' FYE 2005 EBITDA and an enterprise value that was 9.4× Toys' FYE 2005 EBITDA. The equity amount contributed by KKR was $1.3 billion (see Exhibits 17.15 and 17.16). KKR's purchase price was a 63% premium to Toys' share price on the day before the company announced it was exploring a sale of the global toy business. KKR may have decided to offer a high premium based on an analysis of comparable transactions that included acquisition premiums and because of Toys' significant real estate holdings (which KKR may have felt was not fully valued by the market). Regardless, KKR would have completed financial projections that showed growth in cash flow over their investment horizon. Multiples applied against cash flow on the projected future sale date would create a final equity amount, which when compared with the initial KKR equity contribution, would result in an IRR that was acceptable to KKR.

EXHIBIT 17.15 TRANSACTION SUMMARY

($ in millions)	Value
Equity Price per Share	$26.75
Implied Shares Purchased (millions of shares)	220.6
Equity Value	$5,900
Other Transaction Value (Ex Fees)	394
Assumed Debt	2,312
Remaining Cash on Balance Sheet	(1,247)
Enterprise Value	$7,359
Transaction Fees	362
Enterprise Value w/Fees	$7,721
FYE 2005 EBITDA	$780
EV (Excluding Fees) / FYE 2005 EBITDA	9.4x
EV (with Fees) / FYE 2005 EBITDA	9.9x

Note: The model assumes transaction closed on FYE January 29, 2005. Actual deal closed on July 21, 2005.

EXHIBIT 17.16 SOURCES AND USES ($ IN MILLIONS)

Sources		Uses	
Cash on balance sheet	$956	Purchase of common stock	$5900
Senior secured credit facility	700	Purchase of stock options and restricted stock	227
Unsecured bridge loan	1900	Settlement of equity security interests	114

EXHIBIT 17.16 SOURCES AND USES ($ IN MILLIONS)—cont'd

Sources		Uses	
Secured European bridge loan	1000	Purchase of all warrants	17
Mortgage loan agreements	800	Transaction fees	362
Sponsor equity	1300	Severance and bonus payments	36
Total	$6656	*Total*	$6656

Summary of Fees	
Advisory fees and expenses	$78
Financing fees	135
Sponsor fees	81
Others	68
Total	$362

Note: Senior secured credit facility has $2.0 billion of availability.
This exhibit reflects actual sources and uses for the Toys transaction that closed on July 21, 2005: the $956 million cash used is included in the model, which assumes (for simplicity) a closing on January 29, 2005 (see Exhibit 17.18).
Source: Toys "R" Us, Form 10-Q, July 30, 2005.

Determine Target's Capitalization Postacquisition

Postacquisition, Toys had a capitalization of: (1) $2.3 billion of assumed existing debt plus $4.4 billion of new debt for a total of $6.7 billion in debt (see Exhibit 17.17), and (2) $1.3 billion of equity. As a result, equity represented only 16.3% of postacquisition Toys capitalization, and debt represented 83.7% of capitalization. This compares to a preacquisition equity and debt of approximately 65% and 35%, respectively. As a result, Toys' capitalization became significantly more leveraged based on the LBO transaction (see Exhibit 17.18).

EXHIBIT 17.17 LEVERAGE SUMMARY ($ IN MILLIONS)

LEVERAGE ANALYSIS		Cumul. Multiple
Approximate existing debt	$2,312	3.0x
$2 billion senior secured credit facility	700	3.9x
Unsecured bridge loan	1,900	6.3x
Secured European bridge loan	1,000	7.6x
Mortgage loan agreements	800	8.6x
Total	$6,712	8.6x
Remaining cash and short-term investments on balance sheet assumed by the consortium	(1,247)	
Net leverage	$5,465	7.0x

Note: The model assumes transaction closed on FYE January 29, 2005. Actual deal closed on July 21, 2005.

EXHIBIT 17.18 CONSOLIDATED BALANCE SHEET @ TRANSACTION CLOSE

($ in millions)	Actual For the Fiscal Year Ended		Acquisition Adjustments	Adjusted Balance Sheet @ Close
	1/31/2004	1/29/2005		
ASSETS				
Cash and Cash Equivalents	$2,003	$2,203	($956)	$1,247
Accounts and Other Receivables	146	153		153
Merchandise Inventories	2,094	1,884		1,884
Other Current Assets	486	167		167
Total Current Assets	$4,729	$4,407	($956)	$3,451
Net, PP&E	$4,439	$4,339		$4,339
Goodwill, net	348	353	(353)	0
New Goodwill	0	0	2,684	2,684
Other Assets	749	669		669
Total Assets	$10,265	$9,768	$1,375	$11,143
LIABILITIES & STOCKHOLDERS' EQUITY				
Accounts Payable	1,022	1,023		1,023
Accrued Expenses & Other Current Liabilities	1,185	1,126		1,126
Total Current Liabilities	$2,207	$2,149	$0	$2,149
Assumed Debt	3,006	2,312		2,312
Senior Secured Credit Facility	0	0	700	700
Unsecured Bridge Loan	0	0	1,900	1,900
Secured European Bridge Loan	0	0	1,000	1,000
Mortgage Loan Agreements	0	0	800	800
Total Debt	3,006	2,312	4,400	6,712
Deferred Income Taxes	538	485		485
Other Liabilities	540	497		497
Total Liabilities	$6,291	$5,443	$4,400	$9,843
Stockholders' Equity				
New Preferred Stock	$0	$0		$0
Sponsor Equity	0	0	1,300	1,300
Retained Earnings	3,974	4,325	(4,325)	0
Total Stockholders' Equity	$3,974	$4,325	($3,025)	$1,300
Total Liabilities & Stockholders' Equity	$10,265	$9,768	$1,375	$11,143

Note: Cash includes short-term investments. The model assumes transaction closed on January 29, 2005.
Actual deal closed on July 21, 2005.

Note: Goodwill Calculation

Equity Purchase Price (Incl. Fees)	$6,656
Less Tangible Net Worth	3,972
New Goodwill	$2,684

Note: Tangible Net Worth calculated as Retained Earnings - Goodwill

Determine Cash Flow Available for Debt Service

KKR determined the cash flow available for debt service by subtracting CapEx from projected EBITDA and then making adjustments based on changes in working capital and other long-term assets and liabilities and payment of cash taxes. In addition, because KKR expected to receive cash from the future sale of stores, the projected after-tax proceeds of these sales increased cash. The result was a forecast of cash available for debt service through 2015 (see Exhibit 17.19). This amount was then reduced to reflect interest expense netted against interest income to create cash available for debt repayment. Normally, this cash is used to pay down debt and, in the case of Toys, the Exhibit suggests that the $2.3 billion of debt assumed on the date of acquisition is paid off first, and then the senior secured credit facility receives partial repayment. The end result of using available cash flow to retire debt is the reduction in total debt over time and improvement in debt/EBITDA ratios (see Exhibits 17.19 and 17.20). The gradual reduction in debt combined with the increase in EBITDA creates a growth in equity for a financial sponsor, enabling the sponsor to achieve its targeted IRR (see Exhibit 17.1).

The Toys' projected cash flow statement (Exhibit 17.19) shows that there should be $347.9 million in cash available during 2006 to repay a portion of the debt assumed at the time of the acquisition.[2] Payment of this debt reduces total debt from $6.712 billion in 2005 to $6.364 billion in 2006 (see Exhibit 17.20). This total debt amount continues to decrease from debt repayment through 2010, when it reaches $5.423 billion (net debt of $4.176 billion). LBO models typically assume that all excess cash is used to pay down debt. This is because the financial sponsor usually thinks that this is the best use for excess cash. However, if there is a compelling investment opportunity, or if the sponsor wants the company to pay a large dividend, this cash can be diverted, unless lenders include loan covenants that prevent or minimize dividends and other large cash payments (which they usually do).

---

[2] Sometimes, a range of cash flows is projected since it is increasingly difficult to be precise the further out in time the projection continues. A variable cash flow projection will reveal alternative IRR outcomes and the riskiness of the debt brought onto the balance sheet.

EXHIBIT 17.19 CASH FLOW STATEMENT ($ IN MILLIONS)

Base Case

For the FYE January 31	Actual							Projected					
	2003	2004	2005	2006	2007	2008	2009	2010	2011	2012	2013	2014	2015
Consolidated EBITDA				$860.8	$860.0	$877.2	$914.9	$956.9	$992.4	$1,029.3	$1,067.6	$1,107.2	$1,148.4
Net Capex				217.5	209.1	208.1	214.8	222.8	231.1	239.7	248.6	257.8	267.4
EBITDA - Capex				$643.3	$650.9	$669.1	$700.1	$734.1	$761.3	$789.6	$819.0	$849.4	$881.0
(Increase) / Decrease in Working Capital				($0.1)	$1.3	($0.3)	($2.0)	($2.3)	($2.2)	($2.2)	($2.3)	($2.4)	($2.5)
(Increase) / Decrease in Other LT Assets				0.0	0.0	0.0	0.0	0.0	0.0	0.0	0.0	0.0	0.0
Increase / (Decrease) in Other LT Liabilities				0.0	0.0	0.0	0.0	0.0	0.0	0.0	0.0	0.0	0.0
Cash Taxes				(4.3)	(18.9)	(33.0)	(48.0)	(64.4)	(79.1)	(95.4)	(111.3)	(129.7)	(151.5)
Cash on Balance Sheet in Excess of Minimum Balance				0.0	0.0	0.0	0.0	0.0	0.0	0.0	0.0	0.0	0.0
Other Sources / (Uses) of Cash				($4.4)	($17.6)	($33.3)	($50.0)	($66.7)	($81.3)	($97.7)	($113.6)	($132.1)	($154.0)
Proceeds from Store Sales (After-Tax)				217.7	185.8	0.0	0.0	0.0	0.0	0.0	0.0	0.0	0.0
Cash Available for Debt Service				$856.6	$819.1	$635.8	$650.1	$667.4	$680.1	$691.9	$705.3	$717.3	$727.0
Total Interest Expense				$549.2	$530.5	$517.5	$509.0	$498.3	$485.6	$468.9	$448.2	$421.4	$385.5
Interest Income on Cash Balance				40.5	46.8	53.0	59.2	65.5	71.7	77.9	77.9	77.9	77.9
Cash Available for Debt Amortization / Repayment				$347.9	$335.4	$171.3	$200.4	$234.5	$266.2	$301.0	$335.1	$373.9	$419.4
Assumed Debt Repayment				($347.9)	($335.4)	($171.3)	($200.4)	($234.5)	($266.2)	($301.0)	($335.1)	($120.3)	$0.0
Senior Secured Credit Facility Repayment				$0.0	$0.0	$0.0	$0.0	$0.0	$0.0	$0.0	$0.0	($253.6)	($419.4)
Excess Cash After Debt and Credit Facility Repayment				$0.0	$0.0	$0.0	$0.0	$0.0	$0.0	$0.0	$0.0	$0.0	$0.0
Minimum Cash Balance				1,247.0	1,247.0	1,247.0	1,247.0	1,247.0	1,247.0	1,247.0	1,247.0	1,247.0	1,247.0
Ending Cash Balance				$1,247.0	$1,247.0	$1,247.0	$1,247.0	$1,247.0	$1,247.0	$1,247.0	$1,247.0	$1,247.0	$1,247.0
Credit Statistics													
Total Debt / EBITDA	8.61x			7.39x	7.01x	6.68x	6.18x	5.67x	5.20x	4.72x	4.23x	3.74x	3.25x
Net Debt / EBITDA	7.01x			5.94x	5.56x	5.26x	4.82x	4.36x	3.94x	3.51x	3.07x	2.62x	2.16x
EBITDA / Interest Expense				1.57x	1.62x	1.69x	1.80x	1.92x	2.04x	2.20x	2.38x	2.63x	2.98x
(EBITDA-Capex) / Interest Expense				1.17x	1.23x	1.29x	1.38x	1.47x	1.57x	1.68x	1.83x	2.02x	2.29x
Tax Loss Carryforward													
Beginning Balance				$0.0	$0.0	$0.0	$0.0	$0.0	$0.0	$0.0	$0.0	$0.0	$0.0
Additions				0.0	0.0	0.0	0.0	0.0	0.0	0.0	0.0	0.0	0.0
Use of NOLs				0.0	0.0	0.0	0.0	0.0	0.0	0.0	0.0	0.0	0.0
Ending Balance				$0.0	$0.0	$0.0	$0.0	$0.0	$0.0	$0.0	$0.0	$0.0	$0.0

EXHIBIT 17.20 RETURNS SUMMARY ($ IN MILLIONS)
Base Case

	Actual		Projected				CAGR
	2005	2006	2007	2008	2009	2010	'05-'10
Consolidated EBITDA	$780.0	$860.8	$860.0	$877.2	$914.9	$956.9	4.2%
Growth	20.4%	10.4%	-0.1%	2.0%	4.3%	4.6%	
Margin	7.0%	7.9%	8.2%	8.4%	8.5%	8.6%	
Capex		$217.5	$209.1	$208.1	$214.8	$222.8	
Total Interest Expense		$549.2	$530.5	$517.5	$509.0	$498.3	
Total Debt	$6,712	$6,364	$6,029	$5,857	$5,657	$5,423	
Cash and Cash Equivalents	1,247	1,247	1,247	1,247	1,247	1,247	
Net Debt	$5,465	$5,117	$4,782	$4,610	$4,410	$4,176	
Total Debt / EBITDA	8.61x	7.39x	7.01x	6.68x	6.18x	5.67x	
Net Debt / EBITDA	7.01x	5.94x	5.56x	5.26x	4.82x	4.36x	
EBITDA / Interest Expense		1.57x	1.62x	1.69x	1.80x	1.92x	
(EBITDA-Capex) / Interest Expense		1.17x	1.23x	1.29x	1.38x	1.47x	

Returns (Including Sponsor Fee)

EBITDA Multiple	ROI	Gain	ROI w/Fee	Gain
7.00x	13.0%	$1,100.4	14.5%	$1,181.4
7.50x	16.8%	1,531.0	18.4%	1,612.0
8.00x	20.2%	1,961.6	21.8%	2,042.6
8.50x	23.2%	2,392.2	24.8%	2,473.2
9.00x	26.0%	2,822.8	27.6%	2,903.8
9.50x	28.5%	3,253.4	30.2%	3,334.4
10.00x	30.8%	3,684.0	32.5%	3,765.0

II. HEDGE FUNDS AND PRIVATE EQUITY

Calculate Credit Ratios

Lenders in an LBO transaction take considerable risks based on their exposure to highly leveraged companies such as Toys. As a result, they require controls on the company's total amount of debt and on the cash flow available to pay interest when due. As a condition for lending, therefore, two different kinds of credit ratios are imposed by lenders: leverage ratios and coverage ratios.

Leverage ratios limit the amount of total debt and net debt that the target company is allowed to undertake relative to EBITDA. In the Toys transaction, postacquisition total debt/EBITDA during 2005 was 8.61×. Net debt/EBITDA during 2005 was 7.01× (see Exhibit 17.20). Note that these ratios are forecast to reduce each year based on the repayment of debt until 2010, when total debt/EBITDA is 5.67× and net debt/EBITDA is 4.36×.

Coverage ratios require the company to produce cash flow in excess of annual interest payments. For example, EBITDA must exceed interest payments due in any year by a certain ratio. In the Toys transaction, EBITDA/interest expense during 2006 was 1.57×. (EBITDA-CapEx)/interest expense was 1.17× during 2006. Through the repayment of debt, these ratios are forecast to improve each year until 2010, when EBITDA/interest expense increases to 1.92× and (EBITDA-CapEx)/interest expense increases to 1.47×.

Calculate the Equity Value, Internal Rate of Return and Multiple of Investment on Projected Exit Date

To calculate equity value, IRR, and multiple of investment on the projected exit date, start with EBITDA on the projected exit date year (2010 in the Toys case—see Exhibit 17.21) and multiply that EBITDA by a range of enterprise value/EBITDA multiples that might apply as of the exit date. This creates an expected enterprise value. After the enterprise value alternatives are determined, equity value as of the exit date can be calculated by subtracting debt and adding cash. A further step sometimes involves determining the equity value of options held by nonsponsor holders (such as management) and reducing the equity value for the sponsor by this amount.

EXHIBIT 17.21 RETURNS SUMMARY ($ IN MILLIONS)

Base Case

	Exit Multiple	Enterprise Value	Less: Debt	Plus: Cash	Net Debt	Equity Value	Value of Mgmt Options	Net Sponsor Equity Value
Assumed Exit Year	2010							
EBITDA	$956.9							
7.00x		$6,698.3	($5,422.6)	$1,247.0	($4,175.6)	$2,522.7	$122.3	$2,400.4
7.50x		7,176.7	($5,422.6)	$1,247.0	($4,175.6)	$3,001.1	170.1	2,831.0
8.00x		7,655.1	($5,422.6)	$1,247.0	($4,175.6)	$3,479.6	218.0	3,261.6
8.50x		8,133.6	($5,422.6)	$1,247.0	($4,175.6)	$3,958.0	265.8	3,692.2
9.00x		8,612.0	($5,422.6)	$1,247.0	($4,175.6)	$4,436.5	313.6	4,122.8
9.50x		9,090.5	($5,422.6)	$1,247.0	($4,175.6)	$4,914.9	361.5	4,553.4
10.00x		9,568.9	($5,422.6)	$1,247.0	($4,175.6)	$5,393.4	409.3	4,984.0

Sponsor Return

	2005	2006	2007	2008	2009	2010	ROI	Gains
7.00 x	($1,300.0)	$0.0	$0.0	$0.0	$0.0	$2,400.4	13.0%	$1,100.4
7.50 x	(1,300.0)	0.0	0.0	0.0	0.0	2,831.0	16.8%	1,531.0
8.00 x	(1,300.0)	0.0	0.0	0.0	0.0	3,261.6	20.2%	1,961.6
8.50 x	(1,300.0)	0.0	0.0	0.0	0.0	3,692.2	23.2%	2,392.2
9.00 x	(1,300.0)	0.0	0.0	0.0	0.0	4,122.8	26.0%	2,822.8
9.50 x	(1,300.0)	0.0	0.0	0.0	0.0	4,553.4	28.5%	3,253.4
10.00 x	(1,300.0)	0.0	0.0	0.0	0.0	4,984.0	30.8%	3,684.0

Sponsor Return Including Initial Fees

	2005	2006	2007	2008	2009	2010	ROI with Fee	Gains with Fee
7.00 x	($1,219.0)	$0.0	$0.0	$0.0	$0.0	$2,400.4	14.5%	$1,181.4
7.50 x	(1,219.0)	0.0	0.0	0.0	0.0	2,831.0	18.4%	1,612.0
8.00 x	(1,219.0)	0.0	0.0	0.0	0.0	3,261.6	21.8%	2,042.6
8.50 x	(1,219.0)	0.0	0.0	0.0	0.0	3,692.2	24.8%	2,473.2
9.00 x	(1,219.0)	0.0	0.0	0.0	0.0	4,122.8	27.6%	2,903.8
9.50 x	(1,219.0)	0.0	0.0	0.0	0.0	4,553.4	30.2%	3,334.4
10.00 x	(1,219.0)	0.0	0.0	0.0	0.0	4,984.0	32.5%	3,765.0

The most relevant multiple to use in forecasting the exit equity value for the sponsor depends on who the expected buyer is on the exit date (IPO sale, or M&A sale to a strategic buyer or to another financial sponsor) and the multiple used to value the investment on the original acquisition date. Generally, sponsors use the same multiple for entering and exiting an investment, but this depends on the facts and circumstances of the investment.

After a range of equity values is determined, the IRR of the investment can be calculated based on the number of years the investment is expected to be held and the entry and exit equity values derived from the analysis. The IRR is the discount rate which causes the present value of the future cash flow (including the equity value on the exit date) to equal the equity investment at time zero. This IRR can be calculated on most financial calculators by including the time horizon (n), which was 5 years in the Toys case, the original investment (PV), which was -$1.3 billion (without fees) for Toys and the exit equity value (FV), which, assuming a 9.0× multiple, was $4.12 billion for Toys. Assuming no interim dividend payments (PMT), solving for the IRR (i) based on the 9× multiple results in an IRR of 26%.

In Exhibit 17.21, the original equity investment by KKR in Toys during 2005 was $1.3 billion. Assuming a 5-year holding period (an exit during 2010), the sponsor's equity value at exit ranges from $2.4 billion to just under $5.0 billion, depending on the enterprise value/EBITDA multiple used. Since the 2005 multiple (excluding fees) was 9.4×, it is reasonable to assume an exit multiple of between 9.0× and 9.5×, which suggests that the IRR for KKR in the Toys transaction may have been expected to be between 26.0% and 28.5%. Including fees, the expected return may have been 26.7%–30.2%.

If an exit multiple of 9.0× had been used, the expected exit equity value would have been $4.12 billion, producing a gain of $2.82 billion (not including initial fees) since the original equity investment was $1.3 billion. As a result, the expected multiple of investment would have been $4.12 billion/$1.3 billion = 3.17 times (equity exit value/entry equity value).

LEVERAGED BUYOUT ANALYSIS POSTCREDIT CRISIS

Although when KKR initiated the Toys LBO the expected IRRs may have been 26%, or higher, and expected multiple of investment at 3.17 times, or higher, there was considerable risk associated with this transaction. It is likely, therefore, that KKR completed several "stress test" scenarios that projected worsening credit, real estate, and retailing markets. Based on this risk-adjusted analysis, they may have expected lower returns. Indeed, in the postcredit crisis environment, returns for most financial sponsors were significantly diminished. This happened, in part, because creditors were unwilling to provide as much leverage in support of LBO transactions (and the cost of leverage increased). With less leverage available, financial sponsors were required to commit more up-front equity, which reduced returns. In addition, because of a massive inflow of new private equity funding that came from investors during 2006–08, there was significantly more competition for acquisition targets, which also resulted in a reduction in returns. Since 2009, many sponsors have accepted IRRs substantially below 25%, and sometimes as low as 10%–15%, while other sponsors have decided to seek returns from nontraditional sources.

KKR had Toys file a registration statement during 2010 in relation to a potential IPO, but the offering was delayed that year, and again in 2011 and 2012, with the registration formally withdrawn during 2013. In each year, Toys cited market conditions for not launching an offering, and so 10 years after the original purchase by KKR and its partners, there was still no exit for the investment group.

Private Equity Impact on Corporations

The material in this chapter should be cross-referenced with the following case: **Cerberus and the US Auto Industry**.

PRIVATE EQUITY–OWNED COMPANIES: MANAGEMENT PRACTICES AND PRODUCTIVITY

The credit crisis that started in mid-2007 caused private equity acquisition activity to drop substantially. The market was forced to adjust to a deleveraging world when access to debt financing became limited. As a result, the private equity ownership model came under increasing scrutiny and questions arose regarding whether this asset class could create sustainable value without "financial engineering."

In response to this question, the authors of the World Economic Forum's "The Economic Impact of Private Equity Report 2009" publication concluded that private equity-owned companies are, on average, better managed than other forms of companies, including government-, family-, and privately owned firms, even after controlling for characteristics such as country, industry, size, and employee skills. This is because there are very few badly managed firms that are controlled by private equity firms, whereas other companies include a "tail" of very badly managed companies.

Although the results for private equity–controlled companies versus dispersed shareholding companies are not statistically significant, private equity–portfolio companies have slightly higher management practices scores. Private equity–owned company management quickly adopts merit-based hiring, firing, pay, and promotion practices. These companies have tough evaluation metrics, which are focused on both short-term and long-run objectives, and the metrics are well understood by employees and are linked to the company's performance. Private equity–owned companies are also very good at operational management practices such as adoption of lean management, focusing on continuous improvement, and implementing comprehensive performance documentation processes.

The World Economic Forum's publication concluded that private equity–owned companies are more productive than companies with other ownership structures. A key finding of the 2010 version of the World Economic Forum's report on the economic impact of private equity is that the net impact of private equity ownership on employment was almost neutral: although these companies shed jobs at a considerably higher pace immediately after the acquisition is completed, in the subsequent 3 years they added back many of these jobs. In addition, when factoring in productivity and worker earnings, private equity–owned companies compared favorably with other forms of company ownership. See Exhibit 18.1 for a summary of the publication's key findings.

EXHIBIT 18.1 SUMMARY OF PRIVATE EQUITY AND TARGET COMPANY PRODUCTIVITY FROM THE GLOBAL ECONOMIC IMPACT OF PRIVATE EQUITY REPORT, 2010

The evidence supports neither the apocalyptic claims of extensive job destruction nor arguments that there was a large increase in domestic employment. Studies suggest that employment falls more rapidly at target establishments posttransaction. At the same time, private

EXHIBIT 18.1 SUMMARY OF PRIVATE EQUITY AND TARGET COMPANY PRODUCTIVITY FROM THE GLOBAL ECONOMIC IMPACT OF PRIVATE EQUITY REPORT, 2010—cont'd

equity targets engage in more greenfield job creation than controls. Private equity also accelerates the pace of acquisitions and divestitures. These results regarding private equity's impact on employment fit the view that private equity acts as catalysts for change and eventual growth in the economy.

Firms acquired by private equity groups experience productivity growth in the 2-year period after the transaction that is on average 2% points more than at controls. About 72% of this outperformance differential reflects more effective management of existing facilities, including gains from accelerated reallocation of activity among target firms. It was also found that firms acquired by private equity had higher productivity than their peers at the time of the original acquisition by the private equity group. Productivity gains at both targets and controls are shared with workers in the form of higher wages.

Industries where private equity funds have been active grow more rapidly than other sectors, whether measured using total production, value added or employment, and are no more volatile in the face of industry cycles than other industries. In some cases, industries with private equity activity are less volatile (as evidenced in terms of employment).

Source: "The Globalization of Alternative Investments Working Papers Volume 3: The Global Economic Impact of Private Equity Report 2010." World Economic Forum, December 2009.

In summary, the World Economic Forum's conclusions are that private equity firms do more than apply financial engineering to their target companies. Research has demonstrated that private equity–owned companies have high scores on a wide range of management practices and, during the first 2 years after acquisition, productivity grows faster than at control companies. In addition, the research demonstrates that productivity gains at private equity–owned companies are shared more with employees in the form of higher wages as compared to nonprivate equity–controlled companies.

PRIVATE EQUITY–OWNED COMPANY FAILURES

In spite of the favorable research that supports the private equity ownership model, there have been a number of notable failures.

Hawaiian Telecom Communications

Hawaiian Telecom Communications (HTC) (at the time, Hawaii's largest telephone carrier) filed for bankruptcy protection in December 2008. The Carlyle Group purchased HTC from Verizon Communications in 2005 for $1.6 billion, using $425 million in equity and debt financing for the balance. Unfortunately, Carlyle faced problems from the start, as state utility regulators delayed the closing of the acquisition, and billing and customer service issues plagued the company while it was creating a new back-office system. As a result, many customers dropped both cable and wireless services and the company's revenues fell, creating large losses. By February, 2008, three consecutive quarterly losses compelled Carlyle to bring in a turnaround expert as an interim CEO, replacing CEO Michael Ruley. In May, yet another new CEO was brought in. Seven months later, the company filed for Chapter 11 bankruptcy protection.

Washington Mutual, Inc.

An investment group led by Texas Pacific Group (TPG) purchased Washington Mutual, Inc. (WaMu) for $7 billion during April 2008. In September 2008, WaMu, the largest savings and loan association in the United States, was placed in receivership by the Federal Deposit Insurance Corporation (FDIC). The FDIC then sold the banking subsidiaries of the company to JP Morgan for $1.9 billion, after invalidating all debt and equity claims. The holding company (without the banking subsidiaries) subsequently filed for Chapter 11 bankruptcy protection. TPG had invested $1.35 billion in WaMu, and the firm's losses were spread between three of TPG's investment funds: $475 million loss in $15 billion TPG V; $475 million loss in $20 billion TPG VI; and $400 million loss in $6 billion TPG financial partners.

Other Notable Failures

TXU Energy and Harrah's were two very large LBO transactions that were completed during late 2007, utilizing very large amounts of debt. Both companies sought bankruptcy protection during 2014 after many years of posting losses, causing credit facilities to go unpaid. More detailed information on these two failed transactions and other problematic transactions is provided in the section entitled Private Equity Portfolio Companies Purchased during 2006–07.

PRIVATE EQUITY PURCHASE COMMITMENT FAILURES

BCE, Inc.

Eighteen months after Ontario Teachers' Pension Plan, Providence Equity, Madison Dearborn Partners and Merrill Lynch Global Private Equity signed a merger agreement to acquire BCE, Canada's largest telephone company, but the deal collapsed. This would have been the largest private equity–led acquisition in history (at the time of announcement) based on its original valuation of $41 billion. There was an express condition of closing that a solvency opinion be provided. The BCE transaction collapsed when a valuation expert at KPMG issued an opinion that the acquisition would result in an insolvent entity, thereby releasing the four equity providers from their obligation to close the transaction. These firms stated that because of the failure to receive a solvency opinion, they were also released from an obligation to pay a $1.2 billion breakup fee. Because the equity providers walked away from the deal, four banks that had committed to provide $34 billion in debt financing also walked away. These banks were Citigroup, Deutsche Bank, Royal Bank of Scotland Group, and Toronto Dominion Bank. It was estimated that, given the poor condition of the credit markets, if these banks had been forced to provide financing based on the terms of their original commitment, they might have absorbed up to $12 billion in theoretical losses.

The biggest losers from this failed transaction were BCE shareholders, who expected to be bought out at around $34 per share. When the transaction collapsed during December 2008, BCE's share price was $18.29, resulting in a total loss of value to shareholders of approximately $12.6 billion.

Huntsman Corporation

On December 15, 2008, 18 months after an initial agreement was reached, Huntsman Corporation, a manufacturer and marketer of differentiated chemicals, announced that it terminated its $6.5 billion merger agreement with Hexion Specialty Chemicals, a company owned by Apollo Management. Huntsman had sued Hexion and Apollo in an effort to force them to proceed with the leveraged buyout of the company, but Huntsman withdrew the lawsuit based on a settlement agreement totaling $1 billion in payments to Huntsman. This payment obligation was shared between Apollo, who paid $425 million (and an additional $250 million in exchange for 10-year convertible notes issued by Huntsman), and Credit Suisse and Deutsche Bank (originally committed to provide debt financing for the transactions), who paid a $325 million breakup fee.

In spite of the payment by Credit Suisse and Deutsche Bank, Huntsman pursued claims against the banks based on, among other things, an allegation that the banks conspired with Apollo and tortuously interfered with Huntsman's prior merger agreement with Basell. This dispute was settled out of court during June 2009.

Huntsman had reached an agreement to sell their company at $25.25 per share to Basell, a large European-based chemical company, but changed its course when Apollo made a $28 per share offer and advised that it had financing commitments in place with the banks. The company's share price fell to $10 when the LBO transaction with Apollo and Hexion fell through, creating a loss of $3.6 billion for Huntsman shareholders. See Exhibit 16.15 in Chapter 16 for a more complete summary.

PRIVATE EQUITY PORTFOLIO COMPANIES PURCHASED DURING 2006–07

The largest private equity acquisitions during 2006 and 2007 are listed in Exhibit 18.2. During 2008 and 2009, the valuations for all of these companies were marked down considerably below the original acquisition valuations. Evidence of the decline in valuations is provided by Blackstone Group, which is a publicly reporting company. Blackstone posted a fourth-quarter 2008 loss of $415.2 million and a full-year loss of $1.16 billion. During the fourth quarter of 2008, it marked down the equity value of its holdings by 20%, on average, following a 7% reduction during the previous quarter. Valuation declines in portfolio companies drove down Blackstone's own stock price by 88% during a 20 month period following its June 2007 initial public offering (IPO).

EXHIBIT 18.2 LARGE PRIVATE EQUITY TRANSACTIONS DURING 2006 AND 2007

Target Name	Sponsor(s) Involved	Transaction Value ($mm)
TXU	Citigroup, GSCP, KKR, LEH PE, MS PE, TPG	$ 44.2
Equity Office Properties	Blackstone	$ 39.0
HCA Inc.	Bain, KKR, ML Private Equity	$ 33.5
First Data Corp.	KKR	$ 30.8
Alltel Corp.	GS, TPG	$ 27.8
Clear Channel Communications Inc.	Bain, TH Lee	$ 26.8
Hilton Hotels Corp.	Blackstone	$ 26.5
Harrah's Entertainment Inc.	Apollo, TPG	$ 25.6
Kinder Morgan Inc.	GSCP, Carlyle, Riverstone, Management	$ 21.6
Albertsons Inc.	SuperValu, CVS, Cerberus	$ 17.1
Freescale Semiconductor Inc.	Blackstone, Carlyle, Permira, TPG	$ 16.6
Intelsat Ltd.	BC Partners	$ 15.9
Univision Communications Inc.	MDP, Providence, TPG, TH Lee	$ 13.9
VNU NV	Blackstone, Carlyle, KKR, TH Lee, H&F, AlpInvest	$ 11.5
Philips Semiconductors	KKR, Silver Lake, AlpInvest	$ 11.2
Biomet	Blackstone, GSCP, KKR, TPG	$ 10.9
Home Depot Supply	Bain Capital, CD&R, Carlyle	$ 10.3
Total Transaction Value		**$ 383.2**

Source: Thomson Financial

A summary of six of the private equity transactions listed in Exhibit 18.2 follows.

TXU Energy

TXU Energy (TXU) provides electricity and related services to 2.3 million customers in Texas through 41 generating plants. A $44 billion acquisition was announced on February 26, 2007 and closed on October 10, 2007. The principal purchasers were KKR, TPG, and

Goldman Sachs, with Lehman Brothers, Citigroup, and Morgan Stanley as coinvestors. The transaction was announced at the peak time for securing financial leverage, but funded after the credit markets started freezing up. The investment banks considered paying a $1 billion breakup fee to get out of their debt funding commitment, but agreed to fund, taking an estimated $900 million in theoretical or actual debt underwriting losses. See Exhibits 18.3–18.5 for a summary of the transaction. TXU, which was renamed Energy Future Holdings Corporation (EFH) after the acquisition was completed, had a fourth quarter 2008 loss of $8.86 billion, causing KKR to write down the value of their holding by 30%. EFH shut down 15 generating plants in Texas during 2008 (22% of capacity) because they couldn't operate these plants profitably. In spite of these difficulties and a $38 billion debt load, KKR and TPG said that their investment was well positioned to survive an extended downturn. However, debt holders were not as sanguine during March 2009, given the 60 cents on the dollar trading level for senior secured bonds and 48 cents on the dollar trading level for the company's high yield bonds at that time. Loans to EFH represent the largest single position in KKR's fixed income investment vehicle, compounding the firm's overall exposure to the company.

EXHIBIT 18.3 TXU: INVESTMENT SUMMARY

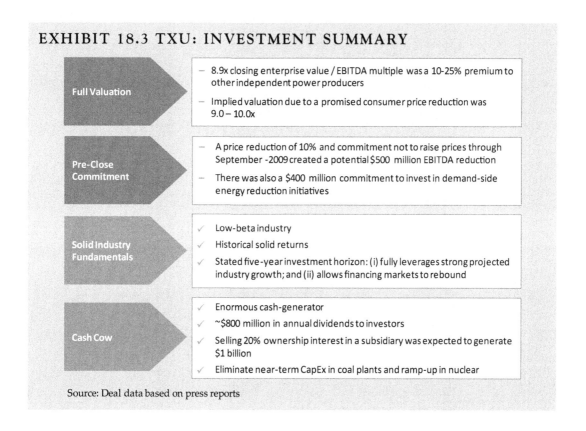

Full Valuation
- 8.9x closing enterprise value / EBITDA multiple was a 10-25% premium to other independent power producers
- Implied valuation due to a promised consumer price reduction was 9.0 – 10.0x

Pre-Close Commitment
- A price reduction of 10% and commitment not to raise prices through September -2009 created a potential $500 million EBITDA reduction
- There was also a $400 million commitment to invest in demand-side energy reduction initiatives

Solid Industry Fundamentals
- Low-beta industry
- Historical solid returns
- Stated five-year investment horizon: (i) fully leverages strong projected industry growth; and (ii) allows financing markets to rebound

Cash Cow
- Enormous cash-generator
- ~$800 million in annual dividends to investors
- Selling 20% ownership interest in a subsidiary was expected to generate $1 billion
- Eliminate near-term CapEx in coal plants and ramp-up in nuclear

Source: Deal data based on press reports

EXHIBIT 18.4 TXU: SOURCES AND USES/CLOSING CAPITAL

$ in MMs

Sources	$	% of Capital	Capital Structure EBITDA Multiple [1]	Interest Rate	Tenor	Uses	$
Revolver ($2,700MM)	$0	0.0%	0.00x	L+3.50%	6 yrs	Purchase of TXU Equity	$32,105
Letter of Credit Facility ($1,125MM)	$0	0.0%	0.00x	3.50%	6 yrs	Existing Debt Assumed	8,000
Term Loan	16,450	36.1%	3.20x	L+3.50%	6 yrs	Refinancing of Existing Debt	4,000
Delay-Draw Term Loan ($4,100MM)	2,150	4.7%	0.42x	L+3.50%	7 yrs	Transaction Fees and Expenses	1,500
Senior Secured Debt	**18,600**	**40.8%**	**3.62x**				
New Senior Unsecured Bridge / HY Notes	11,250	24.7%	2.19x	10.25-11.25%	8-10 yrs		
Existing Senior Unsecured Notes	2,978	6.5%	0.58x	Various	Various		
Pollution / Other Control Bonds	5,022	11.0%	0.98x	Various	Various		
Total Senior Unsecured Debt	**19,250**	**42.2%**	**3.74x**				
KKR Equity	2,500	5.5%	0.49x				
TPG Equity	2,500	5.5%	0.49x				
GS / Lehman / CITI / MS Equity	2,755	6.0%	0.54x				
Total New Cash Equity	**7,755**	**17.0%**	**1.51x**				
Total Transaction Sources	**45,605**	**100.0%**	**8.86x**			**Total Transaction Uses**	**$45,605**

[1] Estimated FYE 2007 EBITDA $5,145MM.

- $12 billion of pre-acquisition debt, but nearly $38 billion post-acquisition
- Substantial senior secured and total leverage of 3.6x and 7.4x, respectively

Source: Company filings

EXHIBIT 18.5 TXU: AVERAGE DEBT MULTIPLES OF LARGE CORPORATE LBO LOANS

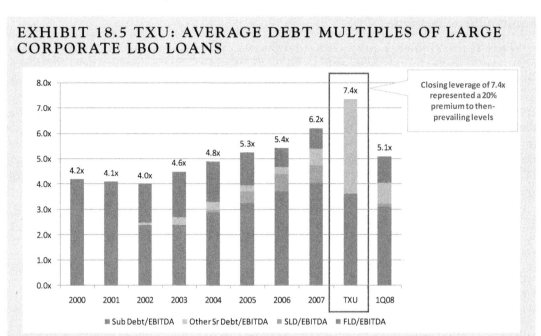

Note: FLD = First Lien Debt; SLD = Second Lien Debt.
Source: S&P's Leveraged Lending Review

TXU Postmortem

TXU filed for bankruptcy protection during 2014, creating the largest private equity fund portfolio company failure in history. The company was purchased during 2007 for $32 billion plus about $13 billion in assumed debt by KKR, TPG, and Goldman Sachs. As of the bankruptcy, these firms had written down nearly all of the $8 billion they originally invested.

Other firms, including Apollo Global Management and Blackstone Group, bought a significant amount of the company's discounted debt prior to the bankruptcy, hoping for profit during the bankruptcy period. Private equity buyers were interested in TXU because it was the biggest utility in a fast-growing electricity market and the only one in Texas that hadn't been broken up as a result of the state's deregulation of the industry. The investors assumed that natural gas prices would rise, and electricity rates in Texas were pegged to gas prices. Since TXU generated most of its electricity with less expensive coal and uranium for nuclear plants, it was positioned to benefit from any gas price increase. Instead, natural gas prices plunged as hydraulic fracturing of shale rock increased, which, in turn, pushed down electricity rates. For years, TXU negotiated to extend deadlines for debt repayments, hoping that natural gas prices would rebound. But with large amounts of debt coming due during the last quarter of 2014, the company, renamed Energy Future, ran out of cash. Energy Future bondholders who were owed about $1.7 billion took control of the reorganized company.

Equity Office Properties

When the $39 billion Equity Office Properties (EOP) transaction was agreed to in February 2007, the buyers were able to take advantage of the "best ever" debt financing environment for LBO transactions (see Exhibit 18.6). EOP (controlled by Sam Zell) was the largest US publicly traded owner and manager of office buildings, with 580 properties boasting over 100 million square feet. The buyer was the real estate arm of The Blackstone Group, which competed with Vornado Realty Trust for over 1 month, before finally winning (see Exhibits 18.7 and 18.8). Within 3 weeks of completing the transaction, Blackstone had sold $20.6 billion of EOP's real estate, leaving them with $19 billion of net assets. See Exhibits 18.9 and 18.10 for a summary of the transaction's financing and valuation.

EXHIBIT 18.6 EQUITY OFFICE PROPERTIES: PREDEAL MARKET ENVIRONMENT

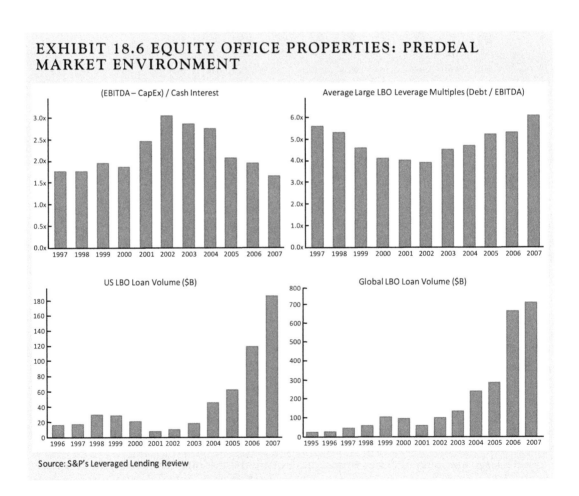

Source: S&P's Leveraged Lending Review

EXHIBIT 18.7 EQUITY OFFICE PROPERTIES (EOP): HOW DID THE BIDDING WAR FOR EOP UNFOLD?

- Throughout 2006, EOP engages several parties regarding a potential sale
- November 2006: EOP accepts an all-cash offer by Blackstone to be acquired for $48.50/share, with a $200 million breakup fee, but before closing, the following events occurred:

Timeline of Events: January 17, 2007 to February 5, 2007		
January 17	**January 25**	**January 31**
Consortium of Vornado, Starwood Capital, and Walton Street submits a bid for $52/share using 40% stock and 60% cash	Blackstone raises its all-cash offer to $54/share and break-up fee increased to $500 mm. EOP board re-affirms support	Vornado submits an offer for $56 using 45% stock and 55% cash
February 4	**February 5**	
Vornado revises bid to include up front cash for 55% of the shares	Blackstone raises its offer to $55.50/share and break-up fee increased to $720 mm. EOP board re-affirms support	

Source: Press reports and company press releases.

EXHIBIT 18.8 EQUITY OFFICE PROPERTIES (EOP): WHY WAS BLACKSTONE'S OFFER SUPERIOR?

On February 7, Vornado withdrew its proposal and EOP shareholders unanimously approved Blackstone's offer of $55.50 per share, a 37.8% premium over the 3 month trading price.

Comparison of Proposals			
	Blackstone Transaction	**Vornado Proposal**	**Considerations / Issues**
Price / Share	$55.50	$56.00	EOP board preferred all cash offer to mix of cash/stock
Form of Consideration	100% cash	55% in cash; 45% Vornado stock	Use of stock adds complexity and valuation risk
Closing	Immediate	Uncertain	Vornado's closing was subject to shareholder approval of stock issuance

EOP's board preferred the greater speed and certainty of closing offered by Blackstone

Source: Press reports and company press releases.

EXHIBIT 18.9 EQUITY OFFICE PROPERTIES: VALUATION ANALYSIS

Valuation Metrics									

NAV & DCF Valuations

Net Asset Value

	Implied Share Price	
Gross Value Net of Liabilities	$45.6	$49.1
Gross Value Net of Liabilities & Transaction Costs	$43.8	$47.2
2007 Nominal Cap Rates	5.4%	5.7%
Values Per Square Ft	$349.0	$367.0

Discounted Cash Flow

	Implied Share Price	
DCF Valuation	$41.3	$46.1
Terminal Value Multiples (2011 EBITDA)	17.5x	18.5x
Discount Rates	7.25%	7.75%

Comparables Valuation

Comparable Companies Analysis

	Multiple		Implied Share Price	
Funds From Operations (FFO)	18.0x	20.0x	$41.0	$45.6
2007 EBITDA	17.5x	18.5x	$44.6	$48.4

Comparable Transaction Analysis

	Multiple		Implied Share Price	
2007 EBITDA	18.0x	19.0x	$46.0	$49.8
	Cap Rate			
2007 Net Operating Income	5.25%	5.75%	$44.4	$50.8

Transaction Pricing Metrics

Offer Price	$55.5
Equity Value	**$24,631**
Net Debt	12,743
Preferred	213
Minority Interest	1,396
Total Transaction Value ($38.983 billion)	**$38,983**
2007 FFO Multiple (Funds from Operations) [1]	**23.8x**
2007 EBITDA Multiple [2]	**20.2x**

(1) Based on First Callconsensus estimate of $2.33 as of February 5, 2007
(2) Based on Wall Street Research

Transaction Premiums

Closing Date		2/9/07
Offer Price		$55.50
Premium to 11/1/06 unaffected price	$42.95	29.2%
Premium to 11/17/06 price	$44.72	24.1%
Premium to 3-month average	$40.26	37.9%
Premium to 6-month average	$38.24	45.1%

Source: Company filings; analyst reports

EXHIBIT 18.10 EQUITY OFFICE PROPERTIES (EOP): HOW WAS THE TRANSACTION FINANCED?

EOP Post-LBO Capitalization ($ in billions)			
Initial		**Post-Asset Sale**	
Equity – Blackstone	$4.3	Equity – Blackstone	$4.3 (est.)
Bridge – GS, Bear, B of A	$3.3	Bridge – GS, Bear, B of A	---
Assumed Debt	$2.3	Assumed Debt	$1.2
New Debt	$29.7	CMBS & Mezzanine[1]	$13.5 (est.)
Total	$39.6	Total	$19.0

$20.6 billion of asset sales in 3 weeks, leaving $19.0 billion of net assets

Note 1: Completed at tight levels with range of LIBOR plus 100 to 300 b.p.
Source: Press reports

Equity Office Properties Postmortem

Blackstone Group ultimately achieved more than a threefold return from its $39 billion buyout of Equity Office Properties Trust. When Blackstone bought Equity Office, the REIT was trading at a discount to private market valuations based on cash flow. Amid a bidding war with Vornado Realty Trust, Blackstone negotiated agreements to sell hundreds of Equity Office's more than 500 properties to reduce the firm's cost before completing its purchase. What looked like a very aggressive purchase was mitigated by the resale of $30 billion of property prior to and within 60 days following the purchase. The approximately $9 billion in holdings left over was marked down to about 65 cents on the dollar as the real estate market tanked shortly after the transaction was completed. However, a highly advantageous capital structure had been secured to finance the remaining property, with 6-year terms, no amortization, floating rate debt, and no covenants. This allowed the investment to remain on Blackstone's books while they waited for the real estate market to recover, which it did, enabling the remaining property to be sold during 2016.

Hospital Corporation of America

Hospital Corporation of America (HCA) is the largest private operator of health-care facilities in the world. As of the transaction date, they owned 169 hospitals and 108 surgery centers in 21 states, the United Kingdom, and Switzerland. The LBO was announced in July 2006 and closed in November 2006, for a total enterprise value of $33 billion. The private equity consortium included Bain Capital, KKR, Merrill Lynch Private Equity, and HCA founder Thomas F. Frist Jr. and members of his family, who contributed $800 million in equity. Exhibit 18.11 summarizes the transaction's valuation and the sources and uses of funds. HCA operated in a difficult industry environment and shareholders had grown frustrated with poor stock market performance. To secure an acceptable internal rate of return (IRR), the buyers relied on a challenging assumption that margins would not decline in the future (see Exhibit 18.12). An overview of the financing commitments is summarized in Exhibit 18.13.

EXHIBIT 18.11 HOSPITAL CORPORATION OF AMERICA: LBO VALUATION, SOURCES, AND USES OF FUNDS

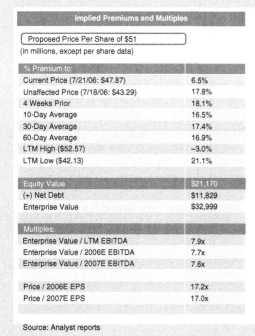

Implied Premiums and Multiples

Proposed Price Per Share of $51
(in millions, except per share data)

% Premium to:	
Current Price (7/21/06: $47.87)	6.5%
Unaffected Price (7/18/06: $43.29)	17.8%
4 Weeks Prior	18.1%
10-Day Average	16.5%
30-Day Average	17.4%
60-Day Average	16.9%
LTM High ($52.57)	−3.0%
LTM Low ($42.13)	21.1%

Equity Value	$21,170
(+) Net Debt	$11,829
Enterprise Value	$32,999

Multiples:	
Enterprise Value / LTM EBITDA	7.9x
Enterprise Value / 2006E EBITDA	7.7x
Enterprise Value / 2007E EBITDA	7.6x
Price / 2006E EPS	17.2x
Price / 2007E EPS	17.0x

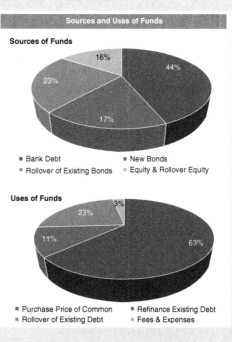

Sources and Uses of Funds

Sources of Funds

- Bank Debt — 23%
- New Bonds — 44%
- Rollover of Existing Bonds — 17%
- Equity & Rollover Equity — 16%

Uses of Funds

- Purchase Price of Common — 63%
- Refinance Existing Debt — 23%
- Rollover of Existing Debt — 11%
- Fees & Expenses — 3%

Source: Analyst reports

EXHIBIT 18.12 HOSPITAL CORPORATION OF AMERICA: TRANSACTION RATIONALE

Buyers' perspective	• Difficult industry environment and depressed valuations made industry attractive to sponsors
	○ Good leveraged buyout (LBO) candidate:
	- Low entry multiple: 7.9× LTM EBITDA of $4.1 billion versus comp range of 8.0×–9.5×
	- Margin improvement through divestiture of underperforming assets
	- Possible multiple expansion through initial public offering (IPO): HCA already had a successful LBO, with an IPO exit in 1993, creating ~39% internal rate of return (IRR) for sponsors
	• Low probability of competition for deal
Management perspective	• Greater operating flexibility in tough industry environment
	• Create shareholder value—best alternative based on review of strategic alternatives
	• Participate in future upside potential of company through equity rollover in transaction
Shareholders' perspective	• Poor stock price performance since 2002 despite share repurchases
	• Offer price likely best offer due to size of company and management involvement
Risks	• Financing—capital markets' appetite for $27 billion of new debt
	• Target IRR difficult to achieve if margins contract 1%–2% due to increasing bad debt and competition
	• Difficulty in gaining shareholder approval due to relatively low 18% premium

EXHIBIT 18.13 HOSPITAL CORPORATION OF AMERICA: SUMMARY OF DEBT FINANCING COMMITMENTS

- The Buyer Group submitted debt commitment letters from Merrill Lynch, Citigroup, Bank of America, and JP Morgan
  - $16.8 billion of senior secured credit facilities, $5.7 billion of senior secured second lien bridge loans
- Financing commitments were not subject to the successful syndication of new credit facilities
- Bridge loan facility committed to by banks, with funding drawn down if bonds not placed prior to closing
  - Funding of bridge conditioned upon delivery of offering memorandum no less than 20 business days prior to funding
  - Company must use commercially reasonable efforts to ensure underwriters have 20 consecutive business days to market the bonds after receipt of offering memorandum
- Commitment letters have the same conditionality as in the Merger Agreement
  - Material Adverse Effect definition conformed, Representations matched Merger Agreement
  - Termination date consistent with Merger Agreement end date
- Equity requirement equal to 15% of pro forma capitalization
  - Equity commitment letters delivered by the Buyer Group, with limited conditionality

Hospital Corporation of America Postmortem

During March 2011, HCA Holdings completed the largest private equity–backed IPO in history. Although analysts warned of long-term risks arising from HCA's large debt and uncertainties surrounding US health-care reform, investor interest was very strong. The company sold 126.2 million shares at $30 per share, raising about $3.79 billion. Based on the IPO valuation, the LBO investors and the Frist family had tripled the value of their 2006 investment. Of course, the final investment returns depended on prices at which shares that were not sold in the IPO are sold in the future. During 2010, HCA completed a $4.3 billion dividend recapitalization, which resulted in the original investors receiving a return of capital that almost paid back the initial investment. And so, the IPO proceeds ($1 billion received by the original investors) and the market value of additional shares not sold represent a significant return for KKR, Bain Capital, Bank of America Merrill Lynch, and the Frist family. Unlike many other buyouts during 2006 that had less predictable income streams, HCA had reported revenue growth of 5%–6% every year it was private, except in 2010, when growth slowed to 2.1%. Net income increased 17% between the buyout date and the IPO date. HCA attributed gains in income to cost-cutting measures and initiatives to improve services for patients. The company sold some hospitals after the buyout and made significant investments in expanding service lines, as well as in information technology. The company's debt load at the time of the IPO was almost unchanged from when it was acquired.

Harrah's Entertainment

Harrah's Entertainment (Harrah's) is the world's largest provider of branded casino entertainment, and its business is operated through 50 casinos in six countries. The company's brand names in the United States are Harrah's, Caesars, and Horseshoe. The $26-billion acquisition of Harrah's by Apollo Global Management and TPG Capital was announced during October 2006 and, after besting a competing offer from Penn National, closed during January 2008, following the Nevada Gaming Commission's granting of final approval. This transaction carried very high debt levels, with total debt at almost 10× EBITDA. In addition, some of the debt utilized PIK toggles (an important feature to keep the company afloat if future cash flow is squeezed). Returns for this transaction are highly dependent on operating improvements and a reduction in CapEx. A key reason why the market accepted such high leverage was because of the creative separation of loans collateralized by Harrah's land from loans provided directly to the casino operations of the company (see Exhibit 18.14). Sources and uses for the LBO transaction are summarized in Exhibit 18.15.

During February 2009, Harrah's massive debt package was restructured to keep the company out of bankruptcy court. Harrah's entered into a debt exchange offer, exchanging their debt for new notes priced at a discount and with longer maturities. The company was required to offer a more senior position in their capital structure to the exchange parties to induce them to complete this transaction. New tax laws associated with the US economic stimulus program allowed Harrah's to delay paying tax up front, when the exchange occurred. Prior to the new law, a company that reduced the principal amount of debt through an exchange was required to pay taxes on the amount reduced, since it was considered taxable income. Now, taxes on cancellation of debt can be deferred for 5 years, and then paid over a subsequent 5-year period. At the time of the exchange, Harrah's loans traded at 58 cents on the dollar and their high-yield bonds traded at 6 cents on the dollar.

EXHIBIT 18.14 HARRAH'S ENTERTAINMENT (HARRAH'S): REAL ESTATE HOLDINGS

- Harrah's owns approximately 350 acres, both developed and undeveloped, in Las Vegas and in other locations around the world
- Harrah's real estate holdings were used to raise $7.5 billion through commercial mortgage-backed securities
- TPG/Apollo leveraged the company's land holdings separately from the casino operations, enabling greater overall leverage
- Sale of unencumbered real estate may become an important source of cash to retire debt in the future

Source: Company filings.

EXHIBIT 18.15 HARRAH'S ENTERTAINMENT (HARRAH'S): SOURCES AND USES

- Harrah's had a presale debt level of $10.7 billion with EBITDA of $2.43 billion, representing a 4.4x leverage multiple

- Post-LBO debt level of $23.9 billion results in a new leverage multiple of 9.8x Debt/EBITDA

$ in millions	Amount	Debt/EBITDA
Senior Secured Term Loan	$7,250	3.0x
Subsidiary Guaranteed Debt	6,775	2.8
Unsecured Senior Notes	2,651	1.1
Unsecured Senior Subordinated Notes	663	0.3
Other Secured Borrowings	6.539	2.7
Other Unsecured Borrowings	31	0.0
Net Leverage	$23,908	9.8x

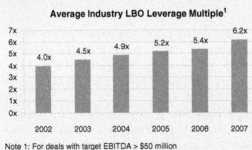

Average Industry LBO Leverage Multiple[1]

Note 1: For deals with target EBITDA > $50 million
Source: S&P's Leveraged Lending Review; company filings

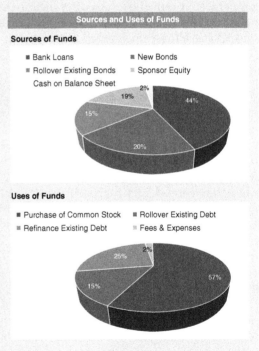

Sources and Uses of Funds

Sources of Funds

- Bank Loans
- New Bonds
- Rollover Existing Bonds
- Sponsor Equity
- Cash on Balance Sheet

Uses of Funds

- Purchase of Common Stock
- Rollover Existing Debt
- Refinance Existing Debt
- Fees & Expenses

Harrah's Entertainment Postmortem

In November 2010, the company canceled plans for a proposed IPO, but changed its name to Caesars Entertainment Corp. In February 2012, the company raised $16.3 million in a small IPO of about 1.4% of its shares. However, during 2000–14, the parent company had posted significant losses each year, and its total liabilities had climbed to $28.2 billion. This led, during November

2014, to a filing for bankruptcy protection and an approach to senior creditors about a plan to convert Caesars into a real estate investment trust largely owned by the creditors, leaving it to a judge to settle a bitter dispute among the company's creditors and the investment firms.

Freescale Semiconductor

Freescale Semiconductor (Freescale) was formed in 2004 when Motorola spun off its semiconductor products division. The company manufactures chips for wireless, networking, and automotive sectors. During September 2006, Blackstone led a consortium bid at $38 per share for Freescale, a 24% premium to the company's preannouncement share price. Another consortium led by KKR quickly topped this by offering $42. Nevertheless, Blackstone's group (including Carlyle, TPG, and Permira) eventually won the bidding in November 2006 with a $40 price, and a total consideration of $17.6 billion (see Exhibit 18.16). A "go-shop" provision allowed the company to solicit other proposals for 50 days, subject to a $300 million breakup fee, but no one else stepped up with a higher price. Leverage, at 5.7× EBITDA, was very high for a technology company acquisition, given the unpredictable cash flow represented by this company (and industry). $3.5 billion of this leverage included "covenant-lite" and "PIK toggle" features. See Exhibit 18.17 for a summary of leverage and sources and uses. This investment became problematic for the buyers: orders from Motorola, the principal customer, dropped significantly; the company's credit ratings were cut; and the pricing of both outstanding loans and bonds fell sharply in the secondary market. The buyers were forced to renegotiate with debt providers, entering into a debt exchange offer that reduced outstanding debt and extended maturities in exchange for higher interest rates and a more senior position in the capital structure.

EXHIBIT 18.16 FREESCALE SEMICONDUCTOR: BUYOUT GROUP COMPETITORS

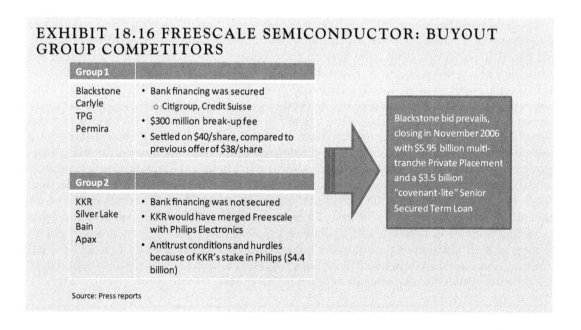

Group 1

Blackstone
Carlyle
TPG
Permira

- Bank financing was secured
  - Citigroup, Credit Suisse
- $300 million break-up fee
- Settled on $40/share, compared to previous offer of $38/share

Group 2

KKR
Silver Lake
Bain
Apax

- Bank financing was not secured
- KKR would have merged Freescale with Philips Electronics
- Antitrust conditions and hurdles because of KKR's stake in Philips ($4.4 billion)

Blackstone bid prevails, closing in November 2006 with $5.95 billion multi-tranche Private Placement and a $3.5 billion "covenant-lite" Senior Secured Term Loan

Source: Press reports

EXHIBIT 18.17 FREESCALE SEMICONDUCTOR: SOURCES AND USES AND LEVERAGE ANALYSIS

Sources and Uses ($ in millions)

Sources		Uses	
Cash on B/S	2,365	Purchase of Common Stock	16,534
Senior Term Loan	3,500	Total Rights/Warrants/Options	675
Private Placement	5,950	Assumed Net Liabilties	1,523
Sponsor Equity	7,150	Other	233
Total	18,965	Total	18,965

EBITDA LTM July 2006:	$ 1,559
Implied EV	$ 15,122
Implied EV/EBITDA	9.7x
Implied EV/Revenues	2.4x

Leverage Analysis ($ in millions)

	Amount	Debt/EBITDA (cumulative)
$3.5b Senior Secured Term Loan	$ 3,500	2.2x
$2.35b Senior Unsecured Notes	2,350	3.8x
$1.6b Senior Subordinated Notes	1,600	4.8x
$1.5 PIK Notes	1,500	5.7x
$0.5m Floating Rate Notes	500	6.1x
Total	9,450	6.1x
Remaining cash on B/S	635	
Net Leverage	$ 8,815	5.7x

Source: Press reports; Capital IQ

Freescale Semiconductor Postmortem

Freescale Semiconductor's $17.6 billion 2006 leveraged buyout won't go down as one of the private equity industry's better deals after the highly indebted semiconductor company fell into distress during 2008. However, this investment was ultimately not a disaster for Freescale's four private equity owners: Blackstone, The Carlyle Group, Permira Funds, and TPG Capital. NXP Semiconductors purchased Freescale in December 2015, paying $11.8 billion in a cash and stock transaction. For Freescale's private equity owners, which collectively owned 66% of the company's shares, the transaction apparently resulted in breaking-even on a deal that once looked like a major mistake. Because a majority of the Freescale acquisition was paid for in NXP stock, the combined company's ability to achieve operational synergies and find new markets will ultimately determine whether the investment is profitable for the private equity firms. Freescale raised nearly $1 billion in a 2011 initial public offering; however, the vast majority of IPO proceeds were used to pay down Freescale debt instead of cashing out shareholders. At the time, Freescale was losing $1 billion a year and had debts exceeding $7.5 billion. Between 2011 and the end of 2014, Freescale's private owners held on to most of their position as the company turned from steep annual losses to a $367 million profit and continued repaying debt. Following the IPO, Freescale's share price increased over 111%, nearly double the performance of the S&P 500 index.

Univision

Univision is a Spanish language television, radio, music, and Internet company. The company was acquired by a consortium comprised of Madison Dearborn Partners, Provident Equity, Saban Capital Group, Texas Pacific Group, and Thomas H. Lee Partners for a total consideration of $13.6 billion. Leading up to the acquisition, Univision's EBITDA margin had grown from 34% to 38.5%, leverage had dropped to a debt to assets ratio of 16%, their television network was the most-watched Spanish language network and their radio stations were in the top 5 in the 16 markets they competed in. The bidding process to acquire Univision started during February 2006, when the board announced their interest in considering alternatives to enhance shareholder value. A broad auction ensued that pitted a range of both financial buyers and strategic buyers. Ultimately, five parties qualified to submit bids, including three private equity consortiums, leading to closure during March 2007 (see Exhibit 18.18). A valuation analysis for the transaction is found in Exhibit 18.19 and a sources and uses analysis is found in Exhibit 18.20. This transaction included covenant-lite debt and a PIK toggle feature. A key criticism of the transaction is that projected EBITDA of $863 million was barely enough to cover combined annual interest costs plus capital expenditures.

EXHIBIT 18.18 UNIVISION: TIMELINE

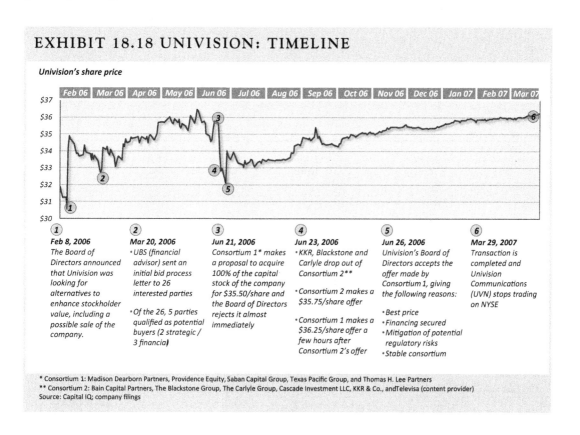

Univision's share price

1	**Feb 8, 2006** — The Board of Directors announced that Univision was looking for alternatives to enhance stockholder value, including a possible sale of the company.
2	**Mar 20, 2006** — • UBS (financial advisor) sent an initial bid process letter to 26 interested parties • Of the 26, 5 parties qualified as potential buyers (2 strategic / 3 financial)
3	**Jun 21, 2006** — Consortium 1* makes a proposal to acquire 100% of the capital stock of the company for $35.50/share and the Board of Directors rejects it almost immediately
4	**Jun 23, 2006** — • KKR, Blackstone and Carlyle drop out of Consortium 2** • Consortium 2 makes a $35.75/share offer • Consortium 1 makes a $36.25/share offer a few hours after Consortium 2's offer
5	**Jun 26, 2006** — Univision's Board of Directors accepts the offer made by Consortium 1, giving the following reasons: • Best price • Financing secured • Mitigation of potential regulatory risks • Stable consortium
6	**Mar 29, 2007** — Transaction is completed and Univision Communications (UVN) stops trading on NYSE

* Consortium 1: Madison Dearborn Partners, Providence Equity, Saban Capital Group, Texas Pacific Group, and Thomas H. Lee Partners
** Consortium 2: Bain Capital Partners, The Blackstone Group, The Carlyle Group, Cascade Investment LLC, KKR & Co., and Televisa (content provider)
Source: Capital IQ; company filings

EXHIBIT 18.19 UNIVISION: TRANSACTION VALUES OVERVIEW ($ IN MILLIONS)

Enterprise Value and Leverage Summary

	Amount	Multiple of LTM EBITDA
Transaction Proceeds (excl. fees)	$12,397	
Approximate Existing Debt	970	
Remaining Cash on Balance Sheet	104	
Enterprise Value	$13,470	19.4x
Transaction Fees	144	
Total Transaction Value	**$13,614**	**19.6x**
LTM EBITDA	$694	

Trading Multiples				Premium Analysis (@ $36.25)		
Total Enterprise Value /					Price	Premium
Comparables	**LTM EBITDA (x)**	**2006E EBITDA(x)**	**2007E EBITDA (x)**	**Strategic Announcement (February 8, 2006)**		
High	14.0x	13.1x	12.2x	One-day prior	$30.54	18.7%
Low	8.2x	7.7x	7.5x	30-day average	$31.36	15.6%
Median	10.8x	10.0x	11.0x			
Univision				**Transaction Announcement (June 26, 2006)**		
Pre-Announcement				One-day prior	$32.95	10.0%
Price	18.0x	14.8x	13.1x	One-week prior	$35.70	1.5%
Univision at $36.25				One-month prior	$36.09	0.4%
Offer	**19.4x**	**16.7x**	**15.1x**	30-day average	$35.23	2.9%

Source: Company filings

EXHIBIT 18.20 UNIVISION: TRANSACTION SOURCES AND USES AND LEVERAGE ANALYSIS

Sources & Uses
($ in millions)

Sources		Uses	
Cash on Balance Sheet	$103.5	Purchase of Common Stock	$11,247
Senior Secured Term Loan Facility	7,000	Purchase of Stock Options	130
Senior Notes	1,500	Purchase of all Warrants	994
Second Lien-Asset Sale Bridge	500	Restricted Stock	26
Sponsor Equity (Approx)	3,437	Merger Related Expenses	144
Total	**$12,541**		**$12,541**

Merger Related Expenses

Share-based compensation expense	$46
Change in control payments to employees	$42
Advisory success fee	$33
Legal fees	$16
Other non-compensation expenses	$4
Other compensation expenses	$3
Total	**$144**

Leverage Analysis

			Cumul. Multiple	
Bank revolving credit facility	$0	(up to $750)	0.0x	
Bank senior secured term loan facility	7,000.0		10.1x	
Bank second-lien asset sale bridge loan	500.0		10.8x	
Senior notes – 9.75%/10.50% due 2015	1,500.0	(with PIK interest)	13.0x	
Senior notes – 7.85% due 2011	525.3		13.7x	Portion of "old" debt
Senior notes – 3.875% due 2008	246.1		14.1x	
Senior notes – 3.5% due 2007	198.4		14.4x	
Total	$9,970		14.4x	
Remaining Cash on Balance Sheet	(104)		-0.1x	
Net Leverage	$9,866		14.2x	

Source: Company filings

Univision Postmortem

The $13.7 billion leveraged buyout of Univision in 2006 came with one of the highest EBITDA/Debt ratios of any of the highly leveraged precrisis large buyout transactions. Even though Univision's specialty in the fast-growing Spanish language market protected it from the worst of the advertising downturn, the company suffered during and following the economic crisis. That opened the door for Televisa, the Mexican media group that lost out to the private equity buyers in their original 2006 bid to buy Univision. During October 2010, Televisa paid $1.2 billion for an initial 5% stake in Univision by taking 15-year Univision debt with a 1.5% coupon that can be converted into an additional 30% equity stake and an option to buy 5% more. The investment valued the company's equity at $2.3 billion. The Mexican group also secured a new programming agreement designed to bring in an extra $50 million of royalties in the first year and considerably more in future years. Locking in Televisa and more of its content should accelerate the ultimate break even for this 2006 investment and may yet produce a profit. Part of Televisa's investment was used to pay down debt to reduce leverage to about 10 times EBITDA. During January 2016, Univision filed a preliminary prospectus for a potential IPO, with shares to be listed on the New York Stock Exchange under the symbol "UVN." Investors, including Thomas H. Lee Partners, Providence Equity Partners, Madison Dearborn Partners, TPG Capital, and Saban Capital Group are hoping for a valuation of at least $20 billion. The prospectus indicated that Univision is "the leading media company serving Hispanic America" and listed as some of its primary assets 59 TV stations in Los Angeles, Miami, New York, and elsewhere, as well as 11 cable brands, Univision broadcasting, 67 radio stations, and several websites. As of mid-2017 the IPO had not yet been launched.

PRIVATE EQUITY VALUE PROPOSITION FOR CORPORATIONS

There are three main areas where private equity investments may bring value to corporations:

- Financial engineering
- Operational engineering
- Governance engineering

Financial engineering refers to efforts to add value by improving a company's capital structure. Improvement means making the capital structure more efficient by reducing the cost of capital. This is achieved by adding leverage from new outside sources.

Operational engineering refers to efforts by private equity firms to improve their portfolio companies through formal and informal consulting services. This consulting may help improve production processes, marketing and product mix decisions, and, ultimately, increase working capital and cash flow.

Governance engineering refers to initiatives by private equity firms to create value in portfolio companies by improving incentives and creating monitoring processes that focus on improvements in cash flow through cost reductions and increases in revenues. Many other areas are monitored as well to determine results against expectations. Managers are directly compensated based on performance in achieving targeted results.

Some portfolio companies respond well to these three forms of engineering, creating significantly more value for a private equity firm than they had previously produced as a public company with a distributed shareholder ownership model. Other portfolio companies have done poorly, unable to operate well with higher leverage, and not able to respond well to the operational and governance models imposed on them by private equity owners.

CORPORATE RATIONALE FOR COMPLETING PRIVATE EQUITY TRANSACTIONS

Companies that have strong cash flow, leverageable balance sheets, low capital expenditures, high-quality assets, and the ability to raise cash through asset sales are good targets for private equity firms. Sometimes, these companies sell to private equity firms simply because their senior management and board can obtain a very high sale premium, and they determine that this is the best way to maximize shareholder value. Examples of additional reasons that companies might consider a sale to a private equity firm are as follows:

Alternative to an Initial Public Offering

Private companies that need new capital to facilitate growth opportunities may consider an IPO, which would result in the sale of 15%–30% of the company. Family-owned companies that have no succession plan when a founder is ready for retirement may also consider an IPO. An alternative to an IPO is a sale to a private equity fund if the owners want a larger reduction in their exposure to the company beyond 30%. A sale to a PE firm would typically result in a reduction in ownership by more than 50%, giving a control position to the PE firm.

Corporate Orphans

Some companies operate multiple business units under a holding company ownership structure. Normally, all of these business units have activities that are somewhat related and benefit from common ownership. However, sometimes, business activities change or markets change and one business unit might not be as related or synergistic with other business units. In this case, a holding company might consider the sale of the "orphan" business. Private equity firms are sometimes the best buyers of an orphan business because they (1) avoid potential antitrust concerns that may arise in a sale to a strategic buyer and (2) minimize disclosure concerns.

Ignored Public Companies

Equity research is a somewhat scarce resource since it is expensive to provide and a series of regulatory changes in the United States during 2003 resulted in more limited coverage of public companies. As a result of the lack of equity analyst coverage, some public companies' shares are not actively purchased by large institutional investors. As a result, their stock price may be negatively impacted. This can happen to an entire industry as well if the industry has suffered a major upheaval. For companies suffering from a sustained weakness in share price that is caused, in part, by limited research coverage and uninformed investors, a private equity buyer might be able to pay a significant premium to the company's current share price if the company has strong cash flow, a leverageable balance sheet, and the other characteristics of a good target, as described above.

Operating or Financial Weakness

If a company has operating weakness in sourcing, distribution, or other operating processes, a private equity firm may be able to bring in new resources to fix these problems. Private equity firms can also significantly bolster a company's access to new sources of financing.

Mandated Divestitures

Sometimes a regulator requires the sale of a business unit as part of an M&A transaction to resolve a restraint of trade concern. The required sale is designed to mitigate concerns that regulators such as the Federal Trade Commission have in relation to their antitrust oversight responsibilities. A private equity firm is frequently the preferred buyer, compared to another company in the same industry, because a strategic buyer might create the same restraint of trade concern that gave rise to the original regulator-mandated sale order.

PRIVATE EQUITY AS AN ALTERNATIVE MODEL OF CORPORATE GOVERNANCE

The two historical models of corporate ownership are (1) dispersed public ownership across many shareholders and (2) family-owned or closely held. Private equity ownership is a hybrid between these two models.

The main advantages of public ownership include giving a company the widest possible access to capital, and, for start-up companies, more credibility with suppliers, customers, and banks. The key disadvantages are that a public listing of stock brings constant scrutiny by regulators and the media, incurs significant costs (listing, legal and—in the United States—Sarbanes–Oxley and other regulatory compliance costs), and a significant focus on short-term financial results from a dispersed base of shareholders (many of whom are not well informed). Furthermore, most investors in public companies have limited ability to influence a company's decision-making because ownership is so dispersed. As a result, if a company performs poorly, these investors are inclined to sell shares instead of attempting to engage with management through the infrequent opportunities to vote on important corporate decisions. This unengaged oversight opens the possibility of managers potentially acting in ways that are contrary to the interests of shareholders.

Family-owned or closely held companies avoid regulatory and public scrutiny. The owners also have a direct say in the governance of the company, minimizing potential conflicts of interest between owners and managers. However, the funding options for these private companies are mainly limited to bank loans and other private debt financing. Raising equity capital through the private placement market is a cumbersome process that often results in a poor outcome.

Private equity firms offer a hybrid model that is sometimes more advantageous for companies that are uncomfortable with both the family-owned/closely held and public ownership models (see Exhibit 18.21). Changes in corporate governance are generally a key driver of success for private equity investments. Private equity firms usually bring a fresh culture into corporate boards and often incentivize executives in a way that would usually not be possible in a public company. A private equity fund has a vital self-interest to improve management quality and firm performance because its investment track record is the key to raising new funds in the future. In large public companies there is often the possibility of "cross-subsidization" of less successful parts of a corporation, but this suboptimal behavior is usually not found in companies owned by private equity firms. As a result, private equity–owned companies are more likely to expose and reconfigure or sell suboptimal business segments, compared to large public companies. Companies owned by private equity firms avoid public scrutiny and quarterly earnings pressures. Because private equity funds typically have an investment horizon that is longer than the typical mutual fund or other public investor, portfolio companies can focus on longer-term restructuring and investments. Private equity owners are fully enfranchised in all key management decisions because they appoint their partners as nonexecutive directors to the company's board and sometimes bring in their own managers to run the company. As a result, they have strong financial incentives to maximize shareholder value. Since the managers of the company are also required to invest in the company's equity alongside the private equity firm, they have similarly strong incentives to create long-term shareholder value. However, the significant leverage that is brought into a private equity portfolio company's capital structure puts pressure on management to operate virtually error free. As a result, if major, unanticipated dislocations occur in the market, there is a higher probability of bankruptcy compared to either the family-owned/closely held or public company model which includes less leverage. While it is generally agreed that debt has a disciplining effect on management and keeps them from "empire building," it does not improve the competitive position of a firm and is often not sustainable. Limited partners demand more from private equity managers than merely buying companies based on the use of leverage. In particular, investors expect private equity managers to take an active role in corporate governance to create incremental value.

EXHIBIT 18.21 PRIVATE EQUITY IS AN ALTERNATIVE TO CLASSIC PRIVATE AND PUBLIC GOVERNANCE MODELS

	Family-owned or closely held	Private Equity	Publicly listed company
	Range of governance models		
Ownership structure	•Single owner or family group	•Private equity fund bundles equity from private investors to speak with one voice	•Many dispersed shareholders, both institutional and retail
Corporate governance	•Controlled and led by founder/owner. May have outside voice on board or management by invitation only	•Direct private equity fund representation on board with significant financial incentives for shareholder value	•Shareholders have weak financial incentives and usually weak voice in management
Capital structure	•Debt tolerance depends on owner – usually low	•High debt-equity ratio	•Low debt-equity ratio
Fund-raising	•Fund-raising through private debt and bank loans	•Fund-raising through private investors, public debt and bank loans	•Fund-raising through public debt and equity markets, bank loans

Source: Farrell, Diana, et al. "The New Power Brokers: How Oil, Asia, Hedge Funds and Private Equity Are Shaping the Global Capital Markets." McKinsey Global Institute October 2007.

PRIVATE EQUITY INFLUENCE ON COMPANIES

In addition to impacting the companies that they purchase, private equity firms also influence other companies' managers and boards, as well as the broader capital markets (see Exhibit 18.22).

Pressure on Corporate Performance

Private equity funds create competitive pressures on companies that want to avoid being acquired. CEOs and boards of public companies have been forced to review their performance and take steps to improve. In addition, they have focused more on anti–takeover strategies. Many companies have initiated large share repurchase programs as a vehicle for increasing earnings per share (sometimes using new debt to finance repurchases). This effort is designed, in part, to make a potential takeover more expensive, and therefore less likely, as well as to increase shareholder value.

Changing Capital Structure

Companies consider adding debt to their balance sheet to reduce the overall cost of capital and achieve higher returns on equity. This strategy is sometimes pursued as a direct response to the potential for a private equity takeover. However, increasing leverage runs the risk of lower credit ratings on debt, which increases the cost of debt capital and reduces the margin for error. Although some managers are able to manage a more leveraged balance sheet, others are ill equipped.

Mergers and Acquisitions

Companies have historically been purchased principally by other companies in their same industry since these companies can find synergies through the acquisition, thereby justifying a large premium to the preannouncement share price of the target company. However, with the availability of low-cost debt financing to private equity firms through mid-2007, a large number of M&A auctions were won by private equity firms, in spite of the fact that they usually could not match the synergy-based rationale for a high purchase price. Instead, private equity firms were competitive, in part, because they included a highly leveraged capital structure assumption in their valuation analysis to justify a high purchase price offer. As shown in Exhibit 18.22, over 19.3% of all M&A transactions completed during 2007 involved a private equity firm. As the access to credit became more difficult following the financial crisis, financial sponsors M&A activity declined to a low of 6.5% in 2009. In the years 2010 and 2011, financial sponsor M&A activity rebounded strongly, but did not reach precrisis levels. In subsequent years, private equity–related M&A transactions have stabilized at about one out of every seven deals.

EXHIBIT 18.22 WORLDWIDE BUYSIDE FINANCIAL SPONSOR ACTIVITY

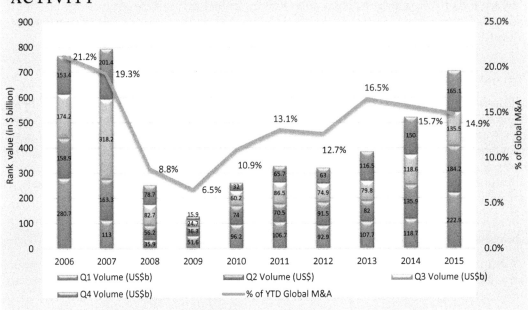

19

Organization, Compensation, Regulation, and Limited Partners

OUTLINE

ORGANIZATIONAL STRUCTURE

A private equity fund is usually structured as a limited partnership that is owned jointly by a private equity firm (General Partner (GP)) and other investors such as pension funds, insurance companies, high net-worth individuals, family offices, endowments, foundations, fund of funds, and sovereign wealth funds (all of which are Limited Partners (LPs)). The GP manages and controls the private equity fund (see Exhibit 19.1).

Private equity investments are often channeled through a new company (NewCo) that receives equity investments from a private equity fund and (usually) management of the target company. NewCo also obtains debt financing from lenders. The proceeds of the debt and equity capital received by NewCo are then used to acquire the target company (see Exhibit 19.2).

The organizational structure of the private equity fund is developed with a view to maximizing incentive compensation for the GP. In this regard, tax considerations are

EXHIBIT 19.1 OWNERSHIP OF A PRIVATE EQUITY FUND

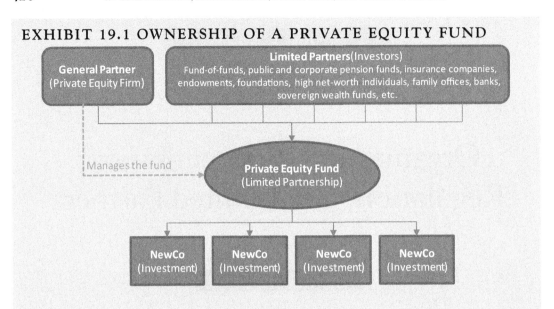

EXHIBIT 19.2 NEWCO FUNDING AND INVESTING

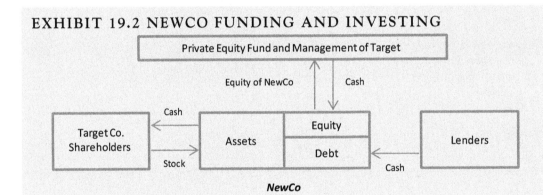

- Target company shareholders sell shares (or assets of target) for cash,
  - Potential for some shareholders to "rollover" and participate in upside,
- Cash paid by NewCo is funded by lenders and private equity fund (and management investments),
  - Cash flow from NewCo/Target Company is used to service debt payments.

Source: Training the Street, Inc.

paramount. The GP earns compensation based on their management of the fund (receiving management fees that usually equal about 2% of the assets under management (AUM) and an interest in the profits of the investment activity, referred to as "carried interest"). Management fees normally require GPs to pay taxes at higher ordinary income tax rates, whereas carried interest is normally considered for tax purposes as an allocation of a portion of the partnership's profits, which allows lower capital gains tax treatment. In the United States, there are periodic attempts to change the tax treatment for carried interest so that it will be taxed at the higher ordinary income tax rate. However, so far, the tax code has not been changed to affect the higher taxes. What has changed, however, is the practice by some firms to reposition management fees by reinvesting these fees in their own funds. During 2015, the IRS proposed changes to the practice by private equity firms to reduce their tax obligations by reclassifying how their management fees are taxed. The proposal would make it harder for firms to convert high-taxed fees into lower-taxed carried interest and by doing so take advantage of a 19.6 percentage-point difference in top tax rates between ordinary income taxes at 39.6% and capital gains taxes at 20%. By obtaining management fee waivers from LPs, some firms have been able to disguise payments for services (which is what management fees are for) by creating investment risk through capital pledges that insert the fees into existing investment funds. Historically, private equity executives sometimes swapped their management fees into additional investments in their funds as a way to satisfy capital pledges they had made to LPs. This practice converted ordinary income taxes that the executives would have paid on income from fees to lower capital gains taxes. Bain Capital and Apollo Global Management, among others, used to offer waivers to its partners, but then discontinued this practice in the face of criticism by others and proposed actions by the IRS.

As discussed in previous chapters, the average carried interest is about 20% of profits. However, GPs and LPs must negotiate how the carried interest will be applied. For example, in the United States a private equity fund is normally required to maintain capital accounts in accordance with the accounting method used by the tax partnership for federal income tax purposes, where each partner has its own capital account. Conceptually, the capital accounts of all partners combined correspond to the consolidated stockholders' equity account in a corporate balance sheet.

The capital account of each partner is credited with the amount of any capital contributions by that partner and increased by the amount of net income of the partnership allocated to that partner. Equally, each partner's capital account is decreased whenever distributions are made to partners. In the event of a net loss from any investment, each partner receives an appropriate loss allocation. All net income and net loss must be allocated since the partnership is not itself a taxpayer. The net worth of a partnership is, in effect, the sum of the interests of all partners.

Closed-End Funds

Most private equity funds are "closed-end" funds, meaning that LPs commit to provide cash for investments in companies and pay for certain fees and expenses, but they cannot withdraw their funds until the fund is terminated. This compares with mutual funds where investors can withdraw their money any time. The GP in a private equity fund usually commits at least 1% (sometimes substantially more) of the total capital, and the balance is committed by LPs. These funds are normally invested over a 4- to 5-year period, and then there is a 5- to 8-year period during which the fund will exit investments and return capital and profits to all partners.

During the period of time that capital is invested, LPs have very limited influence on how the capital is spent as long as the fund adheres to the basic covenants of the fund agreement. Some of these covenants relate to restrictions on how much capital can be invested in any one company and the types of securities in which the fund can invest. In addition to management fees and carried interest, the GP sometimes receives deal and monitoring fees from portfolio companies in which the fund has invested. Some LPs have objected to this arrangement and insist on applying deal and monitoring fees to reduce the management fees or splitting such fees 50/50 or 80/20 with the GP.

Exits

Private equity firms consider alternative exit strategies at the end of the investment holding period, including an IPO, sale to a strategic buyer, sale to a leveraged buyouts (LBO)-backed company, sale to another private equity fund, recapitalization, or sale to management. In addition to these exit strategies, an eventual disposition of the company may be a bankruptcy or other unanticipated outcome.

Exhibit 19.3 shows the exit characteristics of LBO over time. Based on this Exhibit, the most common exit during 2014 was a trade sale to a strategic buyer (50%), followed by sale to another private equity fund in a sponsor-to-sponsor or restructure transaction (33%) and then an IPO (17%).

EXHIBIT 19.3 LEVERAGED BUYOUTS EXIT ALTERNATIVES

	IPO	Sponsor-to-Sponsor/Restructure	Trade Sale	Total Value of Exits ($ Bil.)	Number of Exits
2006	17%	31%	52%	177	955
2007	15%	33%	52%	294	1,215
2008	7%	35%	58%	129	813
2009	17%	33%	50%	91	655
2010	19%	31%	50%	240	1,126
2011	15%	32%	53%	326	1,376
2012	14%	31%	55%	301	1,435
2013	19%	29%	52%	330	1,550
2014	17%	33%	50%	428	1,604

Source: Private Equity Exits in Global Growth Markets Josh Lerner, Andrew Speen, Chris Allen, and Ann Leamon.

COMPENSATION

There are four types of fees and expenses in a typical private equity agreement between GPs and LPs:

1. Management Fee: Usually 2% of total capital commitments until the end of a 4- to 5-year investment horizon, and then 2% of unreturned funded capital thereafter (declining as investments are sold or realized). This fee is payable semiannually in advance. In addition, LPs bear all organizational expenses incurred in the formation of the fund (often subject to a cap).

2. Carried Interest: This is an incentive payment that will be paid only after a certain rate of return is obtained by LPs (see Preferred Returns below). The purpose of this payment is to create an approximate 80/20 split in profits above the return of capital plus Preferred Returns between LPs and GPs (subject to a clawback, as described below). For GPs to receive carried interest, private equity funds must sell their portfolio companies, realizing gains at the time of sale. Alternatively, carried interest may be paid following interim dividends, distributions, partial sales, or recapitalizations before an ultimate sale. Profits or losses are generally recognized at the time of any of these corporate events.

3. Portfolio Company Fees and Expenses: These fees and expenses are paid directly by portfolio companies to the private equity firm. Potential fees and expenses include (1) transaction fees when purchasing and (sometimes) when selling companies; (2) expenses related to proposed but unconsummated investments; (3) tax and accounting, litigation, general legal and annual meeting expenses; (4) advisory and monitoring fees; and (5) director fees.

4. Additional Costs: In some cases, a number of additional costs can be imposed. For example, cash proceeds from the sale of a portfolio company can be retained by the GP for up to 3 months before being distributed to LPs. In addition, distributions of marketable securities can be in kind (including selling restrictions), rather than making a cash distribution, which can create extra costs for LPs. Finally, LPs may have to pay penalties for selling their stakes or for defaults on a capital call.

The payment of fees in the context of unrealized losses in portfolio companies has become an increasingly important issue for the industry. Another issue relates to whether management fees should be included as an expense for purposes of calculating profits that are subject to carried interest. LPs have pressed to include these fees as an expense since they are evaluated by their investors based on a cash out/cash in basis. There is now strong precedent for including management fees as an expense, although this is the subject of ongoing negotiations for some private equity firms.

Preferred Returns

Most compensation arrangements include preferred returns, which must be paid to LPs (after return of capital) before carried interest is paid to GPs. Since LPs invest in private equity funds based on an expectation of higher returns and acceptance of higher risk, a preferred return helps to align interests between all partners by linking carried interest to superior returns.

Carried interest is usually subordinated to a preferred return of 5%–10% payable annually to LPs. A GP catch-up provision can eliminate the negative consequences of a preferred return carve-out for LPs if investment returns are high enough. For example, if there is a preferred return of 8%, 100% of profits (after investor capital is returned) are allocated to LPs until they have received a preferred return of 8% per annum, and then 100% of profits are allocated to the GP until 20% of cumulative profits are received, with the remaining profits (if any) allocated 80% to LPs and 20% to the GP.

Timing Issues

The determination of carried interest and preferred returns is impacted by timing considerations. A private equity fund will normally make a number of different portfolio company investments over a 3- to 5-year investment horizon. Holding periods for each of these investments can vary dramatically, but generally they are for periods of 3- to 7-years. Compensation determination for both carried interest and preferred returns depends on how and when a fund calculates profits. For example, this determination can be made based on the sales date for portfolio companies, or alternatively, based on an averaging or netting process that allows earlier compensation allocations.

Most private equity funds apply an "aggregation" process by netting gains and losses from different portfolio investments as a mechanism to maintain GP focus on all investments in their portfolio (see Clawbacks section). A transaction-by-transaction approach to calculating carried interest is flawed from an alignment of interest perspective. It can create a bias in favor of higher risk and potentially higher return investments. Although the GP will lose its share of capital for a bad investment, since it is compensated at 20% of profits above the preferred return, it might reach for higher return investments (that carry correspondingly higher risk). By aggregating all gains and losses, there is less of an incentive for a GP to make individual portfolio investments that bear disproportionate risk.

A fund must establish in advance whether the preferred return distribution waterfall (in which investor capital is returned first, then any recognized losses, followed by preferred returns and then carried interest) is based on the entire capital commitment from LPs, or only on the percentage of capital that was initially allocated to the portfolio company being sold. Normally, the preferred return is based on the portion of capital initially allocated to fund each investment. This enables a larger carried interest payment to the GP and mitigates the possibility that the GP will alter the optimal timing for sale of a portfolio company.

LPs do not know that their investment will be profitable until their original capital commitment has been recovered. In addition, the exact amount of profit from their investment is not known until the fund is liquidated and wound up. Although the uncertainty associated with interim determinations of a fund's profitability could be reduced by restricting carried interest distributions until after LP capital commitments are fully recovered, almost all private equity funds provide for carried interest payments to GPs coincident with successful portfolio company exits. LPs, therefore, implicitly assume that all remaining unrealized investments will generate proceeds at least equal to their carrying value.

Clawbacks

Most funds have contractual provisions governing allocations and distributions of carried interest before 100% of LP capital commitments have been recovered. Based on this, initial investment gains that result in payment of carried interest to GPs, when followed by investment losses, result in LPs having the ability to recapture some of the carried interest paid. It is not uncommon for a fund to record significant profits during early years, as successful investments are exited, leaving less successful investments to be exited in the later years of a fund. In other words, successful portfolio companies are often sold fairly quickly, while troubled companies usually need time to be fixed before they can be sold. Moreover, when they are sold, the fix often does not restore full value, resulting in capital losses.

A clawback is a contractual provision that adjusts distortions in compensation to GPs based on the timing of gains and losses. Normally, clawback provisions are effective at the time of liquidation and winding up of a fund. Depending on the carried interest formula and the cumulative performance of the fund, the GP may be obligated to return a portion of prior distributions of carried interest. Amounts returned are then distributed to LPs. This mitigates LP risk in terms of sharing early profits, and the risk that a GP might suboptimally sell portfolio companies early in an effort to accelerate earnings.

Usually GPs limit the clawback to after-tax portions of prior distributions of carried interest, because they do not want to return a cash portion that they never received. In practice, the clawback provision usually refers to a hypothetical tax rate, rather than the actual tax paid by the principals who operate the GP, because of different tax determinations that may apply to each principal. Even more important than tax considerations is the triggering event for the clawback. In many cases, the triggering event relates to a circumstance in which the GP receives more than 20% of profits, or if LPs do not receive return of capital plus the full preferred return over the life of the fund.

Since carried interest and other distributions to the GP are normally immediately redistributed to principals of the GP, if a clawback obligation is triggered at the end of the underlying fund, the GP probably will not have sufficient cash to pay the clawback. As a result, LPs often require principals of the GP to guarantee (often on a joint and several basis) the clawback obligations of the GP. Alternatively, sometimes LPs require a portion of carried interest payments to be held as escrow by the GP to satisfy the clawback.

Taxes

Historically, carried interest has been taxed based on the long-term capital gains rate of 20%, rather than the ordinary income tax of up to 39.6% or the corporate capital gains tax rate of 35%. It appears unfair to many that a private equity fund that operates as a partnership is allowed to pay a tax rate that is 15% less than the tax rate that public corporations pay for capital gains. Equally unfair to some is the fact that principals of private equity funds receive compensation through carried interest that is taxed at 19.6% less than the rate that applies to the compensation packages of employees of traditional asset management funds who receive salary and bonus-based compensation, rather than carried interest (assuming they pay the highest marginal tax rate). Although there are efficiency arguments against increasing taxes on managers of private equity funds (it would decrease the number of participants causing less competition and change manager behavior resulting in inefficient allocation of resources), the arguments favoring a more egalitarian tax structure (that are based on the rationale that GPs of a private equity fund are compensated for labor rather than for investing and should, therefore, be taxed accordingly) may someday result in higher taxes for GP principals. However, the tax rates have not yet been changed for carried interest.

REGULATIONS

Historically, in the United States, the SEC has generally not imposed registration requirements on managers of private equity funds because most managers of private equity funds manage 14 or less funds, and therefore, qualify for exemption from registration under the Investment Advisers Act of 1940.

However, the Dodd–Frank Act eliminates these exemptions to a large degree. Under this new regulation, all fund managers who advise funds with more than $150 million AUM or more than $100 million AUM in separate accounts must register with the SEC. Moreover, fund managers who manage less than $100 million and are operating in states without registration requirements must register with the SEC if they manage more than $25 million. In addition, the record-keeping and reporting requirements have been increased significantly. Fund advisers must, among other items, submit reports on the following: amount and types of AUM, use of leverage, counterparty risk exposure, trading and investment positions, valuation policies and practices, side arrangements, and trading practices.

Private equity funds and their managers historically have relied on several key exemptions from the Investment Company Act and the Investment Advisers Act:

1. Investment Company Act: Funds did not need to register with the SEC based on exemptions contained in either Section 3(c)(1) (for funds held exclusively by no more than 100 beneficial owners and that are not offered publicly) or 3(c)(7) (for funds held exclusively by "qualified purchasers" and that are not offered publicly).
2. Investment Advisers Act: Fund managers did not need to register with the SEC as an investment advisor based on exemptions contained in Section 203(b)(3). Under this exemption, private advisors do not need to register with the SEC if they have less than 15 clients (in the case of private equity, less 15 funds), do not advise registered investment companies, and do not hold themselves out to the public as investment advisors.

The Dodd–Frank Act replaced these exemptions, making it clear that, for the purposes of the Investment Company Act, a private equity fund is an "investment company," and a private equity manager is an "investment advisor." However, the Dodd–Frank Act does not subject private equity funds to the full regulatory provisions that apply to public mutual funds.

Perception and Reality

Although there are fewer regulations imposed in the United States on private equity funds compared to mutual funds, private equity funds and fund managers must comply with a number of regulations under federal law, including the following:

1. **Annual Privacy Notices**. Private equity funds are required to have and comply with a privacy policy and send a privacy notice to all LPs who are individuals at the start of the partner's relationship with the fund and annually thereafter. The privacy notice must describe the fund's policy regarding disclosure of current and former LPs' nonpublic information.

2. **Supplemental Filings Pursuant to the Investment Advisers Act of 1940**. All registered investment advisors must file with the SEC certain amendments on an annual basis and offer to provide a brochure with designated information to LPs on an annual basis.

3. **Filings Pursuant to the Securities Exchange Act of 1934**. Filings of Form 13D, Schedule 13G, and Form 4 following certain purchases and sales of securities must be made. In addition, filings may need to be made periodically with the SEC depending on circumstances, including Form 5 (directors, officers, and 10% stockholders regarding beneficial ownership); Form 13F (for holdings of over $100 million of Section 13(f) securities); and Schedule 13G (beneficial owners of public company issuers who are exempt from filing requirements of 13D).

4. **ERISA-Related Filing**. For funds in which more than 25% of the investors are pension plans, annual certification must be given to avoid "plain assets" regulations under the Employee Retirement Income Security Act of 1974. In addition, annual audited, and sometimes quarterly unaudited, financial reports must be delivered to LPs.

5. **Private Placement Limitations**. US private equity funds are typically sold via private placement and must adhere to limitations on private placements imposed by the Securities Act of 1933. Funds can only offer investment opportunities to investors with whom the fund or its sponsor has a preexisting relationship and who are accredited investors (individuals with a minimum net worth of $1.0 million or, alternatively, a minimum income of $200,000 ($300,000 with spouse) in each of the previous 2 years and a reasonable expectation of reaching the same income level in the current year).

6. **Antifraud Rule**. The SEC's antifraud rule applies to registered and unregistered investment advisors. Pooled investment vehicles such as hedge funds and private equity funds are, among other restricted communications or practices, prohibited from making materially false or misleading statements regarding: investment strategies that will be pursued by the pooled investment vehicle, the experience and credentials of the advisor (and associated persons), the risks associated with investing in the pool, the performance of the pool (and other funds advised by the advisor), the valuation of the pool and corresponding investor accounts, and practices the advisor follows in the operation of its advisory business such as how investment opportunities are allocated.

7. **Investment Advisors Act of 1940**. Funds that do not meet the exemptions from the definition of an investment advisor must register as an investment advisor. Once registered, advisors are subject to regulatory reporting requirements; disclosure requirements to investors, creditors, and other counterparties; strong conflict of interest and antifraud prohibitions; robust SEC examination and enforcement authority and record-keeping requirements; and requirements for establishing a comprehensive compliance program.

8. **Investment Company Act of 1940**. As mentioned above, funds that do not meet the exemptions from the definition of an investment company must register as an investment company.

LIMITED PARTNERS

Defaults

When LPs fail to make a scheduled payment, private equity funds must consider how to cover the missed contributions, how to treat the LP, and how and whether to replace the unfunded commitment. Most partnership agreements permit the defaulted amount to be called from other LPs, but there are sometimes caps on the replacement amounts that can be called. Some agreements allow the partnership to borrow to cover the defaulted amount or to offset amounts distributable to cover the defaulted amount.

In the event of a default, the GP generally has sole discretion regarding what measures to take. In theory, the GP may be able to convince a court to require a LP to honor its capital contribution obligations. However, GPs have historically been reluctant to sue their investors based on the concern that this action would have a negative impact on future fund raising. Notwithstanding this aversion to sue, it is possible that under certain circumstances a GP may conclude that its duty to the other LPs requires it to take action to enforce the terms of the partnership agreement.

The GP has a fiduciary duty to all partners (unless waived in the partnership agreement), requiring it to consider what action is in the fund's best interest, including the precedent that their decision will have in future potential defaults, the impact on existing credit facilities (that may trigger acceleration of outstanding loans), the potential effect on D&O (directors and officers) insurance policies (including pricing), audited financial and other reporting obligations, and voting and representation on advisory committees.

Disclosure and Valuations

When private equity fund industry average returns turned negative during 2008 and 2009, many LPs asked for increased and more frequent disclosure. Instead of quarterly mark-to-market disclosure, some investors pushed for monthly disclosure so they could compare valuations with secondary market pricing and make more frequent risk management decisions. During 2016, many private equity funds embraced best practice standards in valuation, including a more consistent practice in the selection of comparables and multiples. However, some GPs resisted International Private Equity and Venture Capital (IPEV) Guidelines because of commercial sensitivities that prevented disclosure of their assumptions. It is clear that GPs will need to be increasingly willing to adopt IPEV Guidelines based on pressure from both LPs and regulators.

IPEV Guidelines require the following valuation process:

1. Determine Enterprise Value of the Investee Company using one or more of the following valuation methodologies: Market Approach, which includes Price of Recent Investment and Multiples; Income Approach, which is completed through a Discounted Cash Flow analysis; and Replacement Cost Approach, which considers Net Asset Value.
2. Adjust Enterprise Value based on factors that a market participant would consider such as surplus assets or excess liabilities to derive an Adjusted Enterprise Value for the Investee Company.

3. Deduct the value of financial instruments ranking ahead of the highest ranking instrument of the Fund in a sale of the Enterprise, including the effect of any instrument that may dilute the Fund's investment to derive the Attributable Enterprise Value.
4. Apportion the Attributable Enterprise Value between the Investee Company's relevant financial instruments according to their ranking.
5. Allocate the amounts derived according to the Fund's holding in each financial instrument, representing their Fair Value.

Fees

Many LPs have pushed for and obtained fee reductions over recent years, as the balance of power has shifted to investors. Some private equity firms have reduced management fees from 2% to 1.5% and performance fees from 20% to 15%, and some have agreed to more favorable clawback arrangements. Competition from secondary market buying opportunities, where some purchases could be made with up to 50% discounts, have forced many private equity firms to become more accommodative in relation to fees.

Secondary Market

A private equity secondary market enables LPs and new investors to buy and sell private equity investments or remaining unfunded commitments to funds. Private equity investments are intended to be long-term investments. However, sometimes LPs need to free up cash, or they become disillusioned with hypothetical losses and want to exit their investment. There is no listed public market for most private equity investments, but the secondary market that is facilitated by investment banks and others has grown substantially. This market creates a certain amount of liquidity to enable LPs to sell their interest in a private equity fund to another party. These sales also remove from the selling LP any remaining unfunded obligations to the fund. Normally, the GP must give consent to any sale (see Exhibit 19.4).

The secondary market has grown considerably (see Exhibit 19.5). Committed capital for secondary buyers exceeded $65 billion during 2016. There was an estimated $40 billion in private equity secondary trades during 2016, with an increasing percentage of these trades completed close to par. Secondary bid spreads declined from 2006 to 2009 but increased and stabilized during 2010 and 2011. During 2012–15, secondary bid spreads increased by more than 10% (see Exhibit 19.6).

During January 2009, Harvard University's endowment fund attempted to sell up to $1.5 billion of its private equity holdings through secondary market transactions, but the indicated pricing from prospective secondary buyers was not acceptable to the fund. Endowment funds from Duke University, Columbia University, and several other universities sold portions of their private equity holdings in secondary transactions. The lack of cash coming out of private equity investments (because of a problematic exit environment), large drops in expected private equity valuations, and the need to fund university expenses all contributed to the focus by many large universities on selling part of their private equity portfolios in secondary markets during 2008 and 2009.

EXHIBIT 19.4 PRIVATE EQUITY SECONDARY MARKET

Note 1: The most basic secondary transaction involves an investor selling its limited partnership interest in a fund. In some instances, however, a portfolio of direct company interests may be sold instead.

EXHIBIT 19.5 SECONDARY LIMITED PARTNER INTERESTS

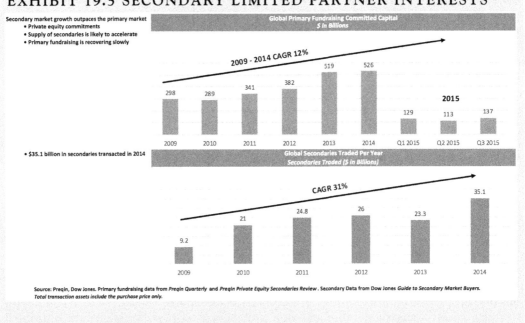

Source: Preqin, Dow Jones. Primary fundraising data from *Preqin Quarterly* and *Preqin Private Equity Secondaries Review*. Secondary Data from Dow Jones *Guide to Secondary Market Buyers*. *Total transaction assets include the purchase price only.*

EXHIBIT 19.6 SECONDARY BID SPREADS OVER TIME

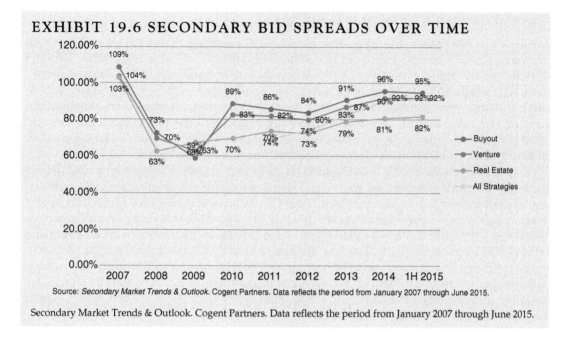

Source: *Secondary Market Trends & Outlook.* Cogent Partners. Data reflects the period from January 2007 through June 2015.

Secondary Market Trends & Outlook. Cogent Partners. Data reflects the period from January 2007 through June 2015.

Historically, the secondary markets were utilized by LPs as a vehicle to sell assets at discounts but without GP encouragement. However, this has changed as GPs have seen the universe of sellers becoming much larger and diverse, with selling interest across the entire spectrum of LPs. Some sellers need to divest private equity interests because of regulatory changes, and other sellers develop a need to diversify their portfolios. Rather than resisting sales, GPs are increasingly facilitating them, especially as a growing universe of buyers have pushed pricing to attractive levels. Many GPs now utilize the secondary market directly to increase their own portfolio flexibility. There are now two new models for GPs in this market:

1. Fund as Seller: GPs use secondary market sales as a strategic tool that involves the sale of interests in illiquid portfolio investments. This enables them to sell long-held underperforming portfolio companies and hard to value illiquid investments that would otherwise keep a fund open beyond its targeted life span. In addition, GPs sometimes sell entire portfolios of direct investments in companies, rather than individual portfolio companies.
2. Stapled Transactions: GPs have used a stapled transaction as a restructuring tool by transferring portfolio companies in an old fund into a new fund, which has new terms and returns. LPs are then offered the option to either cash out or invest in the new fund. If they cash out, GPs will help place their interest with a new LP that is required to invest in the new fund.

Financial Accounting Standards Board 157

Following November 15, 2008, the Financial Accounting Standards Board's (FASB) Statement No. 157 became effective. This statement defines fair value, establishes a framework for measuring fair value in GAAP and expands disclosures about fair value measurements. Although FASB 157 was not specifically promulgated with private equity funds in mind, the statement significantly impacts funds by requiring changes in the method for deriving fair value and the amount of disclosure regarding how fair value is determined. FASB 157 provides a hierarchy of inputs that must be used as the basis for determining value, including comparable company transactions and performance multiples.

Historically, private equity funds valued assets at cost or used the latest round of financing as the basis for determining fair value. This approach is no longer consistent with the fair value determination requirements of FASB 157. As an example of how FASB 157 impacts reported equity value, consider a hypothetical buyout completed this year when a company's EBITDA is $100 million and a private equity fund purchases the company at an enterprise value/EBITDA multiple of 10×, funding the purchase with 60% debt ($600 million) and 40% equity ($400 million). If, next year, the company's EBITDA falls to $66.7 million and comparable companies' multiples drop to 9×, the portfolio company's equity would be wiped out, assuming an unchanged debt amount of $600 million (9 × $66.7 = $600 million, which equals the debt obligation, leaving no equity value).

From 2002 to 2007, a benign interest rate environment, combined with low default rates and ample credit, enabled private equity funds to grow dramatically. Assets under management increased by more than 10 times and individual transaction values increased to more than $40 billion. This remarkable period came to an abrupt halt during the second half of 2007, as the world entered the worst credit crisis in over 75 years. Many of the private equity deals that closed during 2005–07 became big disappointments, with equity values dropping on some of these investments to 50 cents on the dollar, and lower. During 2008 and 2009, bankruptcy courts became busy focusing on private equity portfolio company failures and investors became more cautious in channeling money into private equity funds. In spite of the difficulties faced by the industry, as of mid-2009, private equity funds had over $1 trillion in cash to invest. Many of these funds viewed the low corporate valuations caused by a global recession, combined with their huge war chest of funds, as an excellent opportunity to create strong future investment returns. However, not many deals were completed in 2009. In spite of dire predictions, between 2010 and 2016, the industry enjoyed a resurgence,

Investment Banks, Hedge Funds, and Private Equity, Third Edition
http://dx.doi.org/10.1016/B978-0-12-804723-1.00020-7

with distributions exceeding capital calls, generating strong net positive cash flows. PE funds raised more than $500 billion during 2013–15, and uninvested dry powder exceeded $1.5 trillion by the end of 2016. With ongoing benign debt markets available to finance most transactions, the industry's economic position is strong. However, high asset prices have kept transaction numbers and size at more modest levels.

PRIVATE INVESTMENTS IN PUBLIC EQUITIES

During 2008 and 2009 many private equity funds took the view that the distressed equity values seen in many quality companies represented an excellent opportunity to put cash to work, even though the credit markets were moribund. As a result, investment activity continued (although at a slower pace and in smaller transaction sizes) based, in many cases, on noncontrol acquisitions of common shares in public companies. The term for this type of investment is private investments in public equity (PIPE).

One of the most heavily negotiated issues in large PIPE transactions is the extent to which the investor will be protected if the target company issues new capital on more favorable terms following closing of the investment. Usually this protection is provided for up to a 2-year period of time. In most cases, an equity stake of around 10% is required to gain the right to designate board members. As PIPE investors have sought greater equity stakes in an issuer, standstill provisions restricting additional share accumulations and "hostile" actions by the investor have become routine. The standstill period typically terminates when the investor owns less than a specified percentage (usually 5%) of the outstanding common stock or voting power of the issuer.

Private equity firms often trade liquidity for increased governance rights and better terms. In the United States, most, if not all, PIPE transactions are structured based on the issuance of unregistered securities with trailing registration rights. A registration rights agreement typically requires the issuer to meet a specified timetable for an effective shelf registration and grants the investor additional, but limited, demand and piggyback registration rights. There are typically transfer restrictions that include a lock-up period of up to 3 years during which no issued shares can be transferred other than to specific permitted transferees, including limited partners and existing shareholders.

EQUITY BUYOUTS

Unlike PIPE transactions, which are noncontrol investments, equity buyouts enable private equity firms to achieve control over companies by purchasing most, but not all, of a target company. In an equity buyout, the entire purchase is completed without borrowing any portion of the purchase price. However, the private equity investor expects that, when credit markets permit, they will borrow to fund a future large dividend that reduces their equity exposure. If companies can be acquired at a low enough cost, private equity funds may be able to achieve high returns on their equity investment even without initial leverage. Equity buyouts carry greater risk because firms are investing more of their own capital up front, compared to leveraged buyout transactions. They also lose the tax-shelter benefits of interest payments on debt, which increases the overall cost of capital. However, these issues are mitigated if the original purchase price is low enough.

An advantage of an equity buyout is that this transaction may enable a private equity fund to invest in companies without triggering a change-of-control clause that requires the target company to repay debt. For most leveraged buyouts, a private equity fund needs to raise incremental amounts of debt to repay outstanding recalled loans. An equity buyout that does not trigger debt repayment is a significant benefit because it avoids refunding fees and enables completion of a transaction even in a problematic credit environment.

An example of how a private equity fund may be able to achieve the same internal rate of return (IRR) return through either a leveraged buyout purchase of a target company at 11 times EBITDA or an equity buyout purchase of the same target company (in a depressed valuation environment) at 7 times EBITDA is found in Exhibit 20.1. In this example, to make the comparison more straightforward, it is assumed that the both the equity buyout and leveraged buyout give 100% control of the target company.

DISTRESSED ASSETS

Some private equity firms make loans to troubled companies that are trying to avoid bankruptcy court and need new cash resources. Other firms prowl through bankruptcy courts to find assets that can be purchased at significant discounts. Yet other firms focus on infrastructure spending projects and distressed banks. When markets and businesses blow up, private equity funds are, with lots of available capital, in a good position to make a wide variety of investments in distressed assets and loans at potentially advantageous prices. Broadening their investment toolbox to include nontraditional investment securities and assets has enabled private equity funds to put more money to work, while creating good IRR outcomes. By 2011, PE funds that targeted distressed debt, turnaround investments (which focus on purchasing equity in companies that are in distress), and special situations investments (that focus on event-driven or complex situations) represented 10% of all private equity fundraising.

M&A ADVISORY

Some of the larger private equity firms have attempted to diversify their investment activities by adding M&A advisory services to their business mix. The Blackstone Group, in particular, aggressively focused on providing advice on mergers, acquisitions, and restructurings. Blackstone and other large private equity firms such as Carlyle Group tried to fill the void left by the bankruptcy of Lehman Brothers and the merging of Merrill Lynch into Bank of America and Bear Stearns into JP Morgan. However, after some initial success, conflict of interest concerns over ownership by the firms of many portfolio companies made this business more problematic. Blackstone and Carlyle have spun off their M&A advisory businesses.

EXHIBIT 20.1 A LEVERAGED BUYOUT WITHOUT THE "L"

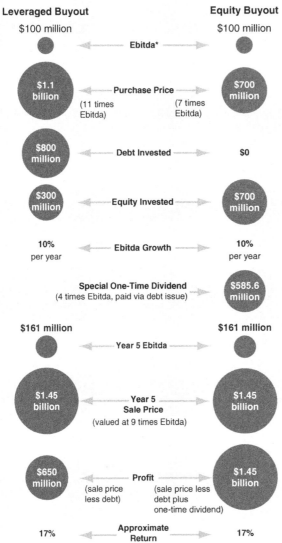

Leveraged buyouts use borrowed money to help improve private-equity returns. What happens to returns if a buyer can't borrow money to fund the initial deal? As one back-of-the-envelope comparison of the "EBO", or equity buyout, makes clear, it all depends on the original purchase price and the recovery of debt markets in the future. In this case, a company's owners use debt to pay a one-time dividend in the fourth year of ownership

Note: Ebitda = earnings before taxes, depreciation and amortization

Source: Lattman, Peter. "Lacking Leverage, Firms Embrace EBOs." *Wall Street Journal* 12 Mar. 2009.

CAPITAL MARKETS ACTIVITY

During June 2009, KKR reached agreement with Fidelity Investments to exclusively sell portfolio company initial public offerings (IPOs) through Fidelity, the world's biggest mutual fund company (with over 12-million brokerage clients). This initiative enabled KKR to bypass investment banking firms, who historically underwrote all of KKR's IPOs.

The arrangement with Fidelity provided a distribution channel to KKR's fledgling capital markets business, which underwrites both stock and bond offerings for the companies it owns. After having paid out billions of dollars in underwriting fees to investment banks over 33 years, KKR decided to build an internal capital markets business to capture a large portion of underwriting fees for itself. This initiative is one of several efforts to diversify KKR's private equity business, which suffered a reported $1.2 billion loss during 2008, based on significant drops in valuations for its portfolio companies.

In the first quarter of 2007, during the height of the leveraged buyout (LBO) boom, private equity firms paid a total of $4.3 billion to investment banks. KKR's promotion of an internal capital markets business enabled the firm to save a considerable amount of underwriting fees, but put it in direct competition with investment banks that are instrumental in bringing many acquisition opportunities to the firm. During 2016, KKR Capital Markets had a platform of approximately 45 professionals offering products that included asset-based lending, high-yield debt, revolving credit, mezzanine capital, leveraged loans, equity-linked securities, and bridge loans. Not all of the other major firms followed KKR's initiative in capital markets, but most have embarked on diversification strategies that make them less reliant on their historical private equity business.

HEDGE FUND AND REAL ESTATE INVESTMENTS

Most of the largest private equity firms conduct hedge fund and real estate investing businesses. At Carlyle, a real estate investment business operated through 9 funds and, as of mid-2016, had invested in 680 properties worldwide, Blackstone is the largest real estate private equity firm in the world as of 2016, with over $105 billion in assets under management.

Hedge fund investment activity at private equity firms suffered a big jolt during the 2007–09 credit crisis. For example, Carlyle Capital Corporation, the hedge fund arm of the Carlyle Group, accrued large losses from its investments in mortgage-backed securities and ended up defaulting on more than $16 billion in related loans during 2008. KKR Financial, the hedge fund arm of KKR, also encountered difficulties during the credit crisis based on bad mortgage-related investments. These investments caused credit rating agencies to lower ratings on KKR Financial and the company's share price dropped precipitously (KKR Financial had completed an IPO on the NYSE during 2004, reducing KKR's ownership of the firm). During March of 2009, KKR Financial disclosed losses of $1.2 billion for the fourth quarter of 2008 based principally on write-downs and realized losses from investing in leveraged loans to KKR's portfolio companies. By 2016, most private equity firms with previously active hedge fund portfolios had scaled back this business and focused more on investing in other hedge funds rather than direct investing. KKR provides hedge fund investment opportunities for its investing clients through KKR Prisma, which constructs and manages customized hedge fund portfolios and fund of-hedge funds. Carlyle and Blackstone are the other private equity firms with the largest exposure to hedge fund investing.

BOOM AND BUST CYCLES

Over the past 30 years, it is clear that credit market conditions are a key determinant of successful private equity portfolio investments. Private equity investors attempt to exploit systematic mispricings in the capital markets when the cost of debt is low compared to the cost of equity (as was the case during 2002–07), private equity firms borrow more money and secure more favorable borrowing terms and conditions. For example, private equity funds were able to borrow at an interest rate spread of around 250 basis points over the benchmark LIBOR during the highly permissive credit markets found in 2006. During 2008, as the credit markets froze up, this interest rate spread increased to 500 basis points. As a result, it can be argued that there was an up to 250 basis point mispricing in the credit markets during 2006, which encouraged private equity funds to do more deals, and larger deals than ever before. This, in turn, led to the bust years of 2008 and 2009, where private equity activity dropped precipitously.

The evidence is strong that boom and bust cycles will continue in private equity. Whenever there is a sustained period of high equity returns and a benign interest rate environment, private equity transactions will increase. This boom cycle is characterized by ample credit and loose debt covenants. However, this will be followed by lower activity when credit is tight and corporate earnings are weak. The resultant bust cycle is characterized by debt defaults and bankruptcies.

ANNEX FUNDS

The 2008/2009 recession forced private equity funds into longer than anticipated holding periods for portfolio companies and created capital shortages for many of these companies. This was especially true for struggling companies that required add-ons or operational improvements prior to a sale of the company by the private equity fund. In an effort to resolve the shortage of capital, private equity firms created annex funds. Annex funds usually take the form of a new parallel investment vehicle to an existing fund and limited partners (LPs) are given the opportunity to participate in the fund. Annex funds usually have a narrow investment mandate, with funds earmarked for well-defined purposes, such as follow-on investments in current portfolio companies, which are often specifically designated. Dilution is a significant concern for the original LPs when they are approached with an annex fund initiative. This is because the annex fund may bring in new investors who may be able to invest in portfolio companies at a lower price than the original LPs. In addition, fees and other terms related to the annex fund are often more favorable. Of course, if original LPs invest in the annex fund, these concerns are mitigated. However, some may not want to increase their exposure to a portfolio company. Without an annex fund, a portfolio company may not be able to exit in a timely way, delaying returns to the original LPs. Because of this, in spite of their concerns, LPs are usually supportive of annex funds.

ASIA–PACIFIC PRIVATE EQUITY

The Asia–Pacific private equity industry posted one of its strongest years on record in 2015, as transaction value reached \$125 billion. Exit activity, at \$88 billion, remained robust, and fund-raising was close to historical averages. Returns from past investments grew across the region, extending the momentum begun in 2014. LPs were cash positive as GPs returned capital with improving returns. See Exhibits 20.2–20.5 for a summary of the industry in this region.

EXHIBIT 20.2 ASIA-PACIFIC PRIVATE EQUITY

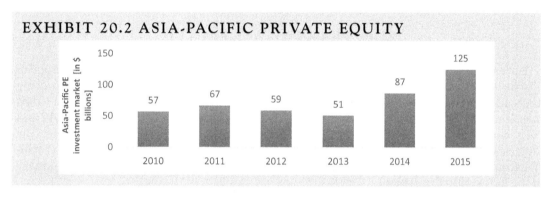

EXHIBIT 20.3 ASIA-PACIFIC PRIVATE EQUITY

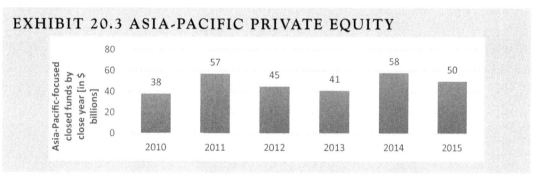

EXHIBIT 20.4 ASIA-PACIFIC PRIVATE EQUITY

EXHIBIT 20.5 ASIA-PACIFIC PRIVATE EQUITY

Average deal Size in Asia-Pacific region [in millions]					
2010	2011	2012	2013	2014	2015
$85	$83	$100	$76	$106	$131

EUROPEAN PRIVATE EQUITY

Since the financial crisis of 2007–08, almost €400 billion has been invested in the European private equity market, involving 28,000 portfolio companies. In 2015, total fundraising approached €47.6 billion, almost reaching the level of 2014. However, the number of funds raising money decreased by 15% to 274 funds, still significantly higher than during 2012 and 2013. During 2015 private equity firms exited from about 2,500 European companies. The most popular exit channels by amount were a sale to a strategic acquirer (29%), sale to financial acquirer (27%), and a public market stock offering (17%). See Exhibit 20.6 for a summary of the industry in this region.

EXHIBIT 20.6 BUYOUT-INVESTMENTS BY EQUITY BRACKET 2011–15

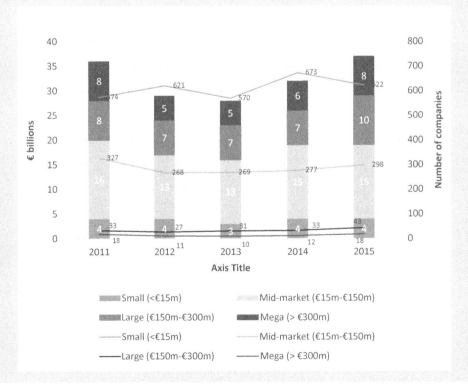

PRIVATE EQUITY INITIAL PUBLIC OFFERINGS

Fortress Investment Group and Blackstone issued IPOs that were listed on the NYSE during 2007. Eighteen months after Blackstone's issuance, its share price dropped to $4.15 from $36.45, and Fortress's stock fell to below $1, after an initial price of $35. During July 2010, KKR completed a reverse merger involving an exchange of stock with an Amsterdam-listed affiliate, creating an NYSE trading stock without conducting a book-building process. Apollo Global Management became an NYSE-traded public company during March 2011, and Carlyle listed on NASDAQ, becoming a public company during May, 2012. Exhibit 20.7 provides risk disclosure for Blackstone's IPO and Exhibit 20.8 suggests factors that caused an decline in these PE firm IPOs.

EXHIBIT 20.7 PRINCIPAL RISKS INCLUDED IN BLACKSTONE INITIAL PUBLIC OFFERING

- Portfolio Companies: ... During periods of difficult market conditions or slowdowns (which may be across one or more industries, sectors or geographies), our funds' portfolio companies may experience adverse operating performance, decreased revenues, credit rating downgrades, financial losses, difficulty in obtaining access to financing and increased funding costs.
- Prior Club Deals: ... Consortium transactions generally entail a reduced level of control by Blackstone over the investment because governance rights must be shared with the other private equity investors. Accordingly, we may not be able to control decisions relating to the investment, including decisions relating to the management and operation of the company and the timing and nature of any exit.
- New Investments and Funds: ... Our funds may be affected by ... reduced opportunities to exit and realize value from their investments, by lower than expected returns on investments made prior to the deterioration of the credit markets and by the possibility that we may not be able to find suitable investments for the funds to effectively deploy capital, which could adversely affect our ability to raise new funds.
- Valuation Uncertainty: ... Because there is significant uncertainty in the valuation of, or in the stability of the value of illiquid investments, the fair values of such investments as reflected in an investment fund's net asset value do not necessarily reflect the prices that would actually be obtained by us on behalf of the investment fund when such investments are realized.
- In the Rearview Mirror, Fortune Returns Are Not As Big As They Appear: Our investment funds' returns in some years benefited from investment opportunities and general market conditions that may not repeat themselves... our current or future investment funds might not be able to avail themselves of comparable investment opportunities or market conditions.
- Dark Side of Leverage: ... The incurrence of a significant amount of indebtedness by an entity could ... give rise to an obligation to make mandatory prepayments of debt using excess cash flow, which might limit the entity's ability to respond to changing industry conditions ... limit the entity's ability to obtain additional financing or increase the cost of obtaining such financing, including for capital expenditures, working capital or general corporate purposes.
- Exiting: ... The ability of many of our investment funds ... to dispose of investments is heavily dependent on the public equity markets ... Large holdings of securities can often be disposed of only over a substantial length of time, exposing the investment returns to risks of downward movement in market prices during the intended disposition period.

Source: Company Filings

EXHIBIT 20.8 FACTORS CONTRIBUTING TO DECLINES IN PRIVATE EQUITY PUBLIC SHARE PRICES

- Macroeconomic conditions
  - High acquisition multiples and the end of cheap financing had a significant impact on these firms
- Opaque business model
  - Difficult to determine "fair value" of shares due to complex financial accounts and subjective accounting
  - Investors don't have access to enough data to make an intelligent decision
- Industry lacks track record in the public market; IPOs priced too high
  - In early 2007, many experts recommended that most investors avoid this "hot part" of the market
  - Blackstone and Fortress went public at peak of PE "fad"
  - Firms are professional investors, making it questionable when they want to sell you a piece of their own firm
- Firms maintained culture of privacy
  - Blackstone declared that management would still retain full control, including decisions on how to allocate large salaries
  - Firms don't disclose enough detail about how funds will be used and don't have to answer to public markets about decisions regarding portfolio companies
- Shareholders lack traditional rights
  - Shareholders don't have traditional voting rights and can't participate in annual shareholder meetings

COMPARISON OF PRIVATE EQUITY FIRMS

A ranking of firms that raised private equity investment capital between 2010 and 2015 is provided in Exhibit 20.9. The 50 largest firms raised more equity capital than the next 250 firms (see Exhibit 20.10). Exhibit 20.11 shows how the 300 largest firms spent funds raised. Finally, Exhibit 20.12 compares the IRR of the 50 largest private equity funds with the IRR of the next 250 largest private equity funds.

EXHIBIT 20.9 RANKING OF PRIVATE EQUITY FIRMS BASED ON PRIVATE EQUITY CAPITAL RAISED BETWEEN 2010 AND 2015

2015 Ranking	Name of Firm	Headquarters	Capital Raised over Last Five Years
1	The Carlyle Group	Washington DC, United	31,906.72
2	TPG	Fort Worth, United States	30,332.95
3	Kohlberg Kravis Roberts (KKR)	New York, United States	29,105.10
4	The Blackstone Group	New York, United States	25,565.89
5	Apollo Global Management	New York, United States	22,200.00
6	CVC Capital Partners	London, United Kingdom	21,178.40
7	EnCap Investments	Houston, United States	21,147.83
8	Advent International	Boston, United States	15,735.37
9	Warburg Pincus	New York, United States	15,243.00
10	Bain Capital	Boston, United States	14,565.47
11	Vista Equity Partners	San Francisco, United States	11,814.00
12	Partners Group	Baar-Zug, Switzerland	11,198.00
13	Silver Lake	Menlo Park, United States	11,074.50
14	Hellman & Friedman LLC	San Francisco, United States	10,900.00
15	Centerbridge Partners	New York, United States	10,496.78
16	Energy Capital Partners	Short Hills, United States	10,436.35
17	Permira Advisers	London, United Kingdom	10,412.49
18	EQT	Stockholm, Sweden	10,382.96
19	NGP Energy Capital Management	Irving, United States	9,832.64
20	Riverstone Holdings	New York, United States	9,164.31
21	Goldman Sachs Principal Investment	New York, United States	9,143.32
22	Ares Management	Los Angeles, United States	8,929.00
23	Neuberger Berman Group	New York, United States	8,844.00
24	Stone Point Capital	Greenwich, United States	3,759.25
25	American Securities	New York, United States	8,640.00
26	BC Partners	London, United Kingdom	8,600.99
27	Clayton Dubilier & Rice	New York, United States	3,539.16
28	General Atlantic	New York, United States	8,510.00
29	Cinven	London, United Kingdom	8,248.70
30	Russian Direct Investment Fund (RDIF)	Moscow, Russia	8,159.58
31	Onex	Toronto, Canada	8,081.11
32	Thoma Bravo	Chicago, United States	8,005.59
33	HgCapital	London, United Kingdom	7,955.59
34	Apax Partners	London, United Kingdom	7,815.29
35	Insight Venture Partners	New York, United States	7,673.96
36	Triton Partners	London, United Kingdom	7,673.48
37	Bridgepoint	London, United Kingdom	7,300.47
38	BDT Capital Partners	Chicago, United States	7,275.00
39	GTCR	Chicago, United States	7,124.23
40	Pamplona Capital Management LLP	London, United Kingdom	6,741.57
41	Tiger Global Management	New York, United States	6,735.00
42	Welsh, Carson, Anderson & Stowe	New York, United States	6,672.00
43	RRJ Capital	Hong Kong, Hong Kong	6,662.00
44	Baring Private Equity Asia	Hong Kong, Hong Kong	6,450.00
45	Sequoia Capital	Menlo Park, United States	6,443.06

Continued

EXHIBIT 20.9 RANKING OF PRIVATE EQUITY FIRMS BASED ON PRIVATE EQUITY CAPITAL RAISED BETWEEN 2010 AND 2015—cont'd

2015 Ranking	Name of Firm	Headquarters	Capital Raised over Last Five Years $ In mm
47	Leonard Green & Partners	Los Angeles, United States	6,250.00
48	Oaktree Capital Management	Los Angeles, united States	6,076.87
49	The Abraaj Group	Dubai, United Arab Emirates	6,001.03
50	Georgian Co-investment Fund (GCF)	Tbilisi, Georgia	6,000.00
51	CDH Investments	Kowloon, Hong Kong	5,663.43
52	JP Morgan Asset Management	New York, United States	5,606.47
53	Brookfield Asset Management	Toronto, Canada	5,172.00
54	New Enterprise Associates	Menlo Park, United States	5,170.00
55	CITIC Private Equity Funds Management	Beijing, China	5,122.75
56	American Capital	Bethesda, United States	5,082.00
57	Providence Equity Partners	Providence, United States	5,000.00
58	Francisco Partners	San Francisco, United States	4,875.00
59	Ardian	Paris, France	4,797.65
60	Cerberus Capital Management	New York, United States	4,750.00
61	TowerBrook Capital Partners	New York, United States	4,690.00
62	Nordic Capital	Stockholm, Sweden	4,654.27
63	Roark Capital Group	Atlanta, United States	4,632.00
64	H.I.G. Capital	Miami, United States	4,616.41
65	Patria Investirnentos	Sao Paulo, Brazil	4,573.00
66	Berkshire Partners	Boston, United States	4,500.00
67	MBK Partners	Seoul, South Korea	4,413.00
68	Affinity Equity Partners	Hong Kong, Hong Kong	4,327.50
69	PAI Partners	Paris, France	4,272.98
70	First Reserve Corporation	Greenwich, United States	4,223.03
71	New Mountain Capital	New York, United States	4,130.00
72	Madison Dearborn Partners	Chicago, United States	4,100.00
73	Avista Capital Partners	New York, United States	4,062.50
74	Caixa Economica Federal	Brasilia, Brazil	4,059.81
75	Hony Capital	Beijing, China	3,912.79
76	HitecVision AS	Stavanger, Norway	3,870.00
77	Andreessen Horowitz	Menlo Park, United States	3,852.20
78	CCMP Capital	New York, United States	3,848.00
79	Equistone Partners Europe	London, United Kingdom	3,758.97
80	Platinum Equity Partners	Beverly Hills, United States	3,750.00
81	Denham Capital Management	Boston, United States	3,665.00
82	Kleiner Perkins Caufield & Byers	Menlo Park, United States	3,653.58
83	Pine Brook	New York, United States	3,595.00
84	Sycamore Partners	New York, United States	3,587.50
85	KPS Capital Partners	New York, United States	3,571.43
86	Montagu Private Equity	London, United Kingdom	3,563.18
87	Accel Partners	Palo Alto, United States	3,548.62
88	Golden Gate Capital	San Francisco, United States	3,500.00

EXHIBIT 20.9 RANKING OF PRIVATE EQUITY FIRMS BASED ON PRIVATE EQUITY CAPITAL RAISED BETWEEN 2010 AND 2015—cont'd

2015 Ranking	Name of Firm	Headquarters	Capital Raised over Last Five Years $ in mm
89	ABRY Partners	Boston, United States	3,500.00
90	China Development Bank (CDB)	Beijing, China	3,497.25
91	Alpinvest Partners	New York, United States	3,471.73
92	Veritas Capital	New York, United States	3,440.60
93	KSL Capital Partners	Denver, United States	3,340.45
94	Littlejohn & Co	Greenwich, United States	3,340.00
95	Yorktown Partners	New York, United States	3,295.53
96	Crestview Partners	New York, United States	3,250.00
97	Summit Partners	Boston, United States	3,250.00
98	ARC Financial Corp.	Calgary, Canada	3,200.98
99	The Jordan Company	New York, United States	3,200.00
100	Bessemer Venture Partners	Larchmont, United States	3,200.00
101	Emerging Capital Partners	Washington, United States	3,173.60
102	Court Square Capital Partners	New York, United States	3,170.00
103	Khosla Ventures	Menlo Park, United States	3,169.00
104	Capital International, Inc.	London, United Kingdom	3,169.00
105	Taoshi Equity Investment Management	Shanghai, China	3,169.00
106	Gávea Investimentos	Rio de Janeiro, Brazil	3,074.20
107	Resource Capital Funds	Denver, United States	3,060.00

Note: "Private equity": For the purposes of the PEI 300, the definition of private equity is capital raised for a dedicated programme of investing directly into businesses. This includes equity capital for diversified private equity, buyouts, growth equity, venture capital, turnaround or control-oriented distressed investment capital. Rankings do not take into account funds of funds, secondaries, real estate, infrastructure, debt (including mezzanine), PIPEs and hedge funds. Source: www.peimedia.com

EXHIBIT 20.10 THE TOP 50 VERSUS NEXT 250

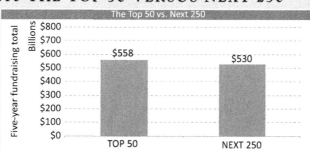

Source: "PEI 300", Private Equity International

EXHIBIT 20.11 BUYOUT VOLUME 2014–15, SPLIT BY INDUSTRY

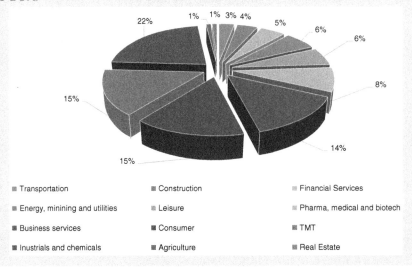

- Transportation
- Energy, minining and utilities
- Business services
- Inustrials and chemicals

- Construction
- Leisure
- Consumer
- Agriculture

- Financial Services
- Pharma, medical and biotech
- TMT
- Real Estate

EXHIBIT 20.12 NET INTERNAL RATE OF RETURN SINCE INCEPTION

The 50 largest private equity firms outperformed the next 250 largest firms and the industry as a whole.

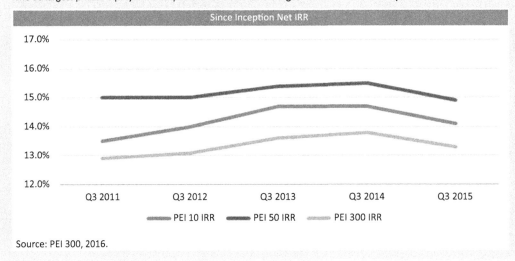

Source: PEI 300, 2016.

PROFILE OF THE CARLYLE GROUP

Founded in 1987, Carlyle is publicly traded on the NASDAQ market. Carlyle Group has three groups of owners: employees, strategic investors, and public unit holders. The Carlyle Group serves more than 1700 investors from 78 countries. As of 2016, the firm had more than 700 investment professionals and over 1700 employees in 36 offices across six continents. Carlyle had almost $188 billion in assets under management (invested across 126 funds and 160 fund of funds vehicles), including more than $4 billion of capital committed by the firm's senior managers. During 2011, Carlyle acquired a majority stake in AlpInvest, a private equity fund-of-funds firm, thereby strongly growing assets under management. Assets are housed within four fund families: leveraged buyouts, real estate, leveraged finance, and growth capital. See Exhibits 20.13 and 20.14.

EXHIBIT 20.13 THE CARLYLE GROUP

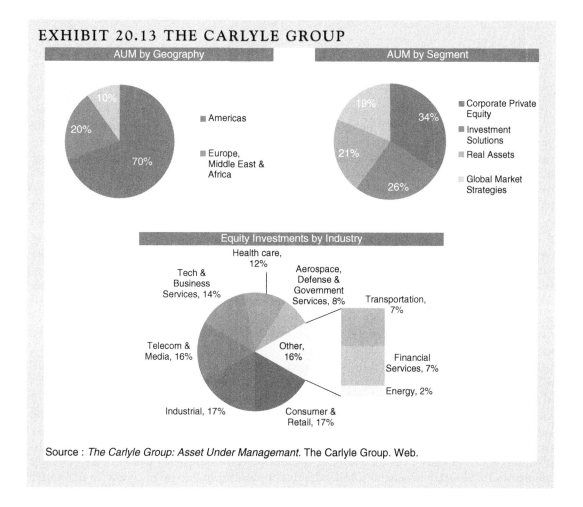

Source : *The Carlyle Group: Asset Under Managemant.* The Carlyle Group. Web.

EXHIBIT 20.14 THE CARLYLE GROUP

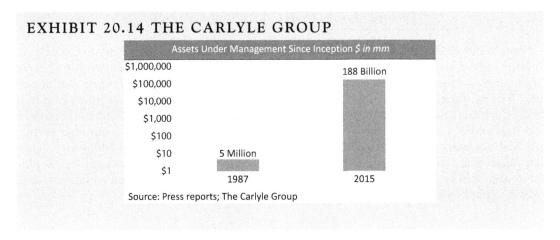

Source: Press reports; The Carlyle Group

FUTURE ISSUES AND OPPORTUNITIES[1]

Coinvesting alongside a GP is continuing to grow in popularity with LPs. LPs like coinvesting because providing additional capital can give them access to a high priority GP while paying a lower fee to the GP. This "shadow capital" invested in PE during 2015 totaled an estimated $161 billion, or the equivalent of 26% of the year's traditional capital raised. Another novel way LPs are choosing to participate in PE is through their increasing use of the secondary market to deploy capital by actively trading shares in existing PE funds. Traditionally, the buying and selling of secondary interests has been the domain of specialist funds created solely for that purpose. The extent to which LPs were active directly in secondaries had been to liquidate a stake in an established fund, either because they needed the cash or because they lost confidence that the GP would generate an expected return. LPs who bought secondaries often sought to take advantage of steep discounts they could command. However, this is now a much more common practice, and almost 60% of LPs now acknowledge having bought or sold assets on the secondary market. Indeed, trading in secondaries has become a potent portfolio management tool. In addition to allowing LPs to use uninvested capital to increase their exposure to PE, secondaries also enable them to better diversify their holdings across several fund vintages.

PE funds have a large amount of uninvested capital, which exceeded $460 billion in 2016, as the pace of investment had lagged fund-raising activity. For GPs, the huge amount of capital directed their way has increased pressure to channel idle dry powder into new deals. Not putting that money to work risks alienating LPs and jeopardizing GPs' chances of raising new funds in the future. But as GPs weigh the investment options they face and contemplate how the money they invest now will fare over the life of their fund, they find themselves caught in another bind. The dry powder available for productive investments has increased already intense bidding battles among GPs. Indeed, with more competition on every deal and shorter

[1] Based, in part, on views expressed by Bain and Company's Global Private Equity Report 2016.

time limits imposed by the banks that bring deals to market, today's auctions often leave potential buyers with little alternative but to accept on good faith the seller's assertions about a target company's market position and growth potential. Small and middle-market PE firms, in particular, often lack the resources and depth to compete for deals, and even many of the best-qualified firms need to exercise self-restraint to avoid being drawn into bidding wars they may ultimately regret having won.

In the United States, PE acquisition multiples now exceed 10 times EBITDA, on average, exceeding even the elevated multiples of 2007. In Europe, buyout multiples are just below 10 times EBITDA. GPs know that the prudent course would be to wait for deal multiples to ease, but LPs expect them to commit to new investments. However, GPs recognize that the surest way to set up LPs for disappointment is to succumb to the pressure to overpay in haste for assets that could then sit for a long time in their portfolios, waiting for returns they might never see. Reluctant to accept either of those unappealing choices, most GPs have tried to weave a cautious path to put capital to work while maintaining strong investment discipline. But their attempts to do so have come up against a third crosscurrent that has stirred up the deal market: deteriorating credit conditions. Although central banks held interest rates close to zero, debt markets have turned choppy, particularly for high-yield bonds and leveraged loans.

Facing more uncertain conditions, banks increasingly have become reluctant underwriters. Worried that they could be left holding risky debt that they cannot syndicate to other investors, they are backing out of PE deals or shunning them altogether. Under the tougher regulatory regime created by the Dodd–Frank Act, US banks are determined to avoid carrying unsold high-yield debt on their balance sheets to avoid triggering steep capital charges that regulators now impose.

The gradual drying up of cheap credit, combined with higher purchase multiples, is changing the calculus of deal making. Even as acquisition multiples on LBOs have increased, leverage multiples have dropped from 5.9 to 5.5 times EBITDA. The result has been to force buyout funds to put more equity capital at risk to close deals. Finding debt to fund bigger buyouts has become particularly problematic. Any deal above $5 billion is more challenging for most private equity firms to do on their own. At $133 billion in 2015, the value of debt financing for buyouts fell for the first time in more than 6 years as the cost of debt on high-yield bonds and leveraged loans increased steeply. While the debt market likely will continue to be challenging, the market will be buoyed somewhat by new sources of debt outside of the traditional bank-led syndication rounds. New loan instruments are gaining in popularity, including unitranche financing, which are loans issued by a single underwriter that takes both senior and subordinated debt positions and stretch senior loans, which combine elements of both asset-based and cash-flow lending. Further supplementing capital that banks are more reluctant to provide are direct-lending funds. In 2015, mezzanine funds raised more than $19 billion in capital, more than twice the amount raised in 2014 and the highest total since 2008.

Buy-and-build strategies have gained in popularity. Under pressure to pay steep acquisition multiples for assets sold through intensely competitive auctions, many GPs are looking to buy businesses they know well—similar to companies already in their portfolios. PE firms have long resorted to buy-and-build strategies, using established portfolio companies as platforms to accelerate growth. Adding bolt-on acquisitions gives PE owners a lot of flexibility to steer their platform portfolio companies in new directions, enabling them to grow their core businesses or opening doors to related ones. Globally, the value of add-on acquisitions by PE-backed companies more than doubled to a record $267 billion in 2015, nearly matching the $282 billion invested in all buyouts during the year. Sizable acquisitions, such as Kraft's acquisition of Heinz in the food industry and Dell's acquisition of EMC in computing, dominated the buyout scene.

By adding on enterprises in the same or related business to a portfolio holding, GPs can target companies that often are too small to attract the attention of big corporate acquirers and can be bought at reduced prices. Particularly as economies slow, owners of smaller companies will be increasingly motivated to sell at lower prices. By bolting on several low-cost businesses, GPs can lower the multiples of their initial platform companies while enhancing their growth prospects. Buy-and-builds also give PE funds more options when it comes time to exit, enabling GPs to sell their holdings in part or in their entirety.

GPs are increasingly targeting acquisitions of small and midsize companies. Even larger PE firms are searching for opportunities among smaller enterprises valued at $250 million or less. At the lower end of the middle market, GPs like the relative bargains that are available, because their small size puts them off the radar of corporate acquirers. Buying these lower-cost assets also affords GPs opportunities to pursue buy-and-build strategies, enabling them to assemble several low-multiple companies into a larger entity that can command a far higher multiple upon exiting. For companies valued at less than $250 million, the median multiple, measured as the ratio of enterprise value to EBITDA on LBOs, was about half that of companies valued at more than $250 million.

Teaming up with strategic buyers to mitigate risk has become a higher priority for GPs. Recognizing the futility of winning bidding wars against strategic acquirers, many GPs are finding ways to partner with big companies in buyouts that suit the needs of both. For PE funds, having a strategic coinvestor provides a built-in exit strategy, enabling them to sell their stakes to the corporate partner when the timing is right. Corporations also find much to like about joining forces with buyout funds. Some are tapping their PE partners for capital to share the risk of acquiring new assets they are not yet ready to integrate into their balance sheets and for expertise to help boost performance. For example, Permira, the Canada Pension Plan Investment Board (CPPIB), and strategic partners Microsoft and Salesforce.com bought Informatica, a data integration software provider, for $5.3 billion. The deal enabled Informatica to reorganize as a privately held company outside the scrutiny of public markets. For the new owners, this partnership brought potential financial returns as well as competitive advantages. Other corporations also are teaming up with PE firms to sell business units, making their PE partners owners of the new subsidiary and retaining a significant minority position in the spun-off enterprise. That is what Walgreens Boots Alliance did by selling a majority stake in its infusion services business to PE firm Madison Dearborn. Creative approaches like these will become more common in the quick-paced, high-stakes dealmaking environment that lies ahead. To succeed, PE firms will need to be nimble in their ability to size up opportunities and be prepared to take advantage of novel ways to put capital to work.

The period immediately following the 2008 global financial meltdown was a time of anxiety about PE's ability to deliver market-beating returns. GPs had paid peak prices prior to the crash to acquire the assets held in their portfolios and rushed to mark them down sharply to their much lower prevailing market value. They put exit plans for their mature assets on hold and stretched out holding periods as they waited for the crisis to pass. Even top-performing GPs were not spared, as first-quartile fund returns converged close to those of the public markets. Stunned by the deep and prolonged downturn and fixated on subpar short-term performance, worried LPs wondered when, if ever, they would see gains from their expensive PE investments. Even as the recovery slowly gained traction after 2010, doubts about PE returns persisted. Deferred asset sales had created a huge exit overhang that would take years to clear, adding to the pressures that would dampen returns. The lingering uncertainty caused recognition that PE is an illiquid, long-term investment, and the PE industry had matured. The outsize returns GPs could earn on once-abundant undervalued assets had dried up. Leveraging their buyouts to boost equity returns was no longer working. Now, however, following many strong years, PE returns have recovered their footing, and GPs and LPs have regained both confidence and a fresh perspective. Both short- and long-term results reflect PE's restored luster and GPs' justifiable claims to have been prudent stewards of their investors' capital.

As the legacy effects of the financial crisis retreat further into the past, PE should consistently perform at a level above public equities, as buyout funds are currently doing in all major regions of the world. While market recovery has led to a general uptick in returns of funds since the 2005 and 2006 vintages that bore the brunt of the economic downturn, returns data for the 2008 and 2009 vintages now coming to fruition suggests that PE performance is again beginning to pull away from the performance of public markets. Top quartile funds have widened their lead in returns by an even greater margin. Comparing successive buyout vintages between 2006 and 2008 reinforces the conclusion that fund returns are trending higher over time. The median IRR, both realized and unrealized, of all three fund vintages took a big hit when the markets tanked from late 2007 through the end of 2008, as GPs wrote down the net asset values of holdings in their portfolios. But all had recovered with the strengthening of public equities markets by the end of 2010. Yet the strength of their rebound followed different trajectories. The median IRR of the 2006 vintage buyout funds was up to 9% by the middle of 2015, while the 2007 funds rose to 10% and the 2008 funds climbed to 12%. Median top-quartile fund returns followed much the same track—up to 17% for the 2006 vintage, 20% for the 2007 vintage, and 24% for the 2008 vintage.

The rebound in returns has been met with LPs' renewed enthusiasm and belief in PE. Most LPs have agreed that PE had met or exceeded their expectations and that positive sentiment for this asset class has been strengthening in recent years. With renewed confidence in PE returns comes a heightened awareness of PE's cyclicality and a magnified sensitivity to the economy's vicissitudes. As healthy as PE returns have recently been, those vulnerabilities and the simple fact that the PE industry has matured should temper investors' expectations that returns will remain as strong as they have been. With GPs now paying premium prices for assets, and recognition that a recessionary economy can always return, the risk remains that PE investors will see future waves of downward revaluations and a convergence of PE and public market returns. Future returns will depend on the severity of the cyclical market and economic shifts. But they will also depend on the skills and foresight of GPs to manage their portfolios proactively to withstand future turmoil. Every crest of every wave in the PE cycle is an opportunity for GPs to demonstrate their ability to outperform. GPs have embedded many lessons they learned from the past downturn into their new investment discipline. They are exercising caution when paying high multiples for acquisitions and taking care in their use of debt, which can just as easily eat into returns as enhance them.

GPs are working harder, and paying more, to source, vet, and land deals in every market around the world. Deal teams and operating partners are stretching out holding periods to groom their portfolio companies for successful sales and to optimize their own returns. Business conditions have remained generally healthy, and PE returns continue to outpace those of all other asset classes over the medium and longer terms. But the shifting contours of the competitive landscape have forward-looking PE firms fundamentally reevaluating every facet of their businesses. Clearly, there is more to do than simply adapt to the challenging new realities of the current investment cycle. The maturing PE industry finds itself in the throes of ongoing generational change as PE firms evolve from the charismatic leadership style of their founding partners, who are now aging into retirement, into the dynamic institutions that they will need to become to carry on their legacy. The 20–30 elite PE firms that dominate the industry are well under way with this shift, but the great bulk of middle-market firms that account for a large proportion of deployed PE capital are only beginning the journey. They are now looking to recast themselves into organizations with the people, systems, and disciplines that can surmount formidable new challenges to become enduring institutions.

As PE firms wrestle with new competitive threats, they need to fully consider institutional investors' shifting priorities as well. The LP community has always been a diverse group, representing many investment styles, behaviors, and objectives. That heterogeneity has never been as prominent as it is today and will almost surely become even more so over time. Big LPs with large specialized teams and long PE investment experience have been eyeing new ways to streamline their relationships with GPs. Others are coinvesting alongside GPs or even building and managing their own PE portfolios. Still others are relying on their research skills to find novel investment themes, find GPs that share their outlook and back those who they are convinced can deliver results. For all of their diversity, however, many LPs remain deeply committed to PE as their top-performing asset class.

There is a growing inclination among many investors to shrink the number of PE funds in which they invest, writing bigger checks to fewer GPs. For large LPs such as CalPERS, paring back the number of their relationships with GPs significantly reduces their administrative burden and presents an opportunity to negotiate more favorable management fees, while freeing up time for due diligence and fund tracking. Bigger brand name GPs have far greater marketing strength than their smaller rivals and bring to bear their substantial economies of scale, offering a broader array of funds to absorb more capital from LPs looking to pool their commitments with fewer PE firms. LPs also know that they can more easily eliminate smaller GPs from their commitment allocations without putting a dent in their portfolios' overall returns. LPs' preference in investing with bigger, well-known funds has been gaining momentum over the recent PE cycle.

LPs still see significant benefits from investing in smaller PE funds. Since 2009, new funds looking to raise up to $1 billion accounted for 75% or more of all funds raised. Smaller funds remain popular in large measure because PE fundamentally remains an entrepreneurial business. A sizable subset of LPs want to sign up with GPs that can identify promising pockets of opportunity and demonstrate that they can deliver top-quartile results. Many LP investors have clear targets for how they want to allocate their money, and they are willing to back smaller or new GPs that offer funds matching the specific risk and sector exposure they are looking for.

Over the next investment horizon, many large investors see slowing GDP growth nearly everywhere they look. And while they expect that PE will continue to outperform public equity markets on a relative basis, they recognize that returns on all asset classes are unlikely to continue posting the strong double-digit gains racked up over recent years. In due course, the extraordinary fund-raising conditions which have produced large capital inflows to GPs will give way to a more competitive scramble to win the backing of LPs.

As LPs' allocations to PE begin to stabilize, the industry will reach a new normal of positive cash flow, with the ratio of distributions to contributions well below their peak of recent years. A tighter balance between GPs' supply of new funds and LPs' demand will continue to favor the largest and best-performing GPs. Large GPs that have a less impressive track record and mid-market PE firms hoping to grow to mega-fund status will encounter more resistance from LPs when the current excess of capital subsides. They will no longer be able to siphon off some of the spillover that LPs have been willing to send their way. Sponsors of smaller and mid-market funds that have underperformed in the past may still be able to garner some capital, but they will be at a distinct disadvantage compared with their more sharply focused peers as fund-raising conditions slightly soften.

A past history of success will always be crucial, but the ability of GPs to clearly communicate how their investment approach differentiates them from their peers will be essential to winning investor confidence and financial backing. Indeed, a sound, differentiated strategy is increasingly viewed as the platform on which successful and durable future performance can be built. It will be the centerpiece of the once-in-a-generation transition that many PE firms are now wrestling with as they set their sights on rising to the industry's top tier. The fundamentals of a good strategy cannot be put in place overnight and GPs need to commit themselves to continually refining their strategy as a crucial part of doing business.

As today's favorable fund-raising conditions slow over the coming years, GPs will need to be able to demonstrate to LPs that they have a sharply honed and differentiated strategy for achieving superior performance. There are many ways to do this, and no firm can excel at all of them. Successful firms will identify and focus on areas in which they have a natural advantage and build their strategies around them. Many PE firms are testing novel pathways to differentiation that show promise and will become increasingly important in the years ahead. Some firms are sharpening their focus on their investment sweet spots, enabling them to zero in on deals with characteristics that best match the firm's unique strengths, capabilities, and past patterns of success. This is allowing them to effectively communicate both internally and with LPs the types of deals they will target and to build their expertise to capitalize on these deals. Other PE firms are developing thematic investment insights to capitalize on broad macro trends and gain an investment edge. They are applying their in-depth understanding of key trends to identify and evaluate businesses and sectors that will see long-term sustainable growth. Finally, more PE firms are mobilizing their talent and resources to develop repeatable approaches for creating value across their fund portfolios. They are adopting value-creation models that reflect their firms' unique philosophy and distinctive investment preferences while ensuring that their methods for enhancing the value of their portfolio companies are consistent and focused.

THE NEW LANDSCAPE

Over time, the most successful private equity firms may fall into one of the two categories: global private equity firms that have scale and have diversified their investment and advisory activities; and smaller "niche" private equity firms that have a well-defined, differentiated strategy based on their operating/investing model or industry expertise. The middle tier firms that do not have an area of specialization or differentiation may find it more difficult to raise funding and meet investment objectives.

For as long as credit limitations exist, private equity firms will need to rely increasingly on effective management of portfolio companies to deliver expected returns. Successful firms will create greater industry specialization and develop expertise in the areas of working capital, sales force management, pricing, procurement, and other operational areas. Firms will need to either build this capability or acquire it to be successful. Without these operational skills and industry specialization, sole reliance on leverage and financial engineering will likely result in failure.

Some firms will become successful in identifying different parts of the capital structure to pursue in an effort to achieve the best risk-adjusted returns. Other firms will learn how to better control relationships with the executives who run their portfolio companies. These firms will find ways to better align the interests of owners and managers based on increasing communication and a greater effort to collaborate, rather than police.

Leveraged transactions will remain smaller, and the limited supply of large deals will cause some private equity firms to revise their strategy and focus increasingly on distressed transactions, other types of debt transactions, and PIPE investments. Relationships with LPs will change, as they require greater alignment in economics, including reductions in management fees, tighter fund documentation, and limitations on "style drift," in exchange for improvements in carry. The new landscape will likely have fewer private equity firms, lower returns, a broader array of investments across the capital structure, and greater operational capability.

CASE STUDIES

Investment Banking in 2008 (A): Rise and Fall of the Bear

Posit: People think a bank might be financially shaky. Consequence: People start to withdraw their money. Result: Pretty soon it IS financially shaky. Conclusion: You can make banks fail. Sneakers (1992)

Gary Parr, deputy chairman of Lazard Frères & Co. and Kellogg class of 1980, could not believe his ears.

"You can't mean that," he said, reacting to the lowered bid given by Doug Braunstein, JP Morgan head of investment banking, for Parr's client, legendary investment bank Bear Stearns. Less than 18 months after trading at an all-time high of $172.61 a share, Bear now had little choice but to accept Morgan's humiliating $2-per-share, Federal Reserve-sanctioned bailout offer. "I'll have to get back to you."[1]

Hanging up the phone, Parr leaned back and gave an exhausted sigh. Rumors had swirled around Bear ever since two of its hedge funds imploded as a result of the subprime housing crisis, but time and again, the scrappy Bear appeared to have weathered the storm. Parr's efforts to find a capital infusion for the bank had resulted in lengthy discussions and marathon due diligence sessions, but one after another, potential investors had backed away, scared off in part by Bear's sizable mortgage holdings at a time when every bank on Wall Street was reducing its positions and taking massive write-downs in the asset class. In the past week, those rumors had reached a fever pitch, with financial analysts openly questioning Bear's ability to continue operations and its clients running for the exits. Now Sunday afternoon, it had already been a long weekend, and it would almost certainly be a long night, as the Fed-backed bailout of Bear would require onerous negotiations before Monday's market open. By morning, the 85-year-old investment bank, which had survived the Great Depression, the savings and loan crisis, and the dot-com implosion, would cease to exist as an independent firm. Pausing briefly before calling CEO Alan Schwartz and the rest of Bear's board, Parr allowed himself a moment of reflection.

How had it all happened?

BEAR STEARNS

Founded with just $500,000 of capital in 1923 by Joseph Bear, Robert Stearns, and Harold Mayer, Bear Stearns needed to show its soon-to-be trademark tenacity and agility in the market merely to survive its first decade. Originally conceived as an equity trading house to take advantage of a roaring 1920s bull market, Bear instead relied on its trading in government

---

[1] Kate Kelly, "Bear Stearns Neared Collapse Twice in Frenzied Last Days," *Wall Street Journal*, May 29, 2008. http://online.wsj.com/article/SB121202057232127889.html.

securities to last through the Great Depression, managing not only to avoid layoffs but also to continue paying employee bonuses. Despite the sagging national and global economy, Bear grew from its seven original employees to 75 by 1933 and began to expand with the acquisition of Chicago-based Stein, Brennan.[2]

The firm quickly developed a reputation as a maverick in the white-shoe culture of New York investment banking. Unlike more polished firms, who catered to the world's most prestigious companies and earned most of their revenues from equity underwriting and advisory services, Bear had a cutthroat, renegade culture that stemmed from its dominant position in bond trading, where the slightest turn in the market can make the difference between a profitable trade and a losing one. CEO Salim "Cy" Lewis reinforced this trader's culture after joining the company in 1938 as head of the firm's institutional bond trading department, running the firm almost as a holding company of independent profit centers that frantically sought his approval. Imposing at six foot four, Lewis's audacity, brash demeanor, and relentless work ethic set the tone at Bear until his death in 1978, when he suffered a stroke at his own retirement party at the Harmonie Club in New York City.[3]

In stark contrast to the WASP-y, cliquish atmosphere of its competitors, Bear set the standard for diversity among its employees, valuing initiative and tenacity over pedigree in its hiring. As Lewis's successor, Alan "Ace" Greenberg, put it, "If somebody with an MBA degree applies for a job, we will certainly not hold it against them, but we are really looking for people with PSD degrees," meaning poor, smart, and with a deep desire to become very rich.[4]

"It was unique," said Muriel Siebert, founder of brokerage house Muriel Siebert & Co. "It didn't matter what your last name was. They had a mixture of all kinds of people and they were there to make money." Long before its clubbier competitors embraced hiring diversity, the scrappy, trading-focused Bear had cultivated a roster of Jewish, Irish, and Italian employees who lacked the Ivy League pedigrees required for positions at white-shoe firms such as Morgan Stanley or Lehman Brothers.

When it went public in 1985, the firm diversified its operations, becoming a full-service investment bank with divisions in investment banking, institutional equities, fixed-income securities, individual investor services, and mortgage-related products.[5] Bear's investment banking unit got off to a rough start, battered by the collapse of the mergers and acquisitions boom in the second half of the decade. The firm remained resilient, however, drawing inspiration from its leader on one of the worst trading days in history: October 19, 1987, or Black Monday. As the Dow Jones fell more than 500 points, Greenberg—who did not play golf— pantomimed a golf swing and announced to the assembled throng of traders that he would be taking the following day off.[6]

[2] Bear Stearns Companies, Inc., "Company History," http://www.answers.com/topic/the-bear-stearns-companies-inc?cat=biz-fin.

[3] Kris Frieswick, "Journey Without Maps," *CFO Magazine*, March 2005. http://www.cfo.com/article.cfm/3709778/1/c_3710920.

[4] Max Nichols, "One of Our Most Remarkable Leaders," *Oklahoma City Journal Record*, April 12, 2001. http://findarticles.com/p/articles/mi_qn4182/is_20010412/ai_n10145162.

[5] Bear Stearns, "Company History."

[6] Kate Kelly, "Fear, Rumors Touched Off Fatal Run on Bear Stearns," *Wall Street Journal*, May 28, 2008. http://online.wsj.com/article/SB121193290927324603.html.

By the time James Cayne succeeded Greenberg as CEO in 1993, the firm found itself at the top of the equity underwriting league tables in Latin America and its research department had flourished. Its *Early Look at the Market: Bear Stearns Morning View* became one of the most widely read pieces of market intelligence.

LONG-TERM CAPITAL MANAGEMENT

Long-Term Capital Management, or LTCM, was a hedge fund founded in 1994 by John Meriwether, the former head of Salomon Brothers's domestic fixed-income arbitrage group. Meriwether had grown the arbitrage group to become Salomon's most profitable group by 1991, when it was revealed that one of the traders under his purview had astonishingly submitted a false bid in a US Treasury bond auction. Despite reporting the trade immediately to CEO John Gutfreund, the outcry from the scandal forced Meriwether to resign.[7]

Meriwether revived his career several years later with the founding of LTCM. Amidst the beginning of one of the greatest bull markets the global markets had ever seen, Meriwether assembled a team of some of the world's most respected economic theorists to join other refugees from the arbitrage group at Salomon. The board of directors included Myron Scholes, a coauthor of the famous Black-Scholes formula used to price option contracts, and MIT Sloan professor Robert Merton, both of whom would later share the 1997 Nobel Prize for Economics. The firm's impressive brain trust, collectively considered geniuses by most of the financial world, set out to raise a $1 billion fund by explaining to investors that their profoundly complex computer models allowed them to price securities according to risk more accurately than the rest of the market, in effect "vacuuming up nickels that others couldn't see."[8]

One typical LTCM trade concerned the divergence in price between long-term US Treasury bonds. Despite offering fundamentally the same (minimal) default risk, those issued more recently—known as "on-the-run" securities—traded more heavily than those "off-the-run" securities issued just months previously. Heavier trading meant greater liquidity, which in turn resulted in ever-so-slightly higher prices. As "on-the-run" securities become "off-the-run" on the issuance of a new tranche of Treasury bonds, the price discrepancy generally disappears with time. LTCM sought to exploit that price convergence by shorting the more expensive "on-the-run" bond while purchasing the "off-the-run" security.

By early 1998 the intellectual firepower of its board members and the aggressive trading practices that had made the arbitrage group at Salomon so successful had allowed LTCM to flourish, growing its initial $1 billion of investor equity to $4.72 billion (Exhibit C1.1). However, the miniscule spreads earned on arbitrage trades could not provide the type of returns sought by hedge fund investors. To make transactions such as these worth their while, LTCM had to employ massive leverage to magnify its returns. Ultimately, the fund's equity component sat atop more than $124.5 billion in borrowings for total assets of more than $129 billion. These borrowings were merely the tip of the iceberg; LTCM also held off-balance-sheet derivative positions with a notional value of more than $1.25 trillion.

[7] Roger Lowenstein, *When Genius Failed: The Rise and Fall of Long-Term Capital Management* (New York: Random House, 2000).

[8] Roger Lowenstein, *When Genius Failed: The Rise and Fall of Long-Term Capital Management* (New York: Random House, 2000).

EXHIBIT C1.1 VALUE OF $1 INVESTED IN LONG-TERM CAPITAL MANAGEMENT VERSUS S&P 500

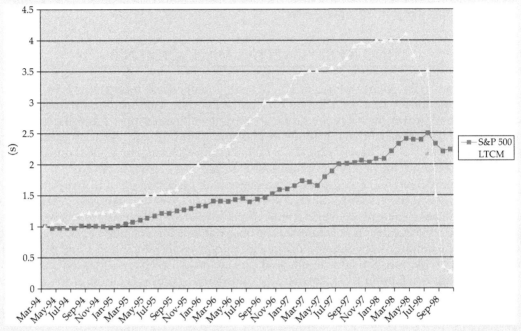

Source: Roger Lowenstein, *When Genius Failed: The Rise and Fall of Long-Term Capital Management* (New York: Random House, 2000).

The fund's success began to pose its own problems. The market lacked sufficient capacity to absorb LTCM's bloated size, as trades that had been profitable initially became impossible to conduct on a massive scale. Moreover, a flood of arbitrage imitators tightened the spreads on LTCM's "bread-and-butter" trades even further. The pressure to continue delivering returns forced LTCM to find new arbitrage opportunities, and the fund diversified into areas where it could not pair its theoretical insights with trading experience. Soon LTCM had made large bets in Russia and in other emerging markets, on S&P futures, and in yield curve, junk bond, merger, and dual-listed securities arbitrage.

Combined with its style drift, the fund's more than 26× leverage put LTCM in an increasingly precarious bubble, which was eventually burst by a combination of factors that forced the fund into a liquidity crisis. In contrast to Scholes's comments about plucking invisible, riskless nickels from the sky, financial theorist Nassim Taleb later compared the fund's aggressive risk-taking to "picking up pennies in front of a steamroller," a steamroller that finally came in the form of 1998's market panic. The departure of frequent LTCM counterparty Salomon Brothers from the arbitrage market that summer put downward pressure on many of the fund's positions, and Russia's default on its government-issued bonds threw international credit markets into a downward spiral. Panicked investors around the globe demonstrated a "flight to quality," selling the risky securities in which LTCM traded and purchasing US Treasury securities, further driving up their price and preventing a price convergence on which the fund had bet so heavily.

None of LTCM's sophisticated theoretical models had contemplated such an internationally correlated credit market collapse, and the fund began hemorrhaging money, losing nearly 20% of its equity in May and June alone. Day after day, every market in which LTCM traded turned against it. Its powerless brain trust watched in horror as its equity shrank to $600 million in early September without any reduction in borrowing, resulting in an unfathomable 200× leverage ratio. Sensing the fund's liquidity crunch, Bear Stearns refused to continue acting as a clearinghouse for the fund's trades, throwing LTCM into a panic. Without the short-term credit that enabled its entire trading operations, the fund could not continue and its longer-term securities grew more illiquid by the day.[9]

Obstinate in their refusal to unwind what they still considered profitable trades hammered by short-term market irrationality, LTCM's partners refused a buyout offer of $250 million by Goldman Sachs, ING Barings, and Warren Buffet's Berkshire Hathaway.[10] However, LTCM's role as a counterparty in thousands of derivatives trades that touched investment firms around the world threatened to provoke a wider collapse in international securities markets if the fund went under, so the US Federal Reserve stepped in to maintain order. Wishing to avoid the precedent of a government bailout of a hedge fund and the moral hazard, it could subsequently encourage, the Fed invited every major investment bank on Wall Street to an emergency meeting in New York and dictated the terms of the $3.625 billion bailout that would preserve market liquidity. The Fed convinced Bankers Trust, Barclays, Chase, Credit Suisse First Boston, Deutsche Bank, Goldman Sachs, Merrill Lynch, JP Morgan, Morgan Stanley, Salomon Smith Barney, and UBS—many of whom were investors in the fund—to contribute $300 million apiece, with $125 million coming from Société Générale and $100 million from Lehman Brothers and Paribas. Eventually the market crisis passed, and each bank managed to liquidate its position at a slight profit. Only one bank contacted by the Fed refused to join the syndicate and share the burden in the name of preserving market integrity.

That bank was Bear Stearns.

Bear's dominant trading position in bonds and derivatives had won it the profitable business of acting as a settlement house for nearly all of LTCM's trading in those markets. On September 22, 1998, just days before the Fed-organized bailout, Bear put the final nail in the LTCM coffin by calling in a short-term debt in the amount of $500 million in an attempt to limit its own exposure to the failing hedge fund, rendering it insolvent in the process. Ever the maverick in investment banking circles, Bear stubbornly refused to contribute to the eventual buyout, even in the face of a potentially apocalyptic market crash and despite the millions in profits it had earned as LTCM's prime broker. In typical Bear fashion, Cayne ignored the howls from other banks that failure to preserve confidence in the markets through a bailout would bring them all down in flames, famously growling through a chewed cigar as the Fed solicited contributions for the emergency financing, "Don't go alphabetically if you want this to work."[11]

Market analysts were nearly unanimous in describing the lessons learned from LTCM's implosion; in effect, the fund's profound leverage had placed it in such a precarious position

---

[9] Roger Lowenstein, *When Genius Failed: The Rise and Fall of Long-Term Capital Management* (New York: Random House, 2000).

[10] Andrew Garfield et al., "Bear Stearns' $500m Call Triggered LTCM Crisis," *London Independent*, September 26, 1998. http://findarticles.com/p/articles/mi_qn4158/is_19980926/ai_n14183149.

[11] Andrew Garfield et al., "Bear Stearns' $500m Call Triggered LTCM Crisis," *London Independent*, September 26, 1998. http://findarticles.com/p/articles/mi_qn4158/is_19980926/ai_n14183149.

that it could not wait for its positions to turn profitable. While its trades were sound in principal, LTCM's predicted price convergence was not realized until long after its equity had been wiped out completely. A less leveraged firm, they explained, might have realized lower profits than the 40% annual return LTCM had offered investors up until the 1998 crisis, but could have weathered the storm once the market turned against it. In the words of economist John Maynard Keynes, the market had remained irrational longer than LTCM could remain solvent. The crisis further illustrated the importance not merely of liquidity but of perception in the less regulated derivatives markets. Once LTCM's ability to meet its obligations was called into question, its demise became inevitable, as it could no longer find counterparties with whom to trade and from whom it could borrow to continue operating.

The thornier question of the Fed's role in bailing out an overly aggressive investment fund in the name of market stability remained unresolved, despite the Fed's insistence on private funding for the actual buyout. Though impossible to foresee at the time, the issue would be revisited anew less than 10 years later, and it would haunt Bear Stearns.

With negative publicity from Bear's $38.5 million settlement with the Securities and Exchange Commission (SEC) regarding charges that it had ignored fraudulent behavior by a client for whom it cleared trades and LTCM's collapse behind it, Bear Stearns continued to grow under Cayne's leadership, with its stock price appreciating some 600% from his assumption of control in 1993 until 2008. However, a rapid-fire sequence of negative events began to unfurl in the summer of 2007 that would push Bear into a liquidity crunch eerily similar to the one that felled LTCM.

THE CREDIT CRISIS

Beginning in the late 1990s, consistent appreciation in US real estate values fueled a decade-long boom in the housing market. During this period, the mortgage business was revolutionized from its traditionally local focus with banks lending directly to homebuyers to a global industry with banks issuing mortgages and then selling them to a diverse pool of investors. Eager to add new products that provided underwriting fees, investment banks began "securitizing" the mortgages, slicing them into various securities differentiated on the basis of the geography of the underlying mortgages, the estimated default risk, and whether the purchaser of the security would receive the interest accruing on the mortgages or the payback of the principal. Investment banks then sold these securities to various investor groups depending on their preferences regarding risk, interest rate exposure, and myriad other factors. Issuance of these collateralized debt obligations, or CDOs, grew to a peak of $421.6 billion in 2006 and $266.9 billion in 1H 2007 in the United States alone (Exhibit C1.2).[12] In the process, the structure of the mortgage industry changed (Exhibit C1.3).[13]

[12] Securities Industry and Financial Markets Association, "Global CDO Market Issuance Data," http://www.sifma.org/research/pdf/SIFMA_CDOIssuanceData2008.pdf.

[13] IMF Global Financial Stability Report, "Financial Market Turbulence: Causes, Consequences, and Policies," 2007.

EXHIBIT C1.2 US QUARTERLY COLLATERALIZED DEBT OBLIGATION ISSUANCE ($ IN BILLIONS)

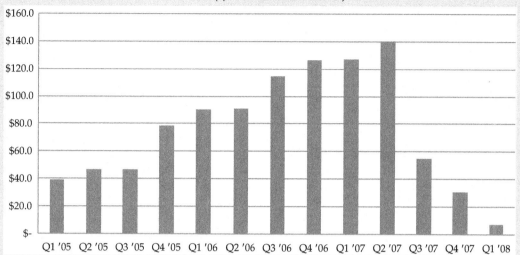

Source: Securities Industry and Financial Markets Association, "Global CDO Market Issuance Data," http://www.sifma.org/research/pdf/SIFMA_CDOIssuanceData2008.pdf.

EXHIBIT C1.3 MORTGAGE MARKET FLOWS AND RISK EXPOSURES

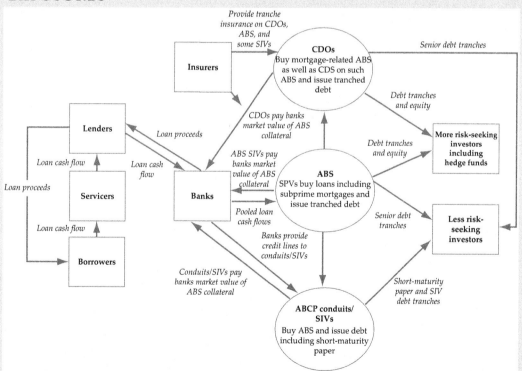

Notes: *ABCP*, asset-backed commercial paper; *ABS*, asset-backed security; *CDO*, collateralized debt obligation; *CDS*, credit default swap; *SIV*, structured investment vehicle; *SPV*, special purpose vehicle.
Source: IMF Global Financial Stability Report, "Financial Market Turbulence: Causes, Consequences, and Policies," 2007.

Previously, small, mostly regional banks had conducted mortgage lending using the funds deposited by their retail customers, which limited the total dollar amount any one bank could lend. More importantly, banks had to rely on their own due diligence to make sure that mortgage terms remained reasonable—that the homebuyer had sufficient income and credit history to repay the loan, or that the appraisal on the property justified the amount lent. The surge of investor appetite for CDOs in the early 2000s allowed lenders to issue mortgages and then immediately securitize them through investment banks, who sold the various tranches of those securities in the mortgage bond market. One can easily recognize the sea change in incentives for lenders; without the loan resting on the bank's balance sheet, the best way to boost profits was to originate more—rather than safer—mortgages before flipping them to investment banks, which reissued them through CDOs. Issuance ballooned.

However, the suddenly lucrative CDO market suffered from inherent limitations on the base of potential homebuyers. Moreover, with interest rates remaining historically low and stable for the better part of a decade, investors—particularly hedge fund investors, who entered the CDO market in earnest in 2004 and 2005[14]—began seeking higher returns by taking on additional risk. The twin pressures of investors seeking higher returns and lenders trying to grow their market led to the boom in higher-risk mortgages to less creditworthy homebuyers, or "subprime" mortgages (Exhibit C1.4).

EXHIBIT C1.4 SUBPRIME ISSUANCE AND SHARE OF MARKET

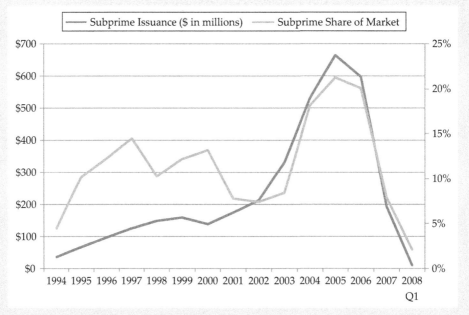

Source: Ellen Schloemer et al., "Losing Ground: Foreclosures in the Subprime Market and Their Cost to Homeowners," Center for Responsible Learning, December 2006. http://www.responsiblelending.org/pdfs/foreclosure-paper-report-2-17.pdf.

[14] Peter Cockhill and James Bagnall, "Hedge Fund Managers Expand Into CDOs and Private Equity," *Hedgeweek*, October 1, 2005. http://www.hedgeweek.com/articles/detail.jsp?content_id=12879.

Officially referring to loans that did not meet the more stringent guidelines of Fannie Mae or Freddie Mac, subprime mortgages were geared toward riskier homebuyers with lower incomes and spottier credit histories. As a result, such mortgages frequently carried higher interest rates, not only increasing investor return but also the likelihood of homeowner default. One common subprime structure was the "2/28" adjustable rate mortgage (ARM), a floating rate loan that featured a low interest rate for the first 2 years before resetting to a significantly higher rate for the final 28 years of the loan, often 500 or more basis points over LIBOR. The long historical trend in rising real estate values and the ready availability of credit in the market convinced many that they could refinance their mortgages before the ARM adjusted to the higher interest rate, allowing them in effect to gain significant equity in the home without significant cash outlay.

The sudden pullback in US housing prices in the summer of 2006 changed all of that (Exhibit C1.5). With the collapse of housing markets in Arizona, California, Florida, and the northeast corridor of the United States, many owners found themselves holding negative equity, meaning the appraised value of the property was less than the mortgage debt outstanding on their loan (Exhibit C1.6). Foreclosures spiked, and suddenly wary lenders stopped issuing new loans almost entirely.

EXHIBIT C1.5 S&P/CASE-SHILLER HOME PRICE INDEX (SPSC20R) APPRECIATION SINCE 2000

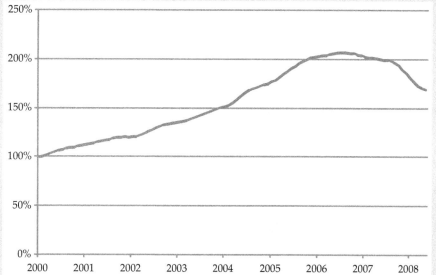

Source: Schloemer et al., "Losing Ground: Foreclosures in the Subprime Market and Their Cost to Homeowners."

EXHIBIT C1.6 FOUR-QUARTER HOUSING PRICE CHANGES BY STATE (2Q 2007–1Q 2008)

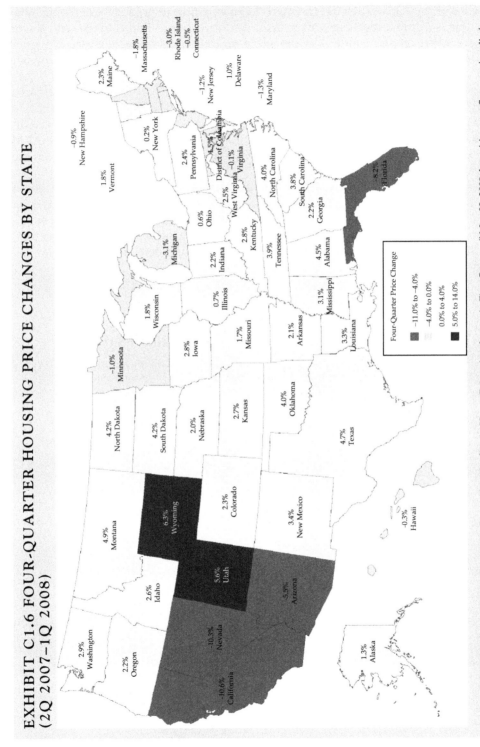

Source: Office of Federal Housing Enterprise Oversight, "Decline in House Prices Accelerates in First Quarter," May 22, 2008. http://www.ofheo.gov/media/hpi/1q08hpi.pdf.

BEAR STEARNS ASSET MANAGEMENT

Like many of its competitors, Bear Stearns saw the rise of the hedge fund industry during the 1990s and began managing its own funds with outside investor capital under the name Bear Stearns Asset Management (BSAM). Unlike its competitors, Bear hired all of its fund managers internally, with each manager specializing in a particular security or asset class. Objections by some Bear executives, such as copresident Alan Schwartz, that such concentration of risk could raise volatility were ignored, and the impressive returns posted by internal funds such as Ralph Cioffi's High-Grade Structured Credit Strategies Fund quieted any concerns.

Cioffi's fund invested in sophisticated credit derivatives backed by mortgage securities. When the housing bubble burst in 2006, Cioffi's trades turned unprofitable, but like many successful Bear traders before him he redoubled his bets, raising a new Enhanced Leverage High-Grade Structured Credit Strategies Fund that would use 100× leverage (as compared to the 35× leverage employed by the original fund).[15] The market continued to turn disastrously against the fund, which was soon stuck with billions of dollars worth of illiquid, unprofitable mortgages. In an attempt to salvage the situation and cut his losses, Cioffi launched a vehicle named Everquest Financial and sold its shares to the public. But when journalists at the *Wall Street Journal* revealed that Everquest's primary assets were the "toxic waste" of money-losing mortgage securities, Bear had no choice but to cancel the public offering. With spectacular losses mounting daily, investors attempted to withdraw their remaining holdings. To free up cash for such redemptions, the fund had to liquidate assets at a loss, selling that only put additional downward pressure on its already underwater positions. Lenders to the fund began making margin calls and threatening to seize its $1.2 billion in collateral, leading to a hastily arranged conference with creditors in which Bear trader and copresident Warren Spector claimed that lenders from Merrill Lynch and JP Morgan Chase did not understand the fund's operations and that Cioffi would turn it around.

In a less turbulent market it might have worked, but the subprime crisis had spent weeks on the front page of financial newspapers around the globe, and every bank on Wall Street was desperate to reduce its own exposure. Insulted and furious that Bear had refused to inject any of its own capital to save the funds, Steve Black, JP Morgan Chase head of investment banking, called Schwartz and said, "We're defaulting you."[16]

The default and subsequent seizure of $400 million in collateral by Merrill Lynch proved highly damaging to Bear Stearns's reputation across Wall Street. In a desperate attempt to save face under the scrutiny of the SEC, Cayne made the unprecedented move of using $1.6 billion of Bear's own capital to prop up the hedge funds. The bailout later revealed deeper problems at the bank when a front-page *Wall Street Journal* article claimed that Cayne had been absent at the height of the scandal, off on a 10-day golf and bridge-playing vacation in Nashville without a cell phone or email device. The article further alleged ongoing marijuana usage by Cayne, who denied the specific 2004 incident identified in the article but refused to make a blanket statement denying any such usage in the past.

[15] Bryan Burrough, "Bringing Down Bear Stearns," *Vanity Fair*, August 2008. http://www.vanityfair.com/politics/features/2008/08/bear_stearns200808.

[16] Bryan Burrough, "Bringing Down Bear Stearns," *Vanity Fair*, August 2008. http://www.vanityfair.com/politics/features/2008/08/bear_stearns200808.

By late July 2007, even Bear's continued support could no longer prop up Cioffi's two beleaguered funds, which paid back just $300 million of the credit its parent had extended. With their holdings virtually worthless, the funds had no choice but to file for bankruptcy protection. The following day, Cayne returned from Nashville and set about trying to calm shareholder fears that Bear was not standing on solid financial ground. Spector would not survive the weekend, with Cayne forcing him out in a sort of public bloodletting to show that things were once again under control. Ironically, his departure may have done more harm than good. After opening an August 3 conference call with a statement of assurance that the company had $11.4 billion in cash and was "taking the situation seriously," Cayne turned the call over to chief financial officer Samuel Molinaro, Jr., and stepped out to speak with an attorney regarding Spector's resignation. When the conversation turned to Q&A, an equity research analyst's question posed to Cayne met with deafening silence. Cayne later returned to the room, but callers were not told this, contributing to the impression of Cayne as a disinterested, absentee CEO.[17]

THE CALM BEFORE THE STORM

On November 14, just 2 weeks after the *Journal* story questioning Cayne's commitment and leadership, Bear Stearns reported that it would write down $1.2 billion in mortgage-related losses. (The figure would later grow to $1.9 billion.) CFO Molinaro suggested that the worst had passed, and to outsiders, at least, the firm appeared to have narrowly escaped disaster.

Behind the scenes, however, Bear management had already begun searching for a white knight, hiring Gary Parr at Lazard to examine its options for a cash injection. Privately, Schwartz and Parr spoke with Kohlberg Kravis Roberts (KKR) & Co. founder Henry Kravis, who had first learned the leveraged buyout market while a partner at Bear Stearns in the 1960s. Kravis sought entry into the profitable brokerage business at depressed prices, while Bear sought an injection of more than $2 billion in equity capital (for a reported 20% of the company) and the calming effect that a strong, respected personality like Kravis would have upon shareholders. Ultimately the deal fell apart, largely due to management's fear that KKR's significant equity stake and the presence of Kravis on the board would alienate the firm's other private equity clientele, who often competed with KKR for deals. Throughout the fall, Bear continued to search for potential acquirers, with private equity firm J.C. Flowers & Co., JP Morgan Chase, and Berkshire Hathaway CEO Warren Buffett all kicking the tires before ultimately passing. With the market watching intently to see if Bear shored up its financing, Cayne managed to close only a $1 billion cross-investment with CITIC, the state-owned investment company of the People's Republic of China.

Meanwhile, a battle raged within the firm, with factions pitted against each other on how to proceed with Bear's mortgage holdings, which were still valued at $56 billion despite steady price declines. With traders insisting that any remaining mortgage positions be cut, head mortgage trader Tom Marano instituted a "chaos trade," essentially a massive short on

---

[17] Kate Kelly, "Bear CEO's Handling of Crisis Raises Issues," *Wall Street Journal*, November 1, 2007. http://online.wsj.com/public/article_print/SB119387369474078336.html.

the ABX, a family of subprime indexes. They also shorted commercial mortgage indexes and the stocks of other financials with mortgage exposure, such as Wells Fargo and Countrywide Financial.

Bear's executive and risk committees met in late September 2007 to review the trades, just after negotiations to sell a 10% stake in Bear to Allianz SE's Pacific Investment Management Co. had failed. With Cayne recovering from an infection, all eyes turned to Greenberg, who had become increasingly active throughout the crisis. Uncomfortable with the size of Bear's remaining mortgage holdings and the potential volatility of the chaos trade, the veteran trader insisted that the firm reduce its exposure. "We've got to cut!" he shouted, invoking the firm's historical aggressiveness in trimming unprofitable positions.

Despite the fact that the hedges had returned close to half a billion dollars, Schwartz followed Greenberg's advice, requesting trades to offset specific assets in Bear's portfolio instead of the broader, more market-based chaos trade.

Morale sunk to demoralizing lows as fall turned to winter, with bankers squabbling over a greatly diminished bonus pool and top Bear executives clamoring for Cayne's dismissal as CEO. Top performers at Bear demanded that Schwartz oust Cayne or else face a mass exodus. Matters worsened on December 20, when Bear posted the first quarterly loss since its founding some 85 years earlier. The next day it received an email from colossal bond manager PIMCO indicating its discomfort with exposure to the financial sector and its desire to unwind billions of dollars worth of trades with Bear. An emergency conference call to Bear alumnus and PIMCO managing director William Powers convinced the fund to hold off on any such drastic moves at least until a meeting with Bear executives, but Powers's admonition came through loud and clear: "You need to raise equity."[18]

In an attempt to stem the tide of quality employees fleeing what appeared to be a sinking ship, Schwartz conversed with the board and received approval to ask for Cayne's resignation, which he tendered on January 8. Cayne remained chairman of the board, with Schwartz stepping in as the new CEO. Schwartz immediately turned his sights to the Q1 numbers, desperate to ensure that Bear would post a quarterly profit and hopefully calm the growing uneasiness among its shareholders, employees, creditors, and counterparties in the market.

RUN ON THE BANK

Bear's $0.89 profit per share in the first quarter of 2008 did little to quiet the growing whispers of its financial instability (Exhibit C1.7). It seemed that every day another major investment bank reported mortgage-related losses, and for whatever reason, Bear's name kept cropping up in discussions of the by-then infamous subprime crisis. Exacerbating Bear's public relations problem, the SEC had launched an investigation into the collapse of the two BSAM hedge funds, and rumors of massive losses at three major hedge funds further rattled an already uneasy market. Nonetheless, Bear executives felt that the storm had passed, reasoning that its almost $21 billion in cash reserves had convinced the market of its long-term viability (Exhibit C1.8).

---

[18] Kate Kelly, "Lost Opportunities Haunt Final Days of Bear Stearns," *Wall Street Journal*, May 27, 2008. http://online.wsj.com/article/SB121184521826521301.html.

EXHIBIT C1.7 CONDENSED CONSOLIDATED STATEMENTS OF INCOME, THREE MONTHS ENDED (US$ IN MILLIONS, EXCEPT SHARE AND PER SHARE DATA)

	February 29, 2008	February 28, 2007
REVENUES		
Commissions	330	281
Principal transactions	515	1,342
Investment banking	230	350
Interest and dividends	2,198	2,657
Asset management and other income	154	168
Total revenues	3,427	4,798
Interest expense	1,948	2,316
Revenues, net of interest expense	1,479	2,482
NONINTEREST EXPENSES		
Employee compensation and benefits	754	1,204
Floor brokerage, exchange, and clearance fees	79	56
Communications and technology	154	128
Occupancy	73	57
Advertising and market development	40	37
Professional fees	100	72
Other expenses	126	93
Total noninterest expenses	1,326	1,647
Income before provision for income taxes	153	835
Provision for income taxes	38	281
Net income	115	554
Preferred stock dividends	5	6
Net income applicable to common shares	110	548
Basic earnings per share	$0.89	$4.23
Diluted earnings per share	$0.86	$3.82
Weighted average common shares outstanding		
Basic	129,128,281	133,094,747
Diluted	138,539,248	149,722,654
Cash dividends declared per common share	$0.32	$0.32

EXHIBIT C1.8 CONDENSED CONSOLIDATED BALANCE SHEETS, THREE MONTHS ENDED (US$ IN MILLIONS, EXCEPT SHARE AND PER SHARE DATA)

	February 29, 2008	February 28, 2007
ASSETS		
Cash and cash equivalents	20,786	21,406
Cash and securities deposited with clearing organizations or segregated in compliance with federal regulations	14,910	12,890
Securities received as collateral	15,371	15,599
Collateralized agreements		
Securities purchased under agreements to resell	26,888	27,878
Securities borrowed	87,143	82,245
Receivables		
Customers	41,990	41,115
Brokers, dealers, and others	10,854	11,622
Interest and dividends	488	785
Financial instruments owned, at fair value	118,201	122,518
Financial instruments owned and pledged as collateral, at fair value	22,903	15,724
Total financial instruments owned, at fair value	141,104	138,242
Assets of variable interest entities and mortgage loan special purpose entities	29,991	33,553
Net PP&E	608	605
Other assets	8,862	9,422
Total assets	398,995	395,362
LIABILITIES AND STOCKHOLDERS' EQUITY		
Unsecured short-term borrowings	8,538	11,643
Obligation to return securities received as collateral	15,371	15,599
Collateralized financings		
Securities sold under agreements to repurchase	98,272	102,373
Securities loaned	4,874	3,935
Other secured borrowings	7,778	12,361

Continued

EXHIBIT C1.8 CONDENSED CONSOLIDATED BALANCE SHEETS, THREE MONTHS ENDED (US$ IN MILLIONS, EXCEPT SHARE AND PER SHARE DATA)—cont'd

	February 29, 2008	February 28, 2007
ASSETS		
Payables		
Customers	91,632	83,204
Brokers, dealers, and others	5,642	4,101
Interest and dividends	853	1301
Financial instruments sold, but not yet purchased, at fair value	51,544	43,807
Liabilities of variable interest entities and mortgage loan special purpose entities	26,739	30,605
Accrued employee compensation and benefits	360	1,651
Other liabilities and accrued expenses	3,743	4,451
Long-term borrowings (includes $9018 and $8500 at fair value as of February 29, 2008 and November 30, 2007, respectively)	71,753	68,538
Total liabilities	387,099	383,569
STOCKHOLDERS' EQUITY		
Preferred stock	352	352
Common stock	185	185
Paid-in capital	5,619	4,986
Retained earnings	9,419	9,441
Employee stock compensation plans	2,164	2,478
Accumulated other comprehensive income (loss)	25	−8
Shares held in RSU trust	−2,955	−
Treasury stock, at cost	−2,913	−5,641
Total stockholders' equity	11,896	11,793
Total liabilities and stockholders' equity	398,995	395,362

Instead, on Monday, March 10, 2008, Moody's downgraded 163 tranches of mortgage-backed bonds issued by Bear across 15 transactions.[19] The credit rating agency had drawn

[19] Sue Chang, "Moody's Downgrades Bear Stearns Alt-A Deals," *MarketWatch*, March 10, 2008. http://www.marketwatch.com/news/story/moodys-downgrades-bear-stearns-alt-deals/story. aspx?guid=%7B9989153A-B0F4–43B6-AE11-7B2DBE7E0B9C%7D.

sharp criticism in its role in the subprime meltdown from analysts who felt the company had overestimated the creditworthiness of mortgage-backed securities and failed to alert the market of the danger as the housing market turned. As a result, Moody's was in the process of downgrading nearly all of its ratings, but as the afternoon wore on, Bear's stock price seemed to be reacting far more negatively than competitor firms.

Wall Street's drive toward ever more sophisticated communications devices had created an interconnected network of traders and bankers across the world. On most days, Internet chat and mobile email devices relayed gossip about compensation, major employee departures, and even sports betting lines. On the morning of March 10, however, it was carrying one message to the exclusion of all others: Bear was having liquidity problems.

At noon, CNBC took the story public on *Power Lunch*. As Bear's stock price fell more than 10% to $63, Ace Greenberg frantically placed calls to various executives, demanding that someone publicly deny any such problems. When contacted himself, Greenberg told a CNBC correspondent that the rumors were "totally ridiculous," angering CFO Molinaro, who felt that denying the rumor would only legitimize it and trigger further panic selling, making prophesies of Bear's illiquidity self-fulfilling.[20] Just 2 h later, however, Bear appeared to have dodged a bullet. News of New York governor Eliot Spitzer's involvement in a high-class prostitution ring wiped any financial rumors off the front page, leading Bear executives to believe the worst was once again behind them.

Instead, the rumors exploded anew the next day, as many interpreted the Federal Reserve's announcement of a new $200 billion lending program to help financial institutions through the credit crisis[21] as aimed specifically toward Bear Stearns. The stock dipped as low as $55.42 before closing at $62.97 (Exhibit C1.9). Meanwhile, Bear executives faced a new crisis in the form of an explosion of novation requests, in which a party to a risky contract tries to eliminate its risky position by selling it to a third party. Credit Suisse, Deutsche Bank, and Goldman Sachs all reported a deluge of novation requests from firms trying to reduce their exposure to Bear's credit risk. The speed and force of this explosion of novation requests meant that before Bear could act, both Goldman Sachs and Credit Suisse issued emails to their traders holding up any requests relating to Bear Stearns pending approval by their credit departments. Once again, the electronically linked gossip network of trading desks around the world dealt a blow to investor confidence in Bear's stability, as a false rumor circulated that Credit Suisse's memo had forbidden its traders from engaging in any trades with Bear.[22] The decrease in confidence in Bear's liquidity could be quantified by the rise in the cost of credit default swaps on Bear's debt. The price of such an instrument—which effectively acts as 5 years of insurance against a default on $10 million of Bear's debt—spiked to more than $626,000 from less than $100,000 in October, indicating heavy betting by some firms that Bear would be unable to pay its liabilities.[23]

---

[20] Burrough, "Bringing Down Bear Stearns."

[21] Chris Reese, "Bonds Extend Losses After Fed Announcement," *Reuters News*, March 11, 2008. http://www.reuters.com/article/bondsNews/idUSNYD00017820080311.

[22] Kelly, "Fear, Rumors Touched Off Fatal Run on Bear Stearns."

[23] Kelly, "Fear, Rumors Touched Off Fatal Run on Bear Stearns."

EXHIBIT C1.9 SHARE PRICE AND TRADING VOLUME

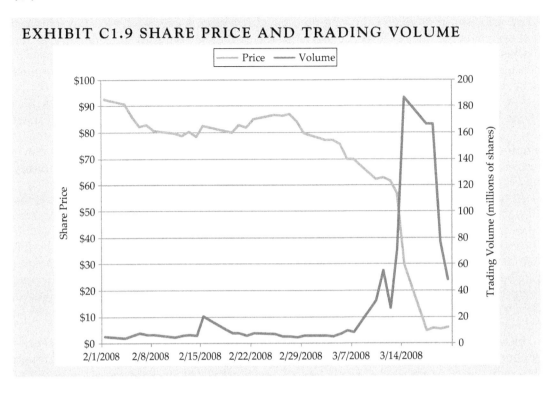

Internally, Bear debated whether to address the rumors publicly, ultimately deciding to arrange a Wednesday morning interview of Schwartz by CNBC correspondent David Faber. Not wanting to encourage rumors with a hasty departure, Schwartz did the interview live from Bear's annual media conference in Palm Beach. Chosen because of his perceived friendliness to Bear, Faber nonetheless opened the interview with a devastating question that claimed direct knowledge of a trader whose credit department had temporarily held up a trade with Bear. Later during the interview, Faber admitted that the trade had finally gone through, but he had called into question, Bear's fundamental capacity to operate as a trading firm. One veteran trader later commented, "You knew right at that moment that Bear Stearns was dead, right at the moment he asked that question. Once you raise that idea, that the firm can't follow through on a trade, it's over. Faber killed him. He just killed him."

Despite sentiment at Bear that Schwartz had finally put the company's best foot forward and refuted rumors of its illiquidity, hedge funds began pulling their accounts in earnest, bringing Bear's reserves down to $15 billion. Additionally, repo lenders—whose overnight loans to investment banks must be renewed daily—began informing Bear that they would not renew the next morning, forcing the firm to find new sources of credit. Schwartz phoned Parr at Lazard, Molinaro reviewed Bear's plans for an emergency sale in the event of a crisis, and one of the firm's attorneys called the president of the Federal Reserve to explain Bear's situation and implore him to accelerate the newly announced program that would allow investment banks to use mortgage securities as collateral for emergency loans from the Fed's discount window, normally reserved for commercial banks (Exhibit C1.10).[24]

---

[24] Burrough, "Bringing Down Bear Stearns."

EXHIBIT C1.10 DIFFERENCES IN REGULATION— COMMERCIAL BANKS VERSUS INVESTMENT BANKS

	Commercial Banks	Investment Banks
General business model	Accept deposits and lend them out in a variety of products, provide financial services for individuals and businesses	Underwrite equity and debt offerings, trade stocks and bonds, provide advisory (e.g., M&A) services
Federally insured?	Yes	No (pre-2008)
Primary source of assets at risk	Depositors	Shareholders
Restrictions on leverage	Significant—10% capital ratio considered "well-capitalized"	None
Primary oversight	Federal Reserve	Securities and Exchange Commission
Restriction of activities	Prohibited from investing in real estate and commodities; new activities require Fed approval	None

Bear executives struggled to placate an increasingly mutinous employee base. Bruce Lisman, head of equities, stood on his desk and implored traders to remain focused and weather the storm, pointing out Bear's historical resilience. Greenberg once again pretended to swing a golf club on the trading floor, as if to suggest that Bear had survived far greater crises.

Regardless of their effect on employees, such assurances had no effect on the market. The trickle of withdrawals that had begun earlier in the week turned into an unstoppable torrent of cash flowing out the door on Thursday. Meanwhile, Bear's stock continued its sustained nosedive, falling nearly 15% to an intraday low of $50.48 before rallying to close down 1.5%. At lunch, Schwartz assured a crowded meeting of Bear executives that the whirlwind rumors were simply market noise, only to find himself interrupted by Michael Minikes, senior managing director.

"Do you have any idea what is going on?" Minikes shouted. "Our cash is flying out the door! Our clients are leaving us!"[25]

Hedge fund clients jumped ship in droves. Renaissance Technologies withdrew approximately $5 billion in trading accounts, and D.E. Shaw followed suit with an equal amount. That evening, Bear executives assembled in a sixth floor conference room to survey the carnage. In less than a week, the firm had burned through all but $5.9 billion of its $18.3 billion in reserves and was still on the hook for $2.4 billion in short-term debt to Citigroup. With a panicked market making more withdrawals the next day almost certain, Schwartz accepted the inevitable need for additional financing and had Parr revisit merger discussions with JP Morgan CEO James Dimon that had stalled in the fall. Flabbergasted at the idea that an agreement could be reached that night, Dimon nonetheless agreed to send a team of bankers over to analyze Bear's books.

[25] Kelly, "Fear, Rumors Touched Off Fatal Run on Bear Stearns."

Parr's call interrupted Dimon's 52nd birthday celebration at a Greek restaurant just a few blocks away from Bear headquarters, where a phalanx of attorneys had begun preparing emergency bankruptcy filings and documents necessary for a variety of cash-injecting transactions. Facing almost certain insolvency in the next 24 h, Schwartz hastily called an emergency board meeting late that night, with most board members dialing in remotely. Cayne missed most of the conversation while playing in a bridge tournament in Detroit.

Bear's nearly 400 subsidiaries would make a bankruptcy filing impossibly complicated, so Schwartz continued to cling to the hope for an emergency cash infusion to get Bear through Friday. As JP Morgan's bankers pored over Bear's positions, they balked at the firm's precarious position and the continued size of its mortgage holdings, insisting that the Fed get involved in a bailout they considered far too risky to take on alone. Fed officials had been gathered down the hall for hours, and discussions continued into early Friday morning between the Fed and JP Morgan as Schwartz and Molinaro ate cold pizza, the decision now out of their hands.

Its role as a counterparty in trillions of dollars' worth of derivatives contracts bore an eerie similarity to LTCM, and the Fed once again saw the potential for financial Armageddon if Bear were allowed to collapse of its own accord. An emergency liquidation of the firm's assets would have put strong downward pressure on global securities prices, exacerbating an already chaotic market environment. Facing a hard deadline of credit markets' open on Friday morning, the Fed and JP Morgan wrangled back and forth on how to save Bear. Working around the clock, they finally reached an agreement wherein JP Morgan would access the Fed's discount window and in turn offer Bear a $30 billion credit line that, as dictated by a last-minute insertion by Morgan general counsel Steven Cutler, would be good for 28 days. As the press release went public, Bear executives cheered; Bear would have almost a month to seek alternative financing.

BEAR'S LAST WEEKEND

Where Bear had seen a lifeline, however, the market saw instead a last desperate gasp for help. Incredulous Bear executives could only watch in horror as the firm's capital continued to fly out of its coffers. On Friday morning, Bear burned through the last of its reserves in a matter of hours. A midday conference call in which Schwartz confidently assured investors that the credit line would allow Bear to continue "business as usual" did little to stop the bleeding, and its stock lost almost half of its already depressed value, closing at $30 per share.[26]

All day Friday, Parr set about desperately trying to save his client, searching every corner of the financial world for potential investors or buyers of all or part of Bear. Given the severity of the situation, he could rule out nothing, from a sale of the lucrative prime brokerage operations to a merger or sale of the entire company. Ideally, he hoped to find what he termed a "validating investor," a respected Wall Street name to join the board, adding immediate credibility and perhaps quiet the now deafening rumors of Bear's imminent demise. Sadly,

[26] Kelly, "Bear Stearns Neared Collapse Twice in Frenzied Last Days."

only a few such personalities with the reputation and war chest necessary to play the role of savior existed, and most of them had already passed on Bear.

Nonetheless, Schwartz left Bear headquarters on Friday evening relieved that the firm had lived to see the weekend and secured 28 days of breathing room. During the ride home to Greenwich, an unexpected phone call from New York Federal Reserve President Timothy Geithner and Treasury Secretary Henry Paulson shattered that illusion. Paulson told a stunned Schwartz that the Fed's line of credit would expire Sunday night, giving Bear 48 h to find a buyer or file for bankruptcy. The demise of the 28-day clause remains a mystery; the speed necessary early Friday morning and the inclusion of the clause by Morgan's general counsel suggest that Bear executives had misinterpreted it, although others believe that Paulson and Geithner had soured both on Bear's prospects and on market perception of an emergency loan from the Fed as Friday wore on. Either way, the Fed had made up its mind, and a Saturday morning appeal from Schwartz failed to sway Geithner.

All day Saturday, prospective buyers streamed through Bear's headquarters to pick through the rubble as Parr attempted to orchestrate Bear's last-minute salvation. Chaos reigned, with representatives from every major bank on Wall Street, J.C. Flowers, KKR, and countless others poring over Bear's positions in an effort to determine the value of Bear's massive illiquid holdings and how the Fed would help in financing. Some prospective buyers wanted just a piece of the dying bank, others the whole firm, with still others proposing more complicated multiple-step transactions that would slice Bear to ribbons. One by one, they dropped out, until J.C. Flowers made an offer for 90% of Bear for a total of up to $2.6 billion, but the offer was contingent on the private equity firm raising $20 billion from a bank consortium, and $20 billion in risky credit was unlikely to appear overnight.[27]

That left JP Morgan. Apparently the only bank willing to come to the rescue, Morgan had sent no fewer than 300 bankers representing 16 different product groups to Bear headquarters to value the firm. The sticking point, as with all the bidders, was Bear's mortgage holdings. Even after a massive write-down, it was impossible to assign a value to such illiquid (and publicly maligned) securities with any degree of accuracy. Having forced the default of the BSAM hedge funds that started this mess less than a year earlier, Steve Black cautioned Schwartz and Parr not to focus on Friday's $32 per share close and indicated that any Morgan bid could be between $8 and $12.[28]

On its final 10Q in March, Bear listed $399 billion in assets and $387 billion in liabilities, leaving just $12 billion in equity for a 32× leverage multiple. Bear initially estimated that this included $120 billion of "risk-weighted" assets, those that might be subject to subsequent write-downs. As Morgan's bankers worked around the clock trying to get to the bottom of Bear's balance sheet, they came to estimate the figure at nearly $220 billion. That pessimistic outlook, combined with Sunday morning's *New York Times* article reiterating Bear's recent troubles, dulled Morgan's appetite for jumping onto what appeared to be a sinking ship. Later, one Morgan banker shuddered, recalling the article. "That article certainly had an impact on my thinking. Just the reputational aspects of it, getting into bed with these people."[29]

[27] Burrough, "Bringing Down Bear Stearns."

[28] Burrough, "Bringing Down Bear Stearns."

[29] Burrough, "Bringing Down Bear Stearns."

On Saturday morning, Morgan backed out and Dimon told a shell-shocked Schwartz to pursue any other option available to him. The problem was, no such alternative existed. Knowing this, and the possibility that the liquidation of Bear could throw the world's financial markets into chaos, Fed representatives immediately phoned Dimon. As it had in the LTCM case a decade ago, the Fed relied heavily on suasion, or "jawboning," the longtime practice of attempting to influence market participants by appeals to reason rather than a declaration by fiat. For hours, Morgan's and the Fed's highest-ranking officials played a game of high-stakes poker, with each side bluffing and Bear's future hanging in the balance. The Fed wanted to avoid unprecedented government participation in the bailout of a private investment firm, while Morgan wanted to avoid taking on any of the "toxic waste" in Bear's mortgage holdings. "They kept saying, 'We're not going to do it,' and we kept saying, 'We really think you should do it'," recalled one Fed official. "This went on for hours… They kept saying, 'We can't do this on our own'."[30] With the hours ticking away until Monday's Australian markets would open at 6:00 p.m. New York time, both sides had to compromise.

On Sunday afternoon, Schwartz stepped out of a 1:00 emergency meeting of Bear's board of directors to take the call from Dimon. The offer would come somewhere in the range of $4–$5 per share.

Hearing the news from Schwartz, the Bear board erupted with rage. Dialing in from the same bridge tournament in Detroit, Cayne exploded, ranting furiously that the firm should file for bankruptcy protection under Chapter 11 rather than accept such a humiliating offer, which would reduce his 5.66 million shares—once worth nearly $1 billion—to less than $30 million in value. In reality, however, bankruptcy was impossible. As Parr explained, changes to the federal bankruptcy code in 2005 meant that a Chapter 11 filing would be tantamount to Bear falling on its sword, because regulators would have to seize Bear's accounts, immediately ceasing the firm's operations and forcing its liquidation. There would be no reorganization.

Even as Cayne raged against the $4 offer, the Fed's concern over the appearance of a $30 billion loan to a failing investment bank, while American homeowners faced foreclosures compelled Treasury Secretary Paulson to pour salt in Bear's wounds. Officially, the Fed had remained hands-off in the LTCM bailout, relying on its powers of suasion to convince other banks to step up in the name of market stability. Just 10 years later, they could find no takers. The speed of Bear's collapse, the impossibility of conducting true due diligence in such a compressed time frame, and the incalculable risk of taking on Bear's toxic mortgage holdings scared off every buyer and forced the Fed from an advisory role into a principal role in the bailout. Worried that a price deemed at all generous to Bear might subsequently encourage moral hazard—increased risky behavior by investment banks secure in the knowledge that in a worst-case scenario, disaster would be averted by a federal bailout—Paulson determined that the transaction, while rescuing the firm, also had to be punitive to Bear shareholders. He called Dimon, who reiterated the contemplated offer range.

"That sounds high to me," Paulson told the JP Morgan chief. "I think this should be done at a very low price." It was moments later that Braunstein called Parr. "The number's $2."

---

[30] Burrough, "Bringing Down Bear Stearns."

Under Delaware law, executives must act on behalf of both shareholders and creditors when a company enters the "zone of insolvency," and Schwartz knew that Bear had rocketed through that zone over the past few days. Faced with bankruptcy or Morgan, Bear had no choice but to accept the embarrassingly low offer that represented a 97% discount off its $32 close on Friday evening. Schwartz convinced the weary Bear board that $2 would be "better than nothing," and by 6:30 p.m., the deal was unanimously approved.

After 85 years in the market, Bear Stearns ceased to exist.

Investment Banking in 2008 (B): A Brave New World

THE AFTERMATH OF BEAR STEARNS

Furious Bear Stearns shareholders found a loophole in the hastily arranged merger documents. In the rush to consummate the deal, JP Morgan had accidentally agreed to honor Bear's trades for up to a year irrespective of shareholder approval of the merger. This oversight created the terrifying specter of Morgan failing to acquire Bear but nonetheless remaining on the hook for billions in potential losses from Bear trades gone awry. Holding negotiating leverage for the first time since the crisis began, newly minted Bear CEO Alan Schwartz pushed JP Morgan CEO James Dimon to up the final offer price from $2. In the ensuing week-long fracas, Bear once again appeared headed for bankruptcy, this time via a Chapter 7 liquidation that would have put downward pressure on securities prices around the world. With the Fed's reluctant approval, Morgan finally increased its bid to $10 per share for a total transaction value of $1.2 billion. The Fed lent JP Morgan $30 billion, taking Bear's mortgage holdings as collateral. Morgan assumed responsibility for the first $1 billion of any potential losses, leaving US taxpayers with $29 billion in exposure to Bear portfolios. The transaction was so difficult to value that Gary Parr's Lazard approved fairness opinions on both the $2 and $10 per share offers within the span of 1 week.

As Dimon began the herculean undertaking of integrating two financial colossi with sprawling, overlapping operations and profoundly different cultures, market observers attempted to make sense of the shocking speed with which Bear went from a viable investment bank to a party with whom no one in the market wanted to trade. Some observers pointed to its extreme leverage and its excessive exposure to risky subprime securities, but many Bear executives, largely off the record, claimed that Bear had fallen victim to a pernicious group of rumor-mongering hedge funds that had taken out massive short positions on Bear's stock in an effort to depress its stock price. So convinced were Bear executives that so-called "shorts" were out to get them that mortgage head Tom Marano rebuffed an offer of help from Citadel Investment Group CEO Kenneth Griffin, claiming, "There's such concern that you're short that I wouldn't even go there."[1] While others pointed out the irony of the notoriously vicious Bear accusing others of sharp practices and foul play, these rumors gained steam on July 15, when the Securities and Exchange Commission (SEC) subpoenaed more than 50 hedge funds (including Citadel, a major Bear client) as part of an investigation into the bank's demise. Additionally, the SEC took the unprecedented step of temporarily banning short sales of financial institution stocks. Unfortunately, this ban on short selling effectively shut down a large portion of the convertible securities market, as 659 convertible securities issued during the first 8 months of 2008 came

---

[1] Kate Kelly, "Bear Stearns Neared Collapse Twice in Frenzied Last Days," *Wall Street Journal*, May 29, 2008, http://online.wsj.com/article/SB121202057232127889.html.

from financial companies, including Bank of America and Citigroup. The shutdown stemmed from the fact that hedge funds acted as the principal investors in convertible securities, simultaneously selling convertible issuer stock as a hedge to their purchase of the convertible note or preferred stock to create a theoretically market-neutral position. The ban caused massive losses in hedge fund portfolios and dissuaded them from making additional investments, denying would-be issuers access to needed capital.

The SEC's emergency order also placed a ban on so-called "naked" shorting, or selling shares in a company without a formal agreement to borrow the shares for the sale. In effect, this reduced the total amount of short interest that could accumulate in a stock. The irony that many of these newly protected financial institutions' trading operations had significant short positions themselves was not lost on financial journalists, one of whom dubbed the emergency order "Operation Stocks Go Up Always."[2] The SEC defended the order on the grounds that unusual market conditions required an extreme response, and that the unique vulnerability of financial institutions to rumors of creditworthiness differentiated such institutions from more traditional operating companies.

At the heart of the rumors that consumed Bear Stearns were novation orders, requests sent by Bear clients to other investment banks asking them to assume contracts agreeing to buy or sell securities to Bear in exchange for a fee. Bear managers alleged that the concentration of such requests at three major banks (Goldman Sachs, Credit Suisse, and Deutsche Bank) represented an attempt to flood those banks' credit departments, resulting in delays in clearing that further fueled the gossip that Bear's credit was no good. If so, it worked; both Goldman and Credit Suisse did delay such requests, and the rumor got back to the market with devastating speed. Allegations that a group of hedge fund managers had toasted Bear's collapse at a breakfast the Sunday morning of the deal and planned a subsequent attack on Lehman Brothers further fueled such speculation.[3] Lehman survived the summer, however, largely because the Fed's acceleration of its emergency lending program allowed it and other banks to access the discount window that had been closed to Bear. Many opined that Bear came up just a week short, for the ability to pledge mortgage securities as collateral against such emergency loans might have allowed it to survive as an independent bank.

Perhaps the greatest amount of speculation surrounded the topic of the Fed's role in the bailout and whether New York Fed President Timothy Geithner acted appropriately; he had prevented a major financial market meltdown, but had he gotten the best possible deal for American taxpayers, now on the hook for $29 billion in potential losses from Bear's mortgage holdings? Geithner's palpably tense interrogation by the Senate Banking Committee on April 3 revealed widespread legislator sentiment that the bailout had benefited Wall Street at the expense of Main Street.[4] Defenders pointed out that Henry Paulson forced a painfully low share price (albeit one that climbed after the offer) so as to discourage banks from taking on similar risk, but critics questioned the Fed's involvement in the first place.

[2] David Gaffen, "Four at Four: Operation Stocks Go Up Always," *Marketbeat*, July 15, 2008, http://blogs.wsj.com/marketbeat/2008/07/15/four-at-four-operation-stocks-go-up-always.

[3] Bryan Burrough, "Bringing Down Bear Stearns," *Vanity Fair*, August 2008, http://www.vanityfair.com/politics/features/2008/08/bear_stearns200808; http://www.vanityfair.com/politics/features/2008/08/bear_stearns200808?printable=true&currentPage=all.

[4] Gary Weiss, "The Man Who Saved (or Got Suckered by) Wall Street," *Portfolio.com*, June 2008, http://www.portfolio.com/executives/features/2008/05/12/New-York-Fed-Chief-Tim-Geithner.

Whatever the implications, bankers and regulators sighed with relief at Bear's rescue, assuming that the Fed's bailout of the beleaguered bank had averted crisis while its insistence that JP Morgan assume responsibility for the first billion dollars in losses from the loan had dissuaded further irresponsible risk-seeking. In truth, the worst was yet to come, for the tangled roots of 2008's global financial meltdown lay in the previous decade of financial and banking deregulation.

GRAMM–LEACH–BLILEY AND THE FALL OF GLASS–STEAGALL

On April 6, 1998, Citicorp announced its plans for the largest corporate merger in history by joining with the Travelers Group. The $70 billion deal would merge America's second-largest commercial bank with a sprawling financial conglomerate offering banking, insurance, and brokerage services. Just a year earlier, Travelers had become the country's third-largest brokerage house with its 1997 acquisition of Salomon Brothers, the investment banking firm that first inspired the industry's shift away from traditional advisory services to proprietary trading. Touting the pressures of technological change, diversification, globalization of the banking industry, and both individual and corporate customers' desire for a "one-stop shop" as justification, both companies lobbied hard for the merger's regulatory approval.[5]

The proposed transaction violated portions of 1933's Glass–Steagall Act, part of sweeping securities and banking regulations enacted in the wake of the Great Depression. The Act prohibited the combination of a depository institution, such as a bank holding company, with other financial companies, such as investment banks and brokerage houses. Citigroup successfully obtained a temporary waiver for its violation of the Act, completed the merger, and then intensified the decades-old effort to repeal Glass–Steagall. Inspired by a desire to make US investment banks competitive with foreign deposit-taking investment banks such as UBS, Deutsche Bank, and Credit Suisse First Boston, a Republican Congress and President Clinton passed the Gramm–Leach–Bliley Financial Services Modernization Act in 1999, permitting insurance companies, investment banks, and commercial banks to compete on equal footing across products and markets. The subsequent Commodity Futures Modernization Act of 2000 further deregulated the industry by weakening regulatory control over futures contracts and credit default swaps.

Both liberated and revolutionized, the banking industry embarked on a decade of acquisitions that concentrated the world's financial power in fewer and fewer hands. Acquisitions of investment banks by commercial banks became commonplace, with FleetBoston buying Robertson Stephens, Bank of America buying Montgomery Securities, Chase Manhattan buying JP Morgan (and the combined entity JPMorgan Chase acquiring Bank One and, later, Bear Stearns), PNC Bank purchasing Harris Williams, Orix buying a controlling interest in Houlihan Lokey, and Wells Fargo buying Barrington (Exhibit C2.1). As international banking barriers fell and the global markets grew less segmented, the drive for consolidation accelerated, spurred on by the apparent success of the "universal bank" model.

---

[5] "Financial Powerhouse," NewsHour with Jim Lehrer transcript, April 7, 1998, http://www.pbs.org/newshour/bb/business/jan-june98/merger_4-7.html.

EXHIBIT C2.1 MAJOR BANK MERGERS SINCE 1997

Year	Acquirer	Target	Name of Merged Entity	Transaction Value
1997	U.S. Bancorp	First Bank System, Inc.	U.S. Bancorp	
	NationsBank Corp.	Boatmen's Bancshares	NationsBank Corp.	$9.6 billion
	Washington Mutual	Great Western Financial Corp.	Washington Mutual	
	First Union Corp.	Signet Banking Corp.	First Union Corp.	
	National City Corp.	First of America Bank	National City Corp.	
1998	NationsBank Corp.	Barnett Banks, Inc.	NationsBank Corp.	
	First Union Corp.	CoreStates Financial Corp.	First Union Corp.	
	NationsBank Corp.	BankAmerica Corp.	Bank of America Corp.	
	Golden State Bancorp	First Nationwide Holdings, Inc.	Golden State Bancorp	
	Norwest Corp	Wells Fargo Corp.	Wells Fargo Corp.	
	Star Banc Corp.	Firstar Holdings Corp.	Firstar Corp.	
	Banc One Corp.	First Chicago NBD Corp.	Bank One Corp.	
	Travelers Group	Citicorp	Citigroup	$140 billion
	SunTrust Bank	Crestar Financial Corp.	SunTrust Banks, Inc.	
	Washington Mutual	H.F. Ahmanson & Co.	Washington Mutual	
1999	Fleet Financial Corp.	BankBoston Corp.	FleetBoston Financial Corp.	
	Deutsche Bank AG	Bankers Trust Corp.	Deutsche Bank AG	
	HSBC Holdings plc	Republic New York Corp.	HSBC Bank USA	
	Firstar Corp.	Mercantile Bancorp., Inc.	Firstar Corp.	
	AmSouth Bancorp.	First American National Bank	AmSouth Bancorp.	$6.3 billion
2000	Chase Manhattan Corp.	JP Morgan & Co.	JP Morgan Chase & Co.	
	Washington Mutual	Bank United Corp.	Washington Mutual	$1.5 billion
	Wells Fargo & Co.	First Security Corp.	Wells Fargo & Co.	
2001	Firstar Corp.	U.S. Bancorp	U.S. Bancorp	
	First Union Corp.	Wachovia Corp.	Wachovia Corp.	
	Fifth Third Bancorp	Old Kent Financial Corp.	Fifth Third Bancorp	
	Standard Federal Bank	Michigan National Bank	Standard Federal Bank N.A.	
	FleetBoston Financial Corp.	Summit Bancorp	FleetBoston Financial Corp.	
2002	Citigroup Inc.	Golden State Bancorp	Citigroup Inc.	
	Washington Mutual	Dime Bancorp, Inc.	Washington Mutual	
2003	BB&T Corp.	First Virginia Banks, Inc.	BB&T Corp.	
	M&T Bank	Allfirst Bank	M&T Bank	

EXHIBIT C2.1 MAJOR BANK MERGERS SINCE 1997—cont'd

Year	Acquirer	Target	Name of Merged Entity	Transaction Value
2004	New Haven Savings Bank	Savings Bank of Manchester, Tolland Bank	NewAlliance Bank	
	Bank of America Corp.	FleetBoston Financial Corp.	Bank of America Corp.	$47 billion
	JP Morgan Chase & Co.	Bank One	JPMorgan Chase & Co.	
	Banco Popular	Quaker City Bank	Banco Popular	
	Regions Financial Corp.	Union Planters Corp.	Regions Financial Corp.	$5.9 billion
	SunTrust	National Commerce Financial	SunTrust	$6.98 billion
	Wachovia	SouthTrust	Wachovia	$14.3 billion
2005	PNC Bank	Riggs Bank	PNC Bank	$0.78 billion
	Capital One Financial Corp.	Hibernia National Bank	Capital One Financial Corp.	$4.9 billion
	Bank of America	MBNA Corp.	Bank of America Card Services	$35 billion
2006	Wachovia	Westcorp Inc.	Wachovia	$3.91 billion
	NewAlliance Bank	Cornerstone Bank	NewAlliance Bank	
	Capital One Financial Corp.	North Fork Bank	Capital One Financial Corp.	$13.2 billion
	Wachovia	Golden West Financial	Wachovia	$25 billion
	Regions Financial Corp.	AmSouth Bancorp.	Regions Financial Corp.	$10 billion
2007	Citizens Banking Corp.	Republic Bancorp	Citizens Republic Bancorp	$1.048 billion
	Banco Bilbao Vizcaya Argentaria	Compass Bancshares	Banco Bilbao Vizcaya Argentaria	$9.8 billion
	Bank of America	LaSalle Bank	Bank of America	$21 billion
	State Street Corp.	Investors Financial Services Corp.	State Street Corp.	$4.2 billion
	Bank of New York	Mellon Financial Corp.	Bank of New York Mellon	$18.3 billion
	Wachovia	World Savings Bank	Wachovia	$25 billion
	Bank of America	U.S. Trust	Bank of America Private Wealth Management	
2008	JPMorgan Chase	Bear Stearns	JPMorgan Chase	$1.1 billion
	Bank of America	Merrill Lynch	Bank of America	$50 billion
	JPMorgan Chase	Washington Mutual	JPMorgan Chase	$1.9 billion
	Wells Fargo	Wachovia	Wells Fargo	$15.1 billion
	5/3 Bank	First Charter Bank	5/3 Bank	
	PNC Financial Services	National City Corp.	PNC Financial Services	$5.08 billion

Advocates of the universal bank model argued that customers preferred to do all of their business—whether life insurance, retail brokerage, retirement planning, checking accounts in the case of an individual consumer or payroll services, mergers and acquisitions (M&A) advisory, underwriting, and commercial lending in the case of a corporate customer—with one financial institution. There was some evidence that such mergers between commercial and investment banks had on average destroyed value[6] and antitying legislation prevented universal banks from making, for example, a loan's approval contingent on a company's agreement to retain the investment banking arm of the bank for more lucrative M&A activity. However, the perception that traditional "pure-play" investment banks would struggle to compete with combined banking entities that could provide a full range of banking products led to rapid consolidation in the industry.

This consolidation created an uphill battle for the remaining pure-play bulge bracket investment banks: Lehman Brothers, Merrill Lynch, Goldman Sachs, Morgan Stanley, and Bear Stearns. As public companies, pure-play banks faced pressure to deliver return on equity comparable to that of universal banks, even as those banks put competitive pressure on traditional advisory businesses such as M&A, underwriting, and sales and trading. In response, pure-play banks resorted to the two advantages they had over nondepository institutions: unlimited, unregulated leverage capacity, and increasing reliance on proprietary trading to deliver earnings. Their successful efforts in 2004 to convince the SEC to abolish the "net capital" rule—which restricted the amount of debt their brokerage units could take on—demonstrated this growing appetite for leverage.[7] These two synergistic effects slowly but decisively transformed pure-play investment banks from advisory institutions to disguised hedge funds, a process PIMCO manager Paul McCulley has referred to as the rise of the "shadow banking" industry.[8] By the winter of 2008, increased leverage and proprietary trading would ravage the investment banking industry, leading to the collapse, merger, or restructuring of all five major pure-play banks on Wall Street.

LEHMAN BROTHERS

By late 2007, the 150-year-old Lehman Brothers had become one of the five largest investment banks in the United States, and appeared poised to continue its stellar growth with record earnings of $1.1 billion and $1.3 billion in Q1 and Q2 2007, respectively. Since the turn of the century, Lehman had grown increasingly reliant on its fixed income trading and underwriting division, which served as the primary engine for its strong profit growth throughout the first half of the decade (Exhibit C2.2). Meanwhile, the bank significantly increased its leverage over the same time frame, going from a debt-to-equity ratio of 23.7× in 2003 to 35.2× in 2007 (Exhibit C2.3). As leverage increased, the ongoing erosion of the mortgage-backed industry in the summer of 2007 began to impact Lehman significantly. The firm's stock price

---

[6] J.F. Houston and M. Ryngaert, "The Overall Gains from Large Bank Mergers," *Journal of Banking and Finance* 18 (1994): 1155–1176; D.A. Becher, "The Valuation Effects of Bank Mergers," *Journal of Corporate Finance* 6 (2000): 199–214; and J.F. Houston, C. James, and M. Ryngaert, "Where Do Merger Gains Come From? Bank Mergers from the Perspective of Insiders and Outsiders," *Journal of Financial Economics* 60 (2001): 285–332.

[7] Stephen Labaton, "Agency's '04 Rule Let Banks Pile Up New Debt," *New York Times*, October 2, 2008, http://www.nytimes.com/2008/10/03/business/03sec.html.

[8] Paul McCulley, "Global Central Bank Focus," *PIMCO.com*, August/September 2007, http://www.pimco.com/LeftNav/Featured+Market+Commentary/FF/2007/GCBF+August-+September+2007.htm.

EXHIBIT C2.2 LEHMAN BROTHERS' FINANCIAL PERFORMANCE SINCE 1999

	Sales ($ in Millions)	Total Net Income ($ in Millions)	Net Margin (%)	Earnings per Share ($)
1999	18,925	1,174	6.2	2.04
2000	26,313	1,831	7.0	3.19
2001	22,340	1,311	5.9	2.19
2002	16,696	1,031	6.2	1.73
2003	17,146	1,771	10.3	3.17
2004	20,456	2,393	11.7	3.95
2005	31,476	3,260	10.4	5.43
2006	45,296	3,960	8.7	6.73
2007	57,264	4,192	7.3	7.26

	Total Assets ($ in Millions)	Current Liabilities ($ in Millions)	Long-Term Debt ($ in Millions)	Total Liabilities ($ in Millions)	Shareholders' Equity ($ in Millions)
1999	222,225	185,251	30,691	215,942	6,283
2000	259,093	216,079	35,233	251,312	7,781
2001	285,407	238,647	38,301	276,948	8,459
2002	298,304	250,684	38,678	289,362	8,942
2003	354,280	297,577	43,529	341,106	13,174
2004	413,654	342,248	56,486	398,734	14,920
2005	463,962	393,269	53,899	447,168	16,794
2006	583,628	484,354	81,178	565,532	18,096
2007	814,213	668,573	123,150	791,723	22,490

EXHIBIT C2.3 INCREASE IN LEVERAGE AMONG BULGE BRACKET INVESTMENT BANKS

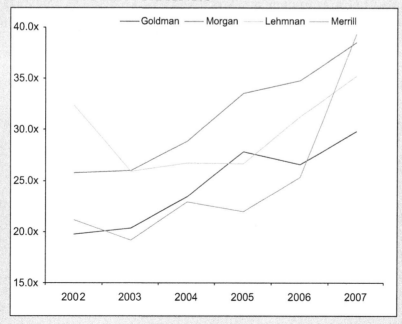

began to fall from its June 2007 peak of $81.30 to an August low of $51.57. The bank closed BNC Mortgage, its subprime mortgage arm, and began a layoff of more than 2000 employees worldwide. However, Lehman executives remained optimistic, with CFO Chris O'Meara stating, "I think the worst of this credit correction is behind us."[9]

Lehman's 2007 annual report in December noted a distinct change in the bank's outlook. More than 6000 layoffs had continued throughout the fall, and the bank wrote down $830 million in subprime-related mortgages as part of a $3.5 billion package of write-downs in the fourth quarter.[10] Lehman still beat analysts' earnings estimates of $1.42 per share, but newly appointed CFO Erin Callan[11] alluded to potential further write-downs, stating, "We're trying not to be too optimistic… that this is the bottom."[12]

The new year brought little salve to the company's growing wounds. In January 2008, Lehman exited its domestic wholesale mortgage lending unit, cutting an additional 1300 jobs, a measure that did little to stanch the hemorrhaging of cash from the firm's ongoing subprime exposure. As Bear collapsed in mid-March, Lehman stock fell 48% on news that Standard & Poor's had revised its outlook on the firm from "stable" to "negative," noting that revenues would likely decline by more than 20% after write-downs.[13] A week later, Lehman reported net income of $489 million in its first quarter 10Q, down 57% year-over-year, with $30 billion in cash and $64 billion in highly liquid assets. As rumors flew that the same aggressive shorts that had allegedly brought down Bear planned to make a run at Lehman, the firm announced the sale of $4 billion in convertible preferred stock. Lehman stock rose 11% on the news, as investors assumed that the injection of capital would allow the firm to avoid Bear's fate. Warning signs remained, however, as Oppenheimer & Co. analyst Meredith Whitney prognosticated, "While this capital raise is expensive on a near-term historical basis, it will only get progressively more expensive to raise capital as the year evolves."[14]

Despite the cash infusion, Lehman continued to slip down the path first trod by Bear. In a move eerily reminiscent of Bear's ill-fated efforts to prop up its faltering Bear Stearns Asset Management (BSAM) hedge funds a year earlier, Lehman bailed out five of its own short-term debt funds by taking $1.8 billion worth of their assets onto its books.[15] Meanwhile, it announced another 1500 layoffs and its plans to raise an additional $6 billion in new capital

[9] Dan Wilchins, "Lehman Earnings Fall Amid $830 Million Writedown," *Reuters News*, December 13, 2007, http://www.reuters.com/article/businessNews/idUSWEN294620071214.

[10] Jessica Dickler, "Lehman Layoffs, the Tip of the Iceberg," *CNNMoney.com*, September 21, 2008, http://money.cnn.com/2008/09/15/news/companies/lehman_jobs.

[11] Effective December 1, 2007, O'Meara transitioned into a new role as global head of risk management.

[12] Wilchins, "Lehman Earnings Fall."

[13] John Spence, "S&P Puts Negative Outlook on Goldman, Lehman," *MarketWatch*, March 21, 2008, http://www.marketwatch.com/news/story/sp-puts-negative-outlook-goldman/story.aspx?guid=%7BE3B0D7FE-7498-48D7-BE29-FB95B33D0A41%7D.

[14] Yalman Onaran, "Lehman Sells $4 Billion Shares to Help Calm Investors," *Bloomberg.com*, April 1, 2008, http://www.bloomberg.com/apps/news?pid=20601087&sid=aUd7LP996GL0.

[15] "Lehman Says It Bailed Out Money Market, Cash Funds," *MP Global Financial News*, April 10, 2008, http://www.mpgf.com/mp-gf/pop/news.aspx?newsID=6081.

via a combined common and convertible preferred stock sale in June 2008, even as it estimated a $3 billion loss in Q3 based on mortgage-related write-downs. The following week, Lehman's board of directors replaced Joseph Gregory as COO with Herbert H. McDade, and terminated Erin Callan's brief tenure as CFO, replacing her with Ian Lowitt.

With the company's stock price in freefall throughout the summer of 2008, CEO Richard Fuld contemplated a go-private transaction, abandoning the idea when it became clear that the company could not arrange the necessary financing to consummate the deal. In a desperate move, Fuld then attempted to locate buyers for $30 billion worth of Lehman's illiquid commercial mortgage holdings and launched merger discussions with government-owned Korea Development Bank (KDB) and China's Citic Securities, whose cross-investment with Bear a year earlier failed to turn market sentiment in the firm. KDB contemplated a two-stage process wherein it would buy a 25% stake from Lehman directly before purchasing an additional 25% in the open market. Ultimately, talks stalled when Lehman refused to budge on price, demanding a 50% premium to its nebulous book value.[16] Discussions with Citic similarly stalled, as had a potential acquisition by Royal Bank of Canada, who passed in July when it could not get comfortable with the firm's tenuous liquidity position.[17] Rapidly running out of potential white knights, Lehman limped toward a September earning report in which analysts predicted an additional $4 billion in write-downs, bringing the total to $12 billion.

Six months after the tumultuous weekend that consumed Bear, Lehman stock fell 30% on September 9, 2008, reducing its market capitalization to $6.8 billion, down from $54.7 billion at the beginning of 2007 (Exhibit C2.4). The share price collapse continued the following day as Lehman announced a $3.9 billion loss in Q3 and its intentions to restructure by spinning off $30 billion of its commercial real estate portfolio into a separate, publicly traded entity, selling 55% of investment advisory subsidiary Neuberger Berman, and selling $4 billion of its European real estate holdings to Black Rock. These moves would eliminate the goodwill from Lehman's 2003 acquisition of Neuberger, improve the firm's Tier 1 ratio,[18] and increase its tangible book value by more than $3 billion.[19] However, with the stock price closing at just over $3 per share, these efforts merely bolstered suspicions that the embattled bank would have to seek a buyer. More perniciously, rumors circulated that other market players had begun refusing to honor Lehman's trades, effectively crippling its ability to remain in business, with such speculation further fueled by the Fed's acknowledgment that it had met with various Wall Street firms and the SEC in an effort to resolve Lehman's liquidity crisis.

---

[16] Henny Sender and Francesco Guerrera, "Lehman's Secret Talks To Sell 50% Stake Stall," *Financial Times*, August 20, 2008, http://www.ft.com/cms/s/0/586ed.412-6ee6-11dd-a80a-0000779fd18c.html.

[17] "Royal Bank of Canada Considered Buying Lehman," *Reuters UK News*, September 7, 2008, http://uk.reuters.com/article/asiaPrivateEquityNews/idUKL722941620080907.

[18] The Tier 1 capital ratio is the ratio of a bank's core equity capital to its total risk-weighted assets, a metric regulators frequently use to evaluate a bank's financial strength.

[19] "Lehman Plans Sale, Spin-Off of Assets," *Reuters News*, September 10, 2008, http://www.reuters.com/article/topNews/idUSN1040161420080910.

EXHIBIT C2.4 INVESTMENT BANK STOCK PERFORMANCE SINCE 1999

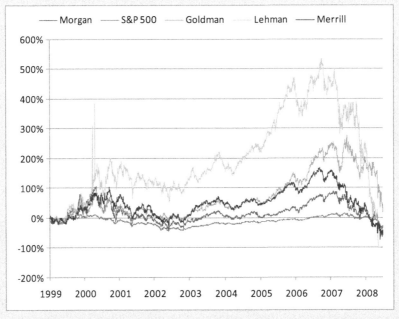

Unfortunately, the political dominos from Bear's bailout had fallen against Lehman. The public outcry over taxpayer assumption of $29 billion in potential Bear losses made repeating such a move politically untenable just weeks before one of the most contentious presidential elections in history. The surreal scene of potential buyers traipsing into an investment bank's headquarters over the weekend to consider various merger or spin-out scenarios repeated itself once again, with the hard deadline of the next day's market open forcing Lehman to consider any and all offers. This time, the Fed refused to back the failing bank's liabilities, attempting instead to play last-minute suitors Bank of America, HSBC, Nomura Securities, and Barclay's off each other, jawboning them by arguing that failing to step up to save Lehman would cause devastating counterparty runs on their own capital positions. Meanwhile, Lehman hired Weil, Gotshal, and Manges to prepare an emergency bankruptcy filing in case negotiations faltered.

The Fed's desperate attempts to arrange its second rescue of a major US investment bank in 6 months failed when it refused to backstop losses from Lehman's toxic mortgage holdings. Complicating matters was Lehman's reliance on short-term repo loans to finance its balance sheet; like Bear, Lehman financed more than 25% of its assets with repos.[20] Unfortunately, such loans required constant renewal by counterparties, who

[20] Prince of Wall Street, "Goldman's Contrarian Move," April 7, 2008, https://www.istockanalyst.com/article/viewarticle+articleid_1692967.html.

had grown increasingly nervous that Lehman would lose the ability to make good on its trades. With such sentiment swirling around Wall Street, the last bidder at the table, Barclay's, dropped out when it determined that it could not obtain timely shareholder approval for the acquisition. After Barclay's threw in the towel, Lehman announced the largest Chapter 11 filing in US history, listing assets of $639 billion and liabilities of $768 billion.[21]

The second domino had fallen. It would not be the last.

MERRILL LYNCH

Long considered the Irish Catholic bastion on Wall Street, Merrill Lynch grew to prominence on the strength of its massive retail brokerage operations, which allowed its investment banking arm to place underwritten securities directly with brokerage clients. Its 1978 acquisition of White Weld & Co. bolstered its investment banking operations, which flourished in the last decades of the twentieth century alongside its private client services and sales and trading arms. Like Lehman, however, it had grown increasingly reliant on its proprietary trading arm following the deregulation of the banking industry, which fueled its more than 13% annual stock price return from 2000 to 2006 (Exhibit C2.4). Merrill similarly exhibited a significant increase in leverage over the same time frame, going from a 19.2× leverage ratio in 2003 to a 39.3× ratio in 2007 (Exhibits C2.3 and C2.5).

At the height of the credit boom in late 2006, Merrill announced its $1.3 billion acquisition of First Franklin, one of the largest originators of subprime residential mortgage loans. The deal closed in January 2007 and brought Merrill's mortgage portfolio to more than $70 billion.[22] Analysts met the deal with mixed reviews; some noted that it had plugged gaps in Merrill's business lines and expanded its client base, while others expressed concern that Merrill had missed the lending boom, buying at a high price and overlooking the significant integration and absorption issues First Franklin would pose.[23]

The first cracks began to appear with the default of the Bear Stearns hedge funds during the summer of 2007. As one of the funds' key lenders, Merrill seized $800 million of the funds' assets and began an auction process, managing to sell off some of the higher-grade products but struggling to generate bids on the toxic lower-rated tranches. Bear's subsequent decision

[21] Drew G.L. Chapman, "Lehman Brothers Holdings, Inc.'s Bankruptcy Filing Raises Pressing Issues for Hedge Funds," DLA Piper Alternative Asset Management Alert, September 17, 2008, http://www.dlapiper.com/files/upload/Alternative_Asset_Management_ Alert_Sep08.html. Given the strict federal regulations for insolvent brokerage houses, Lehman's retail brokerage operations did not file, but continued business as usual while the firm sought an outside buyer.

[22] Merrill Lynch press release, "Merrill Lynch Announces Agreement to Acquire First Franklin from National City Corporation," September 5, 2006, http://www.ml.com/index.asp?id=7695_7696_8149_63464_70786_70780 and Gabriel Madway, "National City Completes First Franklin Sale to Merrill," MarketWatch, January 2, 2007, http://www.marketwatch.com/news/story/national-city-completes-first-franklin/story.aspx?guid=%7BB1E0DE9C-7FA0-48C3-98FF-6F43EA09D169%7D.

[23] Shaheen Pasha, "Merrill Strategy Threatened by Bad Loan Market," CNNMoney.com, February 21, 2007, http://money.cnn.com/2007/02/21/news/companies/merrill_acquisitions/index.htm.

EXHIBIT C2.5 MERRILL LYNCH'S FINANCIAL PERFORMANCE SINCE 1999

	Sales ($ in Millions)	Total Net Income ($ in Millions)	Net Margin (%)	Earnings per Share ($)
1999	34,586	2,887	8.3	3.11
2000	43,885	3,979	9.1	4.11
2001	38,232	−335	−0.9	−0.45
2002	27,368	1,708	6.2	1.77
2003	26,432	3,836	14.5	3.87
2004	31,165	4,436	14.2	4.38
2005	45,000	4,815	10.7	4.86
2006	64,500	7,097	11.0	7.18
2007	64,865	−8,637	−13.3	−10.73

	Total Assets ($ in Millions)	Current Liabilities ($ in Millions)	Long-Term Debt ($ in Millions)	Total Liabilities ($ in Millions)	Shareholders' Equity ($ in Millions)
1999	360,966	294,121	54,043	348,164	12,802
2000	474,709	386,182	70,223	456,405	18,304
2001	510,348	412,989	76,572	489,561	20,787
2002	533,021	427,227	81,713	508,940	24,081
2003	582,645	467,259	86,502	553,761	28,884
2004	750,703	596,728	122,605	719,333	31,370
2005	816,516	645,415	135,501	780,916	35,600
2006	1,026,512	802,261	185,213	987,474	39,038
2007	1,286,177	988,118	266,127	1,254,245	31,932

to bail out the funds ended the auction process, but the fiasco highlighted Merrill's significant exposure to the subprime crisis.[24]

Soon thereafter, Merrill announced a $4.5 billion loss from CDOs and US subprime mortgage-backed securities, which it later revised to $7.9 billion. As losses in the firm's credit portfolios mounted, chairman and CEO Stan O'Neal made the mistake of approaching Wachovia Corporation about a potential merger without notifying his board of directors. Infuriated, the board dismissed O'Neal, naming NYSE Euronext CEO John Thain as his replacement in December. The appointment came on the heels of Merrill's announcement that it would write down an additional $11.5 billion in mortgage-backed securities and take a $2.6 billion loss on hedges related to CDOs. The company's stock price slid 46% to $48.57 in February 2008, down from its $89.37 high in May 2007.

[24] Ivy Schmerken, "Credit Crisis in Sub-Prime Mortgages Affects Hedge Funds Trading in Other Asset Classes," September 30, 2007, http://www.advancedtrading.com/ems-oms/showArticle.jhtml?articleID=201805585.

Desperate to stop the bleeding, Merrill announced layoffs of 2900 employees, having already eliminated 1100 positions worldwide since the previous summer. Its first-quarter 2008 results—which included an additional $3.09 billion in mortgage-related write-downs—did little to comfort a market with memories of Bear's implosion fresh in its mind. Moody's Investors Service placed the bank's long-term debt on review for a possible downgrade based on its forecast of an additional $6 billion in write-downs in coming quarters.[25]

Troubles continued in the second quarter, when Merrill suffered $3.5 billion in losses from US super-senior CDOs and negative credit valuation adjustments of $2.9 billion related to hedges. The bank also lost $1.7 billion in its investment portfolios and $1.3 billion from residential mortgage exposures. Amidst the staggering losses, Thain attempted to avoid Bear's fate by raising capital while it was still available. In July 2008 Merrill sold its 20% stake in Bloomberg L.P. back to Bloomberg Inc. for $4.425 billion and began negotiations to sell a controlling interest in Financial Data Services, its in-house provider of administrative functions for mutual funds, retail banking products, and other wealth management services.

Even the injection of capital from the Bloomberg transaction could not guarantee Merrill's ongoing independence after more than $52 billion in cumulative write-downs. Complicating matters, Merrill held billions in credit default swaps with troubled insurance giant AIG as the counterparty, exposure that further weakened Merrill's tenuous financial position. The bank's situation turned critical in early September when it became clear that Lehman Brothers would not survive the month. In a last-ditch effort to salvage some shareholder value, Thain reached out to Bank of America CEO Ken Lewis.

Bank of America's investment banking efforts had achieved only middling success following its 1997 acquisition of San Francisco-based boutique Montgomery Securities and the later integration of the remnants of Robertson Stephens, which came in its 2004 acquisition of FleetBoston Financial. While certain groups had excelled—the healthcare and real estate industry groups, and the debt underwriting and private equity placement product groups, for example—the bank had struggled to attract the top-tier talent necessary to compete with other bulge bracket banks. By 2008 the bank had begun to shrink its investment banking operations, laying off more than 1100 employees in the wake of mortgage-related write-downs. Lewis's comment in 2007 that he had "had all the fun I can stand in investment banking" contributed to perceptions of the bank's faltering commitment to building the investment banking unit's brand, and prompted defections by junior bankers pessimistic on the group's future.[26]

However, Merrill presented what Lewis later described as "the strategic opportunity of a lifetime." During the very same cataclysmic weekend that claimed Lehman, talks accelerated, with Bank of America finally agreeing to pay $50 billion to acquire Merrill Lynch, a price less than half of Merrill's market capitalization at its 2007 peak. The transaction more than doubled the size of Bank of America's investment banking unit and created the largest retail brokerage unit on Wall Street, while significantly increasing Bank of America's exposure to mortgage-backed securities. Standard & Poor's immediately reduced its long-term

[25] Louise Story, "At Merrill, Write-Downs and More Layoffs," *New York Times*, April 18, 2008, http://www.nytimes.com/2008/04/18/business/18merrill.html.

[26] "Will BofA Retreat From Investment Banking?" October 18, 2007, http://dealbook.blogs.nytimes.com/2007/10/18/will-bofa-retreat-from-investment-banking.

counterparty credit rating on Bank of America from AA to AA-, and put the bank's credit ratings on CreditWatch with "negative implications."

And then there were two.

GOLDMAN SACHS AND MORGAN STANLEY

Unlike its peers, Goldman largely avoided excessive exposure to the mortgage industry and wrote down just $2 billion in residential mortgages and leveraged loans. Observers expressed skepticism at Goldman's seeming imperviousness to the most catastrophic market environment in history. "I'm not sure what to think; it's almost too good to be true," said Robert Lagravinese of Trinity Funds. "I'm not sure how they avoid every problem that every other investment bank has. No one is that good, smart, or lucky."[27]

During the summer of 2008, Goldman reduced its leveraged loan exposure to $14 billion from $52 billion 6 months earlier and reduced its residential and commercial real estate holdings by $6.4 billion over the same period. However, the company could not ignore its eroding profits, posting the first quarterly loss in its history in the fourth quarter of 2008 driven largely by losses in its proprietary trading operations (Exhibit C2.6).

Meanwhile, Morgan Stanley, ironically created in 1938 when the passage of Glass–Steagall forced JP Morgan to divest its investment banking operations, found itself plagued by exposure to the widening credit crisis (Exhibit C2.7). By the fourth quarter of 2007, the firm had written down $10.3 billion in mortgage-related securities, trailing only Merrill, Citigroup, and UBS in write-downs. CEO John Mack called the results "embarrassing," and dismissed copresident Zoe Cruz, who had headed Morgan Stanley's institutional-securities business. In December 2007 the bank attempted to shore up its liquidity position by raising capital from a foreign wealth fund, joining Citigroup and UBS, who had sold $7.5 billion in equity to an Abu Dhabi fund and $11.5 billion in equity to a Singaporean fund, respectively. Morgan sold 9% coupon convertible preferred shares amounting to roughly 9.9% of the company to China Investment Corporation for $5 billion.[28]

After Lehman declared bankruptcy in September 2008, Morgan Stanley and Goldman Sachs found themselves under pressure from investors who felt that the credit crisis had revealed the untenability of their more than 20× leverage multiples. One week after Lehman's Chapter 11 filing, both firms announced that they would reorganize as bank holding companies. The move meant that the banks would for the first time become deposit-taking institutions regulated by the Federal Reserve, the FDIC, and either state or federal bank regulators and would have to delever their balance sheets significantly. On September 23, Berkshire Hathaway announced a $5 billion purchase of perpetual preferred stock in Goldman (priced with a 10% dividend and warrants to purchase $5 billion of common stock at a strike price of

---

[27] Joseph A. Giannone, "Goldman Earnings Fall By Half, Yet Beat Views," *Reuters News*, March 18, 2008, http://www.reuters.com/article/businessNews/idUSWNAS527620080318.

[28] John Spence, "Morgan Stanley Write-Downs Grow by $5.7 Billion," *MarketWatch*, December 19, 2007, http://www.marketwatch.com/news/story/morgan-stanley-sets-57-bln/story.aspx?guid=%7BA49D1DF8-A341-409C-9574-E035AF79EFC9%7D.

EXHIBIT C2.6 GOLDMAN SACHS'S FINANCIAL PERFORMANCE SINCE 1999

	Sales ($ in Millions)	Total Net Income ($ in Millions)	Net Margin (%)	Earnings per Share ($)
1999	25,363	2,708	10.7	5.57
2000	33,000	3,067	9.3	6.00
2001	31,138	2,310	7.4	4.26
2002	22,854	2,114	9.3	4.03
2003	23,623	3,005	12.7	5.87
2004	29,839	4,553	15.3	8.92
2005	43,391	5,626	13.0	11.21
2006	69,353	9,537	13.8	19.69
2007	87,968	11,599	13.2	24.73

	Total Assets ($ in Millions)	Current Liabilities ($ in Millions)	Long-Term Debt ($ in Millions)	Total Liabilities ($ in Millions)	Shareholders' Equity ($ in Millions)
1999	271,443	240,346	20,952	261,298	10,145
2000	315,805	267,880	31,395	299,275	16,530
2001	343,234	293,987	31,016	325,003	18,231
2002	394,285	336,571	38,711	375,282	19,003
2003	461,281	382,167	57,482	439,649	21,632
2004	612,075	506,300	80,696	586,996	25,079
2005	806,811	678,802	100,007	778,809	28,002
2006	987,177	802,415	148,976	951,391	35,786
2007	1,317,270	1,076,996	197,474	1,274,470	42,800

$115). The following day, Goldman issued an additional $5 billion of equity in a public offering. Despite Goldman's lower reliance on repo lending (it had financed just 14.8% of its balance sheet with repos) and limited exposure to the mortgage-backed securities industry, the fall in prices of its marketable securities and the drought in M&A activity forced Goldman to announce layoffs of 3200 employees.[29]

Goldman applied for a New York state bank charter, differentiating it from competitors such as Citigroup and Bank of America, who operated under a national bank charter. (Morgan Stanley applied for a national bank charter at the same time.) The firm also accepted $10 billion (as did Morgan Stanley) from the controversial $700 billion federal bailout passed in early October 2008, and Goldman Sachs also benefited from the bailout of AIG, which enabled the insurance company to make payments on debt held by Goldman. Morgan Stanley similarly tapped new funding with a $9 billion investment by Japan's Mitsubishi UFJ Financial Group

---

[29] Prince of Wall Street, "Goldman's Contrarian Move."

EXHIBIT C2.7 MORGAN STANLEY'S FINANCIAL PERFORMANCE SINCE 1999

	Sales ($ in Millions)	Total Net Income ($ in Millions)	Net Margin (%)	Earnings per Share ($)
1999	34,343	4,791	14.0	4.10
2000	44,593	5,484	12.3	4.73
2001	43,333	3,630	8.4	3.16
2002	32,449	3,086	9.5	2.70
2003	34,550	4,174	12.1	3.66
2004	39,017	4,634	11.9	4.15
2005	46,581	4,532	9.7	4.20
2006	70,151	6,335	9.0	5.99
2007	84,120	2,563	3.0	2.37

	Total Assets ($ in Millions)	Current Liabilities ($ in Millions)	Long-Term Debt ($ in Millions)	Total Liabilities ($ in Millions)	Shareholders' Equity ($ in Millions)
1999	385,240	349,953	29,004	378,957	6,283
2000	452,240	402,008	42,451	444,459	7,781
2001	521,249	461,912	50,878	512,790	8,459
2002	572,927	507,614	56,371	563,985	8,942
2003	659,560	577,976	68,410	646,386	13,174
2004	829,334	719,128	95,286	814,414	14,920
2005	996,600	869,341	110,465	979,806	16,794
2006	1,248,902	1,085,828	144,978	1,230,806	18,096
2007	1,227,254	1,014,140	190,624	1,204,764	22,490

in common and perpetual noncumulative convertible preferred stock. Both firms announced plans to build out deposit-taking businesses, essentially making them commercial banks with diversified investment banking operations.

As 2008 came to a close, the landscape of the investment banking industry had dramatically changed. While investment banking clients would always require advisory work, underwriting services, and sales and trading services, the days of the 30× leveraged pure-play investment bank ended during a 6-month period when Bear Stearns collapsed into the arms of JP Morgan, Lehman Brothers filed for bankruptcy protection, Merrill Lynch merged into Bank of America, and Goldman Sachs and Morgan Stanley converted to bank holding companies. With the newfound prohibition on aggressive leverage and a regulation-induced reduction in risk-taking, the latter two firms would be challenged to deliver their previous return on equity and would likely come to resemble their chief remaining competitors: JP Morgan, Citigroup, Bank of America, Credit Suisse, Deutsche Bank, and UBS.

Freeport-McMoRan: Financing an Acquisition

A November 19, 2006, press release announced Freeport-McMoRan Copper & Gold's (NYSE: FCX) acquisition of Phelps Dodge, creating the world's largest publicly traded copper company. FCX chief executive officer Richard Adkerson said, "This acquisition is financially compelling for FCX shareholders, who will benefit from significant cash flow accretion, lower cost of capital, and improved geographic and asset diversification. The new FCX will continue to invest in future growth opportunities with high rates of return and will aggressively seek to reduce debt incurred in the acquisition using the substantial free cash flow generated from the combined business."[1] The press release went on to note that "FCX has received financing commitments from JPMorgan and Merrill Lynch." This was the culmination of weeks of work "inside the wall" at the two investment banks. However, the public announcement was only the beginning of a new stream of work that would take place "outside the wall" in the sales and trading divisions at these firms.

METALS HEATING UP

At the time of the announced merger, FCX described itself as a company that "explores for, develops, mines, and processes ore containing copper, gold, and silver in Indonesia, and smelts and refines copper concentrates in Spain and Indonesia."[2] Phelps Dodge was described as "one of the world's leading producers of copper and molybdenum and is the largest producer of molybdenum-based chemicals and continuous-cast copper rod."[3] The merger of these two companies took place after an unprecedented run in the value of copper, based in part on the rapid growth in demand from China (see Exhibit C3.1), resulting in the world's largest publicly traded copper company.

[1] FCX company press release, November 19, 2006.

[2] FCX company press release, November 19, 2006.

[3] FCX company press release, November 19, 2006.

EXHIBIT C3.1 COPPER SPOT PRICE VERSUS FCX STOCK, SEPTEMBER 2001 TO DECEMBER 2006

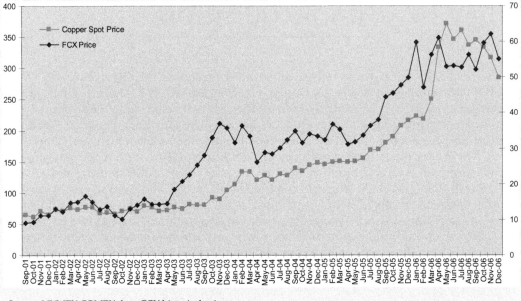

Source: NYMEX COMEX data; FCX historical prices.

These two merger candidates came together only after a tumultuous series of events in the mergers and acquisitions (M&A) landscape within the mining industry. Just months earlier, in June 2006, Phelps Dodge announced a three-way merger between itself and two Canadian mining companies, Inco and Falconbridge, for $56 billion.[4] At the time, this would have created the world's largest nickel producer and largest publicly traded copper producer. J. Steven Whisler, CEO of Phelps Dodge, made the following proclamation at the time of the announced merger:

> This transaction represents a unique opportunity in a rapidly consolidating industry to create a global leader based in *North America*—home of the world's deepest and most liquid capital markets. The combined company has one of the industry's most exciting portfolios of development projects, and the scale and management expertise to pursue their development successfully. The creation of this new company gives us the scale and diversification to manage cyclicality, stabilize earnings, and increase shareholder returns. At the same time, we are committed to maintaining an investment-grade credit rating throughout the business cycle.[5]

[4] Phelps Dodge company press release, June 26, 2006.

[5] Phelps Dodge company press release, June 26, 2006.

The Phelps Dodge announcement came months into Falconbridge's implementation of a "poison pill" defense in an ongoing attempt to protect itself from a takeover by Swiss mining giant Xstrata, which had accumulated more than 20% of Falconbridge's stock.[6]

Eventually, the attempted combination between Phelps Dodge, Inco, and Falconbridge fell apart after Xstrata upped its bid for Falconbridge,[7] causing Falconbridge's board of directors to accept this higher bid and reject Phelps Dodge and Inco.[8]

As the events with Xstrata unfolded, Companhia Vale do Rio Doce (CVRD), a Brazilian mining company, made an unsolicited all-cash offer for Inco of C$86 per share; Phelps Dodge, on the other hand, had made a partial-equity bid of C$86.89. In spite of the lower price, analysts prophetically suggested that investors would favor the all-cash bid of CVRD at the time.[9] By early September, Phelps Dodge and Inco had decided to go their separate ways, and CVRD soon claimed victory in acquiring Inco.[10] Having been left at the altar now twice, analysts predicted that Phelps Dodge "could soon find itself transformed from a bidder to a target in the deal-making that has engulfed the global mining industry."[11]

Whisler attempted to reassure his investor base when his company announced that it was terminating its combination agreement with Inco:

> We are very confident about the prospects of Phelps Dodge. The market fundamentals for copper and molybdenum are excellent, and at current prices we are generating significant amounts of cash. Throughout the past several months, management and the board have focused on our fundamental responsibilities to build long-term value for all our shareholders while managing our balance sheet prudently and maintaining investment-grade credit in this cyclical industry. While we regret the proposed three-way combination could not be completed on acceptable terms, the future of Phelps Dodge remains very bright.[12]

ENTER FREEPORT-McMoRAN

On November 19, 2006, FCX and Phelps Dodge signed a definitive merger agreement in which the acquirer, FCX, would purchase the larger Phelps Dodge for $25.9 billion in cash and stock. The joint press release announced the following transaction details:

---

[6] "Falconbridge Protects Against 'Creeping Takeover' by Xstrata," *Metal Bulletin*, September 23, 2005.

[7] "Falconbridge Gets $52.50-Per-Share Offer from Xstrata," *Stockwatch*, May 17, 2006.

[8] "Falconbridge Yields to Xstrata," *Steel Business Briefing*, August 11, 2006.

[9] "In the Battle to Control Inco, CVRD Looks Ready to Rumble," *American Metal Market*, August 11, 2006.

[10] "Phelps Leaves CVRD as Sole Bidder for Inco," *Financial Times*, September 6, 2006.

[11] "Phelps Leaves CVRD as Sole Bidder for Inco," *Financial Times*, September 6, 2006.

[12] Phelps Dodge company press release, September 5, 2006.

FCX will acquire all of the outstanding common shares of Phelps Dodge for a combination of cash and common shares of FCX for a total consideration of $126.46 per Phelps Dodge share, based on the closing price of FCX stock on November 17, 2006. Each Phelps Dodge shareholder would receive $88.00 per share in cash plus 0.67 common shares of FCX. This represents a premium of 33 percent to Phelps Dodge's closing price on November 17, 2006, and 29 percent to its one-month average price at that date.

The cash portion of $18 billion represents approximately 70 percent of the total consideration. In addition, FCX would deliver a total of 137 million shares to Phelps Dodge shareholders, resulting in Phelps Dodge shareholders owning approximately 38 percent of the combined company on a fully diluted basis.

The boards of directors of FCX and Phelps Dodge have each unanimously approved the terms of the agreement and have recommended that their shareholders approve the transaction. The transaction is subject to the approval of the shareholders of FCX and Phelps Dodge, receipt of regulatory approvals and customary closing conditions. The transaction is expected to close at the end of the first quarter of 2007.

FCX has received financing commitments from JPMorgan and Merrill Lynch to fund the cash required to complete the transaction. After giving effect to the transaction, estimated pro forma total debt at *December 31, 2006, would be approximately $17.6 billion, or approximately $15 billion net of cash.*[13]

The initial reaction to the merger announcement among Wall Street analysts was mixed (see Exhibit C3.2 and Exhibit C3.3 for stock price performance):

In our view this transaction makes sense for both companies... Freeport is basically a single mine company, with its only significant asset located in Indonesia (asset has a long life, but limited growth opportunities). Phelps Dodge has a geographically diverse operating base and also has a growth profile, targeting increased output of 20 percent by 2009 but a relatively short reserve life. Hence for Freeport, this deal spreads the company's operating risk and gives the company a growth profile. In our view this deal also highlights the scarcity of copper reserves globally, with one large producer acquiring another, instead of building large-scale copper mines.[14]

There are several positives surrounding this transaction: (1) an improved cost position (vs. PD stand-alone); (2) long reserve life; (3) a more diversified geographic footprint; (4) an attractive growth profile; and (5) enhanced management depth. We do not see any anti-trust issues surrounding this transaction. For PD shareholders specifically—the 33 percent premium to Friday's close and departure of *CEO* Steven Whisler from the combined entity is the antidote we believe they were looking for—post the failed three-way merger attempt for two nickel producers earlier in the year. For *FCX—we are surprised—we believed FCX was more of a seller than a buyer of assets.*[15]

[13] FCX company press release, November 19, 2006.

[14] Credit Suisse Equity Research, November 20, 2006.

[15] Bear Stearns Equity Research, November 20, 2006.

We assign a one-third likelihood that Freeport acquires Phelps Dodge as announced. Two-thirds likelihood that Freeport collects the $750 million breakup fee. The deal appears very accretive to *FCX and likely to attract higher bidder.*[16]

EXHIBIT C3.2 PHELPS DODGE STOCK PERFORMANCE, JANUARY 3, 2006 TO MARCH 19, 2007

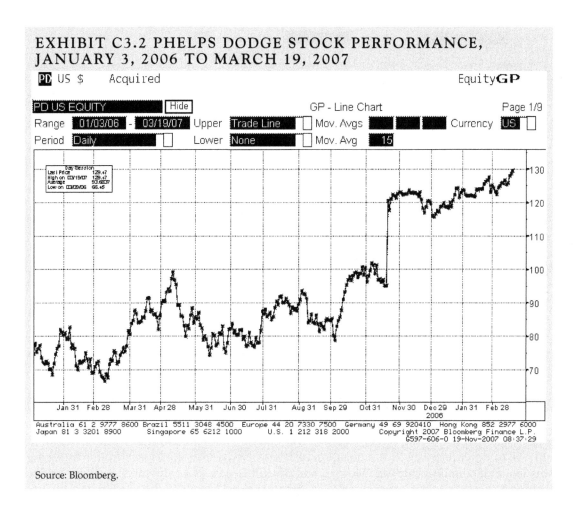

Source: Bloomberg.

<hr/>

[16] Prudential Equity Research, November 21, 2006.

EXHIBIT C3.3 FCX STOCK PERFORMANCE, JANUARY 3, 2006 TO MARCH 19, 2007

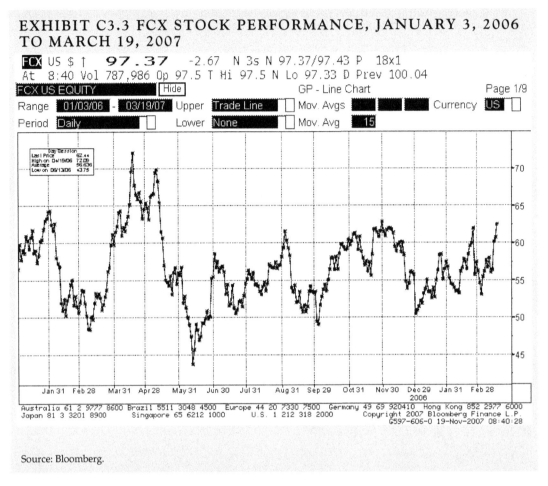

Source: Bloomberg.

As the companies initially projected in their joint press release, the shareholders ultimately approved the merger on March 14, 2007, under the announced terms.[17] Of course, one of the worst kept secrets on Wall Street was that the smaller FCX still had a tremendous amount of work to do in financing the acquisition of Phelps Dodge. An initial step in this financing was the joint commitment by JPMorgan and Merrill Lynch to a combined $6 billion bridge loan prior to approval of the merger. FCX announced on March 15 the pricing of a total of $17.5 billion in debt financing for the Phelps Dodge acquisition, including $6 billion in high-yield senior notes offered in the public debt market (the bridge loan would be drawn down only if this public offering failed) and $10 billion in senior secured term loans. In addition, a $1.5 billion senior secured revolving credit facility was provided, which was to be undrawn at closing.[18] JPMorgan and Merrill Lynch jointly underwrote the note offerings and term loans and led the credit facility. Finally, on March 19, in conjunction with the closing of the

[17] FCX press release, March 14, 2007.

[18] FCX press release, March 15, 2007.

Phelps Dodge acquisition, FCX announced a public offering of common stock and convertible preferred stock. The initial press release indicated an offering of "approximately 35 million shares of common stock" and 10 million shares of mandatory convertible preferred stock at $100.00 per share.[19] Total proceeds from these two equity-related transactions were expected to be approximately $5 billion. The market received these financings positively, marking up FCX nearly 3% on a day when the S&P 500 increased just over 1%. At least one Wall Street analyst portrayed the announcement as an expected positive:

> Management clearly communicated its intention to do an equity transaction. Likewise, the size of the transaction is consistent with our expectations. While diluting existing shareholders is not a positive, we believe this equity deal is a prudent transaction in terms of reducing some of the financial risk. We estimate the combination of the equity transaction and free cash flow at current copper prices has the potential to reduce *FCX's debt burden by $5 billion, or 31 percent of the $16 billion in debt taken on from this transaction, with the magnitude of debt reduction to translate into higher multiples over time.*[20]

FCX's two equity-related transactions (common stock and mandatory convertible preferred) were led by JPMorgan and Merrill Lynch as joint bookrunners. The two firms equally shared fees and league table credit for these transactions. Each quarter, league tables ranking the major investment banks by underwriting proceeds from various categories (debt, equity, convertible bonds, etc.) are released. At the end of the first quarter of 2007 (1Q07), JPMorgan ranked first in US convertibles, with a 23.9% market share and nearly $6 billion in proceeds from convertible issuance. Merrill Lynch ranked third in US convertibles at the end of 1Q07 with nearly $4 billion, a 15.8% market share. For common stock underwriting at 1Q07, JPMorgan was first at just over $5.1 billion in underwriting proceeds, with a 16.2% market share; Merrill Lynch was second at over $4.3 billion, with a 13.7% market share.[21]

ROLE OF THE INVESTMENT BANKS

Throughout the flurry of activity centered around FCX, from merger advisory to debt and equity underwriting, there was a consistent theme: JPMorgan and Merrill Lynch were involved at nearly every step of the way. Typically, when a company needs advisory or financial assistance, it holds a "bake-off" between investment banks, where firms are invited to present their credentials, preliminary valuation, and view of investor demand. Companies will choose an investment bank (or banks) for a variety of reasons, but over time, they usually focus on existing relationships, in addition to factors such as execution capability, independent research function, and league table rankings. In the case of FCX, it had well-established ties to both JPMorgan and Merrill Lynch and placed its trust in them for both M&A advisory and underwriting responsibilities.

Investment banks typically talk about two sides of a "Chinese wall" of information. Coverage, M&A, and capital markets teams within the investment banking function are responsible for all

---

[19] FCX press release, March 19, 2007.

[20] Credit Suisse Equity Research, March 19, 2007.

[21] Thomson Equity Capital Markets Review, First Quarter 2007.

of the due diligence and valuation work. As a result, they are considered to be insiders working on the "private side" of the wall (or inside the wall) because of the sensitive information that they receive. Generally, an investment bank's sales and trading group sits on the "public side" of this wall, working with investors and having access only to information that has been made publicly available. When a company issues a press release describing a merger and/or financing, it is generally the first time that an individual in sales and trading will hear of it.

Inside the Wall

Prior to the public announcements of the transactions surrounding the merger, the investment banking coverage teams at JPMorgan and Merrill Lynch were actively coordinating the entire process, from the acquisition to all aspects of the capital raising. The metals and mining industry coverage team at each bank was primarily responsible for knowing FCX's general needs and priorities. From there, each bank's M&A group was responsible for advising the company on merger valuation, mix of cash and stock, timing, and likely shareholder reaction. The leveraged finance group at each bank was responsible for the analysis behind making the bridge financing commitment to the company (which was never drawn down because the banks successfully placed high-yield notes with institutional investors). The bridge loan was particularly important to enable FCX to show committed financing to Phelps Dodge. The equity capital markets groups at JPMorgan and Merrill Lynch were responsible for all aspects of the equity offering: advising the company regarding the optimal structure, size, pricing, and timing of the financing (the "origination" function), as well as working with colleagues in their firm's institutional equity sales area to determine potential investor interest (the "placement" function).

The investment banks and FCX needed to determine a permanent financing structure based on expected credit ratings. Essentially, FCX's management first had to decide on the optimal capital structure and acceptable equity dilution levels before selecting the best financing alternatives. Ratings advisory professionals who were part of the debt capital markets group at JPMorgan advised the company on the credit ratings process and the expected ratings outcomes based on the selected capital structure. All of the information about financing terms and conditions, as well as pricing, was fed back to each bank's M&A team, which assessed the impact to earnings per share (EPS), expected valuation, and likely investor reaction.

There are several forms of risk that investment banks must consider when advising clients and executing transactions. *Capital risk* is the financial risk associated with a bank's financing commitment in relation to an acquisition. If the bank commits to providing a loan, it undertakes considerable risk. Large banks mitigate this risk by syndicating up to 90% of these loans to a wider group of banks and money managers. However, banks are forced to keep the debt that they are unable to syndicate to others. During the first half of 2007, banks had committed more than $350 billion in loan commitments to facilitate acquisitions of companies by private equity firms. Because of severe dislocation in the mortgage-backed securities market starting in mid-2007, these loans became very difficult to syndicate, leaving huge unanticipated risk positions that resulted in billions of dollars in reported losses (see Exhibit C3.4). Banks set aside capital (usually cash invested in risk-free securities) commensurate with the risk they undertake in their underwriting and lending commitments. *Reputation risk* is less tangible, but no less important. This is the risk that comes from associating the investment banking firm with the company for which it is raising capital. Serious problems experienced by the company may have a residual effect on the investment bank's reputation.

EXHIBIT C3.4 BANKS ON A BRIDGE TOO FAR? AS RISK RISES IN LEVERAGED BUYOUTS, INVESTORS START TO BALK; WARNING FROM OVERSEAS

By Robin Sidel, Valerie Bauerlein, and Carrick Mollenkamp

The nation's largest financial institutions have spent the past year relying on robust capital markets to offset woes in their retail-banking operations. Now, that big revenue stream may be starting to dry up.

A sudden retrenchment in debt markets is likely to nip at profits at the big banks that have been financing the leveraged-buyout (LBO) boom around the globe. The latest deal bonanza, in which private equity firms buy public companies and load them up with debt, has created several new financing techniques that mint money for the banks, but can also leave them holding more risk.

For JPMorgan Chase & Co., Citigroup Inc., and Bank of America Corp., the biggest players in the leveraged-loan business, a slowdown in deal financings comes as they grapple with difficult issues. Among them, a tricky interest-rate environment that makes it less lucrative to make loans, a slowdown in mortgage and home-equity lending, and fierce competition to acquire deposits, even as banks are still struggling to assess the fallout from the turmoil in subprime housing.

Banks won't "lose money, but what will happen is that they won't make as much and earnings may decline," said Ganesh Rathnam, a banking analyst at Morningstar Inc. in Chicago.

As they have raced to finance LBOs, the banks have also steadily taken on more risk. Although much of it is typically parceled out to investors, the banks can be left holding the bag, as happened when investors balked at the US Foodservice deal.

In the United States, so-called covenant-lite deals accounted for about 26% of first-quarter deals versus 4.6% in European leveraged-loan issues. The pace began to sharply increase in Europe in March, according to Bank of America research. The "cov-lite" deals—where a bank's covenant protections are weakened—have been a result of the cheap financing, allowing borrowers to reduce financial covenants that typically require borrowers to meet financial hurdles on a quarterly basis.

In particular, regulators are expressing concern about "equity bridge loans" in which private equity firms ask their banks to provide stop-gap financing for some deals. The loans, which carry high interest rates, last from 3–24 months and are repaid once the sale of below-investment-grade, or junk, bonds has occurred.

So far this year, banks have provided $33.38 billion in bridge loans to LBO deals, more than double last year's $12.87 billion, according to Reuters Loan Pricing/DealScan. The volume is the highest since the LBO heyday 20 years ago, when $48.14 billion in bridge loans was issued in 1988.

Of the banks, Citigroup, Deutsche Bank AG, and J.P. Morgan have arranged the most bridge loans for LBO deals this year.

Regulators expect to take another look at guidance they issued in 2001 on leveraged lending to see if it still fits. At the time, banks kept most leveraged loans on their balance sheets, and regulators thus expected them to consider the borrower's ability to repay principal, not just interest. Banks now typically distribute their loans to institutional investors, so regulators say they may need to consider different criteria. It may be less important for a bank to consider the borrower's ability to amortize a loan, and more important to weigh the "reputational risk" that a loan it sold to investors goes bad, or "pipeline risk"— when adverse financing conditions force it to keep a loan on its balance sheet rather than distributing it.

A report by the Bank for International Settlements said, "The fact that banks are now increasingly providing bridge equity, along with bridge loans, to support the still growing number of corporate mergers and acquisitions is not a good sign." It went on to say: "A closely related concern is the possibility that banks have, either intentionally or inadvertently, retained a significant degree of credit risk on their books."

Source: Wall Street Journal, June 28, 2007.

Outside the Wall

Freeport announced its acquisition of Phelps Dodge in a formal press release that "hit the tape" (published on the news wire services) on November 19, 2006.

After the Phelps Dodge acquisition had been signed, the investment banks' focus soon shifted to syndicating out the bridge loan to raise the capital necessary to complete the transaction. Included in this process was negotiating with credit rating agencies to secure the highest possible ratings on the upcoming bond offerings. On February 28, 2007, S&P upgraded its debt rating on FCX's existing 2014 senior debt from B+ to BB+. It followed this with another upgrade to BBB– on April 4. Just 2 months after this, on June 7, it upgraded FCX's debt rating once again to BBB. Similarly, Moody's had placed the company on positive watch on November 20, 2006. It followed this up with an upgrade from B1 to Ba2 on February 26, 2007, and then to Baa3 on March 27. The credit upgrades resulted from both the more than $5 billion in equity capital raised through the common stock and convertible offering and the significant increase in cash flow that resulted from the merger (see Exhibit C3.5).[22]

EXHIBIT C3.5 BOND RATINGS BY DATE AND RATING AGENCY

Date	Rating Agency	Upgrade
November 20, 2006	Moody's	Positive outlook
February 26, 2007	Moody's	B1 to Ba2
February 28, 2007	S&P	B+ to BB+
March 27, 2007	Moody's	Ba2 to Baa3
April 4, 2007	S&P	BB+ to BBB–
June 7, 2007	S&P	BBB– to BBB

Source: Bloomberg.

After the completion of all debt-related transactions, FCX and Phelps Dodge finalized the acquisition. Once this was complete, it opened the door to the equity and equity-linked capital raising.

Placing the Equity and Convertible Offerings

Institutional salespeople at investment banks are responsible for bringing investment opportunities to the analysts and portfolio managers of large asset managers such as mutual funds, hedge funds, pension funds, and some insurance companies. Their investment ideas come from a variety of sources, including research done by the firm's equity research analysts. The institutional asset managers do not pay investment banks for their

[22] Bloomberg.

investment ideas; rather, they pay commissions on the large trades that they execute. This process is part art and part science. Traditionally, institutional managers conduct a periodic vote to rank each investment bank and attempt to allocate commissions for the next period accordingly.

Shortly after FCX's intention to issue equity and convertible securities was announced, the JPMorgan institutional sales force heard a "teach-in" by the firm's metals and mining industry analyst. Because of JPMorgan's involvement as advisor to Freeport on the acquisition, their equity research analyst was restricted from providing an investment opinion on shares of FCX. However, he was allowed to provide the institutional sales force an overview of the equity and convertible offerings and their uses, as well as answer any related questions that salespeople had. After this presentation, the sales force had the opportunity to hear from FCX's management team regarding both the rationale for the Phelps Dodge acquisition as well as the method of financing chosen. Altogether, this session provided the sales team with enough information to be able to discuss the offerings in detail with their institutional asset manager clients.

The management team at FCX also participated in an investor "roadshow": a series of meetings with institutional investors to discuss the company's current financial position and business activities. For initial public offerings, roadshows typically last 1 or 2 weeks, providing the company a forum to tell its story to new investors. For secondary offerings (follow-on capital raisings from an existing public company) and convertibles, roadshows are considered optional, depending on how well the company is known. In this case, FCX had done a "nondeal" roadshow after the acquisition announcement, educating investors on the transaction, and so only a limited roadshow was scheduled for the equity and convertible financings.

The combined equity and convertible roadshow began on Tuesday, March 20, 1 day after the public announcement regarding closing of the acquisition. Salespeople from both JPMorgan and Merrill Lynch lined up a series of meetings in multiple cities over a 3-day period and then joined a member of the investment banking team and several members of the company's management team on the roadshow. Because of the high demand for meetings and the limited time frame, sales force management had to work with the capital markets syndicate team to decide which investors to see. The decision to meet with investors depended on several factors, such as the size of the investor, quality of relationship with the company, and level of previous interest in it. Current share ownership was also an important consideration.

During this time, salespeople had a series of conversations with their institutional investor clients about the stock and convertible issues and provided feedback to the capital markets syndicate team, who kept track of investor concerns and overall sentiment about the issue. The syndicate team communicated any recurring issues that came up during the feedback process to company management. This feedback loop was particularly important for the price discovery process, as the syndicate team was responsible for establishing a price for the offering. The price discovery process is relatively transparent because the stock is already traded in the open market. However, the key question that remains is how much of a discount (if any) will be applied to the "last sale," or closing price of the stock on the day of pricing. Some investors put in limit orders, which dictate the highest price they would be willing to pay, while others are content with market orders, which indicate a willingness to pay the market-clearing price for the offering. This affects the final pricing decision because investment banks, as well as companies, are reluctant to shut out large and important investors who have submitted limit orders, even though market orders are always preferable.

For the convertible offering, price discovery focuses on the coupon and conversion premium relative to the underlying common stock. Similar to the common stock transaction, the equity capital markets syndicate maintains a book of investor demand and makes a pricing recommendation to the company that is designed to allow the security to trade up modestly. Demand for the convertible comprises approximately half convertible arbitrage hedge funds and half traditional mutual funds or dedicated convertible funds. In smaller transactions and for convertibles that do not have a mandatory conversion feature, allocations tend to be skewed toward convertible arbitrage funds. Convertible arbitrage funds attempt to purchase the convertible instrument while short-selling shares of the common stock in a manner to take advantage of inherent arbitrage opportunities. While companies might have concerns about a large pool of investors shorting their common stock, convertible arbitrage funds provide several advantages: (1) the incremental demand from convertible arbitrage funds allows companies to achieve better pricing in their convertible offerings (cheaper financing) and (2) the demand also ensures more trading liquidity in the convertible security, adding to the attractiveness for traditional long-only investors.

MANDATORY CONVERTIBLE PREFERRED SHARES

FCX's convertible instrument was designed to be converted mandatorily into a predetermined number of the company's common shares in 3 years. As a result, rating agencies assigned "equity content" of up to 90% to this convertible transaction (see Exhibit C3.6 and Exhibit C3.7). For a more traditional optionally converting convertible, rating agencies usually attribute no equity content and, in fact, assume the convertible is more like a bond unless and until it converts in the future into common shares (which will happen only if the investor determines that the value of the common shares the convertible can convert into exceeds the cash redemption value of the original security). The use of a mandatory convertible structure by FCX facilitated the rapid credit rating upgrades previously discussed. The issuance of common stock in conjunction with the convertible enabled convertible arbitrage hedge fund investors to more easily borrow and then short sell FCX common shares, which facilitated stronger demand for and resulted in better pricing of the convertible.

EXHIBIT C3.6 SELECTIONS FROM SECURITIES AND EXCHANGE COMMISSION FILING FOR CONVERTIBLE PREFERRED OFFERING, 3/23 THE OFFERING

Issuer	Freeport-McMoRan Copper & Gold Inc.
Securities offered	25,000,000 shares of 6¾% mandatory convertible preferred stock (28,750,000 shares if the underwriters exercise their overallotment option in full), which we refer to in this prospectus supplement as the "mandatory convertible preferred stock."
Initial offering price	$100.00 per share of mandatory convertible preferred stock.
Option to purchase additional shares of mandatory convertible preferred stock	To the extent the underwriters sell more than 25,000,000 shares of our mandatory convertible preferred stock, the underwriters have the option to purchase up to 3,750,000 additional shares of our mandatory convertible preferred stock from us at the initial offering price, less underwriting discounts and commissions, within 30 days from the date of this prospectus supplement.
Dividends	6¾% per share on the liquidation preference thereof of $100.00 for each share of our mandatory convertible preferred stock per year. Dividends will accrue and cumulate from the date of issuance and, to the extent that we are legally permitted to pay dividends and our board of directors, or an authorized committee of our board of directors, declares a dividend payable, we will pay dividends in cash or, subject to certain limitations, in common stock on each dividend payment date. The expected dividend payable on the first dividend payment date is $2.30625 per share, and on each subsequent dividend payment date is expected to be $1.6875 per share.
Dividend payment dates	February 1, May 1, August 1, and November 1 of each year prior to the mandatory conversion date (as defined below), and on the mandatory conversion date, commencing on August 1, 2007.
Redemption	Our mandatory convertible preferred stock is not redeemable.
Mandatory conversion date	May 1, 2010.
Mandatory conversion	On the mandatory conversion date, each share of our mandatory convertible preferred stock will automatically convert into shares of our common stock, based on the conversion rate as described below. Holders of mandatory convertible preferred stock on the mandatory conversion date will have the right to receive the dividend due on such date (including any accrued, cumulated, and unpaid dividends on the mandatory convertible preferred stock as of the mandatory conversion date), whether or not declared (other than previously declared dividends on the mandatory convertible preferred stock payable to holders of record as of a prior date), to the extent we are legally permitted to pay such dividends at such time.

Continued

EXHIBIT C3.6 SELECTIONS FROM SECURITIES AND EXCHANGE COMMISSION FILING FOR CONVERTIBLE PREFERRED OFFERING, 3/23 THE OFFERING—cont'd

Conversion rate	The conversion rate for each share of our mandatory convertible preferred stock will not be more than 1.6327 shares of common stock and not less than 1.3605 shares of common stock, depending on the applicable market value of our common stock, as described below.
	The "applicable market value" of our common stock is the average of the daily closing price per share of our common stock on each of the 20 consecutive trading days ending on the third trading day immediately preceding the mandatory conversion date.
	The following table illustrates the conversion rate per share of our mandatory convertible preferred stock subject to certain antidilution adjustments.

Applicable Market Value	Conversion Rate
Less than or equal to $61.25	1.6327
Between $61.25 and $73.50	$100.00 divided by the applicable market value
Equal to or greater than $73.50	1.3605

Optional conversion	At any time prior to May 1, 2010, you may elect to convert each of your shares of our mandatory convertible preferred stock at the minimum conversion rate of 1.3605 shares of common stock for each share of mandatory convertible preferred stock. This conversion rate is subject to certain adjustments.
Ranking	The mandatory convertible preferred stock will rank with respect to dividend rights and rights on our liquidation, winding up, or dissolution: senior to all of our common stock and to all of our other capital stock issued in the future unless the terms of that stock expressly provide that it ranks senior to, or on a parity with, the mandatory convertible preferred stock.
Use of proceeds	We intend to use the net proceeds from the offering to repay outstanding indebtedness under our Tranche A term loan facility and Tranche B term loan facility.
Listing	The mandatory convertible preferred stock has been approved for listing on the New York Stock Exchange.

EXHIBIT C3.7 CONVERTIBLE PREFERRED MECHANICS

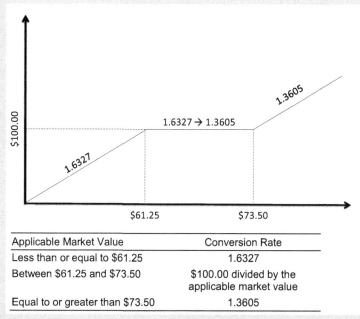

Applicable Market Value	Conversion Rate
Less than or equal to $61.25	1.6327
Between $61.25 and $73.50	$100.00 divided by the applicable market value
Equal to or greater than $73.50	1.3605

As of the mandatory conversion date, for each $100 mandatory convertible preferred share purchased by investors, they will receive 1.6327 FCX shares if FCX share price is less than or equal to $61.25 on that date. If FCX share price is between $61.25 and $73.50, investors will receive between 1.6527 and 1.3605 FCX shares. If FCX share price is equal to or greater than $73.50, investors will receive 1.3605 FCX shares.

FCX POSTALLOCATION

Shares of FCX closed on Thursday, March 22, 2007, at $61.91. On March 23, the company priced 47.15 million shares of stock at $61.25 per share (proceeds of approximately $2.9 billion), along with 28.75 million shares of 6¾% mandatory convertible preferred stock at $100.00 per share (proceeds of approximately $2.9 billion). Net proceeds to FCX, after underwriting discount and expenses, totaled $5.6 billion.[23] By the end of trading on March 23, FCX shares closed up 39 cents from the prior close to $62.30, a nearly 2% gain from the transaction price (see Exhibit C3.8). By most accounts, this was a successful offering for both the company and investors. FCX was interested in the quality of the investor base. Generally, if a company has an opportunity to allocate newly issued shares to investors it believes will be long-term holders, it is willing to make some concession on price, which was the case with the FCX offering.

[23] FCX press release, March 28, 2007.

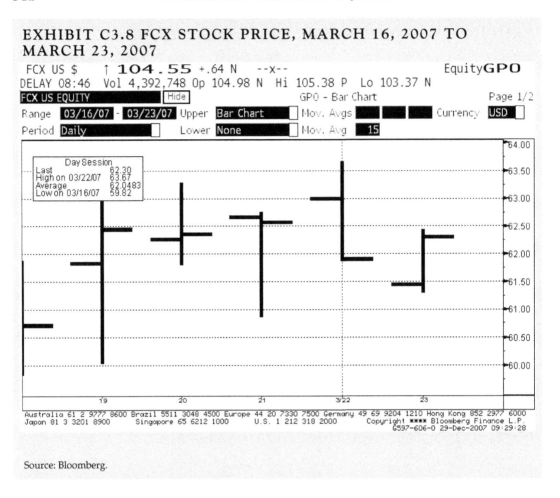

EXHIBIT C3.8 FCX STOCK PRICE, MARCH 16, 2007 TO MARCH 23, 2007

Source: Bloomberg.

The convertible ended the trading day at 101.5, having been offered to investors at 100 (the "par" price). As was the case with the equity offering, FCX had an interest in making sure that it did not leave significant money on the table for the convertible transaction. At the same time, it wanted to ensure that both offerings—common shares and convertible—were placed with appropriate investors who were willing to take long-term positions (see Exhibit C3.9 and Exhibit C3.10 for posttransaction price action).

EXHIBIT C3.9 FCX EQUITY, MARCH 1, 2007 TO DECEMBER 28, 2007

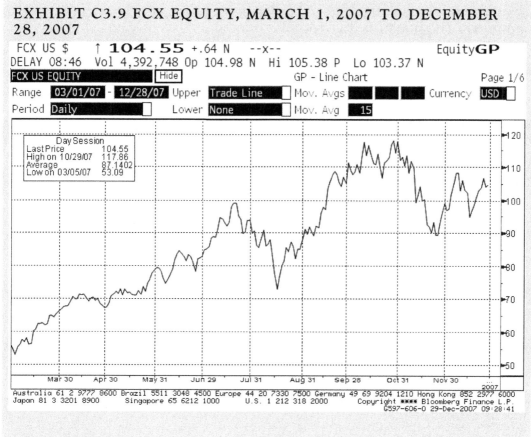

Source: Bloomberg.

EXHIBIT C3.10 FCX CONVERTIBLE PREFERRED, MARCH 23, 2007 TO DECEMBER 14, 2007

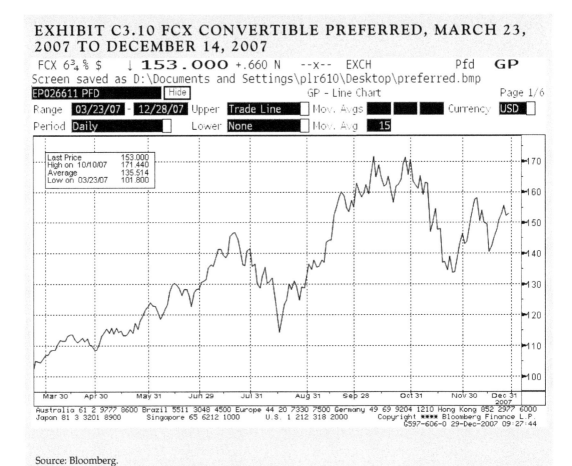

Source: Bloomberg.

The Best Deal Gillette Could Get? Procter & Gamble's Acquisition of Gillette

January 27, 2005, was an extraordinary day for Gillette's James Kilts, the show-stopping turnaround expert known as the "Razor Boss of Boston." Kilts, along with Procter & Gamble chairman Alan Lafley, had just orchestrated a $57 billion acquisition of Gillette by P&G. The creation of the world's largest consumer products company would end Kilts's 4-year tenure as CEO of Gillette and bring to a close Gillette's 104-year history as an independent corporate titan in the Boston area. The deal also capped a series of courtships between Gillette and other companies that had waxed and waned at various points throughout Kilts's stewardship of Gillette. But almost immediately after the transaction was announced, P&G and Gillette drew criticism from the media and the state of Massachusetts concerning the terms of the sale. Would this merger actually benefit shareholders, or was it principally a wealth creation vehicle for Kilts?

A DREAM DEAL

Procter & Gamble was known for its consumer products such as soap, shampoo, laundry detergent, and food and beverages, as well as products for health and beauty care.[1] The company owned a portfolio of approximately 150 brands—ranging from Ace bleach to Zest soap—including some of the world's most recognizable: Pampers, Tide, Folgers, Charmin, Crest, Olay, and Head & Shoulders.[2] Gillette was best known for its razor business, but the company controlled two other brands—Oral-B toothbrushes and Duracell batteries—that produced at least $1 billion in annual revenue (see Exhibit C4.1). Whereas P&G was particularly skilled in marketing to women,[3] Gillette's core customer segment was men (with the memorable marketing tagline "The Best a Man Can Get"). Gillette had expanded into female product lines with its Venus razor, and P&G also had several brands—Head & Shoulders dandruff shampoo among them—that targeted male customers, but the two companies were naturally stronger in distinct gender segments. They also performed better in different regions of the globe. Gillette understood how

---

[1] Naomi Aoki and Steve Bailey, "P&G to Buy Gillette for $55B Latest in String of Deals for Old-Line Hub Firms," *Boston Globe*, January 28, 2005.

[2] James F. Peltz, "P&G-Gillette Union Could Hit Shoppers in Pocketbook," *Los Angeles Times*, January 29, 2005.

[3] Aoki and Bailey, "P&G to Buy Gillette for $55B."

to operate successfully in India and Brazil, while P&G brought expertise in the Chinese market.[4]

EXHIBIT C4.1 P&G'S AND GILLETTE'S BILLION DOLLAR BRANDS

21 "Billion Dollar Brands"

Baby & Family Care	Bounty, Charmin, Pampers
Beauty Care	Always, Olay, Pantene, Head & Shoulders, Wella
Fabric & Home Care	Ariel, Downy, Tide
Oral Care	Crest, Oral-B
Snacks & Beverages	Folgers, Pringles
Blades & Razors	Gillette, Mach 3
Batteries	Duracell
Small Appliances	Braun
Pet Food	IAMS
Health Care	Actionel

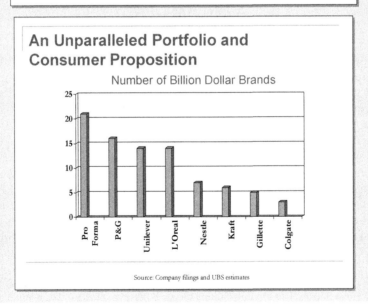

An Unparalleled Portfolio and Consumer Proposition

Number of Billion Dollar Brands

Source: Company filings and UBS estimates

---

[4] Steve Jordon, "Billion-Dollar Brands Buffett Says 'Dream Deal' Should Make the Most of Magic in Household Names of Products Made by P&G and Gillette," *Omaha World-Herald*, January 29, 2005.

Gillette was no stranger to overtures from both strategic and financial investors. The company had successfully defended itself against four takeover attempts in the late 1980s, three from Ronald Perelman and his cosmetics company Revlon, and one from Coniston Partners.[5] Yet the P&G proposal promised to be different. While some of the same key drivers (including an array of excellent brands) that had interested Perelman and Coniston likely drove P&G's interest in Gillette, the two companies also saw new opportunities that had not previously existed, including the chance to combine complementary business lines and the ability to create an industry leader that could better negotiate with mass merchandisers.

A combined firm would capitalize on the core marketing competencies of both companies and be able to more effectively reach both male and female consumer segments worldwide. The combination would also enable the entities to better negotiate with large retailers such as Wal-Mart and Target. Throughout the 1990s, as mass retailing increased in geographic scope and customer base, the retailers' reach had forced more consumer products group (CPG) companies to channel their sales through superstores. In 2003, Wal-Mart accounted for 13% of Gillette's sales, enough to be listed in accounting statements filed with the Securities and Exchange Commission (SEC) as a substantial business risk.[6] Preserving a Wal-Mart relationship was so important that many of the larger and more successful CPG firms had gone so far as to establish permanent offices in what had become known as Vendorville, a community of hundreds of CPG companies near Wal-Mart's headquarters in Arkansas. Wal-Mart's reach and market clout enabled it to negotiate significant pricing concessions from CPG firms. Its buyers were able to say to retailers: "If you'd like to reach our 138 million customers per week, here's the deal."[7] CPG companies therefore had to bow to ever-mounting price pressure from Wal-Mart and other large retailers. The acquisition of Gillette by P&G could counterbalance this pressure and allow the combined firm to better control pricing and product placement in superstores nationwide.

As early as 2002, Kilts had approached P&G about a possible merger, and he began courting P&G anew in late 2004 (see Exhibits C4.2 and C4.3). On November 17, 2004, representatives of senior management from Gillette and P&G met with representatives from Merrill Lynch (representing P&G) and UBS, and Goldman Sachs (representing Gillette) to discuss a possible merger between the companies. The following day, Lafley met with McKinsey & Company consultants to receive their assessment of a combined firm. After receiving the blessing of both the bankers and the consultants, the two companies appeared close to completing a transaction. However, the deal fell apart in early December 2004, largely because Gillette's leadership believed that the valuation P&G had offered to Gillette shareholders (approximately $50 per share) was too low.

---

[5] Steve Jordon, "Buffett Calls It a 'Dream Deal'," *Omaha World-Herald*, January 28, 2005.

[6] Mike Hughlett and Becky Yerak, "P&G, Gillette Deal a Matter of Clout; Combined, Firm Can Fight Retail Squeeze," *Chicago Tribune*, January 29, 2005.

[7] Greg Gatlin, "Deal Is No Blue-Light Special for Wal-Mart," *Boston Herald*, January 29, 2005.

EXHIBIT C4.2 KEY DEAL DATES COMPARED WITH STOCK PRICE OF P&G AND GILLETTE

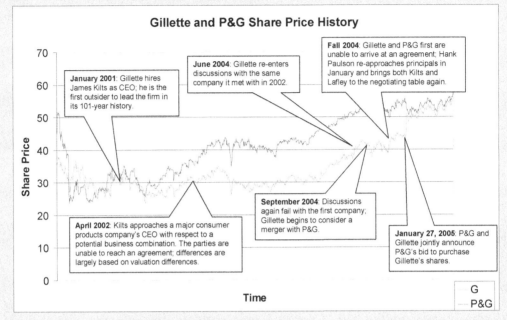

Gillette and P&G Share Price History

January 2001: Gillette hires James Kilts as CEO; he is the first outsider to lead the firm in its 101-year history.

June 2004: Gillette re-enters discussions with the same company it met with in 2002.

Fall 2004: Gillette and P&G first are unable to arrive at an agreement; Hank Paulson re-approaches principals in January and brings both Kilts and Lafley to the negotiating table again.

April 2002: Kilts approaches a major consumer products company's CEO with respect to a potential business combination. The parties are unable to reach an agreement; differences are largely based on valuation differences.

September 2004: Discussions again fail with the first company; Gillette begins to consider a merger with P&G.

January 27, 2005: P&G and Gillette jointly announce P&G's bid to purchase Gillette's shares.

Yet hope remained that the two companies would be able to bridge the valuation divide. On January 4, 2005, Hank Paulson (board chairman and CEO of Goldman Sachs) called Lafley to remind him of the long-term strategic value of the merger and asked that P&G to reconsider its offer. One week later, P&G's board of directors authorized Lafley to resume discussions with Gillette. Lafley then asked Rajat Gupta (former managing director of McKinsey & Company) to phone Kilts. The two met 2 days later, on January 13, 2005, to explore the possibility of reaching an agreement between the two companies.[8] Paulson and Gupta successfully bridged the gap between Lafley and Kilts. Instead of the original offer (0.915 P&G shares for every Gillette share), Lafley now offered 0.975 P&G shares for every Gillette share, which was accepted by Kilts and Gillette's board of directors.

[8] Proxy Statement filed under Section 14A.

EXHIBIT C4.3 TIMELINE OF THE TRANSACTION

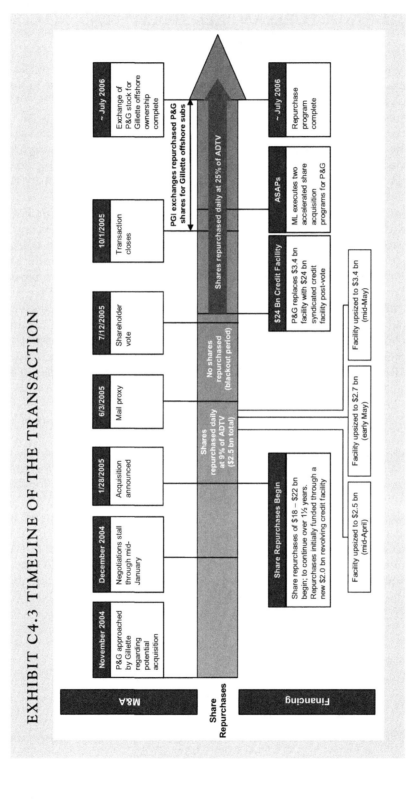

DEAL STRUCTURE: AN "ALL-STOCK," 60/40, NO-COLLAR ACQUISITION

A key concern of any acquisition involves how the consideration paid to complete the transaction will be structured. Acquisitions may be completed using one of three forms: all-cash, all-stock, or a hybrid of the two. Each option provides costs and benefits to both the buyer (acquiring company) and the target (purchased company). In an all-cash deal, the acquiring company typically pays the target company's shareholders a fixed price (per share) in cash. The benefit of this arrangement lies in its efficiency and transparency. Because companies are often acquired for a premium over their current stock price, a cash offer creates an immediately recognizable gain and allows shareholders to easily reallocate their newfound cash.

However, cash transactions have negative consequences as well. First, the target company's shareholders must pay taxes if there is a capital gain. Second, a cash payment requires the acquiring company to dip into its corporate coffers. This can adversely impact a company's bond rating and stock price, since credit rating services are wary of a firm greatly increasing its debt load or significantly reducing its cash resources.

Because of the negative tax and leverage consequences of all-cash deals, acquiring firms often provide the target company's shareholders with shares of the acquiring company instead. Yet all-stock deals also have drawbacks. For one, the target company's shareholders may not wish to hold the stock of the acquiring company. Doing so requires additional time and effort to analyze the financial health and future opportunities of the new firm. Second, the acquiring company may be concerned about diluting the value of its shares in the marketplace. Because both all-cash and all-stock transactions present problems, acquiring firms sometimes create a blended offer that contains elements of both cash and stock.

P&G's offer for Gillette, for example, was a modified all-stock deal (see Exhibits C4.4 and C4.5). Under the terms of the agreement, P&G would issue 0.975 shares of its stock for each share of Gillette. This would avoid triggering a taxable event for Gillette's shareholders and would allow P&G to retain more of its cash. However, P&G also agreed to begin repurchasing $18–$22 billion of P&G stock over an 18-month period. This stock repurchase program sweetened the deal for Gillette shareholders. It provided them with a wholly tax-free transaction as well as an opportunity to continue to participate in the combined company if they wished or to sell stock back to P&G for cash.[9] P&G's share repurchases would result in reduced shareholder dilution. By the end of the 18-month buyback period, the transaction would be comprised of about 60% stock and 40% cash.[10]

[9] Proxy Statement filed under Section 14A.

[10] Jordon, "Buffett Calls It a 'Dream Deal'."

EXHIBIT C4.4 TRANSACTION SUMMARY

Structure	0.975 shares of P&G for each share of Gillette
Consideration	100% stock acquisition
Implied offer price	$54.05, based on P&G closing price of $55.04 on January 26, 2005 (20.1% premium to Gillette share price of $45 on that date)
Tax treatment	Tax-free reorganization
Breakup fee	$1.9 billion
Closing	October 1, 2005
Share repurchase	P&G to repurchase $18–$22 billion of P&G shares by June 2006
Dilution	Expected to be dilutive in 2006, break even in 2007, and accretive in 2008
Synergies	More than $1 billion of cost synergies expected to be achieved over a 3-year period
Enterprise value	Approximately $57.2 billion, including $2.3 billion of Gillette net debt assumption

EXHIBIT C4.5 TERMS AND OVERVIEW OF THE DEAL

Rationale

- Merger accomplished via an all-equity deal
- Transaction followed by $18–$22 billion share repurchase program over 12–18 months
  - Equivalent to ~60%–65% stock and ~35%–40% debt-financed acquisition
- $18–$22 billion of debt in P&G International (PGI), along with all international subsidiaries of P&G and Gillette
- Transaction financed with portion of cash
- Simultaneous announcement of buyback to help support P&G stock price
- Offshore entities receive their fair share of the economic cost of the deal
  - Future cash flow of PGI used to pay down offshore debt
- All international business aligned to facilitate business synergies and efficiencies

Process

- PGI borrows and buys P&G shares
- Acquisition Co. (parent subsidiary) exchanges P&G shares for Gillette shares
- Periodically, PGI exchanges repurchased P&G shares for shares of Gillette offshore subsidiaries
- By ~July 2006 PGI will have borrowed $18–$22 billion, repurchased $18–$22 billion of P&G stock, and exchanged it all for international subsidiaries of Gillette
- Ongoing PGI debt will be supported by all international cash flows of the combined entities

This buyback, however, could still impact P&G's credit standing with major rating agencies. Shortly after announcing the details of the acquisition and buyback programs, P&G was notified by Standard & Poor's, Moody's, and Fitch Ratings that "borrowings associated with [the] announced stock repurchase program have resulted in the re-examination and possible downgrading of its credit rating."[11] However, when P&G began issuing debt to complete the share buyback program in August 2005, it continued to enjoy the fourth-highest investment-grade credit ratings at both Moody's Investors Service (Aa3) and Standard & Poor's (AA–).[12]

Another notable aspect of the acquisition included the deal protections agreed by both companies' boards of directors, including a breakup fee of $1.9 billion, or approximately 3% of the value of the transaction. Under this provision, if Gillette's board received and accepted a competing offer, the new acquirer would be required to pay $1.9 billion to P&G. Although the companies agreed to a breakup fee, they did not employ a collar on the 0.975 P&G shares offered. A collar, common in many mergers and acquisitions, creates a ceiling and a floor on the value of the shares offered to complete the transaction. By creating a definitive price range, the collar assuages shareholders' (from both companies) fears regarding potential fluctuations in the acquiring company's share price, while the transaction awaits shareholder approval (a process often 3 to 6 months in length). Since both companies would have received protection from a collar, it was surprising that it was not employed.

VALUATION OF THE DEAL

Based on P&G's closing price on January 26, 2005, its offer of 0.975 P&G shares for every share of Gillette translated into an implied offer price of $54.05 per share. This price fell somewhere in the middle of a series of valuations prepared by investment bankers ranging from $43.25 to $61.90 (see Exhibit C4.6). A valuation based on public market reference points, including Gillette's 52-week trading range and a present value of Wall Street price targets, would have priced Gillette's stock at $43.25 to $45.00. A valuation analysis based on discounted cash flows was more favorable. One such valuation that incorporated only the cash flows from Gillette in its current form valued the shares at $47.10. A second valuation that took into account the potential cost savings resulting from the combination of Gillette and P&G valued the stock at $56.60. Cost savings were expected to be realized in purchasing, manufacturing, logistics, and administrative costs. A third valuation that incorporated total synergies (both cost savings and capitalizing on complementary strengths) valued the stock at $61.90 per share. This valuation included not only the cost savings, but also potential revenue synergy opportunities that a combined firm might realize, including the increased market power that a combined firm would wield in dealing with large retailing firms such as Wal-Mart. Finally, a sum-of-the-parts valuation established a price of $52.50 per share (see Exhibit C4.7).

---

[11] Proxy Statement filed under Section 14A.

[12] Ed Leefeldt, "P&G Leads U.S. Borrowers with $24 Billion Stock-Buyback Loan," *Bloomberg News*, August 5, 2005.

EXHIBIT C4.6 VALUATION OF THE DEAL

$ Per Share

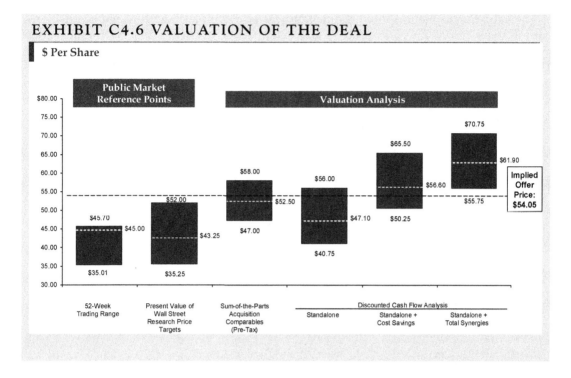

EXHIBIT C4.7 SUM-OF-THE-PARTS VALUATION

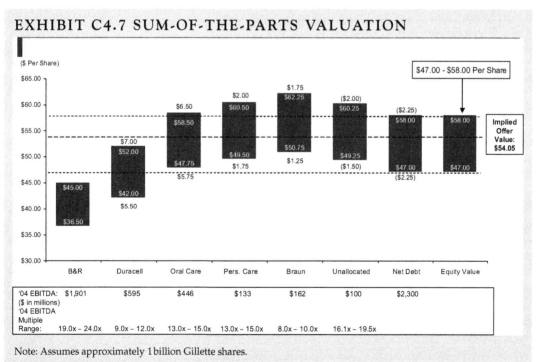

Note: Assumes approximately 1 billion Gillette shares.

The valuation of the proposed acquisition was also compared with recent acquisitions, both in the sector and across similarly sized companies, to ensure that the compensation paid to Gillette's shareholders was in line with recent transactions (see Exhibit C4.8). The total transaction value at the implied offer price of $54.05 per share was $57.177 billion (see Exhibit C4.9).

EXHIBIT C4.8 COMPARISON WITH OTHER ACQUISITIONS

Announcement Date	Acquiror	Target	Transaction Value ($ in Billions)	Premium to Share Price	
				1 Day Prior (%)	1 Week Prior (%)
06/25/2000	Philip Morris	Nabisco	19.2	69.9	103.2
08/22/1994	Johnson & Johnson	Neutrogena	1.0	63.0	76.3
11/03/2004	Constellation Brands	Robert Mondavi	1.4	49.9	52.3
03/18/2003	P&G	Wella	7.0	44.5	47.3
10/23/2003	Tchibo	Beiersdorf	13.0	51.2	45.7
06/06/2000	Unilever	Bestfoods	23.7	44.4	39.9
12/04/2000	PepsiCo	Quaker Oats	15.1	22.2	24.0
Average				49.3	55.5
At 0.975× exchange ratio					
01/26/2005	P&G	Gillette	57.2	20.1	20.1

KEY STAKEHOLDERS: BEANTOWN, WALL STREET, DC, AND MAIN STREET

The turbulence associated with an acquisition can cause a host of negative effects, and leaders navigating a company through an acquisition can face opposition from managers, employees, politicians, shareholders, and regulators. Top management might be forced out as a result of the acquisition or asked to take lower-profile positions. Employees often fear the consequences of consolidation, including work force reductions mandated by cost-saving synergies (see Exhibit C4.10). Politicians, in turn, are concerned about the long-term social and economic impact that reduced employment can have on a community. Shareholders fear that the price brokered for their shares may not be adequate compensation. Finally, regulators evaluate every aspect of the transaction to determine whether the combined or separate entities have violated applicable state and federal laws, including antitrust laws. The approval of each of these stakeholder groups is essential, and managing the diverse interests of each group can be as challenging as managing the initial financial and strategic interests driving the acquisition.

EXHIBIT C4.9 TRANSACTION VALUES AND MULTIPLES

Offer and Transaction Values

P&G share price (01/26/2005)	$55.44
Proposed exchange ratio	0.975x
Implied offer price per share	$54.05
Total Gillette shares & options outstanding	1,068.379 [a]
Gross offer value	$57,750 [a]
Less: Option proceeds	(2,893) [a]
Net offer value	$54,857 [a]
Plus: Net debt assumed	2,321 [a]
Transaction value	$57,177 [a]

[a] In millions.

Offer Premiums

	Stock Prices	Offer Price $54.05
Current 01/26/2005	$45.00	20.1%
30-day average	$44.58	21.3%
90-day average	$44.00	22.8%

Transaction Multiples

		Gillette Multiples		
	Gillette Results	Market $45.00	Offer Price $54.05	P&G Market Multiples
Revenues				
12/2004A (LTM)	$10,366 [a]	4.6x	5.5x	3.0x
06/2005E	$10,581 [a]	4.5	5.4	2.9
EBITDA				
12/2004A (LTM)	$3,013 [a]	15.8x	19.0x	13.1x
06/2005E	$3,149 [a]	15.1	18.2	12.4
P/E				
06/2005E	$1.78	25.2x	30.3x	21.3x
06/2006E	$2.01	22.4	26.9	19.3

[a] In millions.

EXHIBIT C4.10 GILLETTE'S PRESENTATION TO ITS EMPLOYEES

P&G / Gillette Transition
5 Guiding Principles to the Integration Process

- 1. Maintain P&G and Gillette business momentum
- 2. Field the best team
- 3. Treat people with dignity/respect
- 4. Move quickly, making decisions promptly, objectively, and fairly
- 5. Communicate openly and proactively

4/29/2005

Gillette – Proctor & Gamble

P&G wants to field the *best possible team* ... with members from BOTH companies
- There will be job losses
- Losses are estimated at approximately 4% of the combined company's work force of 140,000
- Many will occur at the corporate office ... but NO decisions have been made
- We've implemented special severance protection
  - Change of control measures
  - Fully vested stock option plan

The Razor Boss of *Boston*: James Kilts, Gillette Chief Executive Officer

Former Nabisco executive James Kilts was a turnaround expert who had orchestrated the sale of Nabisco to Philip Morris in 2000. He was named CEO of Gillette in January 2001 and immediately set on a course to turn it around. Kilts succeeded in resurrecting the company's stagnant stock price by pursuing a policy of "slash and earn." Under this policy, he reduced overhead expenses and invested the savings in promoting the company's razors, blades, and batteries.[13] The strategy performed remarkably well, and Gillette's stock rose 50% under Kilts's stewardship (see Exhibit C4.2). In total, it was estimated that he created about $20 billion in shareholder value.[14]

[13] Greg Gatlin, "Boston Blockbuster; Hub Icon Gillette Sold in $56B Deal," *Boston Herald*, January 28, 2005.

[14] Naomi Aoki, "Kilts' Many Options," *Boston Globe*, February 2, 2005.

Gillette's board of directors' 2001 executive search effort had yielded a CEO who restored investor confidence in the company and crafted a strategy that would enhance the value of its well-known and respected brands. In its recruiting efforts, Gillette's board had offered Kilts an extensive executive compensation package customary for a capable leader with a "knack for rescuing ailing companies."[15] However, though investors had not balked at the structure of Kilts's package in 2001, interest in his compensation increased after the P&G transaction was announced in 2005.

Kilts's compensation package allowed him to realize impressive financial gains in the event that the company was sold. The package included stock options and rights and a one-time $12.6 million "change-of-control" payment.[16] Kilts was also compensated by P&G with options and restricted stock valued at $24 million. His total compensation package amounted to more than $164 million (see Exhibit C4.11). To some business leaders, this amount did not seem outlandish.[17] After all, the figure represented less than 1% of the total value that he had created during his tenure as Gillette's CEO. Yet Kilts took on fierce criticism from the Boston media and some political leaders, including Secretary of the Commonwealth of Massachusetts William Galvin and US Congressman Barney Frank (D-Mass), when the acquisition was announced. Kilts, expressing frustration over this criticism, would refer to himself as Boston's piñata.[18] The moniker reflected his irritation at the negative press attention he received over a deal that he felt would provide many stakeholders with tangible benefits. In a press conference defending the acquisition and his compensation, he pointed out that Massachusetts would retain a key manufacturing plant located south of Boston, job losses would be less than 5%, and Gillette's razor business would continue to be run from the Boston area.

EXHIBIT C4.11 SEVERANCE AND CHANGE IN CONTROL BENEFITS (GILLETTE'S OFFICERS)

Name and Principal Position	Net Equity Award	All Other Payments and Benefits	Estimated Aggregate Dollar Value
James M. Kilts, Chairman, President and CEO	$125,260,167	$39,272,025	$164,532,192
Edward F. DeGraan, Vice Chairman	29,711,715	15,655,483	45,367,198
Charles W. Cramb, Senior VP	16,258,040	10,174,097	26,432,137
Peter K. Hoffman, VP	10,695,578	9,567,625	20,263,203
Mark M. Leckie, VP	9,426,564	7,528,840	16,955,404
All other executive officers as a group (12)	96,073,693	79,795,179	175,868,872

[15] Naomi Aoki, "Kilts' Many Options," *Boston Globe*, February 2, 2005.

[16] Naomi Aoki, "Kilts' Many Options," *Boston Globe*, February 2, 2005.

[17] Naomi Aoki, "Kilts' Many Options," *Boston Globe*, February 2, 2005 citing Shawn Kravetz, president of Boston money management firm Esplanade Capital.

[18] Jenn Abelson, "'Boston's Pinata' Slams Media, Politicians for P&G Deal Attacks," *Boston Globe*, September 9, 2005.

The Rainmakers: Investment Bankers and Power Brokers

The investment bankers that had assisted in the transaction (Goldman, Merrill, and UBS) equally split a $90 million acquisition completion fee for their merger advisory services.[19] In addition, each investment bank provided its client a fairness opinion (see Exhibit C4.12). Fairness opinions are drafted by investment banks "to assure the directors of companies involved in a merger, acquisition, or other deal that its terms are fair to shareholders."[20] This can be problematic, however, because "the bank affirming the fairness of the transaction is often the same one that proposed the deal—and that stands to reap millions in fees if it goes through."[21] This was precisely the case in the P&G–Gillette transaction. Hank Paulson of Goldman Sachs had been directly responsible for bringing the two parties back to the negotiating table in January 2005. His firm netted a $30 million fee for assisting the companies with the transaction after rendering a fairness opinion in support of the transaction. Merrill Lynch and UBS also received fees of $30 million each after providing fairness opinions, putting them in the same position as Goldman Sachs.

EXHIBIT C4.12 EXCERPTS OF GOLDMAN SACHS'S FAIRNESS OPINION SENT TO GILLETTE'S BOARD OF DIRECTORS

Ladies and Gentlemen:

You have requested our opinion as to the fairness from a financial point of view to the holders of the outstanding shares of common stock, par value $1.00 per share (the "Company Common Stock"), of The Gillette Company (the "Company") of the exchange ratio of 0.975 of a share of common stock, without par value (the "P&G Common Stock"), of The Procter & Gamble Company ("P&G") to be received for each Share (the "Exchange Ratio") pursuant to the Agreement and Plan of Merger, dated as of January 27, 2005 (the "Merger Agreement"), among P&G, Aquarium Acquisition Corp., a wholly owned subsidiary of P&G, and the Company.

* * *

We have acted as financial advisor to the Company in connection with and have participated in certain of the negotiations leading to, the transaction contemplated by the Merger Agreement (the "Transaction"). We expect to receive fees for our services in connection with the Transaction, substantially all of which are contingent upon consummation of the Transaction, and the Company has agreed to reimburse our expenses and indemnify us against certain liabilities arising out of our engagement.

* * *

In connection with this opinion, we have reviewed, among other things, the Merger Agreement; certain publicly available business and financial information relating to the Company and P certain financial estimates and forecasts relating to the business and financial prospects of the Company prepared by certain research analysts that were publicly available; certain internal financial information and other data relating to the business and financial prospects of the Company, including financial analyses and forecasts for the Company prepared by its management (the "Company Forecasts"), and certain cost savings and operating synergies projected by the managements of the Company and P&G to result from the Transaction (collectively, the "Synergies"), in each case provided to us by the management of the Company and not publicly available; and certain financial information and other data relating to the business of P&G provided to us by the managements of the Company and P&G and which were not publicly available, which information did not include

---

[19] Brett Arends, "Gillette Shareholders OK P&G Takeover," *Boston Herald*, July 13, 2005.

[20] Gretchen Morgenson, "Mirror, Mirror, Who Is the Unfairest?," *New York Times*, May 29, 2005.

[21] Gretchen Morgenson, "Mirror, Mirror, Who Is the Unfairest?," *New York Times*, May 29, 2005.

EXHIBIT C4.12 EXCERPTS OF GOLDMAN SACHS'S FAIRNESS OPINION SENT TO GILLETTE'S BOARD OF DIRECTORS—cont'd

forecasts for P&G. In such connection, we also have reviewed certain financial estimates and forecasts relating to the business and financial prospects of P&G prepared by certain research analysts that were publicly available, as adjusted and provided to us by the management of the Company following their discussions with the management of P&G as to public guidance expected to be given by P&G contemporaneously with the announcement of the Transaction (the "P&G Adjusted Street Forecasts"). We have held discussions with members of the senior management of the Company and P&G regarding their assessment of the strategic rationale for, and the potential benefits of, the Transaction and the past and current business operations, financial condition and future prospects of the Company and P&G (including as a result of the significant stock buyback being announced by P&G contemporaneously with the Transaction). In addition, we have reviewed the reported price and trading activity for the Company Common Stock and the P&G Common Stock, compared certain publicly available financial and stock market information for the Company and P&G with similar financial and stock market information for certain other companies the securities of which are publicly traded, reviewed certain financial terms of certain recent publicly available business combinations in the consumer products industry specifically and in other industries generally, considered certain pro forma effects of the Transaction, and performed such other studies and analyses, and considered such other factors, as we considered appropriate.

* * *

Our opinion is necessarily based on economic, monetary, market and other conditions as in effect on, and the information made available to us as of, the date hereof.

Based upon and subject to the foregoing, it is our opinion that, as of the date hereof, the Exchange Ratio pursuant to the Merger Agreement is fair from a financial point of view to the holders of the Company Common Stock.

Very truly yours,

/s/ Goldman, Sachs & Co.

The investment bankers and top management at Gillette and P&G faced substantial criticism for the consideration paid to the firms. However, Gillette spokesperson Eric Kraus advised those investigating the bankers' role in the transaction that "virtually no financial expert thinks the deal is anything but excellent for Gillette shareholders."[22] Though Kraus's statement reminded the investment community how much support the transaction enjoyed, it did not appease the investigating appetite of regulators in the United States and abroad.

The Regulators: International, National, and Local

Mergers and acquisitions face scrutiny from regulators at multiple levels of government. For publicly traded companies, the regulatory process begins with the SEC. Each firm is required to disclose its plans to merge (or be acquired) in a series of forms. Form 8-K is filed

[22]Gretchen Morgenson, "Mirror, Mirror, Who Is the Unfairest?," *New York Times*, May 29, 2005.

whenever a publicly traded company has a material event and is often accompanied by Form 425, which is filed whenever a public company makes an important announcement. The net effect of filing both of these forms is that they put investors on notice as to a major decision reached by the board of directors.

Once the information concerning a proposed merger or acquisition is publicly available, regulators begin to scrutinize the transaction to ensure that economic and financial fairness is achieved. Often in a consolidation, two firms with similar business models are forced to divest assets (or entire business lines) to satisfy the antitrust and consumer-watchdog concerns voiced by federal regulators in the United States and by regulators at the European Commission (EC). In Europe, the EC is responsible for approving transactions between public companies and is charged with investigating the impact that a merger or acquisition would likely have on consumers and employees in Europe. As a result of the EC's investigation, "P&G offered to improve the conditions of its proposed disposals" to include not only its electronic toothbrush business in the United Kingdom, but also other brands elsewhere in Europe.[23]

In the United States, the Federal Trade Commission (FTC) is responsible for investigating the possible effects of a merger or acquisition. The FTC derives its authority to investigate such transactions from the Clayton Act and the Federal Trade Commission Act. The Hart–Scott–Rodino Act requires prospective acquirers to notify the FTC of a potential transaction and allow 30 days for a review. While investigating P&G's acquisition of Gillette, the FTC found that there might be anticompetition problems within the at-home teeth-whitening products, adult battery-powered toothbrushes, and men's antiperspirants/deodorants markets.[24] As a result of the FTC's ruling, the two companies began divesting themselves of business lines that might run afoul of anticompetition laws.[25] Gillette sold its Rembrandt teeth-whitening products to Johnson & Johnson and its Right Guard, Soft & Dri, and Dry Idea deodorant brands to Dial. P&G, for its part, sold its Crest SpinBrush line to Church & Dwight.

Companies intending to merge can also face scrutiny from state governments. The state of Massachusetts, under Secretary Galvin, attempted to subpoena records and information from Gillette to investigate whether the sale of Gillette ran contrary to Massachusetts laws. Under state law, it is the Secretary's duty to prohibit fraud "in connection with the offer, sale, or purchase of any security (and is) expected to prohibit fraud by any person who is paid for advising (another) as to the value of the securities or their purchase or sale."[26] Yet mergers and acquisitions are "expressly removed from the scope of the Uniform Securities Act,"[27] the law under which Galvin was attempting to subpoena Gillette. Therefore, a state court in Massachusetts determined that in spite of Galvin's concerns about the impact of the acquisition on employees and shareholders in Massachusetts, the state did not have the authority to further subpoena Gillette regarding its acquisition by P&G. The court left open the possibility

[23] Tobias Buck and Jeremy Grant, "EU Officials Back P&G/Gillette Merger," *Financial Times*, July 15, 2005.

[24] *In the Matter of the Procter & Gamble Co.*, Federal Trade Commission Docket No. C-4151 (2005).

[25] Jenn Abelson, "Gillette Selling Its Deodorants to Dial," *Boston Globe*, February 21, 2006.

[26] *Galvin v. Gillette*, 19 Mass. L. Rep. 291 (2005).

[27] *Galvin v. Gillette*, 19 Mass. L. Rep. 291 (2005).

that Galvin could subpoena the investment banking firms advising Gillette and P&G during the transaction, as the law did not exempt those firms. Hank Paulson of Goldman Sachs was ultimately subpoenaed by Galvin and gave testimony to state lawyers in June 2005. Though Galvin raised a series of questions about the deal and the fairness opinion, as of April 2006 he had not brought suit against Goldman Sachs or any other investment banks involved in the transaction.

The White Squire from *Omaha*: Warren Buffett, Gillette Investor

To help deal with the scrutiny caused by the acquisition of Gillette, the company turned to Warren Buffett, one of its most notable brand investors. Buffett's involvement in the P&G–Gillette transaction stemmed from his longstanding investment in Gillette, dating back to the 1980s. Though Gillette had successfully fended off several hostile takeover attempts between 1986 and 1989, the defensive efforts it had employed had placed it in financial peril at the time. The firm was saddled with $1 billion in debt as a result of measures deployed defending against these takeover attempts, and remained a possible acquisition target.[28] But the company still had a series of strong brands, which attracted Buffett. In 1989, Buffett agreed to purchase $600 million of convertible securities that could later be converted into an 11% interest in Gillette stock. Buffett's purchase provided the cash infusion Gillette desperately needed to retire debt, and also placed a large number of shares in the hands of an investor friendly to Gillette's board. With such a large concentration of shares controlled by one friendly investor, Gillette was able to ensure that any attempt to take over the company would have to be approved by its new "white squire."[29] This became Gillette's "insurance policy" against any future corporate raiders.

Buffett had executed a well-timed entrance into what would become a booming industry. Consumer product firms were favored by investors throughout the 1990s, and Buffett saw his Gillette investment appreciate more than tenfold during that decade. However, the stock languished during the late 1990s, and investors lost patience with former Gillette CEOs Al Zeien and Michael Hawley. Buffett was reportedly instrumental in Hawley's removal and he initiated the search that led to the selection of James Kilts as Gillette's new CEO in 2001.

When Gillette again turned to Buffett for assistance in 2005, instead of asking him to invest additional funds in the company, Gillette sought his blessing of its sale to P&G. So powerful was Buffett's reputation throughout the investment community that Gillette's board of directors felt certain that his approval would assuage investors' fears and pave the way toward a quick approval of the deal. Buffett, who participated (via remote video) in the initial press conference announcing the agreement between P&G and Gillette, declared the transaction a "dream deal" that would "create the greatest consumer products company in the world."[30] Although Buffett already held 10% of Gillette's stock, he announced his intention to purchase more stock of both P&G and Gillette so that, after the acquisition, he would

---

[28] Steven Syre, "As Firm's Chief Shareholder, Buffett Likes What He Sees," *Boston Globe*, January 29, 2005.

[29] Steven Syre, "As Firm's Chief Shareholder, Buffett Likes What He Sees," *Boston Globe*, January 29, 2005.

[30] Steven Syre, "As Firm's Chief Shareholder, Buffett Likes What He Sees," *Boston Globe*, January 29, 2005.

own 3.9% of P&G stock. His comments and commitments on the heels of the announcement seemed to calm investors in both companies.

CONCLUSION

The complementary strengths of the two firms were clear, as was their motivation for combining. Though management was unable to secure the full cooperation of all stakeholders, it was able to successfully leverage the support of one of the world's most respected investors. Additionally, P&G made overtures to the Massachusetts community to reduce fears that the acquirer would lay off Gillette's employees at the company's state-of-the-art production facility near Boston. However, despite the key synergies, the complementary strengths, and the support of Warren Buffett, the deal still raised questions on Main Street, Wall Street, and in the offices of elected officials.

A Tale of Two Hedge Funds:
Magnetar and Peloton

It was the best of times, it was the worst of times... *Charles Dickens*

WHAT A YEAR

Magnetar Capital had returned 25% in 2007—only its third year in business. This return was achieved with significantly lower risk than the S&P 500. Investors were happy; assets under management were among the largest of any hedge fund manager and growing.

On the other hand, the team at Magnetar recognized that investors can have short memories. Magnetar needed to consistently generate new ideas to meet investor return objectives. Formerly well-respected hedge funds such as Peloton, Thornburg, and Carlyle Capital were closing at a record pace due to illiquidity. Even the world's largest banks were not immune to a crisis, as Bear Stearns and Lehman Brothers had proven. Magnetar's diversification, low leverage, and capital call restrictions offered additional stability, but could not in themselves be relied upon to produce future success.

Magnetar employed approximately 200 of some of the smartest investment professionals in the world. It was the job of Alec Litowitz, chairman and chief investment officer, to provide guidance to his team, evaluate and prioritize (and allocate resources to) their ideas, and generate new ideas of his own. Although Litowitz preferred to limit exposure by separating risk capital across multiple businesses and trades, he knew that much of Magnetar's returns in 2007 had come from one brilliant trading strategy. This strategy was based on the view that certain tranches of collateralized debt obligations (CDOs) were systematically mispriced (see Exhibit C5.1). Magnetar made dozens of bets across multiple securities to capitalize on this observation. At the same time, the firm undertook comparatively little risk. According to the *Wall Street Journal*, "Mortgage analysts note that Magnetar's trading strategy wasn't all luck—it would have benefited whether the subprime market held up or collapsed."[1]

Recent turmoil in the markets had caused new mispricings—and therefore new investment opportunities. Magnetar would seek to locate and prioritize them.

---

[1] Serena Ng and Carrick Mollenkamp, "A Fund Behind Astronomical Losses," *Wall Street Journal*, January 14, 2008.

EXHIBIT C5.1 A FUND BEHIND ASTRONOMICAL LOSSES (ABRIDGED)

The trading strategy of a little-known hedge fund run by an astronomy buff contributed to billions in losses on Wall Street, even as the fund itself profited from the subprime-mortgage crisis.

Even as it helped to spawn collateralized debt obligations (CDOs) that would later wrack Wall Street with painful losses, Magnetar, which has around $9 billion in assets, itself made a tidy profit. Its funds returned 25% across a range of stock and debt strategies last year, thanks largely to the way it hedged these trades.

In this case, Magnetar swooped in on securities that it believed could become troubled but were paying big returns. CDOs are sliced based on risk, with the riskiest pieces having the highest yield but the greatest chance of losing value. Less-risky pieces have lower yields, and some pieces were once considered so safe that they paid only a bit more than a US Treasury bond.

Magnetar helped to spawn CDOs by buying the riskiest slices of the instruments, which paid returns of around 20% during good times, according to people familiar with its strategy. Back in 2006, when Magnetar began investing, these were the slices Wall Street found hardest to sell because they would be the first to lose money if subprime defaults rose. Magnetar then hedged its holdings by betting against the less-risky slices of some of these same securities as well as other CDOs, according to people familiar with its strategy. While it lost money on many of the risky slices it bought, it made far more when its hedges paid off as the market collapsed in the second half of last year.

Magnetar hedged itself by buying credit default swaps that act as a form of protection—similar to an insurance policy—against losses on the CDOs. It isn't clear which CDOs it hedged against, but these swaps broadly soared in value when the CDOs dived last year.

Mortgage analysts note that Magnetar's trading strategy wasn't all luck—it would have benefited whether the subprime market held up or collapsed.

Source: Serena Ng and Carrick Mollenkamp, "A Fund Behind Astronomical Losses," *Wall Street Journal*, January 14, 2008.

WHAT A NIGHTMARE

An ocean away, Ron Beller was contemplating some very different issues than was Alec Litowitz. Beller's firm, Peloton Partners LLP (also founded in 2005), had been one of the top-performing hedge funds in 2007, returning in excess of 80%. In late January 2008, Beller accepted two prestigious awards at a black-tie EuroHedge ceremony. A month later, his firm was bankrupt (see Exhibit C5.2).

EXHIBIT C5.2 PELOTON FLEW HIGH, FELL FAST (ABRIDGED)

When hedge fund chief Ron Beller's investments in US mortgages turned against him, he got a rude awakening to Wall Street's unsentimental ways. Bankers who had vied for his business reeled in credit lines and seized the fund's assets. In a matter of days, Peloton Partners LLP, once one of the world's best-performing hedge fund operators, lost some $17 billion. In its sheer speed, Peloton's demise offers an illustration of the delicate relationships on which the financial industry is built, and the breakneck pace at which they have been unraveling.

There is a widespread weakness in the hedge fund business: high-flying managers sometimes fail to fully factor in broader risks, such as what happens when troubled banks pull back the borrowed money many funds need to make their investments. Peloton was particularly susceptible because it borrowed heavily to boost returns. For every dollar of client money, Peloton had borrowed at least another nine dollars to buy some bonds.

... In mid-February, Messrs. Beller's and Grant's investments took a hit when Swiss bank UBS AG said it had marked down the value of highly rated mortgage securities similar to those that Peloton held.

Peloton had $750 million in cash and believed its funding from banks was secure. That provided a level of comfort to Messrs. Beller and Grant that Peloton could cover banker demands, known as margin calls, to put up more collateral as the value of its investments fell.

But by Monday, February 25, further sharp drops had left Peloton scraping for cash to meet margin calls from lenders, including UBS and Lehman Brothers Holdings Inc. When Peloton traders tried to sell securities to raise money, brokers were unwilling to bid, according to people familiar with the situation.

Mr. Beller and his team worked around the clock to assemble a rescue plan, persuading investors to provide a $600 million loan. But the financial lifeline, which included some 25 parties, depended on Peloton's banks agreeing to postpone certain margin calls. Some banks were reluctant to sign off on such an unusual deal at a time when they were dialing back risk amid the financial crisis. On Wednesday morning, February 27, yet another sharp drop in Peloton's mortgage investments killed a rescue. Mr. Beller at one point collapsed on a couch in distress.

Mr. Beller and his team made one final effort to sell Peloton's portfolio, including to other hedge funds, working late into Wednesday night. By 4 a.m. Thursday morning, Mr. Beller threw in the towel and went home, exhausted.

The next day, lenders seized Peloton's assets, bringing a chaotic end to the fund. Mr. Beller later likened the situation to the final scene in Quentin Tarantino's movie "Reservoir Dogs," when several actors, guns trained on each other, simultaneously blow each other away.

Source: Carrick Mollenkamp and Gregory Zuckerman, "Peloton Flew High, Fell Fast; Winning Hedge Fund Lost on Bets as Credit Crunch Moved at Breakneck Speed," *Wall Street Journal*, May 12, 2008.

Beller shorted the US housing market before the subprime crisis hit and was paid handsomely for his bet. After the crisis began, however, he believed that panicking investors were throwing out the proverbial baby with the bath water. Beller felt that prices for highly rated mortgage securities were being unfairly punished, so he decided to go long AAA-rated securities backed by Alt-A mortgage loans (between prime and subprime). As was common at Peloton, he levered up the investments at an average of 9×.

The trade moved against Beller in a big way on February 14, 2008, when UBS disclosed that the bank owned $21.2 billion of high-rated Alt-A securities, and the market speculated that UBS would need to sell those securities in a hurry.[2] Over the next 2 weeks, Alt-A backed AAA securities dropped by 10%–15%. Beller did what any fund manager would do: he lined up additional funding from investors, liquidated positions where possible to raise cash, and tried to persuade his banks to delay their margin calls. Unfortunately, the banks were not providing any bids on his securities. Banks were also unwilling to delay margin calls at a time when they too were dealing with enormous losses from their own mortgage-related holdings. Investors, meanwhile, would only guarantee the new money if the banks agreed to delay the margin calls. It was a perfect storm. The firm ran out of liquidity, lost $17 billion, and was forced to close.

MAGNETAR'S STRUCTURED FINANCE ARBITRAGE TRADE

Magnetar had made more than $1 billion in profit by noticing that the equity tranche of CDOs, and CDO-derivative instruments were relatively mispriced. It took advantage of this anomaly by purchasing CDO equity and buying credit default swap (CDS) protection on tranches that were considered less risky.

Magnetar performed its own calculation of risk for each tranche of security and compared that with the return that the tranche offered. By conducting such an analysis, investors could find a glaring irregularity: two classes of securities had very similar risks but significantly different yields. More importantly, this mispricing was occurring across multiple ABS CDOs (see The Collateralized Debt Obligation Market section). Successful investors developed a long/short strategy to take advantage of the anomaly. Using this strategy, they could replicate the same basic trade many times across many securities. Further, they could put large sums of money to work while having little effect on market prices, undertaking little risk, and locking in a return that was nearly certain. This was the type of trade about which hedge funds dream.

Specifically, astute investors noticed that the equity and mezzanine tranches of ABS CDOs had very different yields. This did not seem to make sense. After all, an ABS CDO simply consisted of slim mezzanine tranches of multiple ABS notes, which were then packaged together and sold in different tranches. It was unlikely that holders of the mezzanine tranche would get paid off while the equity holders would not. Either both securities would be paid, or neither would be paid. Since the risk was similar, the yield should also be similar. Instead, due to illiquidity in the equity tranche and the market's misunderstanding of correlation across tranches, the yield of the equity tranche was often much higher than that of the mezzanine tranche.

Successful investors such as Magnetar capitalized on this observation by buying CDS protection on the mezzanine tranche and going long the equity tranche. In some cases, the market was so spooked by the equity tranche that few buyers existed and the entire CDO deal was at risk of not getting funded. As the *Wall Street Journal* reported, "In all, roughly $30 billion

[2] Jody Shenn, "Alt-A Mortgage Securities Tumble, Signaling Losses," *Bloomberg News*, February 28, 2008.

of these constellation CDOs were issued from mid-2006 to mid-2007, with Magnetar as their lynchpin investor."[3]

Magnetar did not need to form a view on absolute prices; it only needed to realize that the two tranches were *relatively* mispriced. Trades could be structured to generate cash on an ongoing basis because the current yields flowing in from the equity long positions were so much higher than the current yields being paid on the mezzanine short positions. Meanwhile, in the event of high defaults, the principal balance on the mezzanine shorts would be higher than that of the equity longs, so the strategy would have a large payoff if prices of the overall underlying collateral took a turn for the worse. The strategy would only lose money if the equity got wiped out while the mezzanine tranche stayed intact. Magnetar reasoned that the probability of this scenario was remote.

Rating agencies based their CDO credit ratings primarily on historical data, which showed that a nationwide housing downturn was unprecedented. However, astute investors recognized that this cycle was very different from the previous ones and therefore the historical data used by the agencies could not be relied upon as the sole predictor of future events. This recognition was the catalyst for Magnetar's trade on the pricing anomalies in the ABS CDO space. Its strategy was very different from the well-publicized bearish bet on housing established during 2007 by John Paulson of Paulson & Company, who personally made $3.7 billion when the market crashed.[4] Paulson took a position on the market, whereas Magnetar focused on locating relative pricing anomalies that should profit no matter what happened in the market. Strategies such as Magnetar's are consistent with the objectives of many hedge funds: to earn returns that are uncorrelated with the market.

THE 2007–08 FINANCIAL CRISIS

In the aftermath of the 2001 recession, concerns about deflation and the economy caused the Federal Reserve to bring interest rates to 40-year lows. These low interest rates were partially responsible for the housing bubble. Because they significantly lowered a borrower's monthly home payment, borrowers often bought larger houses than they could afford. "Teaser rates" would sometimes increase after a short initial period. Other loans were based on variable rates rather than the fixed rates of traditional home mortgages. Consumers often brushed aside fears that rates would increase because they believed the housing market could only increase in value. Millions of Americans became homeowners for the first time, as homeownership reached an all-time high of 70%.[5] Moreover, the housing boom was only one part of a broader increase in leverage across the economy that had been ongoing for 30 years (see Exhibit C5.3).

[3] Ng and Mollenkamp, "Fund Behind Astronomical Losses."

[4] Andrew Clark, "The $3.7bn King of New York," *The Guardian*, April 19, 2008.

[5] Roger M. Showley, "Working Families See Little Hope For Homes," *San Diego Union–Tribune*, March 23, 2006. http://www.signonsandiego.com/news/business/20060323-9999-1b23owners.html.

EXHIBIT C5.3 US CREDIT MARKET DEBT/GDP

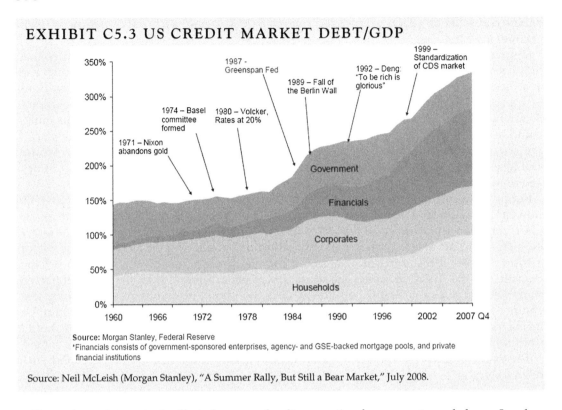

Source: Morgan Stanley, Federal Reserve
ᵃFinancials consists of government-sponsored enterprises, agency- and GSE-backed mortgage pools, and private financial institutions

Source: Neil McLeish (Morgan Stanley), "A Summer Rally, But Still a Bear Market," July 2008.

Beyond pure interest rate effects, however, lending practices became extremely loose. Lenders granted loans with no money down and no proof of income. These practices did not result from banks becoming more generous or consumers more creditworthy. Financial innovation was largely to blame, in the form of CDOs. Despite all the benefits CDOs offered, they created a principal-agent problem. Banks are the most capable entities for assessing a borrower's risk and determining a fair interest rate. However, when banks can securitize all of their loans within a few months and transfer most of the risk to someone else, their economic incentive changes. The new focus becomes making as many loans as possible to collect origination fees. The bankers who granted the original home loans were likely more concerned with their annual bonuses (which were based on fee income) than the ultimate performance of the loan.

While large investment banks originated some loans themselves, many home loans were originated by small regional banks, which then sold the loans to major investment banks. The investment banks then securitized the loans into CDOs, which were sold to investors. Still, the investment banks held large inventories of loans and CDOs for three reasons. First, the securitization procedure took time, so loans in the process of being securitized were owned by banks temporarily. Second, banks held inventories because their trading divisions made markets in the security. Finally, when an investment bank created a CDO, it often kept a small "holdback" amount. These three forms of exposure led to investment banking losses of $300 billion between July 2007 and July 2008. Some predict the total will rise to $1 trillion before the carnage is over.[6]

---

[6] Peter Goodman, "Uncomfortable Answers to Questions on the Economy," *New York Times*, July 22, 2008.

THE COLLATERALIZED DEBT OBLIGATION MARKET

A CDO is a general term that describes securities backed by a pool of fixed-income assets. These assets can be bank loans (collateralized loan obligations, CLOs), bonds (collateralized bond obligations, CBOs), residential mortgages (residential mortgage-backed securities, or RMBSs), and many others. A CDO is a subset of asset-backed securities (ABS), which is a general term for a security backed by assets such as mortgages, credit card receivables, auto loans, or other debt.

To create a CDO, a bank or other entity transfers the underlying assets ("the collateral") to a special purpose vehicle (SPV) that is a separate legal entity from the issuer. The SPV then issues securities backed with cash flows generated by assets in the collateral pool. This general process is called securitization. The securities are separated into tranches, which differ primarily in the priority of their rights to the cash flows coming from the asset pool. The senior tranche has first priority, the mezzanine second, and the equity third. The allocation of cash flows to specific securities is called a "waterfall" (see Exhibits C5.4 and C5.5). A waterfall is specified in the CDO's indenture[7] and governs both principal and interest payments.

EXHIBIT C5.4 INTEREST WATERFALL OF A SAMPLE COLLATERALIZED DEBT OBLIGATION

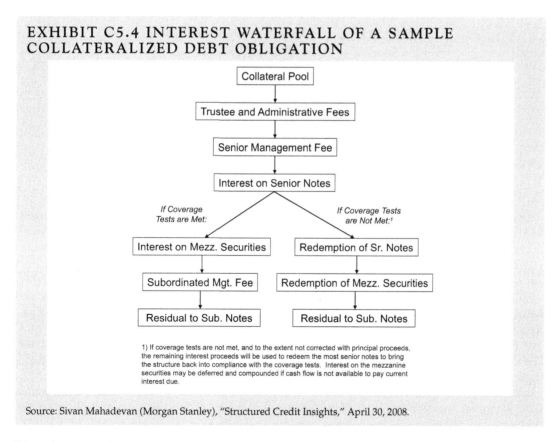

1) If coverage tests are not met, and to the extent not corrected with principal proceeds, the remaining interest proceeds will be used to redeem the most senior notes to bring the structure back into compliance with the coverage tests. Interest on the mezzanine securities may be deferred and compounded if cash flow is not available to pay current interest due.

Source: Sivan Mahadevan (Morgan Stanley), "Structured Credit Insights," April 30, 2008.

[7] An indenture is "the legal agreement between the firm issuing the bond and the bondholders, providing the specific terms of the loan agreement." http://www.financeglossary.net.

EXHIBIT C5.5 PRINCIPAL WATERFALL OF A SAMPLE COLLATERALIZED DEBT OBLIGATION

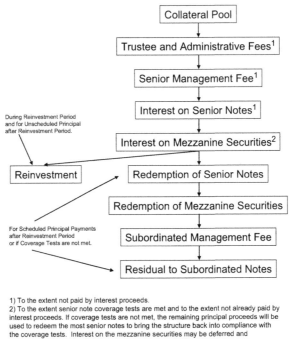

1) To the extent not paid by interest proceeds.
2) To the extent senior note coverage tests are met and to the extent not already paid by interest proceeds. If coverage tests are not met, the remaining principal proceeds will be used to redeem the most senior notes to bring the structure back into compliance with the coverage tests. Interest on the mezzanine securities may be deferred and compounded if cash flow is not available to pay current interest due.

Source: Sivan Mahadevan (Morgan Stanley), "Structured Credit Insights," April 30, 2008.

One may observe that the creation of a CDO is a complex and costly process. Professionals such as bankers, lawyers, rating agencies, accountants, trustees, fund managers, and insurers all charge considerable fees to create and manage a CDO. In other words, the cash coming from the collateral is greater than the sum of the cash paid to all security holders. Professional fees to create and manage the CDO make up the difference.

CDOs are designed to offer asset exposure precisely tailored to the risk that investors desire, and they provide liquidity because they trade daily on the secondary market. This liquidity enables, for example, a finance minister from the Chinese government to gain exposure to the US mortgage market and to buy or sell that exposure at will. However, because CDOs are more complex securities than corporate bonds, they are designed to pay slightly higher interest rates than correspondingly rated corporate bonds.

CDOs enable a bank that specializes in making loans to homeowners to make more loans than its capital would otherwise allow, because the bank can sell its loans to a third party. The bank can therefore originate more loans and take in more origination fees. As a result, consumers have more access to capital, banks can make more loans, and investors a world away can not only access the consumer loan market but also invest with precisely the level of risk they desire.

The Structured Credit Handbook provides an explanation of investors' nearly insatiable appetite for CDOs:

> Demand for [fixed income] assets is heavily bifurcated, with the demand concentrated at the two ends of the safety spectrum... Prior to the securitization boom, the universe of fixed-income instruments issued tended to cluster around the BBB rating, offering neither complete safety nor sizzling returns. For example, the number of AA- and AAA-rated companies is quite small, as is debt issuance of companies rated B or lower. Structured credit technology has evolved essentially in order to match investors' demands with the available profile of fixed-income assets. By issuing CDOs from portfolios of bonds or loans rated A, BBB, or BB, financial intermediaries can create a larger pool of AAA-rated securities and a small unrated or low-rated bucket where almost all the risk is concentrated.[8]

CDOs have been around for more than 20 years, but their popularity skyrocketed during the late 1990s. CDO issuance nearly doubled in 2005 and then again in 2006, when it topped $500 billion for the first time. "Structured finance" groups at large investment banks (the division responsible for issuing and managing CDOs) became one of the fastest-growing areas on Wall Street. These divisions, along with the investment banking trading desks that made markets in CDOs, contributed to highly successful results for the banking sector during the 2003–07 boom. Many CDOs became quite liquid due to their size, investor breadth, and rating agency coverage.

RATING AGENCIES

Rating agencies helped bring liquidity to the CDO market. They analyzed each tranche of a CDO and assigned ratings accordingly. Equity tranches were often unrated. The rating agencies had limited manpower and needed to gauge the risk on literally thousands of new CDO securities. The agencies also specialized in using historical models to predict risk. Although CDOs had been around for a long time, they did not exist in a significant number until recently. Historical models therefore couldn't possibly capture the full picture. Still, the underlying collateral could be assessed with a strong degree of confidence. After all, banks have been making home loans for hundreds of years. The rating agencies simply had to allocate risk to the appropriate tranche and understand how the loans in the collateral base were correlated with each other—an easy task in theory perhaps, but not in practice.

CORRELATION

The most difficult part of valuing a CDO tranche is determining correlation. If loans are uncorrelated, defaults will occur evenly over time and asset diversification can solve most problems. For instance, a housing crisis in California will be isolated from one in New York,

---

[8] Arvind Rajan, Glen McDermott, and Ratul Roy, *The Structured Credit Handbook* (Hoboken, NJ: John Wiley & Sons, 2007), 2.

so the CDO simply needs to diversify the geographic makeup of its assets to offer stable returns. With low correlation, an AAA-rated senior tranche should be safe and the interest rate attached to this tranche should be close to the rate for AAA-rated corporate bonds, or even US treasuries. High correlation, however, creates nondiversifiable risk, in which case the senior tranche has a reasonable likelihood of becoming impaired. Correlation does not affect the price of the CDO in total because the expected value of each individual loan remains the same. Correlation does, however, affect the relative price of each tranche: any increase in the yield of a senior tranche (to compensate for additional correlation) will be offset by a decrease in the yield of the junior tranches.[9]

If a security related to the housing market contained geographically diverse collateral, it was generally assumed to have low correlation. This is because there had not been a nationwide housing crisis in recent history and local downturns had been isolated. As the *Wall Street Journal* reported, "Upbeat mortgage specialists kept repeating that home prices never fall on a national basis or that the Fed could save the market by slashing interest rates."[10] Because of the market's confidence in this assumption, senior tranches typically received very high debt ratings—often AAA—and correspondingly paid low interest rates.

COLLATERALIZED DEBT OBLIGATION MARKET EVOLUTION

Although the market for new CDO origination was essentially dead by mid-2008, hedge funds considered whether it would resurface. After all, CDOs provided liquidity and unique access to risk that investors would continue to seek. It would take some time for banks to work through their existing backlog of underwritten but unsold new-issue leveraged loans, but they had made significant progress over the past year: the original backlog of $338 billion was now down to $105 billion (see Exhibit C5.6). Once this backlog was clear, would CDO origination slowly ramp up again? What strategies should hedge funds use to be ahead of the market?

While some funds thought that the market for new CDO origination would soon return, others had doubts. Many CDO investors, especially hedge funds, relied on leverage to earn their targeted absolute returns. For instance, in 2006 and the first half of 2007, an investor might have purchased the senior tranche of a CDO even though it only yielded 50 basis points above the London Interbank Offered Rate (LIBOR). However, the investor would then have leveraged the investment 25× to earn a return commensurate with the equity tranche, or 1250 basis points above LIBOR. Because of this practice, some investors feared that the CDO origination market would not return until investment banks provided their hedge fund clients with ample and cheap debt funding, as was the case before the summer of 2007—a practice that might not return for a considerable time.

---

[9] Todd Buys, Karina Hirai, Wendy Kam, Charles Lalanne, and Kazuhiro Shibata, "Correlation of Risky Assets and the Effect on CDO Pricing in the Credit Crunch of 2007," student paper, Kellogg School of Management, June 5, 2008.

[10] Gregory Zuckerman, "Trader Made Billions on Subprime," *Wall Street Journal*, January 15, 2008.

EXHIBIT C5.6 LEVERAGED BUYOUT-RELATED LEVERAGED LOANS

Estimated new-issue backlog has declined since the start of the year

	Volumes in billions ($)			
	Total	Pro rata	Institutional Loans	Bonds
Original Pipeline-June 2007	338.0		227.4	110.6
2007 Completed Pipeline	55.0		33.0	22.0
2007 Cancelled	51.0		34.9	16.1
End of 2007 Pipeline	232.0		159.5	72.5
2008 Completed Pipeline	29.4		17.3	12.1
2008 Estimated private sales	15.0		15.0	
2008 Cancelled/Uncertain	35.0		22.2	12.8
Remaining Pipeline	152.7	35.0	70.0	47.7
Remaining Pipeline excluding pro rata	117.7			
Hexion/Huntsman	11.9		6.0	6.0
Pipeline excluding Huntsman	105.8	35.0	64.0	41.7

Note: All information is based on public news and analyst estimates.

Source: JPMorgan.

Note: This backlog tracks LBO-related leveraged loans on deals that have been underwritten by major investment banks but have not yet closed.

Source: Peter Acciavatti (JP Morgan), "Midyear 2008 High Yield and Leveraged Loan Outlook and Strategy," June 28, 2008.

BANK DEBT AND THE COVENANT-LITE CRAZE

The market for corporate bank debt was similar to the housing bubble in at least one respect: frothy credit markets and a push for financial innovation spawned lending practices that strayed widely from historical norms. Fueled by the leveraged buyout (LBO) boom, covenant-lite corporate bank debt allowed companies to operate with no maintenance covenants[11] for leverage (debt/EBITDA) or interest coverage (EBITDA/cash interest) ratios. Sponsors (LBO firms) demanded loose terms by playing lenders against each other and by using their clout as enormous fee generators for the bank. By mid-2007 covenant-lite deals had ballooned and were increasingly considered the norm (see Exhibit C5.7). As in the residential mortgage market, securitization also played a major role.

---

[11] Maintenance covenants are specified in a loan indenture and measured quarterly on an LTM (last 12 months) basis. The leverage covenant typically specifies a certain ratio of debt to LTM EBITDA above which the company cannot go. The coverage covenant specifies a certain ratio of LTM EBITDA to LTM cash interest below which the company cannot go. Most bank loans contained covenants such as these before 2006 and the first half of 2007.

EXHIBIT C5.7 EXPLOSION IN COVENANT-LITE LOAN ISSUANCE

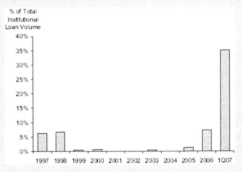

Source: Morgan Stanley, "Focusing on Recoveries," April 11, 2007.

Lenders knew they could pass off large portions of weak covenant-lite loans by syndicating them into CLOs. These CLOs were bought by third parties who often did not bother to do the same level of diligence as would a bank that intended to hold the loan to maturity. Investors often analyzed loan information at a summary level only, instead of reviewing each loan individually. This practice masked the problems of the worst loans, many of which were LBO-backed covenant-lite deals. Rating agencies often gave investors a false sense of security and helped them to justify performing scant due diligence. A study by Fitch indicates that covenant-lite loans were nearly 50% more prevalent in CLOs than in the market as a whole.[12]

Further complicating matters, PIK toggles enabled a company simply to add additional debt instead of paying interest in cash. "Equity cures" were also permitted, so in cases where a company did have maintenance covenants, a technical default could be "cured" by a small equity contribution that would be added to bank-defined EBITDA.[13] As the *Wall Street Journal* reported, "Bankers began marketing debt deals for companies that… didn't have comfortable cash flow. There was Chrysler, burning cash rather than producing it. And there was First Data Corp., whose post-takeover cash flow would barely cover interest payments and capital spending."[14]

The downturn rippled throughout the financial industry starting in mid-2007. It put a premium on liquidity and drove down the prices of leveraged securities in general and leveraged bank loans in particular. Bank loans were hit particularly hard because of the large inventory held by investment banks, which needed to liquidate investment holdings to improve their balance sheets.

The bank loan market bottomed during February 2008 (see Exhibit C5.8), before coming back somewhat by the summer of 2008. Exhibit C5.9 shows that to justify bank debt

[12] Fitch Ratings, "CLOs More Concentrated in Shareholder-Friendly and Covenant-Light Loans," December 21, 2006.

[13] EBITDA (earnings before interest, taxes, depreciation, and amortization) is not a standardized term defined by generally accepted accounting principles (GAAP). However, it is a common measure of cash flow used by banks to determine whether a borrowing company is in compliance with its covenants. A common "maintenance" covenant states that total debt cannot exceed a specified multiple of the company's last 12 months of EBITDA.

[14] Greg Ip and Jon Hilsenrath, "Debt Bomb: Inside the 'Subprime' Mortgage Debacle," *Wall Street Journal*, August 7, 2007.

EXHIBIT C5.8 BANK LOAN PRICES DURING 2008

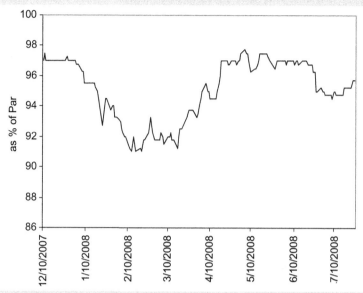

Note: LCDX 9 is a standardized, tradable tranche of the North American loan credit default swap index.
Source: Markit LCDX Analytics, http://www.markit.com/information/products/category/indices/lcdx/analytics.html.

EXHIBIT C5.9 HISTORICAL ANNUAL DEFAULT RATES

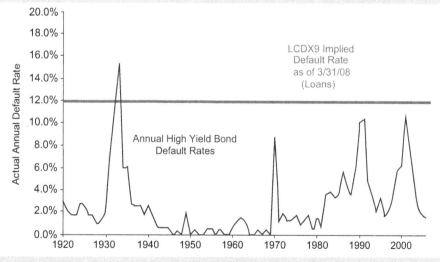

Source: Kellogg student/faculty presentation by Ares Management, Spring 2008.

valuations, an investor needed to assume that default rates would hit levels not seen since the Great Depression and stay there until maturity of the loans. With this in mind, some investors increased their exposure to the bank loan market. Nontraditional players such as private equity firms entered the market, often purchasing loans in large private transactions directly from banks rather than on the open market. The Blackstone Group reported that it achieved a 20% return on a $7.8 billion investment in leveraged loans that it made in Q2 2008.[15]

Instead of investing in the overall bank loan market, some hedge funds were more intrigued with covenant-lite loans. Although new cov-lite loans were unlikely to be brought to market, many existing cov-lite loans were heavily traded. Cov-lite loans, it was thought, would have limited near-term defaults because companies would keep operating until they ran out of cash. However, once those defaults ultimately occurred, the question is whether recovery rates would be significantly lower than the historical average of 82% (see Exhibit C5.10). Since cov-lite loans did not exist in large numbers until 2005 and there have been no defaults of cov-lite loans in the past, it is difficult for investors to know what recovery rates to use in their valuations. Cov-lite loans trade at a discount to cov-heavy (traditional) loans, and this spread continues to widen (see Exhibit C5.11). Funds who bet that there would be a flight to quality away from cov-lite loans have profited handsomely. The exhibit also shows that, paradoxically, cov-lite loans have

EXHIBIT C5.10 LOAN RECOVERY RATES BY DEFAULT YEAR

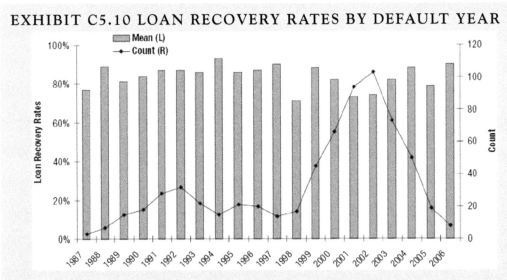

Note: Count means the number of loans in the sample size. Includes all defaulted loans, not just those that were classified as leveraged loans when they were originated.
Source: Emery, Cantor, Keisman, and Ou, (Moody's), "Moody's Ultimate Recovery Database," April 2007.

[15] Pierre Paulden and Jason Kelly, "Blackstone Gains 20 Percent Buying $7.8 Billion of LBO Loans," *Bloomberg News*, August 6, 2008.

EXHIBIT C5.11 B-RATED LEVERAGE LOANS

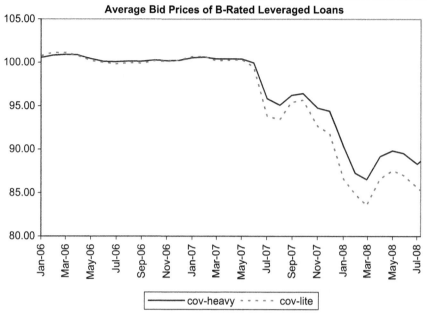

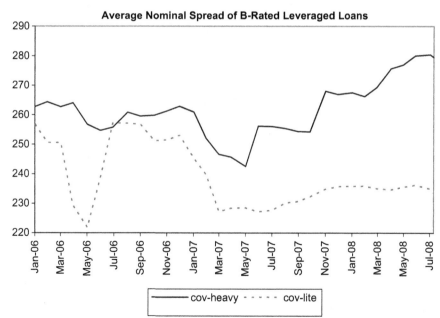

Source: S&P LCD, August 11, 2008, author analysis.

lower nominal coupons than cov-heavy loans. This is because lending practices were very loose during 2006 and the first half of 2007, when most of the cov-lite deals were originated.

Although the spread widened, investors still profited by taking a position that the spread would widen further. As of August 11, 2008, B-rated cov-lite loans traded at prices 336 basis points below cov-heavy loans. To analyze whether the spread should widen even more, one must make assumptions about future default rates and recovery rates (see Exhibit C5.12).

EXHIBIT C5.12 DEFAULT RATE AND RECOVERY RATE DISCOUNT NECESSARY TO JUSTIFY COVENANT-LITE VALUATIONS

Difference in Recovery Rate	Annual Default Rate					
	3%	4%	5%	6%	7%	8%
−5%	244	264	283	303	323	343
−10%	303	343	383	423	463	503
−15%	363	423	483	543	603	663
−20%	423	503	583	663	743	822
−25%	483	583	683	783	882	982
−30%	543	663	783	902	1,022	1,142
−35%	603	743	882	1,022	1,162	1,302
−40%	663	822	982	1,142	1,302	1,461
−45%	723	902	1,082	1,262	1,441	1,621
−50%	783	982	1,182	1,381	1,581	1,781

Basis point discount from non-cov-lite loans.

Assumptions: 8% discount rate

5-year loan life

46 bp avg. coupon discount for cov-lite

Note: Shaded combinations of default rates and recovery rate differentials are above the current 336 bps average spread between cov-lite and cov-heavy loans, indicating that a wider spread is necessary to justify assumptions. Source: Stephen Carlson, "Covenant-Lite Bank Loans: What Will Be Their Implications in a Period of Significant Defaults, and Are Markets Correctly Pricing the Risk?" student paper, Kellogg School of Management, August 2008.

Some funds believed that the best way to play cov-lite bank debt was through a relative value trade. One can look at the yields on secured cov-lite bank loans and compare them with the yields on unsecured bonds of the same company. If the two yields are close, a long secured bank loan/short unsecured bond trading opportunity may exist because bank debt will typically recover more than bonds in a bankruptcy. As companies become more risky, the spread between bonds and secured bank debt of the same company should widen (see Exhibit C5.13). In such capital structure arbitrage trades, investors are betting on the difference in recovery rates among various securities. Default rates will be identical because the two securities are issued by the same company.

Exhibit C5.13 includes all companies that have (1) first lien cov-lite bank debt, (2) unsecured bonds, (3) easily accessible prices, and (4) bank debt that will mature prior to bonds.

EXHIBIT C5.13 BANK VERSUS BOND YIELD PREMIUM ON COMPANIES WITH COVENANT-LITE BANK DEBT

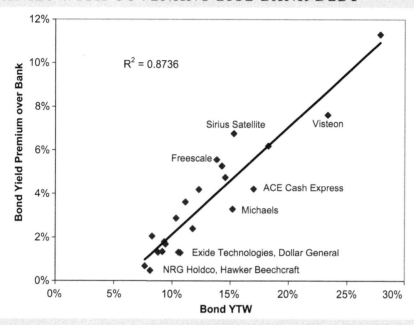

Note: YTW, yield to worst. The lowest potential yield that can be received on a bond without the issuer actually defaulting. The yield to worst is calculated by making worst-case scenario assumptions on the issue by calculating the returns that would be received if provisions, including prepayment, call or sinking fund, are used by the issuer. This metric is used to evaluate the worst-case scenario for yield to help investors manage risks and ensure that specific income requirements will still be met even in the worst scenarios.

Yield to worst is calculated on all possible call dates. It is assumed that prepayment occurs if the bond has call or put provisions, and the issuer can offer a lower coupon rate based on current market rates. If market rates are higher than the current yield of a bond, the yield to worst calculation will assume no prepayments are made, and yield to worst will equal the yield to maturity. The assumption is made that prevailing rates are static when making the calculation. The yield to worst will be the lowest of yield to maturity or yield to call (if the bond has prepayment provisions); yield to worst may be the same as yield to maturity but never higher. Refer definition from Investopedia, http://www.investopedia.com/terms/y/yieldtoworst.asp.

Source: Stephen Carlson, "Covenant-Lite Bank Loans: What Will Be Their Implications in a Period of Significant Defaults, and Are Markets Correctly Pricing the Risk?" student paper, Kellogg School of Management, August 2008.

Companies on the right side of the line represent long bank debt/short bond opportunities. This position is especially compelling for companies that also have low absolute interest rates (NRG Holdco and Hawker Beechcraft). Companies on the left side represent the reverse strategy. Investors could also follow a related strategy by analyzing second-lien bank debt and unsecured bonds in the same company. In a bankruptcy, second-lien debt is paid off before unsecured bonds up to the point at which the collateral value is recovered (see Exhibit C5.14). After that point, second-lien debt has the same priority as other unsecured creditors. Therefore, in normal circumstances, second-lien debt should have a lower yield than unsecured bonds.

EXHIBIT C5.14 LEVERAGED LOANS AND JUNK BONDS

Loans

The bank loans referenced in this case are leveraged loans. A bank loan is classified as leveraged if any of the following occur:[16]

- The company to whom the loan is being made has outstanding debt rated below investment grade, meaning below Baa3/BBB– from Moody's and S&P.
- The company's debt/EBITDA ratio is 3.0 times or greater.
- The loan bears a coupon of +125 bps or more over LIBOR

Leveraged loans generally grant lenders collateral in all (or most) assets of a company. In some leveraged loans, there is an agreement that separates lenders into two classes: first lien and second lien. These two classes agree on contractual subordination terms of the second lien to the first lien.

Some leveraged loans may have traditional, full covenants, whereas others may be covenant-lite.

Bonds (Junk)

(Junk) bonds are typically unsecured and, therefore, have a lower claim on the assets of a company in a bankruptcy scenario. Although each bankruptcy is different and can have its own idiosyncrasies, bondholders in bankrupt companies typically receive much lower recovery rates than do holders of bank loans. The mean recovery rate for bank loans is 82% while the mean recovery rate for senior unsecured bonds (the most common type of bond) is 38%.[17]

This anomaly and many others exist because large holders of bank debt (including many troubled banks that have large investment banking arms) have been forced to sell bank debt for regulatory or liquidity reasons. Bonds, on the other hand, are less frequently held by banks, so the bond market has consequently not experienced the same forced selling pressure that the secured bank debt market has seen. What can hedge funds do to exploit this opportunity? What are the risks they face if they make the wrong bet? How can they best set up trades to hedge their exposure? What is the catalyst that will bring the market back to normal levels? Hedge funds that can accurately answer these questions stand to gain handsomely.

---

[16] Timothy Aker (Prudential), "Leveraged Loans: Capturing Investor Attention," July 2006.

[17] Emery, Cantor, Keisman, and Ou (Moody's), "Moody's Ultimate Recovery Database," April 2007.

Kmart, Sears, and ESL: How a Hedge Fund Became One of the World's Largest Retailers

THE UNUSUAL WEEKEND

January 11, 2003, was the weirdest Saturday that Eddie Lampert could remember. Most Greenwich billionaires do not spend their weekends lying in bathtubs in cheap motels eating cold chicken. Unfortunately, the setting was not only odd; it was quite ominous. Lampert was fully clothed, blindfolded, and handcuffed.

The previous day, Lampert, 42, had sat in his office at ESL Investments, the multibillion dollar hedge fund he controlled. The fund's clients included savvy institutions and famous names such as Michael Dell and David Geffen, but Lampert himself was the single largest investor. He had spent much of his time that Friday poring over documents related to Kmart's Chapter 11 bankruptcy. Lampert had access to experienced attorneys, bankers, and accountants who specialized in restructurings, but he insisted on personally understanding every detail of the complicated swap of defaulted debt for new equity. On first glance, Lampert thought he smelled a great opportunity that rival retailers and private equity shops were missing. He had already accumulated a sizeable amount of Kmart's defaulted debt for less than half of its face value. But before he really took the plunge and started buying larger amounts in the biggest trade of his career, he wanted to study the upside potential and downside protection in excruciating detail. After all, it was his reputation, and largely his money, on the line.

Lampert discovered within hours that money and reputation are not the most serious assets that one can have on the line, as he took an unexpected plunge of a different sort. When he left his low-rise Greenwich office building and walked to his car in the parking garage around 7:30 p.m., four men unknown to Lampert approached, and one suddenly drew a pistol. Lampert soon found himself locked in the trunk of a car that had been parked near his. Presumably, Kmart's bankruptcy was the last thing on his mind as he tried to determine which direction the vehicle was headed on Interstate 95. He would soon have to apply his considerable intelligence to negotiations of a different kind.

FLASH FORWARD: NOVEMBER 2004

Lampert had always been somewhat secretive and tried to avoid much press coverage for ESL Investments, but since talking his kidnappers into letting him go free in exchange for a small amount of money, he had become extremely tight-lipped. (Lampert never actually turned over the money, and his inept kidnappers later found themselves in police custody after using Lampert's credit card to order pizza.)

Despite Lampert's desire to stay out of the limelight, he was not the sort of person to turn down a compelling investment, even if it meant an explosion of press coverage. Since his kidnapping, Lampert had gone from being a talented manager of a hedge fund to also serving as chairman of Kmart Holdings, the new company that emerged from the bankruptcy of the venerable retailer. Then, on November 17, 2004, Lampert announced that he had reached an agreement with the board of Sears to acquire the famous company for approximately $11 billion in cash or Kmart stock. The financial community was surprised, and research reports from Wall Street analysts revealed a wide divergence of opinion on the wisdom of the combination. Lampert's preference for a low profile became hopeless as it became clear that, despite his day job managing a hedge fund that did not even have a website, he would soon be the chairman of the nation's third largest retailer. *BusinessWeek* featured Lampert in several major articles, following a cover story whose copy deadline apparently predated the announcement of the acquisition by days if not hours. The title posed the flattering question: "The Next Warren Buffett?"[1]

Case Focus

The idea of a hedge fund manager becoming chairman of Kmart and Sears was laughable just a decade ago. This case examines some of the notable and rapid changes in the capital markets over the last 20 years that have made such an idea a reality. In particular, the case explores the emergence of financial buyers (principally private equity funds and hedge funds) as strong competitors to strategic buyers (companies buying other companies in the same industry) in the mergers and acquisitions (M&A) market. The case presents two key questions: First, as a strictly financial buyer, should ESL have acquired a controlling stake in Kmart's defaulted debt in 2002? Second, as a largely strategic buyer, should Kmart under ESL's control have acquired Sears (announced in November 2004 and consummated in March 2005)?

THE RISE AND FALL OF KMART

Kmart was founded in 1899 as S. S. Kresge Company, and at various times in the last 20 years had owned Borders Books, Walden Book, The Sports Authority, and OfficeMax. After mismanaging its Internet efforts and finding itself unable to keep its supply chain as low cost as rivals Wal-Mart and Target, Kmart by mid-2000 was suffering from stagnant same-store sales, comparatively low sales per square foot, and complaints from customers that the stores were disorganized and run-down. Wal-Mart and Kmart each had $32 billion in sales in 1990; since that time Kmart's sales had been essentially flat, while Wal-Mart's had grown to over $250 billion.[2] (See Exhibit C6.1 for sales comparisons.) One

---

[1] *BusinessWeek*, November 22, 2004.

[2] COMPUSTAT database.

of the *Wall Street Journal*'s epitaphs for Kmart remarked on the decades-long role played by Wal-Mart in the demise:

> In the late 1970s, Wal-Mart's sales were 5% of Kmart's; it had 150 stores to Kmart's 1000 or so, mostly in urban locations. Wal-Mart, meanwhile, invaded rural America, where it quietly perfected a format of using technology to reduce inventory, keep shelves stocked and offer the lowest prices. By the time it began meeting Kmart head on, Wal-Mart enjoyed a significant price advantage that a series of Kmart executives failed to overcome.[3]

The recession of 2001, especially following the 9/11 attacks, hit Kmart very hard. CEO Charles Conaway instituted price cuts to match Wal-Mart on selected goods in early 2001 and then decided on a bold holiday season strategy: Kmart would dramatically cut its advertising budget and use the savings to match Wal-Mart's low prices on almost everything. The plan was executed; the results were disastrous. With reduced marketing, Kmart did not draw many new customers. Those that did come were surprised and gleeful at the reduced prices. In December 2001, with the stock trading below $5 per share (see Exhibit C6.2), Kmart sold millions of items below cost, and below the already marked-down value recorded as inventory on its balance sheet. As details on the scope of the holiday season losses were still emerging, Kmart faced a cash crunch, and after a vendor announced Kmart had fallen behind on payments, the 103-year-old company filed for Chapter 11 bankruptcy on January 22, 2002. In early March, the company fired Conaway and set ambitious plans to emerge from bankruptcy by July 2003.

Not long afterward, hedge funds specializing in trading distressed debt started studying Kmart's assets, but none of them had the capital or the confidence to amass a controlling stake in the defaulted bonds. With the company in bankruptcy, shareholders had lost all of their investment. The question that remained was the value of Kmart's assets now

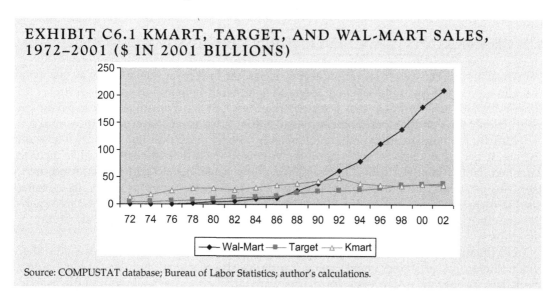

EXHIBIT C6.1 KMART, TARGET, AND WAL-MART SALES, 1972–2001 ($ IN 2001 BILLIONS)

Source: COMPUSTAT database; Bureau of Labor Statistics; author's calculations.

---

[3] "Kmart to Buy Sears for $11.5 billion," *Wall Street Journal*, November 18, 2004.

EXHIBIT C6.2 KMART DAILY CLOSING PRICES, JANUARY 2001 TO JULY 2002

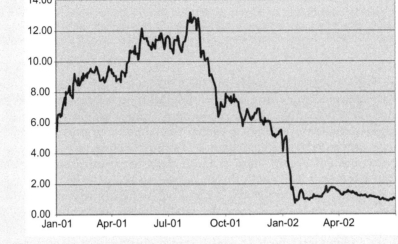

Source: Bloomberg.

belonging exclusively to its creditors, including bondholders. Clearly, the bonds would never be paid off at their face value, but holders would have a clear legal claim on assets, with each creditor's share depending on the number of bonds held and the level of seniority of the bond covenants.

BANKRUPTCY AND INEFFICIENT FINANCIAL MARKETS

In most bankruptcy cases, bondholders receive either cash from sale of assets in the event of liquidation or equity in the new company that successfully emerges from bankruptcy. In either case, each step of the process generally requires both court approval and broad agreement among the bondholders. The complexities that arise from these procedures make it very difficult for mainstream investment managers who focus on traditional equity valuation and credit spread analysis to understand the risks and rewards sufficiently well to include defaulted debt in their portfolios. Furthermore, many pension fund and mutual fund managers are prohibited by the guidelines of their funds to own bankrupt assets, or in some cases to own any "junk" or "high-yield" securities, those bonds for which the ratings agencies Standard & Poor's and Moody's have signified the issuer has a higher probability of bankruptcy.

The difficulty of analyzing competing claims on assets, forging agreements with other bondholders, and satisfying a bankruptcy court gave rise to a small industry of bankruptcy specialists. Twenty years ago, such specialists were largely attorneys who found themselves in high demand when corporations considered snapping up assets at cheap prices following the bankruptcy of a competitor or a company that had a strong position in an adjacent market. Acquiring assets during a bankruptcy was seen as just one piece of a corporation's M&A strategy. Bankruptcy was considered an opportunistic time to acquire businesses that had strong synergies with existing, healthy lines. Since most companies in the same industry experienced the same business cycle, however, the timing of a rival's bankruptcy often found the industry's survivors in a weak position and unable or unwilling to commit cash to an acquisition. This timing mismatch encouraged financial buyer interest in bankruptcy-related activity.

FINANCIAL BUYERS VERSUS STRATEGIC BUYERS

Among Warren Buffett's many skills evident in the 1960s and 1970s was the ability to "keep his powder dry" and build up cash for deployment in a countercyclical manner in several different industries. Thus, when companies were either bankrupt or distressed, Buffett was often the only player who could commit cash on short notice to acquire cheap assets. In many cases, these assets did not have any synergies with Buffett's other holdings. In these instances, Buffett was a pure *financial* buyer, as opposed to a *strategic* buyer. Despite the fact that strategic buyers should theoretically have been willing to offer a higher price for the assets because of the synergies that would come from merging them with similar operations, those bidders found themselves without the ability to acquire at the moment when the assets were available at the most attractive price. On the other hand, pension funds, endowments, and mutual fund managers always had cash to deploy and theoretically should have been able to match Buffett on price, but these managers had neither the expertise, nor in many cases the flexibility, to acquire large, illiquid, and complex assets.

Eddie Lampert's transition from a hedge fund manager to the chairman of Kmart and acquirer of Sears was an example of a financial buyer who had also become a strategic buyer. In 2002, with cash positions under pressure and risk appetites very low, potential corporate buyers of Kmart's assets preferred to stay away from the bankruptcy proceedings, despite the many synergies that might have been available in combining Kmart with another big box retailer. ESL had large holdings in several public companies, but Lampert also had lots of cash on hand that could be deployed opportunistically, regardless of what part of the cycle the macroeconomy or the retail industry was in.

PRIVATE EQUITY

Private equity is usually defined to include venture capital (VC) funds, leveraged buyout (LBO) funds, and mezzanine funds. VC funds seek out small, early-stage companies that are generally several years away from having the size and track record to launch a successful public equity offering. VC funds thus pursue a portfolio of high-risk, high-reward investments, with the full understanding that the majority of their individual investments may fail. Mezzanine funds, a very small portion of the private equity market, typically provide subordinated debt financing to growth companies that require relatively small amounts of debt that is junior to senior debt.

LBO funds have a very different profile from VC funds in that they seek to acquire mature businesses that they can use as vehicles to produce an attractive medium-term return on investment. LBO shops have been able to produce attractive returns because of two market inefficiencies. First, despite many attempts to bring them together, the incentives of managers and shareholders have never been perfectly aligned in public companies. Shareholder activism takes an immense amount of energy and organization, and the more widely dispersed a company's ownership is, the more difficult it is for shareholders to make sure that managers are always acting in the best interest of the owners. Thus, publicly owned companies may in some cases not be managed as effectively as private companies. Or, to put it differently, managers may be maximizing something other than profit. For instance, managers may be maximizing employment, executive compensation and perks, or perhaps even political clout. By taking a public company private and either directly managing it or closely supervising its management, LBO funds believe they can return a company to its *raison d'être* by cutting costs and running the business for cash.

The second inefficiency that LBOs claim to address is that certain types of companies, even when well managed, are perennially undervalued by the public equity markets. There are certain fixed costs associated with being a public company, including ongoing required reports to shareholders and disclosures to the Securities and Exchange Commission (SEC), National Association of Securities Dealers (NASD), New York Stock Exchange (NYSE), and other regulatory bodies. Such costs have increased dramatically due to more aggressive regulators and stock exchanges on top of new accounting demands following passage of the Sarbanes–Oxley bill in 2002. These costs are borne disproportionately by shareholders in smaller companies. In addition, one LBO manager argues, "Many mid-cap companies have begun to feel orphaned by the public equity markets and have a difficult time attracting research coverage and investor interest."[4]

LBO funds have been notably active in the market for M&A in recent years. During the recession of 2001 and its aftermath, traditional corporate strategic acquirers to a large degree shunned M&A as a potential avenue for growth and efficiency, and their shareholders for the most part seemed to approve of this newfound caution after the obvious excesses that characterized some of the acquisitions of the late 1990s. LBO funds, on the other hand, found themselves flush with cash during this period due to their increasing acceptance among institutional investors. The private equity industry had still not deployed the large amount of cash that had been raised during the period 1997–2000, and the decline in new LBO funds during 2001–02 was much less dramatic than the overall slowdown in the M&A market. Overall, the amount of funds raised by private equity sponsors from 1999 to 2004 was comparable to the total amount raised by the industry in its entire history up to 1998 (see Exhibit C6.3).

When an LBO fund seeks to take a public company private, or to acquire a large division of a public company that seeks a divestiture, the "buy-out" of the entity is generally done with an infusion of some equity from the fund's cash reserves, but that thin equity slice is stretched over a large asset with borrowed funds. By tapping the high-yield bond market,

[4] Paul Finnegan presentation at Kellogg Private Equity Conference, March 2005.

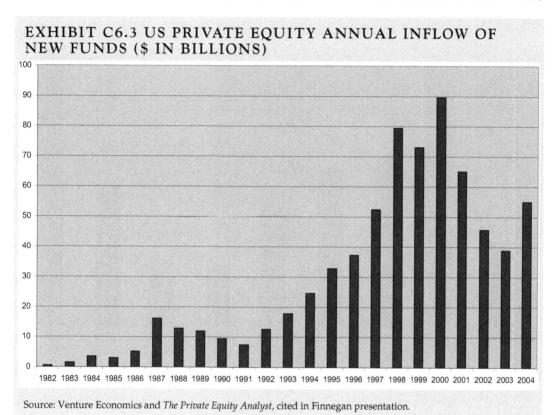

EXHIBIT C6.3 US PRIVATE EQUITY ANNUAL INFLOW OF NEW FUNDS ($ IN BILLIONS)

Source: Venture Economics and *The Private Equity Analyst*, cited in Finnegan presentation.

LBO funds are often able to leverage their equity infusion many times to complete large transactions with mostly borrowed money. By setting up separate legal entities, the LBO funds ensure that they cannot be held liable (beyond the loss of their equity investment) if companies under their control ultimately fail. High-yield bond investors are willing to lend money to these entities because they earn a high interest rate, the LBO funds have a good track record of managing businesses for cash, and in the event of business failure and default the bondholders will at least recognize some value as they will become the new owners of the company's assets.

In addition to experiencing only a limited slowdown in new commitments of capital, LBO funds over the period 2001–04 benefited from historically low interest rates. While the reduction of short-term and long-term rates from 2001 to 2003 was symptomatic of the general economic malaise that caused potential strategic buyers to retreat from M&A activity, it was beneficial for LBO shops because of their reliance on borrowing to fund acquisitions that cost many times their available cash (See Exhibits C6.4 and C6.5). In effect, lowered interest rates meant that LBO funds operated in the M&A market with a much higher leverage multiplier.

EXHIBIT C6.4 VALUE OF COMPLETED LEVERAGED BUYOUT TRANSACTIONS ($ IN BILLIONS)

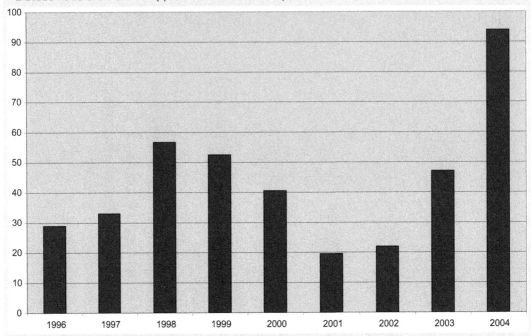

Source: Standard & Poor's, cited in Finnegan presentation.

EXHIBIT C6.5 LIBOR AND TREASURY RATES, 2000–05

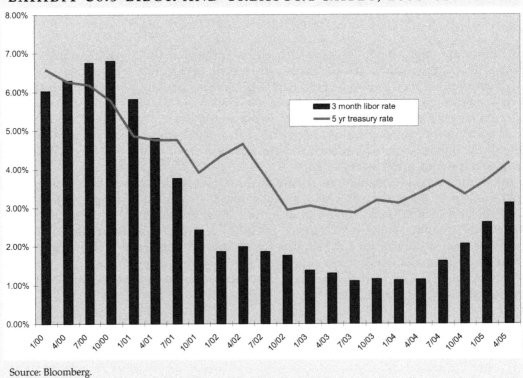

Source: Bloomberg.

HEDGE FUNDS

The line between some types of hedge funds and LBO funds blurred in the last few years, but most hedge fund strategies remained quite distinct from the LBO investing model. Many hedge funds could be thought of as unrestricted mutual funds. Regulators allowed hedge funds to operate outside the limitations of the Investment Company Act of 1940 as long as they did not market their services to, or accept money from, small or unsophisticated investors. In 2005 the SEC was planning new regulations for the industry (the scope of which remained unclear), but for many years hedge funds had been completely unregulated, except that they could accept funds only from large institutions or accredited individual investors who met a high standard of net worth. The regulatory philosophy regarding the hedge fund industry in the United States had essentially been that rich and sophisticated investors were free to have their money managed by whomever they wished and to choose any level of risk that suited their appetite. Small investors, on the other hand, were protected and well served by the myriad of regulations that covered mutual fund managers.

The freedom of hedge fund managers from "long-only" decisions that face traditional managers has given rise to many different investing strategies that are unavailable to mutual funds. The most basic variation on an equity mutual fund is a "long-short" equity hedge fund, in which managers take long positions in stocks that they like and also take short positions in stocks that they feel will decline over the short- or medium term. Most such funds hope to be market-neutral, which is to say that since they hold long and short exposures in roughly equal amounts, their returns over time will have limited correlation to the stock market at large. This suits the goals of many of such funds' investors since one of the reasons investors shift assets to hedge funds is because of their preference for absolute return rather than relative return. Long-short managers are expected to deliver a positive return every year, regardless of whether the stock market goes up or down.

The early years of the hedge fund industry, before institutional money starting pouring in since the early 1990s, was dominated by long-short and other hedging strategies, so the name "hedge fund" stuck even as it became a misnomer for many funds carrying that classification. It is important to note that the main distinction between hedge funds and mutual funds is not that all hedge funds are hedged, or that mutual funds cannot hedge any of their investments. In fact, some mutual funds are allowed to buy put options to protect (hedge) against some of their downside risk or to sell covered call options to generate income in return for giving up some of the potential upside in their investments. The distinction between the two types of funds is simply whether or not they are open to the general public, and therefore whether they are subject to large amounts of regulation. Hedge funds' investing styles range from completely hedged, low-risk strategies that seek simply to generate returns of 6%–8% in any market condition to unhedged, highly leveraged speculation on currencies, commodities, or even weather and natural disasters.

Hedge funds on average do not carry any more risk (as measured by standard deviation of returns over time) than the average equity mutual fund, but no mutual fund manager would be allowed to take the risks undertaken by the small minority of hedge funds that carry very high risk but offer very high-potential rewards. For instance, in 1992 George Soros, head of the Quantum Fund, became known as "the man who broke the Bank of England" when he borrowed at least $10 billion to short the British pound while buying German marks, betting that Great Britain would eventually be forced to remove itself from the European Monetary System. When the size of his bets forced British officials to admit that their stated policies were unsustainable, the Quantum Fund made a quick profit of more than $1 billion. While such hedge fund trades capture headlines, they are not the norm for an industry in which most funds market themselves by pointing out that their historical returns exhibit less volatility than the stock market.

Hedge fund strategies that bear limited correlation to the broad stock and bond markets include convertible arbitrage, risk arbitrage, and distressed debt trading. Convertible arbitrage involves investing in corporate debt that is convertible into a company's stock and usually selling short common stock in the same company, trying to find an arbitrage between the value of two different securities issued by the same corporation, or else trying through constant readjustment of the position to realize the "volatility" or "optionality" value embedded in the convertible security. Risk arbitrage involves betting on whether announced mergers or acquisitions will be consummated as planned. By taking long positions in a target company and short positions in a would-be acquirer, a trader is taking the view that an acquisition will go ahead, because the spread in the price of the two company's common stock will reflect some possibility of the deal falling apart until it actually happens and the spread narrows to the exact terms laid out in the acquisition agreement. Traders realize that they cannot know for sure what will happen in the future, but they translate the spread in prices into the market's opinion of the implied probability of the deal going through. Then they can do their own estimation of the probability of deal success based on all of the available facts and potential complications such as shareholder proxy votes, antitrust concerns, or even volatile personalities in the executive suites of the acquirer or the target. If, for example, the market believes there is a 70% chance of success, but the trader believes it is closer to 50% or 90%, the trader will take a position to exploit the difference.

For many years, hedge funds active in the distressed arena tried to buy defaulted or near-default bonds and then resell them weeks or months later at a profit. While managers of such funds felt they had the expertise sufficient to risk capital in the complicated and esoteric world of bankruptcy, they were generally looking for exit strategies by reselling distressed bonds at a profit as a company moved to the later stages of restructuring. This stands in contrast to some current hedge fund investors who are attracted to restructurings because of the potential to acquire longer-term control over attractive assets. The blurring of the line between LBO and hedge funds began when hedge funds specializing in bankruptcy started hanging onto their distressed investments through the entire restructuring process, leaving them with substantial, and sometimes controlling, stakes in companies when upon emergence from bankruptcy bondholders' claims are transformed into equity in the new entity.

ESL: THE HEDGE FUND THAT COULD NOT BE CATEGORIZED

ESL Investments, so named after the initials of its manager, Edward S. Lampert, had always been an atypical hedge fund in that it tended to buy big chunks of companies' common stock and then stick with its investments for a few years at a time. ESL for the most part did not pursue short-term trading strategies, and it also did not specialize in distressed debt. Instead, Lampert hewed closer to the line of Warren Buffett in acquiring substantial but noncontrolling stakes in public companies that he perceived could provide an attractive return. In some important respects, however, he differed from Buffett. First, Lampert tended to buy stakes in companies that were in worse shape than those Buffett favored. Buffett acquired unhealthy companies only if he was going to take full control and use the assets as springboards for other investments. As far as minority stakes in public companies went, Buffett bought stakes in such companies as Coca Cola and Gillette because he believed they had great management and excellent long-term prospects.

Two of Warren Buffett's most famous quotes show Lampert's deviation from the Buffett model. Buffett wrote that "it's far better to buy a wonderful company at a fair price than a fair company at a wonderful price." Buffett also said many times over the years that his "favorite holding period is forever." Lampert, since leaving a plum job working for Robert Rubin in risk arbitrage at Goldman Sachs, had shown himself very willing to take minority positions in fair companies selling at a discount to benefit from potential improvements in operating businesses. While certainly having a much longer holding period than most of his hedge fund peers, he had also shown no indication of preferring unlimited holding periods. Many of his investments had been in companies that were limping along, neither near death nor extremely successful, where management was able to respond with energy and action to his recommendations.

2002–03 DECISION: SHOULD ESL SEEK TO GAIN CONTROL OF KMART DURING BANKRUPTCY?

ESL, as a hedge fund investing on behalf of its clients, should pursue a single goal: to maximize return on investments in any market condition without unacceptable levels of volatility. In 2002, ESL was a financial buyer seeking to earn high returns from a Kmart acquisition despite having no synergies with other investments.

For years before its bankruptcy filing, Kmart had been consistently beaten by competitors with much more advanced supply chain technologies (Wal-Mart) and superior marketing and store design (Target, Old Navy, and others). Attempts to compete despite a clearly inferior cost structure led to increasing leverage over time. Kmart's balance sheet was ill-equipped to handle the recession of 2001, and the problem was exacerbated by poor decisions on the part of management.

As Lampert and his associates at ESL pondered the risks and rewards of a big infusion of cash into such a troubled entity, they pored over its balance sheet (See Exhibit C6.6). The operating business was in shambles, but could a large reduction in debt and a new, energized management team make Kmart a viable operation? No one had delusions that Kmart could take Wal-Mart on head to head, but Kmart retained many assets, including one that was becoming increasingly difficult for Wal-Mart to find: real estate.

In studying the potential downside of an investment, the ESL team likely took comfort from the fact that if the operating business just could not be salvaged after an all-out effort, Kmart would still retain value even in liquidation because of its real estate holdings. Kmart owned some of its big-box retail locations, but most of them were on long-term below-market

EXHIBIT C6.6 KMART BALANCE SHEET, JANUARY 1999 TO JANUARY 2003 ($ IN MILLIONS)

	JAN 2003		JAN 2002		JAN 2001		JAN 2000	JAN 1999
Assets								
Cash and short-term investments	2,088.00		613.00		1,245.00		401.00	344.0
Receivables	301.00		473.00		0.00		0.00	0.00
Inventories—total	3,23 8.00		4,825.00		5,822.00		6,412.00	7,101.00
Prepaid expense	27.00		191.00		0.00		0.00	0.00
Other current assets	157.00		0.00		817.00		811.00	715.00
Total current assets	5,811.00		6,102.00		7,884.00		7,624.00	8,160.00
Property, plant, and equipment—total (gross)	159.00		10,896.00		12,309.00		11,942.00	11,554.00
Depreciation, depletion, and amortization (accumulated)	6.00		6,004.00		6,148.00		5,385.00	5,144.00
Property, plant, and equipment—total (net)	153.00		4,892.00		6,161.00		6,557.00	6,410.0 0
Other assets	120.00		244.00		253.00		449.00	534.00
Total assets	6,084.00		11,238.00		14,298.00		14,630.00	15,104.00
Liabilities								
Debt—due in one year	51.00		68.00		84.00		68.00	66.00
Accounts payable	820.00		1,287.00		103.00		2,288.00	2,204.00
Income taxes payable	37.00		42.00		40.00		73.00	249.00
Accrued expense	778.00		504.00		138.00		265.00	337.00
Other current liabilities	90.00		219.00		259.00		1,105.00	1,220.00
Total current liabilities	1,776.00		2,120.00		624.00		3,799.00	4,076.00
Long-term debt—total	477.00		1,269.00		2,076.00		3,914.00	3,759.00
Deferred taxes	0.00		0.00		0.00		0.00	0.00
Investment tax credit	0.00		0.00		0.00		0.00	0.00
Other liabilities	1,639.00		8,150.00		8,139.00		834.00	965.00
Equity								
Common stock	1.00		519.00		503.00		487.00	481.00
Capital surplus	1,943.00		1,922.00		1,695.00		1,578.00	1,555.00
Retained earnings	249.00		(2,742.00)		1,261.00		4,018.00	4,268.00
Less: Treasury stock—total dollar amount	1.00		0.00		0.00		0.00	0.00
Total common equity	2,192.00		(301.00)		3,459.00		6,083.00	6,304.00
Total stockholders' equity	2,192.00		(301.00)		3,459.00		6,083.00	6,304.00
Total liabilities and stockholders' equity	6,084.00	AG	11,238.00	TL	14,298.00	TL	14,630.00	15,104.00
Common shares outstanding	89.59		519.12		503.30		486.51	481.38

Source: COMPUSTAT.

leases that could have considerable present value in the event that Kmart wanted to (or had to) sell the leases to other businesses. Later, in response to considerable speculation among Wall Street analysts that ESL just wanted to realize the inherent real estate value of Kmart or Sears and then look for an exit strategy, Lampert would remark that no "retailer should aspire to have its real estate be worth more than its operating business"[5] and emphatically declare his commitment to making Kmart's retail operations strong and viable. But at the time of the decision to plunge into Kmart's defaulted debt, Lampert must have considered the effective "put option" that the real estate represented if things did not work out. In fact, some analysts later decided that the real estate holdings of Kmart alone were worth several times what ESL had paid to acquire control of the company in 2002–03. For instance, in July 2004, Deutsche Bank released a 25-page study of retailers' real estate holdings, which showed that Kmart's shares at that time, despite having already quadrupled since emergence from bankruptcy, were still trading at a minimum 24%, and perhaps as high as 133%, discount to the net asset value of Kmart's real estate holdings including favorable long-term leases.[6] In other words, the analysts believed that even if Kmart were to send all its employees home and shut its doors to business, the company would still be worth much more than the equity market value of the company.

LAMPERT'S KMART PLAY

Based on ESL's analysis of the situation, Lampert decided to plunge into the Kmart restructuring despite ESL's lack of experience in both bankruptcy proceedings and running businesses with majority control of a company's common stock. During the spring of 2002, ESL began quietly accumulating Kmart's defaulted bonds. Trading in distressed debt occurs through private, unpublished transactions, so the exact timing and size of Lampert's trades are unknown. Sometime during the summer of 2002, ESL informed Kmart, then operating under a bankruptcy trustee and a new CEO, that the fund had accumulated more than $1 billion in face value of the company's defaulted debt.[7] In September 2002, ESL was able to gain a voice in the restructuring process through a seat on the Financial Institutions Committee, a statutory body appointed by the bankruptcy court. Lampert pushed for the restructuring to move more quickly than it had been up to that time and argued that the company could emerge from Chapter 11 within a shorter time frame than the management team thought. UBS Investment Bank provided the following commentary:

> In early November, Mr. Lampert met with Kmart's then Chairman and CEO Jim Adamson to emphasize the importance of early emergence and to make clear his opinion that the process was moving too slowly; he specifically pressed Mr. Adamson to file a plan of reorganization by Thanksgiving. When the Company did not meet such a timetable, Mr. Lampert's attorney demanded Mr. Adamson's resignation.

[5] News conference, November 17, 2004. Transcript available in company's SEC filings at http://www.sec.gov.

[6] *Gold in Them Thar Retailers*, Deutsche Bank, July 26, 2004.

[7] ESL's role during restructuring in 2002–03 was largely out of the public eye. This account is consistent with recently published articles and also relies on a timeline created by UBS Investment Bank.

With Lampert's support, Julian Day was appointed the new CEO of Kmart in January 2003, and the bankruptcy process started moving at a faster pace. ESL continued to buy Kmart debt in privately negotiated transactions throughout the period. During final preparations for emergence from bankruptcy in March and April of 2003, many of Kmart's creditors, both banks and bond investors, made it clear that they would prefer to receive cash and end their involvement with Kmart, as opposed to receiving equity in the new company. ESL took advantage of the bank lenders' preference to cut their losses, buying many of their claims for approximately 40% of their face value. Holders of Kmart bonds likely received an even lower recovery value on sales to Lampert's fund. Ultimately, ESL controlled 51% of the new Kmart's equity when it emerged from bankruptcy, after debt was transformed into equity. Lampert became the company's chairman and was also able to nominate three additional directors to the board of directors of Kmart Holdings, whose new stock soon began trading on the NASDAQ National Market. As Lampert made several small sales of Kmart real estate leases to other retailers and managed the retail business for cash, the market realized that Kmart could be a viable business now that it was stripped of almost all of its debt. As a result, the stock started trading up dramatically (See Exhibit C6.7).

EXHIBIT C6.7 KMART DAILY CLOSING PRICES, MAY 2003 TO MARCH 2005

Source: Bloomberg.

NOVEMBER 2004 DECISION: SHOULD KMART (UNDER ESL'S CONTROL) ACQUIRE SEARS?

The Sears chain had been almost entirely based in malls for decades, but after seeing its sales growth eroded by stand-alone "big box" retailers during the 1990s, management in the last few years started experimenting with an "off-mall" concept called Sears Grand. After good results from the early phases of testing, Sears was ready in 2004 to expand the idea at a rapid clip. The chain found that much of the demographic that once constituted reliable consumers at its urban and close suburban mall locations had moved farther away from cities to far suburbs and rural areas. Lampert's desire to sell 50 Kmart locations coincided exactly with Sears management's desire to roll out the off-mall Sears Grand concept nationwide at a fast pace.

During 2002, Lampert had built a substantial minority position in Sears stock, in keeping with his history of acquiring minority stakes in underperforming companies. Owning nearly 10% of the company, he was familiar with its challenges, but also with the opportunities available if the chain could reestablish relationships with its traditional customer base by following them out to neighborhoods and communities without any large malls. After Kmart and Sears closed the deal for the transfer of 50 stores in September 2004, wheels must have begun turning in the heads of each chain's management. The deal seemed to create significant value for each counterparty, and Kmart, a struggling chain, still had 1400 stores left, hundreds of them in the exact types of locations Sears hoped to target with Sears Grand. Sears's sales per square foot were $80 higher than Kmart's, so converting dozens of stores at a time in the right neighborhoods could provide tens of millions of dollars in additional value.

However, in making these new outlays of cash to acquire locations, Sears would clearly be taking a risk as it increased its leverage (See Exhibits C6.8 and C6.9). It would also for the first time be entering the off-mall arena, thus exposing itself to Wal-Mart and Target. Kmart's bankruptcy had come about largely due to being overleveraged and competing with Wal-Mart during a recession, so the additional risk Sears was taking on even with just 50 new locations could not be taken lightly. To acquire additional Kmarts that would have higher operating value as Sears Grands would mean more borrowing.

With Lampert as chairman of Kmart and the second largest shareholder in Sears, and also having recently completed a real estate deal that both sides found to be highly advantageous, it is reasonable to suspect that Lampert stayed in close contact with the top management of Sears throughout September and October of 2004. When the question of combining the two companies was first raised is not known, but it is hard to imagine that Lampert himself was not considering the idea. Then, in the first week of November, a sudden and unexpected flurry of news provided a catalyst.

On November 5, 2004, to Lampert's and Sears's surprise, Vornado Realty Trust announced in a regulatory filing that it had acquired a 4.3% stake in Sears common stock. Vornado was a large real estate investor that had a reputation for buying cheap real estate assets. Sears stock jumped 23% on the news, as speculation swirled that Vornado might purchase the rest of the company at a premium to acquire its real estate. (Unlike Kmart, Sears actually owned most of its store locations.) (See Exhibit C6.10).

EXHIBIT C6.8 SEARS INCOME STATEMENT ($ IN MILLIONS)

	Dec 2003	Dec 2002	Dec 2001
Sales	41,124	41,366	40,990
Cost of goods sold	26,202	25,646	26,234
Selling, general, and administrative expense	10,951	11,510	10,758
Operating income before depreciation	3,971	4,210	3,998
Depreciation and amortization	909	875	863
Interest expense	1,027	1,148	1,426
Nonoperating income (expense) and special items	3,414	266	−486
Pretax income	5,449	2,453	1,223
Income taxes—total	2,007	858	467
Minority interest	45	11	21
Income before extraordinary items	3,397	1,584	735
Extraordinary items and discontinued operations	0	−208	0
Net income (loss)	3,397	1,376	735
Earnings per share (primary)—excluding extraordinary items	11.95	4.99	2.25
Earnings per share (primary)—including extraordinary items	11.95	4.34	2.25
Common shares used to calculate primary EPS	284.30	317.40	326.40
Earnings per share (fully diluted)—excluding extraordinary items	11.86	4.94	2.24
Earnings per share (fully diluted)—including extraordinary Items	11.86	4.29	2.24

Source: COMPUSTAT.

Now came the moment of decision for Lampert and the Sears board of directors. Both controlled retailers that had struggled against Wal-Mart and whose real estate had been undervalued by the market for several years. But now the market had woken up rather suddenly to the real estate argument, and a decision had to be made. How would Sears respond if Vornado or other "vulture investors" made a bid for the company? Could either of the chains, each at one time the nation's largest retailer, succeed against competitors with lower-cost structures and higher sales per square foot?

As a financial buyer, Lampert had not previously been interested in acquiring more than 10% to 15% of Sears. But now he found himself as a potential strategic buyer, and the timing of his decision was being forced by the emergence of a financial buyer (Vornado) that had much more experience than ESL did in real estate investments. (See Exhibit C6.11 and Exhibit C6.12.)

EXHIBIT C6.9 SEARS BALANCE SHEET ($ IN MILLIONS)

	Dec 2003	Dec 2002	Dec 2001
Assets			
Cash and short-term investments	9,057	1,962	1,064
Receivables	2,689	31,622	28,813
Inventories—total	5,335	5,115	4,912
Other current assets	1,115	1,284	1,316
Total current assets	18,196	39,983	36,105
Property, plant, and equipment—total (gross)	13,124	12,979	13,137
Depreciation, depletion, and amortization (accumulated)	6,336	6,069	6,313
Property, plant, and equipment—total (net)	6,788	6,910	6,824
Intangibles	1,653	1,648	C
Deferred charges	24	277	C
Other assets	1,062	1,591	1,388
Total assets	27,723	50,409	44,317
Liabilities			
Debt—due in one year	2,950	4,808	3,157
Notes payable	1,033	4,525	3,557
Accounts payable	3,106	7,485	7,176
Income taxes payable	1,867	0	0
Accrued expense	609	C	C
Other current liabilities	4,194	1,779	1,694
Total current liabilities	13,759	18,597	15,584
Long-term debt—total	4,218	21,304	18,921
Deferred taxes	0	0	0
Investment tax credit	0	0	0
Other liabilities	3,345	3,755	3,693
Equity			
Common stock	323	323	323
Capital surplus	3,493	3,463	3,437
Retained earnings	10,530	7,441	6,582
Less: Treasury stock—total dollar amount	7,945	4,474	4,223
Total common equity	6,401	6,753	6,119
Total stockholders' equity	6,401	6,753	6,119
Total liabilities and stockholders' equity	27,723	50,409	44,317
Common shares outstanding	230.38	316.73	320.4

Source: COMPUSTAT.

EXHIBIT C6.10 SEARS DAILY CLOSING PRICES, JANUARY 2004 TO MARCH 2005

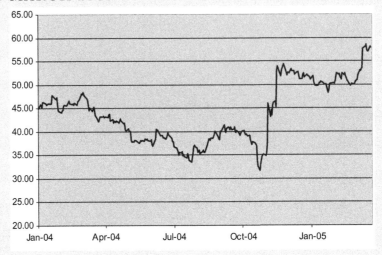

Source: Bloomberg.

EXHIBIT C6.11 SELECTED QUOTES FROM EDWARD S. LAMPERT, CHAIRMAN OF KMART HOLDINGS, AT KMART–SEARS JOINT NEWS CONFERENCE, NOVEMBER 17, 2004 (EMPHASIS ADDED)

"This truly is a historic day and something that we've been working on very diligently to make happen. The combination of Kmart and Sears, as you can see, will jointly have roughly $55 billion in revenues, nearly 3500 store locations consisting of roughly 1500 Kmart locations and 870 or so Sears locations on the mall… The terms of the deal are that Kmart shares are going to be converted to 1 share of Sears Holdings Corporation, and the Sears shares will receive for 55 percent of the Sears a half a share of the combined company, and for 45 percent of the Sears share $50 in stock. There will be an election. Shareholders will have an opportunity to elect either stock or cash, and the stock portion of the merger will be tax-free to shareholders. As part of the merger agreement, ESL and its affiliates, our affiliates, have elected to receive all stock in the merger, and we think that is something that is a very important sign of our confidence in the combined company…

"We are going to need really the best of us, but the best of both the Kmart team as well as the Sears team. I think that there is going to be a lot of work to do in converting Kmart stores into Sears stores where appropriate, bringing Sears products into Kmart stores…

"Given the large ownership that we will have on the Board, we will be able, similar to what Kmart has been able to do for the last couple of years, we will be able to manage the business strategically and for the long term without having to worry about figuring out how to make monthly same-store sales, hit a specific target, and without giving any type of quarterly earnings guidance and then trying to manage the business to that guidance.

"In terms of the *strategic perspective* behind the merger, I think it is pretty obvious that scale is very important to compete effectively…we need to have a very low-cost structure in order to compete with our biggest competitors. And I think that while we need to have a low-cost structure, it needs to be consistent with the reputation and quality of service that Sears has always provided and the type of service that we at Kmart aspire to achieve.

"Clearly, the Kmart locations are very significant, 1500 off-the-mall locations in high-traffic areas. Sears has the best offerings…in hard lines, with Craftsman, Kenmore, DieHard.…The issue for Sears, however, has been with competitors opening hundreds of stores a year; the ability to actually be closer to the customer is something that Sears has started to move towards with the launching of the Sears Grand stores. But the time—the time and capital required to get there quickly—is both prohibitive and risky, and I think that the ability to take the Kmart store base and determine whether we want to convert those Kmart stores over to the Sears nameplate and to bring Sears products into the Kmart stores is a great opportunity.

"The other factor with competitors opening so many stores and Sears not having been opening stores off the mall is Sears has had to spend a significant amount of money, both in marketing and capital expenditures, just to stay even. That same capital which has been running roughly, call it $900 million or $1 billion a year can now be really directed at very, very high return on investment opportunities, both in the conversion process as well as helping to upgrade, whether it is the fixtures or the appearance of the existing Kmart stores.

"From a Kmart perspective, in addition to the products, which is something that we've aspired to and we've been working towards and we did this really with the relaunch of our apparel brands; *we clearly need to find at Kmart points of differentiation with our major competitors.* This has been something that has been talked about. It has been talked about before the Company went into bankruptcy, when it was in bankruptcy and since it has emerged…

"*The combined cost of goods sold of the two companies is roughly $40 billion.* We purchase roughly $40 billion of merchandise from around the world. And I think that the ability to sort of work together to really get best practices from both organizations and work with our supplier base to really help drive their business and help them save money, so that we can save money for our customers, is a big opportunity. In terms of SG&A of the two companies, the combined SG&A is roughly $12 billion. And as you will see when we discuss the synergy opportunity, the opportunity both on the purchase of merchandise as well as the SG&A is fairly significant when you think of those numbers…

"Sears stores in general are roughly $80 per square foot more productive than Kmart stores. And if you talk about roughly 100 million square feet of real estate that Kmart has, if we could ever achieve that level of productivity in the Kmart stores, either as Sears or as Kmart, you're talking about an $8 billion opportunity. So I think that the financial dimensions are very, very significant and they blend very well with the strategic dimensions.

"Finally, I think that as a board and a management team, *we're going to have an ability and a willingness to monetize noncore and nonproductive assets.* We want to make sure that the businesses that we run are going to be able to produce real economic value for the shareholders over time, and at the same time I think we want to make sure that we stay focused on the biggest opportunities…

"I think finally before I turn the podium over, I don't think any retailer should aspire to have its real estate be worth more than its operating business. There's been a lot of speculation about real estate strategy, real estate value, and I think that there is some truth to the notion that there are certain retailers whose real estate is worth more than its operating business. I think while that may have been true at Kmart at one point in time, we've worked very, very hard to improve the profitability of each of our stores and to make those stores worth a lot more as an operating business than as real estate. The more money the store makes, the more valuable they are as operating businesses, and that's something that I think the combined company can do very, very well.

Continued

EXHIBIT C6.11 SELECTED QUOTES FROM EDWARD S. LAMPERT, CHAIRMAN OF KMART HOLDINGS, AT KMART–SEARS JOINT NEWS CONFERENCE, NOVEMBER 17, 2004 (EMPHASIS ADDED)—cont'd

"To the extent that we have stores that can't produce the type of profit that we're looking for, we would have to consider other alternatives. I think *well-run retailers over time should be able to earn a 10 percent EBITDA to sales ratio*. I think when you look at Home Depot, you look at Target, you look at The Gap, they all achieve that metric. And again, that's not something we think that we're going to be able to do anytime soon, but that's something that we're going to work towards. We're going to work towards best-in-class financial metrics and best-in-class customer metrics."

Source: Press conference transcript, available in SEC filings at http://www.sec.gov.

EXHIBIT C6.12 SELECTED QUOTES ON KMART ACQUISITION OF SEARS, NOVEMBER 17–19, 2004

Tom Peters, management author: "If you think they'll be able to take on Wal-Mart, I've got a nice bridge." (*Wall Street Journal, 11/18/04*)

Burt Flickinger, retail consultant: "This is cause for celebration for competitors." (*WSJ*)

Emme P. Kozloff, Sanford Bernstein retail analyst: "Wal-Mart is in a good position. It could take advantage of the inevitable disarray at Kmart over the next year to take market share. And it's always harder to get customers back that have defected." (*WSJ*)

Michael B. Exstein and Shirley Lee, Credit Suisse First Boston retail analysts: "In the near term, we do believe that the opportunities for cost savings and improvements are real, not to mention significant opportunities for the combined entity to monetize some of its real estate (i.e., overlapping/'nonstrategic' store locations). As a result, we believe Sears shares will continue to rally on today's news given these two points. In the longer term, however, we believe that the integration (such as systems and logistics) and execution challenges before the combined entity is [sic] enormous and far more complex than any combination attempted in the retail industry to date. Prior to today's announcement, many would consider Sears and Kmart to be the industry laggards with uncertain business models. It is not clear to us how the combination of such two [sic] retailers could work long term." (*CSFB Retail Industry Flash, 11/17/04*)

Kozloff, McGranahan et al., Sanford Bernstein retail research team: "The merger of Sears and Kmart has strong strategic rationale for two beleaguered retailers: real estate for Sears, brands for Kmart. Sears is currently trapped in a capital-consuming but obsolete on-mall real estate footprint. Kmart real estate helps level the playing field with other hard line players. However, the integration promises to be complex, difficult and lengthy; near-term risk is substantial and probability of success is mixed. Execution will be the key to making the merger work, and the track records of the two companies are not encouraging. The task of integrating supply chains, systems and two disparate cultures is enormous. We expect existing Kmart locations that have appropriate demographic trade areas to be candidates for conversion to the Sears 'mini-grand' format. Management sees 'several hundred' candidates over time, although the pace is likely to be measured and returns carefully monitored. Our demographic analysis suggests roughly 300 potential conversions over time. Potential synergies—revenue, purchasing and cost—are powerful (pegged by company at $500 million) and, if realized, will create value." (*Bernstein Research Weekly Notes, 11/19/04*)

Source: http://www.sec.gov/Archives/edgar/data/319256/000095012304013859/y68947fe425.htm.

McDonald's, Wendy's, and Hedge Funds: Hamburger Hedging? Hedge Fund Activism and Impact on Corporate Governance

GROWING HEDGE FUND ACTIVISM

Are hedge funds heroes or villains? Management of Blockbuster, Time Warner, Six Flags, Knight-Ridder, and Bally Total Fitness might prefer the "villain" appellation, but Enron, WorldCom, Tyco, and HealthSouth shareholders might view management as the real villains and hedge funds as vehicles to oust incompetent corporate managers before they run companies into the ground or steal them through fraudulent transactions. Could the pressure exerted by activist hedge funds on targeted companies result in increased share prices, management accountability, and better communication with shareholders? Or does it distract management from its primary goal of enhancing long-term shareholder value?

Hedge funds have been compared to the corporate raiders of the 1980s, who initiated hostile takeovers by using large amounts of debt to acquire target companies and then ousted management (and often thousands of employees as well). However, activist hedge funds typically use only their own equity to invest, without leveraging the target company, and generally work with existing management to effect change rather than dumping management and employees. And if hedge funds cannot engender support among the other major shareholders, they are usually forced to back down. Another difference between corporate raiders and hedge funds involves "greenmail"—forcing a company to buy out a large hostile shareholder at a premium price to escape unwanted attention. Raiders frequently initiate greenmail, but hedge funds never do.

Following corporate scandals at Enron and WorldCom, some observers believe activist hedge funds serve as catalysts for positive change at targeted underperforming companies. Even if hedge funds do not get everything they want, when they initiate an activist campaign, target companies are frequently compelled to make changes that benefit all shareholders. Others think that, although hedge fund strategies may improve a company's share price in the short term, they may not always enhance the company's long-term viability. The evidence is mixed. Some studies suggest that target companies benefit from a more than 5% rise in share price after the campaign is initiated. Other studies propose that activism has little impact on share values and earnings in the long run. Only a small percentage of hedge fund assets are allocated to activist projects, but this activity is increasing and has been well publicized through proxy fights and "hostile 13-D" letters. When filed with the Securities and Exchange Commission (SEC), these letters become public vehicles for criticizing management in an effort to effect change (Exhibit C7.1).

EXHIBIT C7.1 13-D LETTERS AS A PUBLIC VEHICLE

SEC Regulation 13-D requires every investor who acquires a beneficial ownership of more than 5% of a publicly traded security to file a holdings report with the SEC. The filing includes information on the investor's background and future plans. Since it warns of a changing shareholder base, it allows the target company to initiate potential defensive actions such as share repurchases, preferential share reallotments (poison pills), and announcements of strategic changes, acquisitions, and debt loading if the target is concerned about a hostile action.

13-D filings and attached letters can also become a public vehicle for criticizing management. For example, Daniel Loeb, a hedge fund activist who managed a $3.5 billion fund called Third Point, was known for being rather blunt and abrupt in his 13-D filings and statements to management, earning him the nickname "Wall Street's Merchant of Venom."[1] In a 13-D letter to Star Gas's CEO, Loeb stated, "Do what you do best: Retreat to your waterfront mansion in the Hamptons."[2] To another CEO, Loeb stated, "I also have excellent news, which I would like to share with you and the board: After significant reflection regarding the time commitments and constraints that such a responsibility would entail, I have decided to volunteer to serve on the company's board of directors..."[3] He told yet another CEO, "Since you ascended to your current role of Chief Value Destroyer, the shares have dropped over 45 percent..."[4]

Assets under management by hedge funds exceeded $1 trillion in 2005, almost 3% of global financial assets. More than 8000 hedge funds and approximately 1750 fund of hedge funds shared these assets. Because hedge funds have been particularly active stock traders, they have accounted for up to 50% of daily New York Stock Exchange trading volume. Hedge fund assets have grown at an annual rate of 26% since 1990, with approximately 40% of total assets concentrated in the top 50 hedge funds. High net worth investors represent nearly 75% of the asset base, but starting in 2001 more than 50% of the growth in this industry has come from institutional investors, with further "institutionalization" expected to provide most of the future growth. In February 2006 the hedge fund industry was required, for the first time, to register with the SEC (Exhibit C7.2).

[1] Nichola Groom, "McDonald's Investors Unswayed by Activist Proposal," *Reuters*, January 19, 2006.

[2] James Altucher, "Activist Track: The Softer Side of Loeb," *TheStreet.com, Inc.*, August 23, 2005.

[3] James Altucher, "Activist Track: The Softer Side of Loeb," *TheStreet.com, Inc.*, August 23, 2005.

[4] James Altucher, "Activist Track: The Softer Side of Loeb," *TheStreet.com, Inc.*, August 23, 2005.

EXHIBIT C7.2 SEC HEDGE FUND REGULATION

Historically, hedge funds were not required to register with the SEC and had minimal regulatory oversight. However, in February 2006 the SEC required hedge funds to register in an effort to deter or detect fraud at early stages. During 2005 the SEC had taken action against 20 hedge funds, a significant increase over previous years, with the most common violation related to misrepresentation of management experience and investment performance track record. On its website, the SEC advises investors to seek out a hedge fund's prospectus, valuation methodology of the fund's assets, impact on returns from both management and performance fees, limitations on redemption of shares (timing/lockups), management background, and asset allocation.

A TALE OF TWO ACTIVISTS: CARL ICAHN AND WILLIAM ACKMAN

Well-known hedge fund activist Carl Icahn evolved from a feared corporate raider and greenmailer during the 1980s to a ubiquitous hedge fund manager with $2.5 billion in assets and a personal net worth of $8.5 billion. Icahn's image as a feared and disliked corporate raider has transformed in some quarters to a "white knight." He has pushed through corporate change at Fairmont Hotels, Blockbuster, Kerr-McGee, Hollywood Entertainment, Siebel Systems, RiteAid, UnumProvident, and Time Warner. In late December 2005 he called Time Warner's sale of a 5% stake in its AOL division to Google a "disastrous decision," making a potential AOL merger with other companies, such as eBay, Yahoo, or Microsoft, difficult.[5] Icahn said, "This joint venture is short-sighted in nature and may preclude any consideration of a broader set of alternatives that would better maximize value and ensure a bright future for AOL."[6] In spite of these statements, he ultimately backed down from his threatened proxy battle to gain board seats as a prelude to breaking up the company, following Time Warner's agreement to boost its stock buyback effort and implement a $1 billion cost reduction program. The most likely reason he aborted this effort was lack of support from other significant institutional investors.

Icahn's activism initiatives have principally focused on threatening or initiating proxy fights (asking shareholders to vote on key initiatives he has advocated), pushing companies to distribute more cash to shareholders through dividends and share repurchases, and reducing CEO compensation. In regard to proxies, Icahn has said, "We need to ensure we have the best minds possible focused on business issues, and shareholders cannot trust that corporations being advised by management consultants and investment bankers, neither of which are compensated based on the results they achieve for businesses over time, are going to come up with the best decisions for the company."[7] Concerning CEO compensation, he has argued, "CEO comp eats into earnings, creates a cycle of invisible

[5] Verne Kopytoff, "Icahn Rips into AOL's $1 Billion Google Deal," *San Francisco Chronicle*, December 20, 2005.

[6] Verne Kopytoff, "Icahn Rips into AOL's $1 Billion Google Deal," *San Francisco Chronicle,* December 20, 2005.

[7] Deborah Solomon, "Fighting for a Fair Share," *New York Times Magazine,* June 5, 2005.

dilution and further waste of cash through share buybacks at any level to prevent dilution, and perhaps worst of all, stratifies the company, making the CEO a demi-god in the organization for, basically, being highly paid."[8]

Inherent in Icahn's activist behavior was the view that many corporations were sitting on too much cash. S&P 500 corporations held more than $615 billion in cash at the end of 2005, the most in more than 25 years. This cash pile was equal to 40% of long-term debt, which was also the highest percentage in 25 years. Icahn and other hedge fund activists wanted companies to pay out cash to shareholders through share repurchases (if the share price is weak) or through increased dividends. They also wanted companies to take on more risk by borrowing to increase leverage, creating pressure on management to become more efficient and accountable.

Another well-known activist, William Ackman, cofounded Gotham Partners in 1993 shortly after graduating from business school at the age of 26. This fund, which made investments in both private equity and public markets, was liquidated nearly a decade later, before Ackman started Pershing Square Capital Management in early 2004. He launched Pershing with $10 million of his own capital and $50 million from a strategic investor. The Pershing fund was opened to new investors in early 2005, adding more than $200 million to the prior base. With net returns of 42% in 2004 and 40% in 2005, funds under management exceeded $1 billion from performance and additional investment in early 2006. Pershing took significant positions in both Sears and Kmart before their merger in the fall of 2004. It then drew substantial media attention in the latter half of 2005 after building equity positions through options in both McDonald's and Wendy's, prior to squaring off with each firm's management team regarding comprehensive restructuring and recapitalization plans. Ackman felt that neither company was managing its cash and other resources optimally, so he took large equity stakes believing he could then persuade management to make changes to enhance shareholder value. He explained, "It has become an environment in which boards of directors are more receptive as they are much more aware of potential for personal liability. Management is more willing to listen as mutual funds vote proxies for value-additive transactions and hedge funds are willing to take a much more active and influential role in corporate governance."[9]

PERSHING SQUARE'S INITIAL INVOLVEMENT: WENDY'S AND McDonald's

Wendy's

By mid-April 2005, Pershing Square had acquired nearly a 10% stake in Wendy's and encouraged the restaurant chain to spin off its Tim Hortons doughnut chain, enabling it to operate autonomously from Wendy's and to unlock shareholder value. At that point, Tim

---

[8] Deborah Solomon, "Fighting for a Fair Share," *New York Times Magazine*, June 5, 2005.

[9] William Ackman, Pershing Square Capital Management, interview with the author, December 19, 2005.

Hortons was Wendy's most significant growth driver, representing nearly 50% of overall operating profits. Many shareholders believed Wendy's stock price did not fully reflect the contribution of that unit until Pershing and others pressed for the spinoff. In his April 2005 earnings note, Lehman Brothers restaurant analyst Jeff Bernstein valued stand-alone Wendy's (excluding Tim Hortons) at a price/earnings (P/E) multiple of 14× versus stand-alone Tim Hortons at a 24× P/E multiple. Wendy's stock rose 15% during the 2-week period following Ackman's advocacy of a spinoff.

In mid-July, Pershing submitted a detailed proposal to Wendy's management recommending not only the spinoff of Tim Hortons but also the sale of a large portion of the company's restaurants to franchisees, a major share repurchase, and management avoidance of any large acquisitions. However, in spite of Ackman's 10% ownership of the company, Wendy's management refused to discuss these recommendations with him.

In late July, Wendy's announced it would sell 15%–18% of Tim Hortons in a tax-free spinoff during the first quarter of 2006 and also disclosed authorization for an additional $1 billion in stock repurchases; an increase in the company's dividend by 25%; the reduction of debt by $100 million; and a program to sell more than 200 real estate sites, close 60 poorly performing stores, and sell hundreds of company-owned restaurants (reducing company ownership levels from 22% to as low as 15%).

While Pershing's activism appeared to have accelerated management's initiatives, Wendy's stated in its late-July strategic initiative press release, "The board of directors and management began in 2004 a thorough review of the company's operations and strategic plan with its long-term, independent financial advisor, Goldman Sachs. The resulting initiatives announced today are a comprehensive approach to manage the company for the future."[10] Despite this public statement, which ignored Ackman's efforts, many investors acknowledged that his vocal push motivated management to proactively restructure. From the initiation of Ackman's campaign for change at Wendy's starting in mid-April 2005 until early March 2006, Wendy's stock appreciated by 55%, from $39 to nearly $61.

McDonald's

At the end of 2005, McDonald's was one of the few major restaurant chains that owned large amounts of real estate. Most restaurant chains principally used operating leases and off-balance sheet financing to support their restaurant businesses and limit their actual real estate ownership. With thousands of well-positioned real estate properties, McDonald's carried a significantly higher property value on its balance sheet than any competitor. At the end of 2005 the real estate carrying value was approximately $30 billion (property and equipment before accumulated depreciation and amortization), equal to almost two-thirds of the company's equity market value of $45.6 billion. McDonald's 2005 year-end balance sheet is shown in Exhibit C7.3.

---

[10] Wendy's press release, July 29, 2005.

EXHIBIT C7.3 McDonald's BALANCE SHEET, 2005

	December 31	
	2005	2004
ASSETS		
Current assets		
Cash and equivalents	$ 4,260.40	$ 1,379.80
Accounts and notes receivable	795.90	745.50
Inventories, at cost, not in excess of market	147.00	147.50
Prepaid expenses and other current assets	646.40	585.00
Total current assets	5,849.70	2,857.80
Other assets		
Investments in and advances to affiliates	1,035.40	1,109.90
Goodwill, net	1,950.70	1,828.30
Miscellaneous	1,245.00	1,338.40
Total other assets	4,231.10	4,276.60
Property and equipment		
Property and equipment, at cost	29,897.20	30,507.80
Accumulated depreciation and amortization	(9,989.20)	(9,804.70)
Net property and equipment	19,908.00	20,703.10
Total assets	29,988.80	27,837.50
LIABILITIES AND SHAREHOLDERS' EQUITY		
Current liabilities		
Notes payable	544.00	—
Accounts payable	689.40	714.30
Income taxes	567.60	331.30
Other taxes	233.50	245.10
Accrued interest	158.50	179.40
Accrued payroll and other liabilities	1,184.60	1,188.20
Current maturities of long-term debt	658.70	862.20
Total current liabilities	4,036.30	3,520.50
Long-term debt	8,937.40	8,357.30
Other long-term liabilities	892.30	976.70
Deferred income taxes	976.70	781.50
Shareholders' equity		
Preferred stock, no par value; authorized— 165.0 million shares; issued—none		
Common stock, $0.01 par value; authorized— 3.5 billion shares; issued—1,660.6 million shares	16.60	16.60

EXHIBIT C7.3 McDonald's BALANCE SHEET, 2005—cont'd

Additional paid-in capital	2,797.60	2,186.00
Unearned ESOP compensation	(77.40)	(82.80)
Retained earnings	23,516.00	21,755.80
Accumulated other comprehensive income (loss)	(733.10)	(96.00)
Common stock in treasury, at cost; 397.4 and 390.7 million shares	(10,373.60)	(9,578.10)
Total shareholders' equity	15,146.10	14,201.50
Total liabilities and shareholders' equity	29,988.80	27,837.50

Note: Dollars in millions, except per share data.
Source: McDonald's Corporation 10-K Filing.

McDonald's had benefited from its 90% ownership in Chipotle, a Mexican restaurant that posted double-digit revenue growth from 1998 to 2005. However, even with a strong performance from this business, as of January 2006, McDonald's share price had not broken out of the low- to mid-$30s price range that it had traded within since early 2001—well below its all-time high of $48 in late 1999. To unlock the value of Chipotle from the relatively weaker value of the parent company, McDonald's decided to spin off 20% of the subsidiary through an initial public offering (IPO).

Since 2003, McDonald's had not increased or altered its long-term annual targets for system-wide sales and revenue growth of 3%–5%, operating income growth of 6%–7%, and return on invested capital in the high teens. This led to analyst commentary and McDonald's management discussions regarding a range of strategic options to improve the business. Exhibit C7.4 through Exhibit C7.7 show McDonald's historical performance and relative valuation.

EXHIBIT C7.4 McDonald's HISTORICAL REVENUE AND EBITDA PERFORMANCE

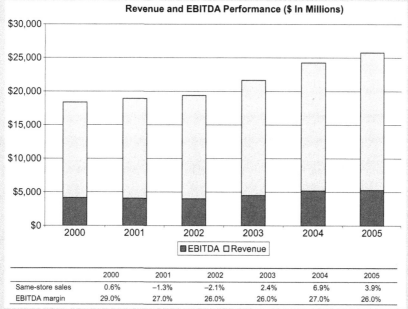

Revenue and EBITDA Performance ($ In Millions)

	2000	2001	2002	2003	2004	2005
Same-store sales	0.6%	−1.3%	−2.1%	2.4%	6.9%	3.9%
EBITDA margin	29.0%	27.0%	26.0%	26.0%	27.0%	26.0%

Note: 2005 EBITDA is an estimate because 2005 10-K had not been filed with depreciation and amortization results as of the writing of this case.

EXHIBIT C7.5 McDonald's STOCK PRICE PERFORMANCE SINCE ALL-TIME HIGH IN NOVEMBER 1999

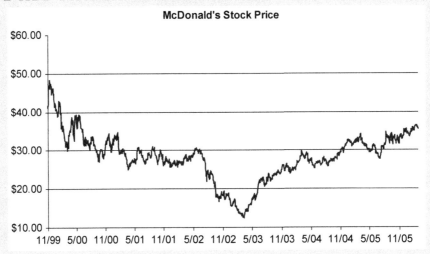

EXHIBIT C7.6 McDonald's FIVE-YEAR RELATIVE STOCK PRICE PERFORMANCE VERSUS PEERS

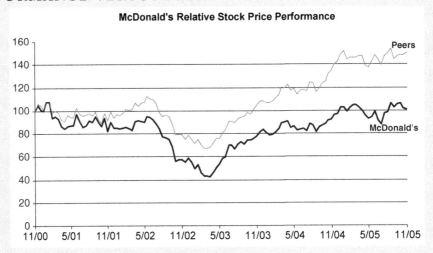

EXHIBIT C7.7 McDonald's RELATIVE VALUATION

Despite McDonald's strong real estate outlets, number-one market share position in the industry, and leading brand, McDonald's traded at a discount to peers (November 2005).

EV/EBITDA (2006 Estimates in November 2005)

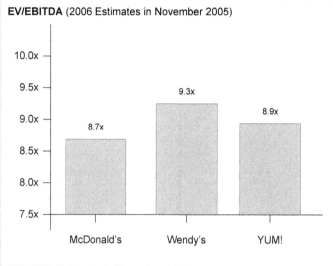

P/E (2006 Estimates in November 2005)

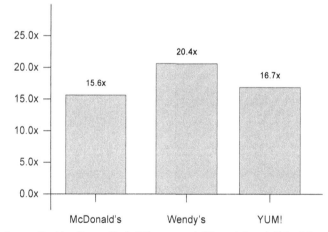

Source: Pershing Square Capital Management, "Presentation: A Value Menu for McDonald's," November 2005.

In the late 1990s, when Ackman's Gotham Partners fund held a small stake in McDonald's, he researched the topic of spinning off restaurants and real estate. In late September 2005, Ackman resumed his focus on McDonald's by acquiring call options on 4.9% of the company's stock (approximately $2 billion in value if options were exercised to acquire shares). After establishing this equity position, he met with McDonald's management and pushed for a recapitalization of the company. He indicated that the result of this recapitalization would be a share price increase of up to $15 per share, nearly a 50% boost to the stock price at that time.

Ackman viewed McDonald's as three separate entities (highlighted in Exhibit C7.8):

EXHIBIT C7.8 PERSHING'S VIEW OF McDonald's AS THREE SEPARATE ENTITIES

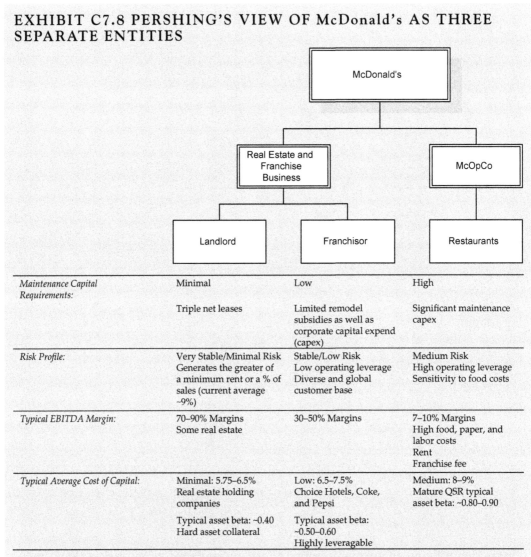

	Landlord	Franchisor	Restaurants
Maintenance Capital Requirements:	Minimal	Low	High
	Triple net leases	Limited remodel subsidies as well as corporate capital expend (capex)	Significant maintenance capex
Risk Profile:	Very Stable/Minimal Risk Generates the greater of a minimum rent or a % of sales (current average ~9%)	Stable/Low Risk Low operating leverage Diverse and global customer base	Medium Risk High operating leverage Sensitivity to food costs
Typical EBITDA Margin:	70–90% Margins Some real estate	30–50% Margins	7–10% Margins High food, paper, and labor costs Rent Franchise fee
Typical Average Cost of Capital:	Minimal: 5.75–6.5% Real estate holding companies Typical asset beta: ~0.40 Hard asset collateral	Low: 6.5–7.5% Choice Hotels, Coke, and Pepsi Typical asset beta: ~0.50–0.60 Highly leveragable	Medium: 8–9% Mature QSR typical asset beta: ~0.80–0.90

Notes: Typical margins are illustrative of restaurant EBITDA margins and assume the payment of a market rent and franchisee fee similar to a franchisee.

Typical betas are Pershing approximations based on selected companies' Barra predictive betas. Average cost of capital estimates are illustrative estimates based on average asset betas.

Source: Pershing Square Presentation, November 2005.

1. Franchising operation: representing nearly 75% of the 32,000 McDonald's restaurants
2. Restaurant operation: company restaurant ownership of remaining 25% ("McOpCo")
3. Real estate business: land ownership of roughly 37% of all restaurants and 59% of all buildings

McDonald's franchising operation received fees equivalent to 4% of individual non–company-owned restaurant unit sales. The company's real estate business received annual rent payments of 9%–10%, with higher rates outside the United States and in high-priced areas such as New York City. Both franchise fees and rent payments provided stable cash flow, which amply supported the company's debt service requirements, share repurchase program, and capital improvement program.

Ackman's proposal to McDonald's recommended a large IPO of McOpCo (the company-owned restaurant operation), which historically underperformed the franchise system average returns by a nearly 2 percentage point margin.[11] Pershing's full proposal[12] included the following provisions:

Step 1. Initiate an IPO of 65% of McOpCo—which owned about 8000 restaurants—raising $3.3 billion after taxes.
Step 2. Issue nearly $14.7 billion in debt secured against McDonald's real estate holdings.
Step 3. Use the IPO proceeds and debt proceeds to the following:
a. Refinance the existing debt of "pro forma" McDonald's, a newly organized company operating as a real estate business ("Prop Co") and a restaurant franchise business ("Fran Co") ($5 billion).
b. Repurchase 316 million shares at an estimated $40 per share($12.6 billion).
c. Fund transaction costs and related fees ($300 million).

Exhibit C7.9 through Exhibit C7.13 provide more details regarding Ackman's full proposal to McDonald's.

EXHIBIT C7.9 McOpCo IPO PROCESS

STEP 1: IPO OF 65% MCOPCO

- IPO 65% of McOpCo

- IPO generates estimated $3.27 billion of after -tax proceeds

  o Assumes a 7x EV/FY 2006E EBITDA multiple

  o Assumes $1.35 billion of net debt allocated to McOpCo

STEP 2: ISSUE DEBT AND PURSUE LEVERAGED SELF-TENDER

- Issue $14.7 billion of financing secured against pro forma McDonald's ("PF McDonald's") real estate

- Debt financing and IPO proceeds used to:

  o Refinance all of the existing $5 billion of net debt at PF McDonald's

  o Repurchase 316 million shares at $40 per share

  o Pay $300 million in fees and transaction costs

continued

[11] Jeremy Grant, "Pershing Drops Push for McDonald's Shake-Up," *Financial Times*, January 25, 2006.
[12] Pershing Square Capital Management, "Presentation: A Value Menu for McDonald's," November 2005.

EXHIBIT C7.9 MCOPCO IPO PROCESS—cont'd

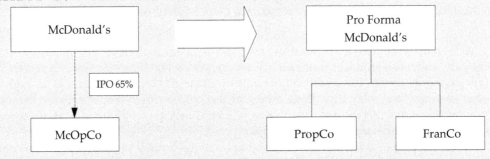

- At the time of IPO, McOpCo signs market lease and franchise agreements with PF McDonald's

- Resulting PF McDonald's is a world-class real estate and franchise business
  - o McOpCo financials deconsolidated from PF McDonald's
- Leverage is placed only on PropCo
- FranCo is unlevered, maximizing its credit rating

Source: Pershing Square Presentation, November 2005.

EXHIBIT C7.10 TRANSACTION TRANSFORMATION ESTIMATES

Improves Operating and Financial Metrics at Every Level

- Significantly improves Pro Forma (PF) McDonald's EBITDA and free cash flow margins
- Enhances return on capital and overall capital allocation for PF McDonald's
- Improves ability of PF McDonald's to pay significant ongoing dividends

	McDonald's Standalone FY 2006E	Pro Forma McDonald's FY 2006E	Typical Mature QSR
Revenue	$20,816	$7,393	
EBITDA	5,594	4,464	
EBITDA margin	26.9%	60.4%	15–20%
EBITDA—Capex	4,335	3,739	
EBITDA—Capex margin	20.8%	50.6%	7.5–12.5%
EBITDA—Maintenance capex	4,651	4,025	
EBITDA—Maintenance capex margin	22.3%	54.4%	10–15%
FCF	3,059	2,440	
FCF margin	14.7%	33.0%	5–10%

Note: Capex projections are net of proceeds obtained from store closures. Dollars in millions.
Source: Pershing Square Presentation, November 2005.

EXHIBIT C7.11 COMPARABLE COMPANIES

PF McDonald's operating metrics are much closer to those of a typical real estate C corporation or a high-branded intellectual property business such as PepsiCo or Coca-Cola than they are of a typical quick service restaurant (QSR).

	Pro Forma McDonald's	Typical Real Estate C Corp	High-Branded Intangible Property			
			Choice Hotels	PepsiCo	Coca-Cola	Typical Mature QSR[a]
2005E operating metrics:						
EBITDA margins	60%	~70–80%	66%	23%	31%	~15–20%
EBITDA—Capex margins	50%	~65–75%	61%	18%	27%	~7.5–12.5%
EPS growth	9%	NA	16%	11%	9%	~10–12%
Trading multiples:						
Adjusted enterprise value[b]						
CY 2006E EBITDA	13.0x	~13x–16x	15.1x	12.3x	12.6x	~8.5x–9.5x
CY 2006E EBITDA—Capex	15.5x	~17x–20x	16.0x	15.5x	14.2x	~12x–15x
Price						
CY 2006E EPS	21.1x	NA	24.3x	20.1x	18.8x	~15x–19x
CY 2006E FCF[c]	20.9x	~20x–25x	24.0x	20.8x	18.9x	~16x–20x
Leverage multiples:						
Net debt/EBITDA	3.4x	~5x–10x	1.7x	0.0x	NM	~0.5x–1.8x
Total debt/enterprise value	24%	~35–60%	11%	4%	4%	~7.5–20%

[a] Typical mature QSR based on YUM! Brands and Wendy's.

[b] Adjusted for unconsolidated assets.

[c] FCF denotes net income plus D&A less capex.

Notes: Stock prices as of November 11, 2005. Projections based on Wall Street estimates. Assumes PF McDonald's price of ~$47.50.

EXHIBIT C7.12A McOpCo VALUATION SUMMARY AND POTENTIAL IPO PROCEEDS

McOpCo would likely be valued at $6.0–$7.1 billion of equity market value or 6.5× to 7.5× EV/2006E EBITDA.

McOpCo Financial Summary	FY 2006E
Company-operated revenues	$15,429
Segment EBITDA, pre-G&A	1,690
EBITDA margin, pre-G&A	11.0%
Assumed G&A for McOpCo	560
Assumed G&A as % of total G&A	25.0%
EBITDA post-G&A	$1,130
EBITDA margins	7.3%
Net income	$308
EPS	$0.24

McOpCo Valuation Summary	Low	High
EV/2006E EBITDA multiple range	6.5×	7.5×
McOpCo enterprise value	$7,343	$8,472
Net debt (12/31/05)	1,350	1,350
Equity value of McOpCo	$5,993	$7,122
Ending shares outstanding	1,274	1,274
Price per share	$4.70	$5.59
Estimated after-tax IPO proceeds	$3,042	$3,497

Source: Pershing Square Presentation, November 2005.
Note: Dollars in millions, except per share data.

EXHIBIT C7.12B PF McDonald's VALUATION SUMMARY

Based on relevant publicly traded comparable companies, including several real estate holding C corporations, PF McDonald's should trade in the range of 12.5× to 13.5× EV/CY 2006E. This implies a 37%–52% premium over the recent stock price of $33.

PF McDonald's Summary Financials	FY 2006E
Franchise revenue	$2,275
Real estate revenue	5,118
Total revenue	$7,393
Franchise EBITDA, pre-G&A	$2,275
Real estate EBITDA, pre-G&A	3,869
Less: Allocated G&A	1,680
Assumed G&A as % of total G&A	75.0%
Total EBITDA	$4,464
EBITDA margins	60.4%
Net income	2,141
EPS	$2.27

PF McDonald's Valuation	Low	High
EV/2006E EBITDA multiple range	12.5×	13.5×
Enterprise value	$55,799	$60,263
Less: Net debt (12/31/05E)[a]	14,650	14,650
Plus: Remaining stake in McOpCo[b]	2,097	2,493
Equity value	$43,247	$48,106
Ending shares outstanding (12/31/05E)[c]	957.3	957.3
Price per share	$45	$50
Premium to recent price[d]	36.9%	52.3%
Implied P/FY 2006 EPS multiple	19.9×	22.2×
Implied P/FY 2006 FCF multiple[e]	19.8×	21.9×
Implied FCF/dividend yield	5.1%	4.6%
Memo: share buyback:		
Incremental debt issued		$9,685
Less transaction fees and expenses[f]		($300)
Approximate cash received from IPO, after tax		$3,270
Total funds available for repurchase		$12,654
# of shares repurchased (in millions)		316
Average price of stock purchased		$40

[a] Assumes $1.35 billion of net debt allocated to McOpCo and $5.0 billion of net debt allocated to PF McDonald's. In addition, assumes $9.7 billion of incremental leverage placed on PF McDonald's.

[b] Represents 35% of market equity value of McOpCo.

[c] Assumes incremental leverage and after-tax proceeds from McOpCo IPO (net of fees and expenses) are used to buy back approximately 316 million shares at an average price of $40.

[d] Assumes recent stock price of $33.

[e] P/FY 2006E FCF multiple adjusted for PF McDonald's 35% stake in McOpCo.

[f] Fees and expenses associated with the IPO and financing transactions.

Source: Pershing Square Presentation, November 2005.

Note: Dollars in millions, except per share data.

EXHIBIT C7.13 COMPARISON OF PRO FORMA McDonald's AND REAL ESTATE HOLDING CORPORATIONS

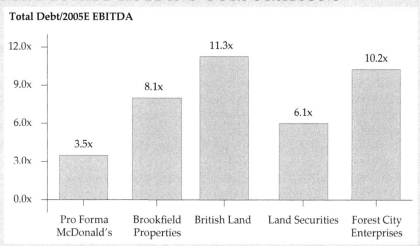

Total Debt/2005E EBITDA

A review of large REITs indicates that these businesses support investment grade ratings with a debt-to-enterprise value of 36% on average, as compared to Pro Forma McDonald's, which would have a debt-to-enterprise value of 25%.

Company Name	Total Debt/ Enterprise Value	Moody's Rating	Moody's Outlook	S&P Rating	S&P Outlook
Simon Property Group Inc.	47.2%	Baa2	Stable	BBB+	Stable
Equity Office Properties Trust	50.9%	Baa3	Stable	BBB+	Stable
Vornado Realty Trust	37.4%	Baa3	Stable	BBB+	Stable
Equity Residential	38.4%	Baa1	Stable	BBB+	Stable
Prologis	31.5%	Baa1	Stable	BBB+	Stable
Archstone-Smith Trust	33.5%	Baa1	Stable	BBB+	Stable
Boston Properties Inc.	36.0%	NR	NR	BBB+	Stable
Kimco Realty Corp.	25.2%	Baa1	Stable	A–	Stable
AvalonBay Communities Inc.	27.3%	Baa1	Stable	BBB+	Stable
Median total debt/EV	36%				
Average total debt/ EV	36%				
PF McDonald's total debt/EV	25%				

Notes: Stock prices as of 11/11/2001.
PF McDonald's EV assumes valuation multiple of 13× EV/FY 2006 EBITDA.
Total debt includes preferred.
Source: Pershing Square Presentation, November 2005.

McDonald's MANAGEMENT AND FRANCHISEES RESPOND

In late October 2005, after a Pershing team made its presentation to McDonald's management, Ackman had a follow-up meeting with the McDonald's board of directors. To help build his case, he cited precedent transactions and suggested that a restructuring would attract new dividend/income-focused investors and real estate investors. Two independent investment banking advisors for McDonald's reviewed the Pershing proposal in regard to valuation and credit impact, and the McDonald's management team analyzed friction costs (property tax revaluations, legal, financing structure) and governance/alignment issues. Although McDonald's advisors agreed with most of Pershing's views on the McOpCo IPO valuation, they disagreed with the suggestion that a recapitalization would create a new pro forma entity that would trade at a higher P/E multiple.

In November, McDonald's CFO rejected Pershing's suggestions, stating, "The proposal is an exercise in financial engineering and does not take into account McDonald's unique business model. While we remain open to ideas, we simply will not jeopardize the long-term health of our company, nor our relationships with customers, franchisees, and suppliers."[13] Management also asserted that it was focusing on enhancing shareholder value by developing plans to sell more company-owned restaurants to franchisees in underperforming markets like the United Kingdom. McDonald's CEO reiterated that the company's "unmatchable" competitive advantage was its "three-legged stool": the company, its franchisees, and its suppliers. Exhibit C7.14 highlights McDonald's rejection rationale.

EXHIBIT C7.14 RATIONALE FOR McDonald's REJECTION OF PERSHING'S PROPOSALS (2005 AND 2006)

- Valuation potential short of proposal's forecasts, not taking into account unique model
- Alignment and conflict issues would surface between parent company and franchisees
- More leverage would result in negative rating agency decision to downgrade debt, possibly increasing borrowing rates up to 150bps, which would impact franchisee borrowing costs
- Unlikely valuation multiple expansion potential
- High friction costs from IPO spinoff
- Possible higher rents and less income for franchisees
- Already returning value to shareholders via increased dividend and large share repurchases

[13] Bethany McLean, "Taking on McDonald's," *Fortune*, November 15, 2005.

A large franchisee group regarded Pershing's proposal as "injurious" to restaurant owners.[14] The head of the national group of franchisees encouraged members to ignore Ackman's plan, stating in a letter distributed in late December, "While on the surface some of the ideas he is floating might seem to benefit us, we have serious concerns regarding the long-term impact of his approach and the unintended consequences that this might have for us and our system." McDonald's CFO characterized the plan as a "threat" to the company's relationship with franchisees that would lead to "unhealthy restaurant-level cash flow" and "loss of franchisee equity." McDonald's argued that franchisees were more comfortable knowing that corporate headquarters was not only a landlord but also a knowledgeable restaurant mentor.

Ackman believed that franchisees thought he wanted to sell the real estate their restaurants sat on, resulting in their having a new landlord. In fact, he wanted McDonald's to continue to be their landlord. Prior to unveiling a revised "franchisee-friendly" proposal, Ackman spoke with more than a dozen franchisees in an effort to earn their support to put more pressure on McDonald's management. He also suggested that dropping restrictions on the number of stores each franchisee could own would make franchisees more effective at running their stores because of economies of scale. Ackman pointed out that managers at company-owned stores lacked motivation without direct equity compensation, unlike franchisees. Finally, he reminded franchisees that a more profitable pricing structure would emerge as a result of reducing the number of company-owned stores because company stores did not have to pay 3%–4% franchisee fees.

RATING AGENCY CONCERN

Credit rating agencies had significant concerns about Ackman's proposal. They felt that adding more debt to McDonald's in combination with a company-owned restaurant spinoff and a large share repurchase would result in ratings downgrades to just above high-yield/junk-bond status as a result of significant new debt service requirements. McDonald's had been rated A/Stable by Standard & Poor's and A2 by Moody's since 2003 for senior unsecured debt. A Standard & Poor's rating agency director stated, "If McDonald's leveraged up their balance sheet to do a share repurchase, their credit rating would be under great pressure. The lower the credit rating, the higher their interest rate becomes and the more expensive it becomes to finance expansion."[15] Many analysts believed that the massive amount of incremental debt recommended by Ackman's initial proposal would seriously erode earnings. An estimated 20 cents from every dollar operating profit would be used to service debt, leaving the company with less cash to invest in existing stores and for expansion.[16]

---

[14]Julie Jargon, "McD's, Ackman Lobby for Franchisee Backing," *Crain's Chicago Business*, December 1, 2005.

[15]Julie Jargon, "Ackman 101: Debt Could Squeeze Growth at McDonald's," *Crain's Chicago Business*, December 12, 2005.

[16]Julie Jargon, "Ackman 101: Debt Could Squeeze Growth at McDonald's," *Crain's Chicago Business*, December 12, 2005.

UNLOCKING McDonald's REAL ESTATE VALUE

The Pershing team valued McDonald's total real estate, including leaseholds, at $46 billion, substantially higher than its recorded book value of $30 billion ($20 billion after depreciation and amortization). The $46 billion valuation was nearly equal to the company's enterprise value of $52 billion ($46 billion market capitalization at that time plus $6 billion net debt). This implied a substantial disconnect between how investors viewed McDonald's and how Ackman viewed it. The question was whether the market was ignoring most of the company's real estate value and even its brand value by focusing instead principally on earnings.

Vornado Realty Trust, which owned nearly 90 million square feet of office and retail space principally in the Northeast, had purchased a 4.3% stake in Sears prior to its merger with Kmart and had acquired a more-than-30% stake in Toys "R" Us at the time of its buyout. Both of these acquisitions were premised on the assumption that the equity market was undervaluing the real estate component of these retailers. In an early November 2005 filing with the SEC, Vornado indicated that it had acquired a 1.2% stake in McDonald's during the third quarter of 2005 and implied that it viewed that company's real estate undervalued. Vornado had used a combination of puts and calls to obtain its stake, transacted exclusively through private negotiations during the third quarter of 2005. It asserted that, although McDonald's carried $30 billion of real estate on its books, the true worth was not being adequately recognized by the market at current terms.[17] A popular and simple method of valuing real estate is to apply a capitalization rate (cap rate) to the net operating income of the property. While cap rates vary by market, property type (residential, commercial, industrial, etc.), and economic conditions, analysts believed a 7% cap rate was appropriate for McDonald's real estate portfolio. Using this cap rate resulted in a McDonald's total real estate value (land, buildings, and leaseholds) of nearly $64 billion prior to subtracting net rent (Exhibit C7.15).[18] Although Vornado did not disclose its exact valuation view, it might not have been very different from this level.

Vornado was focused on transferring all or most of McDonald's real estate assets into an REIT (real estate investment trust), which would be required to distribute almost all unpaid earnings and profits tied to real estate. Deutsche Bank estimated that an REIT distribution would be equal to $20 billion pretax—or a nearly-$16-per-share payout after taxes (equal to 45% of McDonald's stock price in February 2006). An REIT is a publicly traded trust or corporation that pools capital from investors to buy or manage income properties and mortgages. REITs tend to trade with valuations reflecting broader market conditions and act as a liquid means of investing in real estate. They are generally not taxed on income, provided their

---

[17] Nicholas Yulico, "McDonald's REIT Could Be a Sizzler," *TheStreet.com, Inc.*, November 9, 2005.

[18] Nicholas Yulico, "McDonald's REIT Could Be a Sizzler," *TheStreet.com, Inc.*, November 9, 2005 (Lou Taylor, Deutsche Bank equity research analyst).

EXHIBIT C7.15 McDonald's REIT VALUATION ESTIMATION

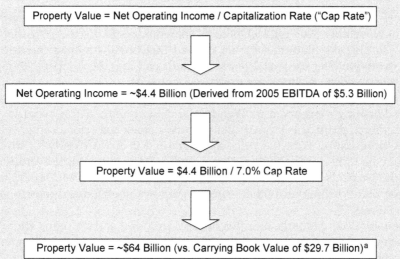

Property Value = Net Operating Income / Capitalization Rate ("Cap Rate")

Net Operating Income = ~$4.4 Billion (Derived from 2005 EBITDA of $5.3 Billion)

Property Value = $4.4 Billion / 7.0% Cap Rate

Property Value = ~$64 Billion (vs. Carrying Book Value of $29.7 Billion)[a]

Although PF McDonald's would not be configured as an REIT and would not have the tax advantages of an REIT, it would have several superior credit characteristics:

• REITs are required to pay 90% of earnings through dividends, whereas PF McDonald's would have much more credit flexibility

• PF McDonald's would have significant brand value to support its cash flows and overall credit

[a] 10-K filing for fourth quarter ending December 31, 2005. Net book value of $19.9 billion after depreciation and amortization.
The $64 billion of property value includes net rental income from franchises, which inflates property value and might not reflect true market value. Capitalization rate estimate provided by Deutsche Bank analyst Lou Taylor.
Source: Nicholas Yulico, "McDonald's REIT Could Be a Sizzler," *TheStreet.com, Inc.*, November 9, 2005.

dividend payout is at least 90% of taxable income and certain other provisions are also met. While a $20 billion special REIT dividend would attract attention and strong investor interest, a popular criticism of this new REIT formation was the likelihood of its involving significant costs from transfer taxes, property tax reassessment expenses, and capital gains taxes on particular properties. Moreover, loss of control and the future value of lease renewals tend to be top concerns for REIT transfers.

There were distinct differences in the proposals offered by Pershing and Vornado. Pershing argued that, since McDonald's company-operated restaurant business was very capital intensive and yielded low margins, part of McOpCo should be sold through an IPO. However, Pershing would keep all of McDonald's real estate and use it as a vehicle for issuing collateralized debt to fund a large share repurchase. Vornado, on the other hand, was focused on spinning off McDonald's real estate assets into an REIT and did not advocate either an IPO of McOpCo or a share repurchase.

AFTERMATH OF McDonald's REJECTION

In the week following management's rejection of Ackman's proposal, Pershing hosted a conference in November 2005 for McDonald's shareholders to discuss potential options for McDonald's. In his presentation, Ackman praised McDonald's management for its strong operational execution over the past 2 years, but indicated that the company should be doing more for its shareholders, maintaining pressure for change.

Lehman Brothers restaurant analyst Jeff Bernstein later explained, "Hedge funds were happy with Pershing's proposal to Wendy's and have reaped the benefits. Long-term holders are mixed about the impact, yet Wendy's stock was not doing well, so many should have been happy with the price appreciation. It made Wendy's further consider whatever they had previously contemplated. McDonald's has adopted and will continue to adopt certain aspects of Ackman's proposal. However, some of McDonald's stockholders are saying that Pershing and others should stop pressuring management since fundamentals are strong."[19]

In mid-January 2006, 3 months after his original proposal and 2 months after its rejection, and after speaking to more than a third of McDonald's largest investors, Ackman revised his plan based on the following key points:

- Sell off 20% of McOpCo, the company-operated franchises, in an IPO instead of the previous 65% target (tax-free benefit if stake sold is 20% or lower).
- Use the IPO funds along with existing cash balances to boost expansion of restaurants in China and Russia.
- Triple the current dividend to $2, retire all unsecured debt, and repurchase more shares than currently targeted by the company.
- Refranchise 1000 stores in mature markets over the next 2–3 years (retire lower-performing franchisees and start new ones in replacement).
- Provide more disclosure around financial performance of company-owned stores.

Basically, Ackman dropped the two most controversial parts of his previous proposal ($12.6 billion in share repurchases and $14.7 billion in new debt issuance backed by real estate), while reducing the percentage of the McOpCo IPO and increasing the company's dividend.

McDonald's quickly rejected Ackman's second proposal, asserting there was nothing "fundamentally new" about it. Ackman responded, "If something is not done to boost McDonald's share price, it could become the target of a leveraged buyout. With $50 billion in leverageable real estate and a robust commercial mortgage-backed securities market, McDonald's is going to be bought if it languishes at $30 per share."[20] He remained resolute in pushing for a McOpCo IPO to create a separate restaurant operating company, indicating that this would

---

[19] Jeff Bernstein, Lehman Brothers restaurant equity research analyst, interview with the author, December 21, 2005.

[20] Christine Richard, "Pershing Sq Scraps Debt Issuance in McDonald's Plan," *Dow Jones Newswires*, January 18, 2006.

result in greater transparency and efficiency, and an expansion in the company's P/E multiple. Exhibit C7.16 highlights quotes and outside criticisms relating to hedge fund activism and Pershing Square's McDonald's proposal.

EXHIBIT C7.16 PERSHING'S PROPOSAL—OUTSIDE CRITICISMS AND COUNTERARGUMENTS

Mr. Ackman is clearly passionate about the company and we respect that. We also appreciate his candor in acknowledging that his previous ideas presented publicly were not workable. But the fact is, with his latest presentation, he has not presented anything fundamentally new beyond what we've discussed with him previously and what we have evaluated. Ackman's proposal will not deliver the value already being created by our current strategy.[21] *Mary Kay Shaw, vice president of investor relations, McDonald's.*

The typical hedge fund manager's idea of long-term planning is figuring out where to have dinner tonight. Their strategy is to buy stock in a company whose assets—such as real estate or cash—aren't reflected in the price of the stock, and browbeat management until they force the sale of those assets, with proceeds distributed to them and other shareholders. Then they grab their money, and move on to their next quarry.[22] *Dan Miller, Chicago Sun-Times (regarding Pershing/McDonald's).*

Ackman was off-base in arguing that McDonald's has been a "slacker." In fact, the company's U.S. operations are the envy of the industry. After all, franchisees want to see the company put their own skin in the game first.[23] Peter Oakes and Scott Waltmann, Piper Jaffray analysts.

The company is going to get to these [earnings] levels by themselves regardless of the push Ackman is putting on. In the end it's going to be a slow process...I'm OK with that as a shareholder because I think we get to the same place eventually.[24] *Herb Achey, U.S. Trust.*

By creating a separate restaurant company, you may create some kind of diametrically opposing forces that in the long run could be detrimental, not beneficial, to shareholders.[25] *Scott Rothbort, LakeView Asset Management.*

If McDonald's leveraged up their balance sheet to do a share repurchase, their credit rating would be under great pressure. The lower the credit rating, the higher their interest rate becomes and the more expensive it becomes to finance expansion.[26] *A Standard & Poor's Director.*

We think the greatest long-term risk of a McOpCo spinoff is its potential damage to franchise-company relations. With its current ownership of 2,000 *U.S.* stores, McDonald's communicates to franchisees its focus on the bottom line and not just sales. Conversely, by not having any involvement in restaurant operations as the proposal suggests, McDonald's would likely tarnish the franchisees' trust of the company. Overall, spinoff would threaten the three-legged stool.[27] *Mark Wiltamuth & Dana Greenberg, Morgan Stanley.*

On the surface, there is a lot of merit to the argument. Ackman's view is that the market is misvaluing the company and I'm inclined to agree with him. The guy has got very good arguments, and I think the company owes its shareholders a reasoned response.[28] *Leon Cooperman, Omega Advisors.*

[21] McDonald's press release, January 18, 2006.
[22] Dan Miller, "Greedy Mac Attack Bad for Business," Chicago Sun-Times, December 2, 2005.
[23] Nichola Groom, "McDonald's Investors Unswayed by Activist Proposal," Reuters, January 19, 2006.
[24] Nichola Groom, "McDonald's Investors Unswayed by Activist Proposal," Reuters, January 19, 2006..
[25] Deepak Gopinath, "Hedge Fund Rabble-Rouser," Bloomberg Markets, October 2005.
[26] Jargon, "Ackman 101."
[27] Mark Wiltamuth and Dana Greenberg, Morgan Stanley Equity Research North America, November 1, 2005.
[28] "McDonald's Rejects Shareholder Plan to Restructure," Reuters, January 18, 2006.

THE TRUCE

During a year-end earnings conference call in late January 2006, McDonald's CEO said, "The system is a bastion of credibility for a company that is, at its core, a franchising operation. Abandoning it or restructuring it—as hedge-fund activist William Ackman has proposed recently—is out of the question." However, notwithstanding this strong statement, the CEO announced that McDonald's would shift some underperforming stores to more profit-focused owners by selling nearly 1500 company-owned stores in 15–20 countries to "development license ownership" over the next 3 years, including 800 stores in the United Kingdom. The CEO also committed to providing better information comparing the performance of company-operated restaurants and franchised restaurants. The day following McDonald's agreement to sell underperforming company-owned restaurants and to provide better financial transparency, Ackman dropped his activist campaign, stating, "We are supporting McDonald's because they're doing the right thing. They've pretty much given us everything we wanted. The only thing we didn't get, which we felt would have given more instant value, would've been a true separation for McOpCo" (the IPO).[29] Exhibit C7.17 contrasts the cash payout differences between Pershing's two proposals and McDonald's management's final decision.

EXHIBIT C7.17 DIFFERENCES BETWEEN PERSHING SQUARE'S PROPOSAL AND McDonald's MANAGEMENT'S PLAN ($ IN BILLIONS)

	Pershing Proposal (September 2005)	Pershing Revised Proposal (January 2006)	McDonald's Management's Plan
Dividends	Unspecified	$1.7	$5–6 total dividends and share repurchases payout in 2006 and 2007[a]
Share repurchases	$12.6	Unspecified	
IPO proceeds (posttax)	$3.3	$1.3	None
Secured debt issue	$14.7	None	None
Debt reduction	$5.0	None	None
Transaction fees	$0.3	Unspecified (less than $0.3)	Minor amount for refranchising

[a] *2005 payout was dividends of $850 million and repurchases of $1.2 billion ($2.05 billion total).*

RETROSPECTIVE

In November 2005, when asked about the likelihood of Pershing's proposal actually being executed by McDonald's, Ackman responded, "I'm the most persistent person, especially when I believe I'm right. I don't think this will have to be taken to a proxy contest. It's an

[29] Nicholas Yulico, "McDonald's Placates Pershing," *TheStreet.com, Inc.*, January 25, 2006.

intellectual contest. We have the ability to share our ideas." Pershing's option on up to 4.9% of the company's stock represented the second largest shareholding in McDonald's after Dodge & Cox at 5.5%. The top 10 stakeholders combined, excluding Pershing, accounted for 30% of outstanding shares. Vornado and Pershing combined represented slightly more than 6% of shares; however, their full level of backing by other investors, whether hedge or mutual funds, was not publicly determinable.

In December, Ackman explained, "If businesses are undervalued and if there are simple things to do, the shareholder base becomes more perceptive. McDonald's had done nothing in 5 years and Wendy's had not done much prior to the summer. We convinced Wendy's to restructure and the stock is up $17 in the last few months since Pershing stepped in. McDonald's management was more willing to discuss our thoughts and we will see how that turns out."

Ackman went on, "We do our homework to find a deep discount between price paid and actual value. Our approach is to talk to management first without going public." Pershing considered only public companies because Ackman believed it took different skill sets to invest in private and public companies. He added, "Pershing focuses on high-quality businesses, and so if you are wrong on timing, you can still make up for it on attractive quality as the company becomes more valuable with each day that passes." Wendy's stock was up 55% since Pershing first established its equity position; however, McDonald's stock was up to only 20%. Ackman still believed that his original transformational strategic plan for McDonald's would push the share price to $45–50 per share, a 37–52% premium to the stock price at the time of his initial proposal.

Separately, two of the most anticipated IPOs of early 2006 included Chipotle (McDonald's stake) and Tim Hortons (Wendy's stake). The Chipotle IPO broke the 5-year largest opening day gain record when it was launched during January 2006, doubling on the first day of the offering, and Tim Hortons IPO traded up 42% during its opening day in late March 2006.

Porsche, Volkswagen, and CSX: Cars, Trains, and Derivatives

Family members knew something was very wrong when Adolf Merckle, who had guided the family holding company, VEM Vermögensverwaltung GmbH, through successful investments in dozens of firms in industries from pharmaceutical drugs to cement, left the house one afternoon in January 2009 and failed to return. That night their fears were confirmed when a German railway worker located Merckle's body near a commuter train line near his hometown of Blaubeuren, about a 100 miles west of Munich.

It was no secret that the financial crisis had taken a toll on Merckle's investments following his frank comments to the media in 2008. Merckle, known in Germany as a savvy investor, had lost hundreds of millions of Euros after being caught on the wrong side of a short squeeze of epic proportions. In a short squeeze, investors who are shorting a company's stock, or betting against the rise in its price, are forced into the market to buy back stock to cover their short position if the price unexpectedly increases. Merckle's misplaced bet against Volkswagen's stock had been one significant cost among several that eventually led to talks between the Merckle family and thirty creditors about the viability of VEM.

USING DERIVATIVES TO OBTAIN CONTROL POSITIONS

Volkswagen Equity Derivatives

Merckle's was not the only large bet against Volkswagen's stock. A number of hedge funds, including Greenlight Capital, SAC Capital, Glenview Capital, Tiger Asia, and Perry Capital, lost billions of Euros in a few hours based on their large short positions in Volkswagen's stock following the news on October 26, 2008, that Porsche AG had obtained a large long synthetic position in Volkswagen stock through cash-settled options. Porsche's news release that day showed it had a 74.1% equity position in Volkswagen, a combination of its known ownership of 42.6% of Volkswagen stock and cash-settled options on shares representing an additional 31.5% of the company. The funds and other investors quickly realized that, factoring in the nonborrowable 20% ownership held by the German state of Lower Saxony, just 5.9% of Volkswagen shares remained on the market for short sellers to buy to cover their short positions. In the next 2 days, this short squeeze produced a fivefold increase in Volkswagen's share price, as demand for shares from hedge funds exceeded the supply of borrowable shares. In addition, there was upside pressure on Volkswagen's share price because the company's stock was included in the DAX Index (a capitalization-weighted index), and as the share price increased, index funds were required to purchase more stock.

Porsche's effort to obtain majority control over Volkswagen through derivative contracts created one of the most dramatic run-ups in a large company's share price in history. The result of this shrewd strategy on the part of Porsche's CFO, Holger Härter, was gaining control over Volkswagen without allowing hedge funds and other third parties to drive the price upward. The consequence of this strategy was major losses at hedge funds that had shorted Volkswagen's stock.

CSX Equity Derivatives

A similar situation had taken place overseas just a few months previously. During the summer of 2008 a court ruled that two UK-based hedge funds, The Children's Investment Fund Management (TCI) and 3G Capital Partners (3G), had been illegally plotting a bid for control of American railroad company CSX Corporation without disclosing their intentions. Another court ruled that TCI and 3G violated Securities and Exchange Commission (SEC) disclosure requirements by disguising their takeover intentions regarding CSX when they entered into equity derivatives called total return swaps (TRS) with multiple investment banks.[1] TRS are agreements in which one party makes interest payments based on a set rate—fixed or variable—while the other party makes payments based on the return of an underlying asset, which includes both the income it generates and any capital gains or losses. Regulation 13D requirements mandated that stock ownership of greater than 5% must be disclosed, but the hedge funds took the position that equity swaps did not give them beneficial control over shares, and so there was no disclosure obligation. The ruling against the hedge funds moved equity swaps into new territory. Equity swaps are a form of "synthetic shares," which endow the holder with the economic benefits of share ownership without the voting rights.

However, it was not a total victory for CSX. Although the hedge funds had their hands slapped for the disclosure violations, they ultimately prevailed in obtaining seats on CSX's board. The court acknowledged it was too late to reverse the funds' actions, as it was prohibited from denying shareholders the right to vote for a new board of directors. Though the court battle carried on into the fall, a federal appeals judge ultimately granted TCI and 3G a total of four seats, replacing two CSX-backed directors with dissident nominees, including TCI's Christopher Hohn.[2]

While many US companies had already expanded the definition of equity ownership to include anyone who held derivatives on a company's stock, this ruling forced the SEC to regulate the meaning of ownership more stringently under American law.

---

[1] The court held that the two hedge funds had violated provisions of Section 13(d) of the Securities Exchange Act of 1934 and Rule 13d-3(b) by using cash-settled swap transactions in a way that, given the circumstances, improperly evaded disclosure obligations related to the formation of a group "beneficial owner."

[2] "CSX Accedes Seats to Dissidents," *Directorship*, September 17, 2008. http://www.directorship.com/csx-fills-board.

These two stories demonstrate the rapidly increasing importance of equity derivatives such as cash-settled options and equity swaps. Porsche and the hedge funds had used equity derivatives for similar control purposes but ended up with dramatically different results. Porsche's use of these instruments in its pursuit of ownership in Volkswagen resulted in a significant swing in market capitalization and huge losses for short-selling hedge funds, while TCI and 3G's pursuit of ownership in CSX resulted in legal wrangling and condemnation by a US federal judge, as well as an increase in the hedge funds' control when they were granted seats on the company's board.

Comparing the two stories provides a framework for comprehending the uses of equity derivatives; assessing the growing regulatory, economic, and legal risks associated with these instruments; and learning valuable lessons regarding their use as a vehicle to achieve beneficial ownership of a company's stock. This analysis provokes the following questions: Should there always be public disclosure of equity derivatives? Should CEOs actively consider using derivative contracts? Are investment banks complicit, or just doing their jobs for clients, when they act as counterparties to derivative contracts? Are hedge funds playing fair in their use of equity derivatives? How can hedge funds get burned by equity derivatives? Should regulators make derivative disclosure requirements absolute?

CSX COLLIDES WITH TCI AND 3G

Background

CSX Corporation—a Jacksonville-based rail and transport conglomerate—was a descendant of Chessie Systems, which started in 1836 and owned such famous rail lines as the Chesapeake and Ohio and Baltimore and Ohio railroads. CSX was the result of Chessie's 1980 merger with Seaboard Coast Line Industries (formed in 1958), and a flurry of mergers and divestments that cumulatively added line capacity in addition to terminal and switching operations. Through its coal business, CSX delivered about 1.9 million carloads of coal, coke, and iron ore to electric utilities and manufacturers in 2007. Almost 100% of revenue came from its rail and intermodal businesses.

CSX primarily operated in North American nerve centers via its principal operating company, CSX Transportation (CSXT), which delivered merchandise, coal, and automobiles via its approximately 21,000-route-mile rail network. CSXT was one of the largest railroads in the eastern United States, serving thousands of production and distribution facilities through track connections to more than 230 short-line and regional railroads in 23 states.[3] Michael Ward, CEO of CSX, was widely hailed as an innovator and leader in the transport segment, delivering returns far exceeding the S&P during the 5 years prior to the recent economic downturn. In addition, *Railway Age* named him Railroader of the Year in 2008.

Since 2003, when money manager Christopher Hohn founded the TCI hedge fund with $3 billion initially under management, TCI had taken public stances against management at

---

[3] CSX Company Report, Datamonitor 2008.

Deutsche Börse, ABN Amro, and South Korean cigarette maker KT&G. Its activist approach paid off in 2005 when it led a successful movement to oust the leadership of German stock exchange operator Deutsche Börse. An activist strategy did not work in 2007, however, when the Japanese government forced TCI to unwind its position in the electric utility JPower on national security grounds. The forced sale resulted in a ¥12.5 billion ($127.3 million) loss for the fund.

Hohn first gained recognition as a money manager for hedge fund Perry Capital in London, where he had overseen European investments. Since starting TCI, he posted strong results, predominantly by one-off, large-scale trades in European and Asian equities. In 2006, when the S&P Hedge Fund Index rose just 3.9%, TCI's returns topped 40% and won the fund a top award from EuroHedge, a London newsletter that ranked Europe's best-performing hedge funds. Yet Hohn had some "rough edges," according to acolytes and detractors alike.[4] He was known for a demanding style, combative emails to target companies, and a staccato, bullying way of speech.

3G Capital had been cofounded in 2004 by Pavel Begun and Corey Bailey to be a long term–oriented fund with no more than 10 investment positions. The name derived from the three Gs in their firm-wide objective: to invest in good business, run by good management, and available at a good price.

TCI and 3G Take a Position

2007 ended with TCI and 3G actively calling for change at CSX, pushing for the railroad to improve performance by changing senior management, including separating the chairman and chief executive roles, both held by Michael Ward. They also sought to add five independent directors to its board and link management compensation to performance. In response, CSX stated that it was the only major railroad that already had 100% performance-based annual and long-term incentive plans.[5]

In February 2008, CSX wrote to TCI, calling the investor's interest in pushing change "not in good corporate governance, but in achieving effective control of the company." CSX had amended its bylaws to provide that a special meeting would be called only after the company received a written request from shareholders representing at least 15% of its voting power.

The following month CSX filed a lawsuit against TCI and 3G, alleging a violation of Regulation 13D of the Securities and Exchange Act, which requires disclosure for ownership positions greater than 5% of a target company. CSX had learned the hedge funds had initially entered into TRS with eight counterparties, which in aggregate gave TCI and 3G economic upside on a position of more than 14% of CSX's shares, with a notional value of more than $2.5 billion at the time. It was alleged that "most if not all" of the TRS counterparties accumulated an equivalent position in CSX shares to hedge these positions. See Exhibit C8.1 for a chronology of the lawsuit.

---

[4] Laura Cohn, "A Little Fund With Big Demands," *BusinessWeek*, May 23, 2005. http://www.businessweek.com/magazine/content/05_21/b3934161_mz035.htm.

[5] Performance-based earnings exclude time-based stock options and restricted stock.

EXHIBIT C8.1 CHRONOLOGY OF CSX PROXY FIGHT WITH TCI/3G

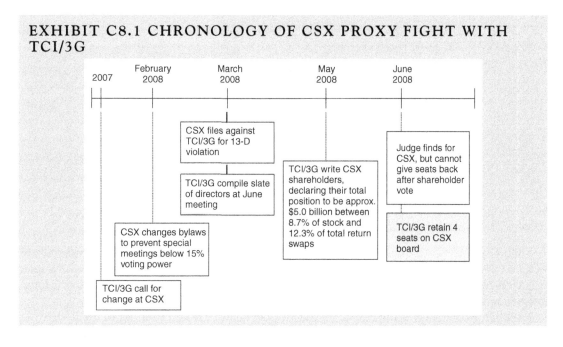

TCI and 3G, meanwhile, formed a group to nominate a slate of directors to stand for election at the CSX annual meeting in June 2008. Later in May, the two investors went on the offensive with CSX shareholders, writing that the funds had increased their position to a 21% interest in the company based on a $2.0 billion share holding (8.7% of CSX stock) combined with a notional value of $2.8 billion in TRS on the company's stock (12.3% of CSX stock).[6] The funds' stated goal was to persuade shareholders to vote the slate of candidates proposed by the funds onto the company board at the next election and accept the funds' recommendations (which they said could help CSX achieve $2.2 billion in annual productivity gains within 5 years).[7]

In the CSX TRS, the underlying asset, or reference asset, was CSX common shares owned by the party receiving the set rate payment.[8] For the period of the transaction, the TRS receiver of reference asset returns had a synthetic long position in the market risk of the reference asset.

In the CSX TRS, TCI and 3G made interest payments to eight investment banks, which made payments back to the hedge funds based on the returns of CSX shares. A key benefit of the TRS for TCI and 3G was that they gained equity exposure to CSX without actually owning the shares that underlined the TRS. Hedge funds preferred these swaps because they got the benefit of a large exposure with a minimal cash outlay and, until the 2008 court ruling, without a legal requirement to disclose their position. See Exhibit C8.2 for a diagram of the CSX TRS.

---

[6] Dan Slater, "Judge Kaplan Reprimands Hedge Funds in Takeover Battle with CSX," June 12, 2008. http://blogs.wsj.com/law/2008/06/12/judge-kaplan-reprimands-hedge-funds-in-takeover-battle-with-csx.

[7] Lisa LaMotta, "CSX Tells Activists To Get Off The Tracks," *Forbes.com*, May 20, 2008. http://www.forbes.com/equities/2008/05/ 20/csx-tci-update-markets-equities-cx_lal_0520markets41.html.

[8] Barron's Dictionary of Financial Terms.

EXHIBIT C8.2 CSX TRANSACTION DIAGRAM

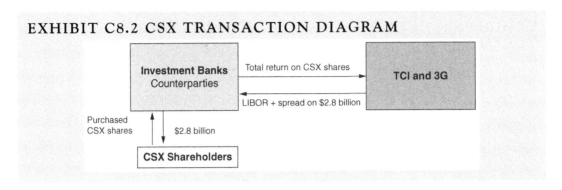

PORSCHE AND VOLKSWAGEN: BROTHERS REUNITED

Following on the American court ruling in 2008 that begrudgingly granted board seats to TCI and 3G, Porsche's strategic use of equity derivatives to gain ownership of Volkswagen was well-received in Germany. Of course, this warm perception was partially due to the long, interwoven history of the firms there.

Ferdinand Porsche was the creator of the VW Beetle in 1931 and founder of the luxury car manufacturer Porsche. The Porsche 64, the company's first product, was built with many of the same components as the Beetle. Ferdinand Porsche was also the grandfather to the board chairmen of both Porsche and Volkswagen.

Porsche primarily made a line of luxury automobiles, including the famous 911, Boxster, and more modern Cayenne SUV, among others. It produced approximately 100,000 cars a year.

Volkswagen, in contrast, made more than 6 million cars a year for major markets in Europe, the Americas, Asia/Pacific, and Africa. Its stable of brands ranged from the middle-market proprietary brand and family-oriented Scania to Audi, Lamborghini, and Bentley.

In recent years, German politicians had begun publicly vilifying foreign investors (who had bought more than 5000 German firms since 1990) and clamoring for more domestic ownership. In 2005, Porsche's CEO, Wendelin Wiedeking, announced the company's intention to purchase 20% of Volkswagen stock to support a "German solution" to the takeover dilemma, matching the 20% held by the state of Lower Saxony.[9] The company increased its holding to 30% in 2007, prompting German legislators to change securities laws, which put pressure on Porsche to make a tender offer. Its hand forced, Porsche publicly disclaimed its interest in majority control and offered the legal minimum for additional shares in Volkswagen, leading to a meager 0.6% increase in its ownership. See Exhibit C8.3 for a chronology of Porsche's position in Volkswagen.

[9] Mike Esterl et al., "As Giant Rivals Stall, Porsche Engineers a Financial Windfall," *Wall Street Journal.com*, November 10, 2008. http://online.wsj.com/article/SB122610533132510217.html.

EXHIBIT C8.3 CHRONOLOGY OF PORSCHE POSITION IN VOLKSWAGEN

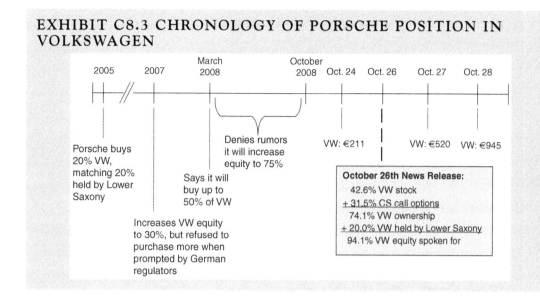

Suddenly, Porsche changed course. Less than a year after its public refusal to ratchet up its ownership in Volkswagen, in March 2008 Porsche's board backed the CEO's goal to increase its net position in Volkswagen up to 50%. Between March and October, Wiedeking and other Porsche officials denied rumors that Porsche would take this position up to 75%.

On Friday, October 24, 2008, Volkswagen's share price closed at €211.

On October 26, Porsche dropped a bombshell, disclosing in a news release that it had obtained 42.6% in Volkswagen equities and cash-settled options accounting for an additional 31.5% of the company. The news meant just 5.9% of Volkswagen equities remained in circulation after considering Lower Saxony's position of 20%, creating a perfect condition for a short squeeze.

By October 28, the price of Volkswagen shares exceeded €1000 ($1125) in intraday trading, creating a total market capitalization of €324 billion ($364 billion) and making it temporarily the most valuable company in the world (see Exhibit C8.4). By entering into option contracts with investment banks before the disclosure was made, Porsche made purchase of Volkswagen shares by others very difficult.

Many hedge funds had entered pairs trades involving Volkswagen stock prior to Porsche's disclosure. They were long Volkswagen preferred shares and short Volkswagen common shares. In addition, many funds were also long Porsche common stock and short Volkswagen common shares.

The hedge funds found themselves in a short squeeze of epic proportions following Porsche's disclosure. To cover their short position, the funds scrambled to purchase Volkswagen shares, bidding up the share price to previously unimaginable levels. The upside share price pressure was exacerbated by index funds that purchased Volkswagen shares to maintain proper

EXHIBIT C8.4 VOLKSWAGEN'S SHARE PRICE

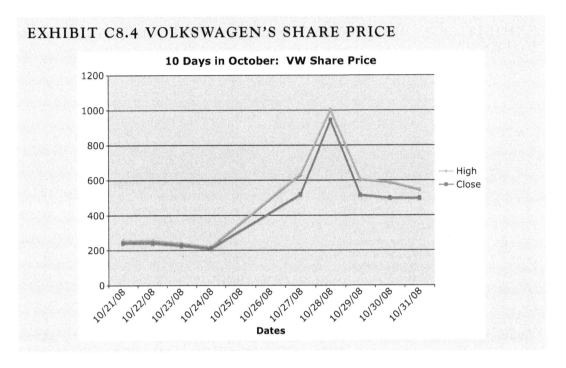

weighting in the DAX Index, as Volkswagen's share of the index grew with the rising share price. The result of this enormous demand was a fivefold increase in Volkswagen's share price and an estimated $15 billion loss for hedge funds that had entered into the pairs trades.

Cash-Settled Options

Cash-settled options are option contracts in which settlement is completed by paying cash equal to the difference between the market value and the contractual value of the underlying security at the time of exercise or expiration. This compares to physically settled options in which actual physical delivery of the underlying security is required.

The cash-settled options on Volkswagen's stock into which Porsche entered were call spread options, which gave Porsche the right to receive a predetermined maximum cash payment if Volkswagen's share price increased during the option period. See Exhibits C8.5 and C8.6. The purchase of cash-settled options on Volkswagen stock by Porsche gave Porsche the right to receive a future payment of cash based on the amount by which Volkswagen's share price exceeded the options' lower strike price on the earlier of the date of exercise or maturity. The cash payment was limited by a cap determined prior to initiation, which was set at the higher strike price. The higher the cap, the higher the cost of the option premium. Investment banks hedged their cash payment exposure by buying a "delta" number of Volkswagen shares, depending on the probability of the shares exceeding the strike price.

EXHIBIT C8.6 CASH-SETTLED OPTIONS: PORSCHE AND INVESTMENT BANKS

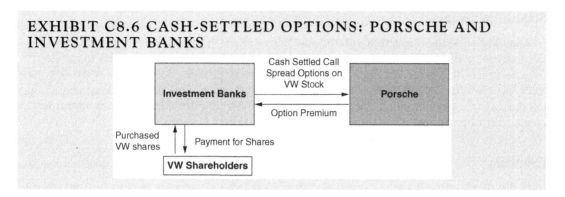

EXHIBIT C8.5 CASH-SETTLED OPTIONS

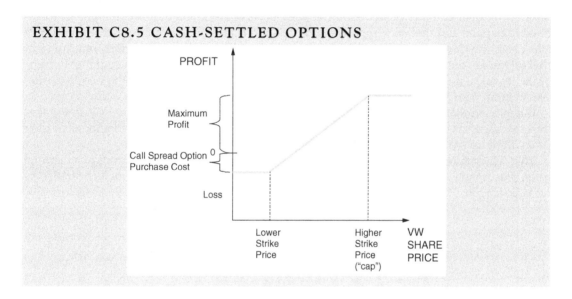

Porsche began purchasing cash-settled options tied to Volkswagen stock in 2005, when the share price was less than €100. If the price rose, Porsche could exercise the options and receive the difference between the lower strike price and the higher market price (creating a cap on the cash received). It could then use the cash to buy Volkswagen shares. Alternatively, Porsche could request that its investment banking counterparties deliver the shares to Porsche based on a value equal to the cash settlement value of the options when exercised (although the banks could decline to alter the contract in this way).

German law did not require an investor to disclose ownership of any size holding of cash-settled options, allowing Porsche to build a large stake in Volkswagen while keeping the rest of the market unaware of this activity.

Banks that were counterparties to Porsche hedged their exposure by holding actual Volkswagen shares, removing them from circulation.

Stealth by Swaps

As with the hedge funds that entered into TRS in their bid for influence at CSX, Porsche's derivatives created a synthetic form of ownership. In both cases, counterparties to the derivatives contracts held common shares as a hedge while the paying party for the derivative contract assumed the economic risks and benefits of ownership. This form of silent acquisition via derivatives was becoming more common as both companies and investors attempted to create control positions in corporate shares while avoiding disclosure.

Dilemma

In the aftermath of Porsche's effort to control Volkswagen, German politicians initially dismissed calls for a public inquiry into Porsche's strategic use of the cash-settled options to skirt disclosure. Their comments seconded the view of most Germans that this merger was destined to happen and that no sympathy for hedge funds and their mounting losses should be felt. Later, the German securities regulator Bundesanstalt für Finanzdienstleistungsaufsicht (BaFin) found "there was no evidence of wrongdoing."[10] Even if BaFin had found that Porsche broke its rules, it could have imposed fines of no more than €200,000 for the nondisclosure and €1 million for violating the mandatory bid rule.

It appeared that Porsche's CEO had made a careful and smart calculation, assuming that the costs were far outweighed by the benefits of his strategy—much like TCI and 3G in their proxy fight for seats on the board at CSX.

That was before January 5, 2009, when Adolf Merckle threw himself in front of a German train, presumably distraught by the extreme losses his firm had suffered from its bearish bets on Volkswagen.

---

[10] Chris Reiter, "Porsche May Delay VW Stake Increase as Debts Mount," *Bloomberg.com*, March 31, 2009. http://www.bloomberg.com/apps/news?pid=newsarchive&sid=aI48e1cKDQog.

The Toys "R" Us LBO

"I don't want to grow up, I'm a Toys 'R' Us kid" was the famous marketing slogan of Toys "R" Us (the "Company"), the world's leading specialty toy retailer for much of the 1980s and 1990s. Private equity industry veterans may have had a similar attitude regarding the maturation of their industry. In its infancy, the industry had consisted of relatively few firms and lucrative investing opportunities that far exceeded capital in the industry. By 2005, however, a record amount of capital had been committed to the industry and aggregate transaction values had reached a new high. The industry had become intensely competitive and the best investing opportunities were being chased by too much capital, making it difficult for investors to match historically lofty returns. While private equity executives would have preferred that the industry not grow up, they continued to find investment opportunities that provided compelling value to themselves and their limited partners.

In 2006 $252 billion of capital was committed to the private equity industry, compared to $90 billion in 2000—an absolute increase of 181% (Exhibit C9.1). As the amount of committed capital increased, so did the need for more investment opportunities. In 2006 there was more than $233 billion of aggregate transaction value in private equity deals, compared to $41 billion in 2000—an absolute increase of 475% (Exhibit C9.2). An increasing supply/demand imbalance led to an increase in the average purchase price multiple in leveraged buyouts (LBOs), which reached a record high of 8.6× EBITDA in 2006 (Exhibit C9.3).

CASE FOCUS

This case simulates the experience of a private equity investor evaluating a potential investment. It requires the reader to (1) determine the risks and merits of an investment in Toys "R" Us, (2) evaluate the spectrum of returns using multiple operating model scenarios, and (3) identify strategic actions that might be undertaken to improve the risk/return profile of the investment. The case discusses the participants in the Toys "R" Us LBO and emerging trends in the private equity industry.

EMERGENCE OF CLUB DEALS IN A MATURING INDUSTRY

In the past, the largest private equity funds were able to minimize competition with smaller funds because of the distinct advantage their fund size provided. As of November 2004, the largest single private equity fund, raised for JP Morgan's Global 2001 Fund, was approximately $6.5 billion.[1] That amount would be greatly overshadowed by the capital raised by private equity firms just a few years later, however. As of January 2007, for example, both Kohlberg Kravis & Roberts (KKR) and Blackstone had raised single private equity funds with

---

[1] "The New Kings of Capitalism," *The Economist*, November 25, 2004.

EXHIBIT C9.1 US PRIVATE EQUITY COMMITTED CAPITAL ($ IN BILLIONS)

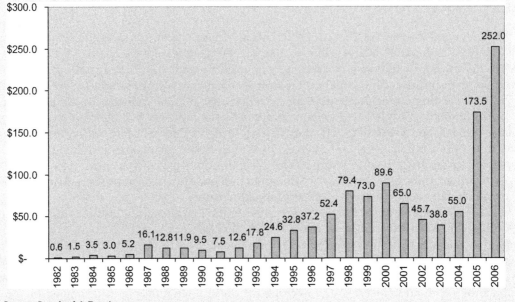

Source: Standard & Poor's.

EXHIBIT C9.2 VALUE OF LEVERAGED BUYOUT TRANSACTIONS ($ IN BILLIONS)

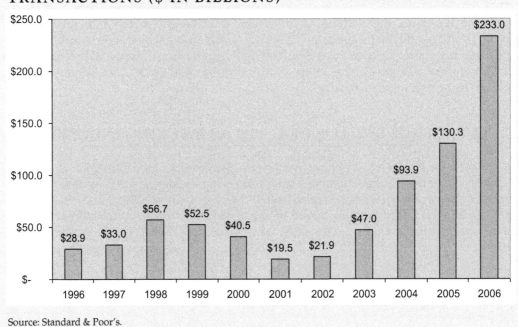

Source: Standard & Poor's.

EXHIBIT C9.3 BUYOUT ACQUISITION MULTIPLE

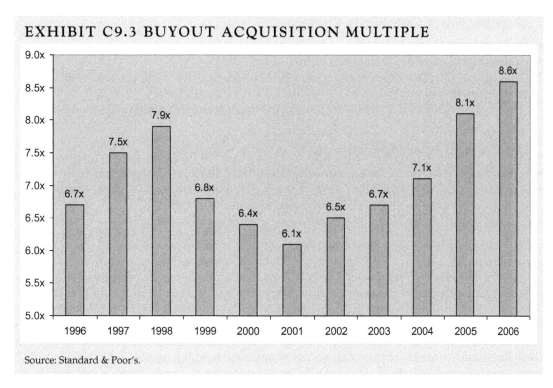

Source: Standard & Poor's.

approximately $16.0 billion of committed capital.[2] JP Morgan's Global 2001 Fund would not rank in the top 10 largest funds raised as of January 2007.[3]

Historically, private equity firms preferred to complete acquisitions without other financial partners to ensure complete control over acquired companies. In an industry that required a precise strategy to create value, partnering issues (e.g., agreeing on strategic decisions, capital structure, and investment exits) could prove problematic. However, as the asset class grew and competition for traditional private equity transactions increased, private equity firms turned to club deals.

A club deal was an acquisition completed by two or more private equity firms that allowed them to acquire companies that were too large for one private equity firm to acquire. Many funds set concentration limits on the percentage of committed capital that could be invested in a single asset. Club deals expanded the universe of potential acquisitions by bringing together the capital of multiple firms, enabling very large acquisitions. By allowing large private equity firms to target companies beyond the reach of smaller private equity firms, club deals reduced competition and increased potential returns.

Although there was competition between consortia—for example, more than one club chasing an asset—this competition was below the level observed in the traditional small/middle private equity market. Chasing bigger assets through club deals allowed the largest funds to more efficiently allocate their time (the industry's most precious resource) as they put money to work.

[2] "The Uneasy Crown," *The Economist*, February 8, 2007.

[3] "The Uneasy Crown," *The Economist*, February 8, 2007.

Club deals offered the following advantages:

- Limited competition
- Allowed for greater deployment of capital
- Leveraged multiple sources of expertise while conducting due diligence and evaluating an investment
- Spread expenses incurred while evaluating the investment and reduced "busted" deal costs

Disadvantages included the following:

- Limited ability to control an investment—potential for strategic disagreements
- Interfered with limited partners' desire for risk diversification because they became owners of the same asset through participation in multiple funds
- Created potential regulatory issues regarding anticompetitive behavior

Specific charges included submitting separate bids to gauge a competitive price with an agreement to "club up" in the future and "clubbing up" at the beginning of a process to reduce the field of potential buyers. In October 2006 the Department of Justice began an inquiry into potential anticompetitive behavior by private equity firms. Justice Department officials sent letters requesting information on deals and auctions to Kohlberg, Kravis & Roberts, Silver Lake Partners, and other firms.[4]

According to *Buyouts* magazine, of the 845 private equity deals completed in 2005, 125 were club deals, meaning that private equity shops were teaming up nearly 15% of the time.[5] Recent high-profile club deals included SunGard Data Systems, Hertz Corporation, and HCA. Barring a major change in the regulatory environment or problems in existing club deals, club deal activity was likely to continue to increase.

DIVIDENDS AND FEES PAID TO PRIVATE EQUITY FIRMS

Another trend that was gaining popularity in the private equity industry involved rapidly accessing the capital markets after closing a deal to raise cash to pay a large dividend to the private equity owners. Firms typically used the debt markets to finance these dividends, creating more highly levered, riskier companies. In some cases, dividends paid to private equity firms within 1 year of their original investment equaled the original equity commitment. In the Hertz LBO transaction, Clayton, Dubilier & Rice, Carlyle Group, and Merrill Lynch collected $1 billion in bank-funded dividends 6 months after buying rental car company Hertz for $15 billion.[6] About 4 months later, Hertz issued an initial public offering to pay off the debt and to fund an additional dividend, resulting in total dividends paid to the owners that equaled 54% of their original investment of $2.3 billion (still leaving them with 71% ownership).

[4] "Justice Department Probing Buyout Funds," *MSNBC.com*, October 10, 2006.

[5] Mark L. Mandel, "Wielding a Club," *New York Law Journal*, June 29, 2006.

[6] "Gluttons at the Gate," *BusinessWeek*, October 30, 2006.

Private equity funds also took cash out of their portfolio companies to pay large "advisory" fees to themselves. These fees exceeded $50 million on large transactions during the buyout phase and annual fees often continued throughout their ownership.

US RETAIL TOY INDUSTRY IN 2005

In 2005 sales in the US retail toy industry totaled $21.3 billion, down 4% from $22.1 billion in 2004.[7] While some categories—plush, vehicles, and games and puzzles—had large declines in sales in 2005, there was growth in certain subcategories. It is difficult to track consistent data across multiple sources as category and subcategory definitions varied. However, it is important to note that, in aggregate, dollar sales in the industry declined for a third consecutive year. See Exhibit C9.4 for growth by category.

Video game sales continued to outperform traditional toy sales in 2005 as younger children increasingly chose video games over traditional toys. In addition, the video game market benefited from the increased acceptance of video gaming among adults. In 2004 the average video game player was 29 years old.[8] Video game sales were expected to continue to outperform the traditional toy market.

EXHIBIT C9.4 US RETAIL TOY INDUSTRY ($ IN BILLIONS)

Category	2004 ($)	2005 ($)	Growth (%)
Action figures and accessories	1.25	1.30	4.0
Arts and crafts	2.50	2.40	−4.0
Building sets	0.60	0.70	16.0
Dolls	2.76	2.70	−2.0
Games/puzzles	2.64	2.40	−9.0
Infant/preschool	3.13	3.10	−1.0
Learning and exploration	0.37	0.39	5.0
Outdoor and sports toys	2.78	2.70	−3.0
Plush	1.53	1.30	−15.0
Vehicles	1.96	1.80	−8.0
Other	2.60	2.50	−4.0
Total traditional toys	22.12	21.29	−3.8
Total video games	9.91	10.50	6.0

Source: NPD Group Press Release, February 2006.

[7] NPD Group Press Release, February 13, 2006.

[8] Citigroup Equity Research, "Toy Industry Outlook," September 22, 2004.

EXHIBIT C9.5 PROJECTED POPULATION GROWTH (IN MILLIONS)

Age Cohort	2005	2010E	Total Growth (%)	Implied CAGR (%)
Ages 5 and under	20,311	21,426	5.5	1.1
Ages 6–8	11,782	12,228	3.8	0.7
Ages 9–12	15,744	15,986	1.5	0.3

Source: NPD Group, October 2006.

EXHIBIT C9.6 US TOY RETAIL MARKET SHARE (%)

	2003	2005
Mass market share	48.6	54.0
Toy stores	25.1	20.0

Source: NPD Group Press Release, February 2006, and Doug Desjardins, "Toy Market Still Full of Surprises," DSN Retailing Today, September 6, 2004.

After a period of robust growth in the 1990s, analysts and industry experts in 2005 were expecting 0%–2% growth in the traditional toys and games market over the next 3–5 years. This stabilization was based in part on a view that the worst of the price competition was behind the industry and continued consolidation should improve the competitive dynamic. In addition, favorable demographic trends were expected to help the industry. See Exhibit C9.5 for growth estimates by age cohort.

According to the NPD Group, the mass/discount channel continued to gain share from other toy retailers in 2005, accounting for 54% of total toy sales, while toy stores represented 20% (the vast majority of this was Toys "R" Us). Clearly the mass/discount channel—specifically Wal-Mart and Target—were growing at the expense of the specialty toy retailers (see Exhibit C9.6).[9] Toys "R" Us was the largest specialty toy retailer in the industry, and while it struggled in a difficult operating environment, it was better equipped to compete with the mass/discount channel than its peers. For example, two other leading specialty toy retailers, KB Toys and FAO Schwarz, filed for Chapter 11 protection in 2004. Online toy sales continued to increase as well, generating more than $1.3 billion in 2005, a 2.6% increase over the prior year, and accounting for approximately 6% of sales for the year.[10]

The retail toy industry was highly competitive. Competitors included discount and mass merchandisers, electronics retailers, national and regional chains, and local retailers. Competition was principally based on price, store location, advertising and promotion, product selection, quality, and service. Advantages in financial resources, lower merchandise acquisition costs, and/or lower operating expenses were usually passed along to customers in an attempt to preserve or gain market share. Discount and mass merchandisers increasingly used aggressive

[9] JP Morgan Equity Research, "Toy Retailing: The Shakeout Goes On," May 5, 2003.

[10] NPD Group Press Release, February 13, 2006.

pricing policies and enlarged toy-selling areas during the holiday season to build traffic for other store departments (e.g., toys were used as a loss leader).

Success in the retail toy industry depended on a company's ability to identify, originate, and define product trends, as well as anticipate, gauge, and react to changing consumer demands in a timely manner. If a retailer misjudged the market for products, it might have significant excess inventories for some products and missed opportunities for others. Sales of toys and other products depended upon discretionary consumer spending, which was affected by general economic conditions, consumer confidence, and other macroeconomic factors. A decline in consumer spending would, among other things, negatively impact sales across the toy industry and result in excess inventories, requiring discounting to move old inventory.

Electronics retailers became more relevant competitors in toy retailing by capitalizing on "age compression," the acceleration of the trend of younger children leaving traditional play categories for more sophisticated products such as cell phones, DVD players, CD players, MP3 devices, and other electronics products. The age compression pattern tended to decrease consumer demand for traditional toys or at least increase competition for purchases within the segment of 5- to 12-year-olds.

An article in *DSN Retailing Today*[11] examined the competitive environment in the industry during 2003–04:

> Retailers can't afford a repeat of the 2003 holiday season when a slow economy and price wars between Wal-Mart and Target produced a nightmare scenario. Toys "R" Us reported a 5% decline in fourth quarter same-store sales, and KB Toys reported a 10% decline in sales in 2003.
>
> In the aftermath, Toys "R" Us closed its Kids "R" Us and Imaginarium divisions, and KB filed for Chapter 11 bankruptcy and closed nearly 500 stores. FAO Schwarz fared worst of all and liquidated its 89-store Zany Brainy chain and sold its flagship stores in New York City and Las Vegas.

* * *

> Toy industry analyst Chris Byrne doesn't expect the specialists to fare any better during the upcoming [2004] holiday season. "The business model for toy retail is really changing, and we could be seeing the end of the specialty toy store," said Byrne.
>
> He said the specialists are not being hurt just by mass merchants, noting that other chains are stealing away business in core categories, such as video games and action figures. "What we're seeing is more and more category specialists," said Byrne. "Places like Best Buy and GameStop have become great places to buy toys."

EUROPEAN RETAIL TOY INDUSTRY

In 2005 traditional toy sales in Europe (excluding video games) grew 3% to €13.3 billion from €12.9 billion.[12] The market had been stable over the previous few years, and in most European countries there was increased demand for infant/preschool toys, building sets,

---

[11] Doug Desjardins, "Toy Market Still Full of Surprises," *DSN Retailing Today*, September 6, 2004.

[12] Toy Industries of Europe, Facts & Figures, July 2006.

and action figures.[13] Analysts and industry experts expected European traditional toy sales to outpace sales in the United States. Including video games, growth was expected to be in the 3%–6% range. Exhibit C9.7 shows market share by country in Europe.

While the industry drivers and demand trends in Europe were similar to those in the United States, the competitive landscape was different. On average, the specialty toy retailers had better market share across Europe than in the United States. Exhibit C9.8 shows distribution channel market share across Europe.

EXHIBIT C9.7 EUROPEAN TRADITIONAL TOY SALE MARKET SHARE BY COUNTRY (%)

Country	2004	2005
UK	22.8	24.0
France	19.6	19.6
Germany	18.1	17.0
Italy	8.0	7.9
Spain	6.3	6.5
Poland	2.0	2.0
Hungary	0.6	0.6
Czech Republic	0.5	0.5
Others	22.1	21.9
Total	100.0	100.0

Source: Toy Industries of Europe, Facts & Figures, July 2006.

EXHIBIT C9.8 DISTRIBUTION CHANNEL BY COUNTRY (%)

	France	Germany	Spain	Italy	UK	Europe
Toy specialist	44.3	40.8	46.0	34.0	26.9	36.2
Mass merchant/ discount stores	42.9	14.2	30.8	39.0	10.6	24.0
General merchandise	3.3	5.5	5.8	13.2	27.0	13.2
Department stores	1.9	15.7	11.8	7.6	3.3	6.5
Mail order	3.5	6.7	0.0		3.5	3.9
Other	4.1	17.1	5.6	6.2	28.7	16.2
Total	100.0	100.0	100.0	100.0	100.0	100.0

Source: Toy Industries of Europe, Facts & Figures, July 2006.

[13] Toy Industries of Europe, Facts & Figures, July 2006.

INFANT, TODDLER, AND PRESCHOOL MARKET

The US market for infant, toddler, and preschool products was approximately $34 billion in 2005 and consisted primarily of the following segments: home furnishings and accessories ($8 billion), clothing ($17 billion), baby-care supplies ($6 billion), and traditional toys ($3 billion).[14] Traditional toys in this market segment overlapped with sales in the broader traditional US toy market. The mass/discount retailers and Babies "R" Us (the Company's specialty baby/juvenile stores) were the clear market share leaders in this segment, with the remaining market share distributed across a highly fragmented, specialty retailer base and department/grocery stores. This market had shown steady growth over the previous few years and analysts and industry experts estimated it would continue to grow at a 3%–6% rate. Growth was expected to come from an anticipated increase in the infant population and increased spending per child.

This market segment had become more attractive to retailers as competition in the traditional toy market intensified, and it was insulated from age compression as it focused on very young children. In addition, it did not have the same price competition as the traditional toy market because retailers were better able to differentiate based on perceived product quality and shopping experience.

OVERVIEW OF TOYS "R" US

Toys "R" Us was a worldwide specialty retailer of toys, baby products, and children's apparel. As of January 29, 2005, it operated 1499 retail stores worldwide.[15] These consisted of 898 locations in the United States, including 681 toy stores and 217 Babies "R" Us stores. Internationally, the Company operated, licensed, or franchised 601 stores (299 operated stores, 2 of which were Babies "R" Us, and 302 licensed or franchised stores, 7 of which were Babies "R" Us). See Exhibit C9.9 for a breakdown of owned and leased stores. The Company also sold merchandise through its Internet sites.

The retail business began in 1948 when founder Charles Lazarus opened a baby furniture store, Children's Bargain Town, in Washington, D.C. The Company changed its name to Toys "R" Us in 1957. The first Babies "R" Us stores opened in 1996, expanding the Company's presence in the specialty baby/juvenile market. The Company was among the market share leaders in most of the largest markets in which its retail stores operated, including the United States, the United Kingdom, and Japan. See Exhibit C9.10 through Exhibit C9.13 for consolidated and segment financial results.

The Company's worldwide toy business was highly seasonal, with net sales and earnings highest in the fourth quarter, which included the all-important holiday sales of November and December. More than 40% of net sales from the Company's worldwide toy business and

---

[14] Data compiled from various packaged facts industry reports.

[15] Toys "R" Us FYE 2005 10-K Filing. Note all financial data related to the Company is from the 2005 10-K Filing.

EXHIBIT C9.9 TOYS "R" US PROPERTY SUMMARY

	Owned	% of Total	Ground Lease	% of Total	Leased	% of Total	Total
Stores							
Toys "R" Us	315	46.3	155	22.8	211	31.0	681
International[a]	80	26.8	23	7.7	196	65.6	299
Babies "R" Us	31	14.3	76	35.0	110	50.7	217
Total	426	35.6	254	21.2	517	43.2	1197
Distribution centers							
US	9	75.0	0	0.0	3	25.0	12
International	5	62.5	0	0.0	3	37.5	8
Total	14	70.0	0	0.0	6	30.0	20
Operating stores and distribution centers	440	36.2	254	20.9	523	43.0	1217

[a]Excludes 302 licensed or franchised stores in international markets.
Source: Toys "R" Us FYE 2005 10-K Filing.

a substantial portion of its operating earnings and cash flows from operations were generated in the fourth quarter. See Exhibit C9.14 for quarterly results from the fiscal year ending January 29, 2005.

Toys "R" Us—United States

The Company sold toys, plush, games, bicycles, sporting goods, VHS and DVD movies, electronic and video games, small pools, books, educational and development products, clothing, infant and juvenile furniture, and electronics, as well as educational and entertainment computer software for children. Its toy stores offered approximately 8000–10,000 distinct items year round, more than twice the number found in other discount or specialty stores selling toys. The Company sought to differentiate itself from competitors in several key areas, including product selection, product presentation, service, in-store experience, and marketing. This became increasingly important as discount retailers and other specialty retailers increased competition.

Toys "R" Us—International

Toys "R" Us—International operated, licensed, and franchised toy stores in 30 foreign countries. These stores generally conformed to prototypical designs similar to those used by Toys "R" Us in the United States. As noted above, as of January 29, 2005, the Company operated 299 international stores, 2 of which were Babies "R" Us, and licensed or franchised 302 international stores, 7 of which were Babies "R" Us. International added 33 new toy stores in calendar year 2004, including 26 licensed or franchised stores, and closed 10 stores, including 5 licensed or franchised stores. The division intended to add 41 new toy stores in 2005,

EXHIBIT C9.10 CONSOLIDATED FINANCIAL RESULTS ($ IN MILLIONS, EXCEPT PER SHARE DATA)

	For the Year Ended		
	2/1/2003	1/31/2004	1/29/2005
Net sales	$11,305	$11,320	$11,100
Growth		0.1%	−1.9%
Cost of sales	(7,799)	(7,646)	(7,506)
Gross margin	$3,506	$3,674	$3,594
Growth		4.8%	−2.2%
Margin	31.0%	32.5%	32.4%
SG&A	($2,724)	($3,026)	($2,932)
Growth		11.1%	−3.1%
Margin	−24.1%	−26.7%	−26.4%
Reported EBITDA (pre-restructuring charges)	$782	$648	$662
Growth		−17.1%	2.2%
Margin	6.9%	5.7%	6.0%
D&A	($339)	($368)	($354)
Restructuring and other charges	0	(63)	(4)
EBIT	$443	$217	$304
Growth		−51.0%	40.1%
Margin	3.9%	1.9%	2.7%
Interest expense	($119)	($142)	($130)
Interest and other income	9	18	19
Pretax income	$333	$93	$193
Growth		−72.1%	107.5%
Margin	2.9%	0.8%	1.7%
Income tax (expense)/benefit	(120)	(30)	59
Net income	$213	$63	$252
Growth		−70.4%	300.0%
Margin	1.9%	0.6%	2.3%
Diluted EPS	$1.02	$0.29	$1.16
Growth		−71.6%	300.0%
Adjusted consolidated EBITDA			
Reported EBITDA (pre-restructuring charges)	$782	$648	$662
Add-back of one-time items in Toys "R" Us—U.S.[a]	0	0	118
Adjusted consolidated EBITDA	$782	$648	$780
Growth		−17.1%	20.4%
Margin	6.9%	5.7%	7.0%

[a] EBITDA for FY 2005 adjusted by adding back $132 million in inventory markdowns and excluding $14 million related to a lawsuit settlement—$118 million net add-back in FY 2005.

Source: Toys "R" Us FYE 2005 10-K Filing

EXHIBIT C9.11 CONSOLIDATED BALANCE SHEET ($ IN MILLIONS)

	For the Year Ended	
	1/31/2004	1/29/2005
ASSETS		
Cash and cash equivalents	$1,432	$1,250
Short-term investments	571	953
Accounts and other receivables	146	153
Merchandise inventories	2,094	1,884
Net property assets held for sale	163	7
Current portion of derivative assets	162	1
Prepaid expenses and other current assets	161	159
Total current assets	$4,729	$4,407
Property, plant, and equipment		
Real estate, net	$2,165	$2,393
Other, net	2,274	1,946
Total PP&E	$4,439	$4,339
Goodwill, net	348	353
Derivative assets	77	43
Deferred tax asset	399	426
Other assets	273	200
Total assets	$10,265	$9,768
LIABILITIES AND STOCKHOLDERS' EQUITY		
Short-term borrowings	$0	$0
Accounts payable	1,022	1,023
Accrued expenses and other current liabilities	866	881
Income taxes payable	319	245
Current portion of long-term debt	657	452
Total current liabilities	$2,864	$2,601
Long-term debt	2,349	1,860
Deferred income taxes	538	485
Derivative liabilities	26	16
Deferred rent liability	280	269
Other liabilities	225	212
Minority interest in Toysrus.com	9	0
Total liabilities	$6,291	$5,443
Stockholders' equity		
Common stock	$30	$30
Additional paid-in capital	407	405
Retained earnings	5,308	5,560
Accumulated other comprehensive loss	(64)	(7)
Restricted stock	0	(5)
Treasury shares, at cost	(1,707)	(1,658)
Total stockholders' equity	$3,974	$4,325
Total liabilities and stockholders' equity	$10,265	$9,768

Source: Toys "R" Us FYE 2005 10-K Filing

EXHIBIT C9.12 CONSOLIDATED STATEMENT OF CASH FLOW ($ IN MILLIONS)

	For the Year Ended		
	2/1/2003	1/31/2004	1/29/2005
CASH FLOWS FROM OPERATING ACTIVITIES			
Net earnings	$213	$63	$252
Adjustments to reconcile net earnings to net cash from operating activities:			
Depreciation and amortization	$339	$368	$354
Amortization of restricted stock	0	0	7
Deferred income taxes	99	27	(40)
Minority interest in Toysrus.com	(14)	(8)	(6)
Other non-cash items	(9)	1	2
Non-cash portion of restructuring and other charges	0	63	4
Changes in operating assets and liabilities:			
Accounts and other receivables	8	62	(5)
Merchandise inventories	(100)	133	221
Prepaid expenses and other operating assets	(118)	28	76
Accounts payable, accrued expenses,and other liabilities	109	117	(45)
Income taxes payable	48	(53)	(74)
Net cash provided by operating activities	$575	$801	$746
CASH FLOWS FROM INVESTING ACTIVITIES			
Capital expenditures, net	($395)	($262)	($269)
Proceeds from sale of fixed assets	0	0	216
Purchase of SB Toys, Inc.	0	0	(42)
Purchase of short-term investments and other	0	(572)	(382)
Net cash used in investing activities	($395)	($834)	($477)
CASH FLOWS FROM FINANCING ACTIVITIES			
Short-term borrowings, net	$0	$0	$0
Long-term borrowings	548	792	0
Long-term debt repayment	(141)	(370)	(503)
Decrease/(increase) in restricted cash	(60)	60	0
Proceeds from issuance of stock and contracts to purchase stock	266	0	0
Proceeds from exercise of stock options	0	0	27
Net cash (used in)/provided by financing activities	$613	$482	($476)
Effect of exchange rate changes on cash and cash equivalents	($53)	($40)	$25
CASH AND CASH EQUIVALENTS			
(Decrease)/increase during year	$740	$409	($182)
Beginning of year	283	1,023	1,432
End of year	$1,023	$1,432	$1,250

Source: Toys "R" Us FYE 2005 10-K Filing

EXHIBIT C9.13 FINANCIAL PERFORMANCE BY SEGMENT ($ IN MILLIONS)

	For the Year Ended						For the Year Ended		
	2/1/2003	% of Total	1/31/2004	% of Total	1/29/2005	% of Total	2/1/2003	1/31/2004	1/29/2005
NET SALES BY SEGMENT							GROWTH BY SEGMENT (%)		
Toys "R" Us—U.S.	$6,755	59.8	$6,326	55.9	$6,104	55.0		-6.4	-3.5
Toys "R" Us—International	2,161	19.1	2,470	21.8	2,739	24.7		14.3	10.9
Babies "R" Us	1,595	14.1	1,738	15.4	1,863	16.8		9.0	7.2
Toysrus.com	340	3.0	371	3.3	366	3.3		9.1	-1.3
Kids "R" Us	454	4.0	415	3.7	28	0.3		-8.6	-93.3
Consolidated net sales	$11,305	100.0	$11,320	100.0	$11,100	100.0		0.1	-1.9
OPERATING EARNINGS BY SEGMENT							MARGIN BY SEGMENT (%)		
Toys "R" Us—U.S.	$256	49.4	$70	20.4	$4	0.9	3.8	1.1	0.1
Toys "R" Us—International	158	30.5	166	48.4	220	51.9	7.3	6.7	8.0
Babies "R" Us	169	32.6	192	56.0	224	52.8	10.6	11.0	12.0
Toysrus.com	(37)	-7.1	(18)	-5.2	1	0.2	-10.9	-4.9	0.3
Kids "R" Us[a]	(28)	-5.4	(67)	-19.5	(25)	-5.9	-6.2	-16.1	-89.3
Segment operating earnings	$518	100.0	$343	100.0	$424	100.0	4.6	3.0	3.8
Corporate/other expenses[b]	(75)		(63)		(116)				
Restructuring charges	0		(63)		(4)				
Reported operating earnings	$443		$217		$304		3.9	1.9	2.7
ADJUSTED EBITDA BY SEGMENT							MARGIN BY SEGMENT (%)		
Toys "R" Us—U.S.[c]	$447	55.1	$264	39.3	$322	37.4	6.6	4.2	5.3
Toys "R" Us—International	210	25.9	227	33.8	295	34.3	9.7	9.2	10.8
Babies "R" Us	197	24.3	223	33.2	262	30.5	12.4	12.8	14.1
Toysrus.com	(33)	-4.1	(16)	-2.4	1	0.1	-9.7	-4.3	0.3
Kids "R" Us[a]	(10)	-1.2	(27)	-4.0	(20)	-2.3	-2.2	-6.5	-71.4
Adjusted segment EBITDA	$811	100.0	$671	100.0	$860	100.0	7.2	5.9	7.7
Corporate/other expenses[b]	(75)		(63)		(116)				
Add-back: other D&A	46		40		36				
Consolidated adjusted EBITDA	$782		$648		$780		6.9	5.7	7.0

[a] Includes markdowns of $49 million and accelerated depreciation of $24 million in 2003 related to the closing of all stores.

[b] Includes corporate expenses, the operating results of Toy Box, and the equity in net earnings of Toys "R" Us — Japan. Increase in amount is due to our strategic review expenses and Sarbanes-Oxley Section 404 compliance totaling $29 million. In addition, we incurred charges of $8 million relating to our 2004 restructuring of the Company's corporate headquarters operations, and a $19 million increase in incentive compensation costs.

[c] EBITDA for FY 2005 adjusted by adding back $132 million in inventory markdowns and excluding $14 million related to a lawsuit settlement—$118 million net add-back in FY 2005.

Source: Toys "R" Us FYE 2005 10-K Filing

EXHIBIT C9.14 QUARTERLY FINANCIAL RESULTS ($ IN MILLIONS)

	5/1/2004	% of Total	7/31/2004	% of Total	10/30/2004	% of Total	1/29/2005	% of Total	FYE 1/29/2005
					For the Quarter Ended				
Net sales	$2,058	18.5	$2,022	18.2	$2,214	19.9	$4,806	43.3	$11,100
COGS	(1,330)	17.7	(1,441)	19.2	(1,475)	19.7	(3,260)	43.4	(7,506)
Gross margin	$728	20.3	$581	16.2	$739	20.6	$1,546	43.0	$3,594
SG&A	(643)	21.9	(661)	22.5	(682)	23.3	(946)	32.3	(2,932)
D&A	(86)	24.3	(86)	24.3	(88)	24.9	(94)	26.6	(354)
Restructuring (charges)/income	(14)	NM	(31)	NM	26	NM	15	NM	(4)
Operating earnings	($15)	-4.9	($197)	-64.8	($5)	-1.6	$521	171.4	$304
Reported EBITDA (includes one-time items)	$85	12.8	($80)	-12.1	$57	8.6	$600	90.6	$662

Note: EBITDA is defined as operating earnings with an add-back of D&A and restructuring charges (does not exclude one-time items)

Source: Toys "R" Us FYE 2005 10-K Filing

including 31 licensed or franchised stores. As of January 29, 2005, Toys "R" Us—Japan, Ltd., a licensee of the Company, operated 153 stores, which were included in the 302 licensed or franchised international stores. The Company had a 48% ownership in the common stock of Toys "R" Us—Japan.

Babies "R" Us

In 1996 the Company opened its first Babies "R" Us stores. The acquisition of Baby Superstore, Inc. in 1997 added 76 locations, and the continued expansion of this brand helped Babies "R" Us become the leader in the specialty baby/juvenile market. Babies "R" Us stores targeted the prenatal and infant markets by offering juvenile furniture such as cribs, dressers, changing tables, and bedding. In addition, the Company provided baby gear such as play yards, booster seats, high chairs, strollers, car seats, toddler and infant plush toys, and nursing equipment. As of January 29, 2005, Babies "R" Us operated 217 specialty baby/juvenile retail locations, all in the United States. Based on demographic data used to determine which markets to enter, the Company opened 19 Babies "R" Us stores in calendar year 2004. As part of its long-range growth plan, it planned to continue expanding its Babies "R" Us store base in 2005.

Toysrus.com

Toysrus.com sold merchandise to the public via the Internet at www.toysrus.com, www.babiesrus.com, www.imaginarium.com, www.sportsrus.com, and www.personalizedbyrus.com. The Company launched its e-commerce website in 1998. To improve customer service and order fulfillment, the Company entered into a strategic alliance with Amazon.com and launched a cobranded toy store in 2000.

CHALLENGING TIMES FOR TOYS "R" US

During 2003–04, the Company's performance and prospects were hurt by developments in the retail toy industry. Discount and mass merchandisers with greater financial resources and lower operating expenses had reduced pricing and profit margins for other players in the retail toy industry, and the Company's toy sales had decreased because of changing consumer habits, including age compression. On November 17, 2003, the Company announced plans to close all 146 of the freestanding Kids "R" Us stores, with final closings completed by January 29, 2005.

The Company's consolidated net sales decreased 1.9% to $11.1 billion in fiscal year end (FYE) January 29, 2005, from $11.3 billion in FYE January 31, 2004, and $11.3 billion in FYE February 1, 2003. The decrease in net sales was primarily the result of declines in comparable store sales at the Toys "R" Us—US division, which posted comparable store sales declines of 3.7% for FYE 2005, following comparable store sales decreases of 3.6% and 1.3% in FYE 2004 and FYE 2003, respectively (see Exhibit C9.15).

EXHIBIT C9.15 COMPARABLE STORE SALES PERFORMANCE (%)

	For the Year Ended		
	February 1, 2003	January 31, 2004	January 29, 2005
Toys "R" Us—US	−1.3	−3.6	−3.7
Toys "R" Us—International	5.9	2.1	0.6
Babies "R" Us	2.7	2.8	2.2

Note: This does not reflect sales from new store openings or store closings, comparable stores year over year.
Source: Toys "R" Us FYE 2005 10-K Filing.

These decreases in net sales were partially offset by net sales increases in the Babies "R" Us division of 7.2% to $1.9 billion in FYE 2005, and net sales increases in the international division of 10.9% (these figures include the effect of currency translation) to $2.7 billion in FYE 2005, primarily due to the addition of 19 Babies "R" Us stores in the United States and 7 wholly owned international stores in 2004. In addition, comparable store sales at Babies "R" Us and international divisions showed favorable increases.

TOYS "R" US STRATEGIC REVIEW AND SALE

Facing both difficult industry trends and weak performance of US toy stores during the 2003 holiday season, Toys "R" Us decided to conduct a strategic evaluation of its worldwide assets and operations. The Company retained Credit Suisse First Boston (CSFB) as its financial advisor. The Company and CSFB considered several alternatives, including the following:

- Maintaining status quo and refocusing management on reviving domestic performance at Toys "R" Us
- Unlocking value in a faster-growing asset by selling the global Toys "R" Us business or spinning off Babies "R" Us
- Pursuing the sale of consolidated Toys "R" Us

The Company and CSFB initially decided to separate the US toy retailing business and Babies "R" Us by running a thorough sale process for its toy retailing business. However, participants in the auction determined it would be too difficult to uncouple the businesses. One participant said, "It would be like selling your kitchen to one buyer and your dining room to another."[16] With no compelling bids for any of the individual businesses after an extended period of time, pressure increased for Toys "R" Us to sell the portfolio of businesses together.

[16] "Toys 'R' Us Narrows Suitors to Four," *Wall Street Journal*, March 1, 2005.

Ultimately, a consortium that included Cerberus, Goldman Sachs, and Kimco Realty Corp. submitted a bid for the entire business. Subsequently KKR teamed up with Bain Capital Partners and Vornado Realty Trust (Bain and Vornado initially joined to bid on the toy business) and submitted a rival bid. On March 17, 2005, the Company announced that it had reached a definitive agreement to sell the entire worldwide operations to the consortium of KKR, Bain Capital, and Vornado Realty Trust for $26.75 per share in a $6.7 billion transaction.[17] The acquisition price represented a 122.5% premium over the stock price on the day before the announcement of the strategic review on January 7, 2004, and a 62.9% over the stock price on August 10, 2004, the day before the Company announced it was seeking to divest its toy retailing business.

The $26.75 per share winning bid for Toys "R" Us represented an aggregate value of $6.7 billion, including all transaction fees. It is important to note that as part of the transaction, the consortium assumed the Company's existing debt and cash not used in the transaction. Exhibit C9.16 summarizes the sources and uses for the transaction. Based on adjusted EBITDA of $780 million during FYE January 29, 2005, Exhibit C9.17 shows the implied purchase price and leverage multiples (including all assumed debt and cash) for the Toys "R" Us transaction.

EXHIBIT C9.16 SOURCES AND USES ($ IN MILLIONS)

Sources		Uses	
Cash on balance sheet	$956	Purchase of common stock	$5,900
Senior secured credit facility	700	Purchase of stock options and restricted stock	227
Unsecured bridge loan	1,900	Settlement of equity security interests	114
Secured European bridge loan	1,000	Purchase of all warrants	17
Mortgage loan agreements	800	Transaction fees	362
Sponsor equity	1,300	Severance and bonus payments	36
Total	$6,656	Total	$6,656

Summary of Fees	
Advisory fees and expenses	$78
Financing fees	135
Sponsor fees	81
Other	68
Total	$362

Note: Senior secured credit facility has $2.0 billion of availability.

Source: Toys "R" Us, Form 10-Q, June 30, 2005

[17] Toys "R" Us Company Press Release, March 17, 2005.

EXHIBIT C9.17 ENTERPRISE VALUE AND LEVERAGE SUMMARY ($ IN MILLIONS)

	Amount	Multiple of FYE 2005 Adj. EBITDA
Transaction proceeds (excl. fees)	$6,294	
Approximate existing debt assumed by the consortium	2,312	
Remaining cash and short-term investments on balance sheet	(1,247)	
Enterprise value	$7,359	9.4x
Transaction fees	362	
Total transaction value	$7,721	9.9x
2004 adjusted EBITDA	$780	
LEVERAGE ANALYSIS		Cumul. Multiple
Approximate existing debt	$2,312	3.0x
$2 billion senior secured credit facility	700	3.9x
Unsecured bridge loan	1,900	6.3x
Secured European bridge loan	1,000	7.6x
Mortgage loan agreements	800	8.6x
Total	$6,712	8.6x
Remaining cash and short-term investments on balance sheet assumed by the consortium	(1,247)	
Net leverage	$5,465	7.0x

Note: Assumes transaction closed on January 29, 2005 for simplicity.

As part of this transaction, John H. Eyler, Jr. (chairman, CEO, and president of Toys "R" Us) and Christopher K. Kay (executive vice president and chief operations officer) were to leave the Company. The consortium appointed Richard L. Markee (a Company veteran) as interim CEO, with the expectation of filling out the management team over time. This was somewhat unusual, as financial sponsors typically preferred to back an in-place management team to lead a company through the initial period after an LBO. This action was particularly note-worthy given the pressures of operating a business in a difficult industry with a significant amount of new leverage.

Markee had served as president of Babies "R" Us since August 2004. Prior to that, he had been vice chairman of Toys "R" Us Inc., president of Toys "R" Us Domestic, president of Specialty Businesses and International Operations, president of Babies "R" Us, and chairman of Kids "R" Us.

THE TOYS "R" US CLUB

The Toys "R" Us Club featured two of the premier private equity firms in the world and a leading real estate investment trust (REIT). The two private equity firms—KKR and Bain Capital—had also partnered in several deals, including a $11.4 billion buyout of SunGard Data Systems, which had closed in August 2005. Including the Toys "R" Us deal, KKR had become the most active participant in club deals, having participated in 10 announced club deals valued at $95.3 billion during the previous 2 years.[18]

The Toys "R" Us Club was particularly interesting because of the diverse core competencies of each member. KKR was known for structuring highly complex transactions with expert use of financial engineering, a skill that was of particular importance given the recent performance issues at Toys "R" Us. Bain Capital, while also skilled at financial engineering, had built a reputation for in-depth industry research capabilities, especially in retail. The consortium leveraged Bain Capital's resources to understand and analyze the nature of the industry downturn and to forecast the future viability of both the Company and the industry. The inclusion of Vornado highlighted the club's focus on understanding the value of the Company's real estate portfolio. While it historically had been rare for an REIT to be involved in a typical private equity deal, as private equity firms began to target companies with large real estate portfolios, there was an increased need for expertise in valuing real estate.

Kohlberg Kravis & Roberts

Established in 1976 and led by cofounding members Henry Kravis and George Roberts, KKR had completed more than 140 transactions valued at approximately $215 billion[19] and created $68 billion of value from $26 billion of invested capital, a multiple of 2.5 times.[20] KKR historically had been involved with the highest-profile, largest transactions in the private equity industry, including those involving RJR Nabisco, SunGard Data Systems, and HCA.

Bain Capital

Established in 1984, Bain Capital was one of the world's leading private investment firms with approximately $40 billion in assets under management. Since its inception, Bain Capital had completed more than 200 equity investments. The aggregate transaction value of these investments exceeded $17 billion.[21] Bain Capital had been founded by three ex-Bain & Company partners, Mitt Romney, T. Coleman Andrews, and Eric Kriss. Less than 1 year before its acquisition of Toys "R" Us, Bain Capital had completed the acquisition of another specialty retailer, the Canadian dollar store chain Dollarama.

---

[18] "KKR Tops 'Club' Buyout Deals," *CNN Money.com*, October 17, 2006.

[19] KKR, http://www.kkr.com.

[20] KKR, http://www.kkr.com.

[21] Bain Capital, http://www.baincapital.com.

Vornado Realty Trust

Vornado Realty Trust was a fully integrated REIT. The firm was one of the largest owners and managers of real estate in the United States, with a portfolio of approximately 60 million square feet in its major platforms, primarily in the New York and Washington, D.C. metro areas.[22]

THE ASSIGNMENT

Your private equity firm has been approached by KKR, Bain, and Vornado to join the consortium. You have been asked by a senior member of your firm to prepare a presentation that summarizes the Toys "R" Us investment opportunity. You should

- use the provided operating model template to develop assumptions that drive a base case operating model and analyze the returns for the investment group
  - use the operating model to generate input for an LBO model, which will calculate relevant returns, financial data, and credit statistics
  - focus on developing a reasonable set of projections on which to base your investment recommendation

The presentation should include the following (a template has been included for guidance):

- Risks and merits of the transaction
- Summary of the industry dynamics, including the major issues and potential catalysts for improvements
- A list of key due diligence questions/requests you want to ask the Company
- Summary of the debt in the transaction indicates whether you feel comfortable with the capital structure proposed by the consortium
- Downside case(s) that stress test the investment under various difficult operating outcomes: quantify the risk/return profile of the transaction and evaluate this profile
- Potential exit alternatives for this investment
- Recommendation whether or not to join the consortium

For the purpose of your evaluation assume that you are not able to change the consortium's proposed capital structure.

---

[22] Vornado Realty Trust, http://www.vno.com.

Cerberus and the US Auto Industry

INTRODUCTION

In August 2005, General Motors Acceptance Corporation (GMAC) announced that it had entered into an agreement to sell a 60% equity interest in its commercial mortgage subsidiary, GMAC Commercial Holding Corp (GMACCH), to a high-profile investor group led by private equity giant Kohlberg Kravis Roberts & Co. (KKR). The KKR-led group later upped its ante in March of the following year, increasing its investment to almost $9 billion for a 78% stake in the mortgage business's equity. Less than 2 weeks after this announcement, Cerberus Capital Management—a multistrategy, $22 billion New York hedge fund led by manager Stephen Feinberg—made its own announcement, stealing KKR's headlines. With Citibank's private equity division and a large Japanese bank on board, Cerberus agreed to buy a 51% controlling interest of GMAC in a deal that would net the cash-starved General Motors (GM) $14 billion over 3 years.

In May 2007, Cerberus acquired 80.1% of Chrysler LLC from Daimler-Benz AG for about $7.8 billion. At the time, Cerberus was hailed as a hero—the private equity firm that saved the American car industry. But 2 years later, Cerberus's dream had turned into a nightmare. Both GM and Chrysler declared bankruptcy, causing massive losses for Cerberus and the firm's coinvestors, including the investment arm of Abu Dhabi, as well as hedge funds such as York Capital and Eaton Park.

"WHAT'S GOOD FOR GENERAL MOTORS?"

General Motors—A Power

At his confirmation hearing as the newly appointed Secretary of Defense in 1953, Charles E. Wilson, former CEO and president of GM, is often misquoted as having boldly claimed, "What's good for GM is good for the country." (In response to a question about potential conflict of interest, Wilson had actually stated his belief that "what's good for the country is good for GM and vice versa.") The difference was semantic. At the midpoint of the century, GM was a dominant force in the US economy. Half a century ago "the only thing standing between [GM] and virtually limitless profits was the possibility of labor unrest,"[1] noted (ominously, as it were) historian David Halberstam. The first American corporation to boast profits of more than $1 billion (in 1955), GM was one of the largest employers in the world for much of the twentieth century, with automobile market share in the United States reaching 47.7% in 1978.

---

[1] David Halberstam, "The Fifties" (New York: History Channel: A&E Home Video, 1994).

General Motors—Hard Times

How times have changed. In 2006, GM reported sales of $207.3 billion, a 6.5% year-over-year increase. And while GM showed an improvement over 2005's operating loss of more than $10 billion, GM's operations remained in the red with losses of nearly $2 billion in 2006. Operating margins had fallen from 5.2% in 1995 to 1.7% in 2004 before the company announced the sizable annual loss from 2005 (see Exhibits C10.1 and C10.2 for General Motors Balance Sheet and Income Statement). Its business had eroded over the previous decade under the weight of enormous employee liabilities, rapidly declining market share, and a deteriorating macroeconomic environment. In the first 5 months of 2006, GM's market share in the United States fell to 23.8%. February 2006 may have marked the low point, as the once-proud giant of American economic strength slashed its annual dividend from $20 to $10. Headlines involving GM over the preceding several years had invariably focused on restructuring-related manufacturing closings, layoffs, and divestitures. Pension, healthcare, and other employee benefit costs swelled along with the rapidly aging work force at the once-powerful corporation, causing deterioration in profitability. In addition, increased competition from foreign automakers, unsaddled with the labor agreements and pension obligations of their US counterparts, significantly reduced GM's market power (see Exhibit C10.3: General Motors Two-Year Stock Chart).

Effect on Suppliers

Labor and healthcare costs and rising raw material and transportation prices were also forcing many of GM's major suppliers into financial distress. Coupled with the lower production at GM and other major US automakers as a result of restructuring, these ballooning cost structures had forced large US suppliers, including Delphi Automotive (a former unit of GM and the largest US auto parts supplier) and Dana Corporation, to file for bankruptcy protection. The implications to GM of its suppliers' distress were significant. Strapped for cash and in the midst of restructuring, the companies, most prominently Delphi, often found themselves asking for wage concessions from their workers. Labor stoppage, and thus production stoppage, at any of its suppliers would have dire consequences for GM. With protecting production its top priority, GM had spent billions of dollars subsidizing its suppliers through extended financing.

CEO Wagoner's Tough Task Remaking Company

G. Richard Wagoner joined the GM treasurer's office in 1977 as an analyst before steadily climbing his way up the corporate ladder to become GM's chairman and CEO in May 2003. Wagoner had a reputation for success in making tough decisions, and his storied career had given him a true sense of purpose in turning around this once-great company. "I feel a tremendous sense of responsibility to the job that I have,"[2] he told the *Detroit Free Press* in a September 2006 interview, and given his history with the company, it was hard not to believe him. However, soon after taking the job, Wagoner was faced with some of the toughest challenges in GM's history.

---

[2] "Interview with Rick Wagoner," *Detroit Free Press*, September 10, 2006.

EXHIBIT C10.1 GENERAL MOTORS BALANCE SHEET, 2004–06 ($ IN MILLIONS)

	2004	2005	2006
ASSETS			
Cash and equivalents	13,148	15,187	23,774
Short-term investments	6,655	1,416	138
Accounts receivable	6,713	7,758	8,216
Inventory	11,717	13,851	13,921
Finance dividends, loans and leases, short-term	220,712	203,821	0
Finance dividends, other current assets	26,390	19,436	349
Deferred tax assets	8,883	7,073	10,293
Other current assets	8,399	8,797	7,789
Total current assets	302,617	277,339	64,480
PP&E	76,575	80,020	85,374
Accumulated depreciation	(39,405)	(41,554)	(43,440)
Net PP&E	37,170	38,466	41,934
Long-term investments	7,126	3,726	1,969
Goodwill	600	757	799
Other intangibles	234	362	319
Finance dividends, loans and leases, long-term	1,763	1,873	–
Finance dividends, other long-term assets	73,939	93,747	21,774
Deferred tax assets, long-term	17,639	22,849	32,967
Other long-term assets	41,259	41,411	21,950
Total assets	482,347	480,530	186,192
LIABILITIES			
Accounts payable	24,257	26,182	26,931
Accrued expenses	46,202	42,665	35,225
Short-term borrowings	1,478	955	3,325
Current portfolio, long-term debt	584	564	2,341
Finance dividend debt, current	91,043	82,054	4,423
Finance dividends, other current liabilities	4,573	3,731	1,214
Other current liabilities	2,426	4,452	–
Total current liabilities	170,563	160,603	73,459
Long-term debt	30,460	31,014	33,067
Minority interest	397	1,039	1,190
Finance dividend debt, noncurrent	176,714	171,163	5,015
Finance dividends, other noncurrent liabilities	27,799	39,887	925
Pension and other post-retirement benefits	32,848	40,204	62,020
Other noncurrent liabilities	16,206	22,023	15,957
Total liabilities	454,987	465,933	191,633
Common stock	942	943	943
APIC	15,241	15,285	15,336
Retained earnings	14,062	2,361	406
Treasury stock	–	–	–
Comprehensive income	(2,885)	(3,992)	(22,126)
Total common equity	27,360	14,597	(5,441)
Total liabilities and equity	482,347	480,530	186,192

Source: Capital IQ.

EXHIBIT C10.2 GENERAL MOTORS INCOME STATEMENT, 2004–06 ($ IN MILLIONS, EXCEPT PER SHARE DATA)

	2004	2005	2006
Revenue	161,545	158,221	172,927
Finance dividend revenue	31,972	34,383	34,422
Gain (loss) on sale of investment	–	–	–
Total revenue	193,517	192,604	207,349
Cost of goods sold	150,224	162,173	157,782
Finance dividend operating expense	17,991	17,875	1,350
Interest expense – Finance division	9,500	12,895	14,301
Gross profit	15,802	(339)	33,916
SG&A	11,863	13,222	25,081
Other operating expenses	273	497	500
Operating income	3,666	(14,058)	8,335
Interest expense	(2,480)	(2,873)	(2,644)
Income (loss) from affiliates	702	595	184
Other nonoperating income	–	–	–
EBT excluding unusual items	1,888	(16,336)	5,875
EBT including unusual items	1,888	(16,336)	(15,461)
Income tax expense	(916)	(5,878)	(5,882)
Restructuring charges			(6,200)
Impairment of goodwill			(828)
Gain (loss) on sale of assets			(2,910)
Asset writedown			(700)
Earnings from continuing operations	2,804	(10,458)	(1,978)
Extraordinary item and accounting charge	–	(109)	–
Net income	2,804	(10,567)	(1,978)
Basic EPS	4.96	(18.70)	(3.50)

Source: Capital IQ.

Rising oil prices; the failure of unparalleled incentives to meaningfully drive auto sales; bankruptcy of suppliers, including Delphi; and enormous, crippling, long-tailed liabilities all conspired to drive GM's credit ratings into a downward spiral. This, in turn, created pressure on GMAC, the company's most successful business unit and its financing arm.

EXHIBIT C10.3 GENERAL MOTORS STOCK CHART, 5/2006 TO 4/18/2007

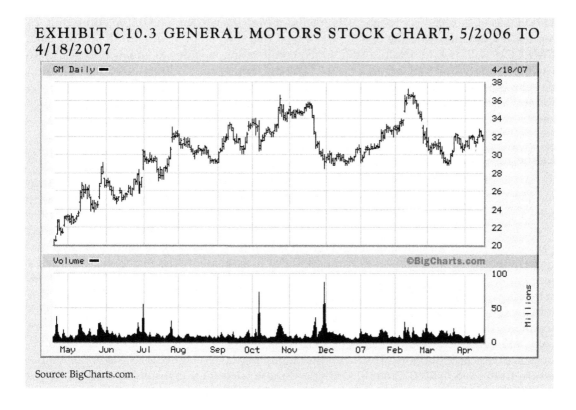

Source: BigCharts.com.

CERBERUS CAPITAL MANAGEMENT TO THE RESCUE...MAYBE

While the automotive division suffered, GMAC boasted a healthy EBITDA of $20 billion and net income of $2.4 billion on $34 billion in sales in 2005. As a wholly owned subsidiary of GM since 1919, GMAC provided automotive and commercial financing, insurance and mortgage products and services, and real estate services. Despite being the crown jewel of GM, GMAC saw its credit rating downgraded to junk in the spring of 2005 as a result of its association with GM. Following the downgrade, widespread speculation began in the press and on Wall Street that a sale of all or part of the finance arm would be a centerpiece to GM's restructuring, under the assumption that a sale would potentially allow the finance company to obtain its own independent debt rating (presumably investment-grade). After all, GMAC was much more than an auto financing company; greater than 50% of its business focused on nonautomotive businesses. Spokeswoman Toni Simonetti responded to speculation at the time, "We are exploring how we would attain a separate rating for GMAC. We would probably look at and evaluate any and all options that would lead to that."[3] Supporting analysts' predictions was the announcement of the sale by GMAC of 78% of its real estate finance unit to the KKR-led consortium. This sale, which accounted for about

[3] "Will GM Part with GMAC?," *CNNMoney.com*, May 25, 2006, http://money.cnn.com/2005/05/25/news/fortune500/gm_gmac/index.htm.

11% of GMAC's 2005 net income, was seen as a precursor to the sale of the entire unit. In a press release following the deal, it was noted that "in conjunction with the equity sale, GMACCH will seek to obtain a standalone credit rating in order to enhance its ability to fund its operations on an ongoing basis."[4] Shortly thereafter, GM announced that it would be selling a 51% stake in the remaining parts of GMAC to a consortium led by Cerberus Capital Management that included Citigroup and Aozora Bank Ltd. (a Japanese bank 62% owned by Cerberus).

Cerberus—New Beast of the Investment Community

Cerberus Capital Management L.P. was a private, highly secretive investment firm located in New York with reportedly more than $22 billion under management. Led by founder and manager Stephen Feinberg, Cerberus grew from a fringe vulture fund in the early 1990s to a multistrategy behemoth that defied definition, as its business straddled private equity, venture capital, and hedge fund investing. Cerberus began its life as a distressed-debt shop with around $10 million under management. The firm quickly earned a reputation as a tough investment firm that, like its founder, shied away from the spotlight. It became increasingly difficult to remain below the radar as the firm's assets quickly grew into the billions in the late 1990s. Named after the three-headed dog that guarded the gates to Hades, the underworld in Greek mythology, by the end of 2006 Feinberg's investment company owned controlling stakes in 45 diverse companies that boasted combined revenues in excess of $60 billion.[5] The firm's marketing materials claimed a 22% average annual return from 1998 to 2005. Among Cerberus's more successful investments were software firm SSA Global; communications services provider Teleglobe International Holdings; and Vanguard Car Rental USA, the parent of car rental brands National and Alamo.[6] The firm also had stakes in supermarket retailer Albertson's and Air Canada. Historically, Cerberus had taken a benign approach to the management of its portfolio companies, preferring friendly takeovers and deals that included the current stakeholders in the future strategic decision-making process. Though almost half the company's investments were in the manufacturing and services sectors, Cerberus's portfolio included stakes in companies from the healthcare, retail, financial services, and transportation industries as well (see Exhibit C10.4 for a breakdown of its operating professionals).

The Deal and Its Details

In successfully winning the bidding for GMAC, Cerberus launched itself from a behind-the-scenes operator to a front-row participant by beating out a competing group led by KKR. In exchange for $14 billion in cash over 3 years, Cerberus would take control of more than

---

[4] KKR press release, August 3, 2005.

[5] Charles Duhigg,"Can Private Equity Build a Public Face?," *New York Times*, December 24, 2006 and Cerberus website.

[6] "What's Bigger than Cisco, Coke or McDonald's?," *BusinessWeek Online*, October 3, 2005.

EXHIBIT C10.4 CERBERUS OPERATING PROFESSIONALS

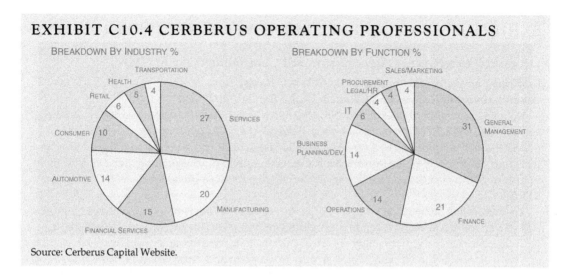

Source: Cerberus Capital Website.

$300 billion worth of leases, loans, mortgages, and insurance policies.[7] An excerpt from the press release discussed several terms of the deal (see Exhibit C10.5 for full press release):

> The $14 billion in cash that GM is to receive as part of the transaction includes $7.4 billion from the Cerberus-led consortium at closing and an estimated $2.7 billion cash distribution from GMAC related to the conversion of most of GMAC and its U.S. subsidiaries to limited liability companies. In addition, GM will retain about $20 billion of GMAC automotive lease and retail assets and associated funding with an estimated net book value of $4 billion that will monetize over three years.

In addition, GM and the consortium agreed to invest $1.9 billion of cash in a new GMAC preferred equity ($1.4 billion from GM and the balance from the consortium). Because a large goal of the deal for both parties was a decrease in GMAC's unsecured exposure to GM, Citigroup provided GMAC with a new $25 billion syndicated asset-backed funding facility. GM planned to continue receiving a 49% share of common dividends and other value generated by GMAC. A pretax charge of approximately $1.2 billion was taken by GM in the second quarter of 2006 associated with the sale. Finally, GM retained an option, exercisable for 10 years after closing, to reacquire GMAC's auto finance operations subject to certain conditions including an investment-grade credit rating at GM. (The option is summarized in Exhibit C10.6 and the postacquisition GMAC credit profile, revenue diversification, and bond spreads are provided in Exhibit C10.7.)

Roadblocks and Hurdles

In addition to regular state and federal regulatory issues, additional hurdles delayed the deal's closing. In July 2006, GM cleared the first major hurdle to a sale when the Pension Benefit Guaranty Corporation (PBGC) said that it would not impose GM's pension liability on the buyer of GMAC. In a public filing with the Securities and Exchange Commission, GM announced that the PBGC had given assurance that Cerberus would not be held responsible for the automaker's pension obligations. The agency, through a spokesperson, stated its satisfaction that the sale of a majority stake in GMAC was not an attempt to evade pension liabilities.

[7] "Cerberus to KKR: Eat Our Dust," *BusinessWeek Online*, April 24, 2006.

EXHIBIT C10.5 GMAC SALE PRESS RELEASE (APRIL 2, 2006)

General Motors Reaches Agreement to Sell Controlling Stake in GMAC

Cerberus-Led Consortium to Buy 51% of GMAC Equity
General Motors to Receive $14 Billion in Cash Over 3-Year Period

Detroit—General Motors Corp. (NYSE: GM) today announced it has entered into a definitive agreement to sell a 51% controlling interest in General Motors Acceptance Corporation (GMAC) to a consortium of investors led by Cerberus Capital Management, L.P., a private investment firm, and including Citigroup Inc., and Aozora Bank Ltd. GM expects to receive approximately $14 billion in cash from this transaction over 3 years, including distributions from GMAC, with an estimated $10 billion by closing.

The transaction strengthens GMAC's ability to support GM's automotive operations, improves GMAC's access to cost-effective funding, provides significant liquidity to GM, and allows GM to continue to participate in the profitability of GMAC over the long term through its 49% ownership stake.

"We look forward to working with Cerberus to maintain and grow GMAC's traditional strong performance and contribution to the GM family," said GM chairman and chief executive officer Rick Wagoner. "This agreement is another important milestone in the turnaround of GM. It creates a stronger GMAC while preserving the mutually beneficial relationship between GM and GMAC. At the same time, it provides significant liquidity to support our North American turnaround plan, finance future GM growth initiatives, strengthen our balance sheet, and fund other corporate priorities.

"Over the last nine months we have been aggressively implementing our North American turnaround plan," Wagoner said. "We've made some big moves, such as the health-care agreement with the United Auto Workers union; the manufacturing capacity plan; changes to our salaried health-care and pension plans; an accelerated attrition plan for hourly employees; and a complete overhaul of our marketing strategy. These bold initiatives are designed to immediately improve our competitiveness and position GM for long-term success and today's transition is a further step in that direction."

The GM board of directors approved the sale in a special meeting on Sunday, which followed extensive consideration of this transaction and alternative strategies over the past several months. Speaking for the GM board, presiding director George Fisher stated, "This transaction along with the other progress GM has been making on its turnaround plan, is an important milestone. While there is still much work to be done, the GM board has great confidence in Rick Wagoner, his management team and the plan they are implementing to restore the company to profitability."

The transaction is subject to a number of US and international regulatory and other approvals. The companies expect to close the transaction in the fourth quarter of 2006.

GM to Receive $14 Billion in Cash

The $14 billion in cash that GM is to receive as part of the transaction includes $7.4 billion from the Cerberus-led consortium at closing and an estimated $2.7 billion cash distribution from GMAC related to the conversion of most of GMAC and its US subsidiaries to limited liability companies. In addition, GM will retain about $20 billion of GMAC automotive lease and retail assets and associated funding with an estimated net book value of $4 billion that will monetize over 3 years.

GM also will receive dividends from GMAC equivalent to its earnings prior to closing, which largely will be used to fund the repayment of various intercompany loans from GMAC. As a result of these reductions, GMAC's unsecured exposure to GM is expected to be reduced to approximately $400 million and will be capped at $1.5 billion on an ongoing basis.

Continued

EXHIBIT C10.5 GMAC SALE PRESS RELEASE (APRIL 2, 2006)—cont'd

GM and the consortium will invest $1.9 billion of cash in new GMAC preferred equity—$1.4 billion to be issued to GM and $500 million to the Cerberus consortium. GM also will continue to receive its 49% share of common dividends and other value generated by GMAC.

GM will take a noncash pretax charge to earnings of approximately $1.1 billion to $1.3 billion in the second quarter of 2006 associated with the sale of 51% of GMAC.

Citigroup Providing $25 Billion Syndicated Funding Facility

Citigroup will arrange two syndicated asset-based funding facilities that total $25 billion which will support GMAC's ongoing business and enhance GMAC's already strong liquidity position. Citigroup has committed $12.5 billion in the aggregate to these two facilities. The funding facilities are in addition to Citigroup's initial equity investment in GMAC.

"Citigroup has a 90-year relationship with GM and this transaction represents both an opportunity to demonstrate our ongoing commitment to its long-term success as well as an attractive investment opportunity. We are pleased to be part of this unique and strong partnership, led by Cerberus," said Michael Klein, chief executive officer of the Global Banking Unit of Citigroup Corporate and Investment Banking.

The GMAC board of directors will have 13 members—six appointed by the consortium; four appointed by GM; and three independent members. GMAC will continue to be managed by its existing executive management.

GM expects that the introduction of a new controlling investor for GMAC, new equity capital at GMAC, and significantly reduced intercompany exposures to GM will provide GMAC with a solid foundation to improve its current credit rating. GM and GMAC expect that these actions will delink the GMAC credit ratings from those of GM.

EXHIBIT C10.6 GM CALL OPTION SUMMARY

- GM call option term of 10 years on global auto finance business
  - Does not include mortgage and insurance operations
- Can exercise if GM ratings are investment-grade or are higher than GMAC's ratings
- Exercise price greater of
  - fair market value
  - 9.5 times the global auto finance business net income

Source: GMAC Financial Services Fixed Income Investor Presentation, December 1, 2006.

A major motivating factor for Cerberus's investment in GMAC was the assumption that it would be able to transfer GMAC's industrial bank charter to the consortium. It was widely believed (and more or less confirmed by spokespeople from both parties) that a failure to transfer the charter by the end of 2006 would result in a potential deal-breaking roadblock. When the Federal Deposit Insurance Corporation (FDIC) announced a 6-month moratorium on approving new applications for industrial banking charters in the summer of 2006 (largely in response to retailing giant Wal-Mart's application for its own private bank), it placed a

EXHIBIT C10.7 GMAC CREDIT PROFILE, REVENUE DIVERSIFICATION, AND 5-YEAR BOND SPREADS

Strengthened Credit Profile

- New $2.1 billion (face) layer of preferred equity injected
- $1 billion GM equity contribution in March 2007
- Essentially all 2007–08 "after-tax earnings" to be retained by GMAC
- All 2009–11 after-tax profit distributions to Cerberus to be reinvested in GMAC as preferred equity
- Certain unsecured exposure to GM in the United States capped at $1.5 billion
- Eliminated potential risks related to GM pension liability
- Substantial committed funding facilities
  - $10 billion Citibank secured facility in place
  - New $6 billion wholesale bridge facility
- Improved access to unsecured funding at lower cost of borrowing

Gross Revenue—Business Diversification

- Notably strong growth in diversified revenues, with about 50% of revenue being contributed by mortgage and insurance operations

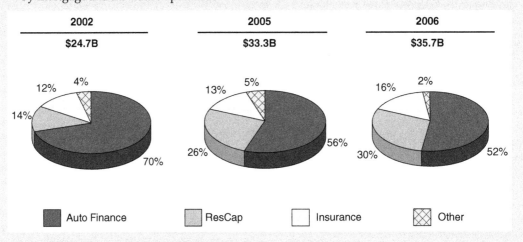

Gross revenue reflects gross financing revenue plus insurance premiums and service revenue plus mortgage banking income plus investment income and other income. Gross revenue is not net of interest and discount expense and provision for credit losses.

GMAC 5-Year Unsecured Bond Spreads

- GMAC bond spreads have narrowed to the lowest level since early 2004
  - Market acknowledges credit delinkage with GM
  - Nonetheless, GMAC 5-year spreads still 90 bps above those of the BBB– composite

Continued

EXHIBIT C10.7 GMAC CREDIT PROFILE, REVENUE DIVERSIFICATION, AND 5-YEAR BOND SPREADS—cont'd

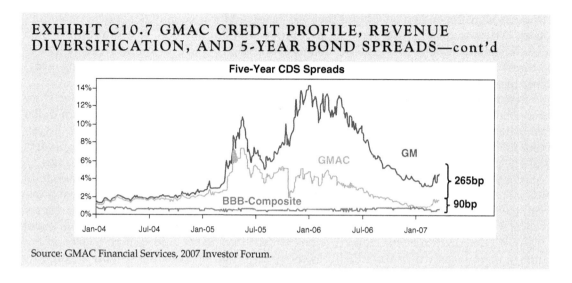

Source: GMAC Financial Services, 2007 Investor Forum.

potentially crippling barrier in front of the deal. In mid-November 2006, however, the FDIC voted to allow GM to transfer its charter to the Cerberus-led group, clearing a major condition for the deal.

Another hurdle was only partially overcome when, in late November 2006, rating services Fitch and Standard & Poor's both upgraded GMAC one notch, to BB+. S&P also removed GMAC from CreditWatch, where it had been since October 2005. At the same time, Moody's confirmed GMAC's unchanged rating at Ba1, leaving in place their negative rating outlook. Moody's noted that GM's call option on GMAC's automotive operations represented an upside ceiling on GMAC's rating. It acknowledged, however, that GMAC's negative rating outlook could improve to stable should the firm strengthen its liquidity profile. As a significant customer, GM would still have an effect on GMAC's future rating status; however, the agencies were explicit in stating that GMAC's rating was no longer directly linked to GM's rating. Although this was a positive development, GMAC's rating as of the end of 2006 was still substantially lower than the company had hoped.

GENERAL MOTORS' SUPPLIER RELATIONSHIPS

More so than almost any other industry in the United States, automakers' relationship with their suppliers has been fraught with difficulty and discontent on both sides for the better part of the past 2 decades. While the US auto industry faced a perfect storm of adverse business conditions, suppliers felt an almost exponential flow-through effect. As Detroit's Big Three scrambled to reduce capacity, lay off workers, and cut costs, GM and the other auto manufacturers pushed for deeper and deeper price concessions from suppliers. As a result, major suppliers, such as Dana Corporation, Collins & Aikman, and Delphi Automotive, were all forced into bankruptcy. The financial crisis for US auto manufacturers revealed the downside of the symbiotic relationship between car makers and their suppliers; while many suppliers were dependent on GM for their existence, GM was equally dependent on its suppliers. GM's top priority was ensuring that production did not stop, as a shutdown would lead to estimated weekly losses in the billions of dollars.[8] As such, its solution essentially was to throw money at the problem through subordinated loans and extended financing—anything to prevent production stoppage.

These bailouts and infusions of capital were an effective band-aid in keeping Big Three production going. However, the dynamics of raising financing changed as the trillion-dollar hedge fund industry became an important new source of cash for the industry. Private investment funds descended on the distressed supplier industry like never before, buying up debt and offering debt financing, including second-lien loans, to these beleaguered companies.

Second-lien loans offered hedge funds—who are "not necessarily driven by internal credit risk ratings"[9]—greater security than other forms of debt, with only slightly lower returns. With the same rights and covenants as a bank loan, this class of debt, as its name suggests, is second in line in terms of repayment priority.[10] Second-lien loans offered returns of about 10%–15% compared to less-secured mezzanine debt rates in the mid-to-high teens and traditional bank loans with substantially lower returns. Second liens are usually secured by either incremental dollars against the same collateral pool as first liens or, more often, by an alternative pool of collateral. In this second scenario, for example, should the first-lien loan be secured by working capital assets (receivables, inventory, etc.), the second-lien loan would use fixed assets (property, plant, and equipment) as collateral (see Exhibit C10.8).[11]

Hedge funds brought much needed funding to the auto suppliers, but they often also introduced disparate priorities to those of the suppliers' traditional providers of debt. With enormous capital behind them, funds such as Appaloosa Management, Davidson Kempner, and legendary buyout investors Carl Ichan and Wilbur Ross swooped into the troubled sector and threw their considerable weight around. Their approach to providing financing and their exposure to—and perspective on—troubled suppliers were often at odds with those of traditional lenders. David Tepper was one of the most active players through his hedge fund, Appaloosa Management. After investing nearly 10% in Delphi's equity immediately following its bankruptcy filing at the end of 2005, Appaloosa became an active player in the supplier's bankruptcy proceedings, leading an equity committee as a voice in the firm's restructuring.[12] The Appaloosa-led committee (partnered with several investors, including Cerberus) reached an agreement in December 2006 to invest $3.4 billion in Delphi and reorganize the company.[13]

---

[8] "GM Boosts Profit But Not Recovery," *Boston Globe*, October 25, 2006.

[9] "Capital Eyes: Completing the Capital Structure with a Second-Lien Loan," Bank of America e-newsletter, April 2003.

[10] "Capital Eyes: Completing the Capital Structure with a Second-Lien Loan," Bank of America e-newsletter, April 2003.

[11] "Capital Eyes: Completing the Capital Structure with a Second-Lien Loan," Bank of America e-newsletter, April 2003.

[12] Micheline Maynard, "Equity Firms to Invest up to $3.4 Billion in Delphi," *International Herald Tribune*, December 18, 2006.

[13] David Welch, "Bankruptcy Becomes Delphi," *BusinessWeek Online*, January 15, 2007.

EXHIBIT C10.8 SECOND-LIEN LOANS AT A GLANCE

Secondary Lien Loans	Asset-Based	Cash Flow-Based
Priority	Secondary credit behind senior lenders.	Secondary credit behind senior lenders.
Structure	Assets serve as collateral —such as accounts receivable, inventory, machinery, equipment, real estate, and intellectual property.	Financing is based on company's going concern value instead of asset liquidation values.
Term	3–5 years.	3–7 years.
Pricing	LIBOR plus 5%–12%.	LIBOR plus 5%–15%.
	Pricing is typically a function of asset quality and supportability of advance rates.	Pricing is typically a function of size, availability of credit ratings, and financial sponsor support.
		Secondary market liquidity afforded to larger tranches ($50 million+) with acceptable risk ratings; minimum B3 (Moody's) or B–(S&P), and equity sponsor support will drive more competitive pricing. Increased leverage or weaker enterprise valuation will typically increase spreads.
Benefits	Additional source of financing, with no equity dilution or additional covenants.	Additional source of financing, with no equity dilution or additional covenants.
	Also offers flexibility in loan amortization schedule.	Also offers flexibility in loan amortization schedule.

Source: GE Commercial Finance.

CERBERUS BUILDS AN EVEN BIGGER AUTO STAGE

In May 2007, Cerberus added to its auto industry investment portfolio by agreeing to acquire 80.1% of Chrysler Holdings for about $7.8 billion from Daimler-Benz, nearly a decade after the German company had paid approximately $36 billion for Chrysler. In this ground-breaking transaction Cerberus stood to gain not only a large, iconic auto manufacturer but also Chrysler Financial, enabling the potential combination of GMAC and Chrysler Financial. This gave Cerberus an approximately 11% market share in auto loans, more than double the market share of Ford Motor Credit, the next largest auto lender. As a result, Cerberus expected to achieve the combined benefits of dominant market share and significant cost and operating synergies. Cerberus was now positioned to create even more meaningful future earnings from its original investment in GMAC.

THE DREAM BECOMES A NIGHTMARE

After acquiring Chrysler, Cerberus piled about $20 billion of debt onto the company's balance sheet, mortgaging all available plants and property to secure this debt. When gasoline prices shot up to $4 a gallon in 2008, consumers started buying smaller cars and hybrids—unfortunately, Chrysler's model line was heavily skewed toward "gas-guzzling" trucks, SUVs, and minivans. At the same time, the subprime mortgage crisis worsened and credit tightened, making it harder for consumers to fund large purchases such as cars. In addition, Chrysler Financial had a difficult time borrowing to fund car loans, given the parent company's increasingly dire financial condition. By summer of that year, Cerberus's plan to turn Chrysler Financial into a highly profitable finance firm had unraveled. Banks forced the company to discontinue leases and loans to customers with marginal credit. This, in turn, negatively impacted Chrysler's ability to sell cars and trucks. During August 2008, Chrysler's sales dropped 35%. In September, Lehman Brothers collapsed and Wall Street fell into turmoil. With customers staying away from dealerships, Chrysler slashed production, revenue plunged, and the company raked up huge losses every day.

By November, Chrysler's sales were in a free fall and Chrysler Financial practically stopped providing loans altogether, leaving dealers with no financing source. At this point, Cerberus came to the realization that an auto financing business was viable only if it is connected with a healthy car company. At the end of March 2009, the US government gave Chrysler 30 days to finalize a deal to merge with Fiat, which required an agreement with the United Auto Workers (UAW) to achieve significant cost cutting. By the middle of April, the only major hurdle was the resolution of $6.9 billion in debt obligations. The US Treasury offered $2.25 billion in cash in exchange for giving up the debt. However, the 45 banks and hedge fund creditors refused to agree, throwing the company into bankruptcy court and destroying any remaining value for Cerberus and its partners.

The action by the banks and hedge funds angered President Obama, who stated that these creditors "decided to hold out for the prospect of an unjustified, taxpayer-funded bailout."[14] Rep. John Dingell, a Michigan Democrat, called the creditors "rogue hedge funds" and "vultures," who "will now be dealt with accordingly in court."[15] The bankruptcy court strategy by the Obama administration was to give the UAW's retiree health fund cash at more than 50 cents on the dollar and majority ownership of Chrysler, while limiting the cash payment to the bank and hedge fund creditors to $2 billion and not providing any equity ownership in Chrysler (even though the creditor claims exceeded the UAW claims prior to entering bankruptcy court). The creditors indicated their intention to argue in court that this outcome meant that the United States was overriding contract law, bankruptcy law, and constitutional protections against the seizure of private property.

In June 2009, GM followed Chrysler into bankruptcy court after a majority of its bondholders refused to exchange their $27 billion in debt for equity in the company. Prior to this event, GMAC's effort to survive included converting to a bank holding company as it accepted $7 billion in federal bailout funds and then changing the name of its online bank to Ally Bank, because this name "conveys the sense of a trusted partner,"[16] according to new chief marketing officer Sanjay Gupta. GM's bankruptcy weighed heavily on GMAC and forced GM and

[14] White House press release, "Remarks By the President on the Auto Industry," April 30, 2009, http://www.whitehouse.gov/the_press_office/remarks-by-the-president-on-the-Auto-Industry.

[15] Neil King Jr. and Jeffrey McCracken, "Chrysler Pushed Into Fiat's Arms," *Wall Street Journal.com*, May 1, 2009.

[16] Aparajita Saha-Bubna, "GMAC Will Change the Name of Its Bank," *Wall Street Journal.com*, May 15, 2009.

Cerberus to significantly reduce their combined ownership of the company, opening the door for majority ownership by the Treasury.

The original separation of GMAC from GM was intended to preserve and eventually increase GMAC's credit ratings so that it could borrow funds at a competitive rate. This effort ultimately proved unsuccessful, as did the effort to achieve scale and profitability by combining GMAC with Chrysler Financial. Cerberus's dream investment in the US auto industry turned into its worst nightmare.

H. J. Heinz M&A

In December 2012, Jorge Paulo Lemann, a cofounder and partner at investment firm 3G Capital, proposed to Warren Buffett that 3G and Berkshire Hathaway acquire H. J. Heinz Company. After negotiating the purchase price, Heinz agreed to continue discussing the acquisition. Although the food industry was mature, 3G and Berkshire Hathaway saw opportunities for Heinz both in expanding into emerging markets and realizing operational efficiencies in production. Investment bankers representing both sides agreed that the acquisition was valued fairly. But was this, in fact, a fair deal? What could be the future consequences for shareholders, management, employees, and citizens of Pittsburgh, where Heinz had long been headquartered? Also, what was the role of activist investors in bringing Heinz to this deal stage?

PROXY FIGHT

Six years prior to the acquisition talks, in 2006, the market overall was booming: companies signaled record profits; merger and acquisition (M&A) activity was strong; and markets were showing signs of recovery from the dot-com crash of the early 2000s. The story was the opposite for Heinz: quarterly losses piled up and shareholders demanded immediate changes. Pressure for improvement was fierce, especially from Nelson Peltz, the outspoken activist investor who had recently acquired a 5.4% stake in Heinz through his investment fund, Trian Fund Management L.P. Peltz demanded that the company either be sold, or shed noncore assets, aggressively repurchase stock, and trim the fat that had built up under the watch of William Johnson, Heinz's CEO. Peltz demanded that he receives five board seats to add real management oversight to the weakening company. In June 2006, Heinz announced a massive restructuring that eliminated more than 2700 employees, closed 15 factories, and initiated a $1 billion share buy-back. Heinz's effort to retain control of the company by embarking on this turnaround plan was only partially successful. Ultimately, Peltz was able to secure two board seats on the twelve-person board. The foundation had been paved for a potential sale of the company down the road.

MARKET CONDITIONS

Following the 2008–09 financial crisis that devastated the worldwide economy, the US economy revived slowly. The GDP growth rate oscillated around 2%, and many economists predicted a slight GDP rebound to 3%. As consumer confidence grew, there was moderate growth in consumer spending and an increase in inventory. Although dissenting opinions existed, many economists and economic indicators pointed to the fact that the United States was on the road to recovery.

Within the food and beverage industry, many companies began to see a rebound in consumer purchasing. Some executives saw growth opportunities by expanding their customer base to new geographic markets (including China, Russia, India, and the Latin America region), while others saw growth opportunities by leveraging economies of scale across fixed production lines. M&A activity increased from lows in 2008, as investors continued to pressure management to divest noncore product lines in search of more efficient businesses and to expand growth and margins through acquisitions.

THE ACQUISITION

Jorge Paulo Lemann and Warren Buffett, who had known each other for years, jointly decided that the Heinz turnaround that was started by Peltz had been successful and there was significant potential for continued global growth. 3G informed CEO Johnson that it and Berkshire Hathaway were interested in jointly acquiring Heinz. Johnson then presented the investors' offer of $70.00 per share of outstanding common stock to the Heinz board. At a meeting on January 15, 2013, the board appointed a transaction committee and voted to retain Centerview and Bank of America Merrill Lynch as advisors. Heinz's board and advisors discussed the trends that were negatively impacting Heinz, including low international GDP growth. They also discussed alternatives to a sale, including remaining a stand-alone company or pursuing acquisition by another company in the food and beverage industry. After updating its strategic plan and financial projections, Heinz informed 3G that without better financial terms it would not continue to discuss the possibility of an acquisition. Two days later, 3G and Berkshire Hathaway returned with a revised proposal of $72.50 per share, for a total transaction value of $28 billion (including Heinz's outstanding debt). A week after the new proposal, Heinz agreed to continue discussing the acquisition.

Following a 40-day "go-shop" period[1] (permitting Heinz some time to look for other investors), Heinz, 3G, and Berkshire Hathaway agreed to sign the deal on February 13, 2013. On that day, Bank of America Merrill Lynch and Centerview presented to the Heinz board their opinions that the acquirers' offer was fair from a financial perspective. The transaction committee of the board also provided its approval of the acquisition after receiving a fairness opinion from Moelis & Company, allowing execution of a merger agreement and a press release announcing the transaction.

---

[1] A go-shop is a provision in a merger that allows a target to solicit interest from potential buyers of the company for a limited period of time (usually less than 2 months) after signing a definitive agreement with an initial buyer. The right to solicit includes the ability to exchange confidential information about the target with a potential buyer based on the completion of a confidentiality agreement. If a better offer emerges from the go-shop process, the target company board is able to exercise a "fiduciary out" and terminate the merger agreement with the initial buyer. This may be subject to payment of a breakup fee.

KEY DATES[2]

December 12, 2012	Jorge Paulo Lemann, partner at 3G Capital, proposes to Warren Buffet that Berkshire Hathaway and 3G acquire Heinz. Buffet responds positively.
December 18, 2012	William Johnson, CEO of Heinz, meets with Lemann and Alexandre Behring, a managing partner at 3G. They discuss the food and beverage industry without proposing an acquisition.
January 10, 2013	Behring tells Johnson that 3G and Berkshire Hathaway are interested in jointly acquiring Heinz. Johnson responds that he will inform the Heinz board if Behring will provide a written proposal, but that Heinz is not for sale.
January 14, 2013	3G and Berkshire Hathaway provide a nonbinding proposal in which they offer to acquire Heinz at $70.00 per share for outstanding common stock.
January 15, 2013	Heinz board meets to discuss the proposed acquisition, then appoints a transaction committee and votes to retain advisors (Centerview and Bank of America Merrill Lynch).
January 20, 2013	Heinz updates its financial projections and strategic plan.
January 22, 2013	Heinz informs 3G that it will not advance discussions without improved financial terms.
January 24, 2013	3G and Berkshire Hathaway provide a revised nonbinding proposal for $72.50 in cash per outstanding common share.
January 30, 2013	Heinz board decides the proposal is an attractive option and allows continued discussions.
February 1, 2013	3G and Berkshire Hathaway send a proposed term sheet to Centerview.
February 7, 2013	New draft term sheet is provided that includes a 40-day "go-shop" period.
February 8, 2013	All parties agree to sign by February 13.
February 13, 2013	Moelis & Company presents a fairness opinion to the transaction committee, which then recommends to the Heinz board that the company be sold. The other advisors present fairness opinions, and the board approves the transaction.
February 14, 2013	Heinz, 3G, and Berkshire Hathaway issue a press release announcing the transaction.
March 30, 2013	Heinz announces that shareholders approved the acquisition.

[2] Heinz Proxy Statement, http://www.sec.gov/Archives/edgar/data/46640/000119312513089866/d491866dprem14a.htm.

THE HISTORY OF HEINZ

The H. J. Heinz Company was established in 1869 when founder Henry J. Heinz began selling bottled horseradish in Sharpsburg, Pennsylvania. The company was incorporated in 1900 and has been headquartered in Pittsburgh, Pennsylvania, since then. In 1896, Heinz was selling more than 60 products, including ketchup, allowing the company to adopt the slogan "57 Varieties." As one of the first food-processing companies in the United States, Heinz allowed customers who were used to preparing their own food to buy preprepared and packaged foods such as beans, soups, pickles, and condiments. Heinz was first listed on the New York Stock Exchange in 1946. It began acquiring other companies in 1978, starting with Weight Watchers International. Heinz had historically placed great emphasis on its headquarters location in Pittsburgh and has demonstrated loyalty to its employees there. The Heinz mission statement is: "As the trusted leader in nutrition and wellness, Heinz—the original Pure Food Company—is dedicated to the sustainable health of people, the planet and our Company."

William Johnson, Heinz's CEO during the acquisition, began working at Heinz in 1982 and became CEO in 2000, when he replaced Tony O'Reilly, the company's first CEO from outside the Heinz family. Heinz announced that at the completion of the acquisition, Bernardo Hees would become the CEO, after transitioning from his previous role as the CEO of Burger King, a portfolio company of 3G.

PRODUCT OVERVIEW

Most consumers associate Heinz with the ubiquitous glass ketchup bottle stamped "57," but Heinz sold hundreds of other products. Its range of products included condiments, frozen food, soups, infant nutrition, and more. Some of its products popular in the United States included Classico pasta sauces, Bagel Bites, and TGI Friday's frozen appetizers. Although many Heinz products were considered staples in the United States, 60% of the company's sales were generated from markets outside the United States.[3] Heinz divided its business segments into North America, US Foodservice, Europe, Asia/Pacific, and the "rest of the world." Heinz had been able to adapt to different cultural climates in a variety of global markets. For example, in Italy, Heinz was known for the baby food Plasmon, and in the United Kingdom, Heinz Beans was very popular. One challenge of selling products in so many different regions was that Heinz's earnings were sensitive to exchange rate variations. Heinz's sales in the "rest of the world," which principally represented developing countries, had expanded rapidly, with 108.3% sales growth in 2012 (see Table C11.1).[4]

[3] Heinz 2012 10-K.

[4] Heinz 2012 10-K.

TABLE C11.1   Heinz Sales by Market Segment ($ in Billions)

Market Segment	Sales in 2011	Sales in 2012
Europe	3.25	3.44
Asia/Pacific	2.32	2.57
North America	3.27	3.24
US Foodservice	1.41	1.42
Rest of the world	0.47	0.98

Source: *Heinz 2012 10-K.*

GROWTH OPPORTUNITIES

Although the food industry was mature, investors had been pleased with Heinz's entrance into the emerging markets, even though these markets represented less than 9% of the company's revenue.[5] Competition in emerging markets was disaggregated. Traditional competitors had entered at approximately the same pace as Heinz, but a clear market leader had not yet been crowned. According to some economists, the BRIC countries (Brazil, Russia, India, and China) were expected to overtake the G7 countries (the United States, the United Kingdom, France, Germany, Italy, Canada, and Japan) in economic growth by the year 2027, fueling strong potential growth in product sales.

Earnings growth for Heinz was expected to be based on the use of improved technology and supply chain management. The company planned on investing less in product R&D as it focused increasingly on improving production procedures to optimize plant capacity utilization and minimize or repurpose waste. Raw material providers and distribution channels were expected to continue to consolidate, creating cost-reduction opportunities for the mainstream food producers, including Heinz.

BUYER OVERVIEW

3G Capital was an investment firm with offices in New York and Rio de Janeiro. 3G's expertise was in the retail and consumer sector. Brazilian cofounders Jorge Paulo Lemann, Carlos Alberto Sicupira, Marcel Herrmann Telles, and Roberto Thompson Motta all acted as board members. 3G acquired Burger King in September 2010 for $4 billion, and two of 3G's cofounders were board members of Burger King. The firm had previously invested in Jack in the Box and Wendy's, but sold its shares prior to its acquisition of Burger King.

Berkshire Hathaway, a holding company, was established in 1955 by Warren Buffett and was headquartered in Omaha, Nebraska. Ranking ninth on *Forbes*'s list of biggest publicly owned companies, Berkshire owned companies in a variety of industries, including insurance, railroad, and retail. Berkshire's portfolio included several food and beverage companies, including Dairy Queen, The Pampered Chef, and See's Candies. Berkshire Hathaway owned 18% of Coca-Cola and a portion of Mars, Inc.

[5] Heinz 2012 10-K.

INVESTMENT BANKERS

For Buyers

J.P. Morgan, Lazard, and Wells Fargo were retained by 3G and Berkshire Hathaway to advise on the transaction and to provide fairness opinions.

For Heinz

Bank of America Merrill Lynch, Centerview, and Moelis & Co. were retained by the Heinz board to advise on the transaction and to provide fairness opinions.

TRANSACTION DYNAMICS

Structuring

Berkshire and 3G considered various forms of legal ownership, ultimately settling on a reverse triangular merger whereby Hawk Acquisition Sub, a fully owned holding corporation of Hawk Acquisition Holding, which was controlled by Berkshire Hathaway and 3G, would merge with Heinz. Immediately after the merger, Hawk Acquisition Sub would be renamed Heinz, as the surviving entity. This structure helped avoid triggering major change in control and due-on-sale clauses embedded within existing Heinz contracts and agreements.

Termination Fees

Heinz agreed to pay a breakup fee of $750 million in cash in the event that the merger agreement was terminated by the company, or if the merger was not completed by November 13, 2013, or if its shareholders did not approve the merger. The buyers agreed to a reverse termination fee of $1.4 billion to protect shareholders in the event that the buyers failed to complete the transaction.

Commitment to Pittsburgh

When Heinz attempted to acquire Hershey Food Company in the early 2000s, the deal fell apart when many Hershey stakeholders expressed concerns about a possible relocation away from Hershey, Pennsylvania, after Heinz was silent regarding this possibility. The Heinz board learned from this experience and considered the impact of potentially transitioning Heinz out of Pittsburgh following sale of the company (including the impact on naming rights to the Heinz football stadium). During merger negotiations, CEO Johnson confirmed that there were no plans to relocate operations outside of the original company headquarters in Pittsburgh.

Synergies

Many M&A transactions generate significant value from merger synergies, which can vary in size for every transaction. The schedule in Table C11.2 provides an overview of typical synergies for different industries.

TABLE C11.2 Median Announced Synergies as a Percentage (%) of Target Sales

Health care	9.9%	Service	4.9%	Food	3.2%
Finance	8.6%	Construction	4.4%	Retail	3.0%
Chemicals	8.0%	Communications	4.4%	Autos	2.9%
Mining	7.3%	Beer	4.2%	Oil	2.4%
Household	5.1%	Technology	4.0%	Wholesale	2.0%
Average	5.0%				

Source: *Adapted from FactSet and Jens Kengelbach, Dennis Utzerath, Christoph Kaserer, and Sebastian Schatt, Boston Consulting Group and Technische Universität München, "Divide and Conquer: How Successful M&A Deals Split the Synergies," March 2013, http://www.bcg.de/documents/file130658.pdf.*

In the Heinz transaction, both buyers had investments in related business: Berkshire Hathaway owned See's Candies, The Pampered Chef, Mars Inc., and Dairy Queen, while 3G Capital owned Burger King Holdings. Despite these complimentary portfolio companies, the buyers estimated virtually zero synergies in the Heinz acquisition. Heinz management and the buyers repeatedly stated that Heinz would continue to operate as an independent portfolio company.

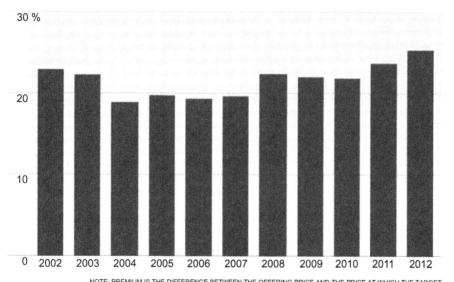

NOTE: PREMIUM IS THE DIFFERENCE BETWEEN THE OFFERING PRICE AND THE PRICE AT WHICH THE TARGET COMPANY'S STOCK CLOSED AT ON THE DAY BEFORE THE DEAL WAS ANNOUNCED.

FIGURE C11.1 Historical acquisition premiums. *Dealogic 2013.*

ACQUISITION PREMIUM

Fig. C11.1 depicts historical acquisition premiums: the acquisition price compared to the target company's share price 1 day prior to announcement of the acquisition. For comparative purposes, Heinz's acquisition price was approximately 20% above the company's previous day closing share price.

EQUITY ANALYST COMMENTARY ON THE ACQUISITION

The packaged food industry has been ripe for value-enhancing transactions—both marriages and divorces—for quite some time. To that end, H. J. Heinz announced that it is to be acquired by Berkshire Hathaway and Brazilian private-equity firm 3G Capital in a $28 billion deal ($72.50 per share). Our initial take is that this is a fabulous deal for Heinz shareholders, representing a nearly 30% premium to our stand-alone $56 fair value estimate and a 20% premium to the closing price the day before the announcement. We are raising our fair value estimate to the takeout price, as we don't anticipate any roadblocks to the deal's completion. *Erin Lash, CFA, Morningstar Equity Research, H.J. Heinz Company, February 14, 2013.*

Apparently, Warren Buffett likes ketchup…a lot. Berkshire Hathaway and 3G announced their acquisition of HNZ for $72.50, representing a 20% premium to yesterday's closing price. We view this acquisition as a good deal for HNZ shareholders and believe it also has positive valuation implications for the group considering: (1) the price paid (a rich multiple, particularly for a financial transaction), (2) that the buyer is Berkshire Hathaway, and (3) that Heinz's recent fundamentals (minimal EBIT growth in the past 12 months) have been challenged. *Edward Aaron, CFA, RBC Capital Markets, Price Target Revision Comment, February 14, 2013.*

Heinz satisfies Berkshire's preference for companies with strong brands, cash flow discipline, and good management. There is also potential for a step-up in profit margins three years from now as the company comes to the completion of its information systems overhaul and starts reaping the benefits of the scale it is building in emerging markets. This bid has positive implications for valuation across the staples space. Low borrowing costs give private equity a lot of firepower, and they like companies like these because the strong and consistent cash flows allow for a high degree of financial leverage. Campbell, Unilever, Nestle, and Kraft Foods have all been considered potential candidates for a Heinz merger in the past, but we would be highly surprised if any one of them tried to top the Berkshire/3G bid. Cost synergies with Kraft and Campbell in the U.S. would theoretically be significant, but not internationally. Neither Unilever nor Nestle appear interested strategically. We think private equity would have a hard time topping this particular bid given the size of the deal and the financial firepower of Berkshire. *Robert Moskow, Credit Suisse, H.J. Heinz Company Research Report, February 14, 2013.*

COMPETITOR OVERVIEW

Heinz, one of the leading food products company in the world, competed with companies on multiple fronts. Although few competitors offered exactly the same robust line of products, the following companies posed continued threats to Heinz's market share.

Campbell

Founded in 1922, Campbell Soup Company, together with its consolidated subsidiaries, produced and marketed convenience food.[6] The Company was headquartered in Camden, New Jersey. Campbell had 11 operating segments based on product type and geographic

[6] The information in this paragraph has been adapted from Campbell 2012 10-K.

location and reports the results of operations in the following segments: US Simple Meals, Global Baking and Snacking, International Simple Meals and Beverages, US Beverages, and North America Foodservice.

ConAgra Foods

ConAgra Foods, Inc. was one of North America's largest packaged food companies.[7] Its portfolio included consumer brands found in 97% of US households. The company had the largest private brand packaged food business in North America and a strong commercial and foodservice business. Consumers could find recognized brands such as Banquet, Chef Boyardee, Egg Beaters, Healthy Choice, Hebrew National, Hunt's, Marie Callender's, Odom's Tennessee Pride, Orville Redenbacher's, PAM, Peter Pan, Reddi-wip, Slim Jim, Snack Pack, and many other ConAgra Foods brands and products, along with food sold by ConAgra Foods under private brands, in grocery, convenience, mass merchandise, club stores, and drugstores. The company also had a strong commercial foods presence, supplying frozen potato and sweet potato products, as well as other vegetable, spice, bakery, and grain products to a variety of well-known restaurants, foodservice operators, and commercial customers. The company's recent acquisitions included Banquet, Chef Boyardee, PAM, Marie Callender's, and Alexia.

Nestlé

Nestlé was the world's number-one food and drinks company in terms of sales. Nestlé was also the world leader in coffee (Nescafé).[8] It also made coffee for the home-brewing system, Nespresso. Nestlé was one of the world's top bottled water makers (Nestlé Waters), one of the biggest frozen pizza makers (DiGiorno), and a big player in the pet food business (Friskies, Purina). Its most well-known global food brands included Buitoni, Dreyer's, Maggi, Milkmaid, Carnation, and Kit Kat. The company owned Gerber Products and Jenny Craig. North America was Nestlé's most important market.

Kraft Foods

Kraft Foods Group was one of the largest consumer packaged food and beverage companies in North America and one of the largest worldwide among publicly traded consumer packaged food and beverage companies, with net revenues of $18.3 billion and earnings from continuing operations before income taxes of $2.5 billion in 2012.[9] The company manufactured and marketed food and beverage products, including refrigerated meals; refreshment beverages; and coffee, cheese, and other grocery products, primarily

[7] The information in this paragraph has been adapted from ConAgra Foods Company Fact Sheet, http://www.conagrafoods.com/news-room/company-fact-sheet and "ConAgra Foods: What Do We Do?" https://www.youtube.com/watch?v=gVz5UagmjwI.

[8] The information in this paragraph has been adapted from Nestlé S.A. Company Profile, http://biz.yahoo.com/ic/41/41815.html.

[9] The information in this paragraph has been adapted from Kraft 2012 10-K.

in the United States and Canada, under a host of iconic brands. Its diverse brand portfolio consisted of many of the most popular food brands in North America, including two brands with annual net revenues exceeding $1 billion each—Kraft cheeses, dinners, and dressings and Oscar Mayer meats—plus more than 25 brands with annual net revenues of between $100 million and $1 billion each.

General Mills

General Mills, Inc., incorporated in 1928, was a leading global manufacturer and marketer of branded consumer foods sold through retail stores.[10] The Company was also a leading supplier of branded and unbranded food products to the foodservice and commercial baking industries. It manufactured products in 16 countries and marketed them in more than 100 countries. Its joint ventures manufactured and marketed products in more than 130 countries worldwide. Product categories in the United States included ready-to-eat cereals; refrigerated yogurt; ready-to-serve soup; dry dinners; shelf stable and frozen vegetables; refrigerated and frozen dough products; dessert and baking mixes; frozen pizza and pizza snacks; grain, fruit, and savory snacks; and a wide variety of organic products including granola bars, cereal, and soup. In Canada, its product categories included ready-to-eat cereals, shelf stable and frozen vegetables, dry dinners, refrigerated and frozen dough products, dessert and baking mixes, frozen pizza snacks, refrigerated yogurt, and grain and fruit snacks. In markets outside the United States and Canada, its product categories included superpremium ice cream and frozen desserts, refrigerated yogurt, snacks, shelf stable and frozen vegetables, refrigerated and frozen dough products, and dry dinners.

Smucker

The J.M. Smucker Company was established in 1897 and incorporated in Ohio in 1921.[11] It operated in the manufacturing and marketing of branded food products globally, although the majority of its sales were in the United States. Net sales outside the United States represented approximately 9% of consolidated net sales for 2013. The company had three reportable segments: US Retail Coffee; US Retail Consumer Foods and International, Foodservice, and Natural Foods. The two US retail market segments in total comprised more than 75% of consolidated net sales in 2013 and represented a major portion of its strategic focus. The International, Foodservice, and Natural Foods segments represented sales outside of the US retail markets and had grown recently primarily as a result of contribution from the acquisition of the North American foodservice coffee and hot beverage business from Sara Lee Corporation in January 2012. The company's principal products were coffee, peanut butter, fruit spreads, shortening and oils, baking mixes and ready-to-spread frostings, canned milk, flour and baking ingredients, juices and beverages, frozen sandwiches, toppings, syrups, and pickles and condiments.

---

[10] The information in this paragraph has been adapted from General Mills 2013 10-K.

[11] The information in this paragraph has been adapted from Smucker 2010 10-K.

Kellogg Company

The Kellogg Company, founded in 1906 and incorporated in Delaware in 1922, was engaged in the manufacture and marketing of ready-to-eat cereal and convenience foods.[12] Its principal products were ready-to-eat cereals and convenience foods, such as cookies, crackers, savory snacks, toaster pastries, cereal bars, fruit-flavored snacks, frozen waffles, and veggie foods. These products were mainly manufactured in-house in 18 countries and marketed in more than 180 countries. Its cereal products were generally marketed under the Kellogg's name and were sold to the grocery trade through direct sales forces for resale to consumers. It also marketed cookies, crackers, chips, and other convenience foods, under brands such as Kellogg's, Keebler, Cheez-It, Murray, Austin, and Famous Amos, to supermarkets in the United States.

The Hershey Company

The Hershey Company was incorporated under the laws of the State of Delaware on October 24, 1927, as a successor to a business founded in 1894 by Milton S. Hershey.[13] It was the largest producer of quality chocolate in North America and a global leader in chocolate and sugar confectionery. Its principal product groups included chocolate and sugar confectionery products; pantry items, such as baking ingredients and toppings; beverages; and gum and mint refreshment products. The company marketed its products in approximately 70 countries worldwide. It operated under a matrix reporting structure designed to ensure continued focus on North America and on continuing its transformation into a more global company. Its business was organized around geographic regions and strategic business units; this structure was designed to enable the company to build processes for repeatable success in its global markets.

Groupe Danone

Groupe Danone was a société anonyme, a form of limited liability company, organized under the laws of the Republic of France.[14] It was incorporated on February 2, 1899. Under Groupe Danone's bylaws, revised in 1941, the company's existence was to last 141 years, until December 13, 2040, except in the event of earlier dissolution or extension. In 1997 the group's management decided to focus on three core activities on a worldwide basis (fresh dairy products, beverages, and biscuits and cereal products). The group had since completed several significant divestitures in grocery, pasta, ready-to-serve meals, and confectionery activities, mainly in France, Belgium, Italy, Germany, and Spain.

---

[12] The information in this paragraph has been adapted from Kellogg Company Profile, http://www.buyandhold.com/StockMgr? request = display.profile&symbol = k.

[13] The information in this paragraph has been adapted from Hershey Company Profile, http://www.buyandhold.com/StockMgr? request = display.profile&symbol = HSY.

[14] The information in this paragraph has been adapted from Groupe Danone 20-F SEC Filing, April 2, 2007.

PepsiCo, Inc.

PepsiCo, Inc. was incorporated in Delaware in 1919 and was reincorporated in North Carolina in 1986.[15] It was a leading global food and beverage company with brands that were respected household names throughout the world. Through its operations, authorized bottlers, contract manufacturers, and other partners, the company made, marketed, sold, and distributed a wide variety of convenient and enjoyable foods and beverages, serving customers and consumers in more than 200 countries and territories. Its products were brought to market through direct-store-delivery, customer warehouse, and distributor networks. It owned numerous valuable trademarks, including Aquafina, Aunt Jemima, Cap'n Crunch, Cheetos, Cracker Jack, Doritos, Duyvis, Frito-Lay, Fritos, Gatorade, Izze, Mother's, Mountain Dew, Müller, Naked, Pepsi, Propel, Quaker, Rice-A-Roni, Ruffles, 7UP, Sierra Mist, SoBe, Stacy's, SunChips, Tostitos, and Tropicana. Joint ventures in which it participated either owned or had the right to use certain trademarks, such as Lipton, Müller, Starbucks, and Sabra.

Unilever plc

Unilever was one of the world's leading suppliers of food, home, and personal care products with sales in more than 190 countries.[16] Its products were present in 7 out of 10 homes globally and were used by more than 2 billion people on a daily basis. It generated annual sales of more than €50 billion in 2012. More than half of the company's footprint was in the faster-growing developing and emerging markets (55% in 2012). Its portfolio included some of the world's best known brands, including Knorr, Persil/Omo, Dove, Sunsilk, Hellmann's, Lipton, Rexona/Sure, Wall's, Lux, Rama, Pond's, and Axe.

Mondelēz International, Inc.

Mondelēz International was one of the world's largest snack companies, with global net revenues of $35.0 billion and earnings from continuing operations of $1.6 billion in 2012.[17] Beginning on October 1, 2012, following the spinoff of its North American grocery operations to their shareholders, Mondelēz International was a "new" company in name and strategy, yet it carried forward the values of its legacy organization and the heritage of its iconic brands. The company manufactured and marketed food and beverage products for consumers in approximately 165 countries around the world. It held the number one position globally in biscuits, chocolate, candy, and powdered beverages, as well as the number two position in gum and coffee. Its portfolio included nine brands with annual revenues exceeding $1 billion each, including Oreo, Nabisco, and LU biscuits; Milka, Cadbury Dairy Milk, and Cadbury chocolates; Trident gum; Jacobs coffee; and Tang powdered beverage. It changed its name from Kraft Foods Inc. to Mondelēz International, Inc. following a spinoff on October 2, 2012.

[15] The information in this paragraph has been adapted from PepsiCo 2012 10-K.

[16] The information in this paragraph has been adapted from "Unilever Completes Sale of Wish-Bone and Western brands to Pinnacle Foods," press release, October 1, 2013.

[17] The information in this paragraph has been adapted from Mondelēz International 2012 10-K.

EXHIBIT C11.1 HEINZ FINANCIAL AND MARKET INFORMATION

HEINZ SHARE PRICE: JANUARY 22, 2007–JANUARY 22, 2013

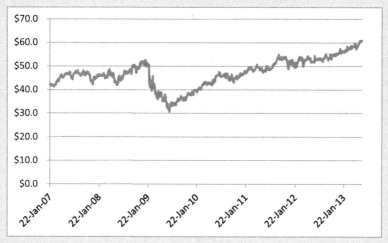

Source: Yahoo!Finance.

HEINZ SHARE PRICE: NOVEMBER 1, 2012–APRIL 1, 2013

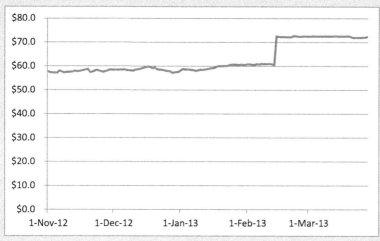

Source: Yahoo!Finance.

EXHIBIT C11.2 DISCOUNTED CASH FLOW ANALYSIS[18]

Cost of equity for heinz and its competitors

Company	Beta[a]		Data	Rate (%)
Campbell	0.848		10-year treasury yield	1.8
ConAgra Foods	0.677		Market risk premium	6.0
General Mills	0.688			
Groupe Danone	0.736			
Hershey	0.780			
Kellogg	0.665			
Kraft	0.897			
Mondelēz	1.030			
Nestle S.A.	0.821			
PepsiCo	0.657			
Unilever	0.772			
Smucker	0.817			
Mean	0.782			
Median	0.776			
Heinz	0.651			

[a] Represents levered beta.

Source: FactSet.

EXHIBIT C11.2 DISCOUNTED CASH FLOW ANALYSIS[18]—cont'd

Cost of debt for heinz (US$ in thousands)

Debt	2013	2012
Japanese yen credit agreement due October 2012 (variable rate)	–	186,869
Other U.S. dollar debt due May 2013–November 2034 (0.94%–7.96%)	25,688	43,164
Other non-U.S. dollar debt due May 2013–May 2023 (3.50%–11.00%)	56,293	64,060
5.35% U.S. dollar notes due July 2013	499,993	499,958
8.0% Heinz finance preferred stock due July 2013	350,000	350,000
Japanese yen credit agreement due December 2013 (variable rate)	163,182	199,327
U.S. dollar private placement notes due May 2014–May 2021 (2.11%–4.23%)	500,000	500,000
Japanese yen credit agreement due October 2015 (variable rate)	152,983	–
U.S. dollar private placement notes due July 2016–July 2018 (2.86%–3.55%)	100,000	100,000
2.00% U.S. dollar notes due September 2016	299,933	299,913
1.50% U.S. dollar notes due March 2017	299,648	299,556
U.S. dollar remarketable securities due December 2020	119,000	119,000
3.125% U.S. dollar notes due September 2021	395,772	395,268
2.85% U.S. dollar notes due March 2022	299,565	299,516
6.375% U.S. dollar debentures due July 2028	231,396	231,137
6.25% British pound notes due February 2030	192,376	202,158
6.75% U.S. dollar notes due March 2032	435,185	435,112
7.125% U.S. dollar notes due August 2039	628,082	626,747
Total long-term debt	4,749,096	4,851,785
Hedge accounting adjustments	122,455	128,444
Less portion due within one year	(1,023,212)	(200,248)
Total long-term debt	3,848,339	4,779,981
Weighted-average interest rate on long-term debt	4.70%	4.28%

Source: Heinz 2012 10-K.

Heinz taxes

Tax Rate History	2013	2012	2011
U.S. federal statutory tax rate	35.0%	35.0%	35.0%
Effective tax rate	18.0%	19.8%	26.2%

Source: Heinz 2012 10-K.

Heinz financial forecast (US$ in millions, except per share data)

For Fiscal Year Ending April	2013E	2014P	2015P	2016P	2017P	2018P
Revenue	11,675	12,141	12,657	13,112	13,744	14,446
EBITDA	2,057	2,195	2,340	2,453	2,613	2,789
EBIT	1,705	1,834	1,965	2,061	2,202	2,355
Fully diluted earnings per share	$3.58	$3.78	$3.83	$4.00	$4.29	$4.60

Source: Heinz 2012 10-K.

[18] Note that prevailing interest rates at the time of the transaction were low by historical standards. The actual cost of capital that was used by the company reflected a higher interest rate than the rate implied by outstanding debt. Students should calculate WACC based on information in Exhibit C11.2 as the lower bound for WACC, but a sensitivity analysis should also be completed based on realistic long-term expectations for interest rates and consideration of the issuance by the company of $8 billion of preferred shares with a 9% dividend to Berkshire Hathaway.

EXHIBIT C11.3 HEINZ HISTORICAL FINANCIAL STATEMENTS (US$ IN THOUSANDS, EXCEPT PER SHARE DATA, UNLESS OTHERWISE SPECIFIED)

Consolidated statements of income

	12 Months Ended		
	Apr. 28, 2013	Apr. 29, 2012	Apr. 27, 2011
Sales	11,675	11,508	10,559
Cost of products sold	7,333	7,513	6,614
Gross profit	4,195	3,995	3,944
Selling, general, and administrative expenses	2,534	2,492	2,257
Operating income	1,662	1,502	1,688
Interest income	28	35	23
Interest expense	284	293	273
Other expense, net	(62)	(8)	(21)
Loss from continuing operations before income tax	1,344	1,236	1,416
Provision for income taxes	242	245	371
Income from continuing operations	1,102	991	1,046
Loss from discontinued operations, net of tax	(75)	(51)	(40)
Net income	1,027	940	1,006
Less: Net income attributable to the non-controlling interest	14	17	16
Net income attributable to H. J. Heinz Company	1,013	923	990
Average common shares outstanding—basic (millions)	321	321	320
Average common shares outstanding—diluted (millions)	323	323	323
Earnings before interest, taxes, depreciation, and amortization	2,057	1,947	1,862

Source: Heinz 2012 10-K.

EXHIBIT C11.3 HEINZ HISTORICAL FINANCIAL STATEMENTS (US$ IN THOUSANDS, EXCEPT PER SHARE DATA, UNLESS OTHERWISE SPECIFIED)—cont'd

Consolidated balance sheets

	12 Months Ended	
	Apr. 28, 2013	Apr. 29, 2012
Cash and cash equivalents	2,477	1,330
Receivables (net of allowance)	1,074	994
Inventories	1,333	1,329
Prepaid expenses	252	229
Total current assets	5,136	3,882
Property, plant,and equipment, net	2,459	2,484
Goodwill and intangible assets	4,495	4,684
Other non-current assets	850	933
Total assets	12,939	11,983
Short-term debt and current portion of long-term debt	2,160	247
Payables	1,493	1,349
Accrued liabilities	1,019	951
Income taxes	114	102
Total current liabilities	4,787	2,648
Long-term debt	3,848	4,780
Deferred income taxes	679	818
Non-pension post-retirement benefits	240	231
Other non-current liabilities	507	581
Total long-term debt and other non-current liabilities	5,274	6,411
Non-controlling interest	77	166
Capital stock	108	108
Additional capital	609	595
Retained earnings	7,907	7,567
Treasury shares, at cost	(4,647)	(4,666)
Accumulated other comprehensive loss	(1,175)	(845)
Total equity	2,849	2,811
Total liabilities and equity	12,939	11,983

Source: Heinz 2012 10-K.

Continued

EXHIBIT C11.3 HEINZ HISTORICAL FINANCIAL STATEMENTS (US$ IN THOUSANDS, EXCEPT PER SHARE DATA, UNLESS OTHERWISE SPECIFIED)—cont'd

Consolidated statements of cash flows

	12 Months Ended		
	Apr 28, 2013	Apr 29, 2012	Apr 27, 2011
OPERATING ACTIVITIES:			
Net income	1,027	940	1,006
Adjustments to reconcile net income to cash provided by operating activities:			
Depreciation	302	296	255
Amortization	47	47	43
Deferred tax (benefit)/provision	(87)	(95)	154
Pension contributions	(69)	(23)	(22)
Asset write-downs/impairments	56	59	0
Other items, net	85	75	98
Changes in current assets and liabilities, excluding effects of acquisitions:			
Receivables (incl. proceeds from securitization)	(166)	172	(91)
Inventories	(49)	61	(81)
Prepaid expenses and other current assets	14	(12)	(2)
Accounts payable	169	(72)	233
Accrued liabilities	72	(20)	(61)
Income taxes	(9)	66	51
Cash provided by operating activities	1,390	1,493	1,584
INVESTING ACTIVITIES:			
Capital expenditures	(399)	(419)	(336)
Proceeds from disposals of PP&E, net	19	7	(605)
Proceeds from divestitures	17	4	2
Sale of short-term investments	0	57	0
Change in restricted cash	4	(39)	(5)
Other items, net	(14)	(11)	(6)
Cash used for investing activities	(373)	(402)	(950)
FINANCING ACTIVITIES:			
Net proceeds/(payments) on short-termdebt	1,090	(43)	(193)
Dividends	(666)	(619)	(580)
Purchase of treasury stock	(139)	(202)	(70)
Exercise of stock options	113	83	155
Acquisition of subsidiary shares from non-controlling interests	(80)	(55)	(6)
Earn-out settlement	(45)	0	0
Other items, net	2	1	28
Cash provided by/(used for) financing activities	257	(363)	(483)
Effect of exchange rate changes on cash and CE	(128)	(122)	90
Net increase in cash and cash equivalents	1,146	606	241
Cash and cash equivalents at beginning of year	1,330	724	483
Cash and cash equivalents at end of year	2,477	1,330	724

Source: Heinz 2012 10-K.

EXHIBIT C11.4 COMPARABLE COMPANY METRICS

Growth analysis

	Revenue Growth (%)				EBITDA Growth (%)				EPS Growth (%)			
	2011	2012	2013(E)	2014(E)	2011	2012	2013(E)	2014(E)	2011	2012	2013(E)	2014(E)
Campbell	(0.2)	4.5	5.1	2.1	(7.8)	9.9	1.4	3.3	(4.3)	8.6	(1.7)	5.5
ConAgra Foods	7.8	16.8	13.4	0.3	3.0	19.0	18.0	5.6	5.1	17.4	7.7	10.9
General Mills	11.9	6.7	3.2	3.7	5.3	4.4	5.3	5.2	3.2	5.1	8.2	7.8
Groupe Danone	13.6	8.0	3.3	4.5	9.7	4.3	(2.5)	7.2	6.6	4.2	(4.2)	6.9
Hershey	7.2	9.3	6.7	6.2	8.5	10.4	9.9	8.6	10.6	14.9	14.6	10.7
Kellogg	6.5	7.6	4.5	2.7	(1.6)	5.0	7.5	4.8	2.4	(0.3)	11.8	7.6
Kraft	—	—	(0.4)	2.4	—	—	9.8	12.3	—	—	1.7	14.0
Mondelēz	10.5	(35.6)	1.2	4.3	9.3	(37.6)	(0.1)	10.2	13.4	(39.3)	12.0	9.3
Nestlé S.A.	(23.8)	10.2	1.7	4.3	(9.3)	9.9	2.7	5.8	(4.8)	9.6	1.8	6.7
PepsiCo	15.0	(1.5)	1.4	4.2	8.3	(5.6)	3.5	6.8	6.5	(6.8)	5.6	8.5
Unilever	1.6	12.2	1.2	1.6	(2.0)	12.4	4.6	3.7	(6.1)	12.6	1.2	5.7
Smucker	14.5	6.7	(0.5)	3.0	1.5	8.5	4.4	4.7	0.9	13.5	8.6	8.5
Mean	5.9	4.1	3.4	3.3	2.3	3.7	5.4	6.5	3.0	3.6	5.6	8.5
Median	7.8	7.6	2.4	3.3	3.0	8.5	4.5	5.7	3.2	8.6	6.7	8.1
Heinz	8.6	8.8	1.9	4.4	2.9	1.7	7.4	6.4	9.5	8.1	4.0	5.2

Source: FactSet.

Continued

EXHIBIT C11.4 COMPARABLE COMPANY METRICS—cont'd

Profitability analysis

	Gross Margin (%)				EBITDA Margin (%)				Net Margin (%)			
	2011	2012	2013(E)	2014(E)	2011	2012	2013(E)	2014(E)	2011	2012	2013(E)	2014(E)
Campbell	38.8	37.3	37.5	37.6	19.3	20.3	19.5	19.8	10.0	10.4	9.6	9.8
ConAgra Foods	22.2	22.9	22.3	22.9	12.9	13.1	13.6	14.4	5.8	5.0	5.6	6.3
General Mills	36.9	36.1	36.2	36.5	19.9	19.5	19.9	20.2	9.4	10.4	10.3	10.5
Groupe Danone	52.5	50.8	49.8	49.8	18.0	17.4	16.4	16.8	8.7	8.0	7.2	7.9
Hershey	42.4	43.8	46.2	47.0	21.4	21.7	22.3	22.8	10.3	9.9	11.8	12.3
Kellogg	41.3	40.1	38.6	39.2	17.8	17.3	17.8	18.2	9.3	6.8	9.2	9.6
Kraft	—	31.8	32.8	32.8	—	16.9	18.6	20.4	—	9.0	9.2	10.2
Mondelēz	35.1	37.4	37.5	38.2	16.0	15.5	15.3	16.2	7.5	8.6	7.9	8.0
Nestlé S.A.	47.4	47.6	47.9	48.0	18.7	18.6	18.8	19.1	11.3	11.5	11.4	11.7
PepsiCo	52.0	52.2	53.0	53.3	19.7	18.9	19.3	19.8	10.6	9.9	10.1	10.4
Unilever	39.9	41.2	42.8	42.8	16.1	16.1	16.6	17.0	9.2	8.8	9.1	9.4
Smucker	34.2	34.6	36.4	36.7	20.2	20.6	21.6	21.9	8.3	9.2	10.4	10.8
Mean	40.2	39.7	40.1	40.4	18.2	18.0	18.3	18.9	9.1	9.0	9.3	9.7
Median	39.9	38.8	38.0	38.7	18.7	18.0	18.7	19.4	9.3	9.1	9.4	10.0
Heinz	35.5	34.3	35.8	36.0	17.3	17.3	17.9	18.2	7.9	9.5	9.6	9.7

Source: FactSet.

Returns analysis

	Return on Assets (%)				Return on Equity (%)				Dividend per Share (%)			
	2011	2012	2013(E)	2014(E)	2011	2012	2013(E)	2014(E)	2011	2012	2013(E)	2014(E)
Campbell	11.5	11.2	9.7	10.1	67.4	69.3	60.4	51.9	1.16	1.16	1.25	1.34
ConAgra Foods	6.7	4.9	4.6	4.8	16.7	15.6	15.9	14.5	0.95	0.99	1.00	1.02
General Mills	7.9	8.5	8.3	8.6	23.9	26.0	24.7	24.6	1.22	1.32	1.52	1.71
Groupe Danone	5.9	5.8	5.2	5.8	13.6	13.6	12.4	13.7	1.39	1.45	1.45	1.55
Hershey	14.5	14.4	16.6	16.6	69.5	68.8	64.2	53.6	1.38	1.54	1.81	2.03
Kellogg	10.4	7.1	8.9	9.2	62.8	45.6	46.1	39.6	1.67	1.74	1.79	1.89
Kraft	–	7.0	7.2	8.2	–	46.0	45.0	47.0	–	0.50	2.03	2.12
Mondelēz	4.3	3.6	3.7	4.0	11.4	8.8	7.8	7.5	1.16	0.52	0.54	0.58
Nestlé S.A.	8.4	8.8	8.3	8.6	15.9	18.0	17.0	17.0	1.95	2.05	2.13	2.25
PepsiCo	10.0	8.8	8.9	9.4	33.2	29.8	29.8	30.9	2.03	2.13	2.24	2.40
Unilever	10.4	10.2	10.2	10.0	29.1	30.0	28.6	28.1	1.17	1.27	1.43	1.50
Smucker	5.3	6.0	6.7	7.0	8.8	10.6	11.8	12.6	1.89	2.05	2.31	2.54
Mean	8.7	8.0	8.2	8.5	32.0	31.8	30.3	28.4	1.45	1.39	1.62	1.74
Median	8.4	7.8	8.3	8.6	23.9	27.9	26.7	26.3	1.38	1.39	1.65	1.80
Heinz	7.6	7.6	9.5	9.9	29.4	31.5	39.2	37.4	1.92	2.06	2.22	2.39

Source: FactSet.

Continued

EXHIBIT C11.4 COMPARABLE COMPANY METRICS—cont'd

Leverage analysis

	Net Debt/EBITDA				Debt/Equity				Assets/Equity			
	2011	2012	2013(E)	2014(E)	2011	2012	2013(E)	2014(E)	2011	2012	2013(E)	2014(E)
Campbell	0.6x	0.5x	0.4x	0.5x	0.4x	0.5x	0.6x	0.5x	5.5x	6.9x	5.7x	4.7x
ConAgra Foods	0.7x	0.3x	0.3x	0.3x	0.8x	1.0x	1.3x	1.2x	2.5x	3.8x	3.2x	2.9x
General Mills	0.5x	0.5x	0.5x	0.5x	1.1x	1.3x	1.4x	1.8x	3.2x	3.0x	3.0x	2.7x
Groupe Danone	0.5x	0.5x	0.5x	0.5x	1.7x	1.9x	2.7x	2.1x	2.3x	2.4x	2.4x	2.3x
Hershey	1.2x	1.2x	1.5x	1.8x	1.6x	2.1x	6.1x	—	5.1x	4.5x	3.4x	3.1x
Kellogg	0.4x	0.4x	0.4x	0.4x	0.5x	0.6x	0.6x	0.6x	6.8x	6.2x	4.4x	4.1x
Kraft	—	0.4x	0.4x	0.4x	0.4x	0.5x	0.5x	—	—	6.5x	6.0x	5.8x
Mondelēz	0.3x	0.3x	0.4x	0.4x	2.7x	2.8x	2.9x	2.1x	2.7x	2.3x	1.9x	1.9x
Nestlé S.A.	1.7x	1.1x	1.0x	1.3x	4.1x	5.0x	6.5x	4.7x	2.0x	2.1x	2.0x	1.9x
PepsiCo	0.6x	0.6x	0.6x	0.6x	1.1x	1.1x	1.1x	0.9x	3.5x	3.3x	3.3x	3.2x
Unilever	1.0x	1.0x	1.1x	1.1x	2.1x	2.3x	2.4x	3.9x	3.2x	2.7x	2.9x	2.7x
Smucker	0.8x	0.7x	0.7x	0.8x	3.0x	3.2x	3.6x	2.5x	1.8x	1.8x	1.8x	1.8x
Mean	0.8x	0.6x	0.6x	0.7x	1.6x	1.9x	2.5x	2.0x	3.5x	3.8x	3.3x	3.1x
Median	0.6x	0.5x	0.5x	0.5x	1.3x	1.6x	1.9x	1.9x	3.2x	3.2x	3.1x	2.8x
Heinz	0.5x	0.5x	0.6x	0.7x	1.8x	1.8x	1.6x	1.3x	3.9x	4.3x	3.9x	3.6x

Source: FactSet.

Valuation analysis 1

	Price/Book				Price/Sales				Price/Earnings to Growth			
	2011	2012	2013(E)	2014(E)	2011	2012	2013(E)	2014(E)	2011	2012	2013(E)	2014(E)
Campbell	9.8x	9.0x	11.6x	8.5x	1.4x	1.4x	1.8x	1.6x	9.8x	9.0x	11.6x	8.5x
ConAgra Foods	2.3x	2.1x	2.6x	2.4x	0.8x	0.8x	0.9x	0.8x	2.3x	2.1x	2.6x	2.4x
General Mills	4.0x	3.5x	4.7x	4.7x	1.7x	1.5x	1.7x	1.8x	4.0x	3.5x	4.7x	4.7x
Groupe Danone	2.1x	2.4x	2.4x	2.7x	1.8x	1.6x	1.5x	1.6x	2.1x	2.4x	2.4x	2.7x
Hershey	11.5x	16.2x	15.7x	16.5x	1.9x	2.3x	2.4x	3.1x	11.5x	16.2x	15.7x	16.5x
Kellogg	8.7x	10.3x	8.3x	6.3x	1.5x	1.4x	1.4x	1.5x	8.7x	10.3x	8.3x	6.3x
Kraft	—	—	7.6x	8.6x	—	—	1.5x	1.7x	—	—	7.6x	8.6x
Mondelez	1.0x	1.2x	1.4x	1.8x	1.1x	1.2x	1.3x	1.7x	1.0x	1.2x	1.4x	1.8x
Nestlé S.A.	3.0x	3.0x	3.1x	3.4x	1.7x	2.1x	2.1x	2.3x	3.0x	3.0x	3.1x	3.4x
PepsiCo	4.9x	5.1x	4.8x	5.7x	1.8x	1.6x	1.6x	2.0x	4.9x	5.1x	4.8x	5.7x
Unilever	4.5x	5.0x	5.5x	5.5x	1.6x	1.7x	1.7x	1.7x	4.5x	5.0x	5.5x	5.5x
Smucker	—	—	2.2x	2.2x	1.8x	1.6x	1.9x	2.0x	—	—	2.2x	2.2x
Mean	5.2x	5.8x	5.8x	5.7x	1.6x	1.6x	1.7x	1.8x	5.2x	5.8x	5.8x	5.7x
Median	4.2x	4.3x	4.8x	5.1x	1.7x	1.6x	1.7x	1.7x	4.2x	4.3x	4.8x	5.1x
Heinz	5.1x	5.5x	7.6x	6.9x	1.5x	1.5x	2.0x	1.9x	5.1x	5.5x	5.6x	5.5x

Source: FactSet.

Continued

EXHIBIT C11.4 COMPARABLE COMPANY METRICS—cont'd

Valuation analysis 2

	Price/Earnings				Enterprise Value/EBITDA				Enterprise Value/Free Cash Flow			
	2011	2012	2013(E)	2014(E)	2011	2012	2013(E)	2014(E)	2011	2012	2013(E)	2014(E)
Campbell	13.0x	13.6x	17.7x	16.3x	8.2x	8.7x	11.5x	10.2x	15.3x	18.4x	47.4x	21.2x
ConAgra Foods	14.5x	13.7x	15.6x	14.2x	7.6x	7.8x	11.6x	9.4x	14.3x	18.6x	24.6x	22.4x
General Mills	16.0x	15.0x	17.5x	17.6x	10.0x	9.6x	10.8x	10.9x	36.1x	18.4x	16.3x	20.3x
Groupe Danone	17.3x	16.8x	16.6x	19.1x	11.8x	10.9x	10.7x	11.9x	22.3x	20.6x	19.1x	31.0x
Hershey	18.5x	21.9x	22.3x	26.5x	9.7x	11.6x	12.0x	14.6x	17.7x	38.1x	20.1x	36.8x
Kellogg	15.5x	15.0x	16.6x	16.6x	10.2x	10.1x	11.2x	11.3x	20.7x	23.7x	22.6x	32.5x
Kraft	—	—	16.5x	19.0x	—	—	11.5x	11.9x	—	—	13.7x	39.9x
Mondelēz	10.2x	10.7x	18.3x	21.9x	10.2x	10.4x	11.2x	13.6x	38.9x	33.1x	36.8x	35.3x
Nestlé S.A.	17.0x	17.6x	17.7x	19.5x	11.2x	12.3x	12.3x	13.1x	23.2x	37.8x	20.9x	28.4x
PepsiCo	15.8x	15.1x	16.7x	19.9x	10.1x	9.6x	10.3x	12.0x	23.4x	22.6x	22.2x	29.5x
Unilever	15.8x	18.2x	18.7x	19.1x	10.3x	11.7x	11.4x	11.3x	22.1x	28.5x	22.0x	25.0x
Smucker	16.0x	16.8x	19.2x	18.8x	8.8x	9.6x	10.6x	10.4x	45.9x	14.3x	19.8x	20.8x
Mean	15.4x	15.8x	17.8x	19.0x	9.8x	10.2x	11.3x	11.7x	25.5x	24.9x	23.8x	28.6x
Median	15.8x	15.1x	17.6x	19.0x	10.1x	10.1x	11.3x	11.6x	22.3x	22.6x	21.5x	29.0x
Heinz	16.7x	15.6x	20.5x	19.2x	10.4x	10.4x	12.8x	12.0x	17.0x	20.2x	24.7x	22.2x

Source: FactSet.

EXHIBIT C11.5 COMPARABLE TRANSACTION METRICS (US$ IN MILLIONS, EXCEPT MULTIPLES)

The following is a list of transactions from the packaged food, beverage, and related industries. Use discretion in choosing comparable transactions for valuation analysis because some of the target companies may be better comparables than others.

Announcement Date	Target	Acquiror	Ent Value ($bn)	Ent Value/LTM EBITDA	Revenue	EBITDA	Net Income	Capex	Cash	Debt	Assets
Dec. 2012	Morningstar Foods, LLC	Saputo Inc.	1.45	9.3x	1,626	156	–	–	–	–	–
Nov. 2012	Ralcorp Holdings, Inc.	ConAgra Foods, Inc.	6.78	12.1x	4,322	560	73	–	352	2,022	4,539
July 2012	Peet's Coffee & Tea, Inc.	Joh A. Benckiser GmbH	0.95	23.2x	383	40	15	–	32	–	230
Feb. 2012	Pringles Business of P&G	Kellogg Company	2.70	11.1x	1,456	243	153	(41)	–	–	581
Dec. 2011	National Beef Packing Co. LLC	Leucadia National Corp.	0.87	3.7x	5,808	300	248	–	20	–	913
Aug. 2011	Provimi SAS	Cargill, Inc.	1.83	8.1x	2,296	224	93	–	304	–	2,162
June 2011	Foster's Group Ltd.	SABMiller Plc	13.12	-122.9x	4,547	(107)	(554)	–	238	4,731	6,908
Nov. 2010	Del Monte Foods Co.	Funds affiliated with KKR & Co. and others	5.30	8.8x	3,713	603	–	–	–	–	–
June 2010	American Italian Pasta Co.	Ralcorp Holdings, Inc.	1.26	8.3x	590	151	80	(11)	36	45	508
Jan. 2010	N.A. Frozen Pizza Business of Kraft	Nestlé S.A.	3.70	12.5x	2,100	296	–	–	–	–	–
Nov. 2009	Birds Eye Foods, Inc.	Pinnacle Foods Group, Inc.	1.37	9.5x	921	144	52	(21)	44	750	747
Sept. 2009	Cadbury plc	Kraft Foods Inc.	21.40	13.3x	5,975	1,609	509	(408)	313	1,618	8,129
Sept. 2008	UST LLC	Altria Group, Inc.	11.50	11.9x	1,991	971	560	–	48	1,280	1,417
June 2008	The Folgers Coffee Company	The J.M. Smucker Company	3.40	8.8x	1,754	386	227	(23)	–	8	629
Apr. 2008	Wm. Wrigley Jr. Company	Mars, Incorporated	23.02	18.4x	5,780	1,251	682	(240)	383	1,130	5,517
Nov. 2007	Post Foods	Ralcorp Holdings, Inc.	2.64	11.3x	1,103	234	117	(21)	–	–	919
Feb. 2007	Pinnacle Foods Group, Inc.	The Blackstone Group, L.P.	2.14	8.9x	1,809	241	(109)	–	–	–	1,765
Aug. 2006	European Frozen Foods of Unilever	Permira Advisors Ltd.	2.20	9.9x	15,200	222	–	–	–	–	–
Aug. 2006	Chef America, Inc.	Nestlé S.A.	2.60	14.5x	22	179	–	–	–	–	–
Oct. 2001	The Pillsbury Company	General Mills, Inc.	10.40	10.1x	6,067	1,005	(114)	(156)	51	230	9,262
Dec. 2000	The Quaker Oats Company	PepsiCo, Inc.	14.01	15.6x	5,096	928	468	(269)	161	774	2,494
Oct. 2000	Keebler Foods Company	Kellogg Company	4.47	10.7x	2,757	449	176	(93)	34	583	1,773
June 2000	Nabisco Holdings Corp.	Philip Morris Companies Inc.	19.02	13.7x	8,913	1,394	378	(222)	140	4,014	11,610
June 2000	International Home Foods	ConAgra Foods, Inc.	2.91	8.5x	2,210	342	1,000	(44)	14	1,150	1,527

Source: FactSet.

Quintiles IPO

Quintiles Transnational Holdings Inc. was the world's largest global provider of biopharmaceutical development and commercial outsourcing services. The company's revenue was generated by running clinical trials and carrying out the subsequent statistical analysis for pharmaceutical development as well as providing postapproval sales, marketing, and commercialization support to pharmaceutical companies. As of December 2012, the company had helped to develop or commercialize the top 50 bestselling biopharmaceutical products and top 20 bestselling biologic products on the market.

At the end of 2012, the majority of the firm was owned by company founder Dennis Gillings and four private equity firms (Bain Capital, TPG Capital, 3i Capital, and Temasek Life Sciences). This ownership structure was established after the company was taken private in a management-led buyout in 2003 and a subsequent recapitalization in 2008. Now the private equity firms were looking to monetize their positions and were considering different strategic alternatives, including a merger or acquisition (M&A) sale to strategic or financial buyers, an initial public offering (IPO), or capital restructuring through special dividends.

At the end of January 2013, Quintiles hired a leading investment bank to analyze these alternative options. You are the bank's associate tasked with carrying out the analysis of these possible strategic options, including exploring a possible public offering of 10.6 million shares from selling shareholders and 13.1 million new shares from the company. Consider the timing of the potential IPO, based on macroeconomic trends at the time, as well as the potential benefits and downsides to this option versus other exit options for the private equity owners.

QUINTILES TRANSNATIONAL HISTORY[1]

February 1982: Dennis Gillings, professor at the University of North Carolina (UNC), signs his first consulting contract. His team of part-time staff working in a trailer on the UNC campus provides statistical and data management consulting for pharmaceutical customers. Quintiles is formally incorporated in North Carolina, cofounded by Gillings and Gary Koch.

January 1987: Quintiles begins its global expansion, opening its UK operations to serve customers in Europe.

November 1992: Quintiles Laboratories Ltd. opens in Atlanta, Georgia, growing from one small room offering safety testing to a global network with a full-service offering, including biomarkers to esoteric evaluations.

August 1993: Quintiles establishes operations in Asia, opening a location in Tokyo to expand services to Japanese customers.

[1] Company history adapted from Quintiles Facebook page.

April 1994: Quintiles goes public, completing an IPO of Quintiles stock.

May 1996: Quintiles establishes its consulting practice with the acquisition of a globally recognized healthcare policy research and management consulting company.

November 1996: Quintiles combines with Innovex Ltd., a UK-based contract pharmaceutical company specializing in sales and marketing services for major pharma companies. The addition of Innovex makes Quintiles the world's largest full-service biopharmaceutical services company and enables the company to provide services across a product lifecycle.

January 1999: Quintiles acquires Hoechst Marion Roussel's drug development facility in Kansas City and employs about 500 of its staff. In addition, Quintiles partners with HMR over 5 years to support ongoing HMR projects.

July 2002: Quintiles signs landmark partnership agreement with Eli Lilly and Company to commercialize Cymbalta. Quintiles makes an initial $110 million investment and provides a dedicated primary care team comprising 500 representatives, 50 managers, four regional trainers, and a national trainer based in-house.

April 2003: Quintiles becomes a private company through a management buyout led by founder and chairman Dennis Gillings, with principal equity funding coming from Gillings and private equity firm One Equity Partners and debt capital from Citicorp. At the time of the transaction, Gillings said: "I felt that Wall Street undervalued the company and that equity analysts' lack of understanding affected the stock price and hurt employee morale. Being private is beneficial because we won't be subject to short-term volatility and pressure to make quarterly earnings."

January 2008: Quintiles reorganized through a sale of the company to Gillings and a new group of private equity firms, including Bain Capital, TPG, 3i, Temasek (a Singapore-based fund), and certain other shareholders and members of management.

November 2011: Quintiles acquires Outcome Sciences, positioning Quintiles as the industry powerhouse in late-phase and real-world research.

December 2012: The Quintiles management team and the board of directors consider different strategic alternatives as the largest shareholders of the company look to monetize their positions (see Table C12.1).

TABLE C12.1   Quintiles Insider Ownership of Common Shares as of December 2012

	Number	% of Common Shares
Dennis B. Gillings	27,681,669	23.9
Bain Capital	26,481,659	22.9
TPG Funds	26,481,658	22.9
Affiliates of 3i	17,497,087	15.1
Temasek Life Sciences	11,271,069	9.7
DIRECTORS AND OFFICERS:		
John Ratliff	1,055,000	0.9
Michael Mortimer	750,000	0.6
Derek Winstanly	619,500	0.5
Kevin Gordon	120,000	0.1
Others	3,807,748	3.3
Total inside ownership	115,765,390	100.0

FactSet.

REVENUE STREAMS

Quintiles operated in the contract research organization (CRO) industry. Biopharmaceutical companies outsourced research and development (R&D) functions to contract research organizations for a variety of reasons, including (1) the complexity of clinical trials and regulatory requirements; (2) the efficiency of using third parties to access regions across the globe for patient recruiting and research site start-up; (3) the need for sophisticated data management and biostatistical support; (4) access to laboratory and diagnostic infrastructure, and integration of biomarkers and genomics into trials; and (5) therapeutic experience and expertise. Large CROs such as Quintiles added value to biopharma by offering these services and helping to reduce cost and frequency of trial failure.

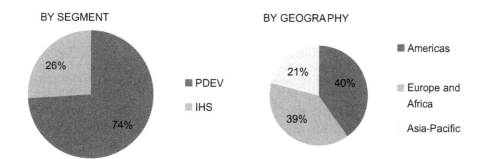

FIGURE C12.1   Quintiles revenue. *PDEV*, product development; *IHS*, Integrated Healthcare Services.

Quintiles had helped to develop or commercialize 85% of the central nervous system drugs, 76% of oncology drugs, and 72% of cardiovascular drugs across the new molecular entities, and new biologic applications approved from 2004 through 2011.[2] The company offered a diverse mix of service offerings, operating across two business segments:

- Product development (PDEV), which was the core CRO segment, was focused primarily on late-stage (Phase IIb–IV) clinical trials
- Integrated Healthcare Services (IHS), which included sales, commercialization, marketing strategy, outcomes-based research, and payer and provider services

As shown in Figure C12.1, 74% of Quintiles's revenue was generated through the PDEV segment and 26% was from the IHS segment.[3]

[2] Quintiles Preliminary Prospectus, as filed with the Securities and Exchange Commission on April 26, 2013.

[3] Quintiles Preliminary Prospectus, as filed with the Securities and Exchange Commission on April 26, 2013.

Also shown in Figure C12.1, Quintiles had a geographically diverse portfolio, deriving 40% of revenues in the Americas, 39% in Europe and Africa, and 21% in Asia–Pacific (approximately 14% of which came from Japan).

PRODUCT DEVELOPMENT SEGMENT OVERVIEW

The market served by the PDEV segment consisted primarily of biopharmaceutical companies, including medical device and diagnostic companies, that were seeking to outsource clinical trials and other product development activities. Quintiles management estimated that the total biopharma spending on drug development was $91 billion in 2011, of which an estimated $48 billion was the addressable market (clinical development spending excluding preclinical spending).[4]

The PDEV segment can be divided into

- early-stage development (Phases I and IIa)
- late-stage development (Phases IIb–IV)

Quintiles did not compete in the preclinical portion of the clinical trial process of the early development market. Quintiles's scale and breadth of services allowed it to compete effectively in clinical trial management, lab services, data analysis and reporting, biostatistics, and consulting.

Global biopharmaceutical R&D spending grew at a 6.5% CAGR from 2004 to 2010 and is expected to grow at 1.5% CAGR through 2018.[5] R&D spending dropped in 2009–10 as a result of the financial crisis. A steady recovery in biopharma R&D emerged in 2011 and was expected to continue over the next decade because of

- steady recovery in the biopharma pipeline
- improved biotech funding, which would serve as future pipeline growth
- more stable macroeconomic environment

There was also a trend of consolidation of R&D budgets toward higher-probability compounds with the goal of greater R&D productivity ahead of a looming "patent cliff," referring to the large number of blockbuster branded pharmaceuticals that would hit patent expiry in 2011–12. The patent cliff included Pfizer's Lipitor, Bristol-Myers Squibb's Plavix, AstraZeneca's Seroquel, Novartis's Diovan, Merck's Singulair, Forest Laboratories' Lexapro, and Takeda's Actos, putting nearly $70 billion of sales at risk in 2012 (nearly 9% of worldwide biopharma sales).[6] However, worldwide pharma sales were expected to rebound from this patent cliff.

According to the IMS Institute for Healthcare Informatics, worldwide spending for biopharma products was expected to be in the 3%–6% range through 2015.[7] The recovery in global biopharma sales was important because the industry was at the low end of the

[4] Quintiles Preliminary Prospectus, as filed with the Securities and Exchange Commission on April 26, 2013.

[5] Tao Guo, "Transforming Biopharma Innovation via Global Collaboration," Chapter 17 in *Vision 2025: How To Succeed in the Global Chemistry Enterprise* (American Chemical Society, January 1, 2014).

[6] EvaluatePharma, "World Preview 2018: Embracing the Patent Cliff," June 2012.

[7] IMS Institute for Healthcare Informatics, "The Global Use of Medicines: Outlook Through 2015," May 2011.

TABLE C12.2   Worldwide R&D Spend and Relationship to Worldwide Biopharma Sales (US$ in Billions)

	2010	2011	2012	2013	2014	2015	2016	2017	2018
Pharma R&D spend	128.3	134.6	134.2	136.1	138.4	140.9	143.8	146.7	149.4
Growth per year (%)	0.8	4.9	0.3	1.4	1.7	1.8	2.1	2.0	1.8
Worldwide Rx sales	676	716	709	732	760	793	827	857	885
R&D as % of worldwide Rx sales (%)	19.0	18.8	18.9	18.6	18.2	17.8	17.4	17.1	16.9
Generics	59	65	70	74	78	83	88	92	96
Rx excluding generics	616	651	639	659	681	710	739	765	788
R&D as % of Rx excluding generics (%)	20.8	20.7	21.0	20.7	20.3	19.8	19.5	19.2	19.0

Source: *EvaluatePharma, "World Preview 2018: Embracing the Patent Cliff," June 2012.*

historical relationship of R&D to sales, and higher sales growth could spur greater confidence in R&D spending (refer to Table C12.2 for details).

The health of the biopharma development market can be traced to empirical data supported by increasing new molecular entity (NME) approvals, increasing new drug applications (NDAs) filed, and growing biopharma pipelines. The number of NME approvals in the United States reached 39 in 2012, a level not seen since 1997.[8] In addition to the 39 NMEs approved, rare orphan drug approvals reached 13 in 2012, more than doubling since 2006.[9] NDAs reached a peak in 2009 and appeared to have stabilized at 105 in 2011.[10] The cost of failure had led to fewer NDAs since 2009, but higher R&D productivity and pipeline growth led to a gain in NDAs in 2012. A key driver of clinical trial spending was biotechnology funding, as biotech firm cash on hand was required to cover the high costs of drug development. Biotech funding reached nearly $80 billion in 2012, up significantly from $60 billion in 2010.[11].

As shown in Figure C12.2, approximately half of the pipeline drug candidates were in preclinical development. The number of pipeline drug candidates in Quintiles's primary market (Phase II–III) was largely unchanged between 2012 and 2013, while early-stage drug

[8] Quintiles S-1 filings.

[9] US Food and Drug Administration, "FY 2012 Innovative Drug Approvals: Bringing Life-Saving Drugs to Patients Quickly and Efficiently," December 2012.

[10] US Food and Drug Administration, "Summary of NDA Approvals & Receipts, 1938 to the Present," http://www.fda.gov/AboutFDA/WhatWeDo/History/ProductRegulation/SummaryofNDAApprovalsReceipts1938tothepresent/default.htm.

[11] "2012 a Banner Year for New Drugs," *The Burrill Report* 3, no. 2, February 2013.

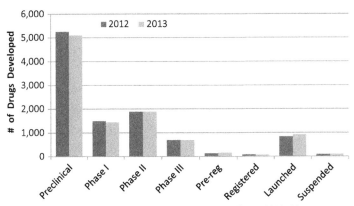

FIGURE C12.2 Global biopharma R&D pipeline by development phase, 2012–13.

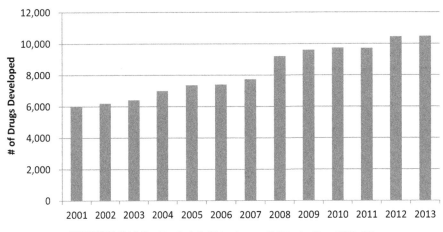

FIGURE C12.3 Total global biopharma R&D pipeline, 2001–13.

candidates had fallen off slightly. As shown in Figure C12.3, as of January 2013, there were approximately 10,500 drugs in active development.

INTEGRATED HEALTHCARE SERVICES SEGMENT OVERVIEW

Quintiles's IHS segment offered a variety of services related to the postapproval market. IHS's biggest offering was in commercialization services, which included salesforce recruiting, training/development and deployment, patient education, market access consulting, brand communication, and medical education. IHS also offered a variety of other consulting services for biopharma, payer, and provider clients in areas such as outcomes and comparative effectiveness research, disease registry, and market access. A combination of cost pressure in healthcare systems around the world and an increasing focus on the appropriateness and efficacy of pharmaceutical therapy provided many opportunities to grow revenues and expand services.

IHS revenue has grown considerably due to the massive salesforce restructuring activity that had been occurring in big pharma in recent years. Historically, pharmaceutical companies had spent approximately 9%–10% of prescription sales revenue on the costs of selling a drug, so given a worldwide prescription sales forecast of $700 billion, there would be $60–70 billion of salesforce spend.[12] Over time, more of this could be outsourced. The other categories of IHS were difficult to forecast because the markets were evolving and the players included many niche consulting firms and vendors.

COMPETITIVE LANDSCAPE

The CRO industry was competitive and fragmented, but it was rapidly consolidating. In 2013 the top 10 players accounted for more than 50% of the market. Within the publicly traded market, the industry leaders comprised four US firms:

- Charles River Laboratories International
- Covance
- Parexel International
- ICON plc

The competition also included one sizable Chinese company, WuXi PharmaTech. In addition, there were several privately held firms including the following:

- Pharmaceutical Product Development
- INC Research
- PRA International

Charles River Laboratories was more of a pure-play in the early-stage market. Covance maintained an early-stage presence, but its growth had been driven primarily by the late-stage product development segment. At the end of 2012, Covance's late-stage product development revenues accounted for 59% of its total revenue, up from 56% in the prior year.

In the IHS segment, the main competitors included privately held inVentiv Health, PDI Inc., and several conglomerates that had marketing service divisions. Parexel had two divisions (consulting and medical communication services, and perceptive informatics) that competed with some of Quintiles's offerings (refer to Table C12.3 for details). Relative to its peers, Quintiles was significantly larger (see Table C12.4).

---

[12] EvaluatePharma, "World Preview 2018: Embracing the Patent Cliff," June 2012.

TABLE C12.3 Quintiles's Competitors

Product Development	Ticker/Private Owner
Charles River Laboratories	CRL
Covance	CVD
Parexel	PRXL
ICON	ICLR
Pharmaceutical Product Development	The Carlyle Group/Hellman & Friedman
WuXi PharmaTech	WX
INC Research	Avista Capital Partners/Teachers' Private Capital
PRA International	Genstar Capital

Integrated Health Services	Ticker/Private Owner
IN THE UNITED STATES	
inVentiv Health, Inc.	Thomas H. Lee Partners
PDI, Inc.	PDII
OUTSIDE THE UNITED STATES	
United Drug plc	UDG-GB
inVentiv	Thomas H. Lee Partners
EPS Corporation	4282-JP
Publicis Selling Solutions	PUB-PAR

Deutsche Bank Research.

TABLE C12.4 Sizing Quintiles Versus Top Contract Research Organization Peers

Company	Total Employees	Number of Countries Served
Quintiles	27,000	100
Parexel	12,700	51
Pharmaceutical Product Development	12,500	46
Covance	11,500	100
ICON	10,000	37
Charles River Labs	7000	15
WuXi PharmaTech	7000	2
PRA International	5000	30

Company filings/websites.

CONCLUSION

Quintiles was larger than its competitors and it served a broad market within the CRO industry. The question was what was the best option for the private equity owners to exit their position? In particular, what would an IPO look like for the company in January 2013? As an investment banker, you are told that the net proceeds from the IPO would be used as follows:

- Approximately $306 million to pay all amounts outstanding under an outstanding term loan
- Approximately $50 million to repay indebtedness under senior secured credit facilities
- $25 million to pay a one-time fee to terminate a management agreement with Dennis Gillings and the private investment firms of Bain Capital Partners, TPG Capital, and 3i Corporation

The remainder of the net proceeds would be used for general corporate purposes, including strategic growth opportunities.

Based on the information in this case, including Exhibits C12.1 through C12.13, you will be asked to determine an IPO valuation for Quintiles's common stock and answer related questions.

EXHIBIT C12.1 QUINTILES'S FINANCIAL HEALTH

Quintiles's Book-to-Bill Ratio

A book-to-bill ratio is the relationship of net new business wins during a period divided by that period's revenue. Quintiles's book-to-bill ratio has remained steady in recent years despite significant volatility in the market and a service revenue base that is significantly higher than its publicly traded peers. Quintiles's book-to-bill ratio has averaged 1.23× over the past 5 years and stood at 1.30× at the end of 2012.[13] Quintiles's peers have reported meaningfully higher book-to-bill ratios in recent quarters. Although these higher book-to-bill ratios are clearly an indicator of strong future revenue growth, some of this higher growth comes at lower profit margins due to the need to staff up for strategic partnerships.

Quintiles's Backlog Visibility

Quintiles maintained a sales backlog that has grown steadily over time, but has exhibited signs of strength in recent years. Quintiles's backlog of nearly $9 billion at the end of 2012 is 36% higher than Covance, the largest publicly traded Contract Research Organization (CRO) peer. And Quintiles's backlog has grown as a result of strong new business win activity amidst an environment in which there is an estimated 20%–30% growth in proposal activity, which can be attributed to biopharma clients increasingly looking to outsource R&D spending and the trend of large and midtier biopharma clients to consolidate CRO partners.

Quintiles's net new business wins increased 11% in 2012 to $4.5 billion, with product development as the primary driver of this growth.[14] Quintiles discloses backlog as a representation, at a particular point in time, of future service revenues from work not yet completed or

EXHIBIT C12.1 QUINTILES'S FINANCIAL HEALTH—cont'd

performed under signed contract. New business in backlog is subject to change order (which can increase or decrease the scope of work) and/or termination. The integrated healthcare services (IHS) segment is subject to shorter sales cycles and faster burn rates, thus making IHS's revenues harder to predict.

Quintiles Backlog

	2008	2009	2010	2011	2012
Backlog ($ in millions)	5,882	6,599	7,153	7,973	8,704
YoY growth (%)		12.2%	8.4%	11.5%	9.2%
Backlog % of forward revenue	201%	220%	217%	216%	228%

Backlog Comps ($ in millions)

	2008	2009	2010	2011	2012
ICON	1,748	1,844	1,927	2,300	2,800
YoY growth (%)		5.5%	4.5%	19.4%	21.7%
Parexel	2,000	2,310	3,000	3,740	4,540
YoY growth (%)		15.5%	29.9%	24.7%	21.4%
Covance	4,333	4,866	6,194	6,138	6,643
YoY growth (%)		12.3%	27.3%	(0.9%)	8.2%
Charles River Laboratories	311	274	220	203	214
YoY growth (%)		(11.9%)	(19.7%)	(7.9%)	5.6%
Peer Group Total	8,392	9,294	11,341	12,381	14,197
YoY growth (%)		10.7%	22.0%	9.2%	14.7%

Source: Quintiles SEC S-1 filing, p. F-14.

EXHIBIT C12.2 INITIAL PUBLIC OFFERING PROCESS OVERVIEW

The process of "going public" (selling publicly traded equity for the first time) is an arduous task that usually requires about 3 months.

1. Before initiating the equity-issuance process, a private firm needs to create a business plan; establish an outside board of directors; prepare audited financial statements and projections; and develop relationships with bankers, lawyers, and accountants.
2. Firms usually hold "bake-off" meetings with various investment bankers to discuss the equity-issuance process before selecting the lead underwriter for the initial public offering. Factors that play an important role in the selection process include the investment bank's proposed compensation package, track record, equity research support, distribution capabilities, and aftermarket market-making support.

[13] FactSet, other company filings, Quintiles Preliminary Prospectus.
[14] Quintiles Preliminary Prospectus, as filed with the Securities and Exchange Commission on April 26, 2013, p. 2.

EXHIBIT C12.2 INITIAL PUBLIC OFFERING PROCESS OVERVIEW—cont'd

3. The equity-issuance process begins with an organizational or "all-hands" meeting, which is attended by all the key participants, including management, underwriters, accountants, and legal counsel for both the underwriters and the issuing firm. The meeting is designed to establish a process and to reach agreement on specific terms.

4. The filing process with the Securities and Exchange Commission (SEC) requires preparation of the prospectus (or S-1). This "registration statement" includes answers to specific questions relevant to the company, copies of the underwriting contract, company charter and bylaws, and a specimen of the security to be sold, as well as financial information, risk disclosures, and other information required by the SEC.

5. Following filing of the registration statement, the SEC prohibits the company from publishing information outside the prospectus. The company can continue established, normal advertising activities, but any increased publicity designed to raise awareness of the company's name, products, or geographical presence to create a favorable attitude toward the company's securities could be considered illegal. This requirement is known as the "quiet period."

6. One of the important features of the registration process is the performance of "due-diligence," the process of providing reasonable grounds that there is nothing in the registration statement that is known to be untrue or misleading. Due-diligence is important because all parties to the registration statement are liable for any material misstatements or omissions. Due-diligence procedures involve such things as reviewing company documents, contracts, and tax returns; visiting company offices and facilities; soliciting "comfort letters" from company auditors; and interviewing company and industry personnel.

7. During this period, the lead underwriter forms the underwriting "syndicate," which comprises a number of investment banks that agree to buy portions of the offering at the offer price less the underwriting discount. In addition to the syndicate members, dealers may be enlisted to sell a certain number of shares on a "best-efforts" basis. The dealers receive a fixed reallowance, or concession, for each share sold.

8. As part of the SEC review process, the registration statement is given to accountants, attorneys, analysts, and industry specialists to "provide full and fair disclosure of the character of securities sold in interstate commerce," as per the Securities Act. Under this Act, the registration statement becomes effective 20 days after the filing date. If, however, the SEC finds anything in the registration statement that is regarded as materially untrue, incomplete, or misleading, it sends the registrant a "letter of comment" detailing the deficiencies.

9. While the SEC is reviewing the registration statement, the underwriter is engaged in "book-building" activities, which involve surveying potential investors to construct a schedule of investor demand for the new issue. To generate investor interest, the preliminary offering prospectus, or "red herring," is printed and offered to potential investors. Underwriters generally organize a 1- or 2-week "roadshow" tour, which allows managers to discuss their investment plans and answer questions from financial analysts, brokers, and institutional investors.

10. By the time the registration statement is ready to be declared effective by the SEC, the underwriters and the offering firm's management negotiates the final offering price and the underwriting discount. The negotiated price depends on perceived investor demand and current market conditions. Once the underwriter and the management agree on the offering price and discount, the underwriting agreement is signed, and the final registration amendment is filed with the SEC. The offering is now ready for public sale.

EXHIBIT C12.3 MACROECONOMIC UPDATES

Equity markets benefited from a relief rally in January 2013, as market participants responded favorably to the last-minute short-term fiscal cliff deal that prevented a series of tax increases and spending cuts from simultaneously taking effect with the new year. Improving data in the US labor and housing markets also boosted investor sentiment during the month, but with the Eurozone mired in recession and a looming budget battle in the United States, potential headwinds remained. Despite these concerns, all major global equity indices were in positive territory to start 2013. For the month, the Standard & Poor's 500, Russell 1000, Russell 2000, MSCI EAFE, and MSCI Emerging Markets Indices returned 5.18%, 5.42%, 6.26%, 5.27%, and 1.38%, respectively. Value stocks significantly outperformed growth stocks during the month, and within the Russell 1000 Index, energy, healthcare, and financials were the top-performing sectors, while the information technology, telecommunication services, and materials sectors lagged.

Key Highlights

- Following the US fiscal cliff deal reached at the end of 2012, Congress approved a temporary extension of the debt ceiling in January, which also contributed to the relief rally during the month. However, policy measures did not address the concerns of major credit rating agencies, which maintained that the United States needed to take additional steps to address the country's budget deficit.
- Economic data continued to show signs of gradual improvement in the US labor market, with initial jobless claims falling to a 5-year low during the month. However, the unemployment rate edged up to 7.9% in January despite moderate gains in private payrolls and a sharp upward revision to the number of jobs added in the prior 2 months.
- Fourth-quarter GDP unexpectedly contracted at an annual rate of 0.1%, the first time the US economy shrank in more than 3 years. The drop in economic output was driven by a significant decline in government spending, which more than offset strong gains in residential investment and capital expenditures and a 2.2% increase in consumer spending.
- The global easing cycle continued as the Fed affirmed its existing level of asset purchases at the January Federal Open Market Committee meeting, while Japan launched a massive easing campaign aimed at fighting deflation.
- European countries continued to struggle with recessionary pressures. The United Kingdom, Germany, Spain, and Belgium reported their economies shrank in the fourth quarter, while the Eurozone manufacturing PMI remained in contraction territory.
- At the same time, China's economy continued to show signs of stabilizing, with real GDP rising 7.9% in the fourth quarter and export growth of 14% in December, significantly exceeding expectations.

Source: Adapted from Natalie Trunow, "January 2013 Equity Market Review," *Calvert News & Commentary*, February 18, 2013, http://www.calvert.com/newsarticle.html?article=20284.

EXHIBIT C12.4 S&P BIOTECHNOLOGY PERFORMANCE VERSUS S&P 500

Source: FactSet prices.

EXHIBIT C12.5 QUINTILES INCOME STATEMENT ($ IN THOUSANDS, EXCEPT PER-SHARE DATA)

	Year Ended December 31,		
	2010	2011	2012
Service revenues	3,321,131	3,591,513	4,061,528
Product development (PDEV) segment	2,462,313	2,657,393	3,002,142
Integrated healthcare services (IHS) segment	858,818	934,120	1,059,386
Reimbursed expenses	936,431	1,125,732	1,290,537
Total revenues	4,257,562	4,717,245	5,352,064
Costs, expenses and other:			
Costs of revenues	3,235,747	3,679,451	4,228,131
Selling, general and administrative	553,483	566,069	642,248
Restructuring costs	24,877	24,106	20,615
Impairment charges	3,086	13,402	—
Income from operations	443,455	447,618	461,071
Interest income	(4,122)	(4,294)	(3,374)
Interest expense	153,452	118,881	147,808
Loss on extinguishment of debt	—	50,551	1,403
Other (income) expense, net	16,977	9,890	(3,929)
Income before income taxes and equity in earnings of unconsolidated affiliates	277,148	272,590	319,163
Income tax expense	88,950	22,296	111,423
Income before equity in earnings of unconsolidated affiliates	188,198	250,294	207,740
Equity in earnings of unconsolidated affiliates	1,110	70,757	2,567
Net income	187,088	179,537	205,173
Net loss (income) attributable to noncontrolling interests	(4,659)	1,445	915
Net income attributable to Quintiles Transnational Holdings Inc.	191,747	178,092	204,258
Earnings per share attributable to common shareholders:			
Basic	1.65	1.53	1.77
Diluted	1.62	1.51	1.73
Weighted average common shares outstanding:			
Basic	116,418	116,232	115,710
Diluted	118,000	117,936	117,796

Source: Quintiles Preliminary Prospectus, as filed with the Securities and Exchange Commission on April 26, 2013.

EXHIBIT 12.6 QUINTILES CASH FLOW STATEMENT ($ IN THOUSANDS)

	Year Ended December 31,		
	2010	2011	2012
OPERATING ACTIVITIES:			
Net income	191,747	178,092	204,258
Adjustments to reconcile net income to net cash provided by operating activities:			
Depreciation and amortization	84,217	92,004	98,288
Amortization of debt issuance costs and discount	9,589	30,016	9,237
Amortization of commercial rights and royalties assets	8,977	0	0
Share-based compensation	17,329	14,130	25,926
Gain on sale of business, property and equipment, net	(725)	(1,113)	(541)
Impairment of long-lived assets	—	12,150	—
Earnings from unconsolidated affiliates	(1,110)	(70,757)	(2,567)
Loss on investments, net	589	161	70
Provision for (benefit from) deferred income taxes	(9,005)	(73,216)	16,595
Excess income tax benefits on stock option exercises	(283)	(41)	(465)
Change in operating assets and liabilities:			
Accounts receivable and unbilled services	2,751	(115,748)	(60,255)
Prepaid expenses and other assets	(11,541)	(22,079)	(27,013)
Accounts payable and accrued expenses	38,914	67,382	58,345
Unearned income	82,334	(52,425)	54,502
Income taxes payable and other liabilities	(9,158)	40,162	(13,120)
Net cash provided by operating activities	404,625	98,719	363,260
INVESTING ACTIVITIES:			
Acquisition of property, equipment and software	(80,236)	(75,679)	(71,336)
Acquisition of businesses, net of cash acquired	—	(227,115)	(43,197)
Proceeds from disposition of property and equipment	2,554	2,976	2,729
Cash paid to terminate interest rate swaps	—	(11,630)	—
Maturities of held-to-maturity securities	1,931	—	—
Purchase of equity securities	(7,056)	(16,054)	(13,204)
Proceeds from sale of equity securities	11,264	252	70
Cash balance divested from deconsolidation of PharmaBio Development Inc.	(100,357)	—	—
Investments in and advances to unconsolidated affiliates, net of payments received	(1,354)	(17,846)	(3,646)
(Payments made for) proceeds from sale of investment in unconsolidated affiliates	(163)	109,140	(577)
Purchase of other investments	—	(5,000)	(161)
Proceeds from other investments	8,500	48	—
Change in restricted cash, net	26,963	19,152	231
Other	(3,480)	(3,082)	(3,142)
Net cash used in investing activities	(141,434)	(224,838)	(132,233)

Source: Quintiles Preliminary Prospectus, as filed with the Securities and Exchange Commission on April 26, 2013.

EXHIBIT C12.7 QUINTILES BALANCE SHEET ($ IN THOUSANDS)

	Year Ended December 31,	
	2011	2012
ASSETS		
Current assets:		
Cash and cash equivalents	458,188	597,631
Restricted cash	2,998	2,822
Trade accounts receivable and unbilled services, net	691,038	745,373
Prepaid expenses	31,328	33,354
Deferred income taxes	46,708	69,038
Income taxes receivable	25,452	17,597
Other current assets and receivables	51,655	74,082
Total current assets	1,307,367	1,539,897
Property and equipment, net	185,772	193,999
Intangibles and other assets:		
Investments in debt, equity and other securities	22,106	35,951
Investments in and advances to unconsolidated affiliates	11,782	19,148
Goodwill	278,041	302,429
Other identifiableintangibles, net	269,413	272,813
Deferred income taxes	78,177	37,313
Deposits and other assets	112,148	127,506
Total intangibles and other assets	771,667	795,160
Total assets	2,264,806	2,529,056
LIABILITIES AND SHAREHOLDERS' DEFICIT		
Current liabilities:		
Accounts payable	70,028	84,712
Accrued expenses	616,890	667,086
Unearned income	398,471	456,587
Income taxes payable	47,039	9,639
Current portion of long-term debt and obligations held under capital leases	20,147	55,710
Other current liabilities	39,558	44,230
Total current liabilities	1,192,133	1,317,964
Long-term liabilities:		
Long-term debt and obligations held under capital leases, less current portion	1,951,708	2,366,268
Deferred income taxes	9,866	11,616
Other liabilities	138,806	162,349
Total liabilities	3,292,513	3,858,197
Shareholders' deficit:		
Common stock and additional paid-in capital, 150,000 authorized, $0.01 par value, 115,764 and 115,966 shares issued and outstanding at December 31, 2012 and 2011, respectively	1,160	4,554
Accumulated deficit	(1,052,526)	(1,341,869)
Accumulated other comprehensive income	22,871	7,695
Deficit attributable to Quintiles Transnational Holdings Inćs shareholders	(1,028,495)	(1,329,620)
Equity attributable to noncontrolling interests	788	479
Total shareholders' deficit	(1,027,707)	(1,329,141)
Total liabilities and shareholders' deficit	2,264,806	2,529,056

Source: Quintiles Preliminary Prospectus, as filed with the Securities and Exchange Commission on April 26, 2013.

EXHIBIT C12.8 ADDITIONAL FINANCIAL NOTES

Employee Stock Compensation

The company accounts for its share-based compensation under the fair value method and uses the Black–Scholes–Merton model to estimate the value of the share-based awards granted and restricted stock issued for recourse notes to its employees and nonexecutive directors using the assumptions noted in the following table. Expected volatility is based on the historical volatility of a peer group for a period equal to the expected term, as the company believes the expected volatility will approximate the historical volatility of the peer group. The expected dividends are based on the historical dividends paid by the company, excluding dividends that resulted from activities that the company deemed to be one-time in nature. The expected term represents the period of time the grants are expected to be outstanding. The risk-free interest rate is based on the US Treasury yield curve in effect at the time of the grant.

The company recognized $25.9 million, $14.1 million, and $17.3 million as share-based compensation expense during the years ended December 31, 2012, 2011, and 2010, respectively. Share-based compensation expense is included in selling, general, and administrative expenses on the accompanying consolidated statements of income based on the classification of the employees who were granted the share-based awards. The associated future income tax benefit recognized was $6.9 million, $4.2 million, and $5.4 million for the years ended December 31, 2012, 2011, and 2010, respectively. As of December 31, 2012, there was approximately $22.6 million of total unrecognized share-based compensation expense related to outstanding nonvested share-based compensation arrangements, which the company expects to recognize over a weighted average period of 1.98 years.

Expected volatility:	33–53%
Expected dividends:	4.82%
Expected term (in years):	2.0–7.0
Risk-free interest rate:	0.29–1.31%

Notes Outstanding

We were obligated under the following debt instruments at December 31, 2012 (in thousands):

Term Loan B-1 due 2018	$174,563
Term Loan B-2 due 2018	1,970,000
Holdings Term Loan due 2017	300,000
Other notes payable	43
	2,444,606
Less: unamortized discount	(22,908)
Less: current portion	(55,594)
	$2,366,104

Contractual maturities of long-term debt at December 31, 2012 are as follows (in thousands):

2013	$55,594
2014	21,756
2015	21,750
2016	21,750
2017	321,750
Thereafter	2,002,006
Total	$2,444,606

EXHIBIT C12.9 QUINTILES DISCOUNTED CASH FLOW ASSUMPTIONS

Company Name	Ticker	Book Value of Equity ($ in thousands)	Shares Outstanding	Share Price ($)	Debt ($ in thousands)	Cash ($ in thousands)	Beta Estimate
Charles River Labs	CRL	600.8	48.406	41.32	666.5	116.7	1.62
Covance	CVD	1,307.2	56.290	66.71	320.0	492.8	1.27
Parexel	PRXL	609.7	60.426	33.85	220.0	213.6	1.60
ICON plc	ICLR	754.6	60.451	29.31	0.0	190.2	1.22
WuXi PharmaTech	WX	578.2	72.797	16.18	64.8	229.8	0.95
Average		810.2	59.486	38.38	262.8	248.6	1.27

Source: FactSet (accessed February 1, 2013).

Assume a pretax cost of debt of 5.9% for Quintiles

Treasury constant maturity bond yields (%)

3 month	0.07
1 year	0.15
2 year	0.27
5 year	0.88
10 year	2.02
20 year	2.79
30 year	3.17

Source: U.S. Department of the Treasury, "Daily Treasury Yield Curve Rates," http://www.treasury.gov/resource-center/data-chart-center/interest-rates/Pages/TextView.aspx?data=yieldYear&year=2013 (accessed January 31, 2013).

Market risk premium estimate:

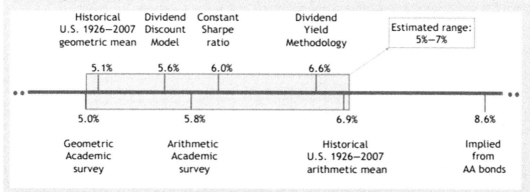

Source: JP Morgan report.

EXHIBIT C12.10 PUBLICLY TRADED COMPETITOR FINANCIALS ($ IN MILLIONS, EXCEPT PER-SHARE DATA)

Company Name	Ent. Value	Revenues						EBITDA						EPS					
		2009	2010	2011	2012	2013P	2014P	2009	2010	2011	2012	2013P	2014P	2009	2010	2011	2012	2013P	2014P
Charles River Labs	2,637	1,203	1,133	1,143	1,130	1,171	1,212	290	253	265	261	270	286	2.38	1.99	2.56	2.74	2.81	3.06
YoY growth (%)			(5.8)	0.9	(1.1)	3.6	3.5		(12.8)	4.7	(1.5)	3.4	5.9		(16.4)	28.6	7.0	2.6	8.9
Covance	4,278	1,963	2,038	2,096	2,172	2,362	2,535	320	288	319	310	353	400	2.60	2.15	2.70	2.70	3.13	3.71
YoY growth (%)			3.8	2.8	3.6	8.7	7.3		(10.0)	10.8	(2.8)	13.9	13.3		(17.3)	25.6	0.0	15.9	18.5
ICON plc	1,975	888	900	946	1,115	1,300	1,419	149	126	78	116	163	187	1.53	1.44	0.52	1.00	1.57	1.88
YoY growth (%)			1.4	5.1	17.9	16.6	9.2		(15.4)	(38.1)	48.7	40.5	14.7		(5.9)	(63.9)	92.3	57.0	19.7
Parexel	1,712	1,247	1,336	1,422	1,618	1,734	1,908	145	163	156	162	212	266	0.68	0.71	0.81	1.05	1.61	2.02
YoY growth (%)			7.1	6.5	13.8	7.2	10.0		12.7	(4.7)	4.0	31.0	25.5		4.4	14.1	29.6	53.3	25.5
WuXi PharmaTech	1,297	270	334	407	500	573	655	76	110	129	141	153	169	0.78	1.09	1.24	1.40	1.53	1.68
YoY growth (%)			23.7	21.9	22.9	14.6	14.3		44.7	17.3	9.3	8.5	10.5		39.7	13.8	12.9	9.3	9.8
Average	2,380	1,114	1,148	1,203	1,307	1,428	1,546	196	188	189	198	230	262	1.59	1.48	1.57	1.78	2.13	2.47

Source: FactSet.

EXHIBIT C12.11 QUINTILES ADJUSTED EBITDA MARGINS VERSUS PEERS

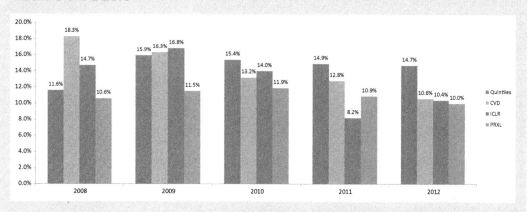

Source: Created using FactSet.

EXHIBIT C12.12 SEQUENCE OF EVENTS IN RELATION TO THE 2003 MANAGEMENT-LED BUYOUT

In an August 1, 2002 executive session, Dennis Gillings requested that the board of directors allow him to share confidential information with certain buyers because he felt that the Quintiles share price didn't reflect its intrinsic value and might not reflect it anytime soon. In an effort to address conflict of interest issues, the board of directors created an ad hoc committee of independent directors, which controlled sharing of financial information with selected prospective buyers. They managed the due-diligence process and safeguarded the interests of minority shareholders. Interested buyers included GF Management Company (a company controlled by Gillings), Citigroup, and One Equity Partners.

During October 2002, Pharma Services Company (PSC), a company formed at the direction of Gillings and One Equity, jointly issued a bid of $11.25 per share. Quintiles then hired Morgan Stanley as its financial advisor.

On November 7, 2002, following a management presentation about the industry trends and Quintiles growth projections, and based on discussions with key management personnel, Morgan Stanley determined that the bid was inadequate, and Quintiles should conduct a formal auction process.

On November 27, Morgan Stanley advised the board that it had received an indication of interest to purchase Quintiles at $14.50, contingent on a 45-day exclusivity period, which the board rejected.

On December 6, the special committee presented and approved a special bonus plan, which changed the compensation plan of existing members of the Quintiles management. The previous plan had contained significant change-in-control payment provisions, which might bias management to support a sale rather than the status quo or other strategic alternatives.

Continued

EXHIBIT C12.12 SEQUENCE OF EVENTS IN RELATION TO THE 2003 MANAGEMENT-LED BUYOUT—cont'd

On January 6, 2003, the special committee received preliminary proposals from seven of 13 bidders ranging from $12 to $16.50 per share, including a $13 bid from PSC and One Equity. Morgan Stanley also indicated an intrinsic share price of $9.75 to $12.75 based on other strategic alternatives available to Quintiles.

On February 6, the special committee invited six bidders, including PSC and One Equity, two strategic bidders (one of which was a significant competitor of Quintiles), and a financial bidder aligned with Quintiles. The special committee also commenced an extensive due-diligence process for these bidders, including follow-up management presentations and data room visits.

On March 10, the special committee received bids from all six bidders ranging from $13.25 to $14 per share, with Pharma Services (combination of PSC and One Equity) bidding at $13.25.

On March 26, 2003, Pharma Services increased its bid to $14.50, while some bidders asked for additional information or exclusivity, which was denied by the board.

In April, Morgan Stanley noted that no bidder was willing to increase its bid beyond $14.50 and that one of the other bidders had expressed uncertainty about maintaining its bid at $14.50 (a 75% premium to the closing price on October 11). The merger agreement was finalized and executed on April 10 with Pharma Services.

Source: SEC filing, p. 2–16, http://www.sec.gov/Archives/edgar/data/919623/000095014403006347/g82646pprem14a.htm.

EXHIBIT C12.13 FIRST PAGE OF QUINTILES INITIAL PUBLIC OFFERING PROSPECTUS

The information in this preliminary prospectus is not complete and may be changed. These securities may not be sold until the registration statement filed with the Securities and Exchange Commission is effective. This preliminary prospectus is not an offer to sell these securities and neither we nor the selling shareholders are soliciting offers to buy these securities in any jurisdiction where the offer or sale is not permitted. *Subject to completion, dated April 26, 2013.*

19,736,842 Shares

Common Stock

Quintiles Transnational Holdings Inc. is offering 13,815,789 shares of common stock. The selling shareholders identified in this prospectus are offering an additional 5,921,053 shares of common stock. This is our initial public offering, and no public market currently exists for our common stock. We anticipate that the initial public offering price will be between $36.00 and $40.00 per share. We will not receive any proceeds from sales by the selling shareholders.

We have applied to list our common stock on the New York Stock Exchange under the symbol "Q."

	Price to Public	Underwriting Discounts and Commissions	Proceeds to Quintiles	Proceeds to Selling Shareholders
Per Share	$	$	$	$
Total	$	$	$	$

The underwriters have an option to purchase up to an additional 2,960,526 shares of common stock from the selling shareholders at the public offering price, less the underwriting discount, within 30 days from the date of this prospectus.

Neither the Securities and Exchange Commission nor any state securities commission nor any other regulatory body has approved or disapproved of these securities or passed on the accuracy or adequacy of this prospectus. Any representation to the contrary is a criminal offense.

The underwriters expect to deliver the shares of common stock to purchasers on or about _____, 2013.

MORGAN STANLEY	*BARCLAYS*	*J.P. MORGAN*
CITIGROUP	GOLDMAN, SACHS & CO.	WELLS FARGO SECURITIES
BofA MERRILL LYNCH		DEUTSCHE BANK SECURITIES
BAIRD	WILLIAM BLAIR	JEFFERIES
PIPER JAFFRAY		UBS INVESTMENT BANK

Source: Quintiles Preliminary Prospectus, as filed with the Securities and Exchange Commission on April 26, 2013.

Index

'*Note*: Page numbers followed by "f" indicate figures, "t" indicate tables and "b" indicate boxes.'

Printed in the United States
By Bookmasters